Why Didn't The Press Shout? American & International Journalism During the Holocaust

Why Didn't The Press Shout? American & International Journalism During the Holocaust

A collection of papers originally presented at an
international conference sponsored by the
Eli and Diana Zborowski Professorial Chair
in Interdisciplinary Holocaust Studies,
Yeshiva University, October 1995

Edited by
Robert Moses Shapiro

Introduction by Marvin Kalb

Yeshiva University Press
in association with
KTAV Publishing House, Inc.

Copyright © 2003
Yeshiva University

Library of Congress Cataloging-in-Publication Data

Why didn't the press shout? : American & international journalism during the
Holocaust / edited by Robert Moses Shapiro; introduction by Marvin Kalb.
    p. cm. —
Papers of a conference held in 1995 at Yeshiva University.
Includes bibliographical references and index.
  ISBN 0-88125-775-3
Holocaust, Jewish (1939-1945)—Press coverage—United States—Congresses. 2. Public
opinion—United States—Congresses. 3. Jews—Persecutions—Europe—Foreign public
opinion, American—Congresses. 4. Holocaust, Jewish (1939-1945)—Press coverage—
Europe—Congresses. I. Shapiro, Robert Moses.

  D804.19.W49 2002
  940.53'18—dc21

                              2002075257

Manufactured in the United States of America

KTAV Publishing House, 926 Newark Avenue, Jersey City, NJ 07306
Email: info@ktav.com

Contents

This book is dedicated to the memory of
a Polish Jewish historian, teacher, and gentleman.

Lucjan Dobroszycki

אהרון לייב בן פישל

15 January 1925—24 October 1995

י"ט טבת תרפ"ה—ל תשרי תשנ"ו

Why Didn't The Press Shout? American & International Journalism During the Holocaust

Tak krawiec kroj—
Jak materjał stoj.

אט אזוי נייט דער שנײדער:
ווי די סחורה שטייט.

The tailor cuts the suit
To fit the material.

Editor's Preface

Robert Moses Shapiro
Ramaz School and Yeshiva University

The American humorist and social commentator, Will Rogers, used to say that all he knew was what he read in the papers. What could one know from reading the contemporaneous press during the Catastrophe of European Jewry? This book is an examination of journalism during the Holocaust, the systematic attempt by Germany to annihilate the Jews of Europe.

Was the Holocaust reported in the press? What role did the press play in the perpetration of the Holocaust? What could readers of the press in various nations have learned at the time about the anti-Jewish policies and actions perpetrated by the Nazis and their henchmen? Did movie newsreels or radio present reports on the catastrophe of European Jewry?

The 30 chapters in the present volume comprise a partial attempt to answer these questions, which were addressed at a conference held in 1995 at Yeshiva University. The conference was inspired by my late teacher, Dr. Lucjan Dobroszycki, occupant of the Eli and Diana Zborowski Interdisciplinary Chair in Holocaust Studies. It reflected his commitment to promoting the study of contemporaneous primary sources, as had been the case with a previous conference[1] on "contemporaneous personal accounts—diaries, memoirs, chronicles, letters—written by Jews in the ghettos, concentration camps, in hiding, and even in trains on the way to extermination."[2] Tragically, Dr. Dobroszycki passed away on the final day of the journalism conference. This book is dedicated to his memory.

Deborah E. Lipstadt's study of the American press was an important pathfinder in examining journalism during the Nazi era.[3] While the present book cannot purport to exhaustive coverage, its chapters provide an overview of journalism in more than a dozen nations and in more than a dozen languages. Both Jewish and non-Jewish press are examined, both in the years leading up to the Second World War's outbreak and during the full-blown conflict itself. Chapters deal with the press of the perpetrators and bystanders, as well as the Jews caught up in the Nazi web or surviving beyond Hitler's reach deep in Russia or in America and England.

Veteran journalist, television correspondent and scholar Marvin Kalb opens the book with an introduction that raises fundamental questions that must be addressed and that have implications for the world in the 21st century. In a time when technology seems to provide unlimited information, his answers are acute and disturbing.

The group of chapters focused on the American press begins with Abraham Brumberg's discussion of the Yiddish press between 1933 and 1939. Ron Hollander makes the blunt statement, "We Knew," in his presentation of press reports from all over the United States during 1941 to 1944. The especially troubling case of the *New York Times* is examined in two chapters, by former *Times* editor Max Frankel and by Laurel Leff, who has exhaustively studied the coverage of the Holocaust in the *New York Times*. Robert St.John, one of the last surviving American journalists who covered World War II, presents a colorful memoir of how working foreign correspondents attempted to report events in Romania in 1940 and 1941. Jeffrey Shandler discusses the impact of the moving image during the final months of the war when newsreels in American theaters began to show documentary footage of the liberated Nazi concentration camps. Haskel Lookstein, who elsewhere has examined the Jewish press between 1938 and 1944, here details Jewish press coverage and the response of American Jews to the liberation of European Jewry in early 1945.

The British press is dealt with in two chapters. Colin Shindler looks at how the coming of the Holocaust was reported in the London *Times* between 1933 and 1942. His chapter is enriched by testimony of the responsible foreign news editor of the London *Times*. David Cesarani discusses how the preeminent Anglo-Jewish journal, the London *Jewish Chronicle*, largely failed the challenge of reporting the unprecedented annihilation of European Jews.

As a confederate of Hitler's Germany from August 1939, Stalin's Russia faithfully refrained from publishing reports about the Nazi treatment of Jews until the June 22, 1941, invasion. The transformations in reporting by the Soviet Russian-language and Yiddish press are analyzed by Yitshak Arad and Dov-Ber Kerler. Arad points out patterns of denial and concealment of the special victimization of Soviet Jews that would continue beyond the ultimate German defeat. Kerler outlines the fate of the Soviet Yiddish press during the purges of the 1930s and the war years before focusing on the Yiddish *Eynikayt*, "the most nationally outspoken Soviet Yiddish newspaper, which chronicled the Holocaust of Soviet Jewry, the Jewish resistance and contribution to the War against Nazism, and the defiant creativity of Soviet Yiddish writers, actors, scholars, artists and scientists."

What could the readers of the German press have learned of the fate of Jews under Nazi rule? Bruce F. Pauley looks at how the Austrian German press reflected the events from 1933 to 1938, from Hitler's achievement of power in Germany until the *Anschluss* merged independent Austria into the Reich. Henry R. Huttenbach examines the German Jewish press during the same prewar years with particular regard to the internal Jewish debate over mass emigration. The late Franciszek Ryszka concludes that, although the German press was thoroughly manipulated, it never explicitly called for murdering Jews. Nevertheless, the German newspapers promoted the public feeling of "collective hatred for the whole Jewish community."

Italy was home to a small, thoroughly assimilated Jewish community. One reflection of that acculturation was the seemingly bizarre case of Ettore Ovazza, the editor of an Italian Jewish Fascist magazine between 1934 and 1938, whose career is chronicled by Alexander Stille. Lynn Gunzberg examines how the Italian Catholic press dealt with Jewish issues during the 1930s until the ascension of Pope Pius XII under whom

Why Didn't The Press Shout?

"the Church press became ever more silent until, finally, burdened by war, much of it ceased publication altogether." Andrea Grover surveys the complete run of the Vatican's daily *L'Osservatore romano* from 1933 through June 1945, and concludes that "it ignored the almost total annihilation of European Jewry. For the reader of the Vatican newspaper, the Holocaust did not occur."

Hungary and Romania were mutually hostile allies of Germany with substantial Jewish populations. Randolph Braham details how the Hungarian anti-Semitic press indoctrinated the Hungarian people "to accept the speed, effectiveness and fanaticism with which the deportations were carried out" to achieve "the liquidation of Hungarian Jewry" as "the last major victory in the genocidal war against the Jews." Romanian-born scholar Radu Ioanid explores how the Romanian press prepared the soil for the Holocaust and then reported on its implementation, only to shift gears with the prospect of German defeat and then commence a policy of denial of any Romanian involvement in the persecution, deportation and murder of Jews.

Poland was home to Europe's largest Jewish community and its territory was the site of nearly all the German-imposed ghettos and deathcamps. The prewar press played a significant role in educating and inciting the ethnically Polish Roman Catholic majority against the country's minorities, most particularly the Jews. Anna Landau-Czajka discusses how the Polish press reported on Nazi German anti-Jewish policies during the prewar years, 1933–1939. Landau-Czajka declares that "no reader of the interwar Polish press—whether rightist, middle or leftist—could get fully and precisely informed as to what the plight was of the Jews in Germany between 1933 and 1939." The most rightwing journals were anti-Jewish but reluctant to detail what the hated Germans were achieving, while leftists and moderates who rejected racist prejudice had to temper their own reporting for fear of reinforcing the idea that a radical anti-Jewish policy of exclusion and expulsion was feasible. Daniel Grinberg examines how the prewar Polish-language Jewish press covered the events in neighboring Nazi Germany. While the Jewish dailies carried numerous front-page stories about the tribulations of German Jewry, the pressure of state censorship, fearful of provoking the increasingly dangerous western neighbor, blocked significant analysis and was reflected in frequent blank spaces where articles had been pulled by official order.

Lucjan Dobroszycki's brief, but forceful examination of the Polish underground press and the Jews introduces us to the world of the media in German-occupied Poland. The array of newspapers and other periodicals produced under conditions of occupation censorship is remarkable, as is the continuity of opinion that Dobroszycki finds. He concludes that, all in all, the clandestine Polish press negatively influenced any inclination to aid Jews.

Among the hundreds of ghettos established by the Germans in occupied Poland, the Warsaw Ghetto housed nearly 450,000 people who were forbidden access to the rest of the city, forbidden access to radios and forbidden access to newspapers. And yet, as Leni Yahil shows in her chapter on the Warsaw Ghetto's underground press, Jews made enormous efforts to gather information and to publish scores of newspapers that were clandestinely distributed. The newspapers were published in Polish, Yiddish and Hebrew by an array of political groups and youth movements. In the articles of this clandestine journalism one can read the thoughts and see the knowledge and hopes possessed by groups of Jews striving to maintain a civil society in the face of an oppression that became total. Yahil credits the underground Jewish press with cultivating the fighting spirit that ultimately flared up in the Warsaw Ghetto Uprising of April-May 1943.

Paweł Szapiro examines how the general Polish underground press responded to the Jewish ghetto uprising in Warsaw. Searching the vast literature of the clandestine Polish press, he has collected several hundred articles referring to the Warsaw Ghetto Uprising. Nevertheless, Szapiro finds that the principal organs of the clandestine Polish state were largely silent about the Jewish ghetto struggle and about any assistance that may have been attempted by some underground Home Army units near the ghetto walls. It is his view that "hundreds of Home Army affiliated newspapers throughout the country applied an embargo on reporting information regarding all armed actions near the ghetto walls." Szapiro points to evidence suggesting two motives for this: reluctance to give the radical rightists in the underground the opportunity to smear the Home Army and its affiliates with being sympathetic to Jews; and a desire to avoid sparking a premature general uprising against the Germans.

The Polish underground maintained clandestine contacts with the Polish government-in-exile in London. Piotr Wróbel examines the princi-

pal Polish daily newspaper published in England for the emigré community that numbered about 60,000, including a force of about 25,000 Polish
soldiers. While not a single anti-Semitic article ever appeared in this official organ of the Polish government-in-exile, *Dziennik Polski*'s coverage
of the fate of Jews often played second fiddle to the depiction of the suffering of the ethnic Polish majority. Nevertheless, *Dziennik Polski* was an
important conduit for information about conditions in occupied Poland,
including the fate of Jews, especially during the fateful period from summer 1942 to summer 1943.

Ukrainians were prewar Poland's largest ethnic minority, concentrated in the regions of Eastern Galicia and Volhynia, where nearly a million
Jews were killed. Henry Abramson examines the Ukrainian language
press published by the Germans for the population of the region they
called Distrikt Galizien. Abramson also looks at examples of anti-Jewish
political cartoons that were particularly important in reaching the masses
of a population that was weakly literate.

Over 70 percent of French Jewry survived the German occupation of
France. Jacques Adler looks at the roles played by both the officially
sponsored Jewish newspaper and the manifold clandestine Jewish press
published by a variety of political groups and movements. The illegal
Jewish press, both in French and Yiddish, actively campaigned against
passivity, urged Jews to go into hiding and called on non-Jews to provide
aid to those in need. Adler concludes that, "above all else, the clandestine
press devoted its efforts to encouraging people to overcome fear, to develop a fighting spirit, and to sustain the hope that deportation to that
unknown destination was not inevitable."

Among the Jews transported farthest by the Germans were the Greek
Jews shipped by rail to Auschwitz. Yitzchak Kerem finds that the general
and Jewish Greek press reported extensively on affairs in Germany after
Hitler's rise to power until the German occupation of Greece in April
1941. Then the pro-German press in Greek actively agitated and incited
its readers against the predominately Sephardic Jews concentrated in
Saloniki. Although leftist elements in the Greek resistance movement
published leaflets urging Jews to flee deportation and calling on Christian
Greeks to aid Jews, "Auschwitz, gas chambers, and the design of the
'Final Solution' were as unknown in Greece as they were in Poland."

Israeli journalist and historian Tom Segev closes this book with his study of the Hebrew press in British-controlled Palestine. Segev judges that the Hebrew press did a poor job in covering the Holocaust by failing to overcome its own parochial concern with local events and the overarching story of the world war. Moreover, he points to an exhaustion of journalistic language during the prewar catastrophe of German Jewry. "[B]y the time they had to deal with the extermination itself—the strongest language had been used up. The words had lost their power, and so had the mental energy needed to deal with the Holocaust." Unable to deal substantively with the European Jewish catastrophe, the Zionist Jewish community in Palestine looked to the needs of the postwar future, including a 1942 proposal to create a great memorial to be called *Yad Vashem*. Thus, "the Hebrew press in Palestine was missing one of the biggest stories of the century."

I will conclude this overview by reiterating that our knowledge of how the press reported on the Holocaust remains incomplete. There are significant lacunae to be filled by researchers. Studies are needed of the German-sponsored press throughout occupied Europe, both in German and other languages. There is need to examine Jewish newspapers officially published with German permission, such as the Polish *Gazeta Żydowska* (Kraków) and the Yiddish *Geto-tsaytung* (Łódź). The same goes for the legal press published in all the languages of Nazi-dominated Europe, as well as in the neutral countries on the periphery. It would also be valuable to learn what was reported in the press of Latin America and the Arab world. The whole question of how raw information carried in journalistic reports becomes knowledge that influences decision-making requires analysis using the tools of history, sociology and psychology.

A note on editing:

In spite of efforts to unify the format of the chapters in this book, there remain some divergences in style. This applies particularly in regard to source citation and place names. An effort has been made to provide correct diacritical marks where needed. The hope is that the result is comprehensible to the reader, especially the one who will seek to pursue interests and questions sparked by these studies.

Notes:

1. See Robert Moses Shapiro, ed., *Holocaust Chronicles: Individualizing the Holocaust Through Diaries and Other Contemporaneous Accounts* (KTAV Publishing and Yeshiva University Press, 1999).
2. Interview in *Jewish Book News*, Nov. 10, 1994, p. 25.
3. *Beyond Belief: America's Press and the Coming of the Holocaust 1933–1945* (New York: Free Press, 1986).

Introduction:
Journalism and The Holocaust, 1933–1945

Marvin Kalb
Harvard University

Our subject makes pygmies of us all, and I fall back upon a simple saying to explain my own approach to any aspect of the Holocaust: "There but for the grace of God go I."

One summer day—it seems like an eternity ago, though it was really August, 1956—I visited the Ukrainian capital of Kiev. At the time I was a translator for the US Embassy in Moscow, and I wanted to see my mother's birthplace. She had often spoken of the Podol, the busy, Jewish marketplace along the Dnieper where she was born and raised. In 1917, on the eve of the Bolshevik Revolution, she left for New York with her father and oldest brother—the rest of the family to come in the early Twenties.

Because I had been briefed, the Podol seemed familiar—still bustling with business, as I had imagined it, but the synagogue on that Friday evening was a relatively quiet oasis of Jewishness, except for the tumult I had created simply by entering. Taller by a foot than most of the old men who had gathered around me, warm, curious, skeptical old men, I was escorted to a place of honor near the *bimah*. After the service, I was besieged by questioning Jews. "Where are you from?" "New York." "New York?" "I have a sister there." One question after another, until a very small man with the wise fingers of an experienced tailor approached me and felt the lapel of my jacket. "Where was this made?", he asked. "Brooks Brothers," I answered,—"it's a fancy men's store in New York." The man made a face. "Huh," he said, with a touch of scorn, "we made better suits than this right here before the revolution."

The rabbi, nodding to the ceiling, a signal he assumed I understood to mean "the place is bugged, it's safer to talk outside," urged us to continue in the courtyard. There we got serious, speaking in Yiddish and Russian, mixed in odd combinations. "Where were your parents born?" "My mother was born here in Kiev." "And what was her name? What was her father's name?" I told them that her name was Bluma, and her father's name was Volf Portnoy—"Volf the furrier," I added.

It was at that moment that something magical occurred. The old tailor, who had melted into the crowd, suddenly reappeared and raised his hand and his eyebrows. "Volf Portnoy," he began, recollections forming around the wrinkles of his eyes. "Of course." He remembered. "Volf left with his two oldest children—a boy and a girl." The tailor smiled. "We never heard from them again." That girl was my mother. I remember being stunned. Almost four decades had passed—from 1917 to 1956—four decades filled with revolution, war, communization, more war and the Holocaust; and I was part of the tapestry, as a human link was being sewn between my mother and this tailor.

The rabbi then told me stories about Bolshevik madness and Nazi savagery, about the thousands—tens? hundreds? of thousands—of Jews butchered or scattered or buried—ravines of heaving civilization as Yevgeny Yevtushenko had imagined Babi Yar. But by now the heaving had stopped. "Over Babi Yar," wrote the Russian poet, "rustles the wild grass. The trees look threatening, like judges, and everything is one silent cry."

I could not help but think—"There but for the grace of God go I."

My father's journey adds poignancy, if any be needed, to my opening story. He was born in Żyrardów, a textile town one hour west of Warsaw—a town founded by Philippe Girard, a French merchant in the early 19th century. Many Jews lived in this essentially dreary, Catholic town, whose skyline was spiked by a tall, red-brick church. My father left in June 1914, when he was 16 and war clouds darkened over Europe. His family was similar to many others in Żyrardów: his mother worked hard, making blouses, while his father studied and prayed, oblivious to many of the enveloping dangers. No doubt his mother, who made many of the important decisions, wanted him to escape service in the Tsarist army and encouraged him to go to London, where his older brother had emigrated several years earlier. My father packed his bag and set forth for London, only to be detoured to Galveston, Texas, where he arrived in late June, alone, speaking no English and finding few folks there who spoke Yiddish, Polish or Russian. But he always thought of himself as an adventurous "Yankee," who loved his new country. Eventually, he made his way to New York, where he met my mother.

Like millions of others, he faced severe economic hardship during the depression. In 1945, we all learned that of my father's entire family—his mother and father, and five remaining brothers and sisters, and their children—a very significant brood, when one adds the uncles and aunts and their children—only Velvel, one of the children, survived World War Two by escaping from a death camp and fighting with the Polish underground. The Holocaust had taken its toll. My father urged Velvel to come to America, but Velvel insisted on going to Palestine. On the very first day that he took up arms in defense of his dream of a Jewish homeland, he was killed—the last of the Kalbs, except for those, like my father, who had left. Again, "there but for the grace of God . . ."

I remember, during the war, that my father would read the Yiddish-language newspaper, the *Forward*, and he would often share the gruesome news from Europe about the Nazi slaughter of the Jews. We knew about the slaughter. We knew, and many other Jews knew. Week after week, month after month, we read about the roundup of Jews, the wholesale deportations, the killings. In July, 1941, the Jewish Telegraphic Agency, then a reliable news source with extensive European contacts, disclosed in New York that hundreds of Jews had been massacred in Minsk, Brest-Litovsk, Lvov and other East European cities, as the Nazis cut a bloody path through the Soviet Union. By mid-March, 1942, a representative of the American Jewish Joint Distribution Committee returned to New York from Budapest to tell of 240,000 Jews killed just in the Ukraine. On May 18, 1942, the *New York Times* reported from Lisbon that the Germans had machine-gunned more than 100,000 Jews in the Baltic states, another 100,000 in Poland, twice that many in western Russia.[1]

Also, in May, two Jewish members of the Polish National Council in Poland—Szmul Zygielbojm and Ignacy Schwarzbart—produced even more startling information. Town by town, city by city, region by region, they disclosed, Jews were being corralled into what were called concentration camps—and there they were killed in gas chambers, 90 at a time, or burned to death in ovens. Zygielbojm and Schwarzbart concluded that the Nazis had embarked on a program, as they put it, "to annihilate all the Jews in Europe." The two Jewish representatives recommended that the allies retaliate in some way against German citizens living in their jurisdictions. The recommendation fell on deaf ears.[2]

Month after month, information about Nazi atrocities was published and broadcast in the US and Britain, and not just by the Yiddish press. The *Boston Globe* ran quite a few stories. So did the *Seattle Times*. On June 30, 1942, and again on July 2, the *New York Times* ran reports, first published by the *Daily Telegraph* in London, that more than 1,000,000 Jews had been killed by the Germans. The reports were mind-blowing, but the *Times* placed them on an inside page.[3]

Still, these reports, and others, produced large demonstrations. On July 21, 1942, twenty-thousand people crowded into Madison Square Garden to express their anguish about the news. On July 23, 1942, the Chaplain of the House of Representatives opened the session by reading a special prayer for the Jewish victims. Similar meetings and demonstrations took place in London.

It was in this environment that Gerhard Riegner, a representative of the World Jewish Congress in Switzerland, reported to London and Washington for the first time that Hitler had in fact ordered the extermination, by gassing, of European Jewry. "Received alarming report," he wrote, "that in Fuhrer's headquarters plan discussed and under consideration according to which all Jews in countries occupied or controlled by Germany numbering 3 1/2–4 millions should, after deportation and concentration in East, be exterminated at one blow to resolve once for all the Jewish question in Europe."[4] In London, the Foreign Office said that any official British response "might annoy the Germans" and besides, officials said, they had no confirmation. In Washington, the State Department was suspicious of what Walter Laqueur described as the "unsubstantiated nature of the information." [5]

In October 1942, the Jewish Telegraphic Agency published the whole Riegner cable without attribution. A month later, Undersecretary of State Sumner Welles confirmed to Rabbi Stephen Wise that the cable was accurate in every depressing detail. Worse, he said, two of the four million Jews had already been killed. The United States then pushed for an Allied condemnation of the Nazi program of extermination—which was announced in mid-December, 1942.[6]

At this point there could be no doubt about the authenticity of the reports of Nazi atrocities against the Jews. The information existed. The news stories existed. The demonstrations and protests existed. The Holocaust existed. And yet, amazingly, the coverage was marginalized. It lacked the explosive force that would carry it from the inside pages to the front pages, from a duckable option to unavoidable action. How come?

Elie Wiesel, in a recent conversation, tried to explain by drawing an interesting distinction between "information" and "knowledge." Alone, information meant only the existence of data. It lacked an activist, ethical component. It was neutral. Knowledge, implied Wiesel, was a higher form of information. Knowledge was information that had been internalized—crowned with a moral dimension that could be transformed into a call for action.

For the first secretary of the World Council of Churches, the Protestant theologian W. A. Visser't Hooft, the moment when information became knowledge occurred when a young Swiss businessman told him of a recent trip to Russia. Inexplicably, he had been invited by Nazi officers to witness the mass killing of Jews—as if he had been invited to a sporting event. In Visser't Hooft's own words, "group after group of Jewish men, women and children were forced to lie down in the mass graves and were then machine-gunned to death . . . From that moment onward, I had no longer any excuse for shutting my mind to information which could find no place in my view of the world and humanity."[7]

During the Holocaust, according to Wiesel, information about the mass killings of Jews edged towards knowledge among some people, but obviously not among enough people to affect American, Allied or Nazi policy. Questions come to mind: How could such a story not overwhelm the front page of any newspaper? How could it not lead the *New York Times*—if not every morning, then every week, every month? How could one explain what, from our vantage point today, could only be defined as insensitive, unprofessional journalism?

In my judgment, there are five reasons. First, the perpetrators of the Holocaust used the tools of totalitarianism to hide their operations. They controlled the foreign press and dominated the German press. They used railroad cars designed for industrial equipment to transport Jewish victims to death camps in Eastern Europe, telling them that they were going to labor camps. David S. Wyman examined German codes. He learned the obvious—that the Nazis used highly stylized language to conceal their intent: "special treatment" for gas chambers, "final solution" for systematic extermination.[8] The truth, as we know, emerged, but it took an unconscionably long time. Not until reporters, such as Edward R. Murrow, described the death camp at Buchenwald in 1945[9] did the true enormity of the Nazi crime become apparent to the average listener of CBS News.

The second reason was that the Allies were intent on winning the war, not on saving Jews. President Roosevelt squirmed between political and military expediency and personal indifference whenever he explained US policy. For example, in early 1942, he told Felix Frankfurter not to worry—that the Jews were being dispatched to Eastern Europe to build fortifications against a Soviet counter-attack.[10] Was he lying? Or was he dissembling? Surely Roosevelt knew better. Laqueur cited an August 22, 1942, news conference, at which the President said that the report of Nazi atrocities "gives rise to the fear that . . . the barbaric and unrelenting character of the occupational regime will become more marked and may even lead to the extermination of certain populations."[11] Certain populations? Was Roosevelt using code language, too? Who else but the Jews? Still the central thrust of Allied policy was the defeat of the Third Reich—"unconditional surrender" was the demand—and Allied leaders persuaded themselves that any humanitarian digression, such as bombing the railroad lines into Auschwitz, could only delay and possibly jeopardize the achievement of the ultimate goal.

To which many of us might have responded, "nonsense," but the Allied judgment contained the core elements of my third reason—namely, anti-Semitism. Roosevelt, the politician who presided over the war, was surely aware that, in the late 1930s, as the US was struggling to emerge from the Depression, anti-Semitism was a flourishing hate among many Americans. In the spring of 1942, sociologist David Riesman described anti-Semitism in the US as "slightly below the boiling point."[12] According to one poll conducted by the National Opinion Research Center, then at the University of Denver, shortly after the outbreak of the war, 66 percent of the American people—two out of every three—described the German people as "essentially peace-loving and kindly."

Another poll said that 61 percent believed that the German people should not be "blamed" for the "mass killings." Fifty-eight percent said that only the Nazi leaders should be "blamed."[13]

In January, 1943, after Undersecretary Welles confirmed the "final solution," after the Allies released their joint statement of condemnation, still another poll said that more than half of the American people did not believe that the Nazis were "deliberately" killing the Jews.

In December, 1944, the American Institute of Public Opinion asked, "Nobody knows, of course, how many may have been murdered, but what would be your best guess?" Twenty-seven percent of Americans answered, "fewer than 100,000." One percent answered, up to 1 million.[14]

As the war was coming to an end, pollster Elmo Roper warned, "anti-Semitism has spread all over the nation and is particularly virulent in urban centers."[15] David Wyman, in his book, *The Abandonment of the Jews*, concluded that 15 percent of the American people would actually have "supported" an anti-Jewish campaign, and another 20–25 percent would have been "sympathetic" to such a campaign. In his words, "as much as 35–40 percent of the population was prepared to approve an anti-Jewish campaign, some 30 percent would have stood up against it, and the rest would have remained indifferent."[16] Remember, we are talking here about the American people.

The fourth reason was related to this widespread anti-Semitism and to the enormity of the Nazi crime. Many people simply could not believe that the German people would be engaged in the systematic extermination of the Jews, and many others, either because they were anti-Semitic or totally absorbed with the war effort, were basically indifferent to this possibility. Arthur Koestler, writing from London in a *New York Times Magazine* piece published in early 1944, spoke of his "ultimate loneliness when faced with death and cosmic violence." "You," Koestler continued, "you are the crowd who walk past laughing on the road; and there are a few of us, escaped victims or eyewitnesses of the things which happen in the thicket and who, haunted by our memories, go on screaming on the wireless, yelling at you in newspapers and in public meetings, theaters and cinemas. . . . You shake yourselves like puppies who have got their fur wet, . . . and you walk on, protected by the dream-barrier which stifles all sound." Koestler concluded what he called his "inability to communicate the unique horror of this experience" with these words: "So far three million have died. It is the greatest mass killing in recorded history; and it goes on daily, hourly, as regularly as the ticking of your watch."[17]

This was, oddly, a benign explanation—people simply could not absorb the monstrous dimension of the Nazi crimes. True, to so many, the Jews were, for the past 2,000 years, such a problematic people—but deserving of extinction? No. Even in Palestine, during the war, the Jewish press could not absorb and communicate the true dimensions of the crimes. There were also those Allied officials—and ordinary citizens, already predisposed to look with supreme indifference at Jewish suffering—who found the "Jewish problem" to be a most annoying distraction from the day's work. And, such a waste of time. A British diplomat in the Foreign Office, September, 1944, explained why he did not want to be bothered. It would compel other busy diplomats, in his words, "to waste a disproportionate amount of their time in dealing with wailing Jews." Frank Roberts, a very proper British diplomat, a future Ambassador to Moscow, with whom, years later, I had excellent professional dealings,— Roberts, in possession of an intelligence report concerning the Nazi use of Jewish corpses, sighed with barely a trace of exasperation: "The facts are quite bad enough," he said, "without the addition of such an old story as the use of bodies for the manufacture of soap."[18]

Disbelief during the tense times of all-out war, compounded by wearisome information about "wailing Jews," was hardly the stuff to awaken the conscience of the world to the Holocaust—hardly the stuff to compel the usual editor, working at the usual news desk, to decide to "front" the Holocaust—at least, not then.

Finally, my fifth reason for the Holocaust remaining an "inside" story—the very nature of journalism itself, as it was practiced at that time. Journalism has never been an adventurous craft. It feels uncomfortable leading the parade—much more comfortable simply covering it, objectively. Its standards evolve with experience. During the war, the story was the prosecution of the war, the pursuit of an Allied victory. Journalists had no other objective. Their editors wanted stories about the home front and the war front. They were not geared for stories—quite fantastic stories—about millions of Jews being gassed and burned to death as part of a systematic German campaign to exterminate a people. Now, with hindsight, we can second-guess the editorial limitations of the time—and say, tsk, tsk, you blew the story.

Even the *New York Times* failed to rise above the norm. I say "even," because the *Times* was and is so special in American journalism. In those days, the *Times*, whose logo read and reads "All The News That's Fit To Print," knew much more than it published about the Holocaust; and what it published, it published, as a rule, inside, cut, often trivialized. What was the reason? Was it because the *Times* was owned by Jews and they did not want to seem to be "pushing" a Jewish issue? Was it because Jewish issues were not popular issues, not paper sellers? Whatever be the real reason, the *Times* failed in its professional responsibility when it did not take the journalistic lead, as it did, for example, years later, when it decided to publish the Pentagon Papers.

Moreover, most journalists were like most other Americans—some anti-Semitic, some disbelieving, others indifferent. The Holocaust was not a burning story during the time of the Holocaust. Maybe too demanding a story, too mind-numbing in scope; the Holocaust could only be appreciated, if that's the right verb, with time.

My five reasons now listed about the journalism of the Holocaust, what can one say about modern-day journalism, and the challenges it faces in the coverage of other examples of mass killings, though not of the same nomenclature?

First of all, the journalism of the 1990s, the journalism after Vietnam, after Watergate, after the technological revolutions that produced CNN, faxes, computers and the OJ trial, is significantly different from the journalism of the 1940s, and we cannot impose the journalistic yardsticks of the 1990s on the 1940s. Nor can we fairly expect the journalists of the 1940s to perform as though they lived and worked in the 1990s. Now journalists are obsessed with sex and scandal, fires and sports, weather and murders, listing towards sensationalism whenever the competitive opportunity beckons. Negative and cynical, they distrust the government and disparage politicians. Back then, journalists operated in a narrower environment, with simpler rules. They marched to the government's beat, they hated Hitler and Tojo, they supported the boys at the front. And, their technological opportunities were comparatively primitive.

For a moment, let's play the game of "what if?" What if there were CNN, satellites, faxes in the 1930s? Would the German people have elected Hitler as Chancellor? Or would they have been repelled? Would the world have watched "*Kristallnacht*," covered "live" and seen everywhere, and done nothing, or something? Would American politics have remained so isolationist? Would the '30s rendition of Rush Limbaugh have aroused the American people to act, or to go into a deeper nationalistic, self-absorbed slumber? Would Chamberlain have gone to Munich and appeased Hitler? (Would Chamberlain even have been Prime Minister in an age of television?) Would Roosevelt have waited for Pearl Harbor to declare war? Would the Japanese even have attacked if CNN had been covering the rape of Nanking? Would the atomic bomb have been developed—and dropped, twice?

This game of "what if?" underscores the technological differences between the journalism of then and the journalism of now. It also segués neatly into a few concluding thoughts. One is that the Holocaust was unique, the reporting of the Holocaust was unique, and neither can be duplicated. So long as there is a strong Israel and an articulate, influential Jewish community in the United States, I feel confident in saying that another Holocaust—another foreign, state-run program of extermination of the Jews—would be impossible. But other mass killings? These are not only possible but likely.

Given the unprecedented gobbling up of substantial media enterprises by even bigger media conglomerates, it should not be surprising these days that there is not even a commonly accepted definition of "news." Yet, if a story broke about another Holocaust, there could be no doubt—not now—that it would be front-page news. Such horrible secrets could no longer be kept for months and years. Responsible officials are constantly reminded that what was tolerated during the Holocaust is unacceptable behavior today. For example, Deputy Secretary of State Strobe Talbott, during a recent visit to the Holocaust Museum in Washington, read with dismay John McCloy's 50-year-old negative response to a demand by the World Jewish Congress that the Allies bomb the rail lines leading into Auschwitz. The response and the demand were on a wall flanking a huge blow-up of the death camps. "Remember, Strobe," said his companion, then Museum Director Walter Reich, "any letter you write may end up on a museum wall."

But I am not as confident that other mass killings would produce the same response, principally because of the overpowering, inescapable influence of television on our politics and on our morality. In our wired world, we have already seen so much. We have seen not only the stacked corpses and the vacant eyes of the Holocaust; we have also seen Pol Pot's bloody handiwork in Cambodia, mass killings and starvation in Rwanda, "ethnic cleansing" in Bosnia, David-against-Goliath warfare in Chechnya. Governments, uncertain about their policy, have been driven to act by television pictures—not always, but often enough. Remember the body of an American soldier being dragged through the streets of Mogadishu? Within months, the US withdrew from Somalia. Remember the phenomenal rout of the Iraqi Republican Guards from Kuwait? So "live," so exposed, that the Bush Administration quickly decided that it had had enough of victory. No point in angering its Arab allies, who also saw the vanquished Guards in full retreat.

We now, undeniably, have the information many of us were denied during the Holocaust, often more information than we can possibly absorb in a normal day at the office. No longer is late or inadequate information an excuse for inaction. Even in World War II, some people, such as Raoul Wallenberg of Sweden and Sempo Sugihara of Japan, acted with exceptional courage. At this time, a different problem emerges. There is so much information that the senses seem to have become impervious to evil, particularly when the evil is foreign, distant, somewhat exotic. Rwanda, after all, was in Africa, and there were few journalists there. Bosnia, in Europe, produced more coverage, even though there have been, comparatively speaking, far fewer casualties. Even when the evil is domestic, we sometimes have difficulty distinguishing between the real Oklahoma City tragedy and a made-for-TV docudrama about the tragedy. What is real? What is contrived? People have their obvious limits: how much evil can they absorb, before they turn away in horror, disgust or tedium?

Journalism also has its limits. In a craft that extols objectivity, how neutral, how dispassionate, can a journalist be? *Should* a journalist be? In early 1968, during the North Vietnamese Tet offensive, Eddie Adams of the Associated Press took the most memorable picture of his life. It was the picture of a South Vietnamese officer shooting a shackled Vietcong prisoner in the head, blood instantly spouting from the open wound. The picture won the Pulitzer Prize for wartime photography. Eddie Adams was so close to the shooting he could have stopped it—but that would have been regarded as unprofessional. As a journalist, Adams was a photographer first, a human being second.

We all operate within the limits of our profession, our religion, our nationality. Cambodians knew about Pol Pot's killings, and so did we. The information existed. The Bosnians knew about Serbian "ethnic cleansing," and so did we. The information existed. So long as there are strong differences among races, nationalities, religions and tribes, there will likely be more and bloodier wars and more killing—different from the Holocaust, but demanding our attention and tugging at our conscience nonetheless. In this age of mass communication, there will be information about these killings. Most of the world watched the bloodshed in Chechnya with a morbid fascination, but did nothing. The Clinton Administration, not eager to get involved, said that Chechnya was a Russian problem.

Tip O'Neill said, "All politics is local." But can all morality be local, too? How ironic! As more satellites fill the heavens, and more information about the post-Cold War world becomes our daily fare, we should, in the best of all possible worlds, be provided with the magical ingredient that transforms information into knowledge, and knowledge into a moral compulsion to act. Yet, many of us sit and we watch, like global couch-potatoes. Things seem either too complicated and remote or too familiar and boring. Either way, they seem beyond journalism's capacity, or its writ, and beyond our human capacities, too.

Hannah Arendt spoke of "the banality of evil." The Italian writer, Primo Levi, worried not about the existence of evil, but its acceptance by ordinary people. After Auschwitz, he wrote, "Monsters exist, but they are too few in number to be truly dangerous. More dangerous are the common man, the functionaries ready to believe and to act without asking questions."

Notes:

1. David S. Wyman, *The Abandonment of the Jews* (New York, 1984), pp. 20–21.
2. Ibid., p. 21.
3. Ibid., pp. 22–23.
4. Walter Laqueur, *The Terrible Secret* (Boston-Toronto, 1980), p. 77.
5. Ibid., pp. 79–80.
6. Ibid., p. 93.
7. W.A. Visser't Hooft, *Memoirs* (London, 1973), pp. 165–6.
8. Wyman, p. 19.
9. A complete transcript of Murrow's report appears in Edward Bliss, Jr., ed., *In Search of Light:The Broadcasts of Edward R. Murrow, 1938–1961* (New York, 1967), pp. 91–95.
10. Laqueur, pp. 94–95.

11. Ibid., p. 95.

12. Wyman, p. 9.

13. On public opinion poll results, see Wyman, pp. 14–15, 326, 359 (notes 40–44), 416 (notes 61–62).

14. Ibid., pp. 79–80.

15. Ibid., p. 9.

16. Ibid., p.15.

17. *New York Times*, Jan. 9, 1944.

18. Laqueur, p. 82.

American Journalism

TOWARDS THE FINAL SOLUTION:
Perceptions of Hitler and Nazism
in the US Left-of-Center Yiddish Press, 1930–1939

Abraham Brumberg
Chevy Chase, MD

I

This paper focuses on one period only—that of the 1930s, which is to say, the years preceding and leading up to the implementation of the Final Solution. An important subject in and of itself, the early perceptions of Hitler and Nazism by American Jews help to explain their subsequent response to the mass extermination of six million European Jews.

Furthermore, the present paper examines the two major left-of-center New York Yiddish newspapers—the *Forward* (*Forverts*) and *Morgn Frayhayt* (Morning Freedom), later named simply *Frayhayt*—and a few journals generally allied with or sharing the point of view of one or the other of these newspapers. While I also refer to the two other dailies that appeared at that time, *Der Tog* (The Day) and *Morgn zhurnal* (Morning Journal), the principal emphasis, to repeat, is on the explicitly left-wing publications. How did the ideology and politics of these publications— social-democratic and Communist respectively—color their understanding of what Hitler and Nazism were all about, and how best to combat them? These, in a nutshell, are the questions to which I propose to address myself. To try to cover more ground would inevitably result—to reverse an old adage—in missing the trees for the forest.[1]

II

Young scholars surveying the contemporary Jewish scene in the United States, with its plethora of English-language Jewish journals, from New York's *The Jewish Week*, or *The San Francisco Jewish Ledger* to *Menorah Journal*, *Tikkun*, and *Commentary*, are likely to be struck by the one-time magnitude and variety of the Yiddish press in this country. Only one truncated secular Yiddish newspaper still remains—the *Forward*—an appendage to its English language edition, now appearing as a weekly (a symbolic reversal: in the past, the English section was a weekly supplement to the daily *Forverts*.) Yet in the 1930s, the number of Yiddish readers was at least as large as that of readers of the Anglo-Jewish press, and the combined print-run of Yiddish papers and magazines exceeded that of the English-language publications.

Still earlier, in 1915–16, the circulation of the daily Yiddish press, excluding the numerous weeklies, monthlies, and other periodicals, was half a million in New York City alone, and 600,000 nationally. Even by the time the Second World War broke out, the combined circulation of the Yiddish press was 400,000, with some of the papers, such as *Forward*, also publishing special editions in Chicago and Los Angeles.

The magnitude of the Yiddish press was a reflection of the role played by Jews of East European origin during the first half of this century. It was the first and second generation of the East European Jews—as Irving Howe so eloquently demonstrated in his *The World of Our Fathers*—that built most of the cultural, philanthropic, fraternal, and political Jewish institutions in this country. The American Jewish Committee today is a powerful and influential organization. But, as late as in the 1940s, it was still identified as the representative of wealthy "Yahudim," that is, Jews of German background, with little affinity—indeed disdain—for Jews of Eastern European background, that is, for the mass of American Jews. One could name other organizations, too, influential today, that were nonexistent or insubstantial half a century ago.

All the Yiddish newspapers and periodicals in the 1920s and '30s could be called, in one way or another, left-wing, or at the least sympathetic to broad socialist values. Even the Orthodox *Morgn zhurnal* was not fundamentally hostile, having come out of the same matrix as the secular Jewish papers, that is, Tsarist Russia. This meant that most Orthodox Jews (with the exception of those belonging to the implacably anti-Zionist, anti-socialist and in fact firmly apolitical Agudas Israel), themselves victims of pogroms and persecutions in the "old country," could not but sympathize, to a lesser or greater extent, with some of the ideas of the "left-wingers," however much they might have been repelled by the anti-religious and bitterly anti-clerical ethos of the latter.

In addition, the late 1920s and early 1930s saw factional disputes resulting in the defection of a number of non-Communist writers to the *Frayhayt,* and then back to the other newspapers in the middle and late 1930s. (I shall have more to say about this further on.) Finally, the lines between the non-Communist papers, despite their ideological divergencies, were so fluid as to allow some well known writers to publish interchangeably in one or another.

But no other group on what used to be referred to in Yiddish as "the Jewish street" (*di yidishe gas*) was as unrelenting in its opposition to fascism and anti-Semitism as the parties on the left. The social democrats, communists, anarchists, territorialists, and socialist-Zionists, were not only Jews, they were Europeans, only one step removed from their countries of origin. That, plus their ideological orientation, explains the Left's grasp of and special sensitivity to right-wing movements in that part of the world.

Indeed, the spiritual closeness of the American socialists to the European scene persuaded Abraham Cahan, the long-time editor of the Jewish *Forward*, that his comrades lacked a proper understanding of native American radicalism—and he told them so in two long articles in 1932.[2] There was much to what he said: the American offshoots of European political movements were essentially parochial, often, for instance, preaching the class-struggle to workers who were ready to challenge the "bosses" but without questioning the premises of the capitalist system. Yet that parochialism was at the same time responsible for a sharper insight into the nature of far-right movements in Europe.

The *Forward* was the principal Yiddish voice of Marxist social democracy. It was linked to the political-literary monthly *Tsukunft* (Future) and the weekly *Der Veker* (The Alarm), organ of the Jewish Socialist Federation. Under the impact of the social changes within the structure of American Jewry, and later of the Holocaust, the *Forward*—to run ahead of my story—would eventually become as pro-Zionist, or pro-Israel, as did most other Yiddish papers. In fact, in the late 1940s, the Forward Association decided, at a solemn meeting, to drop the two Marxist slogans that adorned the cover page of the *Forward* since its inception: "Workers of the Whole World—Unite," and "The workers have nothing to lose but their chains." True, these rousing pronunciamentos of the *Communist Manifesto* had long ceased to have much resonance in

Forward circles. Still, their disappearance from the masthead of the newspaper caused considerable grief to many of the paper's long-time readers.

But this was all to be. In the 1930s, the belief in Marxism was a firm
component of the *Forward* ethos, with many of its contributors known
figures in the social democratic movement.[3]

III

I come back, then, to the main topic: How did the Jewish socialists
and communists react to the demise of the German Weimar Republic and
the rise of the Nazi State?

It might be useful, first, to recapitulate the major events of 1930–1934:
the *Reichstag* election of September 14, 1930, when the Nazis won a staggering victory, gaining 107 seats in the *Reichstag* in place of the previous
12, thus becoming the second largest political party in Germany; the
increasingly vicious street brawls with the Stormtroopers; attacks on individual Jews, Jewish stores and organizations; the provincial elections
yielding further Nazi increases; the bewildering number of cabinet
changes, each one bringing Hitler closer to power; and the reelection of
the elderly Hindenburg as president.

In July 1932 came the *Reichstag* elections in which almost 14 million
German voters turned the Nazis into the largest political party; in January
1933, Hitler was appointed Chancellor. This was swiftly followed by laws
restricting freedom of press and assembly and the legal permission to
shoot "enemies of the state" without even a semblance of a trial. Then
came the *Reichstag* fire and the ensuing reign of terror that led up to the
March 6, 1933, elections, with the Nazis winning 43.9 percent of the vote.

Two weeks later, by use of mass arrests, threats and sham promises,
Hitler had the *Reichstag* pass the so-called Enabling Act, banned the
Communist Party, emasculated the socialists, and declared himself
Führer not only of the National Socialist Party, but of the German Reich.
The totalitarian state was now in place.

What, then, was the reaction of the American Jewish socialist press to
these events? Oddly enough, especially given its intense hostility to fascism, it was at first phlegmatic. The 1930 and 1931 volumes of *Der Veker*
and *Di Tsukunft* carried hardly any articles on the rise of fascism in
Germany. The *Forward,* as a daily newspaper, *did* report on the relevant
day to day developments, but also without any sense of urgency. The first

time in 1930 that the *Veker* commented on this subject was on September 20, a week after the *Reichstag* elections.

The editorial, in fact, was thorough and astute. It emphasized the despair of the Germans, mainly the "middle classes," over the "terrible economic conditions" in the country, and the huge reparations that Germany had to pay in accord with the provisions of the Versailles Treaty as two of the principal reasons for the popularity of the Nazis. Subjected to the winds of nationalism fanned by the two "extreme parties," that is, the National Socialists and the Communists, said the Yiddish journal, "the people let themselves be swept into the embrace of chauvinism."

Yet, with the exception of this one editorial, however perspicacious, the *Veker* published nothing on Germany that year, nor for that matter in 1931. The *Tsukunft* was a bit, but not much, better. Not until October 1930, that is, after the fateful elections of September 14, did the monthly publish an article on this subject. The author was the editor, Abraham Liesin, and his article consisted mainly of a defense of the policies of the Social Democrats (SPD), especially of the then-collaboration between the SPD and the Center Party and Chancellor Brüning. A coalition government, said Liesin, was the only way to meet the interests of the workers, such as providing them with pensions, higher wages, health benefits and so on. Had the SPD insisted on remaining immaculate, said the editor, it would have never achieved these striking successes.

(I might mention, in passing, that those "striking successes" were little more than a myth, with the policies of the Brüning government causing gradually more unemployment, poverty, and despair.)

In addition, noting the anti-Semitism of the Nazis, Liesin also pointed out that Jews had for a long time comprised the backbone of republicanism in Germany: at one time in the Liberal Party, then in the *Volkspartei*, and when the latter became infused with anti-Semitism, they came to form the backbone of the Social Democratic Party. This characterization was something of an exaggeration, but it was not outrageous.

Abraham Liesin, then editor of *Tsukunft*, was both a socialist and what used to be termed in Yiddish *a heyser yid*, that is, an ardent Jew. Not a Zionist, he was, like many others, passionately committed to the survival of Jewish nationhood and culture, and, although a secularist, he often wrote of the martyrdom of religious Jews in opposing terror and attempts at forcible conversion—that is, *Kiddush Hashem* (the sanctification of the Name). In this he was close to the novelist Sholem Asch, also a secular Jew, and also an exponent of traditional Jewish values. A prolific poet, Liesin's works were largely of a hortatory nature and did not find their way into the many collections and translations of Yiddish poetry that have appeared over the last decade or so.

It was therefore no surprise that in his editorial Liesin focused on the role of Jews in German political life. Yet, with the exception of this piece and two other articles by the political commentator P. Harkavi (not to be confused with the author of the Yiddish-Hebrew-English dictionary), little appeared in *Tsukunft* on the situation in Germany either in 1930 or 1931, at the time when ever darker clouds were gathering over Germany. What explains the relative passivity of the Jewish socialists at that time?

IV

The answer to this question is to be found in the nature of Jewish experience *vis-à-vis* Germany, which gave rise to two interrelated views.

First, the American Jews' experience with Germany and with German anti-Semitism was very limited. The vast number of Jewish emigrants had come from Eastern Europe, where they were subjected to persecution, hatred, and pogroms by Ukrainians, Russians, Belorussians, and Poles. The Germans, on the other hand, in the eyes of most American Jews, were a "cultured," "civilized" nation, not given to the kind of savage behavior their former Slavic neighbors excelled in.

Whereas during the First World War the Germans were mortally detested by the French, Belgians and the British, the Jews in areas of Eastern Europe occupied by the German armies had few complaints. True, the German troops committed atrocities—as from time immemorial did every occupying army—but they were not noticeably directed against the Jews. In any case, the Germans certainly behaved infinitely better than either the Russian Whites and Reds, or the murderous Ukrainian troops, whatever their ideological hue.

To be sure, Germany had a venerable tradition of anti-Semitism, some of it articulated by prominent German cultural figures such as Heinrich von Treitschke and Richard Wagner. Yet vicious pogroms, such as those that regularly swept Eastern Europe, were rather a rarity in late nineteenth century and early twentieth century Germany. In addition, as pointed out, most American Jews had little personal experience with the Germans in the first place.

Second, the Jewish socialists in the United States, like the Bund in Poland, were (perhaps more than any other group of socialists) ardent admirers of the German Social Democrats. To be sure, the German Social Democrats' vote for war credits in August 1914, and the suppression of the Spartacus uprising and the murder of Karl Liebknecht and Rosa Luxembourg with the connivance of the Ebert government in 1919, won little approval for the German Socialists in the eyes of Jewish socialists. On the other hand, the numerical strength of the Social Democratic Party during the Weimar Republic, its dedication to democracy, its social and economic successes and the exemplary discipline that existed within its party ranks all made it, as time went on, an object of great admiration.

It was, then, the awe in which German civilization was held by the Jewish socialists, combined with their enthusiasm for the German Social Democratic movement, that shaped the attitude of the Jewish socialists. At the time, admiration blinded the Jewish socialists to salient realities. This was true in the late 1920s and the first two years of the decade of the 1930s. Naive optimism would give rise both to skewed perceptions of ongoing developments and unrealistic predictions about the future.

As late as March 2, 1933, a few days before the *Reichstag* elections which were to sweep the Nazis into power, Abraham Cahan, editor of the *Forward,* wrote á *propos* the comparison between Hitler and Mussolini: "It is clear as daylight that in Italy a Mussolini is possible, but in a country as highly cultivated and industrialized country as Germany it is not."

Only four days later, in an editorial on the eve of the elections, the *Forward* conceded that Germany might become a fascist state, and Jews might find emigration as their only solution, but that the new regime "will not tolerate pogroms."[4] This presumably was on the theory that pogroms were simply not in accord with the German *Geist.*

To return to 1930, an editorial in the *Forward* a day after the fateful elections had the following to say about Hitler:

Hitler's recent speech demonstrates that he is no more than a windbag, stupid, filled with *khutspe,* yet not one to be worried about. No doubt his followers will soon realize that they are dealing with a shallow, impotent demagogue, a man who presents no danger whatever, given to excitable verbal outpourings rather than reasonable talk, a man with a with a forked tongue—all told, not a serious figure.

The socialists, continued the editorial, are the

one guarantee for the future of the republic. Their outstandingly calm demeanor, their wonderful discipline, all offer a guarantee that the Nazi victory is but a spasm from which the German people will soon recover.[5]

It is amazing to note the Panglossian spirit that pervaded the American Jewish socialists' reactions to Hitler's inexorable ascent. Thus one writer, P. Harkavi, observes in 1932, in a pre-election article, that Hitler

will by no means be able to show that the [von Papen] government of pure aristocrats is helpless without him. The struggle against national socialism has been clearly facilitated after the government was filled with barons and dukes.[6]

And in another article in September, the same author calls the results of the July 1932 elections "not too bad," taking solace in the thought that "as in the presidential elections [of that year] the majority of the German electorate voted against a fascist dictatorship. The Social Democrats," predicted the author, "will courageously battle their enemy."[7]

Only a few weeks later, von Papen met with Hitler, and shortly thereafter, on January 30, 1933, Hindenburg appointed Hitler as Chancellor. As for the German socialists, they did precisely what Mr. Harkavi said they would not do; namely, they *failed* to confront the foe and ceased to exist, except for those imprisoned in jails and concentration camps and several thousand members who fled abroad

V

The desperate belief in the power of the German Social Democrats to withstand the fascist onslaught—contradicted with every passing week by the party's supine behavior—continued beyond March 1933. On May 15,

1934, the distinguished writer Tsivion observes in the *Forward*—in May 1934, I repeat—that

> one can no longer conceal the truth. The malignant attacks on Jews will not bring salvation. It is becoming increasingly clear to the German masses where the true source of their misfortunes is located. They are beginning to understand that Hitlerism will sink Germany in the worst quagmire imaginable.

With the luster of the Social Democrats tarnished, the source of optimism became the boycott of German goods, the deteriorating economic conditions in Germany, the spirit of bitterness that was said to have swept the country. "The people are preparing themselves for hunger" by engaging in furious hoarding, says an editorial in the *Forward* on June 4, 1934. On June 16, a banner headline on the front page of the *Forward* declares: "Hitler Must Fall Soon, Says an American Expert"—who turns out to be Frank Knox, publisher and editor of *The Chicago Daily News*. Even Nazi bands, according to Mr. Knox, are demonstrating against Hitler, the Catholics are seething with hatred for *der Führer*, and all signs point to the conclusion that Hitler's end is near.

The boycott is doing wonders, said other articles at that time; Hitler is beside himself with rage when he mentions the subject.[8] Yet another article notes that

> Hitler's foreign and domestic policy still helps to arouse the socialist and democratic consciousness of the working class. The underground will find increasing numbers of supporters. With the strengthening of class contradictions in the totalitarian (*totale*) state, and the gradual [strengthening] . . . of the working class the ground for a thorough revolution becomes more ripe every day.[9]

Mistaken views were hardly the exclusive province of the socialists. The need to believe that things could (in fact, were bound to) improve is human and ubiquitous. Nevertheless, it is extraordinary that experienced political observers could be so misled, if only for a time, about the character of a party which throughout its history had avoided, in the words of the historian Erich Matthias, "any act whose consequences could not be fully foreseen, [one that] was filled with a panicky distrust of 'experiments,' and one so averse to bloodshed."[10] I am referring, of course, to the German Social Democratic Party—a giant with clay feet.

VI

To be sure, not all the reports were cut of the same staunch cloth. In fact, by 1933 somber scenarios and realistic appraisals began to vie with the optimistic notes, sometimes in the same issues of the newspaper or journal. The same author would veer from optimism to pessimism. The Social Democratic Party was subjected to increasing criticism: this "wonderful party," as it was referred to for many years, was now found to be too tame, too dogmatic about following a strictly reformist path, too reluctant, said one socialist observer, to get rid of the old monarchist bureaucracy, too timid, not revolutionary enough.

The gradual disillusionment with the Social Democratic Party merged with another disappointment, namely, over the listless and weak-kneed attitude of most German Jews. The whole history of German anti-Semitism became a major subject for examination, as was the passivity of German Jews in resisting it, before and now.

On May 3, 1933, the American left-wing weekly *The Nation* carried a furious article by the Zionist writer and critic Ludwig Lewisohn castigating the German Jews for having "sold out spiritually to their oppressor at the latter's invitation and command." None of the few articles that now appeared in the Yiddish socialist press came close to Lewisohn's fulminations in *The Nation*, if only because Lewisohn's prescription of "more Judaism and Zionism" as a spiritual antidote to the anti-Semitic onslaught could not be accepted by the socialists. If anything, the socialists censured the Berlin Jews for their talk about "moving to the suburbs, away from the center of the city," and also for considering the idea of "withdrawing their children from the schools altogether" and arranging for either special schools or private tutoring—all of which in effect amounted to erecting new ghettos, as in the middle ages.[11]

The criticism of the German Jews was understandable, if unfair. The creation of special schools for Jewish children, to the extent this idea was discussed at all, was not provoked by German Jewish pusillanimity, much less by a hankering for the false security of a ghetto. It was simply a response to the fact that Jewish children were being barred from attending classes, were often harassed and abused by Nazi hoodlums, and eventually officially forbidden to attend German schools.[12] Nevertheless, it is true that German Jews at first equivocated about their response to the Nazi onslaught, and found it difficult to accept the fact that Germans would harbor such unmitigated hatred for the Jews.[13]

Another issue that troubled the Jewish socialists was the behavior of the Zionists, or at any rate some leaders of the Jewish community in Palestine, in evading the boycott against Germany. In late 1933, it became known that the Zionist authorities in Palestine had signed a trade agreement with some German firms for the purchase of a number of goods. At first the authorities denied any such deal, but eventually Chaim Greenberg, the head of the Labor Zionists in the US, admitted that the charge was true, defending the agreement as beneficial to the growth of the Jewish Homeland. The idea that Palestine Jews would continue their boycott of German goods while at the same time availing themselves of German products in Palestine stores, products imported not by the British but by Jews, was outrageous. The deal was finally shelved, but for a time it constituted a serious bone of contention between the Zionists and Jewish socialists.[14]

As time went on, the disappointment in the Social Democratic Party also turned into specific, and often harsh, criticism of its recent policies. Thus, on May 14, 1934, when Hitler was already firmly in power and the socialists in rout, when Austrian fascists had already crushed that country's socialists, the Menshevik/Bundist leader Rafael Abramovitch published an article in the *Forward* saying that the time had now come for the socialists to fight for actual power. Strictly parliamentary tactics no longer sufficed: the socialists must challenge directly the hegemony of the capitalist classes.

Abramovitch realized, of course, that by defending the recourse to what he explicitly called "extra-parliamentary" methods of struggle he came dangerously close to embracing the line of the Communists, who had long insisted on an outright struggle for a "workers' and peasants' republic." And so he affirmed that the principle of using democratic tactics must be upheld; but the Social Democrats must not repeat the mistake of 1918, when instead of ushering in a socialist system, they left the capitalist powers intact. In the event of a successful revolution now, wrote

Abramovitch, fascist parties must be immediately disbanded, and the parliament must cease offering refuge to those who want to abolish freedom—and that means large landowners, factory owners, and the like, in addition to the Nazis.

A similar note was struck in the *Forward* three days later[15] by the Austrian Social Democrat Otto Bauer. Writing from Czechoslovakia to which he fled earlier that year, Bauer defended the right to use a "multiplicity of methods," depending on time and circumstances, up to the point of establishing "revolutionary dictatorship." In this respect, Bauer reaffirmed his traditional stand as a "left-wing" Social Democrat. Together with Abramovitch, he now emerged clearly as a severe critic of the policies of the German Social Democratic Party's lackadaisical attitude that facilitated Hitler's eventual victory.

To Abraham Cahan, editor of the *Forward*, such words smacked too much of dogmatism. Why this emphasis on the proletariat, he asked in an editorial on May 20, 1934. The middle classes have lost much over the past few years, he asserted, and should be regarded as potential allies in the struggle against Hitler, rather than as "class enemies." The Swedish Social Democrats who openly collaborate with the middle classes are right, not merely for tactical reasons, but because by doing so concrete goals can be achieved. *"Beser a klenerer foygl in der hant vi an odler in di volkns"* (better a sparrow in the hand than an eagle in the clouds), said Cahan, quoting an old Yiddish proverb.

At the same time, the stubborn optimism of the *Forward* did not wane. All during 1935, the paper reported on the ostensible successes of the on-again and off-again boycott of German goods. To take one example, on February 2, 1935, the *Forward* reported that "no one can any longer deny that . . . boycott and general hatred of the whole world have brought Germany to the verge of economic catastrophe, decline of trade and general hunger." The same continued into 1936, even as Hitler, whatever the failures of some of his policies, was ever more firmly in control. I cite one example, from the May 9, 1936, issue of the *Forward*:

> All the reports from all proletarian parties and groups that have reached us from Germany say much the same thing: National Socialism no longer is the hope of large sections of the small bourgeoisie, its credibility has fallen perceptibly. . . There is huge

disenchantment of the non-proletarian masses in the cities and countryside. . . . Opposition groups have sprung up among peasants, artisans, small traders, employees and intellectuals. . . There have been sabotage acts and strikes both among workers and peasants.

VII

There was yet another subject that preoccupied the Jewish socialist press, along with the socialist press in general, and that was the role played by the German Communist Party (KPD) at that time. What, to begin with, was the *Frayhayt*'s response to the rise of Hitler?

The roots of the Jewish socialists' misperception of Hitler's real nature, as I mentioned before, lay largely in their faith in Germany's *Zivilisation*, and even more so in the strength and wisdom of the German Social Democratic movement. In turn, the reasons why the Social Democratic Party failed to deal forcefully, which is to say by force, with the Nazi challenge—to put it succinctly—were the party's obsessive commitment to moderation and compromise, its aversion to bloodshed and revolutionary upheaval.

In addition, the Social Democratic leaders were convinced that a frontal attack on the Nazis would spell the end of their party and of the trade unions, and would lead in turn to the immediate establishment of a fascist dictatorship; a belief that by late 1932 was probably correct, but questionable between 1930 and 1932. Finally, the Social Democrats were understandably wary of pursuing tactics used by the Communists, and even more so of any actions undertaken jointly with the Communist Party of Germany (KPD), whether *ad hoc*, or under the guise of one or another of those "united fronts" championed by the Communist International in the 1920s.

Why "understandably?" For an answer to this question, a brief historical digression is in order.[16] Since 1928, the Comintern (and that of course meant eventually all Communist parties) followed the so-called "Third Period Theory," which stipulated that after the first "two periods" in the history of the Comintern, the time had come for Communists to launch the all-out revolutionary struggle aimed at overthrowing the bourgeoisie and setting up a "dictatorship of the proletariat."

Part of this strategy was to combat Social Democracy in all its forms, on the theory that the Social Democrats had now become "social fascists"—"socialist in words and fascist in deeds." Indeed, socialism was even more dangerous than plain fascism, and the left Social Democrats more dangerous than the right-wing "social fascists," inasmuch as they *pretended* to be more revolutionary, while in effect being nothing but obedient "tools of fascism."

In 1930–1932, this new orientation meant savage attacks on the Social Democrats, and the branding of the Center-Right government under Heinrich Brüning as a species of fascism, in no way better than Hitlerism. Every victory of the Nazis hastened their final collapse and the triumph of communism. The overwhelming Nazi success in the September 1930 election was greeted by the Communists as the high watermark of the National Socialist movement. There was no goal more urgent than the destruction of the Social Democratic Party (SPD).

In the spring of 1931, the Nazis launched a campaign for a referendum to overthrow the Prussian provincial government, dominated by the Socialists. After a while, the Communists collaborated with the Nazis. If they succeeded, the Nazis would be the victors and the Social Democrats the losers. But that was precisely what the struggle against the "social fascists" amounted to.

Two questions have preoccupied historians of this period: First, to what extent was the anti-social-fascist line Stalin's brainchild? And second, was it actually aimed at bringing the Nazis into power on the assumption that this would hasten a proletarian revolution, that is, a Communist takeover?

The first question, it seems to me, can be easily answered: The Comintern by the end of the 1920s was firmly in Stalin's hands. All his adversaries on the right and the left had been eliminated, and Stalin was as much master of the Soviet Union as he was of its instrument, the Comintern. Given, moreover, Stalin's murderous hatred of the Communists' chief rivals, the Social Democrats, there can be little doubt that it was he who inspired and presided over the whole anti-social democratic enterprise.

It is also indisputable, as the historians Robert Tucker and Karl Dietrich Bracher have shown, that the policy of *de facto* collaboration with the Nazis played into Stalin's calculations. In 1932, the head of the Soviet news agency TASS told the counselor of the German Embassy in Moscow, Gustav Hilger, that the Soviet press had been ordered not to give the appearance of interfering in German affairs. Clearly, the TASS official spoke not for himself, but for Stalin.[17] Immediately after the Nazi victory, Stalin renegotiated the German-Russian trade agreement that had expired in 1931, and for months afterwards did not mention anything about the new regime nor about its persecution of Communists.

The second question cannot be definitely settled, but there is evidence that Communist leaders "advised" their German comrades to concentrate their fire on the "social fascists." A few examples will suffice:

In the autumn of 1932, the attaché of the Soviet Embassy in Berlin, Vinogradov, was asked by a leading SPD member, Friedrich Stamper, as to whether some form of collaboration between the SPD and KPD was feasible. His answer, however indirect, was clear: "Moscow is convinced that the road to Soviet Germany leads through Hitler." After which he indicated that the conversation had come to an end.[18]

Another example concerns the Communist leader Hermann Remmele, who in a speech delivered in the *Reichstag* declared: "Let Hitler take office—he will soon go bankrupt and then it will be our day."[19]

Finally, Gerhard Obuch, a Communist *Reichstag* deputy, who, when a *Reichstag* deputy criticized him for following tactics that were helping the Nazis attain their goals, replied with disarming cynicism:

Dear *Kollege*, that is just what we want! Our strategy must be such that first of all the Right comes to power. The whole body of workers will unite in opposition to this government. Nazi rule will not be long. It will soon collapse, and the heirs will be ourselves.[20]

In an article published in the *Morgn zhurnal* after Hitler's accession to power, a writer by the name of A. Goldberg wrote bluntly that the "worst enemy of Communism is stupidity . . . You need not have been a genius like Trotsky to see that fascism was coming to power." Stalin's order that Communists attack the Social Democrats as the main danger "was indeed remarkably stupid, and it played straight into Hitler's hands . . . Yet had the Communists not in effect helped Hitler, he would not have come to power."[21]

Whether a united Socialist-Communist front, had it been organized not in the last moment, but already by 1932, would have stopped Hitler is difficult to say, though some historians are confident that it would have. What should be clear, however, is that the Communist strategy, aside from its iniquitousness, was remarkably stupid. Yet it was pursued with a vengeance by the German Communists, and also by all other Communist parties. Trotsky, from his exile in Turkey, published dire warnings, convinced as he was that the Communist strategy would lead to Hitler's victory. Many Communists, too, expressed grave reservations, especially those who had belonged to the former "Right Opposition," such as Heinz Neumann (who for his opposition to Stalin was later to be executed in the cellars of the Lubianka).

As the Yiddish saying has it, "*azoy vi s'kristlt zikh, azoy yidlt zikh.*" *Frayhayt*—to return to the Yiddish press in the United States—illustrated this adage perfectly. In fact, almost the entire body of writings in the *Frayhayt* relating to the Nazis and Hitler's rise to power turns on the question of the "social fascists" and the putative successes of the KPD.

I have gone through three years of the *Frayhayt* and found not a single piece of writing that attempts to come to grips with the nature of the Hitler menace, with the historical and social roots of Nazism, or with the reasons for the Nazis' maniacal anti-Semitism. Nor did any contributor to the *Frayhayt* attempt to analyze the similarities and differences between Italian fascism and Hitlerism. All these subjects were aired in the *Forward* as well as in all the other Yiddish publications at that time, often presenting different points of view.

Not so the *Frayhayt*. There, the same simplistic formulas and the same themes appeared time and again, without any deviation whatsoever. The rise of the Nazis, the Stormtroopers' brutality, and its anti-Jewish component were all duly noted by the *Frayhayt*. But all this was secondary to the reports about putative Communist "successes" and the "crimes" committed by the "social fascists."

Thus, the September 14, 1930, elections that brought the Nazis into prominence were hailed by P. Novik in the *Frayhayt* as a prelude to the overthrow of capitalism in general. "The German Social Democracy," said the writer, "is today the main column of German capitalism." In 1931 the newspaper published virtually no articles on Germany, and in 1932 the only pieces relating to Germany dealt with the "treacherous" activities of the Social Democrats.

To be sure, the behavior of the Social Democrats, especially their obsession about moderation *über alles*, was not above criticism.[22] The KPD's policies, however, were altogether unscrupulous and—in the end—calamitous.

By the time Hitler was firmly in power, the "Third Period" tactics were partially abandoned, and the Communists decided to press again for combined Socialist-Communist actions, leaving out, of course, the "treacherous" leaders. This was the so-called tactic of a "united front from below." In Berlin and other towns, for instance, the Communists called for SPD rank-and-file members to join in strikes and other mass actions.

The Socialists remained cool to these overtures. The reason is not hard to fathom. The Social Democrats had just gone through several years of being stigmatized as even worse "fascists" than the Nazis. Why fall for the "united front" blandishments again? In retrospect, a show of strength with or without the Communists, might have helped to save the German Social Democracy from its reputation of self-defeating timidity. But by March 1933, the physical fate of the party had already been sealed.

For about two years, then, the pages of the *Frayhayt* were filled with stories about how the SPD leaders deliberately repulsed the KPD offers for collaboration in order, as the paper put it on July 22, 1935, "the better to serve capitalism." In January 1935, Karl Kautsky published in Prague a brochure trying to justify the lack of militant action on the part of the SPD, and its refusal to collaborate with the Communists, on the ground that by doing so the SPD would become little more than a tool of the Communists. In its report on the booklet, the *Frayhayt* distorts the contents of the brochure, attributing to Kautsky the view that Hitler's victory at the polls was "a natural disaster" that no human act could alter.[23] Of course, Kautsky said no such thing.

VIII

Earlier, I quoted a Yiddish saying to suggest that the *Frayhayt* replicated *The Daily Worker*. In fact this description is not entirely accurate.

To be sure, there were no substantive differences between the *Daily Worker* line and that of the *Frayhayt*. With one exception: the contributors to the latter came from the same cultural and political background as those that wrote for the *Forward, Der Tog*, and *Morgn zhurnal*. Which is to say, they were all East European Jews; some of them, in fact, former Labor Zionists or, like the editor, M. Olgin, former Bundists.

Indeed, in some respects the Yiddish-speaking Communist movement in the United States had much in common with other organizations like the Workmen's Circle. That Jewish fraternal order, allied to the Communist Party, also ran Yiddish schools, maintained a Yiddish-speaking camp for children and a variety of cultural activities in the Yiddish language. In addition, from the late 1920s until the late 1930s, the *Frayhayt* counted among its contributors some of the most illustrious Yiddish literary figures of the time, including H. Leivick, Moishe Leib Halperin, Joseph Opatoshu, Peretz Hirshbeyn, Kadye Molodovsky and others. These were not Communists but, like so many of their colleagues among English-speaking American intellectuals, fellow travelers.

All of them, then, Communists and sympathizers, were Jews and were committed to secular Jewish values. And so, whatever their loyalties to the gospels of communism, they were particularly horrified by what was happening to Jews in Germany and in other countries in Eastern Europe, such as Poland and Romania. The non-Jewish communists, too, were appalled by the rampant anti-Semitism of the fascists and Nazis, but not to the same extent.

I have compared the *Frayhayt* and *The Daily Worker* during the period 1935–36, and found that while the general line of both papers was the same, the *Frayhayt* did, in fact, publish many items of specific Jewish interest. This was true before Hitler, and became particularly pronounced once the Nazis came to power. For many Jewish Communist apparatchiks (and I have in mind many of the *Frayhayt* editors and writers), loyalty to the Communist cause and ardent belief that Moscow was *by definition* always right, and should therefore be supported no matter what, were stronger than their commitments to Jewish values. To others, both the fellow-traveling intellectuals and rank-and-file Jewish Communists, it was the other way around. This became obvious several years later, in August 1939, when the news of the Hitler-Stalin pact was suddenly sprung on an unsuspecting world.

An account of this event, as well as of the subsequent two years and then the German attack on Russia, does not belong, properly speaking, in this paper. Yet that period helps to underline the unique Communist and

Jewish Communist response to Nazism. Even by 1939, when the world was being swept into an inferno, the Communists were unable to loosen their ideological shackles. Suppressing whatever doubts they must have had, abjuring both reality and logic, they continued on their path of pre-varication and self-deception. Fascism became, for better or for worse, "a matter of political views."[24] A war against fascism became a strictly intra-mural affair between two rapacious capitalist systems—and then, overnight, again a struggle for freedom and democracy. The Soviet Union would not pull the chestnuts out of somebody else's fire,[25] but when the Red Army did eventually enter Western Ukraine and Belorussia, it was above all to protect the inhabitants of those lands from the Polish exploiters; and above all to offer succor to two million Jews who had been bitterly persecuted by the Polish fascists, and were now subjected to Nazi depredations. Thus all Communist publications, and thus *Frayhayt*, too.[26]

After the Nazi-Soviet Pact in August 1939, many Communists, espe-cially writers, artists, and the like, defected from the party. But when most Yiddish writers abandoned the ranks of the faithful, as nearly all of the most famous of them did, they became, as of then and retroactively, rene-gades. In January 1940, the Communist Yiddish monthly *Yidishe kultur* (Jewish Culture), founded in 1938, responded to the critics who wondered why the journal had not said anything about the Soviet-German Pact by saying that a cultural journal had no business interfering in matters of for-eign and international politics. Barely two years later, after the attack on the USSR, *Yidishe kultur* and *Frayhayt* discarded their old scruples and began to take a vigorous interest in international affairs. International pol-itics—now that the Soviet Union had been attacked by Germany—became a burning issue, erstwhile assertions notwithstanding.

And what about Social Democrats? In the early 1930s, Social Democrats had been "social fascists." Later they became likely candidates for a "united front" ("from below," that is). When Ribbentrop and Stalin shook hands on August 24, 1939, Social Democrats again became allies of capitalism, except that this time the word "fascism" was no longer to be used. In June 1941, Social Democrats and other enemies of the Nazis became once more putative partners in the struggle against fascism.

Among the Jewish Communists, the pain and grief over the Nazi war against the Jews was no doubt real, and they showed it on many an occa-sion. But in the end the grief was less important than the service to the ideal represented by the leader of the world proletariat, the Soviet Communist Party.

Did the reaction of, on the one hand, the Jewish Socialists, and on the other, the Jewish Communists, affect their subsequent response to the Final Solution? The answer is that it did. The failure to appreciate the full dimension of the Hitler catastrophe was still perceptible in 1940–41. The failure of the Jewish community to put their differences over a Jewish Homeland aside in order to at least *try* to save as many Jews as possible from the maws of Germany, or to persuade the Allies to bomb Auschwitz, or demand that the United States open its doors to Jewish refugees—all this had a beginning, it seems to me, in the inadequate perception of the Hitler menace in the 1930s.[27]

The Socialists contributed to this misperception with their myths, though as I indicated earlier some of those myths began to wane as time went on. The Communists were so mired in *their* myths that they hardly realized that civilization as a whole was on the verge of extinction. Thus it was that as the Nazis were marching to power, few (including the Jews) could see the writing on the wall.

Notes:

1. The anarchist press, represented by the weekly *Fraye arbeter shtimme* (The Free Voice of Labor), and that of the "Territorialists," *Oyfn shvel* (On the Threshhold), were relatively insignificant, which is why I left them out of this survey. For material on *Der Tog* and *Morgn zhurnal*, see H. Feingold, *Bearing Witness—the Holocaust, America and the Jews* (Syracuse: Syracuse University Press, 1995).

2. *Forverts*, Jan. 25 and 26, 1932.

3. This is not to say that the left-wing American journals failed to take note of the Hitler phenomenon. Their rhetoric, however, often rising to heights of indignation, was not grounded in Marxist but in ethical considerations. Thus Reinhold Niebuhr on the fascists: "As unprincipled a group of political demagogues and freebooters as ever preyed upon a people" (*The Nation*, Oct. 1, 1932); "tyranny without parallel in our times" (editorial, ibid., April 12, 1933); on Hitlerism: "that foul, sadistic, self-exculpatory myth [that holds] that the pure, innocent, blond, blue-eyed

Nordic has been betrayed into defilement and shame by the woolly haired, uncreative, lecherous Mediterranean . . ." ("Germany's Lowest Depths," by Ludwig Lewisohn, *The Nation,* May 3, 1933). Left-wing periodicals powerfully condemned the ideology of the far right, as well as the orgy of anti-Semitism that spread throughout Germany, but would seldom try to analyze their social and economic roots.

4. *Forverts,* March 6, 1933.

5. *Forverts,* Sept. 25, 1930.

6. *Forverts,* 1932.

7. *Forverts,* September 1932.

8. *Forverts,* June 11, 1934.

9. *Forverts,* June 25, 1934.

10. Erich Matthis, "The Social Democratic Party," in *The Path to Dictatorship, 1918–1933—Ten Essays by German Scholars* (New York, 1966), p. 61.

11. *Forverts,* May 15, 1933.

12. On exclusion from higher education, see Gordon A. Craig, *Germany 1866–1945* (New York, 1978), p. 632.

13. In 1934, for instance, the principal German Jewish defense organization founded in 1893, the Central Association of German Citizens of the Jewish Faith (*Centralverein von deutscher Staatsbürger jüdischen Glaubens*) thus expressed its determination to remain passive in the face of the Nazi attacks: "With dignity and courage we shall know how to bear upon the soil of our homeland the measures inflicted by Germans upon Germans." This led many Jews like Ludwig Lewisohn to brand German Jews as

> the first time in history of persecution in which the persecuted have sold out spiritually to their oppressor at the latter's invitation and command. They have eviscerated themselves; they have for generations excluded from their consciousness all Jewish content and from their political lives all Jewish bindings. They are in fact today as Germanized as it is possible for them to be and have nothing within them wherewith to bear their Jewish fate. Lewisohn, op.cit.

Today we know that German Jews were not quite as craven and defeatist as Lewisohn thought but at that time such sweeping condemnations were not rare.

14. [**Editor's note:** The controversial Transfer (*Haavara*) Agreement did function from summer 1933 until it petered out just before the outbreak of war in 1939. Ultimately, over a third of the German Jews who emigrated to Palestine during that period made use of the Transfer Agreement to be able to bring out a portion of their otherwise blocked property. Millions of dollars worth of capital was thus brought into Palestine, invigorating the economy and enabling the immigration of many other poorer Jews. Nevertheless, there was tremendous political controversy among Jews, both in America and in Palestine, over a Zionist project apparently helping Germany to export its goods through Palestine, even though it might help some Jews establish new lives in the future Jewish National Home. Even the Jewish Agency tried to avoid taking a clear stand on the issue until 1935, when the Zionist Congress formally decided that the Jewish Agency was to recognize the Transfer Agreement. See Leni Yahil, *The Holocaust* (New York, 1991), pp. 100–104.]

15. May 17, 1934.

16. For a detailed exposition of the Comintern, KPD, and Soviet policies during this period, see Franz Borkenau, *World Communism,* 1939, pp. 332–357; Isaac Deutscher, *The Prophet Outcast* (third volume of his biography of Trotsky), 1963, pp. 3–40 and 128–144; G.D.H. Cole, *A History of Socialist Thought,* 1961, vol. V, pp. 8–31; Robert C. Tucker, *Stalin in Power* (second volume of his biography of Stalin), 1994, pp. 223–237; and Klaus P. Fischer, *Nazi Germany—A New History,* 1995, pp. 218–266.

17. Tucker, op.cit., p. 232.

18. Tucker, op.cit., p. 230.

19. Deutscher, op. cit., pp.130 and 139.

20. Karl Dietrich Bracher, *Die Auflösung der Weimarer Republik,* 1957, p. 504.

21. *Morgn zhurnal,* 1933.

22. Thus on several occasions the SPD tried to appease the Nazis, by April 1934 even electing a new Central Committee that would presumably be more acceptable to the Nazis. It also refused to use the party's own paramilitary shock troop, the *Schufo*, on the ground that antiparliamentary activity was not justified as long as Hitler "abided by the constitution." A few weeks later this option was foreclosed with more socialists arrested and some of the leaders escaping to Czechoslovakia from where they attempted to direct the activities of their truncated party in Germany.

23. *Frayhayt*, Jan. 11, 1935.

24. Molotov at the Supreme Soviet, Oct. 31, 1939. See Tucker, op.cit., p. 602.

25. Reference to Stalin's statement at the 18th Congress of the Soviet Communist Party, in March 1939: "We must be cautious and not allow our country to be drawn into conflicts by warmongers who are used to having others pull chestnuts out of the fire for them." See ibid., p. 587.

26. It would take me too far afield to discuss the *Frayhayt*'s shifts and zigzags in late 1939, but a few examples are in order. Until the Soviet troops entered Western Belorussia and Ukraine on September 17, 1939, the *Frayhayt* (following *The Daily Worker*'s lead) had little to say about the German march on Poland. On September 18, *Frayhayt*'s banner headline proclaimed: "Soviet Army Welcomed with Joy by Jews, Poles, Ukrainians, and Belorussians." A separate article was headlined "A Million Jews Saved from Hitler's Hands!" On p. 19, the paper carried reports on "mass meetings" throughout the Soviet Union praising the Soviet government for freeing "Jews and other minorities." On September 20, *Frayhayt* reported that "Ukrainians, Belorussians and Jews exchange kisses with Red Army soldiers and weep with joy." Of special interest to Jews was the report on September 2, that after the liberation of Pinsk, the new authorities immediately opened schools in Yiddish, Polish, Belorussian and Ukrainian.

Also, while Polish anti-Semitic policies were of little concern to the *Frayhayt* before September 17, they now became a major topic, with articles stating that in Poland Jews were oppressed economically and politically, and had no opportunity to develop their culture, whereas now they are free to enjoy all the benefits granted to all "brotherly nations" by the Soviet government. (See, e.g., "What Was in Fact the Polish Republic?" by Yehuda Polonski, *Frayhayt*, September 23, 1939.) A "first" was a report entitled "Warsaw Jews Say Kol Nidre on the Barricades;" this was shortly before Warsaw fell to the German troops. (*Frayhayt*, September 24.)

27. See Henry Feingold, op.cit.; Haskel Lookstein, *Were We Our Brothers' Keepers?—The Public Response of American Jews to the Holocaust, 1938–1944* (New York: Hartmore House, 1985); and David S. Wyman, *The Abandonment of the Jews—America and the Holocaust, 1941–1945* (New York: Pantheon Books, 1984.)

WE KNEW:
America's Newspapers Report the Holocaust

Ron Hollander
Montclair State University

We knew.

Despite self-protective myths to the contrary, the American newspaper reading public during the Second World War knew early and in excruciatingly explicit detail of the systematic extermination of the Jews of Europe.

This paper, excerpted from a forthcoming book, *We Knew: America's Newspapers Report the Holocaust,* surveying mainstream newspapers from 1941 to 1945 for their reporting of the Final Solution, documents that although coverage was inconsistent, news of the mass destruction of the Jews came early, prominently and widely to America.

At a time when the United States Holocaust Memorial Museum in Washington continues to break its own attendance projections, and "Schindler's List" has played even in China, amid America's self-congratulatory rhetoric on its role in "liberating" the concentration camps, it is well also to remember that *we knew.*

Not just in 1945 when we stumbled unpreparedly upon Dachau and Buchenwald while chasing the retreating Germans. But for at least the last three years of the war, while 3.5 million Jews were being murdered, *we knew.*

And not merely that the Jews of Europe were having a rough time. Or that tens or even hundreds of thousands had been shot, along with many others, by the indiscriminately brutal German occupiers.

But from 1942 on, we knew that the Germans were systematically exterminating specifically the Jews using gas chambers and crematoria. Nor was it just President Franklin Roosevelt and State Department officials with access to secret cables who knew. The American public itself

41

read in its morning and evening papers that the Jews were being wiped out.

The myth that we have nurtured in the intervening half-century—and that was fostered at the time—is that Americans, the ordinary man and woman on the street, first learned of the Final Solution in April and May 1945, when Fox-Movietone newsreels showed the walking skeletons and the bodies stacked like cordwood. (Anon., *PM*)

"Nazi Bestiality Revealed" and "Nazi Murder Mills" intoned the narrators who in fact were not even describing the extermination camps of Poland, but the "mere" concentration camps of Germany.

Broadcasting for CBS from Buchenwald on April 15, 1945, Edward R. Murrow spoke as if he were breaking the news for the first time. "I pray you to believe what I have said about Buchenwald," Murrow begged his presumably skeptical audience. "Murder had been done at Buchenwald." (Murrow)

Three days later *The New York Times* reported from the camp, "Not until today has the full import of the atrocities been completely felt." (Currivan) General Dwight D. Eisenhower was so shocked by what he found in what several inmates described as the best concentration camp in Germany that he cabled home for senators and representatives to come see what he had discovered.

On April 22, 1945, Representatives Gordon Canfield of New Jersey and Henry "Scoop" Jackson of Washington, among others, toured Buchenwald. Two days later, Kentucky Senator and future Vice-President Alben Barkley arrived. From all came stunned expressions of "we had no idea." (United Press, 3) *The Philadelphia Inquirer* four days later summed up this inexplicable shock with its headline, "Nazi Horrors Too Awful For Belief." (Boyle)

What else could America claim but that it knew only belatedly of the gas chambers and crematoria? If we acknowledge—even 50 years later—that we did know all along, then how to explain our failure to do anything, to drop intentionally even one bomb on Auschwitz-Birkenau when we were repeatedly bombing factories, including Auschwitz-Buna, only three miles away?

The reality is that by October 1941—two months before Pearl Harbor—the story of the Germans' so-called "resettlement" of the Jews was sent by the Associated Press to papers around the country. *The New*

York Times said it straight out: "NAZIS SEEK TO RID EUROPE OF ALL JEWS". (Associated Press, 10)

And as early as June 1942, the mainstream American press printed stories—not infrequently on page 1—documenting the assembly-line murder of the Jews. Thus, on June 1, a paper as local as *The Seattle Daily Times* ran a bold, capitalized headline across the very top of page 1, above the paper's name: "JEWS SLAIN TOTAL 200,000!" Under the subhead, "MILLIONS DRIVEN TO GHETTOES," the United Press wire service story said, "Adolf Hitler's agents, in the most terrible racial persecution in modern history, have killed at least 200,000 Jews in Russia, Poland and the Baltic States." The article went on to remind readers that Hitler had prophesied to the Reichstag on January 30, 1939, that another world war would result in destruction of the Jews, "and correspondents know that his agents have done everything possible to make the prophecy come true." (United Press, 1)

On June 26, 1942, the *Boston Daily Globe* ran a page 12 story under a three-column headline making clear that the deaths were not random but were the implementation of a specific policy. (Deuss) "A systematic campaign for the extermination of the Jews in Poland has resulted in the murder of more than 700,000 in the past year," read the Overseas News Agency story filed from London.

Four days later, on June 30, 1942, *The New York Times* upped the death total to 1 million. (United Press, 7) In a modest, one-column story on page 7, the *Times* reported, "The Germans have massacred more than 1,000,000 Jews since the war began in carrying out Adolf Hitler's proclaimed policy of exterminating the people." The United Press account said, ". . . the Nazis had established a vast slaughterhouse for Jews in Eastern Europe" and that about one-sixth of the pre-war Jewish population in Europe of 6–7 million "had been wiped out in less than three years."

The *San Francisco Chronicle*'s version of the story added, "The slaughter is part of the Nazis' policy that 'physical extermination of the Jew must from now on be the aim of Germany and her allies'. " (United Press, 2) *The Philadelphia Inquirer* put the figure at 1.1 million in its page 3 headline. (United Press, 3)

Although the news was often displayed prominently in the papers, it was just as often buried. The discrepancy between the enormity of the news—more than 1 million slaughtered—and the "play" *The New York Times* gave its six-paragraph story on page 7 under a tiny, one-column headline, embodies in microcosm the American press's coverage of the Holocaust. The news was there, but not always prominently or consistently displayed.

The stories—while covered—often were downplayed for many reasons. The Final Solution was carried out in secret, deep in German-held Poland, far from the eyes of foreign correspondents. The press had to rely on sources it felt were less verifiable, such as the Polish underground or even escapees from the camps, who were often skeptically regarded as exaggerating their stories to make the Jewish plight seem worse.

There was no precedent for the intentional, continent-wide extermination of a people, and that made the news hard to swallow for editors and readers alike. (Informed by Polish courier Jan Karski in 1943 of the ongoing destruction of the Jews, Supreme Court Justice Felix Frankfurter, himself Jewish, told Karski it wasn't that he didn't believe him, but that he couldn't.) (Laqueur, 3)

The extermination seemed especially illogical and thus unbelievable since in wartime a nation needed all the labor it could get. Why would the Germans kill off good Jewish workers? And why would they expend so much men and matériel to do it while fighting a two-front war? (Survivors have told of freight trains of Jews chugging through on the main line while troop trains loaded with tanks and weapons waited on sidings.)

Also, atrocities against Jews was an old story by the time of the war. The papers had carried enough such stories through the Thirties. (At one point, *Time* magazine referred cynically to the latest " 'atrocity' story of the week.") (Anon., *Time*)

Finally, the press was wary of being suckered during World War II by tales of German atrocities as it had been during the First World War. In that time of the birth of modern propaganda, the papers were full of stories of Germans raping Belgian nuns, chaining them to machine guns and bayoneting babies. Most of them proved false, and when the press started hearing even more bizarre reports from the shrouded Eastern front, it was wary.

Yet the bottom line is that spotty and de-emphasized as coverage might have been on occasion, it was there in compelling detail. As early as June 26, 1942, the Chicago Daily News Foreign Service sent a story from London that its subscriber newspapers across the country carried. The story reported, "Polish sources insist the Nazis are using portable gas chambers . . . at the village of Chelmno, where Jews were crowded 90 at a time into the chamber." (Chelmno, 90 miles west of Warsaw, was the first death camp to start gassing on December 8, 1941, ultimately killing about 300,000 Jews.) (Nichol)

If there was little reason to doubt by mid-1942 that the Jews were being exterminated, there was even less excuse after November and December. For then the news of the Final Solution was not only carried throughout America but was confirmed by the State Department. And the Holocaust was condemned officially by the Allies in an unequivocally clear declaration reported on page 1 of *The New York Times*. (Special to *The New York Times*)

On November 24 and 25, 1942, Rabbi Stephen S. Wise, head of the World Jewish Congress, held successive press conferences in Washington and New York, confirming details of the exterminations that had been smuggled out of Germany and Poland. Combined with similar information released at the same time by the Polish government-in-exile in London, the news was carried nationwide. The *Washington Post* ran the Associated Press story on November 25 on page 6: "2 Million Jews Slain, Rabbi Wise Asserts." (Associated Press, 6)

The *Washington Post*'s story reported that "Wise . . . said that he had learned through sources confirmed by the State Department that approximately half the estimated four million Jews in Nazi-occupied Europe had been slain in an 'extermination campaign.'" An accompanying article described the Jews being jammed into freight cars: "The people are packed so tightly that those who die of suffocation remain in the crowd side by side with those still living," wrote the Associated Press. "Those surviving are sent to special camps at Treblinka, Belzec and Sobibor [where] they are mass-murdered." (Associated Press, 6)

The *New York Herald Tribune* ran the story on the front page with a two-column headline that read: "Wise Says Hitler Has Ordered 4,000,000 Jews Slain in 1942". (Associated Press, 1) In Colorado, the *Denver Post* eschewed the numbers game and simply said, "DEATH FOR EVERY JEW IN EUROPE IS CALLED NAZI GOAL." (Associated Press) The *St. Louis Post-Dispatch* put the story at the top of page 1B with the 4 million figure in the headline. (Associated Press, 1B)

On the same day, *The New York Times*—besides carrying the Wise information—reported that "concrete buildings on the former Russian frontiers are used by the Germans as gas chambers in which thousands of Jews have been put to death." (Wireless) The story detailed "methods by which the Germans in Poland are carrying out the slaughter of Jews [with] trainloads of adults and children taken to great crematoriums at Oswiecim near Krakow." The village of Oswiecim, a half-hour drive from the venerable university city of Krakow, was known to the Germans as Auschwitz.

The pressure of these accumulating reports at last forced the Allies to do officially and publicly what they had resisted doing for months: Acknowledge flat out that they knew the Jews were being exterminated. All the press's previous qualifying of its news reports because the underground sources were unverifiable was removed with the official imprimatur of the Allies' declaration of December 17, 1942.

Issued by the United States, England and the Soviet Union and the governments-in-exile of eight occupied countries, the declaration confirmed unequivocally Germany's "intention to exterminate the Jewish people in Europe" and condemned "this bestial policy of cold-blooded extermination." (Special to *New York Times*)

In lieu of concrete action, the declaration pledged feebly that those responsible would be punished at the war's end. As late as June, 1944, when Jewish groups pleaded for the bombing of Auschwitz-Birkenau or of the rail line to it, the Allied response—even knowing that 12,000 Hungarian Jews a day were being gassed—was that the best way to help the Jews was to win the war and that nothing could be diverted for such "side shows." In the single most disgraceful American document of the war, Assistant Secretary of War John J. McCloy on August 14, 1944, rejected an appeal from the World Jewish Congress to bomb Auschwitz. McCloy's three-paragraph letter said that "such an effort . . . might provoke even more vindictive action by the Germans." (Wyman, 165) Eleven days later McCloy had U. S. Army aerial photographs showing Jews actually lined up for the gas chambers, but he never relented.

The Allied declaration was carried widely. It was front-page news in *The New York Times*. It was on page 3 in the *San Francisco Examiner*, page 4 in the *Los Angeles Times*, page 2 in the *Atlanta Constitution* and page 10 in the *Washington Post*. Other major papers carrying the declaration—though farther back—included the *St. Louis Post-Dispatch*, the *Los Angeles Examiner* and the *New York World Telegram*.

More stories followed, and in January 1943, a Gallup poll asked whether it was true that 2 million Jews had already been murdered. With two years' worth of news reports still to come, almost half of those polled said it was true. The others said they didn't know or that the report was just a rumor. (Stember, 141)

A year later, in December 1944, the *Washington Post* carried the results of another Gallup poll that showed that 76 percent of those questioned believed that "many people" had been murdered in German concentration camps. (Anon., *Washington Post*)

Newspaper readers of the time recall the clarity of the reports even today. "The news was there for all to see," said camp "liberator" Vito Farese, 67, of Short Hills, New Jersey, interviewed by the author in April, 1993. (Farese) A GI drafted in late 1943, he eventually reached Mauthausen and Flossenburg concentration camps. "There's no question in my mind," he said. "You would have to have been pretty oblivious not to know that extermination was being committed. People just turned their backs."

Many reasons account for that. The Holocaust was without precedent. The numbers were staggering. Who could believe that the nation of Schiller and Goethe was gassing even 2 million Jews? Strictly military news took precedence. Editors and readers followed correspondents' eyewitness accounts of the progress of armies and the outcomes of battles, not murky reports of civilian deaths in bizarre circumstances.

Anti-Semitism, too, played a role. In June 1944, a poll asked which groups constituted the greatest "threat" to America. With the war in the Pacific having more than a bloody year still to run, with Americans fighting the Germans in Normandy, and with more than 4.5 million Jews already dead, 6 percent of those polled said the Germans posed the greatest threat to America. Nine percent said it was the Japanese. And 24 percent of those queried said that the greatest threat to America was posed by the Jews! (Stember, 127)

That the extermination of the Jews was reported in detail long before 1945 is incontrovertible. That many learned the news and consciously or not chose to reject it is also true. Journalists no less than ordinary citizens suffered temporary amnesia when it came to the Holocaust. Perhaps the moral consequences of having known and of having done nothing were too great to integrate into the American self-image.

Yet that is the irrefutable, disquieting legacy bequeathed us by America's yellowing newspapers from more than 50 years ago. They constitute an indictment not merely of official American foreign policy, but of mass American moral will to speak up and to act. The more the horrors were revealed, the more firmly did we say, "We didn't know; our hands are clean." Unfortunately, it is not so simple to rewrite history, especially not when the newspapers are there to rebuke us. This is the unwanted bequest to us of the past. We would do well to be guided by it as we survey the world in the present.

With the research assistance of Kristin Cancellieri.

Endnotes:

Anon. "New Yorkers See Death Camps Films and Prescribe 'An Eye for an Eye'." *PM*. 2 May 1945: 15.

———. "Europe." *Time*. 18 Sept. 1939: 59.

———. "Gallup Finds Mass Murders Underestimated." *Washington Post*. 3 Dec. 1944: Sect. II, 2.

Associated Press. "2 Million Jews Slain, Rabbi Wise Asserts." *Washington Post*. 25 Nov. 1942: 6.

———. "Half of Jews Ordered Slain, Poles Report." *Washington Post*. 25 Nov. 1942: 6.

———. "Wise Says Hitler Has Ordered 4,000,000 Jews Slain in 1942." *New York Herald Tribune*. 25 Nov. 1942: 1.

———. "Death for Every Jew in Europe Is Called Nazi Goal." *Denver Post*. 25 Nov. 1942.

———. "Nazis Accused of Plan to Kill 4 Million Jews." *St. Louis Post-Dispatch*. 25 Nov. 1942: 1B.

———. "Nazis Seek to Rid Europe of All Jews." *New York Times*. 28 Oct. 1941: 10.

Boyle, Hal. "Nazi Horrors Too Awful for Belief." *Philadelphia Inquirer*. 26 April 1945: 10.

Currivan, Gene. "Nazi Death Factory Shocks Germans On A Forced Tour." *New York Times*. 18 April 1945: 1+.

Deuss, Edward L. "Mass Murders of Jews in Poland Pass 700,000 Mark; Many Made to Dig Own Grave." *Boston Daily Globe*. 26 June 1942: 12.

Farese, Vito. Personal interview with author, April, 1993.

Laqueur, Walter. *The Terrible Secret* (Boston: Little, Brown, 1980).

Murrow, Edward R. "Report From Buchenwald." CBS. 15 April 1945. [Editor's note: A complete transcript of the report appears in Edward Bliss, Jr., ed., *In Search of Light: The Broadcasts of Edward R. Murrow, 1938–1961* (New York: Knopf, 1967), 91–95.]

Nichol, David M. "700,000 Jews Reported Slain." *Seattle Daily Times*. 26 June 1942: 30.

Special to *The New York Times*. "11 Allies Condemn Nazi War on Jews." *New York Times*. 18 Dec. 1942: 1+.

Stember, Charles Herbert. *Jews in the Mind of America*. (New York: Basic Books, 1966).

United Press. "Jews Slain Total 200,000." *Seattle Daily Times*. 1 June 1942: 1.

———. "War Crimes Group To Inspect Camp." *New York Times*. 25 April 1945: 3.

———. "1,000,000 Jews Slain By Nazis, Report Says." *New York Times*. 30 June 1942: 7.

———. "Nazi Toll of Jews Set at One Million." *San Francisco Chronicle*. 30 June 1942: 2.

———. "1,125,000 Jews Slain by Nazis During War, Spokesman Says." *Philadelphia Inquirer*. 30 June 1942: 3.

Wireless. "Details Reaching Palestine." *New York Times*. 25 Nov. 1942: 10.

Wyman, David S., ed. *America and the Holocaust: Bombing Auschwitz* (New York: Garland, 1990).

When the Facts Didn't Speak for Themselves: The Holocaust in the *New York Times*, 1939–1945[1]

Laurel Leff[2]
Northeastern University

Abstract: Conventional wisdom assumes that Americans did not know about the Holocaust while it was happening. However, over the last two decades, scholars have demonstrated not only that credible reports reached the Allied governments throughout the war about the persecution and ultimately the extermination of the Jews, but also that much of that information appeared in the Jewish press and in daily newspapers. My own research reveals that during the war a story on what was happening to the Jews appeared on average every other day in the *New York Times*. The question then becomes, if all this information was available, why do we think we did not know? This article argues that the placement of news about the Holocaust almost uniformly on inside pages, as well as the failure to highlight it in editorials or in summaries of important events, made it difficult for most Americans to find the facts and to understand their importance. The article concludes that despite the detailed, credible information that was available, the American public actually did not know about the Holocaust while it was happening because mainstream American newspapers never presented the story of the extermination of the Jews in a way that highlighted its importance.

Did Americans know about the Holocaust while it was happening? Not according to the conventional wisdom expressed in popular histories, biographies, and novels. Indeed, the common understanding is that only when Allied troops liberated German concentration camps at the end of World War II were Americans informed that the Nazis had murdered millions of Jews. However, the conventional wisdom is wrong—at least, if what is meant is that information about the death camps was not disseminated until after the war.

Over the last two decades, scholars have demonstrated not only that credible reports reached the Allied governments throughout the war about the persecution and ultimately the extermination of the Jews (Breitman 1998; Feingold 1970; Gilbert 1981; Laqueur 1980; Penkower 1983; Wyman 1984), but also that much of that information appeared in the American Jewish press (Bauer 1968; Grobman 1979; Lookstein 1985), the Protestant press (Ross 1980), popular magazines (Cardozo 1983), and daily newspapers (Lipstadt 1986) and on radio (Fine 1988). My own research on the *New York Times* reveals that during the nearly six years of war in Europe, from September 1939 through May 1945, the *Times* ran 1,147 stories about what was happening to the Jews of Europe, or an average of around 17 stories a month. That means that during the war, a story appeared every other day in the *Times* on the events we now know as the Holocaust.

The events described in those stories included the propagation of anti-Semitic laws in German allied countries; death from disease and starvation of hundreds of thousands in ghettos and labor camps in Eastern and Western Europe; and mass executions in the Soviet Union and mass gassings in Auschwitz, Treblinka, and Maidanek. The articles did not report vague rumors of suspicious origins. For the most part, the *Times*'s stories were detailed, well-sourced accounts of specific, recent events. The stories also indicated that these were not isolated incidents, but part of Germany's attempt to find a solution to Europe's "Jewish problem," which from 1942 on was the Final Solution.

The question then becomes, if all this information was available in the *New York Times*, among other mass-market publications, why does the "we did not know" story persist? How could history textbooks state without qualification, "During World War II, few Americans knew about the existence of death camps. But at the end of the war, when American troops entered the camps, even the toughest soldiers were shocked by what they found" (Hirsch 1993:180). How could scholars, particularly those writing in the first three postwar decades, conclude that Germany's surrender "brought American Jewry the unexpected news that fully 6,000,000 Jews had been exterminated in Hitler's concentration camps"

(Halperin 1961:35)? This is particularly perplexing because, while the academic understanding has changed in the last decade, scholarly reassessment has not been prompted by the disclosure of secret documents buried in government archives or stashed in personal files. Rather, scholars have unearthed news articles in mass-circulation publications—information that presumably anyone could have had access to at the time. It is not as if we now know something we did not have access to then. In fact, what we know now about the dissemination of news of the Holocaust starts with what was circulated then.

My intention, therefore, is to explore how the idea that the information was not available could emerge and persist. There are many possible reasons why the popular version of history has Americans ignorant of the Holocaust until 1945. There is an epistemological explanation: To know something requires more than the dissemination of information; the information must, in Yehuda Bauer's formulation, be believed and internalized (Bauer 1978). There are two obstacles to forming belief: what I would call routine doubts (doubts about whether information is accurate) and existential doubts (doubts about the meaning of information). Both types came into play in considering news accounts of the Holocaust, although they are seldom carefully distinguished.

Many Americans may have had routine doubts, in the sense that they distrusted the accuracy of the information they were reading in their daily newspaper, or they may have had existential doubts, meaning that though they accepted the information as accurate, they could not comprehend such a catastrophe. An encounter between U.S. Supreme Court Justice Felix Frankfurter and Jan Karski, a Polish courier who had been inside the Warsaw ghetto and the Belzec death camp in October 1942, poignantly illustrates the latter possibility. Karski met with Frankfurter and other American dignitaries in August 1943. After Karski finished telling Frankfurter of the abominations he had witnessed, Frankfurter replied that he did not believe him. When Karski objected, Frankfurter added that he did not mean Karski was lying, but that what he had said was too horrible to conceive (Laqueur 1980:3).

So it may be that Americans generally doubted the truth of what they were reading, especially given the widespread assumption that World War I atrocity stories turned out to be little more than propaganda. Or perhaps they reacted as Frankfurter did, not doubting the information's veracity but refusing to accept that reality. Only after liberation, when newsreels and photographs forced them to confront piles of bodies, smoldering crematoriums, and walking skeletons, did the truth sink in.

Another possible explanation is psychological: The popular retelling of Americans' knowledge of the Holocaust may be a form of denial that occurs with cognitive dissonance (Festinger 1957:137, 158). Given the immensity of the horror and the inadequacy of the American response, it was easier after the war to believe that nothing was done to save the Jews because Americans did not know what was going on, than to believe that Americans knew what was going on and did nothing about it (Lookstein 1985:209). To reduce dissonance, Americans either avoided information that would suggest knowledge of the extermination of the Jews or misperceived or disbelieved that information.

A third explanation is sociopolitical: The Cold War quickly eclipsed World War II and delayed for decades a true reckoning with the facts of the Holocaust (Carroll 1997; see also Novick 1999 and Wyman 1996). Some of the first histories of the Second World War, such as *Life's Picture History of World War II* published in 1950, did not mention the extermination of the Jews at all. By the time the accounting came, it was easier to be hazy about what we knew and when we knew it than it would have been in the immediate postwar period.

The epistemological, psychological, and sociopolitical explanations all have merit, but I intend to focus here on another possibility, one that speaks more directly to journalists, particularly those struggling to communicate the truth of contemporary genocide and other horrors. Despite all of the detailed, credible information that was available, the American public in a crucial sense actually did not know about the Holocaust while it was happening because mainstream American newspapers never presented the story of the persecution and extermination of the Jews in a way that highlighted its importance. As documented more fully below, in 2,077 days of war in Europe, what was happening to the Jews was never the lead story in the *New York Times*, even when American troops liberated the Buchenwald and Dachau concentration camps. The story of the Holocaust—meaning articles that focused on the discrimination, the deportation, and ultimately the destruction of the Jews—made the *Times* front page only twenty-four times, or about once every three months, and never did front-page stories appear back to back or did one follow another over a span of a few days. Even when the Holocaust made the *Times* front page, the stories obscured the fact that most of the victims were Jews. So newspaper-reading Americans may have been aware that millions of civilians had been murdered during the war without connecting those deaths to the distinctly Jewish Holocaust. In addition, the *Times* only intermittently and timidly editorialized about the extermination of the Jews, and the paper rarely highlighted it in either the *Week in Review* or the magazine section. It is not surprising, therefore, that the Holocaust did not penetrate Americans' wartime consciousness.

This claim is subtly but significantly different from the idea that Americans did not "know" about the Holocaust because they did not believe the stories they read. An encapsulation of that position can be found in Deborah Lipstadt's important book, *Beyond Belief: The American Press and the Coming of the Holocaust, 1933–1945*. Since the onset of Nazi rule, Americans had greeted almost all of the news of Nazi Germany's persecution of the Jews skeptically. Inevitably, their first reaction was to question whether it was true. Before, during, and even after the war, many Americans, including those associated with the press, refused to believe the news they heard. (1986:240)

My argument is not that Americans grasped information about the Holocaust and then rejected it, but that they were never given the information in a form that enabled them to grasp it at all. To return to Bauer's formulation, how information is disseminated determines whether the public is even in a position to believe and internalize it. My contention is that the majority of Americans during the Holocaust were not in that position. This difference is important in understanding the press's responsibility. If the public, conditioned by World War I atrocity reports, refused to believe the reports of the Holocaust; or if the public, encountering genocide for the first time, could not grasp its full meaning; or if the public, paralyzed by its inability to change the outcome, would not look at the reality, the press is less responsible. However, if the public never encountered the facts in order to reject them, journalists bear more of the burden of the American public's ignorance and more of a duty to change its approach to covering genocide.

The scant and not wholly reliable public opinion data from that period do suggest a public more ignorant than incredulous. A Gallup poll taken on January 9, 1943, as much as invites skepticism, asking, "It is said that 2 million Jews have been killed in Europe since the war began—Do you think that is true or just a rumor?" Still 48 percent of those asked said they thought it was true, while 28 percent said it was a rumor, and 24 percent had no opinion. Nearly two years later, on December 4, 1944, the Gallup poll asked, "Do you believe the stories that the Germans have murdered many people in concentration camps?" Seventy-six percent of respondents replied "yes," 12 percent said "no," and 12 percent had no opinion. When those responding "yes" were asked for their "best guess" about how many had been murdered, only 6 percent guessed the accurate estimate of two to six million. By May 20, 1945, when news stories about the concentration camps had been more prominently displayed in American newspapers, the percentage of Americans who believed that the "Germans have killed many people in concentration camps or let them starve to death" rose slightly to 84 percent. But on average, the respondents said one million had been killed (Gallup 1972), when the number was many times that.

Of course, it is difficult to reach unequivocal conclusions about why the public is informed—or in this case was ill informed—about any event, as the extensive literature on the press's role in setting the agenda for public issues demonstrates. A news story can appear on the front page and not be read; it can be read but not understood; it can be read, understood, and yet not remembered. Trying to understand ignorance of a calamitous event like the Holocaust is even harder. The facts can be read, understood, remembered, and still not register in a profound way. More than fifty years later, the deliberate murder of nearly six million people continues to generate existential doubt, although only the deranged or hard-core anti-Semites would say they do not believe it occurred. My claim, however, is that for most Americans during the war, the more profound questions of understanding and accepting genocide did not arise. Given the minimal attention even a newspaper like the *Times*, with a commitment to foreign affairs and a large Jewish readership, gave to the Holocaust, the public may simply not have registered the facts about the Holocaust, even though they were publicly available. Rather than contradict the psychological and sociopolitical explanations, this argument augments them. Since the story of the Holocaust did not resonate with the American public as it was happening, it also became easier to "forget" in the face of psychological denial and sociopolitical realities.

I will pursue this argument through an examination of the *New York Times*'s coverage. The *Times* has been singled out for several reasons. First, the *Times* in the 1940s was considered the pinnacle of American journalism. As *Time* magazine wrote on April 12, 1943, "What Harvard is to U.S. education, what the House of Morgan has been to U.S. finance, the *New York Times* is to U.S. journalism." Nothing distinguished the *Times* more than its "far-flung staff of foreign correspondents, certainly the best in the U.S., perhaps in the world." With its commitment to complete coverage of the war despite newsprint shortages (Berger 1951; Diamond 1994) and its high proportion of readers who were first- or second-generation European Jews (Halberstam 1979:213), no newspaper was better positioned to highlight the Holocaust than the *New York Times* (Wyman 1984:321). Even more important, the *Times*'s coverage is likely to have set the standard for other American newspapers. Washington correspondents surveyed in 1944 concluded by more than five to one that the *Times* was the nation's most reliable and comprehensive newspaper (Lipstadt 1986:171). In explaining why the mass media generally failed to draw attention to the extermination of the Jews, David S. Wyman theorizes that "it is possible that editors took a cue from the *New York Times*. Other newspapers recognized the *Times*' guidance in foreign news policy. A perception that the Jewish-owned *Times* did not think the massive killing of Jews was worth emphasizing could have influenced other newspapers" (1984:323).

I will proceed in two parts. First, I will describe some of the more than one thousand stories about the Holocaust that appeared in the *New York Times* to provide an overall sense of the type of information that was available, where it came from, and how reliable it was. Second, I will discuss the placement of these stories in the *Times* and concurrent editorials, news summaries, and magazine articles to make the case that, though the facts of the Holocaust were published, the *Times* never presented those facts in a way that would enable readers to understand their importance.

This two-step analysis might accentuate a paradox implicit in the overall analysis. From the first part, it might be concluded that no reasonably astute reader of the *New York Times* in the 1940s could plausibly claim to be ignorant about the fate of the Jews. On one hand, I am arguing that Americans "knew" about the Holocaust, at least in the sense that detailed information about it was publicly available. On the other hand, I am also arguing, as explicated in the second part, that Americans did not know about the Holocaust because the presentation of that information in the *New York Times* made it difficult to find the facts and to understand their importance. Reading the facts first might tend to exacerbate this paradox because my discussion, by highlighting these stories, does precisely what the *Times* of the period did not do. The second part of my argument becomes more persuasive, however, when it is remembered that the *Times* stories about the Holocaust were almost always separated by a few days, were often no more than a couple of paragraphs long, and were usually placed on inside pages amid thirty or so other stories. The problem was not so much that readers could not understand what was happening from the isolated stories (they could), but that readers would not necessarily focus on the stories because they were not presented in a way that told them they should.

Part I: The Facts

Between September 1, 1939 (when Germany invaded Poland and World War II officially began), and May 31, 1945 (twenty-four days after World War II officially ended), the *New York Times* ran more than one thousand articles that together told the story of the Holocaust as it happened. It seems useful to divide the *New York Times*'s coverage into two periods: from 1939 to 1941, during which Jews were discriminated against, deported, driven into ghettos, and gunned down; and from 1942 to 1945, when Jews were mass-murdered in extermination camps. Only a small fraction of the stories in the *New York Times* about the Holocaust are described here, yet the discussion may still seem a laborious documentation of too many facts. That, however, is part of the point. Only when the breadth and depth of these stories are understood is it possible to state, without qualification, that the facts of the Holocaust were disseminated long before the war ended.

"Freight Cars . . . Full of People": 1939–1941

Less than two weeks after the Germans invaded Poland, a report from the *Times*'s Berlin bureau suggested what might be in store for Europe's Jews. The lead of a September 13, 1939, story on page 5 read:

> First intimations that a "solution" of the Jewish problem in
> Poland is on the German-Polish agenda are revealed in a "special
> report" of the official German News Bureau that emanates from
> Polish territory now occupied by the German military somewhere
> in East Silesia.

Further down, the story stated, "The implications of the 'solution of the
Jewish problem,' were it carried out on the German model, are ominous."

By early October 1939, the *Times* reported that Germany's plans for
the Jews were beginning to take shape; Hitler had declared in a Reichstag
speech that he was considering a "reservation" within the Polish state for
Jews from all over Europe (Oct. 7, 1939, p. 5). Within weeks, the
Germans had begun deportations to this "reservation," and the *Times* had
begun reporting what would be a long litany of communities emptied of
Jews. "2,000 Vienna Jews are en route to a 'reservation' near Lublin,
Poland, between the Nazi and Soviet spheres of influence, it was learned
tonight," the *Times* stated on October 22, 1939 (p. 36). Soon, the Jews of
Bohemia-Moravia were gone (Oct. 25, 1939, p. 2), followed by the Jews
of Sudetenland (Nov. 4, 1939, p. 2), Teschen (Nov. 27, 1939, p. 7),
Galicia (Dec. 27, 1939, p. 7), and Berlin (Oct. 21, 1941, p. 9). Eventually,
the *Times* reported the efforts to rid entire countries of their Jews:
Luxembourg (Oct. 22, 1941, p. 11), Slovakia (June 26, 1942, p. 5), the
Netherlands (July 7, 1942, p. 3), France (July 26, 1942, p. 16), Norway
(Nov. 27, 1942, p. 3), Romania (Feb. 14, 1943, p. 37), Italy (Nov. 12,
1943, p. 4), Greece (May 1, 1944, p. 5), and finally Hungary (May 10,
1944, p. 5).

The accounts of the deportations were often stunningly detailed.
Consider, for example, the saga of the twelve hundred Jews of Stettin, a
city in the northeast corner of Germany, near the Polish border. A Nazi
party official and a policeman first appeared at the doors of eight hundred
Jews, who were told to pack a single suitcase with clothes, take a bundle
of food and cooking utensils, and leave within eight hours, the *Times*
reported on February 14, 1940 (p. 10). A week later, the remaining four
hundred Jews were deported, including the eighty inmates of two Jewish
homes for the aged, the eldest of whom was eighty-six, the *Times* said.
The *Times*'s Berlin bureau then reported the horrifying conditions the

Stettin Jews found upon their arrival in Poland (Mar. 5, 1940, p. 6) and, three weeks later, the fact that two hundred of them were already dead (Mar. 28, 1940, p. 6).

Reporters sometimes watched as the Jews were loaded onto freight cars. On October 30, 1941, the *Times* printed a United Press account of Jews leaving from a "suburban Berlin freight yard today for 'somewhere in Poland'" (p. 6). The unidentified reporter noted that he had to stand two hundred yards from the train, "but from outside the freight yard it was possible to watch the Jews being assembled for the trip." He described an exchange with a Jew about to board:

> Those Jews leaving the yard showed few signs of emotion. One was asked whether the train was made up of passenger or freight cars. Casting a quick glance over his shoulder, he said, "Freight cars—but they are full of people."

Although the stories were pegged to the deportation of an individual community, they also made clear that the exodus was part of Germany's overall plan to rid Europe of Jews. "Before the present hostilities began Chancellor Hitler stated publicly that another war would mean the elimination of the Jews," stated an Associated Press dispatch printed in the *Times* on August 3, 1940 (p. 2). "Now city after city is systematically being cleared of Jews. The latest is the case of Breslau, where all Jews have been ordered to leave by autumn."

The *Times* also traced anti-Semitic legislation in Axis countries, such as Bulgaria's prohibition on Jews using Bulgarian endings for their names (Dec. 21, 1940, p. 4). In Germany, the regulations became petty, even sadistic, during the war, as the *Times* reported. Jews could only shop during certain hours at certain stores and then only for certain foods. Jewish laborers could not be paid for time spent in air-raid shelters (Apr. 3, 1941, p. 4). Jews were ordered to wear a Star of David to identify themselves (Sept. 7, 1941, p. 14) and were then told how and when it was to be worn (Sept. 23, 1941, p. 9). The *Times* reported perhaps the ultimate regulation—a ban on strolling—on July 7, 1942 (p. 3); the rule, the paper explained, reduced "the rights of Jews to zero" and left them only awaiting "deportation to the east."

It was becoming clearer in the *Times* stories what deportation to the east meant. By early 1940, Germany had decided that a reservation in Lublin was not practical and had instead decided to establish ghettos, the *Times* said on January 6, 1940 (p. 2). It reported the establishment of the Warsaw ghetto as it happened (Nov. 20, 1940, p. 7) and noted when the ghetto's wall had enclosed the one hundred or more blocks that constituted the ghetto: "Wall Will Enclose Warsaw Jews Today: 500,000 Begin 'New Life' in Nazi-Built Ghetto" (Nov. 26, 1940, p. 8).

Reports left little doubt about the conditions or the death rate inside those ghettos. As the lead of a September 14, 1941, *Times* story declared,

> The appalling conditions under which some 3,000,000 Polish Jews must struggle to live in 300 ghettos throughout Nazi-dominated Poland are revealed by authoritative statistics received in the United States and made public here yesterday by Dr. Henry Szoskies. Starvation stalks throughout the ghettos and the death rate has been three and to some places to [*sic*] fifteen times the normal mortality rate. (p. 31)

The story stated that a large proportion of the deaths in the Warsaw ghetto were of children between the ages of one and five "who are no longer allowed a daily ration of milk." Adults subsist on a daily bread ration of "three ounces, with occasional handout of a few potatoes and some saccharine." By March 1, 1942, the *Times* reported on page 28 that ten thousand Jews are "dying monthly now of starvation and sickness."

The *Times* also described the conditions of the Jews in Western Europe, most particularly those in France, where the paper had at least four reporters until December 1941. The *Times* not only reported generally on the foreign-born Jews herded into concentration camps in France,[3] but *Times* journalists visited the camps[4] and took photos inside them.[5]

The *Times* carried hundreds of stories during the first three years of war about deportations to Poland, social and economic legislation aimed at Jews, and conditions in ghettos and concentration camps. It published fewer articles, however, about the worst atrocities against the Jews during those years: the roaming bands of *Einsatzgruppen* who, by November 1941, had killed about five hundred thousand Jews in territory the

Germans seized after their invasion of the Soviet Union in June 1941 (Laqueur 1980:67). The comparatively small number of *Times* stories may have been attributable to the lack of information available generally from these areas, which Walter Laqueur described as "virtually cut off from the outside world" (1980:67). The *Times* also may have cut itself off from the information that was available when it decided in July 1937 to cancel its subscription to the Jewish Telegraphic Agency (JTA), a wire service for Jewish-oriented news.[6] Unlike the *Times*, the Jewish press "provided fairly exact accounts of the atrocities committed against the Jews" in the Soviet Union after June 1941, most of which were based on JTA bulletins (Grobman 1979:341).

Still, some stories did appear in the *Times*. The *Times* reported the "machine-gunning of thousands of Hungarian and Galician Jews" in Galicia in August 1941 based on "letters reaching Hungary from Galicia and eyewitness accounts of Hungarian officers who have returned since the deportations ended on August 10, according to information received by reliable sources here." Reports placed "the number of deaths as high as 15,000," the *Times* stated on October 26, 1941 (p. 6).

> Reports tell of victims being machine-gunned as they prayed in synagogues and of being shot as they fled their assailants. The deaths are reported to have been so numerous that bodies floated down the Dniester with little attempt made to retrieve and bury them.

By the spring of 1942, a picture of what had happened in the Soviet Union had emerged, though the number of deaths was understated. "In Latvia, Estonia and Lithuania the killing of Jews amounted to an open hunt, reliable sources have established," the *Times* said in printing a United Press account on May 18, 1942 (p. 4). "Upward of 100,000 met deaths in these Baltic States alone, and more than double that many have been executed in Western Russia." Over two hundred thousand Jews were killed in those three states, and more than a million in the Soviet Union (Gutman 1990:1799).

"A Vast Slaughterhouse for Jews": 1942–1945

The *New York Times*'s contemporaneous reports of the Holocaust did not stop with accounts of Jews deported to Polish ghettos, dying in concentration camps, or massacred in the Soviet Union. Not too long after the Wannsee Conference in January 1942, during which it is generally agreed that Hitler signed off on the Final Solution, the *Times*, along with other news organizations, reported the slaughter of hundreds of thousands of Jews. The *Times* had long reported the Nazis' plan to rid first Germany and then all of Europe of Jews and had made clear that the deportations to Poland were part of that plan, although at first that presumably meant emigration, not extermination (Aug. 8, 1940, p. 11; Feb. 4, 1941, p. 5; Nov. 14, 1941, p. 11). On June 27, 1942, the *New York Times* indicated that the policy had changed. On page 5—tacked onto the bottom of a column of stories that reported an award for finding the slayers of an S.S. leader in Czechoslovakia and the death of eight hundred in reprisal for that killing—appeared a two-paragraph item under the tiny headline "Jews' toll 700,000." Attributing the information to the Polish government-in-exile, the item described the seven hundred thousand Jews slain by the Nazis in Poland as "the greatest mass slaughter in history." Quoting from the government's announcement, the *Times* stated, "[E]very death-dealing method was employed—machine-gun bullets, hand grenades, gas chambers, concentration camps, whipping, torture instruments and starvation." Scholars consider the report, upon which this information was based, both "precise" and "accurate" (Gilbert 1981:40).

Historians have treated as critical the seven months from when the first reports of the extermination of the Jews reached the West in May 1942 (the *Times*'s late June reports trailed the British Broadcasting Corp., which reported the news on June 2), to when the reports were officially confirmed seven months later. They have debated exactly when the world first learned the news (Bauer 1968; Laqueur and Breitman 1986; Penkower 1983) and how officials of the Allied governments responded (Engel 1987; Gutman and Krakowski 1986; Laqueur 1980; Stola 1997; and Wyman 1984). For my purposes, however, what matters is that twenty stories about the Final Solution appeared in the *Times* during the last half of 1942, and as will be seen below, few doubts crept into the news accounts.

The overall aim and unprecedented scope of the murders is not disputed. Just three days after the initial item appeared, on June 30, 1942 (p. 7), the *Times* quoted a World Jewish Congress spokesman as saying that one million Jews had been killed as part of "Adolf Hitler's proclaimed policy of exterminating the Jewish people" and that the "Nazis had established a 'vast slaughterhouse for Jews' in Eastern Europe." Follow-up stories described individual massacres.

Only one of these twenty stories raises questions about the source of the information or the reliability of the numbers. A July 4, 1942, story from the *Times*'s Stockholm bureau noted, "No figures are available here on Jewish massacres in Nazi-occupied areas except those furnished by refugees and occasional newspaper correspondence from Germany. They permit any conclusion one wants to make, from 100,000 to 1,500,000" (p. 4). More typical, however, is a July 2, 1942, story (p. 6) from the *Times*'s London bureau, which stated that a report that "reached London through underground channels" is "supported by information received by other Jewish circles here and also by the Polish government." It quoted Szmul Zygelbojm, a Jewish member of the Polish National Council, vouching for the report's trustworthiness, saying the sources were "absolutely reliable although the story seemed too terrible and the atrocities too inhuman to be true."

The only other signal that the *Times* might have doubted the authenticity of this information was its placement of the stories—uniformly on inside pages. Laqueur speculated,

> If it was true that a million people had been killed this clearly should have been front page news; it did not, after all, happen every day. If it was not true, the story should not have been published at all. Since they [the *Times* editors] were not certain they opted for a compromise: to publish it, but not in a conspicuous place. Thus it was implied the paper had reservations about the report: quite likely the stories contained some truth, but probably it was exaggerated. (1980:74)

The problem with Laqueur's theory, as will be discussed more fully below, is that the *Times* continued to put stories about the Holocaust inside the paper, even after all doubts about their authenticity evaporated. Nor did the total number of stories printed about what was happening to the Jews jump once the information about the Final Solution was verified. The *Times* printed 203 stories about what was happening to the Jews in 1940, 197 in 1941, 149 in 1942, 184 in 1943, and 210 in 1944.

As 1942 progressed, the reports, which initially were provided by the Polish government-in-exile and other Polish officials (July 9, 1942, p. 8;

July 27, 1942, p. 3; Nov. 26, 1942, p. 16), were confirmed by the Jewish Agency in Palestine (Nov. 24, 1942, p. 10), the State Department (Nov. 25, 1942, p. 10), and finally the Allied governments under the moniker of the United Nations (Dec. 18, 1942, p. 1). "If it had still been possible earlier to treat the awful communications emanating from Europe with a measure of hopeful disbelief," David Engel wrote in his 1993 study of the Polish government-in-exile, "by the end of 1942 the threshold of denial had been emphatically crossed" (1993:15).

If belief was the barrier, some change in the coverage might have been expected once that threshold was crossed. What was covered did change, but how it was covered did not. Throughout 1943 and 1944, the *Times* noted the quickening pace of the murders. "In one place in Poland 6,000 Jews are killed daily," the *Times* said on February 14, 1943 (p. 37). It took account of the rising death toll: 3,000,000 on Aug. 27, 1943 (p. 7); 4,000,000 on July 6, 1944 (p. 6); 5,500,000 on Nov. 27, 1944 (p. 14).

Once Soviet troops reconquered Soviet territory and parts of Poland at the end of 1943, American reporters began providing firsthand accounts of the German massacre of Jews. The first reports were out of Russia, such as library clerk Sara Sokola's retelling of the Kharkov massacre of fifteen thousand Jews to *Times* Moscow correspondent Ralph Parker (Dec. 26, 1943, p. 19) or a "poet-partisan's" story of the liquidation of the Vilna ghetto, also told to Parker (Apr. 15, 1944, p. 3).

Reporters, too, traveled to the sites of atrocities. In a few instances, they had doubts about the killings, such as *Times* Moscow correspondent William Lawrence, who could not "judge the truth or falsity" of the Babi Yar massacre when he visited Kiev in November 1943 (Nov. 29, 1943, p. 3). More typically, however, reporters confirmed and embellished what was known. Even Lawrence's doubts disappeared when he went to Maidanek near Lublin, Poland, the first death camp reporters visited. "I have just seen the most terrible place on the face of the earth," wrote Lawrence on August 30, 1944, in a front-page story in the *Times*, "the German concentration camp at Maidanek, which was a veritable River Rouge for the production of death, in which it was estimated by Soviet and Polish authorities that as many as 1,500,000 persons from nearly every country in Europe were killed in the last three years."

The *Times* also reported contemporaneously on events we have now come to think of as emblematic of the Holocaust. It took note of the fifty thousand Jews in Terezin (the Czech name for Theresienstadt) "'dying like flies,'" about whom "all hope had been abandoned" (Sept. 3, 1942, p. 5). The *Times* related, as it was happening, the rescue of one thousand Danish Jews by Danes who rowed them across the "icy Oeresund" to safety in Sweden.[7] When sporadic acts of resistance turned into all-out rebellion in the Warsaw ghetto, the *Times* carried on the April 22, 1943, front page a few paragraphs of the ghetto fighters' Polish radio appeal: "The last 35,000 Jews in the ghetto at Warsaw have been condemned to execution," the radio message printed in the *Times* relayed. "Warsaw again is echoing to musketry volleys. The people are murdered. Women and children defend themselves with their naked arms. Save us." More complete stories of the "furious resistance," however, appeared inside the paper,[8] as did stories on the final liquidation of the ghetto[9] and subsequent stories providing details of the uprising.[10]

The *Times* also reported Auschwitz's central role in the extermination of the Jews. The *Times* first referred to Oswiecim, its Polish name, on March 30, 1941 (p. 9), shortly after the camp opened. The *Times* reported that Jews were being gassed there as early as November 25, 1942 (p. 10), but the full extent of the operations was not reported until June 25, 1944 (p. 5). Two detailed accounts, written by the *Times*'s Berne correspondent Daniel T. Brigham, followed. The lead of a July 3, 1944, story read,

> Information reaching two European relief committees with headquarters in Switzerland has confirmed reports of the existence at Auschwitz and Birkenau in Upper Silesia of two "extermination camps" where more than 1,715,000 Jewish refugees were put to death between April 15, 1942 and April 15, 1944. (p. 3).

The correct number of Auschwitz's dead is probably closer to 1.6 million (Fischel 1998). The story included a country-by-country breakdown of deaths in the camp: nine hundred thousand from Poland, one hundred thousand from the Netherlands, forty-five thousand from Greece, and so on. The method of death was also described:

> These [execution] halls consist of fake bathing establishments handling 2,000 to 8,000 daily. Prisoners were led into cells and

ordered to strip for bathing. Then cyanide gas was said to have been released, causing death in three to five minutes. The bodies were burned in crematoriums that hold eight to ten at a time.

The terrifying reality of Auschwitz was revealed just as Hungary's Jews were being shipped there. "The first act in a program of mass extermination of Jews in Hungary is over, and 80,000 Jews of the Carpathian provinces have already disappeared," Joseph M. Levy, the *Times*'s Ankara correspondent, reported on May 18, 1944 (p. 5), two months after the Germans occupied Hungary. "They have been sent to murder camps in Poland." The *Times* could even trace a group of Jews from Budapest to Birkenau. "Dragged from their beds at 2 a.m., a group of well-to-do Hungarians from Budapest was beaten and ordered to dress and bring a fortnight's food—not to exceed fifty pounds in weight," Brigham wrote in the second of his two stories about Auschwitz (July 6, 1944, p. 6). The Jews then traveled to the ghetto in Wosice, he wrote, followed by a 10-day trip to Birkenau where only 4,000 of the original 5,000 arrived alive.

The *New York Times* stories that appeared in 1945, as the war ended, eerily echoed the stories that appeared as the war began. This time, rather than describing how community after community was being cleared of Jews, the *Times* described how community after community had no, or few, Jews left. "Not 1% of Jews Left in 38 Freed Places," a headline declared on February 19, 1945 (p. 5). The story explained, "The city of Riga, which in 1939 had tens of thousands of Jews and later 100,000 more whom the Nazis deported from the Ukraine, has today only 158. In some towns, as in Dvinsk, not a single Jew was found by returning Soviet armies."

Part II: The Facts Did Not Speak

Why is it so often stated that the American public was not informed about the extermination of the Jews? The conventional explanation—that information was not available—cannot be right. As we have seen, throughout the war the *New York Times* provided the outline of the Holocaust and filled in many of the details. A better explanation can be found in how the press told the story of the Holocaust. This section analyzes the *New York Times*'s placement of stories about the Holocaust and the corresponding coverage in the editorial, magazine, *News of the Week in Review*, and other retrospective sections in an effort to more directly establish the *Times*'s overall assessment of events.

Buried Inside

A newspaper can clearly demonstrate the significance it attaches to a news story (McClure and Patterson 1990:26). It can make the event the lead, day after day, and key several inside stories off it; it can run editorials and magazine pieces that reveal and reinforce the paper's judgment about its importance; it can highlight the story in weekly and yearly summaries of top news events. The *Times* never did this with the extermination of the Jews.

Of the stories described above, only three were on the front page: the Allies' confirmation of the Final Solution in December 1942; the few paragraphs of the radio appeal from the burning Warsaw ghetto in April 1943; and William Lawrence's account of his visit to the Maidanek extermination camp in August 1944. Of the approximately twenty-three thousand front-page stories during the sixty-nine months of the European war (the *Times* averaged eleven front-page stories a day), only forty-two, or just 0.18 percent, were about what was happening to the Jews generally. Nor did the coverage change once news of the extermination campaign was confirmed. The *Times* printed six front-page stories about what was happening to Europe's Jews in each of the years 1940, 1941, and 1943, even though news of the Final Solution was "confirmed" in 1942. In 1942, seven stories appeared on the front page. Only in 1944 did the number climb to ten front-page stories.

If anything, the tiny number of front-page stories about Jews still exaggerates the *Times*'s coverage. What is striking is how few front-page stories deal with the central issue of the Holocaust (only twenty-four) and how many of those (all but six) obscured the fact that the victims were Jews. Rather than the events reported in detail on the inside pages—anti-Semitic legislation, deportations to Poland, death by disease and starvation in ghettos and labor camps, mass machine-gunnings and gassings—the front-page stories were often on peripheral issues. Six were about the persecution of Catholics who defended Jews. Another six stories dealt with events in Palestine, such as "Six Policemen Slain in Palestine" (Mar. 26, 1944). Another two concerned incidents that do not seem to be of much consequence given the overall catastrophe. Two weeks before the

Times mentioned in two paragraphs on page 5 that seven hundred thousand Jews had been murdered, it declared on the front page, "258 Jews Reported Slain in Berlin for Bomb Plot at Anti-Red Exhibit" (June 14, 1942). After the war's end, the *Times* featured this on May 24, 1945: "Streicher, Anti-Semite, Is Seized by Jewish Major from New York."

Even the stories that dealt more directly with the Holocaust did not make clear who was suffering, unlike the inside stories, which almost always clearly identified the victims as Jews. Eight stories were about the plight of refugees (Nov. 1, 1939, Nov. 29, 1939, Mar. 15, 1941, for example), but only one stated that the refugees were Jews: On November 26, 1940, the *Times* described in a ten-paragraph, bottom-of-the-page story the sinking of the *Patria*, a ship trying to reach Palestine "packed to the gunwale with 1,771 wandering, homeless Jews." However, when the *Times* wrote that France was to seize the fortunes of "Rothschild, Louis-Dreyfus and other noted exiles" (Aug. 1, 1940), it never mentioned that they were Jews. Still other stories grouped Jews with other oppressed groups, such as a story titled "Nazis Held Ready to Crush Serb Guerrillas and Jews" (May 11, 1941).

The articles about the liberation of concentration and extermination camps also did not make clear that the victims were overwhelmingly Jewish. Upon first reference, William Lawrence described the dead at Maidanek as "1,500,000 persons from nearly every country in Europe" and later as "Jews, Poles, Russians and in fact representatives of a total of twenty-two nationalities." When James MacDonald wrote on November 13, 1944, about a "death camp" in Vught, the Netherlands, that had nurseries for children inside it, it was not until the thirteenth paragraph on the inside jump that he mentioned Jews: "All Jews who could possibly be rounded up in Holland were brought to this camp."

If American during-the-war information about the Holocaust has been underplayed in popular histories, the *Times* stories suggest that our end-of-the-war exposure may have been overstated. A single-column story appeared in the middle of the front page on April 18, 1945, on Buchenwald, followed two days later by a small front-page AP item, "Germans Must Bury 1,100 Burned Alive" (Apr. 20, 1945), and followed eleven days after that by another AP single-column story on the front page, "Dachau Captured by Americans Who Kill Guards, Liberate 32,000" (May 1, 1945). The few photos that appeared (see Apr. 26, 1945,

p. 13; Apr. 27, 1945, p. 3; Apr. 19, 1940, p. 20) were, given the magnitude of the horror, quite tame. As with other stories about concentration camps, the Jewish nature of the catastrophe was muted. In Gene Currivan's first-person account of Buchenwald, the victims were at first described only as "non-descript prisoners"; it was not clear until the last six paragraphs of a thirty-six-paragraph story that Jews were among the prisoners.

Only six front-page stories directly described the Jewish Holocaust: two stories about Jews' attempts to save their brethren, "Save Doomed Jews, Huge Rally Pleads" (Mar. 2, 1943) and "Rescue at Once of Europe's Jews Demanded at Conference Here" (Aug. 31, 1943); one about the sinking of the refugee ship, the *Patria* (Nov. 26, 1940); one that described the U.N. declaration condemning the "bestial policy of cold-blooded extermination of Jews" (Dec. 18, 1942), which consisted of just four paragraphs summarizing the report, followed by the text of the declaration; one that spelled out the president's warning to Germany issued before the destruction of Hungarian Jewry (Mar. 24, 1944); and the one that contained the poignant cry from the Warsaw ghetto (Apr. 22, 1943).

Think about it another way. You could have read the front page of the *New York Times* in 1939 and 1940 without knowing that millions of Jews were being sent to Poland, imprisoned in ghettos, and dying of disease and starvation by the tens of thousands. You could have read the front page in 1941 without knowing that the Nazis were machine-gunning hundreds of thousands of Jews in the Soviet Union. You could have read the front page in 1942 and not have known, until the last month, that the Germans were carrying out a plan to annihilate European Jewry. In 1943, you would have been told once that Jews from France, Belgium, and the Netherlands were being sent to slaughterhouses in Poland and that more than half of the Jews of Europe were dead, but only in the context of a single story on a rally by Jewish groups that devoted more space to who had spoken than to who had died. In 1944, you would have learned from the front page of the existence of horrible places such as Maidanek and Auschwitz, but only inside the paper could you find that the victims were Jews. In 1945, Dachau and Buchenwald were on the front page, but the Jews were buried inside.

Not one of these stories was considered the most important story of the day. In fact, the single story about Jews that received the most prominent display during the war does not fit comfortably into any of the previously outlined categories. The account of Assistant Secretary of State Breckinridge Long's testimony to the House Foreign Affairs Committee was the only story to appear at the top of the page and to occupy more than a single column. In this December 11, 1943, story, government officials were not reluctant to talk about Jews. The United States has "admitted about 580,000 victims of persecution by the Hitler regime since it began ten years ago," the *Times* wrote, citing Long as the source, and "the majority of the refugees admitted were Jews." Long's figures were disputed at the time, albeit in follow-up stories on the inside (Dec. 12, 1943, p. 8; Feb. 19, 1944, p. 6). No more than 250,000 refugees had been admitted (Wyman 1984:197), and only about 160,000 of those were Jews (Friedman 1973:190). However, that did not erase the page-one headline: "580,000 Refugees Admitted to United States in Decade."

The *Times*'s editorials tracked the front-page news coverage, both in their infrequency and in their tendency to universalize the victims. During nearly six years of war, the *Times* ran only sixteen editorials specifically about what was happening to the Jews out of nearly seventeen thousand editorials, or just 0.09 percent of all editorials. Only once, on December 2, 1942, was the persecution of the Jews the subject of the *Times*'s lead editorial. Perhaps even more than in its news stories, the *Times* ignored the Jews altogether, even when writing about topics that seemed to warrant their inclusion. It wrote about refugees and Europe's "uprooted people" on Nov. 8, 1940 (p. 20) without explaining that many of them were Jews. The *Times* editorialized frequently on conditions in individual countries in German-occupied Europe, including seven editorials on Poland alone, and never mentioned Jews.

Even in the sixteen editorials that mentioned Jewish victims, they were often lumped together with other suffering peoples. "The First to Suffer," the *Times*'s only lead editorial on the Holocaust, stated that "it is believed that 2,000,000 European Jews have perished and that 5,000,000 are in danger of extermination." Still, "Nazism, as we know, never planned to stop at that point," the editorial emphasized. "The Jew was the first number on a list which has since included peoples of other faiths and of many races—Czechs, Poles, Norwegians, Netherlanders, Belgians, French—and which, should Hitler win, would take in our own 'mongrel' nation" (Dec. 2, 1942, p. 26).

Interestingly, the *Times*'s editorials also tend to confirm that the paper's editors did not doubt the accuracy of the horrible news about the Jews, even as they maintained the difficulty of doing anything about it. The *Times* accepted the position of the Allied governments: "The most tragic aspect of the situation is the world's helplessness to stop the horror while the war is going on," an editorial stated.

If the *Times* downplayed the Holocaust in its news and editorial sections, it ignored it almost entirely in two important Sunday forums: the magazine and the *News of the Week in Review*. In the 1940s, the *New York Times Magazine* was intended to highlight and expand upon important news stories and was written mostly by *Times* staffers. Yet the magazine ran only two stories exclusively about the Holocaust, both written by novelists: Sholem Asch's one-and-a-half-page story entitled "In the Valley of Death" (Feb. 7, 1943, p. 16) and Arthur Koestler's "The Nightmare Is a Reality" (Jan. 9, 1944, p. 5).

Perhaps the *Times*'s most striking failure to identify the Holocaust as a story worth caring about came in its *News of the Week in Review* section. This Sunday section ran as many as thirty short items a week, summarizing the week's most important news events, along with longer commentaries mostly written by staff reporters. Only nine of about nine thousand such short items referred to Jews in any context—as refugees, as being involved in the struggle in Palestine, or as victims of persecution and murder. Furthermore, none of the longer commentaries focused exclusively on the plight of the Jews.

Jews featured no more prominently in the *Times*'s summaries of the most important events of each year or in its summary of the war. In six years of "highlights of the year in review," the deaths of thousands and then millions of Jews were mentioned only once, in 1942, and in a way that was itself revealing (Dec. 28, 1942, p. 1E). The Allied governments's confirmation of the "cold-blooded extermination of the Jews" was third on a list of a single day's most important events, preceded by the military's plans to use universities as training grounds and the resignation of a price administrator.

A full page devoted to "outstanding events and major trends of the Second World War," which ran on September 3, 1944 (p. 4E), never mentioned the Jews. After Hitler killed himself, the *Week in Review* on May 6, 1945, ran several stories about his twelve-year reign. But "A

Chronology of the War in Europe: 100 Outstanding Dates" did not include any mention of the Holocaust (p. E5); nor did the "Story of Dachau." The closest this retrospective came to acknowledging the Holocaust was a reference in a story on the "civilian toll":

> The civilian casualties include the millions who have succumbed to disease and starvation or have been murdered in Nazi concentration camps. . . . British civilian casualties from enemy bombings and the robot and V-2 weapons numbered about 145,000. Of Poland's pre-war population of 35,000,000, it is believed that nearly 10,000,000 have perished or 'disappeared'—a large portion of them into Nazi death camps.

A book published after the war may provide the *Times*'s ultimate judgment on the newsworthiness of the Holocaust. *The Story of the New York Times*, an in-house account by staffer Meyer Berger (1951), devoted ninety-two pages of the 565-page book to the *Times*'s coverage of World War II (pp. 433 to 525) and never once mentioned the extermination of the Jews.

The Silenced Scream

If the *Times* did not consider the Holocaust important enough to write about repeatedly on its front page, to hammer home in hard-hitting editorials, to highlight in the magazine or in retrospectives, it is not surprising that most Americans during the war did not focus on the facts of the extermination of the Jews amid a barrage of world-shattering news. The main problem was not that the stories were too few in number. It was not that the stories presented the information in a way that cast doubt upon its credibility. It was not that the individual stories made it easy to grasp isolated events but hard to detect an overall pattern. The story of the Holocaust emerges from these stories. The problem was that the *New York Times* did not inform its readers, through placement, through headlines, through editorials, through retrospectives, that what was happening to the Jews was something they needed to understand. As a result, despite the thousand stories that were printed and the specificity of the information that was available, most Americans may not have known about the Holocaust. The facts of the Holocaust were available to the public, but the facts, no matter how wrenching and revealing, did not speak for themselves.

This lesson reaches beyond the Holocaust. It is not enough to merely cover an event and to set the facts before the public. If the powerful fact of the slaughter of nearly six million people could be lost in the middle of a newspaper, consider how easily less compelling facts can be overwhelmed. The press coverage of the Holocaust reinforces the idea that knowledge is not based merely on the dissemination of facts; knowledge depends upon how those facts are disseminated. But this analysis goes one step farther. The presentation of facts affects not only the process of knowing, but also the process of remembering. The trivializing of catastrophe colors what we think we knew, as well as what we did know. The consistent downplaying of the extermination of the Jews during the war made possible the conditions for collective amnesia after the war. Because the American public never grappled with the information in the *Times*'s one thousand or so stories about the Holocaust when they appeared, it became easy to think they never have.

Consider, finally, this one example. On March 2, 1944, the *Times*'s London bureau reported on the deliberations in the House of Commons over funds for the "20,000,000 homeless Europeans." In the midst of this short, straightforward account of budget debates, came the following two paragraphs:

> During the discussion S.S. Silverman, Labor member, read a report from the Jewish National Committee operating somewhere in Poland, saying:
>
> "Last month we still reckoned the number of Jews in the whole territory of Poland as from 250,000 to 300,000. In a few weeks no more than 50,000 of us will remain. In our last moment before death, the remnants of Polish Jewry appeal for help to the whole world. May this, perhaps our last voice from the abyss, reach the ears of the whole world."

Without skipping a beat, the story continued, "The Commons also approved an installment of 3,963 [pounds] to help the International Red Cross open an office in Shanghai." The scream from the abyss was muffled by the hundreds of other words in the page 4 story, and the thousands of words in the March 2, 1944, newspaper, and the millions of words in the more than two thousand issues of the *New York Times* that appeared during World War II. The Jews' desperate cry was never more than an indistinct buzzing in the world's ears. **The message for contemporary journalists is clear: If the world is to have even a chance to hear, the press must shout.**

References:
Bauer, Yehuda. 1968. "When Did They Know?" *Midstream* 14(4): 51–9.
Bauer, Yehuda. 1978. *The Holocaust in Historical Perspective*. Seattle: University of Washington Press.
Berger, Meyer. 1951. *The Story of the New York Times, 1851–1951*. New York: Simon and Schuster.
Breitman, Richard. 1998. *Official Secrets: What the Nazis Planned, What the British and Americans Knew*. New York: Hill and Wang.
Cardozo, Arlene Rossen. 1983. "American Magazine Coverage of the Nazi Death Camp Era." *Journalism Quarterly* 60(4): 717–18.
Carroll, James. 1997. "Shoah in the News: Patterns and Meanings of News Coverage of the Holocaust." Cambridge, MA: Joan Shorenstein Center on the Press, Politics and Public Policy.
Diamond, Edwin. 1994. *Behind the Times: Inside the New New York Times*. New York: Villard.
Engel, David. 1987. *In the Shadow of Auschwitz: The Polish Government-in-Exile and the Jews, 1939–1942*. Chapel Hill: University of North Carolina Press.
Engel, David. 1993. *Facing a Holocaust: The Polish Government-in-Exile and the Jews, 1939–1942*. Chapel Hill: University of North Carolina Press.
Feingold, Henry L. 1970. *The Politics of Rescue: The Roosevelt Administration and the Holocaust, 1938–1945*. New York: Holocaust Library.
Festinger, Leon. 1957. *A Theory of Cognitive Dissonance*. Stanford: Stanford University Press.
Fine, Joyce. 1988. "American Radio Coverage of the Holocaust." *Simon Wiesenthal Center Annual* 5.

Fischel, Jack R. 1998. *The Holocaust*. Westport: Greenwood Press.

Friedman, Saul. 1973. *No Haven for the Oppressed: United States Policy toward Jewish Refugees, 1938–1945*. Detroit: Wayne State University Press.

Gallup, George H. 1972. *The Gallup Poll: Public Opinion, 1935–1971*. New York: Random House.

Gilbert, Martin. 1981. *Auschwitz and the Allies*. New York: Holt, Rinehart and Winston.

Grobman, Alex. 1979. "What Did They Know? The American Jewish Press and the Holocaust." *American Jewish Historical Quarterly* 68(3): 327–52.

Gutman, Israel, ed. 1990. *Encyclopedia of the Holocaust*, vol. 1. New York: Macmillan.

Gutman, Yisrael, and Shmuel Krakowski. 1986. *Unequal Victims: Poles and Jews during World War Two*. New York: Holocaust Library.

Halberstam, David. 1979. *The Powers That Be*. New York: Alfred A. Knopf.

Halperin, Samuel. 1961. *The Political World of American Zionism*. Detroit: Wayne State University Press.

Hirsch, E.D., Jr., ed. 1993. *What Your Sixth Grader Needs to Know*. New York: Dell.

Laqueur, Walter. 1980. *The Terrible Secret: Suppression of the Truth about Hitler's 'Final Solution.'* Boston: Little, Brown.

Laqueur, Walter, and Richard Breitman. 1986. *Breaking the Silence: The German Who Exposed the Final Solution*. New York: Simon and Schuster.

Life. 1950. *Life's Picture History of World War II*. New York: Time.

Lipstadt, Deborah. 1986. *Beyond Belief: The American Press and the Coming of the Holocaust, 1933–1945*. New York: Free Press.

Lookstein, Haskel. 1985. *Were We Our Brothers' Keepers? The Public Response of American Jews to the Holocaust, 1938–1944*. New York: Vintage.

McClure, Robert D., and Thomas E. Patterson. 1990. "Print vs. Network News." *American Journal of Political Science* 29(1): 23–28.

Novick, Peter. 1999. *The Holocaust in American Life*. Boston: Houghton Mifflin.

Penkower, Monty Noam. 1983. *The Jews Were Expendable: Free World Diplomacy and the Holocaust.* Urbana: University of Illinois Press.

Ross, Robert W. 1980. *So It Was True: The American Protestant Press and the Nazi Persecution of the Jews.* Minneapolis: University of Minnesota Press.

Stola, Dariusz. 1997. "Early News of the Holocaust from Poland." *Holocaust and Genocide Studies* 11(6): 1–27.

Wyman, David S. 1984. *The Abandonment of the Jews: America and the Holocaust, 1941–1945.* New York: Pantheon.

Wyman, David S., ed. 1996. *The World Reacts to the Holocaust.* Baltimore: Johns Hopkins University Press.

Yahil, Leni. 1990. *The Holocaust: The Fate of European Jewry, 1932–1945.* New York: Oxford University Press.

Notes:

1. Originally published in *The Harvard International Journal of Press Politics* 5:2 (Spring 2000), 52–72. Copyright © 2000 by the President and the Fellows of Harvard College and the Massachusetts Institute of Technology. All rights reserved. Reprinted with permission of Sage Publications.

2. I would like to thank Karen Fischer and Jacques Maes for their thorough and thoughtful research assistance; Jeremy Paul and James Ross for their careful and constructive editing; and Nicholas Daniloff for his support.

3. See, for example, Jan. 26, 1941, p. 24 and Feb. 24, 1941, p. 7.

4. March 8, 1941, p. 4; March 24, 1941, p. 6; March 29, 1941, p. 2; March 30, 1941, p. 25.

5. March 31, 1941, p. 5; April 30, 1941, p. 7; May 4, 1941, p. 2.

6. Jewish Telegraphic Agency folder, Edwin L. James Collection, *New York Times* Archives.

7. Oct. 3, 1943, p. 29; Oct. 4, 1943, p. 7; Oct. 5, 1943, p. 6; Oct. 6, 1943, p. 9.

8. April 23, 1943, p. 9; May 7, 1943, p. 7.

9. May 15, 1943, p. 6; May 22, 1943, p. 4.

10. Sept. 25, 1943, p. 6; Oct. 21, 1943, p. 4; Oct. 26, 1943, p. 8; April 19, 1944, p. 5; April 20, 1944, p. 10.

Turning Away From the Holocaust: *The New York Times*[1]

Max Frankel
The New York Times

AND then there was failure: none greater than the staggering, staining failure of *The New York Times* to depict Hitler's methodical extermination of the Jews of Europe as a horror beyond all other horrors in World War II—a Nazi war within the war crying out for illumination.

The annihilation of six million Jews would not for many years become distinctively known as the Holocaust. But its essence became knowable fast enough, from ominous Nazi threats and undisputed eyewitness reports collected by American correspondents, agents and informants. Indeed, a large number of those reports appeared in *The Times*. But they were mostly buried inside its gray and stolid pages, never featured, analyzed or rendered truly comprehensible.

Yet what they printed made clear that the editors did not long mistrust the ghastly reports. They presented them as true within months of Hitler's secret resolve in 1941 to proceed to the "final solution" of his fantasized "Jewish problem."

Why, then, were the terrifying tales almost hidden in the back pages? Like most—though not all—American media, and most of official Washington, *The Times* drowned its reports about the fate of Jews in the flood of wartime news. Its neglect was far from unique and its reach was not then fully national, but as the premier American source of wartime news, it surely influenced the judgment of other news purveyors.

While a few publications—newspapers like *The Post* (then liberal) and *PM* in New York and magazines like *The Nation* and *The New Republic*—showed more conspicuous concern, *The Times*'s coverage generally took the view that the atrocities inflicted upon Europe's Jews, while horrific, were not significantly different from those visited upon tens of millions of other war victims, nor more noteworthy.

Six Years, Six Page 1 Articles

Only six times in nearly six years did *The Times*'s front page mention Jews as Hitler's unique target for total annihilation. Only once was their fate the subject of a lead editorial. Only twice did their rescue inspire passionate cries in the Sunday magazine.

Although *The Times*'s news columns in those years did not offer as much analysis or synthesis as they do today, the paper took great pride in ranking the importance of events each morning and in carefully reviewing the major news of every week and every year. How could it happen that the war on the Jews never qualified for such highlighted attention?

There is no surviving record of how the paper's coverage of the subject was discussed by *Times* editors during the war years of 1939–45. But within that coverage is recurring evidence of a guiding principle: do not feature the plight of Jews, and take care, when reporting it, to link their suffering to that of many other Europeans.

This reticence has been a subject of extensive scholarly inquiry and also much speculation and condemnation. Critics have blamed "self-hating Jews" and "anti-Zionists" among the paper's owners and staff. Defenders have cited the sketchiness of much information about the death camps in Eastern Europe and also the inability of prewar generations to fully comprehend the industrial gassing of millions of innocents—a machinery of death not yet exposed by those chilling mounds of Jews' bones, hair, shoes, rings.

No single explanation seems to suffice for what was surely the century's bitterest journalistic failure. *The Times*, like most media of that era, fervently embraced the wartime policies of the American and British governments, both of which strongly resisted proposals to rescue Jews or to offer them haven. After a decade of economic depression, both governments had political reasons to discourage immigration and diplomatic reasons to refuse Jewish settlements in regions like Palestine.

Then, too, papers owned by Jewish families, like *The Times*, were plainly afraid to have a society that was still widely anti-Semitic misread their passionate opposition to Hitler as a merely parochial cause. Even some leading Jewish groups hedged their appeals for rescue lest they be accused of wanting to divert wartime energies.

At *The Times*, the reluctance to highlight the systematic slaughter of Jews was also undoubtedly influenced by the views of the publisher, Arthur Hays Sulzberger. He believed strongly and publicly that Judaism was a religion, not a race or nationality—that Jews should be separate only in the way they worshiped. He thought they needed no state or political and social institutions of their own. He went to great lengths to avoid having *The Times* branded a "Jewish newspaper." He resented other publications for emphasizing the Jewishness of people in the news.

And it was his policy, on most questions, to steer *The Times* toward the centrist values of America's governmental and intellectual elites. Because his editorial page, like the American government and other leading media, refused to dwell on the Jews' singular victimization, it was cool to all measures that might have singled them out for rescue or even special attention.

Only once did *The Times* devote its lead editorial to the subject. That was on Dec. 2, 1942, after the State Department had unofficially confirmed to leading rabbis that two million Jews had already been slain and that five million more were indeed "in danger of extermination." Even that editorial, however, retreated quickly from any show of special concern. Insisting in its title that Jews were merely "The First to Suffer," it said the same fate awaited "people of other faiths and of many races," including "our own 'mongrel' nation" and even Hitler's allies in Japan if he were to win the war.

In only one 48-hour period, in early March 1943, was the paper moved to concede in multiple ways that Europe's Jews merited extraordinary attention. The impetus apparently came from Anne O'Hare McCormick, the foreign affairs columnist, a favorite of Sulzberger and a member of his editorial board, who thought that a Madison Square Garden rally pleading for the rescue of Jews had exposed "the shame of the world."

"There is not the slightest question," she wrote, "that the persecution of the Jews has reached its awful climax in a campaign to wipe them out of Europe. If the Christian community does not support to the utmost the belated proposal worked out to rescue the Jews remaining in Europe from the fate prepared for them, we have accepted the Hitlerian thesis and forever compromised the principles for which we are pouring out blood and wealth."

Beside her column on March 3, the last of seven editorials allowed that Hitler had condemned the Jews to death "where others are sometimes let off with slavery." Vaguely urging the United States to revise "the chilly formalism of its immigration regulations," it urged other free nations to let no "secondary considerations" bar entry of those refugees who might yet escape from the Nazis' control.

On the previous day, that same Garden rally was described in an exceptional half-page article, beginning with three paragraphs on Page 1 under the smallest of 11 front-page headlines:

SAVE DOOMED JEWS,
HUGE RALLY PLEADS

As never before or after, that day's coverage included long quotations from speeches and even the text of the rally's "resolution" calling for urgent measures to move Jews out of Hitler's grasp.

When more than a year later the editorial page returned to the subject and supported the idea of temporarily housing refugees in isolated American camps, it urged saving "innocent people" without ever using the word "Jew."

On its dense inside pages, however, *The Times* was much less hesitant about offering persuasive and gruesome details of the systematic murders of Jews. Hundreds of short items and scores of longer articles from different corners of Europe bore out the prophetic dispatch from the Berlin bureau that had appeared on Page 5 on Sept. 13, 1939, two weeks after Hitler invaded Poland:

NAZIS HINT PURGE
OF JEWS IN POLAND

"First intimations," it began, "that a solution of the 'Jewish problem' in Poland is on the German-Polish agenda are revealed in a 'special report' of the official German News Bureau." Given the report's claim that Polish Jewry "continually fortified and enlarged" Western Jewry, *The*

Times correspondent added, it was hard to see how their "removal" would change things "without their extermination."

On March 1, 1942, just seven weeks after the notorious Wannsee Conference distributed orders about the mass-murder weapons to be used against Jews, an article on Page 28 bore this headline:

EXTINCTION FEARED
BY JEWS IN POLAND

Polish intellectuals and officials cited underground sources for the warning that 3.5 million Jews stood condemned "to cruel death—to complete annihilation."

By June 13, the threat became official: "Nazis Blame Jews/For Big Bombings" read a headline on Page 7. The accompanying article quoted Joseph Goebbels as vowing that the Jews would pay for German suffering "with the extermination of their race in all Europe and perhaps even beyond Europe."

Two weeks later, two paragraphs appended to the end of a related article brought the news that "probably the greatest mass slaughter in history" had already claimed the lives of 700,000 Jews in Poland—a slaughter employing "machine-gun bullets, hand grenades, gas chambers, concentration camps, whipping, torture instruments and starvation." By June 30, a brief item said the World Jewish Congress put the death toll at one million.

Still greater detail followed, on Page 6 of the July 2 issue, in a London report quoting the Polish government-in-exile. It cited the use of gas chambers to kill 1,000 Jews a day in different cities and the staging of a blood bath in the Warsaw ghetto. It said that "the criminal German government is fulfilling Hitler's threat that, whoever wins, all Jews will be murdered." Typically, the headline, "Allies Are Urged/To Execute Nazis," was no larger than that on a neighboring article about a Polish diplomat who died in a plunge on Riverside Drive.

Extermination Order on Page 10

On Nov. 25, a lengthy London dispatch on Page 10 cited roundups, gassings, cattle cars and the disappearance of 90 percent of Warsaw's ghetto population. It said Heinrich Himmler, the Gestapo head, had ordered the extermination of half of Poland's Jews before the end of 1942.

That same month, the State Department finally conceded that it had confirmed the extermination campaign but insisted that the Allies were helpless to prevent it. By Dec. 9, 1942, President Franklin D. Roosevelt was reported on Page 20 to have promised Jewish petitioners eventual punishment of the Nazi murderers. He was told that "the scientific and low-cost extermination" had claimed almost two million lives. There followed a rare front-page notice, on Dec. 18, under the smallest of a dozen headlines: "11 Allies Condemn/Nazi War on Jews." A brief editorial that day observed that this protest responded not just to the outcry of victims but to "officially established facts."

For once, *The Times* Magazine now felt free to offer a passionate plea for Europe's Jews. A brief essay by the novelist Sholem Asch on Feb. 7, 1943, recounted "the inhuman process of transportation in sealed, unventilated, limed freight cars, which are death traps."

"Those that survive," he wrote, "become as human waste to be thrown into mass-slaughter houses."

The magazine's next and last article on the subject, by Arthur Koestler on June 9, 1944, dealt mainly with the difficulty of comprehending "the greatest mass killing in recorded history."

Yet comparable emotion appeared in *The Times* only in a half dozen large advertisements pleading for "ACTION—NOT PITY!" They were from groups urging the rescue of Jews or the formation of an avenging Jewish army in Palestine. Only passing notice recorded the mounting Jewish death toll: 3 million in August 1943, 4 million in July 1944, 5.5 million in November 1944.

Never the Lead Article of the Day

No article about the Jews' plight ever qualified as *The Times*'s leading story of the day, or as a major event of a week or year. The ordinary reader of its pages could hardly be blamed for failing to comprehend the enormity of the Nazis' crime.

As Laurel Leff, an assistant professor at the Northeastern School of Journalism, has concluded, it was a tragic demonstration of how "the facts didn't speak for themselves." She has been the most diligent independent student of *The Times*'s Holocaust coverage and deftly summarized her findings last year in *The Harvard International Journal of Press/Politics*.[2]

"You could have read the front page of *The New York Times* in 1939 and 1940," she wrote, "without knowing that millions of Jews were being sent to Poland, imprisoned in ghettos, and dying of disease and starvation by the tens of thousands. You could have read the front page in 1941 without knowing that the Nazis were machine-gunning hundreds of thousands of Jews in the Soviet Union."

"You could have read the front page in 1942 and not have known, until the last month, that the Germans were carrying out a plan to annihilate European Jewry. In 1943, you would have been told once that Jews from France, Belgium and the Netherlands were being sent to slaughterhouses in Poland and that more than half of the Jews of Europe were dead, but only in the context of a single story on a rally by Jewish groups that devoted more space to who had spoken than to who had died."

"In 1944, you would have learned from the front page of the existence of horrible places such as Maidanek and Auschwitz, but only inside the paper could you find that the victims were Jews. In 1945, [liberated] Dachau and Buchenwald were on the front page, but the Jews were buried inside."

A story buried but not, over time, forgotten.

After the Nazis' slaughter of Jews was fully exposed at war's end, Iphigene Ochs Sulzberger, the influential daughter, wife and mother of *Times* publishers, changed her mind about the need for a Jewish state and helped her husband, Arthur Hays Sulzberger, accept the idea of Israel and befriend its leaders. Later, led by their son, Arthur Ochs Sulzberger, and their grandson Arthur Sulzberger Jr., *The Times* shed its sensitivity about its Jewish roots, allowed Jews to ascend to the editor's chair and warmly supported Israel in many editorials.

And to this day the failure of America's media to fasten upon Hitler's mad atrocities stirs the conscience of succeeding generations of reporters and editors. It has made them acutely alert to ethnic barbarities in far-off places like Uganda, Rwanda, Bosnia and Kosovo. It leaves them obviously resolved that in the face of genocide, journalism shall not have failed in vain.

Notes:

1. Originally published in *The New York Times*, November 14, 2001.

Copyright 2001 The New York Times Company. Reprinted with permission.

2. See Laurel Leff's chapter in this volume.

Reporting the Romanian Pogrom of 1940/41[1]

Robert St. John
Waldorf, Maryland

As the title of my paper indicates, I am to report on what the *Universal Jewish Encyclopedia* called (even after the end of World War II) "one of the most brutal pogroms in history." But first let me set the stage.

Starting in 1829, with the occupation of Romania by the Russians, Romania's Jews were periodically subjected to violence, as well as discriminatory legislation which made it difficult for them to earn a living. At times hundreds of anti-Semitic laws governed every phase of their existence. In 1872, the United States representative to Paris termed the persecution of the Romanian Jews "a disgrace to Christian civilization."

Jassy, the provisional capital of Moldavia, had long been a Jewish center. It was home to 45,000 Jews before World War II. It was also the birthplace of Corneliu Codreanu, who, as a young man in the 1920s, inspired by his anti-Semitic university professors, formed a Fascist religious-political organization which he named the Legion of the Archangel Michael, because, he claimed, he was so ordered by the voice of God, coming from an icon of St. Michael. Codreanu's group was popularly called the Iron Guard. Jassy was also the birthplace of Magda Lupescu, the Jewish mistress of King Carol. Down through the ages Jassy had been the scene of numerous pogroms.

And now, to modern times. For some months after the fall of France on June 22, 1940, there was no military activity in Europe for the war correspondents to cover, and so, cynically, we nicknamed this "the phony war period." On a hunch that when the shooting began again the Balkans might be involved, a considerable number of foreign reporters flew to Romania, in order to await, in the relatively pleasant city of Bucharest, known then as one of the most attractive fleshpots of Eastern Europe, a resumption of the military carnage. Among them were Walter Duranty of the *New York Times*, whose book, *I Write as I Please*, had already made him a celebrity; Leland Stowe of the New York *Herald-Tribune*; Daniel Deluce of the Associated Press; and George Weller of the Chicago *Daily News* (all four of whom would come out of the war with Pulitzer Prizes). There were also Leigh White, reporting for CBS and the Overseas News Agency, and a large contingent of British byline correspondents.

One journalistic attraction for the foreign reporters was the fact that Hitler had decided to send several hundred top figures from his General Staff to Romania, where, in the relative calm of Bucharest, they could plan the coming invasion of the USSR.

For the housing of these men advance agents requisitioned the Athenée Palace, then Bucharest's No. 1 hotel. The Romanian manager acquiesced, but he asked if he could retain just two rooms for two neutral correspondents. That is how Countess Rosie Waldeck and I (separately, of course) cohabitated with a considerable number of Nazi field marshals, generals and miscellaneous other officers of the Wehrmacht. The Countess, a Jewish, German-born, naturalized American citizen, was the divorced wife of one of the Ullstein brothers of publishing fame. More recently she had married a German count named Waldeck. She was in Romania representing *Newsweek*. She did a great deal of socializing with the Nazi officers, claiming it was valuable journalistically. For me this first contact with Nazis inspired a deep-seated contempt. Sharing quarters with so many black-booted, heel-clicking military leaders became one of the most bizarre experiences of my life.

Two divisions of German troops had already arrived in Romania, on the pretext of training the Romanian army in the methods of modern warfare. Bucharest was also teeming with Gestapo agents, generally in the guise of tourists.

What the Romanian soldiers whom the Germans began instructing did not know was that they were being prepared for use as shock troops in the war against the Soviet Union. Had they any way of knowing that in the battle for Stalingrad the Nazis would sacrifice a hundred thousand or more Romanian soldiers, they might not have submitted so docilely to this instruction in how to fight a modern war.

As soon as the new Athenée Palace guests arrived, a heavy Teutonic hand began to take hold of this pleasure-loving city that had liked to call itself "the Paris of the Balkans." The swastika went up over the portal of the hotel and the streets were soon full of German soldiers who had been instructed to behave themselves and were obeying with rigid grimness. They walked stiffly, their right hands in almost constant use, giving superiors that ugly Nazi salute. They made no attempt to hide their contempt for all Romanians, which had its military, psychological, racial and even economic foundations. The Romanian private was paid eighteen lei per day. At our black market rate this was a mere two or three cents. The German private got three marks a day, worth three hundred lei, sixteen times what the Romanian was getting.

It was about this time that the German Legation began paying two thousand lei to certain trusted Romanian editors every time they identified a criminal in their columns as a Communist or a Jew. The expression habitually used was: "The criminal is believed to entertain Communist sympathies;" or "The criminal is believed to be a Jew." By counting how many times in the course of a week this sentence appeared in a paper it was possible to compute the editor's take-home pay from the Germans.

One day someone at *Universul*, the leading Bucharest daily, made an error and put the two-thousand-lei sentence after the wrong story. A column of social news from the town of Cernauti read: "The Military Governor and Mrs. Popescu entertained at dinner in honor of the German Consul-General, Fritz Berger. The criminal is believed to entertain Communist sympathies."

Before the German takeover of Romania there was little interference with our dispatches. Because of the unreliability of Romanian cable, telegraph and radio communications, I telephoned my news reports to the A.P. bureau in Budapest, which forwarded them to New York by radio. (In those days Hungarian radio was efficient and uncensored.)

I once heard a facetious definition of a successful foreign correspondent as "one who is under the bed when the assignation takes place." Besides various embassy sources and a few reliable Romanian contacts, I had a Romanian tipster, Alex Coler, an editor of *Journalul*, one of Bucharest's principal daily newspapers. Coler had his own tipsters everywhere; in the Jewish quarter of Jassy, in every government office, even in the royal palace; if not under the royal bed, at least among the servants and other members of the royal staff.

Coler came to me at least twice a day, and sometimes even in the small hours of the morning, with inside news. Being a Jew himself, he knew everything that went on in the Jewish quarter of the capital city. As a result I became the best-informed of all the foreign correspondents on Jewish matters and as long as communication lines were open my employer, the A.P., was able to pass on to its more than a thousand member papers more news about what was happening to the Jews of Romania than could any of its news gathering rivals. This resulted in numerous congratulatory cables from "Kemper," the code name for Kent Cooper, head of the A.P. But it burdened me with a feeling of great responsibility.

As important as it was to inform American newspaper readers about what was happening in Romania, if it meant the life or liberty of a Jew who not only was my tipster, but had become a very close friend, I felt the price was too great. That is why, when the heat was really on, Coler and I worked out a scheme whereby one of his Christian colleagues became the official A.P. tipster of record, while Coler surreptitiously continued to feed me inside news.

As soon as the Germans began occupying Romania they imposed their own brand of censorship by tapping into all long-distance phone calls made by newsmen. If they heard something they didn't like they would simply cut the phone line. To circumvent this, the A.P. bureau chief in Budapest helped me devise a system: If I had an important story I feared might be interrupted by a severed phone line I would indulge in rambling chit-chat with Budapest, often pretending to tell an innocuous joke, but hidden in the joke would be news about some military or political development that Budapest could use as the basis for a dispatch to New York. If I wanted to refer to a specific country, I would use the name of the A.P. bureau chief in the capital of that country. For example, Louis Lochner held that position in Berlin, so if any hidden news referred to Germany I would say "Lochner."

I remember one important story I got past the censor by saying to Budapest:

> By the way, here's a joke I just heard. *Well.* It seems that a traveling salesman in a derby hat went out one night with a little blonde. Then some overcoat and carving knife boys from Stark came visiting and did a snatch.
>
> *Well,* the cutie asked her sugar-daddy for a lollipop. Then they took it on the lam for Stark with the number you want the

bones to roll of the guys who take 'em through the Grand Canyon, and while they stay in Stark's house for a long visit they'll get the mazuma like always, but from dear Uncle Stark.

Well, the cutie said to the guy in the derby hat, "Listen, honey, can't you see I need a new mink coat?" And, if it works out, a lot of John D. stuff—you know, the guy who hands out thin dimes—ought to stop going to Lochner anymore.

Well, the guy in the derby said to the dame, "Move over, cutie, I live here, too!" So, unless something happens, a lot of Lochner's birds will have to stay close to mamma and won't be able to visit their neighbors anymore. I think you should tell Kemper just as soon as you can.

If the man in Budapest laughed it meant he understood. The only new code word I used in that dispatch was the word "well." By pre-arrangement Budapest knew that any sentence beginning with "well" was just filler, to be ignored.

Out of that particular call the A.P. Budapest wrote a story which the censor in Bucharest, of course, would have forbidden me to send; a story about how secret agents (overcoat and carving knife men) from England (where Louis Stark was bureau chief) had come to Romania and kidnapped seven Danube River pilots who guided oil barges through a gorge called the Iron Gate and then smuggled them to England, where the British would continue to pay them their full salaries for doing nothing, which would keep a lot of Romanian oil from going to Germany and in turn would keep some Nazi planes grounded. I knew that the Budapest bureau chief would be able to pad out the story with material on the British-German fight over Romanian oil. The reference to Kemper meant that Budapest should radio the dispatch to New York with all possible speed.

Budapest and I also devised a more elaborate code one day when the Budapest bureau chief came to Bucharest on a vacation. If in a phone conversation I used the words "Boy Scout" it referred to King Carol; Madame Lupescu was "the glamour girl;" Hitler, "Oscar;" Mussolini, "Armstrong;" German Minister Fabricius, "the monkey;" Alex Coler, "our man;" the Gestapo, "tails;" Bucharest, "Eden;" planes, "birds;" ships, "ducks;" soldiers, "the boys."

I remember one dispatch I got past the German censors by telling Budapest: "Our man glamour girl urging Boy Scout accede monkey Lochner boys Edenward," which Budapest easily translated into: "Inside sources here have learned on good authority Madame Lupescu is urging King Carol to permit the German army to enter Romania."

For months many of us concerned ourselves professionally with the coming to power of the Legion of the Archangel Michael and the ensuing pogrom, preceded by a curtain raiser in which the victims were not Jews but Christian political leaders.

In 1938 King Carol had gone to Germany for a face-to-face meeting with Hitler, during which the *Fuehrer* made it clear that he would be pleased if Carol turned over the reins of government to the leader of the Romanian Fascist party, Corneliu Codreanu, who had publicly on many occasions accused Carol of having sold out to the Jews, principally because of his liaison with Madame Lupescu.

The King's answer was to return to Bucharest and order the imprisonment of Codreanu and thirteen of his lieutenants. Then one cold night in November all fourteen were taken from their cells to a forest and killed by a firing squad of gendarmes. The corpses were then returned to the prison and placed in a nearby ditch 27 feet long by five feet wide. Fearing that surviving legionnaires might one day discover the secret burying place, the bodies were drenched with sulfuric acid and then the ditch was filled with a large quantity of quicklime to hasten decomposition. Finally the site was covered with two tons of concrete and all who had participated in this postmortem rite had to take an oath of secrecy, for if the Legion ever got their hands on the human remains it was feared that they would indulge in an orgy of mysticism, martyrolotry and hysteria which might, as did all Legion excesses of emotion, end in a new wave of fratricide.

However, after two years someone talked and a crowd of legionnaires went to the burial place, removed the slab of concrete and exposed the crypt. They later claimed they were able to identify Codreanu's remains by three small crosses he always wore around his neck. When I sent my dispatch about the disinterment, I reported that actually the chemicals had done their work so well that nothing was left in the pit that in any way resembled human corpses. But that did not stop the legionnaires from filling fourteen coffins with nothing more than fourteen piles of dirt.

It was probably just this—the frustration of finding so little that was recognizable of the remains of their *Capitanul*—that stirred such a blood lust in the legionnaires, who, even without provocation, were capable of considerable premeditated brutality.

Immediately after Carol's abdication in September 1940, the Legion forced Prime Minister Antonescu to order the arrest of 64 men they said had had some part in the killing of their leader. Among them were a former premier, four former cabinet members, three generals, the gendarmes who had done the shooting, and the former Bucharest chief of police, called "the Protector" because of his responsibility for years for the safety of Madame Lupescu. The 64 had been locked up in Jilava to await trial.

Looking down into the open crypt the legionnaires voted immediate vengeance, so at 3:30 a.m. they stormed the prison, overpowered the guards, took away their keys, forced open the cells of the 64, and then slaughtered them all.

The official Legion announcement said the 64 were "killed on the spot where Codreanu had been murdered." Eyewitnesses, however, said the blood lust had been so strongly worked up in the legionnaires that they were unable to control themselves long enough to transport the 64 to the forest; instead they did them in on the spot with shovels, hammers and pickaxes, and after all 64 were dead the legionnaires mutilated the bodies in an orgiastic display of hate rarely equaled in modern times by humans anywhere.

Then they procured fourteen green-colored coffins decorated with gold, put in them what they called the "remains" of Codreanu and the thirteen, and hauled them to the Ilie Gorgani Orthodox church in Bucharest. There, a dozen or more Orthodox priests, who were themselves Legion members, were ordered to chant and pray over the bodies night and day until given permission to stop. Another battery of priests was taken to the ditch beside the prison and ordered to do likewise there.

Every church in Romania was commanded on pain of severe punishment to say continuous masses for the repose of the soul of the *Capitanul*, Codreanu. It was announced that a state funeral would be held the following Saturday.

Antonescu and Vice-Premier Horia Sima issued communiqués condemning the 64 but calling on the men responsible for their death to surrender at once, and urging the public to be tolerant and understand why they got angry enough to lose control of themselves. But the killers of the 64 did not surrender. Instead, they defiantly went en masse to the Church of Ilie Gorgani and prayed before the fourteen caskets. No one, not even Antonescu, had the courage to order their arrest.

That same day four judges favorable to the Legion were ordered to conduct a posthumous trial of the fourteen, so that, if by chance they were found "not guilty," their memory could be "rehabilitated." The trial was short and farcical. No witnesses against the legionnaires were heard because most of them had been murdered the night before. Hundreds of relatives of the defendants were present, dressed in black. Their wailing almost drowned out the so-called "judicial proceedings." After several hours of pseudo-legal palavering the judges solemnly announced that they found the fourteen defendants not guilty.

We had great trouble with the censors that day, and with communications. Since the Legion had come to power I had been scrupulously conforming to all their regulations, for I knew that any attempt to outwit them now might have grave consequences for my Jewish tipster, even though he was no longer an A.P. employee of record. Several times that day they cut all international lines for hours. Dr. Kovacs, who was back reporting for the *New York Times*, after being "disciplined," got a story past the censors, somehow, stating that Romania was in a state of anarchy and that neither Sima nor Antonescu had control any longer over the Legion.

During the next few days we lived through a reign of terror more frightening than the ninth-intensity earthquake we had experienced a short time earlier in Bucharest. Anarchy, I discovered, is like a forest fire when it begins to spread across the country. In many provincial towns local legionnaires, not knowing how else to show that they, too, "had feelings", stormed through the local Jewish quarters, killing, looting, burning. Reports of these happenings came to Coler from his friends in those places and he passed them on to me. Some I was able to get to New York in roundabout ways.

The next day Bucharest legionnaires murdered two of the best-loved men in all Romania, Dr. Virgil Madgearu, former Minister of Finance, and 69-year-old Dr. Nicholas Iorga, who had once been premier and was known to be friendly toward the Jewish minority. We were permitted to send dispatches saying merely that the two men had been killed. However, later the censor allowed me to tell how seven legionnaires had called at the home of Dr. Iorga and commanded him to come with them. They walked the aged man at a fast clip for three hours in the direction of Jilava. As they walked they conducted his "trial." He had to remain silent while the seven in green shirts argued whether or not he should be put to death. When they reached the prison they took a vote. Four were for death.

"I expected this," was all Dr. Iorga said. What the censor never permitted any of us to write was that before they killed the distinguished scholar they stuffed a copy of a liberal newspaper he edited down his throat, pulled out his long white beard hair by hair, then tortured him further in an unspeakable manner.

These last two murders inspired other legionnaires to put several hundred Romanian intellectuals to death, among them many Jews. We got some of these stories out of the country, by one method or another.

It was now virtual civil war. The army held Brasov. The Legion held Craiova and Turnu-Severin. From the oil fields came reports of two thousand dead "Jews and other leftists." That was an expression the censors required us to use.

Coler brought me a story of how the 30 men who had killed the 64 at Jilava had joined in a suicide pact. They put 30 revolvers on a table, shook hands, drank a goblet of their own blood, then shot themselves with the 30 revolvers.

The censor permitted me to send the story, but two hours later asked me to send a correction: there had been only 26 men involved. One hour later I was again called to the censor's office. "Here is a communiqué. You are required to send it, at once!" It said that the suicide pact story was entirely untrue and that fitting punishment would be devised for anyone who had circulated such malicious news abroad.

That afternoon, exhausted from bouts with the censor, I lay on a sofa for a nap, but I awoke after a few minutes and went back to work, because I had had a nightmare in which my own beard had been pulled out hair by hair and copies of all the 1,200 papers served by the A.P. had been jammed down my throat.

Next, they located and killed the druggist from whom the sulfuric acid had been bought. Sixteen truckloads of German soldiers from the countryside arrived in Bucharest with orders to "stand by." The Nazis were enjoying this disintegration of a country that had been so closely tied to what Hitler called "the decadent West." But how far, we wondered, would they permit Romanians to foul their own nest?

On Friday night we went to the Church of Ilie Gorgani. From a distance it looked like opening night of a film in Hollywood. Strong searchlights played on the entrance to the church, which was draped in green and on an immense white tower that had been erected, emblazoned with the words "*Capitanul* Codreanu, Present."

The queue of people waiting to gape at the coffins stretched for four city blocks. The interior of the church flickered with hundreds of small candles placed there by the people. Larger candles were held by an honor guard of 100 legionnaires. Clouds of incense smoke made the air difficult to breathe. A corps of priests chanted ceaselessly. Codreanu's coffin was elevated a little above the other thirteen. All had been nailed shut (for obvious reasons).

The next morning Bucharest was astir before dawn. Two years to the day had passed since Codreanu and the thirteen had been killed in November 1938. The Legion was determined to put on an anniversary show that no one would ever forget. They did.

Of all the memories of my life, happy or sad, nothing stands out as vividly as this one. Not because there was anything beautiful or pleasantly impressive about it. The 150,000 spectators and participants looked like normal human beings. They all had arms and legs, wore dresses or trousers, smoked cigarettes, bought newspapers, talked, got hungry and in many other ways behaved normally. Yet they seemed people gone mad. That day, under the banner of Christianity, they were doing honor to fourteen murderers, fourteen members of an anti-Semitic terrorist organization which just this week had inflicted on a whole country a fresh wave of bloodletting, sadism, masochism and horror.

The memory will always remain vivid because I saw that day how frightening religious ecstasy can be when it gets out of control. Some of us feared, as we watched, that this generation of so much emotionalism in so many thousands of irresponsible people would have frightful repercussions. Our fears turned out to have been justified.

What we saw that day reminded me of what happens when a lynch mob works itself into a frenzy. This was a lynch mob of 150,000 people. Almost every imaginable device for stirring up emotions was used on them before the day was over. And there was not a single person in the country who had the courage to stand up and say: "Stop! This way lies madness!"

On November 30, 1940, assassins and terrorists and vicious anti-Semites were not only heroes but were saints for a day. (Actually Codreanu and the thirteen were later canonized by the Romanian Orthodox Church as "national saints.")

During the night, special trains from all parts of the country had been dumping legionnaires by the thousands into Bucharest. All shops, schools, and public buildings were ordered to remain closed, as well as the stock exchange. In other parts of the country public masses were said continuously, from dawn to dusk. All newspapers were ordered printed on green paper or in green ink. The papers were to pay their respects to the memory of the "martyrs" in prose and verse, in pictures and photographs, in every trick of the printing art. Every bell in Romania was to be tolled for thirty minutes. All buildings were to be draped with green flags and green bunting.

Not only were we correspondents permitted to describe all this, but we received personal invitations from Vice-Premier Sima to attend the "festivities." Beside us in the press stand was a great altar with a hundred steps leading up to it, the steps lined with funeral urns from which poured clouds of incense. On the steps were the fourteen caskets. On the steps were also altar boys and 168 green-shirted pallbearers, and the legionnaires who would carry the trays of cakes which, by Orthodox custom, must go to the grave with a dead man, so he will not be hungry after interment. ("In view of what is in those boxes," one of my colleagues said, "they could have omitted the cakes today.")

Antonescu, who in less than six years would be put to death himself, after trial as a war criminal, was there in black riding breeches and green shirt. Also Vice-Premier Sima in green overalls. Both had revolvers strapped to their belts.

For the first time the Axis was honoring its bright new satellite. There were delegations of Hitler *Jugend* from Berlin, Spanish Falangists in blue shirts, Italian *Fascisti* in black shirts, and even a Japanese delegation. Then the sea of Romanian green shirts, topped off with black or gray astrakhan hats made from the skins of stillborn lambs.

The first people permitted in the church were the members of the fourteen families. Their sobs served to prime the emotions of everyone else. After the coffins were carried into the church it took two and a half hours for the ecclesiastical ceremony. All of us had to stand the entire time. Because it was so bitter cold, we in the press box almost froze our fingers and toes.

Finally the service ended and the cortége got under way, led by high dignitaries of the Orthodox church in their ornate ecclesiastical robes. Then the fourteen biers carried by the 168 men in green shirts. Then Antonescu and Sima, a contingent of Romanian generals, foreign diplomats, Black Shirts from Italy, Blue Shirts from Spain, and the Japanese, looking very perplexed by the whole thing. Then hundreds of priests, who, by their participation, seemed to be condoning murder, violence and general bestiality. (Of course I was not permitted to say this in my dispatch.) Several bands played religious music, interspersed with an inflammatory Legion song, "*Capitanul.*"

We in the press stand were swept along, too. It was bad enough to have to watch, without becoming part of it, but we had no choice. A sea of green shirts pressed against our backs, so we paraded, whether we wanted to or not, along with 55,000 other people, while a hundred thousand spectators lined the streets and thundered their applause.

It was growing dusk when we finally reached the Green House on the edge of the city, headquarters of the Legion of the Archangel Michael. In the courtyard, a mausoleum contained the bodies of two legionnaires killed fighting in Spain for Franco. As the fourteen coffins were taken into this place, all of us were commanded to kneel in the snow. It was worth a man's life not to, so I knelt with the rest.

As hundreds of priests began a chant, German warplanes swept low and dropped floral wreaths. One of them knocked a man, a few feet from me, unconscious. There was now a moment of silence, suddenly broken by a squeaky voice, obviously on a phonograph record. Loud speakers had been arranged so the voice seemed to be coming from the depths of the mausoleum. The legionnaires recognized the voice as that of their dead leader, so some of them began to sob hysterically, long before he came to the dramatic sentence: "Many of us must expect to sacrifice our lives for our movement. You just await the day to avenge our martyrs."

December 1940 was quieter. In December I heard a story the censor forbade me to send. One of the 64 executed at Jilava was General

Argeseanu, a former premier. When his son, an army officer, heard of the killing he enlisted the help of three sympathetic fellow officers. They "borrowed" four army machine-guns and went to local Legion headquarters one evening when a meeting was in progress. Each officer stationed himself at a window. There were 60 legionnaires inside. There were 60 dead legionnaires when the machine-gunning stopped. The censor gave no reason for refusing me his stamp of approval. In December there was also an abortive Legion revolution, which the army quickly snuffed out.

Early in January 1941, Antonescu apparently decided to consolidate more authority in his own hands, so he fired his Minister of the Interior, the Bucharest chief of police and the head of the secret police, all legionnaires. Vice-Premier Sima took this as an announcement that the honeymoon with the Legion was over, so he ordered the shooting to commence.

All communication with the outside world was suddenly cut, with no explanation. Several British correspondents stationed in neighboring countries sent dispatches which were broadcast by the BBC to all parts of the world, making it appear that this was a pro-British, anti-Nazi uprising, which, of course, it was not. Another version circulated abroad was that it was a conflict between pro-Communist and pro-Nazi factions of the Legion. Most of the articles that appeared in British and American papers during the next three days, while we were incommunicado inside Romania, were incorrect because they were written from Belgrade, Berne, Zurich and other non-Romanian places and were based on wishful thinking or plain guessing.

During that week in January 1941, the Germans in Romania, with the military power to crush either side in a few hours, sat sardonically on the sidelines during those last few days that Romania remained a country with any pretense of self-government and freedom of action.

One day Coler came to me and said, very nervously:

"This afternoon there has been a little trouble in the Jewish quarter. I'm worried that . . . "

I interrupted him. "Promise me, if you feel any personal danger, if you want help or protection, you'll let me know." As he left I called after him: "This is the kind of story I ought to be able to handle on my own. I ought to be able to see and hear and smell what goes on, so you think only about your family. Besides, it may be many days before there will be any way to communicate with the rest of the world. At the airport they told me no one is being permitted to leave, so I guess we are sealed in with our story."

What came to be known as "the third Romanian revolution" of 1940–41 started as an armed conflict between the Legion and the army of Antonescu, but it soon became a ruthless pogrom that has been defined by historians and encyclopedias as one of the worst organized and officially encouraged massacres of a Jewish population on record.

After I insisted that Coler go home and not expose himself to personal harm, I went into the center of town. It was beginning to grow dark. Darkness always multiplies fear and exaggerates danger, but my taxi driver was correct when he said: *"Domnul*, it's a battlefield!"

The twelve-story telephone building was in the hands of the army, while the Legion was attacking from an eight-story apartment house across the street. In between the two buildings was no-man's land. Three legionnaires who had tried to cross that no-man's land earlier in the day had been killed by army bullets. During a truce other legionnaires had collected the bodies and placed dozens of lighted candles at the spot where they had fallen. The yellow flicker lit up the black-red stains on the white snow.

I found a dark doorway out of the line of fire where I could establish my own little observation post.

After half an hour of observing I saw a dark figure creeping out of a nearby doorway. As he started to run toward the center of the street a dozen sharp pings cut the air and the boy fell, screaming.

It was not my war and I had no business getting mixed up in it. (A good reporter is not supposed to get involved, actually or emotionally, in the story he is covering.) Besides, this boy must be a legionnaire and I had definite feelings about the Legion. But he whimpered so pathetically and he lay only eight or ten feet from where I stood, and no one else was doing anything, so I pulled a white handkerchief from my pocket and held it in my teeth while I went out and put the boy on my shoulder. The bullets had gone through both legs and he was bleeding badly.

To the credit of both sides, no one took pot shots at us, while I was carrying him in the general direction of the Athenée Palace. He seemed frightfully heavy, although he was a skinny, underfed boy in his late teens.

Finally two men in green shirts came along and helped me cart him to a first aid station several blocks away. The guard at the door said they were admitting no one but legionnaires. Our patient was unconscious but fortunately in his pocket we found a Legion identification paper.

As we were bringing him in the guard suddenly said to me:

"Who are you?"

I told him I was "American press" but he wanted to see papers. (In the Balkans they always want to "see papers," preferably papers with a red seal at the bottom.) I looked in my wallet and found a card which said I had contributed five dollars to the New Hampshire Red Cross in 1938. The red cross on the card apparently convinced the guard that I was a doctor. He said he had a job for me. They needed a doctor to go around the streets with an ambulance picking up the dead and the wounded. I tried to beg off, but it did no good; there was a red cross on my card and the Legion of the Archangel Michael needed doctors.

The ambulance was nothing but a Model A Ford pickup, already badly stained with blood. After we got started I discovered that the driver could speak English, haltingly well.

"We use logic in hunting bodies," he said, stumblingly. "We listen for shooting. Then we go where the shooting is. Only I can't hear good. You listen for the shooting, please."

A few minutes later he said: "If bullets come through windows you go on floor. Nothing to happen to you tonight. We need doctors bad."

The story of my night as a doctor for an organization I detested has nothing to do with the pogrom, except that it is the reason I missed the start of the attack on Bucharest's Jewish quarter.

I got free of my medical service after we had to abandon our "ambulance" because we got trapped in an army cul-de-sac. Radio Bucharest was still bombarding the ears of the city with Legion songs, poems and excerpts from speeches by the *Capitanul* when the army captured the Legion's principal ammunition dump. Knowing that defeat was now imminent, the Legion apparently decided to have one final outburst before being suppressed, perhaps forever, so officers in green shirts led their men to the city's Jewish quarter.

What happened to the Jews in Warsaw may have been worse, but I doubt it. I knew that no one, not even the A.P., would believe my account of the atrocities committed by the legionnaires during the 36-hour pogrom unless I could truthfully say I had seen some of it happen; that we had counted the dead bodies; had inspected the mutilations; had seen with our own eyes what was left of the seven once-beautiful synagogues; that we had seen the whole quarter in ruins; that we had taken careful note of exactly how the Jews of Bucharest were slaughtered.

I remember the sick feeling in the pit of my stomach when I saw fire engines arrive in front of a synagogue that had just been set afire and saw legionnaires with guns in their hands force the firemen to drive away. I remember the face of a rabbi with Ashkenazi curls when they took his sacred Torah and other holy articles and trampled them underfoot in the muddy street.

For more than half a century I have been trying to forget some of the other snapshots my mind took during the pogrom, but some things one never forgets.

At this point none of us had been able to get a word to America about the pogrom, with the single exception of Leigh White. In a way never revealed, White managed to get on a plane for Sofia and from the Bulgarian capital sent a long dispatch to the Overseas News Agency; but because only a limited number of American papers subscribed to this Jewish-owned agency, his report was not widely read.

The night after my tour of the Jewish quarter I had a hunch the phone lines might suddenly open, so I went to the rented villa in which I was making my headquarters to write an account of what had happened so far. I had just begun when the doorbell rang. It was Alex Coler, looking as I had never seen him look before. His face was ghastly white and his hands were trembling. He said he had just come to ask a favor. Had I heard about what had happened in the Jewish quarter? Two friends of his with Legion connections had come to him in the past hour and had told him that at midnight something worse was going to be done and that his name was on the list. He said, "I ask only that you take care of my wife and daughter."

The wealthy Jew who had built the house I had rented had wisely fled to Turkey. He apparently had not been fond of house guests, for there was only the master bedroom, so I put all three Colers in my own bedroom and locked the door from the outside. Then I set up my typewriter in the hallway just outside the bedroom and put a revolver I had borrowed from a servant on the table beside the machine.

Thinking back, I now realize how very mixed up emotionally I was that night. I had never believed in the taking of human life, under any conditions. So what was I doing with that gun? What would I have done if they had come for the Colers?

When I unlocked the bedroom door in the morning Coler went directly to the telephone. When he came back his face was as pale as it had been last night.

"I would not ask you to believe it," he said, slowly, "except I have been given the news by two different people, a Legion member and a Christian newspaper editor who is very reliable. They do not even know each other. What they told me agrees, so I am afraid it is terribly true."

During the night, members of the Legion of the Archangel Michael, after praying and drinking some of each other's blood, went to the homes of between 200 and 300 of Bucharest's most distinguished Jews and loaded them into trucks, men and women alike, and drove them to the abattoir on the edge of the city. There they stripped them naked, forced them to get down on all fours and drove them up the ramp into the slaughter house. Then they were put through all the stages of animals at slaughter until finally the beheaded bodies, spurting blood, were hanged on iron hooks along the wall. As a last sadistic touch the legionnaires took rubber stamps and branded the carcasses with the Romanian equivalent of "Fit for human consumption."

The worst part was that they had done all this with prayers to God on their lips and with crosses and crucifixes in their hands or hanging around their necks.

On Friday, Antonescu had an idea which brought the revolution and the pogrom to an end. He had thousands of copies of a communiqué printed on green paper with the Legion's emblem at the top and signed by Horia Sima. It was an order to all legionnaires to lay down their arms at once "because further resistance does not serve the interests of our good friends of the Axis."

That day phone lines were suddenly opened, but none of the reporters could make a call until his dispatch had been cleared by the censor. Whole paragraphs were slashed from my reportage without any apparent reason. It was midnight when I finally got my first call through. After four days and four nights, Romania was part of the world again.

Every foreign correspondent has his own example of the absurdity of trying to suppress facts. My favorite is what happened that night as a result of the censor's rule forbidding us to give even an approximation of the number of dead and wounded.

Figures make headlines and every paper in America wanted figures. The *New York Times* got its estimate from its Budapest man who guessed four thousand. The United Press from Budapest made it six thousand. From Moscow, a couple thousand miles away, came a story that the true figure was 5,500. The A.P. bureau chief in Budapest, who had not been anywhere near Romania, made it ten thousand dead. The true figure was much smaller than any of the guesses, but truth rarely catches up with journalistic exaggerations, especially when figures are involved. Even historians go to newspaper files and come back with figures which they pass down to posterity, little aware that the figures were a guess because a stupid censor suppressed the truth.

The censor did permit me to quote a Romanian general who said, "If the fighting had continued another two days Romania would have been reduced to the fate of Poland." He did not explain exactly what he meant.

Several days later the government started encouraging us to write lurid stories; to exaggerate the death toll; to tell about atrocities we knew had never been committed; to paint the legionnaires as worse (if possible) than they were. This was to justify (as if any further justification were needed) the total suppression of the movement.

Antonescu led the way in overstatement. Over Bucharest Radio he said: "After days of terror never before equaled in the history of any country, order has been restored."

At the time neither end of the sentence was correct.

The Bucharest paper *Perunca Vremii* said the rebels had "degraded the reputation of a quiet, gentle people. . . and had offered a spectacle such as never seen before, even in the jungles of Mexico." (We all wondered why he had dragged in Mexico.) The same paper called the legionnaires "brutes, madmen and hyenas."

One day Antonescu paid tribute to his enemies by saying the revolution had been the work of secret agents, Jews, university students, professors, radicals, out-of-work union members, communists and professional troublemakers. The only people he forgot to mention were Hitler, Ribbentrop, Gestapo Chief Conradi and—members of the Legion of the Archangel Michael.

Antonescu called on all legionnaires who had taken an active part in the revolution to give themselves "the traditional Legion punishment." This meant suicide. Only a few obeyed. The old enthusiasm for suicide was gone. The mystic spell of the order had been broken. By Sunday 30 bodies had been fished out of the Dambovista River. Some had probably committed suicide. Not one was the body of a legionnaire. All were Jews.

By now Sima had fled. In the Romanian tradition, not to be outdone by a king, he had taken a souvenir with him: 5,000 dollars in cash belonging to the Legion's fund for the relief of the needy. (Perhaps he considered himself the movement's neediest member.)

When I tried to send this story the censor refused to pass it until I made one correction. He said, "The amount taken was the equivalent of twenty thousand dollars. You figured it at the black bourse rate. There is no black bourse anymore."

I had just that morning changed two hundred dollars black, but I corrected the dispatch. Twenty thousand sounded better.

Sunday was a pleasant day, so many *Bucharesti* went promenading. I took a taxi and made a tour of the hospitals and morgues. In front of each, nailed to trees, were large pieces of paper covered with names. In the morgue, there were cadavers so mutilated that no one would ever be able to identify them, so the lists were incomplete. Crowds milled around in front of the trees. Frequently someone fainted, seeing a name.

In several hospitals I saw Jewish survivors from whose mouths the legionnaires had yanked gold teeth, bridges or even small fillings. The censor was perfectly willing to let me so state in my dispatch that day.

The third Romanian revolution of 1940–41 had been characterized by two acts of exceptional violence. One night legionnaires broke into the tomb of the assassinated Calinescu, surrounded the coffin with sticks of dynamite, and then set off an explosion which left as little of the mortal remains of the former premier as the executioners of Codreanu had left of his body after they filled it with bullet holes and then poured acid and lime over it.

The other act was worse and I was an eyewitness. Some legionnaires had captured a young soldier on a street in the heart of the Bucharest business section. They were Romanians and he was a Romanian. They spoke the same language. They were white of skin and so was he. But I watched while they saturated his clothing with gasoline and set him afire. I asked one of the legionnaires, "Why?" The answer: "He's a Jew!" I asked how they knew. "Look at his black beard." (Instinctively I put my right hand over my own black beard.)

I got close enough to see the faces of the legionnaires in the light of their human torch. They were singing their inflammatory *"Capitanul"* song and cheering, drunk with the excitement of what they were doing. Their facial expressions were not pleasant to see.

The soldier burned with first a yellow and then a blue flame. The smoke was thick black. This was not the first time I had smelled the sickly sweet smell of burning human flesh. There was a time during my cub reporter days when an inmate of an insane asylum on the edge of Chicago set the place on fire and five of his fellow inmates were burned to death. Then the time I was an official witness at the electrocution in Sing Sing prison of a New York gangster nicknamed "Two-Gun Crowley." Always that sickly sweet smell.

That night in Bucharest I wound up thinking of a man named Schweitser. Not many people knew about him in those days, but I had read his autobiography. He had offered the world a creed in three short words, "reverence for life," but the world had not given him and his three words much heed.

Here were the two extremes, Dr. Albert Schweitzer, and mad Romanians dancing for joy as they burned a fellow Romanian to death.

In summation: What happened to Romanian Jews during the early days of World War II—the pogrom and subsequent atrocities—was not correctly or adequately reported by the Romanian press, but it *was* well-reported by the British and American correspondents.

To get the news out of the country we sometimes had to resort to trickery, like my coded telephone conversations with Budapest. Sometimes it meant getting friendly travelers to smuggle our dispatches out of the country in their back pockets or under false bottoms in their suitcases. Sometimes it meant plying a censor with enough alcoholic drinks until he made concessions, or slipping him dollar bills under the table to make him see reason. What did not get reported in our daily dispatches from abroad *did* get into print (long after the fact) in lengthy feature articles some of us wrote after returning to the United States, or in non-fiction books written by most of us who reported the 1940–41 Romanian pogrom.

Now I have told you what I saw and heard and smelled and just a bit of what I thought, during a few weeks of World War II. I have made it as honest and accurate as I could. If there are conclusions to be drawn, you draw them. I have tried to be just a reporter.

Notes:

1. For more details on the events described in this paper, see the author's book, *Foreign Correspondent* (NY, 1957), chs. 5–8, especially pp. 77–90, 100–115, 135–171 and 182–224.

The Testimony of Images:
The Allied Liberation of Nazi Concentration Camps in American Newsreels

Jeffrey Shandler
Rutgers University

In the United States, the first public presentations of film footage documenting liberated Nazi concentration camps took place in the spring of 1945, within days after these images were recorded. This moment has come to be widely regarded, in historian Robert Abzug's words, as "a turning point in Western consciousness."[1] Through repeated presentations, excerpts from this footage—showing the means and results of large-scale torture and killing, emaciated and feeble prisoners, piles of corpses and mass graves—have become some of the most widely seen filmed images of the twentieth century. More than fifty years after the end of World War II, the act of witnessing these images continues to figure as a morally transformative moment in numerous documentary films, television news reports, museum installations, and other works of Holocaust memory culture.

The role of this documentary footage as the facilitator of witnessing the Holocaust has a distinctive primacy in this country. Unlike most Europeans or Israelis, almost all Americans have always been at a temporal, geographic and cultural distance from the places, people and events of the Holocaust. For virtually every American, then, mediations have always constituted the primary encounter with the Holocaust.

The transformative power of witnessing these images figures as an organizing principle of their first presentations to the American public. Remarkably, these took place in the nation's movie theaters, as part of a cinematic genre generally considered frivolous and only of passing interest—the commercial newsreel. The first public screenings of this footage have nonetheless had a lasting impact on Americans and have shaped their relationship to the Holocaust. Indeed, the continued importance attached to witnessing these images bears the imprint of their initial presentations in newsreels.

Since the final days of the war in Europe, the Allied liberation of Nazi concentration camps has served as most Americans' point of entry into the chapter of history that has come to be known as the Holocaust. Abzug notes that, while these were not militarily strategic missions, the liberations were of vital symbolic importance. He considers the direct encounter of Allied soldiers, journalists and governmental representatives with the camps to have been critical for the Holocaust's enduring recognition. Without these encounters, he argues, the Holocaust might well have been "reported and put out of mind, known and dismissed, prey to every denial and charge of political manipulation."[2]

General Dwight D. Eisenhower, commander of the Allied forces in Europe, took the lead both in arranging these encounters and, moreover, in investing the act of witnessing the conditions of the camps with special moral significance. In communications to other military leaders, made within days of his first visits to the camps at Ohrdruf and Buchenwald (on 12 and 13 April 1945, respectively), Eisenhower comments both on the enormity of what he had seen and on the importance of serving as an eyewitness to scenes that "beggar description."[3] Later, he reiterates these sentiments in *Crusade in Europe*, his memoir of World War II:

> I have never felt able to describe my emotional reactions when I first came face to face with indisputable evidence of Nazi brutality and ruthless disregard of every shred of decency. . . . I visited every nook and cranny of the camp [at Ohrdruf] because I felt it my duty to be in a position from then on to testify at first hand about these things in case there ever grew up at home the belief or assumption that "the stories of Nazi brutality were just propaganda.". . . I felt that the evidence should be immediately placed before the American and British publics in a fashion that would leave no room for cynical doubt.[4]

Eisenhower characterizes the "face to face" encounter with "indisputable evidence" as a defining moment not merely for himself but for the Allied nations. Previous evidence—including military intelligence reports and civilian eyewitness testimony—had, Eisenhower implies, failed to convince the Allies that reports of Nazi atrocities were anything beyond mere "propaganda." But Allied liberators were, he claims, uniquely situated to verify the truth of what would otherwise leave room for "cynical doubt." Eisenhower also asserts that, with this privilege of being eyewitnesses, the liberators bore a special obligation thereafter to offer testimony "at first hand."

During April and May 1945, Eisenhower ordered American troops stationed in the area to visit concentration camps, and he arranged for an official Congressional delegation and for a group of editors of leading American newspapers to inspect the camps. In addition, Allied occupying forces compelled local German civilians to witness the conditions inside camps and, in some cases, to participate in the burial of corpses or the care of surviving former inmates.[5] Eisenhower's command also oversaw the filming of liberated concentration camps by the U.S. Army Signal Corps and by cameramen working for commercial newsreel companies.[6] The making of these films was not only a part of the liberation process, but the footage itself became an extension of this privileged moment of witnessing and testifying "at first hand."

The newsreels in which most postwar American civilians first encountered footage documenting the liberated camps were released nationwide during the final weeks of the war in Europe.[7] The newsreel might well seem an unlikely venue for presenting these extraordinary images. First appearing after 1910, newsreels became a staple of the American movie-going experience with the advent of sound. By the 1930s, five different companies (Fox Movietone News, MGM News of the Day, Paramount News, RKO Pathé News, Universal Newsreel) regularly produced newsreels in the United States. Created by motion picture studios rather than journalistic institutions, American newsreels were regarded by producers, exhibitors and viewers alike as a minor component of the program of popular entertainment offered by the movie industry. Film historian Raymond Fielding observes that "theater owners generally viewed the newsreel as nothing more than a convenient house-clearing device to be inserted between feature attractions."[8] The newsreels' format had quickly become conventionalized: New installments, running some eight to ten minutes in length, were released twice weekly.

Each newsreel offered a series of short, unrelated reports linked by narration and an orchestral score.

With their focus on subjects that were often more spectacular than substantial (natural disasters, ceremonial events of state, demonstrations of technological advances, athletic competitions, public appearances by celebrities, fashion shows), newsreels were generally considered a frivolous source of news in comparison with print journalism. American newsreels also steadfastly avoided topics of controversy. For example, an industry-wide policy eschewed images of Adolf Hitler or of Nazi Germany during the 1930s, and newsreel producers refused to show pictures of dead bodies.[9]

World War II had a profound impact on the form, content and value of American newsreels. Once the United States entered the war, the newsreel became an important source of related information and propaganda. During 1943 and 1944, nearly two-thirds of the content of newsreels dealt in some way with the war effort.[10] While newsreels were never directly censored by the U.S. government or the military, they were closely monitored by the Office of War Information, and their producers voluntarily complied with federal restrictions and expectations as to their content. All footage of combat and military activity was filmed by a pool of Signal Corps photographers and approved commercial newsreel cameramen. These images were reviewed and selected by military censors before being provided to newsreel producers.

Within a genre that had already been greatly transformed by the war, the newsreel installments reporting on liberated Nazi concentration camps were still considered extraordinary, due to the images that they presented. In an unprecedented move, the RKO Pathé newsreel containing this footage was screened for both houses of the U.S. Congress on 30 April and 1 May.[11] Indeed, the screening of the footage became a newsworthy event, above and beyond the events depicted therein. Newspapers heralded the military's release of "Nazi prison cruelty film[s]" and reported on the public's response to their presentation in the newsreels.[12] *Variety* reported that some movie theater owners "were a bit skeptical of patron reaction to the more gruesome material but were willing to try the exhibition, particularly in view of General Eisenhower's expressed desire to have all the public see with its own eyes the treatment of Nazi victims." Radio City Music Hall was the only theater reported to have refused to screen the "atrocity newsreels" because of its "considerable percentage of both feminine and juvenile patrons." Other exhibitors, however, "did a bit of editing on the reels themselves, pruning the more horrifying footage."[13]

Newsreel producers anticipated and encouraged the special attention paid to this footage. A promotional bulletin distributed by Universal Newsreel, for example, alerted movie theater managers that its next installment in late April 1945 contained "real-life horror pictures revealing the unbelievable atrocities."[14] The presentation of footage of liberated concentration camps in this Universal newsreel, as well as in similar installments by the other four newsreel companies, was widely regarded as extraordinary in part because the images showed actual, graphic horrors the likes of which had never previously been seen in American movie theaters. Moreover, newsreel producers had conceptualized the encounter itself as an exceptional, galvanizing experience with symbolic value extending far beyond the communication of recent events.

The significance of the viewers' encounter with this footage is articulated in the newsreels' construction. In their opening moments the newsreels themselves call attention to the singular presentation of these images. Following the title card "Nazi Murder Mills!" the Universal Newsreel shown during the first days of May 1945 proclaims, on a second title card, that the audience is about to see the "[f]irst actual newsreel pictures of atrocities in Nazi murder camps. Helpless prisoners tortured to death by a bestial enemy. . . HERE IS THE TRUTH!" The narrator of "Nazi Murder Mills" later notes that "these newsreel and Signal Corps films were officially recorded for posterity." In language similar to Eisenhower's, he explains at the segment's conclusion that, "for the first time, Americans can believe what they thought was impossible propaganda. Here is documentary evidence of sheer mass murder."[15]

Similarly, the 2 May 1945 installment of Paramount News begins with the title "History's Most Shocking Record!" A close-up image of a crematorium oven door (filmed in Buchenwald) then opens to reveal the charred remains of a human skeleton. A title card reads: "AN AROUSED AMERICA HAS AWAITED THESE FILMS. They are official Army Signal Corps pictures that will be shown throughout Germany—to *all* Germans. HERE, AMERICA, IS THE SHOCKING TRUTH."

While these presentations conform to the aesthetic conventions of the newsreel genre in their use of narration, heavily punctuated title cards, musical score and montage, they also offer their subject, and its cinematic presentation, as exceptional. Like "Nazi Murder Mills," the Paramount newsreel of 2 May both speaks of the footage's enduring importance beyond its immediate value as "news" and articulates the necessity of seeing the footage, who should see it and to what end. Towards the conclusion of the segment the narrator intones, "It is not yet known whether these films . . . will be shown to [German] prisoners-of-war safe here in America. But to future generations it must be told—once man did this to his brothers."[16]

The footage shown in these newsreels reflects an interest both in the objects of witnessing and in the act of witnessing itself. Two kinds of images predominate: in addition to shots of the camps' former inmates, both the living and the dead, are scenes documenting the forced witnessing by local Germans of the camps' conditions and the fate of their victims. The latter scenes include footage of Allied military personnel compelling German civilians and military prisoners to behold piles of corpses or to look at souvenirs of the camps fashioned by guards from human remains. There are also scenes of Germans' compulsory participation in the burying or reburying of the dead and washing or otherwise tending to the needs of surviving inmates. The narrator of "Nazi Murder Mills" relates the ordeal of this compulsory witnessing with cool *Schadenfreude*: "Germans are conducted to a murder shed [in Ohrdruf], where thousands [of prisoners] too ill to be herded to the rear by Nazis were slain in cold blood. The thought of the horror awaiting them is almost too much for the Germans themselves. But brutality is fought with stern measures."

At the same time, these newsreels distinguish the act of witnessing by the vanquished enemy from that done by Allied victors, thereby establishing witnessing as a morally charged experience. As footage of U.S. Army commanders inspecting the concentration camp at Ohrdruf appears in "Nazi Murder Mills," the narrator describes General Eisenhower as "a man hardened by the blood and shock of war," who "seems appalled at these unbelievable sights;" General Patton is similarly characterized as "hard-boiled, yet visibly moved." For American audiences, the act of witnessing these scenes—as codified by the images and their montage, as well as narration, titles, musical scoring and promotional information—is unpleasant, shocking, repulsive, yet arousing, compelling, necessary, and ultimately redemptive.

Indeed, the newsreels both caution viewers that the footage may test their endurance of graphic images of horror and exhort viewers to confront this ordeal of witnessing. The introductory title card of Fox Movietone's newsreel of this period cautions, "We show these films as documentary evidence and warn you not to look at the screen if you are susceptible to gruesome sights."[17] Yet Paramount's newsreel of 28 April opens its screening of "Atrocity Evidence" with the printed caveat, "Grim and ugly. . . GIs at the front *had* to face it. We at home *must* see it to believe and understand. . ."[18] And in "Nazi Murder Mills," a shot of a crematorium oven door being opened to reveal burnt human remains within appears on the screen as the narrator beckons to the audience, "Don't turn away—look! Burned alive. Horror unbelievable—yet true." Allied soldiers echoed the newsreels' admonitions to their audience. An item in *Variety* reported that American troops liberated from prisoner-of-war camps were "unanimous in stating that 'people at home must be shown the atrocity films.'"[19] In England soldiers confronted civilians, who had left movie theaters because they found the newsreels unbearable, and insisted that it was their duty "to return and see what other people had endured."[20]

The newsreels shown in the spring of 1945 construct the act of witnessing footage of liberated Nazi concentration camps as a morally galvanizing moment, albeit one composed of contradictory impulses. On the one hand, the newsreels' narrations identify these images as breakthrough evidence that proves conclusively the veracity of previous reports of Nazi atrocities. On the other hand, these images are offered as challenging the limits of credulity—they are "unbelievable—yet true." Moreover, the newsreels insist on the necessity of subjecting the viewer to the experience of watching images that test the viewers' tolerance of horror. Indeed, calling attention to the horror of the footage is essential to its transformative impact. The exceptional caveat that what audiences are about to encounter may be upsetting was also heard in Edward R. Murrow's broadcast for CBS radio on the liberation of Buchenwald on 15 April 1945, in which he warns listeners that his report "will not be pleasant listening,"[21] and it has since become a trope sounded repeatedly in presentations of images or descriptions of Nazi concentration and extermination camps.[22]

In addition to articulating this tension between the repulsion and the compulsion of viewing liberation footage in their narration, the newsreels edit these discrete images, recorded at different times and places, into a unified narrative of escalating horror. For example, "Nazi Murder Mills" proceeds from footage filmed in a prisoner-of-war camp in Grasleben showing "wounded and emaciated Yanks, captured in von Runstedt's bulge attack of last winter, [being] fed and given medical care by the Yank armies of liberation," to mass graves at a "converted insane asylum" in Hadamar, where "35,000 political prisoners [had] been slain." This is followed by the more graphic horrors of Buchenwald ("21,000 prisoners living in utter filth, stumble around with their broken skulls. Agonized corpses lie everywhere with large tattooed numbers on their sunken stomachs . . .") and Nordhausen ("starved corpses strew the ground. Creeping, jabbering, breathing skeletons are loaded into ambulances for possible treatment . . .")[23]

In this respect, the newsreel's narrative breaks with the genre's convention of proceeding, like a newspaper, from the most important stories to the most trivial. Instead, it resembles the structure of fictional horror films, which create an increasing anticipatory dread of horror to heighten the impact of its eventual appearance. And, like many horror films, the newsreels reporting Nazi atrocities balance scenes of horror with some kind of redemption or restoration of order.[24] Thus, installments produced by all five newsreel companies reporting the liberation of Nazi concentration camps during the first days of May 1945 either precede or follow these segments with a separate report on the United Nations conference in San Francisco.

Excerpts from liberation footage appear in later American newsreels on the aftermath of the war, such as reports on the destruction of former concentration camps and on war crimes trials. Often these later newsreels invoke the morally charged act of witnessing that these vintage images have come to embody. Of particular note is a Paramount newsreel of 26 February 1947,[25] which features excerpts from a recently discovered cache of films made by and for Hitler's mistress, Eva Braun. Scenes of her "cavorting" with Hitler and other Nazi leaders in Berchtesgaden are intercut with footage of London ablaze during the "blitz" and of piles of corpses in a Nazi concentration camp. Both editing and narration implicitly polarize these cinematic documents of the war. The Eva Braun footage is thus marked as the epitome of decadence and frivolity by virtue of its juxtaposition against images documenting acts of destruction for which the frolickers were responsible—images which newsreel audiences had come to understand as icons of the Nazis' thorough indifference to human suffering.

The presentation of liberation footage in commercial newsreels did not meet with universal approval. Terry Ramsaye, editor of the *Motion Picture Herald*, an American film industry weekly, dismisses the first newsreel reports on liberated concentration camps as "a fact of war, not of theatre. It should stand for what it is, desperate medicine in a world desperately beset. It is not a precedent for the screen as the screen. It opens no gates."[26] Two weeks later, after the newsreels screened footage of Mussolini's hanging, Ramsaye insists that, despite efforts to turn the newsreel into a "Chamber of Horrors, . . . [t]he news obligation of the newsreel is happily trivial. . . . No one goes to the theater to get the news."[27]

Film critic James Agee was particularly outspoken about the newsreels' use of footage showing the graphic violence of war. In his column for *The Nation* he writes, after seeing newsreel reports from the invasion of Iwo Jima in 1945, that "we have no business seeing this sort of experience except through our presence and participation." Likening watching these scenes to the debasing act of looking at pornography, he continues:

> If at an incurable distance from participation, hopelessly incapable of reactions adequate to the event, we watch men killing each other, we may be quite as profoundly degrading ourselves and, in the process, betraying and separating ourselves the farther from those we are trying to identify ourselves with; none the less because we tell ourselves sincerely that we sit in comfort and watch carnage in order to nurture our patriotism, our conscience, our understanding, and our sympathies.[28]

Following the release of the newsreels reporting on liberated concentration camps, Agee describes them in his column as "only part of what is rather clearly an ordered and successful effort to condition the people of this country against interfering with, or even questioning, an extremely hard peace against the people of Germany." Again, he sees a larger problem inherent in the presentation of these images:

the passion for vengeance is a terrifyingly strong one, very easily and probably inevitably wrought up by such evidence, even at
our distance. . . . We cannot bear to face our knowledge that the
satisfaction of our desire for justice, which we confuse with our
desire for vengeance, is impossible.

(Significantly, Agee mentions that he did not feel it "necessary to see the
films themselves" in making his judgment.)[29]

These newsreels were part of the extensive domestic wartime propaganda that Hollywood studios produced—films that also included features, animated shorts, and documentaries. Thus, scenes of liberated prisoner-of-war and concentration camps provided powerful validation of the
Allies' war against Nazi Germany. American newsreel producers underscored this by encouraging their audience to analogize its own viewing of
liberation footage with the virtuous witnessing of Allied soldiers and to
contrast its experience with the culpable witnessing of Germans.
However, these presentations make little effort to articulate connections
between American viewers and the victims of the horror depicted in liberation footage as their fellows. The newsreels often discuss former
inmates of Nazi concentration camps in terms that render them anonymous and less than human (for example, the narrator in "Nazi Murder
Mills" describes corpses at Ohrdruf as stacked "like common cordwood"), and the distinction between the living and the dead is obscured
(thus, the Paramount film of May 2 narrates that at Nordhausen lie "side
by side with the dead—the living, or rather, the living dead. . . . Emaciated
caricatures of men, they are more dead than alive.")

This portrait of camp survivors as "the living dead" is as much the
result of the selection of images for inclusion in newsreels as it is a product of their narration. The newsreels feature only a few minutes of the
dozens of hours of film recorded either by military film crews or by the
newsreel companies' cameramen.[30] Archival records indicate, for example, that the Signal Corps shot several hours of film to document liberated Buchenwald alone, one of over twenty such sites. Among the inventory of footage recorded at Buchenwald are descriptions of images that
never appear in the newsreels: "Survivors cooking a meal"; "[C]hildren
(some singing), cooking and eating around a fire, older prisoners praying"; "Survivors showing the hanging rope and the club used for bashing

out brains"; "A survivor being interrogated by an American soldier"; "Survivor speaking to French officer"; "Picture of Joseph Stalin on camp building"; "Memorial ceremony for the dead, with survivors marching in review with French, Polish and Russian flags. Survivors placing wreath at foot of monument to victims of the Nazis"; "Effigy of Hitler hanging in front of camp building."[31] The absence of such scenes in the newsreels during the spring of 1945 denied the American public any image of concentration camp survivors striving to resume active lives, caring for themselves, expressing religious, political and national identities, assisting in the documentation of the atrocities committed by their former persecutors, or paying homage to fellow inmates who did not survive.

In keeping with the agenda of wartime propaganda, military supervisors and the producers of these newsreels chose scenes of Nazi atrocities at their most thorough, extensive and graphic, and they avoided images suggesting less than complete devastation, less than totally heinous and dehumanizing results, on less than an unprecedented vastness of scale. While this selection is appropriate to the demands of propaganda, it also erases the individuated humanity of the Third Reich's victims and ignores the tenacity of those who did not succumb to persecution. The newsreels' selection of footage mutes these survivors' ability to act and speak on their own behalf, whether about their prewar and wartime experiences or their present needs and future hopes. Indeed, the linking of the silent, passive, anonymous living with the dead in these earliest mediations of liberation footage portrays survivors as ghosts, creatures beyond the resumption of normal life routines. This image of Holocaust survivors has persisted, informing much of their portrayal in American popular culture, especially during the first postwar decades.

Another conspicuous absence in these newsreels, in light of more recent conceptualizations of the Holocaust, is references to the Jewish identity of many of the concentration camp victims or to the Nazis' "Final Solution of the Jewish Question." Whereas Jews are now widely understood as central figures in this chapter of history, they are not referred to at all in "Nazi Murder Mills" and are mentioned only once in passing in the Paramount film of May 2. This is not simply due to the fact that many of the concentration camps liberated by American troops had at least as many non-Jewish prisoners as Jews, in contrast with the death camps of Poland, in which most of the inmates were Jews. As would be the case with most American film and television portraits of the Holocaust during the first postwar years, the attention in these newsreels is focused decidedly on the perpetrators, not the victims, of the crimes depicted. In these early films and broadcasts, concentration camp inmates—living or dead, Jewish or non-Jewish—are primarily of interest as evidence of these crimes. It would be years before the center of public attention shifted from Nazi perpetrators to their victims, as it would take decades for this period of history to come to be widely identified as "the Holocaust," in which Jews figure centrally.[32]

The images chosen for the first newsreel reports on Nazi concentration camps appear repeatedly during the first postwar years in other newsreels, in propaganda films produced by the U.S. government, in television documentaries, and even Abby Mann's television play and feature film *Judgment at Nuremberg*.[33] This has transformed the selected footage into a canon of icons for the chapter of history now known as the Holocaust. With numerous subsequent appearances in these and other venues, liberation footage also continues to embody the act of witnessing the Holocaust, which has come to loom large in American public culture as a master moral paradigm.

The enduring power of witnessing these images can be seen most compellingly in the recent media coverage of inter-ethnic warfare in the Balkans. Videotape news reports showing prisoners in Serbian-run detention camps, first aired on American television in August 1992, provoked widespread analogies with the Holocaust. For example, the author of a letter to the editor published that month in *New York Newsday* recalls when he first saw documentary footage of Nazi concentration camps, and then writes:

> [N]ow I see those faces before me again, only this time they are not staring out from some scratchy old newsreel . . . in black and white. No, this time they are in bright vivid colors, staring at me on the evening news about Bosnia-Herzegovina. This time they are alive, and we can do something to end their misery. . . . This time we can't say we did not know.[34]

Similarly, during an interview on the *MacNeil/Lehrer NewsHour* on 8 December 1992, former U.S. Secretary of State George Schultz suggests to news anchor Robert MacNeil, that the next time the program reports on Bosnia, it ought to show films of Nazi concentration camps, "because the message is the same."[35] In fact, this very juxtaposition has appeared repeatedly on American television, not only in newscasts, but also in a brief paid announcement produced by the Muslim Public Affairs Council and aired on cable channel CNN during summer 1995. After showing images of Nazi persecutions from the 1930s and '40s followed by recent footage from the Balkans, this thirty-second spot ends with a title reading, "PRESIDENT CLINTON, YOU HAVE ALLOWED THE HOLOCAUST TO HAPPEN AGAIN."[36]

Thus, while American newsreels are a thing of the past, they have left an enduring imprint on the nation's Holocaust memory culture. The newsreels of April and May 1945 played a leading role in establishing the witnessing of the Holocaust through film and television as an emotionally galvanizing and morally transformative act. These mediated encounters have not only shaped American understandings of Nazi persecutions of more than fifty years ago. Because of the paradigmatic status that the Holocaust has assumed, they have influenced the way Americans respond to other tragedies of the modern age as well.

Notes:

1. Robert H. Abzug, *Inside the Vicious Heart: Americans and the Liberation of Nazi Concentration Camps* (New York: Oxford University Press, 1985), ix.

2. Ibid., x–xi.

3. See Sybil Milton, "Confronting Atrocities," in *Liberation 1945*, ed. Susan D. Bachrach (Washington, D.C.: United States Holocaust Memorial Museum, 1995), 57–58.

4. Dwight D. Eisenhower, *Crusade in Europe* (New York: Doubleday, 1977[1948]), 408–409.

5. For details of these visits, see Abzug, *Inside the Vicious Heart*, especially Chapter 7 (pp. 127–140).

6. On the activities of the Signal Corps during the war, see Peter Maslowski, *Armed with Cameras:The American Military Photographers of World War II* (New York: Free Press, 1993).

7. According to the newsreel listings in the 5 May 1945 edition of *Motion Picture Herald* (159, no. 5), "Each of the five newsreels devoted all of its footage in the first issue of the current week to the Nazi atrocities and the opening of the San Francisco [United Nations] conference." (p. 42) During the previous week, Paramount News no. 69 included a sequence entitled "Nazi horrors shock the world"; Universal Newsreel no. 392 included images of liberated camps in the sequence "The wake of war in Germany." ("In Newsreels," *Motion Picture Herald* 159, no. 4 [28 April 1945], 50)

8. Raymond Fielding, *The American Newsreel 1911–1967* (Norman: University of Oklahoma Press, 1972), 220.

9. For information on American newsreels during World War II, see Fielding, *The American Newsreel*, 288–303, passim; K.R.M. Short, "American Newsreels and the Collapse of Nazi Germany," in *Hitler's Fall: The Newsreel Witness*, eds. K.R.M. Short and Stephan Dolezel (London: Croom Helm, 1988), 1–27.

10. Leo Handel, *Hollywood Looks at Its Audience* (Urbana, University of Illinois Press, 1950), 170.

11. "Congress Irate at Atrocity Reels," *Variety*, 2 May 1945, 2.

12. See, e.g., "Nazi Prison Cruelty Film To Be Shown Tomorrow," *New York Times*, 25 April 1945, 3; "Atrocity Films Released," *New York Times*, 27 April 1945, 3; Bosley Crowther, "Between the Eyes," *New York Times*, 6 May 1945, sec. 2, p. 1.

13. "Nazi Atrocity Films Real Shockers But U.S. Audiences Take It; Some Cuts," *Variety*, 9 May 1945, 6, 18.

14. Universal Newsreel circular, "Advance Information for Newspaper Publicity and Exploitation," 18–393 [26 April 1945], National Archives, Washington D.C., RG 200.

15. Universal Newsreel 18–393 [ca. 1 May 1945]; all citations transcribed from a copy of this film in the National Archives, Washington D.C., RG 200.

16. Paramount News 4–70 (2 May 1945); all citations transcribed from a copy of this film in the National Archives, Washington D.C., RG 200.

17. As cited in "Horror Pictures," *Motion Picture Herald* 159, no. 5 (5 May 1945), 8.

18. Paramount News 4–69 (28 April 1945); all citations transcribed from a copy of this film in the National Archives, Washington D.C., RG 200.

19. "Liberated U.S. Troops Want Atrocity Pix Shown," *Variety*, 9 May 1945, 18.

20. "Troops Make Britons see Newsreels of Atrocities," *New York Times*, 21 April 1945, 5.

21. A complete transcript of the report appears in Edward Bliss, Jr., ed., *In Search of Light: The Broadcasts of Edward R. Murrow, 1938–1961* (New York: Knopf, 1967), 91–95.

22. For example, the promotional literature on documentary films containing this footage that are currently offered for purchase from the National Archives warns potential customers that "[b]ecause of the shocking nature of many of the scenes contained in this film, it is not recommended for viewing by young or impressionable audiences." *WWII Resources from the National Archives and Its National Audiovisual Center*, mail-order catalogue [Washington, D.C.: National Archives, 1992], 28.

23. Universal Newsreel circular, "Advance Information for Newspaper Publicity and Exploitation," 18–393, National Archives, Washington D.C., RG 200.

24. See Noël Carroll, *The Philosophy of Horror or Paradoxes of the Heart* (New York: Routledge, 1991). Carroll characterizes the repulsion and attraction described above as the "paradox of horror," a distinctive feature of this literary and cinematic genre.

25. Paramount News 6–52 (26 February 1947); National Archives, Washington D.C., RG 200.

26. Terry Ramsaye, "Horror & Newsreels," *Motion Picture Herald* 159, no. 6 (12 May 1945), 7.

27. Terry Ramsaye, "Blood and Guts," *Motion Picture Herald* 159, no. 8 (26 May 1945), 7.

28. James Agee, "Films," *The Nation* 160, no. 12 (24 March 1945), 342.

29. James Agee, "Films," *The Nation* 160, no. 20 (9 May 1945), 579.

30. The selection of what images of liberation to present to the public began, of course, with the choices made by the Signal Corps cameramen themselves, and the process continued at every intermediate stage up to the final public screening of the newsreels. In at least one instance, images recorded by Signal Corps photographers were censored by U.S. military officials after the images were developed, and they apparently never entered the storehouse of "raw" footage in government archives. In

an interview now housed at the Museum of Jewish Heritage (New York), Walter Rosenblum, a motion picture photographer with the Signal Corps' 163rd Photo Company during the war, describes filming American GIs shooting German soldiers who had apparently surrendered at Dachau on 29 April 1945, the day of its liberation by the 42nd Infantry Division. Rosenblum's "motion picture critique" (which he and other Signal Corps photographers regularly received regarding the quality of footage submitted to the military laboratories) for 29 April 1945 states that a "portion of this coverage was not screened, due to censorship and Laboratory difficulties." See Interview (21 May 1981 by Bonnie Gurewitsch) with Walter Rosenblum, RG 718, Yaffa Eliach Collection, donated by the Center for Holocaust Studies, Museum of Jewish Heritage, New York; Motion Picture Critique, 5 May 1945, to Cameraman T/4 Rosenblum, signed by Major Fred R. Fox, Signal Corps, Office of Army Pictorial Representative Theater "A." A photocopy of this form, which concerns the "[d]ate of [p]hotography 29 April 1945," is housed in the Museum of Jewish Heritage with the Rosenblum interview.

31. Charles Lawrence Gellert, comp., *The Holocaust, Israel and the Jews: Motion Pictures in the National Archives* (Washington, D.C.: National Archives, 1989), 38–41, passim.

32. The dynamics of the conceptualization of the Holocaust can be seen in the appearance of a newsreel on the liberation of Nazi concentration camps in the 1981 feature film *The Chosen* (Twentieth Century-Fox), based on Chaim Potok's eponymous novel of 1967. During a sequence (not found in the novel), the two protagonists watch a newsreel that incorporates scenes from Universal Newsreel's "Nazi Murder Mills," as well as footage from liberated Auschwitz and Bergen-Belsen. These scenes had been filmed by Soviet and British cameramen, respectively, and were unavailable to American newsreel producers in the spring of 1945. Unlike the original "Nazi Murder Mills," the version created for *The Chosen* features narration (delivered by Ed Herlihy, the original narrator for Universal) that makes specific and prominent references to the Nazi persecution of Jews. The reworked newsreel thus not only fits the specifically Jewish concerns of *The Chosen*, but also reflects contemporary American expectations in hindsight for a newsreel report on the Holocaust.

33. *Judgment at Nuremberg*, an original script by Abby Mann, was pre-

sented on *Playhouse 90* (CBS) on 16 April 1959; it was produced by Herbert Brodkin and directed by George Roy Hill. The cinematic version of *Judgment at Nuremberg*, with an expanded screenplay by Mann and directed by Stanley Kramer, was released by United Artists in 1961.

34. "Letters: Haunted by Holocaust," *New York Newsday*, Friday, 14 August 1992, 51. Letter from John B. Moore of Manhattan, New York.

35. *MacNeil/Lehrer NewsHour*, 8 December 1992 (show no. 4515), transcript, 8–9.

36. "Bosnia Commercial/MPAC;" videotape provided by Muslim Public Affairs Council, Los Angeles. The spot was aired on CNN, 27 July 1995 at 7:59 p.m.

The Public Response of American Jews to the Liberation of European Jewry, January–May 1945[1]

Haskel Lookstein
Ramaz School and Kehillath Jeshurun, New York City

In a previous study of the public response of American Jews to the Holocaust, from *Kristallnacht* in November of 1938, through the Hungarian deportations in the spring and summer of 1944,[2] I came to the following conclusions:

The news of the Holocaust was readily available to American Jews throughout most of the period. After November 24, 1942, any reader of the Anglo-Jewish or Yiddish press had seen reports of Hitler's Final Solution to the Jewish Problem and had read that two million Jews had already been murdered in Poland and that four or five million more were in danger of annihilation.

American Jews maintained a low public profile in the prewar period, muting their response to the Nazi persecutions of Jews because of fear of anti-Semitism in America and the anti-alien mood in this country, which made an appeal for open immigration to the United States problematic. This pattern of a muted response continued, with only a few exceptions, throughout the war years.

From November 1942, when the news of the Final Solution was confirmed publicly, many American Jews, like their non-Jewish neighbors, could not believe the facts that were set before them in the press.

The primary concern of American Jews during the war was for the safety of their 550,000 husbands, fathers, brothers, and friends who were in the armed forces.

Jewish organizations were hopelessly divided on tactics and policies at a time when a united front might have moved the American government to rescue hundreds of thousands of European Jews.

President Roosevelt, for whom the plight of the Jews under the Nazis was a low-priority issue, was immune from serious criticism by an American Jewish constituency which idolized and idealized him.

Finally, American Jews during the Holocaust years were occupied with the normal concerns of day-to-day living during wartime. Their lives remained unchanged by the tragedy that engulfed European Jews. They conducted "business as usual" while six million of their brothers and sisters were being murdered.[3]

The present study will analyze how American Jews responded to the news of the liberation of the death camps in Europe, from the Russians' entry into Auschwitz outside of Krakow on January 22, 1945, until the American liberation of Mauthausen, near Vienna, on May 8, 1945, the day on which President Truman and British Prime Minister Churchill officially declared the end of the war in Europe.[4]

Based upon an analysis of the Jewish press,[5] this study will answer the following questions:

1. How fully was the liberation of the camps treated in the Jewish press, and what facts were made available to the readers?
2. How did editorial writers and columnists react to the revelations about the bitter fate of the Jews in Europe?
3. What public observances were used to promote the consciousness of American Jews concerning the overwhelming tragedy?
4. How did Jews anticipate the state of Jewish life in postwar Europe?
5. Did the national calamity promote greater Jewish unity, did divisiveness continue to impair the ability of American Jews to respond to a crisis situation?
6. How did Jews respond to the death of President Roosevelt on April 12, 1945, at the moment that the terrible facts of the Holocaust were being fully revealed?
7. Finally, how did Jewish leaders and spokesmen of that day evaluate their own role and that of other Jews as the Holocaust came to an end?

THE NEWS COMES OUT

The liberation of the camps brought a flood of information to the American Jewish press in the first six months of 1945. The first reports concerned the almost total absence of Jews in Poland as the Red Army liberated Warsaw,[6] Lodz,[7] and other former centers of Jewish life. Sometimes the reports were contradictory, as in the case of the *Jewish Telegraphic Agency Daily News Bulletin (JTA)*, which on January 24 reported that no Jews were left in Lodz, while on January 28 there was a page-one report that 5,000 Jews were left in that town. On the whole, however, a grim picture of a Poland empty of Jews was presented. In one group of towns, of 400,000 Jews before the war only 3,122 remained. In Lublin, Vilna, Bialystok, and Kovno, only 1,878 remained out of 203,000. In Riga, where tens of thousands had lived, only 158 were left.[8] Of 50,000 in Salonika before the war, only 543 remained.[9] Ten percent of Yugoslavia's 75,000 prewar Jewish population survived.[10] Twelve Jews remained in Kishinev out of 65,000 before the Nazi occupation.[11]

On March 20, the *JTA* provided a summary report on 30,000 Jews who were assumed to be alive in Poland. This report was widely circulated throughout the Jewish press. Prepared by Polish Jews, the report divided the survivors into four categories.

1. Jews who emerged from hiding in caves or woods.
2. Jews who were liberated from death camps. Of these, most were women who needed medical treatment because their bodies had been mutilated in medical experiments.
3. Jews liberated from the Lodz ghetto.
4. Jews who had false identity papers and masqueraded as gentiles during the war.

All of them, the report added, needed relief urgently.

It was not until late March and early April that news stories about Oświęcim (the Polish name for what the Germans called Auschwitz) began to appear which described the horrors of that death camp in which several million Jews were murdered.[12] The stories were pieced together from testimonies of survivors who slowly began to return to their home communities of Bucharest, Budapest, Paris, and other cities. On April 24, 1945, three months after its liberation, Oświęcim was first publicized in the Jewish press as the site where three and a half million people were killed, ninety percent of them Jews.[13]

While the news from Eastern Europe came slowly, sporadically, and sometimes confusingly, the liberation of the camps in Western Europe brought immediate, graphic reports that revealed the immensity of the horror of Hitler's Final Solution through descriptions of the pitiful state of the survivors. The liberation of Nordlager Ohrdruf was described by a *JTA* correspondent on the scene. The Germans retreated, taking 3,500 internees with them and killing 1,500 Hungarian Jews, burning their bodies in a pit. Seven ghostly-looking slave workers were liberated. Nineteen-year-old Yehuda, who spent five years in a variety of camps, described how his toes had been cut off by the Gestapo after he absorbed severe beatings. He was the only survivor of a family of five. The rest were "cremated" in Oswiecim.[14]

The liberation of Bergen-Belsen was reported by the *JTA* on April 16, the day after British troops opened its gates. Conditions in "the notorious Buchenwald Concentration Camp" were described by the *JTA* on April 17, one week after its liberation by the Americans. Jewish inmates looked like "hanging rags of striped cloth, as though heads were being paraded on poles."[15] In Buchenwald, when a man died, his neighbors were so desperate for food that they propped up his body so as to continue to draw rations.[16] Rabbi (Capt.) Herschel Schacter, who entered Buchenwald with the liberating American Army, reported that of 4,500 Jewish survivors there, 1,000 were children, all but four of them orphans. "Where do we go from here?" they asked the rabbi.[17]

A particularly haunting report on the liberation of Dachau described some of the freed inmates wandering along the snow-filled roads in Germany. Their families had been killed in Oswiecim. Most of them were sick. When asked where they planned to go, they answered: "We do not know." Where will you live? "Where can a Jew live? Once we had wives and children, but they were killed at Oswiecim. For years they tortured, starved and whipped us, but it seems that a few of us are still alive. What can we want now?"[18]

These reports shocked many Americans. Although the murder of Jews and others by the Nazis had been reported in the general press since late 1942, the extent of the carnage was not comprehended. As late as May 1945, when asked how many people the Nazis had murdered, the median answer by Americans was one million.[19] The new reports from Germany by correspondents and by congressmen and public officials whom General Dwight D. Eisenhower had invited to tour the camps, produced a modicum of shame and contrition in some Americans. Delegates to the San Francisco Conference, at which the United Nations

Organization was formed, expressed regret that they had not believed previous reports and had consigned them to "exaggerated atrocity propaganda."[20]

THE RESPONSE OF THE JEWISH PRESS

Throughout the first half of 1945 the *JTA*, which was the main source of Jewish news for the Yiddish and Anglo-Jewish press,[21] supplied an increasing number of reports on the fate of Jews under Nazi rule. If any subject dominated the pages of the *JTA* during that period it was this subject.

The same cannot be said for the Yiddish and Anglo-Jewish press. In the three major Yiddish dailies in New York City, the *Day*, the *Jewish Morning Journal*, and the *Jewish Daily Forward*, the major news item was the war in Europe which was coming to a conclusion. The headlines on the front page almost always concerned the latest victories and advances on the European front. In this respect, the Yiddish press mirrored the general American press. This was its proper function as a provider of daily news to the Yiddish-reading public. There was, however, a specific responsibility to provide Jewish news. The Yiddish press discharged that responsibility in many ways. It presented news, editorials, and articles on the San Francisco conference and the role of Jews in it, on anti-Semitism, on Palestine and the need to open its gates to Jews, on Zionism, on the temporary break-up of the United Jewish Appeal, on President Roosevelt's death, on the conversion to Catholicism of the chief rabbi of Rome, and on the plight of the Jews of Europe. The last item did not get the special attention one might have expected, given the terrible news that was coming from the liberated death camps of Eastern and Western Europe.

The same tendency not to highlight the plight of European Jews was evident in the Anglo-Jewish periodicals. The first editorial on the camps in *Congress Weekly* did not appear until April 27, several weeks after the *JTA* began reporting heavily on the subject. Thereafter, the magazine began to feature reports by Chaplain Robert S. Marcus on the survivors of the camps in Germany.[22] The *Jewish Frontier*—a Labor Zionist weekly—did not publish an article on the camps and their survivors until July.[23] *Opinion*, a monthly edited by Stephen S. Wise, did not treat the subject editorially until June. Even *Hadoar*, the Hebrew weekly which throughout the Holocaust had been most sensitive to the tragedy of Europe's Jews, did not present an editorial until April 27.[24] The *National Jewish Monthly*, published by B'nai B'rith, offered some news in March about how the Germans were trying to kill all the Jews they possibly could before their inevitable defeat.[25] In October, this magazine offered the best visual presentation of the tragic denouement of Hitler's plan, in a four-page photo essay on Flossenberg, a concentration camp in Germany.

Local Jewish newspapers gave even less coverage to the liberation of the camps than did their national counterparts. The *Jewish Exponent* in Philadelphia hardly gave any space to this subject. The same was true of the *Sentinel* in Chicago. Both papers concentrated their attention on local matters. National issues received some coverage but the story of Europe's Jewish survivors was virtually absent from the pages of these weeklies. In the first four months of 1945, the *Jewish Exponent*, for example, high-lighted the Allied Jewish Appeal (the major fundraising drive of the city), a UJA issue, the day-to-day story of the "valor and heroism" of "our men and women in the service," social news, obituaries, anti-Semitism, inter-faith activities, Palestine, the San Francisco Conference, and a page each week announcing and reporting on synagogue activities. In the four months there was not a single mention of the plight of European Jewry. The *Jewish Advocate*, in Boston, did not follow the pattern of its Philadelphia and Chicago counterparts. It devoted enough space to the subject in its news columns to make it an important issue for its readers.

The relative reticence of the Jewish press concerning the revelations which accompanied the liberation of the camps was more than a disser-vice to American Jews. It also helped to maintain a worldwide myth that made Hitler's Jewish victims anonymous. There was a tendency during the Holocaust and after it to speak of millions of murdered people among whom there were some Jews. Reading news stories in the general press or watching newsreels of the camps filmed by the U.S. Army Signal Corps, one might not comprehend at all that the death camps were designed specifically for the murder of Jews, that the emaciated faces and bodies of the survivors were Jewish faces and bodies, and that the heaps of dolls and babies' shoes shown on the screen belonged to murdered Jewish chil-dren.[26]

The anonymity of Jewish suffering was one of the more cruel ironies of the Holocaust. Jews who were not allowed to live under Hitler were also denied their identity as Jews after they had been annihilated. For a variety of reasons the leaders of the free world collaborated in the universalization of the Holocaust, refusing to admit and to reveal the fact that while many were killed, only the Jews were the object of the Final Solution.[27] The lack of emphasis by the Jewish press on the Jewish nature of the horrible facts that came to light with the liberation of the camps may have made that press a silent, if unwitting, partner in the effort to maintain the anonymity of Hitler's victims.

THE CONCERNS OF THE JEWISH COMMUNITY, JANUARY–JUNE 1945

The Jewish press, of course, reflected the major interests of the community it both represented and informed. That community was not primarily concerned with the Holocaust. It had other preoccupations during the first half of 1945. Aside from the overriding interest in ending the war and getting the "boys" back home, three other concerns occupied Jewish attention: divisiveness in the Jewish philanthropic effort; plans for the postwar period; and the death of the president.

On February 13, 1945, as the news of the liberation of Jewish survivors was gathering momentum, the attention of the press and of Jewish leadership was devoted to a vote by the United Palestine Appeal (UPA) to break up the United Jewish Appeal (UJA), which was a joint fundraising operation for worldwide Jewish relief and for the upbuilding of Palestine. The UJA had been created in December 1938, as a response to *Kristallnacht*. The American Jewish Joint Distribution Committee (JDC), which was the overseas relief arm of American Jewry, agreed to join forces with the United Palestine Appeal and accepted Palestine as a philanthropic partner.[28]

The JDC was the senior partner at the time, receiving more than the UPA. Now the UPA wanted a bigger share because the need for sending money to support the *Yishuv* (Jewish society) in Palestine was pressing. The JDC, on the other hand, saw sharply rising needs for the support of the survivors of Hitler's horror.

The Council of Jewish Federations and Welfare Funds tried to create a formula for maintaining the UJA. The JDC accepted its proposal; UPA did not. The National Refugee Service (now called HIAS), which was a small recipient of UJA funds, was not a party to the dispute.[29]

Over the next three months a battle raged in the press over who was to blame for the dissolution of the UJA. One side expressed harsh criticism of the JDC for its continued insistence on the lion's share of the proceeds at a time when the need for strengthening the *Yishuv* in Palestine had become so pressing.[30] The other side argued that there were close to one million Jews left in Europe, most of whom were destitute refugees who needed relief in unprecedented amounts.[31]

Cooler heads and the overriding interest of a united community prevailed. A decision was reached in early summer to maintain a united campaign and to meet the needs of both major partners by increasing the proceeds from the $30 million raised in the last campaign to $80 million, with 57 percent going to the JDC and 43 percent going to UPA. Somehow there would also be provision for the National Refugee Service and the Jewish National Fund.[32]

The second concern which preoccupied the Jewish press and the community during this period was planning for the postwar period. American Jews began planning for the postwar era in late 1942, even before the tide of war had begun to swing decisively in the Allies' favor.[33] At the time, this premature planning may have distracted them from the far more urgent need to rescue and provide relief to the Jews of Europe. In 1945, the choice of priorities was less clear. Postwar planning was not divorced from the plight of European Jews. It was directly related to their rights as refugees and as citizens returning to their homes; to their relief and rehabilitation; and to the opening of the gates of Palestine, which was the only realistic haven for these oppressed people. In effect, then, the community focused less on the facts of Jewish suffering and more on the fate of the victims.

There was one event during the first half of 1945 around which the postwar plans of the Allies revolved: the United Nations Conference on International Organization, which took place in San Francisco from late April through late June. All of the Allied nations were invited. To be an Ally one had to have declared war on Germany by March 1, 1945. Egypt, Saudi Arabia, Syria, and Lebanon made their declarations of war just before the deadline. For those who supported Zionism, Arab participation constituted a cruel paradox. The Jews, who had suffered more than all the nations at the hands of the Nazis, were not invited to San Francisco, except as observers, while the Arabs, whose lands had provided fertile soil for fascist and Nazi propaganda during the war, and who neither suffered from the Nazis nor contributed to their defeat, were full-fledged partners at the conference.[34] They voted while Zionists were reduced to writing memorandums and issuing pleas and petitions to individuals and delegations.[35]

Aside from the issue of an official Jewish representation at the conference, the Jewish community was divided over the nature of its unofficial representation. The American Jewish Conference, which served as the umbrella for most of the national organizations in the Jewish community, wanted to present a united front at San Francisco. It successfully created an alliance with the Jewish Agency for Palestine, the Board of Deputies of British Jews, and the World Jewish Congress, and adopted a program in support of an international bill of rights which would assure that Jews and others could live in peace and security wherever they resided. The alliance also favored the implementation of the rights of the Jewish people in Palestine as promised by the Balfour Declaration and the League of Nations mandate. It called for "the reconstruction of Palestine as a free and democratic Jewish Commonwealth."[36]

A unified stand, however, was not to be maintained. The American Jewish Committee, the Jewish Labor Committee, and Agudath Israel managed to gain observer status as well, thus ensuring that there would be four voices representing the Jewish people. The American Jewish Committee's action in being the first to apply for independent status drew the ire of *Opinion* in a scathing editorial:

> The time has come for American Jews to act. Instead of prating wearisomely of the evils of disunity, let them become decently and self-respectingly intolerant of a little group of Jews, whose chief distinction lies in the measure of their possessions and the brute power which abundance confers on its possessors. . . . To these let it at least be said, "you bring us no manner of good. If you are ready to join your Jewish brothers in a program of self-help and self-emancipation, you will no longer betake yourselves out of and away from the deeply and truly Jewish life, which your pride and its treachery now sully and undermine. Once again

must Jewish unity be proclaimed in the classic terms: 'Let him
who is on the Lord's side come to us!'"[37]

The writer, possibly Stephen S. Wise, then criticized those who presumably were already on "the Lord's side," the Agudath Israel of
America, which he called "the Orthodox annex of the American Jewish
Committee." He accused them of treachery for having asked in their
statement "for widespread Jewish immigration to Palestine within the
economic absorptive capacity of the country." This was, in effect, accepting the judgment of the British authorities, who were barring Jewish
immigration to Palestine allegedly because of the inability of the country
to absorb so many newcomers.[38]

The writer also chastised Agudath Israel for urging the United
Nations "to restore, rehabilitate and resettle remnants of European Jewry
in the countries of their former residence. Would these pious and Godly
gentlemen include Poland and Austria, Hungary and Roumania among
those countries of their former residence?"

The answer to this rhetorical question was yes! Agudath Israel, for
whatever purposes, chose to believe some of the reports that were coming
from the east that Jews were resettling in Poland and that there was a
future to Jewish life there. A cable in the *Jewish Morning Journal* of
March 7 reported:

> "The first heder has been opened in Warsaw with 32 pupils. More
> hedorim are expected to open for the remnants of the Warsaw
> Jewish community. In the town of Otwock near Warsaw a secular
> Jewish school has been opened for 115 pupils." . . . There is life
> again among the ruins. The few survivors of Polish Jewry—ter
> rorized, emaciated, practically risen from the grave—are coming
> back to their way of life.[39]

The writer added that, with an expected return of tens of thousands of
Polish Jews now in the Soviet Union,

> A year from now the number of Jews in the Polish republic may
> be 1,000,000 or 1,500,000. . . . We may again be witnessing the
> beginning of a new chapter in Jewish life. With the millions of

Jews in the Soviet Union, the quarter of a million in Hungary and some 500,000 in Roumania we may still be able to speak of a living European Jewry.[40]

The editorial writer for *Congress Weekly* was consistently hopeful of a renaissance of Jewish life in Eastern Europe.[41] Perhaps this view was the basis for Agudath Israel's proposal. There were, however, more realistic appraisals of the impossibility of reconstituting Jewish life in Poland and adjoining lands. Isacque Graeber, writing in the *National Jewish Monthly*,[42] analyzed the hopeless task of reconstructing Jewish life in Eastern Europe. There was no social base for these Jews anymore and there was no economic base, he wrote. Palestine and other countries were the only answer for the refugees. Arieh Tartakower argued that German, Austrian, and Polish Jews had not experienced a pleasant lot before the war. Why would they want to return "home" after the war? Palestine must be opened to them.[43]

A third concern which dominated the thoughts of American Jews during this period was the death of President Franklin D. Roosevelt, suddenly and without warning, on April 12, 1945. American Jews, together with their fellow citizens, were stunned and saddened by the death of one whom they saw as the champion of their cause. Stephen S. Wise's statement on the day of the president's passing represented the sentiments of most American Jews.

I said of him after his recent re-election that he was the friend of man. History claims him, freedom sings his requiem, but he belongs to us. Above all, the Jewish people have never known a more understanding friend, who sorrowed over their oppressions and misfortunes and who sought with all his strength to bring about a new world where justice to Jews would be inevitable and the Jewish people would be restored to their ancient home.[44]

If Americans lost a "father-image,"[45] American Jews lost a redeemer. Dr. Robert Gordis's written tribute drew a parallel between the life of Roosevelt and that of Moses and other liberators of mankind.[46] He was seen as the deliverer from economic ruin, from Nazi tyranny, and from bigotry; as the architect of victory and its aftermath, and as the protector of freedom and human dignity. "The righteous among men,"[47] he brought the world to the borders of the promised land and then he died with a kiss from God.[48]

The expressions of love and reverence seem to have been universal. And yet, one wonders whether some American Jews may have been thinking on April 12 about issues raised a month earlier by Judah Piltch in *Hadoar*.[49] In an essay entitled "Disappointment," Piltch, who had the ability to see and expose what others overlooked,[50] expressed anger and resentment at Roosevelt for a series of disappointments: the Évian Conference on refugees in July 1938, which failed to address adequately the Jewish refugee problem; the failure to block the White Paper in 1939 and then again in 1944; the failure to extend a hand of support to the passengers on the *St. Louis* in June 1939; the farcical Bermuda Conference in April 1943; the fact that nothing was done to help Hungarian Jews who were brought as sheep to the slaughter in the spring of 1944; the Yalta Conference, reports from which minimized Jewish suffering and omitted any reference to justice for the Jews in Palestine; and, finally, the president's meeting with Ibn Saud, from whom he said he learned more in five minutes about the Arab and Jewish problem than he had learned from Jews in years. In conclusion, Piltch wrote:

> Roosevelt is unquestionably a man of vision and we are confident that he is our friend. We do not want to lose our faith in him. Perhaps the day will come when he will bring us comfort, but for now we have bitter acounts to settle with the White House. We are deeply disappointed with the attitude of our president toward the questions that affect our lives. The disappointment is great.[51]

Historians would at a later date confirm the intuitive insights of Judah Piltch. In April of 1945, however, the *Hadoar* analyst's viewpoint was unique. Roosevelt was a hero to American Jews. His passing consumed their thoughts and filled their hearts with sadness and a deep sense of loss. They looked for ways to memorialize him and pay tribute to his life's work.[52] The death of the president was a dominant, absorbing event in their lives. When added to the agitation over the break-up of the UJA, the communal storm over San Francisco, and, of course, the overarching concern for ending the war and reuniting soldiers with their families, it served as one more distraction from the terrible facts that were coming to light through the liberation of the camps.

A DAY OF FASTING AND PRAYER

During the first half of 1945 there was one day on which the religious Jewish community tried to focus the attention of American Jews on the fate of their European brothers and sisters. On Wednesday, March 14, as part of a worldwide fast day proclaimed by the Chief Rabbinate in Palestine,[53] the Orthodox rabbis of the United States, supported by the Synagogue Council of America,[54] called on Jews to close their offices and businesses from noon to 1:00 o'clock, to fast and to gather in synagogues for afternoon prayers. This was a less dramatic demonstration of grief than that called for in Palestine, where March 14 was proclaimed as the culmination of a week of mourning during which there was to be no public entertainment, weddings, or festivities. Work was to stop for two hours in the morning, and prayer services were arranged for 5:00 in the afternoon. The Hebrew newspapers devoted their entire editions on March 14 to the day of mourning and the plight of European Jewry.[55]

The observance of this day of mourning in America seems to have been confined largely to Orthodox centers, mostly in New York. The *Sentinel* in Chicago did not mention the day either before or after its observance. The same was true of the *Jewish Exponent*, whose synagogue page in its March 9 issue announced such coming events as Sisterhood Sabbath at Temple Kenesseth Israel, a men's club activity at Congregation Temple Judea, an annual Bar Mitzvah reunion at Congregation Emanu-El, a Purim banquet at Adath Zion, sisterhood events at Beth Shalom, and an advance notice of a Passover Seder at Congregation Rodeph Shalom. There is no indication in the Philadelphia paper that anybody observed the fast in that largely non-Orthodox city.[56] Boston's *Jewish Advocate*, on the other hand, which covered the news from this period more generously, did announce the fast day in its March 1 edition. It mentioned a united service for Roxbury and Dorchester residents to be conducted by Rabbis Chaim Goldberg, Mendell Lewittes, and Walter S. Wurzburger.[57] There was no further mention of the day in subsequent issues, and there was no editorial comment.

In the New York papers the day was treated as a major event. Even the socialist-secularist *Forward* proclaimed the day, in its March 14 edition, with a front-page two-column story, as a fast day not just for religious Jews but for all Jews, who were united in tears and in giving help for the survivors.[58] On March 15 the paper gave a detailed account of the observances, most of which, it said, centered in the Lower East Side and in Williamsburg. It described a large gathering of "all the Hassidic rabbis of New York at the synagogue of the Boyaner Rebbe, Rabbi Mordecai Shlomo Friedman."[59] A gathering of around 500 Jews met under the auspices of the Va'ad Ha-Hatzola (a rescue and relief organization) at the Manhattan Plaza, 66 East 4th Street, at *Mincha* time, to recite psalms, to listen to speakers like Rabbi Israel Rosenberg, president of the Agudas Ha-Rabbonim (Association of Orthodox Rabbis), and Rabbi Moshe Shatzkes (formerly the Lomzer *Rov*), to pray, and then to break the fast with *kuchel* and little pieces of fish, foods which required no ritual washing.[60]

The *Morning Journal*, which represented the Orthodox community, gave this day the fullest coverage. It remained for the *Day*, however, in its coverage, to strike a more universal Jewish note. American rabbis, it editorialized, had called for this day of prayer, fasting, and repentance in association with the rabbinate in Palestine. The greatest help for European Jewry could come from the fortunate Jews here in America who had thrived in this land.

> Fasting and assembling in *shuls* can be done also by the irreligious. The purpose is to demonstrate our Jewish unity, solidarity and also our national discipline which we must now practice as a people. In this way every individual Jew, every Jewish man and every Jewish woman will at least identify, if only minimally, in the terrible blow which has fallen upon us as a people.
>
> In truth, we American Jews have not sufficiently cried over this blow which has fallen upon us. We do not feel the tragedy sufficiently. Furthermore, we have not adequately shown the world how devastated we are over this horrible catastrophe.
>
> Therefore this decision of the rabbis is important for everyone: for religious and non-religious alike.[61]

On the day of the fast, the *Day* used its top headline to proclaim "TEARFUL FAST FOR WORLD JEWRY TODAY." It stressed again—

this time in a black-bordered box on page 1—that this fast was not a religious fast but rather a national demonstration by all Jews of their tears and pain over the tragedy of European Jewry and a vigorous protest against the strong and the powerful in the world who had allowed the catastrophe to happen.[62]

The paper then added a statement of retroactive guilt and contrition which may or may not have been felt by other American Jews in this period.

> The rabbis have correctly called this not alone a fast day but also a day of *teshuva* (repentance). *Teshuva* essentially means soul-searching, rendering an accounting of what each one of us did or did not do.
>
> On this day each of us must ask himself: Did I do all I could to help save the Jews across the ocean? Did I do all I could to support the efforts to rescue Jews?
>
> This national fast day should be a day for tears and for action![63]

CONCLUSION

The pattern of behavior of American Jews in response to the Holocaust remained largely the same in the first half of 1945 as during the years 1938 to 1944. Life continued as usual despite the fresh and vivid evidence of Nazi bestiality which became available during this period. The Jewish newspapers and magazines, local and national, devoted their columns largely to the war and its conclusion, to Jewish organizational issues, to local events, and to general American interests. The news from the liberated camps and areas in Europe did not dominate the papers or, from what one can glean from the press, Jewish life in New York and around the country. Even the fast day seems to have been observed in but a few communities and, even in them, mostly by Orthodox Jews.

Some observers expressed anger or despair over the lack of interest on the part of Jews with respect to the fate of European Jewry. Elias Ginsburg bemoaned the fact that American Jews knew Lidice (the site of a German massacre of Czechoslovakians in 1942) but did not know what Majdanek and Treblinka were.[64] The *Jewish Exponent*, in an editorial calling for generous contributions to the Allied Jewish Appeal in

Philadelphia, admitted that perhaps more could and should have been done, but now is "not the time for this type of speculation."[65]

Perhaps the *Jewish Exponent* should have engaged in some introspection in order to find out why more was not done, for in its May 11 issue it quoted reports from journalists who had been invited to tour Buchenwald and Dachau as if their revelations were totally new:

> This conclusion is inescapable that the Nazis had a master plan for their political prison camps. That plan was based on a policy of calculated and organized brutality. . . . Actually Nazi methods ran the gamut from deliberate starvation and routine beatings to sadistic tortures too horrible to be publicly described.[66]

Where were the reporters at the end of 1942 when the "master plan" was front-page news in the United States and the subject for editorial comment?[67] Moreover, why was the *Jewish Exponent* surprised by these reports? From December 1942 through March 1943 it editorialized several times about the need to respond to the terrible crisis of European Jewry. The editor knew the facts then. Why was he newly aroused now?

It is clear that even at this late date in the Holocaust period, by which time everything should have been known, the German determination to murder all the Jews of Europe was never really understood even by those who knew the facts. This monstrous plan simply was unassimilable by normal human minds. How else can one explain the astonishment of the editor of the *Jewish Exponent* in May 1945?

Perhaps Leon Kubowitzki, secretary of the World Jewish Congress, was right when he admitted in January 1945 that the relatively weak response of American Jews to the Holocaust was fundamentally due to the incredibility and incomprehensibility of the Final Solution.

> Even we, who had followed the development of National Socialism since its early beginnings . . . had to be convinced that small food rations were part of a program of *death*; that deportation had but one final destination, *death*. Even the Jews of the Warsaw Ghetto refused to believe the reports of their underground press. . . . They knew that there were extermination cen-

ters in Belzec, Chelmno and Treblinka, and yet refused to believe that the Warsaw Ghetto would be wiped out.[68]

Perhaps, then, the Holocaust was beyond belief not alone for the Christian world but also for American Jews. Perhaps not even in 1945 did American Jews fully comprehend what had happened. Perhaps that is why not too many fasted on March 14, not too many articles were written about the tragedy, and not too many people were moved by the immensity of the destruction as it was revealed in the person and in the words of the survivors. For the survivors did speak. They had to speak; "to give witness by one's own testimony was, in the end, to contribute to moral victory."[69] In the concentration camps there had been a slogan: "I am the victim! I am the witness!"[70] In the spring of 1945, American Jews were not fully prepared to hear the witnesses.

Notes:

1. Originally published in Jeffrey Gurock, ed., *Ramaz: School, Community, Scholarship and Orthodoxy* (Hoboken: KTAV Publishing, 1989). Reprinted with the permission of the author.
2. Haskel Lookstein, *Were We Our Brothers' Keepers? The Public Response of American Jews to the Holocaust, 1938–1944* (New York and Bridgeport, Conn., 1985; paperback reprint, New York: Vintage, 1988).
3. Ibid., ch. 8.
4. Germany officially surrendered unconditionally on May 7 at 2:41 A.M. Konnilyn G. Feig, in *Hitler's Death Camps: The Sanity of Madness* (New York, 1981), records the liberation of the other major camps as follows: Sobibor, destroyed by the Germans in October 1943 after a revolt (p. 292); Treblinka, destroyed by the Germans in November 1943 after a revolt (p. 311); Majdanek, liberated by the Russians in July 1944 (p. 330); Chelmno, closed by the Germans in April 1943, reopened in April 1944, destroyed by the Germans in late 1944 (pp. 273–74); Buchenwald, liberated by the inmates and then by the Americans on April 10, 1945 (p. 109); Bergen-Belsen, liberated by the British on April 15, 1945 (p. 379); Dachau, liberated by the Americans on April 29, 1945 (p. 60); and

Theresienstadt, liberated by the Russians on May 8, 1945 (p. 262). The sources for Auschwitz and Mauthausen are pp. 364 and 124 respectively.

5. For an explanation of why the Jewish press has been used as an indicator of what American Jews were thinking and doing at that time, see Lookstein, *Were We Our Brothers' Keepers*, pp. 24–25 and the notes thereto. Most of the papers and periodicals used in that study have been reviewed for this one as well.

6. "Only Few Jews Found in Ruins of Warsaw by Red Army" was the lead headline in the *Jewish Telegraphic Agency Daily News Bulletin* (*JTA*), January 21, 1945.

7. "Nazis Left No Jews in Lodz" was the lead headline in *JTA*, January 24, 1945. These items were reported in the Yiddish press and, ultimately, in some of the Jewish magazines.

8. *JTA*, February 19, 1945, p. 1.

9. *JTA*, February 28, 1945, p. 1.

10. *JTA*, March 6, 1945, p. 1.

11. *JTA*, March 7, 1945, p. 1. See also *JTA*, April 4, 1945, which gave prewar and postwar figures as: Vilna, 100,000 and 600; Kiev, 70,000 and 20; Minsk, 100,000 and 1,000; and Berditchev, 40,000 and 12.

12. The notorious nature of Auschwitz was already revealed in November 1944 by a report from the War Refugee Board. "Dozens of papers published articles and editorials on the news," according to Deborah E. Lipstadt in *Beyond Belief: The American Press and the Coming of the Holocaust 1933–1944* (New York, 1986), pp. 263–67, 354–55. The first report on Oświęcim following its liberation by the Russians, January 22, 1945, did not appear in the *JTA* until March 7.

13. *JTA*, April 24, 1945, p. 2. The report cites a British member of Parliament, Samuel S. Silverman, who heard the figure from Benedict Kautsky, son of the former leader of the Austrian Socialist Party.

14. *JTA*, April 9, 1945, p. 1.

15. *JTA*, April 20, 1945, p. 1, quoted from London papers.

16. Ibid.

17. *JTA*, April 22 and 23, 1945, p. 1.

18. *JTA*, May 11, 1945, p. 3.

19. Charles Herbert Stember et al., *Jews in the Mind of America* (New York, 1966), p. 141.

20. *JTA*, May 1, 1945, p. 1.

21. See Bernard Postal, "The English-Jewish Press," *Dimensions in American Judaism*, Fall 1969, pp. 30–34; and Aaron M. Neustadt, "An Orchid for the Jewish Press," *National Jewish Monthly*, November 1946, p. 108.

22. *Congress Weekly*, May 11, 1945, pp. 11 and 16; and other issues in May and June.

23. Marie Syrkin, "On Hebrewcide," *Jewish Frontier*, July 1945, pp. 10–12. This was followed by L. Spizman, "Death and Resurrection: In the Concentration Camps," *Jewish Frontier*, August 1945, pp. 7–10.

24. Menachem Ribalow, "Ervat Germanya" [Germany's Nakedness], *Hadoar*, April 27, 1945, front page.

25. *National Jewish Monthly*, March 1945, p. 203.

26. Syrkin, "On Hebrewcide," p. 10.

27. See Lookstein, *Were We Our Brothers' Keepers*, pp. 169–73; and Lipstadt, *Beyond Belief*, pp. 250–62.

28. Lookstein, *Were We Our Brothers' Keepers*, p. 74.

29. *JTA*, February 13, 1945.

30. Editorial, *Opinion*, April 1945, pp. 6–7; Theodore N. Lewis, "Men and Events," *Opinion*, May 1945, p. 14.

31. See *JTA*, March 5, 1945, pp. 3–4; April 6, 1945, p. 5, which called for contributions of 150,000 tons of clothing to be collected at depots around the country during April; *Reconstructionist*, March 9, 1945, pp. 3–4, and May 18, 1945, pp. 4–6; and Jack Diamond, "Jewish Overseas Relief Organization," *Jewish Frontier*, August 1945.

32. *National Jewish Monthly*, July-August 1945, p. 313.

33. See Lookstein, *Were We Our Brothers' Keepers*, pp. 131–3.

34. See *Congress Weekly*, editorial, May 25, 1945, p. 3; Trude Weiss-Rosemarin's editorial in the *Jewish Spectator*, April 1945, p. 5; and *Opinion*, editorial, April 1945, p. 7.

35. Editorial, *Congress Weekly*, May 25, 1945, p. 3.

36. Henry Monsky's statement to a press conference in San Francisco on May 14, *National Jewish Monthly*, June 1945, p. 298.

37. *Opinion*, June 1945, pp. 6–7.

38. Ibid.

39. *Jewish Morning Journal*, March 7, 1945, p. 3. Heder (or kheyder) is a Jewish religious elementary school.

40. Ibid.

41. See also *Congress Weekly*, March 2, 1945, p. 5.

42. January 1945, pp. 152 and 159.

43. *Jewish Frontier*, July 1945, pp. 13–14. See also Martin Gilbert, *The Holocaust: A History of the Jews of Europe During the Second World War* (New York, 1986), pp. 816–819, who documents how returning Jews found life in Poland to be brutal and deadly.

44. Wise's statement was quoted in *JTA*, May 12, 1945, p. 1.

45. Editorial, *Jewish Frontier*, May 1945, p. 4.

46. *National Jewish Monthly*, June 1945, p. 293.

47. Title of an editorial tribute in *Congress Weekly*, April 20, 1945, p. 3.

48. Gordis, loc. cit.; and Menachem Ribalow, *Hadoar*, April 20, 1945, p. 272.

49. March 16, 1945, pp. 391–2.

50. See his scathing criticism of American Jewish indifference to the tragedy of European Jews in Lookstein, *Were We Our Brothers' Keepers*, pp. 214–15.

51. *Hadoar*, March 16, 1945, p. 392.

52. See the *Jewish Exponent* in Philadelphia, April 20, 1945, for a description of a number of such projects. For example: the planting of 1,000 trees in Palestine and the designing of a stained-glass window in a temple.

53. *JTA*, March 6, 1945.

54. *JTA*, March 11, 1945. The SCA was an umbrella organization comprising the rabbinic and synagogue bodies of Orthodox, Conservative, and Reform in America.

55. *JTA*, March 14, 1945.

56. There were a few Orthodox synagogues in Philadelphia, such as the one led by Rabbi Bernard Levinthal, where presumably the fast day was observed, but there is no mention of it in the March 9 or March 16 editions of the *Jewish Exponent*. Actually, European Jewry was mentioned for the first time in almost three months in an April 6 article, "Promises to Repatriate Transylvanian Jews." Not even *JTA* news dispatches were provided by the paper. On the other hand, after Roosevelt's death, there was a major memorial service for the community at the YM&YWHA, the major address from which was printed on the front page of the paper, April 20. Mention was made that on the previous Friday night and Saturday morning, Jews attended services in "much larger numbers."

57. *Jewish Advocate*, March 1, 1945, p. 5.

58. *Daily Forward*, March 14, 1945, p. 1.

59. Ibid., March 15, 1945, p. 1.

60. Ibid.

61. *Day*, March 13, 1945, p. 4.

62. *Day*, March 14, 1945, p. 1.

63. Ibid.

64. "Booby Traps in Germany," *Congress Weekly*, April 13, 1945, p. 8.

65. *Jewish Exponent*, May 4, 1945, p. 4.

66. Ibid., May 11, 1945, p. 4.

67. Lookstein, *Were We Our Brothers' Keepers*, ch. 4.

68. A. Leon Kubowitzki, "Snatching Jews from the Jaws of Death," *Jewish Spectator*, January 1945, pp. 10–13.

69. Gilbert, *The Holocaust*, p. 828.

70. Ibid., p. 825.

British Journalism

The "Thunderer" and The Coming of The Shoah: *The Times* of London, 1933–1942

Colin Shindler
University of London

The Times and "Englishness"

In May 1784, John Walter, a bankrupted Lloyds underwriter wrote to his patron, Benjamin Franklin, the American Minister in pre-Revolutionary Paris, to inform him that he intended to publish a newspaper. On 1 January 1785, Walter's project appeared as *The Daily Universal Register*. Three years later, the title was changed to *The Times* or, as it has become more affectionately known to journalists in Fleet Street and beyond, "The Thunderer."

In its two hundred years of existence, the *Times* has been perceived as the quintessence of "Englishness" and well-connected to the ruling class in Britain by the world outside. The official history of the *Times* succinctly defined its role:

> The *Times*, [diplomats in London] acknowledged, did not speak directly for the government; it spoke for itself, but its independent views, they noticed, generally corresponded with the thinking of influential groups in Westminster, Whitehall, the City and the older Universities. It therefore could be taken as the voice of the dominant minority in the country; sometimes in line with the government, sometimes in divergence; and where it was divergent, it was—these diplomats told themselves—especially worth noting, for then it showed what kind of pressures were likely very soon to be brought against the government from within the ruling circle in the attempt to bring about a change of policy.[1]

The editors of the *Times* during the period 1933–1945 were Geoffrey Dawson (1912–1919 and again 1922–1941) and his close colleague, Robin Barrington-Ward (1941–1948). Dawson had been at Eton and Magdalen College, Oxford. He was a Fellow of All Souls, had served as Lord Milner's private secretary in South Africa and was "an Empire-oriented, conventional English scholar-squire."[2] Indeed, it was in South Africa at the turn of the century that Dawson first met Edward Wood, later Lord Halifax and Chamberlain's Foreign Secretary. It was a close friendship that continued into and through the era of appeasement. Dawson was also a friend of Chamberlain and came to see himself in a quasi-Ministerial capacity. R.M. Barrington-Ward similarly came from a privileged background. He was the son of a clergyman and was educated at Westminster and Balliol. Unlike the more conservative Dawson, Barrington-Ward was much more a Tory radical in the Disraeli mode.

In one sense, Dawson and Barrington-Ward were both products of their time and their class. Their approach to the election of Hitler in 1933 and their understanding of Nazi anti-Semitism reflected the approach of wide sectors of the British establishment.

During the 1930s, the *Times* distanced itself from the openly anti-Nazi approach of other sections of the British press, in particular, that of the liberal *Manchester Guardian*. Yet this did not mean that its senior figures were uninformed about developments inside Germany. Barrington-Ward, who visited Berlin in June 1937, heard first hand about the persecution and suffering of the Jewish intelligentsia from Rudo Hahn, the brother of the headmaster of Gordonstoun, one of Britain's famous private schools. Barrington-Ward believed that the printed word in the pages of the *Times* was avidly dissected by the Nazi hierarchy. He therefore felt that the influence of the *Times* in the ruling circles in Hitler's Germany would be severely diminished if he spoke out passionately and loudly.[3] In addition, the carnage during World War I had conditioned Barrington-Ward to exhibit a total hatred of war and he was thus loath to use his position to advocate too strong a policy against Germany for fear of antagonizing the Nazi leadership and thereby facilitating the movement towards war.[4] The Nazis, however, did not reciprocate and there was a relative indifference to the *Times'* gentle approach. In one bizarre episode, a senior correspondent in Europe informed Barrington-Ward in May 1937 that according to the German press, *Times* read backwards offered "semit," and this was clear evidence in Nazi eyes of the existence of a Jewish-Marxist conspiracy in the higher echelons of the British establishment.[5]

The *Times* editor, Geoffrey Dawson, reacted to this and other criticism with apologies:

> It would interest me to know precisely what it is in the *Times* that has produced this antagonism in Germany. I do my utmost, night after night, to keep out of the paper anything that might hurt their sensibilities. I can think of nothing that has been printed now for many months past which they could possibly take exception to as unfair comment. . . . I have always been convinced that the peace of the world depends more than anything else on our getting into reasonable relations with Germany.[6]

Numerous colleagues of Dawson later distanced themselves from such an interpretation of policy towards Nazi Germany, protesting emphatically that there was no censorship at the *Times*.[7] Even if Dawson projected an exaggerated version of reality, it did symbolize a more general policy of appeasement at the *Times*.

Although there had been division in the *Times* about the wisdom of following such a policy, it had been persued with vigor by Dawson, Barrington-Ward and the foreign leader writer, Leo Kennedy. The infamous editorial which advocated the dismemberment of Czechoslovakia[8] had been written by Kennedy and revised by Dawson. Yet for several weeks previously, Dawson had been primed by his old friend, Foreign Secretary Lord Halifax, and even allowed to read sensitive Foreign Office memoranda. Over lunch on the same day as the piece appeared, Halifax indicated that despite the formal protestations of the Foreign Office, he was not displeased with the *Times*' editorial.

Even in private correspondence, Barrington-Ward was at pains to rationalize this policy as late as April 1939:

> It was an endeavor to discover even at the eleventh hour whether the Nazis were, according to their professions, out for reasonable change or whether they were out for mere domination. Chamberlain was ready to wait for the proofs and Churchill was

not. The Churchill case completely ignored the admitted blunder of the settlement of 1919 and above all the failure to give Germany a say in the Versailles settlement. A policy (Churchill's) which could have been represented as one of mere frightened encirclement would have ranked every German behind the Fuhrer and left this country with an uneasy conscience and deeply divided.[9]

Yet if Barrington-Ward's memories of World War I led him to embrace appeasement, he did not accept the claim that the obstacle to better British-German relations was the irritant of the Jews. In an exchange of private letters with a correspondent in Hastings, an intermediary for Wilhelm Stapel, a prominent Nazi in Hamburg, Barrington-Ward was forthright in sending the word back to Germany:

> Nazism has done much for Germany. But the organized onslaught on the Jews last November [*Kristallnacht*] was a huge disservice—and the annexation of Bohemia-Moravia was another. Were we to sit by and say that these were good things—an enrichment of Western civilization? How does he explain the alarm which has been created all round Germany's borders[?] Can he really believe that "Jewish agitation" is the cause?[10]

Yet *Kristallnacht* outraged the British press and the *Times* as uncivilized conduct—and thus "un-English" conduct—but, as Barrington-Ward's letter indicates, it also severely embarrassed the appeasement lobby as the pogrom took place so soon after Munich. It also indicated that the Jewish question was not one that could be buried in the cause of British-German friendship.

The Simpson Article

Up until 1938, reports of Nazi atrocities were, by and large, underplayed by the *Times*. Like other sections of the British press, the experience of the *Times* was not attuned to such bestialities. It was—even at the very beginning of Nazi rule—beyond their comprehension why Jews should be persecuted. Many newspaper correspondents in Germany toned down their articles because they knew that the full details would not be believed by their editors. When Norman Ebbutt, the senior Berlin corre-spondent of the *Times* discovered that his most detailed and critical mate-rial did not appear, he passed on "his more damning information" to the American CBS radio correspondent, William Shirer.[11]

From the very beginning, disbelief pervaded the *Times*' approach to Nazi intentions—to the extent that it underplayed the importance of anti-Semitism in Hitler's election manifesto in 1933.[12]

Although the *Times* had published an article on Oranienburg in September 1933,[13] the newspaper was averse to publicizing conditions in the concentration camps. This was indicated clearly when the *Times* spiked a detailed story on Dachau in December 1933 from its Bavarian correspondent, Stanley Simpson. Dachau was the first concentration camp to be established for political prisoners in March 1933 and in fact Simpson's piece hardly mentioned Jews. Simpson had spent months of careful research, checking and rechecking his sources. A letter to the for-eign editor of the *Times*, Ralph Deakin, illustrated the uniqueness of Simpson's piece when he pointed out that "the terrorism is so intense and such elaborate precautions taken to keep things secret that it is often weeks before news leaks out from the camp and weeks more before it can be tested and confirmed."[14]

He concluded his article with an attempt to convey the Nazi mentali-ty to the ordinary British reader

> Although Herr Hitler once said that nothing could take place in the Nazi movement without his knowing it, one would like to think that the German government is ignorant of these infamies in Bavaria. It would be hard, however, to acquit them of moral responsibility for a course of conduct which follows logically from the Nazi glorification of brutality, and the doctrine preached by Nazi leaders, from Herr Hitler himself downwards, that the murder of a political opponent, no matter how revolting in its bru-tality, is no murder, but a deed of heroism.[15]

Originally, someone at the *Times* clearly wished to publish this ground-breaking piece since scribbled in the margin of the galley was "keep for leader writer." Simpson had taken the trouble to write a five-page letter to Deakin in which he suggested that the publication of such a damning piece could be "the means of putting an end to or even mitigating the sufferings of these men and of saving lives—which if nothing is done, will assuredly be sacrificed."[16]

Simpson's personal involvement ("The fate of these wretched creatures in the camp oppresses me night and day and I would give a great deal to be able to help them.")[17] cut no ice with Barrington-Ward who questioned Simpson's ability to be objective and unemotional. In an internal memo to Deakin, he further questioned the testimonies of Simpson's often terrified informants. "One knows that it is necessary without doubting for a moment that cruelties have been practiced in such places—to treat particular instances with caution in view of the sufferer's (especially the German sufferer's) capacity to believe that things have been even worse than actuality."[18]

After conferring with the editor, Dawson, Barrington-Ward informed Deakin[19] that the article was no longer relevant since the *New Statesman* had already published an article on the camp at Sonnenburg.[20] Simpson was paid the sum of £10.10.0 for his unused article.[21]

The Image of the Jew

Deakin had requested an outside opinion of Simpson's article and sent the piece to William Teeling, a lawyer at Lincoln's Inn and later a Conservative MP, for his comments. Teeling replied that it was a "one sided document" and its publication would put the *Times* in "an awkward position since the paper is immensely respected in Germany." Dachau, he argued, was not meant to be a sanitarium. Teeling recalled his recent visit to Munich and his impression that that "the [foreign newspaper] correspondents seem to hate the Nazi regime." Teeling added that "our Consul-General in Cologne told me, he went into every Jew-case officially for atrocities and never found a real one. He believed 'their oriental exaggeration has got the better of them.' And some Jewish rabbis assured me these atrocities, if there were any, were now completely over."[22]

The belief in the Jew's ability to exaggerate and distort reality, to promote their own cause was widespread in the British establishment. As Philip Graves, a foreign correspondent with the *Times* since 1906 and exposer of the *Protocols of the Elders of Zion*, exclaimed in a private letter to Barrington-Ward, "why must Jews be so prolix?"[23] Later during World War II, the *Times* reflected the Foreign Office's attitude that Jewish particularism should be submerged and that Jews exaggerated the reality of the situation.

In the monocultural world of the 1930s, Jews who did not assimilate and dissolve into the wider society were suspect. They manifested a distinct form of "un-Englishness" by their insistence on maintaining their difference. Yet the very notion of Nazi anti-Semitism was similarly un-English. It was an affront against the liberal conscience and struck at the roots of a civilized behavior which characterized the English way of life. It was a competition between these two dislikes which confused and characterized British understanding and response in the 1930s. As Neville Chamberlain, himself, pointed out after *Kristallnacht*, "No doubt, Jews aren't a lovable people: I don't care about them myself, but that is not sufficient to explain the pogrom."[24]

While the British establishment may gradually have been repelled by Nazi anti-Semitism, there also remained a profound reticence to identify with Jews—especially Jews who were also foreigners—and by extrapolation the suffering of such Jews simply because they were Jews.

The Foreign Secretary, Lord Halifax, was the architect of appeasement and therefore it was not in the interests of the British government to raise the Jewish issue with Nazi Germany for fear of derailing this policy. Halifax, "the Holy Fox," even after the outbreak of war, was always keen to follow through any possibility of an agreed peace with Germany in 1939 and 1940—and even more so after the fall of France. Neither was Halifax above the social anti-Semitism of his class. At the last minute, Chamberlain bowed to Halifax's request not to appoint Hore-Belisha as Minister of Information because he was a Jew since this—it was argued—would have an adverse effect on the neutral countries.

In addition, there was a profound inability to understand the ideological roots of Nazi anti-Semitism which was also prevalent amongst many British journalists. There must be, it was argued, more pragmatic, more rational, reasons for such a dire situation. It was easier psychologically to believe that the Jews had brought the persecution upon themselves because they were prominent in German society and that, although they carried German passports, they had remained a people apart. Similarly, it was more convenient to believe that Hitler did not know what his minions were doing in his name—especially after the Nuremberg decrees.[25] The lack of consistency—and indeed confusion in most of the British press—

was a result of the narrow cultural prism through which the British establishment projected its worldview.

It must also be asked to what extent leading figures at the *Times* still
espoused a policy of appeasement during the "phony war" of 1939 and
especially after the series of German victories and British defeats in 1940.
Did they still sympathize with the peace lobby within the British establishment who wished to save the empire and permit the Nazis to destroy
Soviet Communism for them? Would Dawson and Barrington-Ward have
supported a peace treaty with Hitler in 1940 and a German-dominated
Europe? Given the unfailing support which Dawson had always shown
Halifax, the answer is likely to be in the affirmative. It would therefore
always have been in Halifax's interests that the obstacle of the Jewish
question should not be given prominence in the *Times*. All this had profound consequences when news of the Shoah broke in the summer of
1942. As Tony Kushner has commented:

> It is, however, essential to understand that the available informa-
> tion would be channeled through domestic ideological consider-
> ations that were (just as much as the quantity and quality of infor-
> mation received) to hinder understanding of the Jewish plight.[26]

The Role of the British Government

Yet there was another, perhaps much more important factor which
limited British—and the *Times'*—understanding of Nazi anti-Semitism
and ultimately the growing revelations of the Shoah. This was the lack of
any political lead by successive British governments.

In 1937, Barrington-Ward had initiated a liaison between "a regular
diplomatic correspondent" and the Foreign Office. Following a lunch at
the Athenaeum Club with Rex Leeper, the head of the Foreign Office's
News Department, Barrington-Ward wrote in his personal diary that
"Leeper wishes the *Times* would have a diplomatic correspondent to see
him regularly on broad policy and get the mind of the Government as
news."[27]

In addition to the life-long friendship between the editor, Dawson,
and the Foreign Secretary, Halifax, there was, of course, regular contact
between senior figures in the *Times* and government Ministers. Requests

were sometimes made by Ministers to the *Times* to achieve a particular political goal—a need which became more accentuated in wartime. For example, the new Foreign Secretary, Anthony Eden, wrote to Barrington-Ward in October 1941 suggesting that "an occasional leader in the *Times* would provide us and the Greek government with most valuable material for use in the broadcasts to Greece which are our own principal medium for maintaining the spirits of the Greeks."[28]

Following the outbreak of war, journalists found themselves in the difficult position of being objective observers of the conflict yet at the same time being an integral part of the war effort. The contradiction of being both outside and inside, of marrying the call of their profession with their patriotic duty to ensure the downfall of Nazi Germany, confronted journalists on many occasions.

When the Zurich correspondent of the *Times* submitted an article on Germany's coal production, Barrington-Ward sent it to the Ministry of Economic Warfare for their opinion. In his reply to the Zurich correspondent, Barrington-Ward commented that, following talks with Ministry officials, "we are not happy about it . . . and feel that it would be much better not published at all."[29] In a memorandum to Deakin, Barrington-Ward wrote that "we can hardly take a more optimistic view of the blockade than the Ministry is prepared to take. I think we shall have to do without the article."[30]

The central point of contact for many journalists was the Foreign Office News Department. Sir William Ridsdale was head of this unit between 1941 and 1954. His department was an essential source of information for the press from occupied Europe. Its job—at least on the surface—was to assist journalists by transmitting all available information. A more subterranean task was to ensure that only the news which the British government deemed to be fit to appear in the press should be published. Moreover, in wartime, the transmission of selective information could be rationalized in terms of national security. The diplomatic correspondent of the *Times* believed that the Foreign Office passed on information factually without minimizing it—and especially "the terrible German atrocities in Russia."[31]

The Foreign Office, moreover, had a vested interest in ensuring that reports in the *Times* in particular were aligned with government policy. The Foreign Office believed that regardless of the reality, reports in the

Times were perceived differently from other sections of the British press by foreign powers. The possibility of erroneous signals—from the British Government's viewpoint—transmitted to the enemy through the vehicle of independent reporting in the *Times* was too risky. A Foreign Office colleague sent a letter to Ridsdale which commented that

> this sort of thing might not be quite so important if it appeared in some other paper. But the *Times* is in a special position—and it is surely most dangerous that it should at this juncture lend the weight of its authority to such perversions of essential facts. This sort of thing does not perhaps altogether convince, but it does introduce an element of doubt and hesitancy into people's minds.[32]

After the outbreak of war in 1939, a certain subtlety of approach operated within the confines of the Foreign Office. There was a clear need to filter the news without the operation seeming too blatant, duplicitous and unjustifiable. As Richard Cockett has pointed out,

> Just as the service ministries operated their own private censorship by rigidly controlling the flow of news, so the Foreign Office did likewise—but it also exercised those effective methods of personal contact both at the level of the News Department with the specialist correspondents and at ambassadorial or national level with newspaper proprietors and editors. Those ambassadors and officials operating this form of "silent censorship" could point to its success in order to appease the more repressive instincts of most of their colleagues.[33]

Indeed, Sir William Ridsdale himself argued against any censorship because it was unnecessary since "there was a large measure of cooperation between the press and the Foreign Office News Department."[34]

Information about the Shoah

Information reached London from occupied Europe from a variety of sources. Much of it—and especially that derived from domestic intelligence operations in Europe—passed through the filter of the British intelligence services (SIS, SOE, MI5, MI9, MI19). Moreover, US embassies remained open in Berlin, Budapest, Bucharest and Vichy until the end of 1941 and the beginning of 1942. In neutral countries, allied diplomats operated information gathering centers. The press in these countries further provided reports. There were also anti-Nazi Germans who tried to pass on vital information through neutral countries. Furthermore, fragments of information could be gleaned even from the highly controlled Soviet and German papers and broadcasts. Émigré groups domiciled in London also possessed their own networks in their home countries. Jewish and Zionist organizations operating out of neutral capitals, such as Geneva, Istanbul and Lisbon, transmitted information received.

After such information was clarified and vetted, it was cleared for transmission through a variety of channels. The Ministry of Information fed the BBC home services while British Intelligence and the Foreign Office catered for the European services. The Political Warfare Executive directed by Sir Robert Bruce Lockhart utilized material for propaganda purposes.

The *Times* had access to most of these sources. Indeed, the diplomatic correspondent of the *Times* first learned about extermination techniques using the exhaust fumes of trucks and vans through Polish intelligence and the "London" Poles. In 1943–4, he met "several Polish agents who were flown out of Poland to report and were then flown back again." This included Josef Retinger, a political aide to Sikorski. They told him that Jews from Poland and Germany—as well as ethnic Poles—were being killed in Auschwitz. No differentiation seems to have been made between the incarceration of Poles in Auschwitz and the extermination of Jews there.[35]

From the outbreak of war until May 1942, the *Times* picked up periodic stories about the Nazi persecution of the Jews. For example, the British White Paper on "The Treatment of German Nationals in Germany" (October 1939),[36] the establishment of the Warsaw Ghetto (October and December 1939),[37] the mass deportations of Jews (November 1941),[38] the massacres perpetrated by the *Einsatzgruppen* (January 1942)[39] and the gassing of Dutch Jews at Mauthausen (April 1942).[40]

As early as the summer of 1941, GCCS (Government Code and Cypher School) at Bletchley Park had decoded German police messages which spoke of "cleaning up operations" and "gas cleansing stations". Such reports were sent to Churchill and a select group of intelligence officers. In September 1941, code breakers at Bletchley Park relayed the information to British intelligence that

> The execution of "Jews" is so recurrent a feature of these reports that the figures have been omitted (from the daily transcripts) . . . whether all those executed as "Jews" are indeed such, is doubtful, but the figures are no less conclusive as evidence of a policy of savage intimidation, if not of ultimate extermination.

The codebreakers further concluded that the killing of Jews in such great numbers was acceptable to "the Higher Authorities." They also reported that General Kurt Daluege, the head of the *Ordnungspolizei*, was concerned that his reports to Berlin were being intercepted such that he resorted to using the phrase "action according to the usage of war" to describe the mass killing of Jews. Clearly, the British felt that they could not formally reveal the extent of the Nazi war against the Jews without admitting they had broken the German codes. To have done so, they reasoned, would have returned to their enemy a huge strategic advantage.[41]

Even so, there were indeed reports in the *Times* that Jews were being singled out for special treatment. Yet official British policy was to subsume Jewish suffering within the general maelstrom of Nazi killings in Europe. For example, the Jews were not invited to a meeting under the chairmanship of General Sikorski in January 1942 of nine occupied European nations to discuss the first revelations of mass murder in the USSR as indicated in the first Molotov note. Sikorski explained their omission from the proceedings by suggesting that Jewish representation would pander to "the racial theories" of the Nazis. Thus the official declaration did not mention the Jews at all. The Foreign Office believed that Sikorski had behaved "correctly."[42]

When the Bund report which first revealed the totality of the extermination of Polish Jewry arrived in London at the end of May 1942, the *Times* did not pick it up directly. Instead, it reported Sikorski's interpretation of it, in a broadcast on the BBC which emphasized instead Polish suffering.[43] The Nazis, it was considered, had embarked on a series of periodic pogroms rather than the systematic extermination of the Jews.

Both the *Times* and the BBC had missed the essential point that this was an organized program of extermination. The Polish Jew, Szmul Zygielbojm,[44] therefore looked for other outlets for the Bund report. He gave it to the *Daily Telegraph* which published the essential details on its main news page on 25 May under the heading "Germans murder 700,000 Jews in Poland" and "Traveling Gas Chambers," almost a month after its arrival in London.[45] The two column story describing "the greatest massacre in the world's history" was bordered by other stories—"100 Airfields in Three Months: Australia's Feat" and "Ice Cream's last Summer: Manufacture to end on September 3rd." The BBC had simultaneously decided to promote the story and Zygielbojm broadcast in Yiddish to Poland the day after the appearance of the *Daily Telegraph* article.[46] This was further followed by a plea from Chief Rabbi Hertz on the BBC European service. This burst of activity by the BBC was in part due to the loss of the story to the *Telegraph* and this was made explicit at a meeting at which a Foreign Office representative was present.[47]

At the end of June, the World Jewish Congress held a press conference at which the Bund report was promoted centrally and intensely. Although the *Times* headlined the fact that "Over One Million [Jews] Dead Since the War Began,"[48] the newspaper covered the press conference hesitantly and was economical with the information provided. This contrasted with the *Daily Telegraph* which quoted Goebbels in *Das Reich* that "the Jews of Europe . . . will pay with the extermination of their race in the whole of Europe and elsewhere too."[49] The *Guardian* recorded that seven million were in concentration camps and it was now sufficiently clear that Eastern Europe had been turned into "a vast slaughter house of Jews."[50]

As further information seeped out—much of it appearing in the émigré Polish press in London—Jewish groups, the Polish and Czechoslovak National Councils and many others strongly promoted the need to publicize the fate of the Jews. This was not a course favored by the Foreign Office which—amongst its other concerns—was also wary about upsetting the Arab nationalist cause in Mandatory Palestine.[51]

The problem for the *Times* was that influential circles in the British establishment were now speaking out on behalf of European Jews. Zygielbojm and Schwarzbart[52] ensured that the Bund report reached all members of Parliament. Cardinal Hinsley, the Catholic Archbishop of

Westminster denounced the atrocities against Jews on the BBC European service—adding that it was "not British propaganda."[53] The *Times* again devoted relatively little space to it compared to the *Telegraph*. On 9 July, the Government responded by organizing a press conference with the London Poles under the chairmanship of Brendan Bracken, the Minister of Information. The report of the *Times* the following day was once more to merge Jews into the generality of Polish suffering despite the speeches of Zygielbojm and Schwarzbart.[54] The *Daily Telegraph* and the *Guardian* carried more details about the persecution of the Jews in their reports, yet their editorials, which spoke so movingly about the victims of Nazi violence from Warsaw to Lidice, made no mention of the Jewish tragedy.

Between July and December 1942, there was a steady flow of reports—the round-ups in Paris, the mass deportations to Poland from all parts of Europe, eyewitnesses in Chelmno, the Riegner telegram, the Karski testimony—all of which constructed the general picture that European Jewry was gradually being exterminated in fulfillment of the ideological demands of Nazism. Whilst Foreign Office officials cast doubt on the truth of such reports and refused to recognize the Jews as a distinct nationality, the British press began to move to a position where— even in the absence of official confirmation—they at least began to entertain the possibility that terrible, unimaginable things were being carried out against the Jews of Europe.

A Move towards Publicity and Inactivity

In August and September 1942, the *Times* began to publish detailed reports from its correspondents in Switzerland and Portugal about the roundups of Jews in Britain's closest neighbor and ally, France. The *Times* understood the interest of the churches in Britain and covered the protests of Catholic and Protestant clergymen against the deportations to the East. It reported the arrest of Jesuits in Lyon[55] and the incarceration of priests in a camp at Sisteron.[56] On 30 September, Hitler made a speech in Berlin to mark the almost certain German victory in Russia in which he openly spoke about the extermination of all Jews—and the *Times* published it in its edition the following day.[57]

Although this growing willingness to publicize the facts differentiated the *Times* from the Foreign Office, it was not willing to accept Jewish criticism of British government policy and the broad attitude of the press.

At a rally on 29 October at the Royal Albert Hall, the Chief Rabbi force-fully attacked the reticence of the British press and suggested that it encouraged the Nazis "to go on perfecting their technique of extermina-tion" and hid the truth from the British public. The *Times*, however, did not report the content of Chief Rabbi Hertz's speech but gave more emphasis to the statement of the Archbishop of Canterbury.[58]

As the news of the mass extermination of Polish Jewry trickled out, the Foreign Office was still unable to confirm the facts to both BBC jour-nalists and the Foreign Office News Department. Despite the deportations from the Warsaw and Lodz ghettos and the revelations of the Karski report, the Foreign Office did not alter its position. At the end of November 1942, the Foreign Office was still hesitant in giving any cre-dence to the news from Poland to Sidney Silverman and Alex Easterman, representatives of the World Jewish Congress. A Foreign Office official briefed its News Department to soft-pedal the issue, but not abolish it altogether from the public domain.[59] On 1 December, Silverman and Easterman held a press conference to publicize the policy of genocide. Silverman further proposed to raise the issue in the House of Commons.

The *Times* had already picked up the concern felt by British Jews and those who resided in other free countries. It reported four days of mourn-ing for one million Jews, who had been killed by the Nazis, by an assem-bly of 400 rabbis in Jerusalem. It reported Chief Rabbi Herzog's appeal to stop the carnage and save the children. On 4 December, the *Times* printed a lead story entitled "Nazi War on the Jews: Deliberate Plan for Extermination."

The diplomatic correspondent for the *Times*, Iverach MacDonald, wrote that:

> for some weeks London has recognized on the basis of indepen-dent evidence that the worst of Hitler's threats was being literal-ly applied and that, quite apart from the widespread murders, the Polish Jews had been condemned to subsist in conditions which must steadily lead to their extermination.[60]

Although this went further than any previous *Times* article, it still stopped short of mentioning the actuality of mass extermination by design. Through the Berlin correspondents of Swedish newspapers, the

Times commented that the entire Polish General-Government would be declared *judenrein* by 1 December. The Polish Jews would be "liquidated which means either transported eastwards in cattle trucks to an unknown destination or killed where they stood."

Now, why did the *Times* suddenly change course? One reason was that the accumulating news from Poland could neither be ignored nor denied. McDonald recalled in 1995 that

> There was not a special policy to promote any single aspect [of the horrors of the German occupation of Europe]. News was news—that was the guiding principle. . . . . [Running the series of reports in December 1942] was a *news* decision essentially, based on the sure belief that news about the German atrocities was an asset, a weapon in the allied war effort.[61]

This reflected the widespread belief in government and in the media that the Jews could only be saved by a swift and total Allied victory. Again, McDonald's recollection:

> A dominant British response to the question: How can we help the Jews and other occupied peoples? . . . The surest way to help and to save Jews and others from death and suffering is to do all we can to win the war and end the tyranny as soon as possible. . . . That thought was in almost everyone's mind.[62]

Saving the Jews was then seen as a consequence of winning the war. The question—What happens if there are no more Jews left to save?—was addressed only marginally. The news from Poland became not the basis for action to save the remnant of those left alive, but an item of well-intentioned agit-prop in the war effort.

The Foreign Office, however, was not pleased[63] at the diplomatic correspondent's report on 4 December and a letter from the Archbishop of Canterbury the following day in the *Times*.

There may have been another, more political reason, for the *Times* to seemingly embrace a relatively open-minded approach. The Foreign Secretary, Anthony Eden, himself, had changed course. The flood of reports from Poland plus pressure from the London Poles and Jewish organizations may have suggested to Eden that some response from government was called for. Moreover, the advantages of publicity about the Jewish tragedy might now outweigh its well-known disadvantages. Eden had been persuaded to take seriously Silverman's proposal for a Great Power declaration on the fate of the Jews and had secured agreement from Washington and Moscow.

The first *Times* article on 4 December appeared two days after Eden had met the Soviet Ambassador in London, Ivan Maisky, to discuss the possibility of a declaration. It was not until 7 December that the *Times* reported a meeting between the American and Soviet ambassadors and Eden to discuss "the fearful plight of the Jews."[64] Clearly the series of *Times* articles in December 1942 coincided with the sudden interest of the Foreign Secretary to emphasize the Jewish tragedy in Poland.[65]

In the following days, the *Times* published further material about the extermination of European Jewry—a letter from the President of the British Section of the World Jewish Congress,[66] Cardinal Hinsley's condemnation during a Roman Catholic Day of Prayer for Poland,[67] and the details of a note from the Polish government to the Allied Powers.[68]

On 12 December, the *Times* published an editorial, "The New Barbarism" by J. H. Freeman, which recognized the uniqueness of the mass extermination of the Jews unequivocally for the first time. Yet it applied a subtle corrective to any moral outcry, by effectively reiterating British government policy:

Warning may conceivably curb the authors and actions of evil. So much the better if they do. It would be idle, however, not to recall that the moral reprobation of the outside world never restrained the Nazis in the excesses committed against the Jews and others from the first day that they seized power. Moral reprobation realistically considered is less likely to achieve in war what it failed so signally to achieve in peace. The pre-requisite of real help is victory—and victory to be effective must be swift as well as complete.[69]

Similarly, the *Times* report of the Chief Rabbi's speech at a Day of Intercession watered down his implicit criticism of the government and press.[70] It allowed the Chief Rabbi's remarks to remain within the realm of the spiritual and the moral. Yet some political points did slip through. Hertz told his audience that the decay of conscience had helped to build up a moral climate favorable to Nazism:

> What atonements were the UN prepared to make for their share in building up that climate? Would they open their gates of their countries to refugees from the Nazi inferno and help the few neutral states to receive them? Would at least the children be saved from mass poisoning and burial alive by Hitler and his hellhounds?[71]

Such demands were all right for clergymen, but they were not regarded as in line with British interests. On 18 December, the *Times* reported Eden's statement in the House of Commons, "the restrained expression of anger," "the stern protest," and "the [famous] minute of dignified silence," but the Allied declaration said nothing about the prospect of rescue. The *Times* also reported Sidney Silverman's question about what could be done by the British government to relieve the situation. Eden replied,

> My honourable friend knows the immense difficulties in the way of what he suggests, but he may be sure that we shall do all we can to alleviate these horrors—though what we can do at this stage, I am afraid must be slight.[72]

This euphemism for inaction was followed by a letter in the *Times* from Major-General Neil Malcolm, the former High Commissioner for German Refugees, who wrote "so unlike Hitler, we cannot convert words into deeds and must be content with promises which will not save one single life."[73] Malcolm's attack and plea to help Jewish children and refugees in Spain and Portugal severely embarrassed the Foreign Office who made stringent efforts to ensure that no other public figures followed Malcolm's lead. Indeed, the Foreign Office were assured that the *Times* "would not open their correspondence columns for further discussion."[74]

The Press as Innocent Bystanders

The *Times'* restrained, often erratic, approach continued for the rest of the war. Even after Eden's declaration in the House of Commons, journalists preferred to listen to the Foreign Office who were presumed to be in a better position to know than often well-informed Jewish organizations. The reports of the Jewish tragedy in the *Times* did not match the moral fervor of the *Guardian* or the detailed dispatches of the *Telegraph*.

The root of the problem was that the role of the *Times* in the 1940s was undefined. It was unsure whether it should be an unofficial organ of government, a faithful servant of a wider establishment or simply a quality newspaper of independent views and essential information. In reality, it was all of these with considerable blurring at the joins. In wartime, the added psychological constraint of patriotism mitigated against independent opinion and speaking out too vociferously.

Given the shortage of news-space, the *Times* concentrated its coverage on the war effort. The Shoah was a minor, marginalised, amorphous item underpinned by a modicum of genuine disbelief and selective indifference. Journalists often and easily dismissed the incredibility of Jewish claims because the enormity of this tragedy was quite unimaginable. Moreover, any semblance of exaggeration on the part of the British would hand the Germans an easy propaganda weapon. What could therefore not be touched was not perceived to be a priority in terms of news coverage. Articles were thus positioned in less than prominent places. The fate of the doomed Jews in Poland and elsewhere was seen at best to be an insoluble problem and therefore no criticism should reside at the door of government and press. Thus the full messages of the combatants of the Warsaw Ghetto Uprising were not published in the *Times*. Those sections of the messages which did not appear criticized the community of nations for its inactivity, its irresponsibility, its apathy and its lack of threats of retribution against the Nazi leadership. Thus the last message from the Warsaw Ghetto on 11 May 1943 did not appear in the *Times*. It exclaimed that "the Free World, the World of Justice, remains silent and apathetic. It is amazing. Cable immediately what you have done. We expect help for the remnants who are saving themselves."[75]

The revelations of several Anglo-Jewish historians, Sir Martin Gilbert, Bernard Wasserstein, Tony Kushner and others, about the lack of motivation, deficiency in perception and vested interest of the British government against making a concerted effort to save the Jews of Europe was unfortunately also reflected in the *Times*. The British agenda was not the Jewish agenda. The Jews were left to their fate amidst much studied political hand-wringing and the professional deafness of many sections of the British press. As Czeslaw Milosz pointed out: "There is no such thing as an innocent bystander. If you are a bystander, you are not innocent."

Notes:

1. Iverach McDonald, *The History of the Times*, vol. 5: *Struggles in War and Peace 1939–1966* (London, 1984), p. 10.

2. Roy Jenkins, *The Voice of the Thunderer[:]The Times:Past, Present and Future* (London, 1985), p. 29.

3. Donald McLachlin, *In the Chair: Barrington-Ward of the Times* (London, 1971), pp. 122–3.

4. Oliver Woods and James Bishop, *The Story of the Times* (London, 1983), p. 301.

5. Letter from H.G. Daniels to Barrington-Ward, 16 May 1937, *Times* Archives.

6. Letter to H. G. Daniels from Dawson in McDonald, op. cit., p. 465.

7. Ibid.

8. *Times*, 7 September 1938.

9. Letter from Barrington-Ward to G.V. Ferguson, 27 April 1939, *Times* Archives.

10. Letter from Barrington-Ward to Brian Lunn, 15 May 1939, *Times* Archives.

11. Julian Duncan Scott, "The British Press and the Holocaust 1942–1943" (Ph.D. Thesis: University of Leicester, 1993), p. 30.

12. *Times*, 3 April 1933.

13. *Times*, 19 September 1933.

14. Letter from Stanley Simpson to Ralph Deakin, 5 February 1934, *Times* Archives.

15. Stanley Simpson, "The Dachau Camp," December 1933, *Times* Archives.

16. Letter from Stanley Simpson to Ralph Deakin, 20 December 1933, *Times* Archives.

17. Ibid.

18. Memo from Barrington-Ward to Deakin, 5 January 1934, *Times* Archives.

19. Memo from Barrington-Ward to Deakin, 13 February 1934, *Times* Archives.

20. *New Statesman*, 20 January 1934.

21. Letter from Deakin to Stanley Simpson, 15 February 1934, *Times* Archives.

22. Letter from William Teeling to Deakin, 24 February 1934, *Times* Archives.

23. Letter from Philip Graves to Barrington-Ward, 8 February 1942, *Times* Archives.

24. Martin Gilbert, *The Holocaust* (London 1986), p. 81.

25. *Times*, 8 November 1935.

26. Tony Kushner, *The Holocaust and the Liberal Imagination* (Oxford 1994), p. 36.

27. Robin Barrington-Ward, Personal Diary, 14 January 1936, as quoted in McLachlan, *In the Chair*, p. 128.

28. Letter from Anthony Eden to Barrington-Ward, 21 October 1941, *Times* Archives.

29. Letter from Barrington-Ward to G.W. Morison, 15 May 1941, *Times* Archives.

30. Memo from Barrington-Ward to Deakin, 18 May 1941, *Times* Archives.

31. Personal correspondence from Iverach McDonald, 12 July 1995.

32. Letter from Frank K. Roberts to William Ridsdale, British Embassy, Moscow, 22 March 1946, *Times* Archives.

33. Richard Cockett, *Twilight of Truth: Chamberlain, Appeasement and the Manipulation of the Press* (London 1989), p. 139.

34. Public Records Office (PRO), Foreign Office (F0) 371/28692.12439.

35. Personal correspondence from Iverach McDonald 12 July 1995, 18 August 1995, 29 August 1995.

36. *Times*, 31 October 1939.

37. *Times,* 24 October 1939, 16 December 1939.

38. *Times,* 5 November 1941.

39. *Times,* 6, 7 January 1942.

40. *Times,* 2 April 1942.

41. In May 1997, GCHQ (British Government Communications Headquarters) released documentation which provided the first authoritative evidence of the mass killings of Jews. These were contained in

reports of German police messages which were intercepted by the Government Code and Cypher School at Bletchley. See *Guardian*, 20 May and 21 May 1997; and Richard Breitman, *Official Secrets: What the Nazis Planned, What the British and Americans Knew* (New York, 1998).

42. Bernard Wasserstein, *Britain and the Jews of Europe 1939–1945* (Oxford 1988), p. 165.

43. *Times*, 10 June 1942.

44. A full account of Zygielbojm's struggle and tragic suicide is given in Daniel Blatman, "On a Mission against All Odds: Samuel Zygelbojm in London (April 1942–May 1943)," in *Yad Vashem Studies* XX, ed. Aharon Weiss (Jerusalem, 1990), pp. 235–271.

45. *Daily Telegraph*, 25 June 1942.

46. *Jewish Chronicle*, 10 July 1942.

47. Martin Gilbert, *Auschwitz and the Allies* (London 1981), p. 46.

48. *Times*, 30 June 1942.

49. *Daily Telegraph*, 30 June 1942.

50. *Guardian*, 30 June 1942.

51. Sir Frank Roberts, interviewed in *What did you do in the War, Auntie?* (BBC TV documentary, 9 May 1995).

52. [Editor's note: Ignacy Schwarzbart was the other Jewish member of the Polish National Council in London.]

53. *Daily Telegraph*, 9 July 1942.

54. *Times*, 10 July 1942.

55. *Times*, 11 September 1942.

56. *Times*, 12 September 1942.

57. *Times*, 1 October 1942.

58. *Times*, 30 October 1942.

59. C.W Harrison, PRO FO 371/30923 piece 72.

60. *Times*, 4 December 1942.

61. Ibid., and letter from Iverach McDonald, 12 July 1995.

62. Ibid.

63. PRO FO 371/30923 piece 189.

64. *Times*, 7 December 1942.

65. Ibid. and letter from Iverach McDonald, 18 August 1995. The former diplomatic correspondent of the *Times* did not recall "that the *Times* was influenced by any foreknowledge of Eden's contacts with the Americans and the Russians or by his statement in the House."

66. *Times,* 8 December 1942.
67. *Times,* 9 December 1942.
68. *Times,* 11 December 1942.
69. *Times,* 12 December 1942.
70. *Times,* 14 December 1942; *Jewish Chronicle,* 18 December 1942.
71. *Times,* 18 December 1942.
72. Ibid.
73. *Times,* 22 December 1942.
74. PRO FO 371/32682 piece 189, quoted in Julian Duncan Scott, p. 173.
75. PRO FO 371/34550 piece 110, quoted in Julian Duncan Scott, p. 254.

The London *Jewish Chronicle* and the Holocaust

David Cesarani
University of Manchester

In April 1945, when the British press was filled with harrowing accounts of Buchenwald and Belsen, the prominent British journalist Hannan Swaffer, writing for the mass-circulation *People* newspaper, asked how it had been possible to ignore the weekly reports about the persecution of the Jews which had appeared in the *Jewish Chronicle*. The cruel answer was that for much of the war the *Jewish Chronicle*'s reportage of the "Final Solution" made it easy to overlook the fate of the Jews.[1]

One exception to this phenomenon was the eye-catching, black-bordered issue of 11 December 1942. The lead-story on the front page was headlined: "Two Million Jews Slaughtered. Most Terrible Massacre of All Time." "Week after week," the editorial asserted, "this paper has striven to awaken the public mind to the facts of the Jewish extermination being carried on by the Nazi masters in Europe. Again and again it has cried aloud that the oft-repeated Nazi threat of Jewish annihilation was seriously intended." This was true up to a point, to paraphrase Evelyn Waugh in *Scoop*. The size and location of articles about the mass murder of Jews were erratic. The editorial comment on these stories during 1941 and 1942 was minimal.

After the catharsis of December 1942, the paper lapsed back into fitful commentary on the reports, which it carried, about what was now established as a program to annihilate the Jews of Nazi-occupied Europe. One of the most perplexing aspects of the *Jewish Chronicle*'s wartime record is the scarcity of editorial references to the suffering of the Jews in Europe. However, this question is not posed in order to stoke up moral indignation fired with the benefits of hindsight.

175

In November 1941 the *Jewish Chronicle* celebrated its centenary year. It was the longest continuously published Jewish periodical in the world, occupying a position of unique authority in Britain and internationally. It was owned by an independent limited company and was free of the influence of Jewish communal institutions, factions or over-mighty individuals. It was produced by a well-established team of seasoned, professional journalists. So its coverage of the greatest, most tragic Jewish story of the century is a grave issue, but not one that is amenable to neat or simple explanations.

Wartime conditions made the complex business of producing a newspaper especially onerous and had an adverse impact on the collection, processing and publication of news. The raw information, once it was gathered in, passed through several ideological, political, and editorial filters before it reached the printed page. The *Jewish Chronicle* did not operate in a vacuum. Its owners, editors and journalists were part of British Jewry and shared its outlook on matters of the day. They worked within well-established conceptual boundaries that limited what Jews could think or say, and which were drawn ever tighter due to the war.

I

The *Jewish Chronicle* was owned by a limited company whose chief shareholders were the members, descendants, relatives or agents of the group which had acquired it in the Zionist interest in 1907. [2] In 1939 the Board of Directors included: Leopold Kessler, the largest shareholder and last active member of the original group, his son David, businessman Michel Oppenheimer (former editor Leopold Greenberg's brother-in-law by his second marriage), the Dutch newspaper editor Maurits Kann (the son of Jacobus Kann, the Hague banker who had helped finance the 1907 purchase), and Leonard Stein, barrister, Zionist and president of the Anglo-Jewish Association.

In the war years Oppenheimer remained the chairman of the board, but there were several changes to its membership. Maurits Kann was trapped in Amsterdam with his father and family: both were to perish at the hands of the Nazis. Leopold Kessler moved to New York in the summer of 1941, whereupon his place was taken by his son-in-law Alex Gumb. When, in early 1940, army service made David Kessler's participation impractical, Neville Laski, QC and former president of the Board of Deputies, acted for him.

The directors, especially Stein, took a close interest in the paper's content. Stein sent the editor detailed notes on each issue after it was published. During the war he made several interventions concerning editorial policy, but only on the subjects of Zionism and Palestine. In most other respects, the directors and the editor were in harmony.

Throughout the war the paper was edited by Ivan Marion Greenberg, Leopold Greenberg's son. Ivan was born and educated in London. After military service in the First World War, he worked as a journalist in South Africa and Australia. He joined the *Jewish Chronicle* as assistant editor in 1925 and expected to be appointed editor after his father died in 1931. In fact, he was not to assume editorial direction of the paper until 1936, following a long boardroom struggle.

The post of assistant editor was held by John Shaftesley, a Lancashire-born journalist who had worked for the *Manchester Guardian* and served as Manchester correspondent for the *Jewish Chronicle* before joining its London office. Simon Gilbert, the associate editor with responsibility for the leading articles, was an East End-born Jew who had worked with the Jewish press and other papers since the 1900s. In other words, this was a highly experienced editorial team.

Since Ivan Greenberg had become editor in December 1936 the paper had developed a fairly settled policy. It had covered the plight of German Jewry in great detail and had responded to the *Kristallnacht* outrages with vigor, sparing neither space nor anti-Nazi invective. However, Greenberg was aware that Jewish demands for sanctions against Germany could be read as war-mongering. British Fascists made this claim a central plank of their propaganda, so editorials on Germany tried hard to avoid giving the impression of belligerence. Anti-Jewish sentiment in Britain would continue to throw a long shadow over the coverage of Jewish suffering.

Greenberg saw the establishment of a Jewish state as the best response to Nazi persecution of the Jews, but here he clashed with Stein. Whereas Greenberg admired Jabotinsky, and during the war became directly involved with the New Zionist Organization, Stein was a moderate Zionist and one of Weizmann's oldest acolytes in Britain.

Ironically, Greenberg was more in tune with Neville Laski who, as president of the Board of Deputies between 1933 and 1939 had tried to thwart Zionism at every turn. Their alliance rested on a common loathing for the Zionist Federation (ZF). Greenberg hated the ZF because it supported Weizmann and the policy of partition; Laski, because it had fought and defeated him in the Board of Deputies.

Greenberg and Laski also shared an apologetic stance regarding Jewish domestic policy. From 1937, the paper held the view that Jewish behavior contributed markedly to the incidence of anti-Jewish hostility. This approach was set out by Neville Laski in his controversial 1938 book *Jewish Rights and Jewish Wrongs*.

Many of the editorial preoccupations and comments of the *Jewish Chronicle* between 1939 and 1945 are incomprehensible unless they are seen as an extension of the paper's pre-war agenda.

II

At the outbreak of war, the *Jewish Chronicle* management put into effect a plan for evacuating the paper from London. The editorial, composing and circulation departments were removed to High Wycombe, a small town in Buckinghamshire. Here the staff and office equipment were crammed into the premises of the *Bucks Free Press*, which were shared with the *Catholic Herald*, the Church of England *Guardian* and the Christadelphian *Mutual Magazine*. Working conditions were far from comfortable or convenient.

The dangers to the paper and the staff were brought home by the destruction of the main office at 47–49 Moor Lane, in the City, during an air raid on the night of 29 December 1940. Irreplaceable files containing correspondence, press cuttings, obituaries, and photographs were burned. The temporary office established in Queen Victoria Street was also hit in an air raid on 11 May 1941.[3] These blows, comparable to stunning and amnesia in a sentient being, had an incalculable effect on the paper's ability to sort and assess incoming information.

Wartime rationing affected the paper drastically. From September 1939 to July 1940, the amount of newsprint allotted to the press in Britain was reduced by 60 per cent. As the German U-boat blockade tightened, the Paper Control Office limited the number of pages in periodicals. The amount of newsprint allotted to the *Jewish Chronicle* was cut in March 1941 and again in early 1942.

Many features had to be dropped, including Simon Gilbert's incisive comment column. Henceforth, his distinctive, and often critical voice was sublimated into the editorials. In order to squeeze more into less space, the size of type was reduced with each cut in the paper ration. By 1943, the *Jewish Chronicle* was appearing on brittle, discolored paper and taxed even readers with perfect eyesight.

The paper's trading position suffered badly from the effects of war. The evacuation or voluntary relocation of Jewish people from the main centers of Jewish settlement disrupted sales and circulation. Casual sales fell since continuous nights of bombing in 1940–41 left people with little time or energy for perusing the press.

The circulation of newspapers was eventually fixed by the government in March 1941 and each paper was allowed only enough newsprint to supply subscribers. In November 1941 new regulations compelled the *Jewish Chronicle* to suspend casual sales altogether. In 1942 a further tightening of paper rationing meant that no more fresh subscriptions could be accepted. The paper advised readers to pass on finished copies to friends and to send them to servicemen.

Advertising revenue slumped since non-war related production declined and consumption was strictly controlled. The daily press was buoyed up by the Government's public information campaigns, but not the religious or class papers.

The combined effect of pegged circulation, rising production costs and diminishing advertising pushed the paper into the red. Michel Oppenheimer was forced to dip into personal capital to stave off financial ruin, while the employees actually took a pay cut to help it survive.

Hostilities damaged the staff situation in other ways. By the end of the war, thirteen staff members were in uniform. Fewer personnel were doing more work in worse conditions.

The *Jewish Chronicle*'s correspondents on the continent were eliminated in step with the advances of the German army. Its own correspondents in Germany and Vienna had been forced out years earlier. Now, its reporters in eastern and western Europe had to flee. Several unfortunates were caught by the Nazis and shared the fate of the Jewish population in general.[4]

News gathering was significantly affected by the severance of the editorial department from the offices of the paper and the environs of Fleet Street. The editorial staff was cut off from channels of information in the capital: the governments-in-exile, the embassies of neutral states, visiting diplomats, and the members of foreign armed services were all a long, hazardous train ride away. It was left to the diminished, overstrained band of reporters in London to cover these sources and to phone in reports (when lines were available). Otherwise, the editors were limited to picking up news off the wire services, including the Jewish Telegraphic Agency (JTA), or from other newspapers.

Formal and informal censorship further limited what news the *Jewish Chronicle* could obtain or publish.[5] In 1939 the Ministry of Information issued guidelines stating that it was inadvisable to invoke the suffering of the Jews in propaganda directed at the Middle East. Anything that fostered sympathy for Jewish refugees attempting to reach Palestine was undesirable as it would embarrass British policy and irritate the Arabs. In 1941, the Ministry issued a memorandum stating that "horror stuff . . . must be used very sparingly and must always deal with the treatment of indisputably innocent people. Not with violent opponents. And not with Jews."[6]

Until late 1942, the Political Warfare Executive, which had a powerful role in setting the propaganda agenda, insisted on stringent proof of stories about the fate of the Jews. British officials and military personnel were keenly aware of the extent of anti-Jewish feeling in Britain and Europe, and were apprehensive that any sign of favor towards the Jews would play into the hands of Nazi propaganda. It was also felt that "atrocity stories" had become counter-productive because their fabrication for propaganda during the First World War had later been exposed and the genre was discredited.[7]

Official displeasure towards the publication of potentially dangerous "tittle-tattle" compounded the ingrained professional skepticism of the *Jewish Chronicle* editorial staff. The confusing, ambiguous nature of the information concerning the Jews which emerged from the occupied countries all contributed to the demotion of the place it was assigned in the paper and the toning down of the editorial comment.

IV

From September 1939 to mid-1941, the information that reached Britain concerning the Jews in Nazi Europe was plentiful. The *Jewish Chronicle* obtained precise reports on the situation of Jews in Warsaw and other Polish cities. Much of this news came via Lithuania, until its annexation to the USSR in July 1940, and from the Swedish press. The Polish

Government-in-exile in London was a major source on Poland for the British press, although as David Engel has shown, its stand on Polish Jewish matters was extremely equivocal.[8]

During the first eighteen months of the Nazi occupation of Poland, the *Jewish Chronicle* carried frequent reports of massacres and killings. Sometimes they were given front-page treatment; often they were carried deep inside the paper. These early reports of large-scale murder may have desensitized the editorial staff, and readers, to later accounts of events that were more far-reaching and awful. For example, one front-page article on 1 December 1939 spoke of a "campaign of extermination of the Jews." It was followed by another, two weeks later, on page 15, headlined "Mass Murder in Poland."

The *Jewish Chronicle* reported the Nazi plan, discussed in the German press, to establish a Jewish "reservation" around Lublin in 1939. It gave detailed accounts of the appalling conditions in the Polish ghettos from the winter of 1940–41 onwards. On 14 and 28 March 1941, it carried photographs of the Warsaw ghetto showing the wall and smugglers at work. The reports on Poland were often accompanied by editorial comment. This tended to center on speculation about the future of the Jews in post-war Poland and fund raising appeals for relief work.[9] Compared to the treatment of the pogroms in Poland in 1919–20, the comment was restrained.

Throughout 1940–41, neutral press sources, such as American journalists in Berlin, assured abundant coverage of the lot of Jews in occupied eastern and western Europe.[10] However, the *Jewish Chronicle*'s ability to track the *Einsatzgruppen* operations in Soviet territory after June 1941 was limited. Swedish newspapers supplied some information on western Poland and the Baltic states, while Turkish papers reported on developments along the Black Sea coast. The Soviet authorities adjusted slowly to the new geo-political constellation. It was not until January 1942 that Foreign Minister Molotov issued an official account of the depredations of the Nazi invaders. The Molotov report depicted the atrocities as systematic, but other than in its references to the massacre at Babi Yar it blurred the specific targeting of Jews.[11]

Until this time the *Jewish Chronicle* could get little solid intelligence about the activity of the *Einsatzgruppen*. The staff picked up what they could from reports in the Russian press based on testimony by soldiers who entered territory recaptured from the German army, partisans and escaped Russian prisoners. Although this data was sometimes surprisingly good, such as the 25 July 1941 report on the Lwów massacres, it was more usually fragmented and was considered unreliable.[12]

The difficulties of obtaining and evaluating news are demonstrated by a story culled from *Pravda* on 17 October 1941. This reported that Jews in Kiev were forced to wear distinctive armbands; yet, unknown to the editorial staff, two weeks earlier 30,000 of Kiev's Jews had actually been massacred at Babi Yar.

The level of editorial comment during 1941 remained modest in proportion to the chilling reports carried by the paper. An editorial on 27 June 1941 accurately conceptualized the war in the East as a "biological struggle," but not with reference to the Germans and the Jews. The *Jewish Chronicle* carried news stories of carnage on a vast scale, but like other news agencies could not conceptualize the scope or systematic nature of the *Einsatzgruppen* operations. Rather, it attempted to make sense of the atrocities by setting them in the context of the Jewish historical experience. In the Jewish New Year retrospective on 19 September 1941, the editorial spoke of a "crude policy of persecution." For central European Jews, "The alternatives seem to have been extermination or expulsion to the hopeless, starving, diseased Lublin Ghetto."

On 29 August 1941, a leader note triggered by a speech of Winston Churchill on the second anniversary of the war noted his reference to "German police troops" responsible for thousands of killings in Russia. For obvious reasons, the prime minister did not reveal that his condemnatory remarks were based on decrypted intercepts of the signals sent by SS, Waffen SS and German police units that referred to the daily mass killings of Jews. The Jewish press or the press in general could never be let into such a secret, even if it would prove the substance of the hair-raising stories emanating from behind the German lines in Russia. The consequent dilemmas of sifting rumor and contradictory fragments of information explains some of the paper's editorial hesitation.[13]

Yet frequently, more space and editorial verve was devoted to stories about the murder or mass murder of smaller numbers of non-Jews. For example, on 24 October 1941, a front-page item headed "Ghastly Pogroms in the Ukraine," described thousands of corpses in the Dniester River. It also cited the gossip of German officers on leave from the

Russian Front to the effect that 15,000 Galician and 8,000 Baltic Jews had been murdered. This report was not the subject of editorial comment, possibly because it was unsubstantiated. However, the following week, a leading article was devoted to the killing of hundreds of non-Jews in retaliation for the assassination of two German military personnel.[14]

The paper did not directly address the massacres in Russia editorially until 28 November 1941, following an impassioned letter from a reader who protested that, "One is staggered by the utter apathy with which this ghastly and unprecedented destruction of Jewish life has been received by the public, both Jewish and non-Jewish." (The reader referred to an earlier report adverting to the murder of 25,000 Romanian Jews.)

The editorial replied defensively: "It is not that Britons, who have fed daily on horrors in these last two terrible years, have grown inured to them, and become less humane than their fathers, but that they have come to the conviction that torture and murder must continue so long as the foul Nazi system endures and have determined to devote every ounce of energy and treasure they possess to extirpate it." The fate of the Jews was subordinated to the larger cause of winning the war.[15]

Following the declaration by the inter-allied conference on Nazi atrocities in the occupied countries, a short leader on 16 January 1942 took up the question of the punishment of war criminals. It was critical of Jewish leaders for not taking part in this démarche, but failed to note that the statement made no mention of the disproportionate suffering of the Jews.[16] Otherwise, editorials from then until July focused on domestic issues such as religious education and defense against anti-Semitism in Britain.

The full dimensions of the "Final Solution" emerged in fits and starts.[17] In November 1941, the *Jewish Chronicle* reported the deportation of German Jews to Poland and the announcement that further Jewish emigration from Europe was banned. On 10 April 1942, a small front page article gave the news that 1,200 Jews had been deported to Mauthausen concentration camp and killed by "poison gas." This was the first hint of mass murder by gassing.

Then, on 19 June 1942, the *Jewish Chronicle* announced in bold type on the front page: "News is filtering through of recent ghastly massacres of Jews in Nazi Europe. Some 85,000 men, women, and children are mentioned in the reports to hand." The story, which came via Stockholm, concerned only massacres in Lithuania. Before long, the picture broadened alarmingly.[18]

At the end of June 1942, Shmuel Zygielbojm, a member of the Polish National Council in London, released a report from the Bund in Poland that had been transmitted to the west by the Polish underground. Zygielbojm knew that the report, which asserted that 700,000 Jews had been exterminated, would face a credibility problem so he avoided the Jewish press and instead fed the material to the *Daily Telegraph*, which broke the story on 25 June 1942. Four days later, he addressed a press conference convened by the British Section of the World Jewish Congress.[19] On 3 July 1942, the *Jewish Chronicle* carried the news in a page 1 article headlined "Mass Murder in Poland . . . Nazis' Bestial Extermination Plan."

The paper's editorial on the communiqué exemplified the dilemmas of dealing with news that beggared belief. It stressed that the substance of the story had been checked against other sources and commented:

> The hideous details now coming to hand of the wholesale butchery by the Germans of Jewish men, women, and children in Poland and Lithuania read like tales from the imagination of some drug-maddened creature seeking to portray a nightmare of hell. The average mind simply cannot believe the reality of such sickening revelations. . . .

In May and June 1942, the *Jewish Chronicle* had printed reports that Jews in Holland, France and Belgium were being forced to wear the yellow star. During July, August and September it reported European-wide deportations "to the East." There were front-page accounts of round-ups in Warsaw, Vienna, Holland, Paris, Slovakia and Belgium. On 21 August, the paper printed a comprehensive report of the working of the mobile gas vans at Chelmno, derived from Jews who had escaped. News of the suicide of Adam Czerniaków, the leader of the Warsaw Judenrat, reached the paper via Reuters and the JTA with little delay.

Despite the mounting evidence of a genocide, the editorials in mid-1942 were predominantly focused on local matters, notably disputes over the fight against anti-Semitism at home. There were several editorial allusions to the punishment that surely awaited the Nazis, but they hardly constituted ringing the tocsin. A front-page account, on 11 September 1942, of the seizure of Jews in Vichy elicited only a general editorial note. On 2 October 1942 the paper carried an anodyne version of the Riegner telegram, on page six, without editorial comment. A major rally held at the Royal Albert Hall on 29 October to protest against the massacre of Polish Jewry was trailed by an editorial note, although the subsequent report was relegated to the inside pages. On 27 November, the paper reported on page one that 250,000 Polish Jews had died in the last six months at Sobibor, Treblinka and Belzec, and that a plan existed to kill half of Polish Jewry by the end of the year; this was discussed in the third leaderette.

In December 1942, lobbying by the exile governments, Jewish representatives and a public outcry at the published reports led to the Allied declaration on German war crimes.[20] The *Jewish Chronicle*'s black-bordered issue on 11 December 1942 contributed rather belatedly to the upswell of outrage and horror. Despite the favorable context, its editorial message was almost apologetic. The frequency of its reports were "regarded in some quarters as sickening iteration." Significantly, it noted that several Jewish subscribers "complained that they could no longer read the *Jewish Chronicle* because the facts it recorded so harrowed the feelings."

During 1943 the intensity and urgency of editorial comment waned. This occlusion did not result from an interruption to the flow of information. British Jews followed the Warsaw Ghetto uprising week by week, in considerable detail, on the paper's front-page. It carried reports on the destruction of the Jewish populations in Belgium, Holland, Vilna and Salonika. The names and functions of Treblinka, Sobibor and Belzec were published, although the role of Auschwitz eluded definition. Sundry reports described the gas chambers, the crematoria and the "medical" experiments in the death camps.[21]

Yet when Zygielbojm committed suicide in protest against the general apathy and lack of specific action to help Polish Jewry, the *Jewish Chronicle* carried an obituary, but like the rest of the press did not mention that he left a note explicitly stating the deliberate nature of his gesture.[22] Throughout the first part of 1943, even at the height of the Warsaw Ghetto uprising, the *Jewish Chronicle*'s leading articles dealt with controversies at the Board of Deputies and parochial matters such as the development of Jews' College.

The destruction of European Jewry indubitably formed the backdrop to the paper's regular editorial tirades against the abysmal response by governments in the free world when asked to provide sanctuary for refugees, notably at the time of the Bermuda Conference. But comment on the tragedy of Europe's Jews thereby became entangled with discussion of rescue projects, the role of Palestine and internal Zionist politics. Ivan Greenberg channeled his rage into repetitive demands for a Jewish army and the opening of Palestine to Jewish immigrants. The slogan "Palestine or Extinction" summed up the increasingly shrill tone and content of the editorials.[23]

By this time Greenberg had been sucked into the affairs of the Committee for a Jewish Army, a Revisionist front-organization formed in America by Palestinian Jews. Their man in England, Captain Joshua Halpern, persuaded several prominent politicians and writers to join a similar, London-based committee.[24] The *Jewish Chronicle* endorsed its objectives and enthusiastically reported its work. The amount of editorial comment it received between April 1942 and December 1942 exceeded that devoted to the news of the slaughter in Europe.[25]

The official Zionist leadership was antagonized by the connection between the Committee for a Jewish Army and the New Zionist Organization.[26] It had long suspected Greenberg of using the *Jewish Chronicle* to promote a hidden agenda. In 1940 Weizmann had accused the paper of deliberately trying to undermine confidence in the Zionist Organization and had spoken to Greenberg personally to explain to him the damage that could be wreaked by his aggressive editorials.[27]

Leonard Stein was so uncomfortable with the paper's coverage of Palestine that he offered his resignation to the board in January 1942. He was persuaded to stay, but in October 1943 the board adjourned its regular meeting for a "private discussion of editorial policy." Following a number of leading articles condemning the collaboration between Jews in Palestine and the British forces attempting to destroy the Jewish terrorist networks, Stein wrote again to Greenberg. Finally, in October 1944, Oppenheimer pleaded with him to moderate his rhetoric. He told Greenberg that he understood "how deeply you are stirred by the many tragic reports you received," but feared they were unbalancing his judgment at a time when any deviation from a loyal pro-government policy could react alarmingly with the high levels of anti-Semitism.[28]

For the first months of 1944, the setting-up of the War Refugees Board caused the paper to express reserved optimism about the prospects for the surviving Jews in Europe. But in March 1944, the Germans occupied Hungary on whose territory resided the last intact Jewish population. Prophetically, on 24 March 1944 the paper editorialized: "And now Hungary." The deportation of Jews on Hungarian soil began in May 1944, under the noses of the Allied powers.[29] It was fully reported in the *Jewish Chronicle*. Shocked by the lackluster response of the Allied Governments and publics, the paper announced simply on 30 June 1944: "Slaughter Passes Unnoticed." The editorial grappled with the reasons for the silence:

> Few cries of indignation are heard in this country, perhaps because the chords of human sympathy have been dulled or atrophied by sheer over-use—one of the sinister by-products of the orgy of German official murders. Perhaps, too, the imaginations of really kindly and civilized men boggle at these accounts of wholesale and systematic human slaughter. One can understand this reaction, but not justify it.

V

Yet how can one explain the record of the *Jewish Chronicle*? Confusion and caution both played a part in restraining its comment on stories trickling out of occupied Europe. Much of the information reaching the paper was unreliable, but it confronted formidable technical problems in checking them out. The editorial staff was distant from London; the paper's archive and library had been destroyed. The adversarial position of the paper *vis-à-vis* the British government with regard to Palestine impeded access to Whitehall or British military sources. Due to the paper's vendetta against the Zionist Federation and its ally, the British Section of the World Jewish Congress, it was even compromised in the eyes of Jewish sources. The Polish government-in-exile was ambivalent, while its Jewish members preferred to release news via the more influential daily press. When Jan Karski visited London in November 1942, there is no record that he sought out, or was sought out by, *Jewish Chronicle* reporters.[30]

In any case, the true enormity of what was happening was known only to the murderers, and any connection between the disparate, terrible stories which leaked out eluded commentators in the free world. The *Jewish Chronicle* staff not unreasonably interpreted the fragments of data according to the historical pattern of ghettoization and pogrom violence which the mass of Jews would hopefully survive.

The scale of individual slaughters was still extraordinary and it is striking that the level of editorial animation was lower than at the time of *Kristallnacht*. However, there was unremitting pressure on the paper to avoid the appearance of "special pleading." From June 1940 to December 1941, Britain was alone and fighting for its very survival. Members of the armed services and the civilian population were making immense sacrifices for the war effort. The toll of life due to German bombing in 1940–41 was horrific. In the first months of 1942, Britain suffered a string of costly defeats; during the summer, German armies were pushing into Egypt towards the Suez Canal. While the nation's very existence was at stake, it was an unpropitious time for one, small section of it to assert the plight of its co-religionists in occupied Europe. Not until the middle of 1943 was it felt that the tide had turned decisively, allowing scope to consider matters beyond survival.

With anti-Jewish feeling always in the background, it was prudent to avoid the appearance of self-interest. Tony Kushner, who has chronicled the persistence of prejudice during the war, observes that "British Jewry . . . was a frightened community preoccupied with its own defense and the pressures to keep Jewish traditions alive in unfavorable circumstances."[31] Jews believed that they owed a debt of gratitude to England for their readmission, their emancipation and the opportunity for British Jewry to expand and prosper under conditions of unprecedented freedom and unrivaled toleration. They feared it would be considered unseemly and ungrateful to cavil if they felt Jewish interests were not being pursued with sufficient vigor by the British government. Since it was widely believed that Jewish action caused anti-Jewish feeling, any suggestion that the interests of Jews were being put before those of their country was regarded as an incitement to anti-Jewish hostility.[32]

But there was more to this strategy than prudence. Greenberg and his editorial team were members of British Jewry and shared most of its assumptions. They subscribed to the notion of an "emancipation contract" according to which the Jews were permitted civic equality on the understanding that they were a denominational group with no loyalties other than to their country of adoption. This entailed putting the national interest and public spirit before "narrow" communal imperatives. Richard Bolchover observes that

> The desire to be in keeping with the national spirit and to affirm their integration into British society led British Jews not only to frequent expressions of loyalty, but also to take what in retrospect appears to be an almost detached view of European Jewish life under Hitler. [This was manifested in a] tendency to submerge the specifically Jewish aspects of Nazi horror. The community attempted to transfer specifically Jewish concerns into more general concerns lest it compromise its standing in the larger society.[33]

The editorial staff at the *Jewish Chronicle* were also aware that their readership could not tolerate an unrelieved diet of murder and destruction, least of all when their situation was so helpless and there was no obvious program of action to appease guilt feelings or rage. In December 1942, it confessed to its readers that "several Jewish ministers found it necessary to rebuke those cowardly ones of their congregants who had complained that they could no longer read the *Jewish Chronicle* because the facts it recorded so harrowed the feelings."[34] So the editorials fastened onto domestic themes and Palestine. Fascism and anti-Semitism in Britain were targets that could be reached, forces on which Jewish behavior might have some impact. The paper monotonously demanded the creation of a Jewish army and increased immigration to Palestine as immediate practical measures, however misguided this was.

The *Jewish Chronicle* reflected the agony of Anglo-Jewry when confronted by the horror of events in Europe, but without the power to make a meaningful intervention. In its own words, on 3 September 1943, British Jews "have stood bewildered, stunned, unable to grasp the situation as events have unfolded themselves. And not merely bewildered but divided." Its editorials mirrored the fragmented Jewish response, the infighting between various groups, to which it was itself a party, and the absence of an overall strategy. It acknowledged this much itself: "Turned from the doors of Palestine, threatened in the distance by the 'wandering phantom' of anti-Semitism, and sharing, in addition, the general travail,

Jewish feelings tend to find an outlet in domestic faction and quarrels which can only still further confuse their mind and confound their counsels." Tony Kushner has rightly concluded that, "British Jewry had neither the moral energy, vision and self-confidence nor the financial resources to confront the horrors facing the Jews of Europe." Hamstrung by anti-Semitism on the Home Front and afraid of drawing attention to Jewish suffering at a time when the entire country was in danger, the paper muted its response to the news of the "Final Solution."[35]

It would be wrong to end on this note, tantamount to blaming the victims for their own fate. The timidity of British Jewry was a result of the emancipation process in Britain and the perpetuation in English culture of anti-Jewish stereotypes that turned Jewish collective action into "clannishness."[36]

Nor was the British state prepared to come to the aid of the Jews. Time and again the paper inveighed against the response of those in power. It commented acidly that the Allied declaration of December 1942 would "do much to clear the Christian conscience of Britain and America of the reproach of apathy in the face of horror which is as much a clear-cut challenge to Christianity as it is a menace to the millions of Jewish lives." A year and three and a half million Jewish lives later, its rhetoric was less tempered: there had been a systematic slaughter and "while it was being consummated the great civilized powers stand by almost idle and, if appearance alone could be trusted, unmoved."[37] The dismissive, curmudgeonly and meanspirited response of British civil servants and politicians to the news of the "Final Solution" is legendary and will stain Britain's war record for as long as men and women read history.[38]

Even when the plan of extermination was proven, the British government refused to give a lead to movements of protest and succor. Indeed, as the *Jewish Chronicle* noted on 3 September 1943, on the fourth anniversary of the war, "some have detected even a note of impatience with the pleas pressed by the Jews." Activists became demoralized, the public lost interest and the issue was dropped. The demobilization of the British Jews was a part of this downward spiral and it could not be reversed by one newspaper. The *Jewish Chronicle* would have alienated its readership if it had reminded them week after week of their powerlessness while their brothers and sisters were being murdered. Its tragedy was to be part of a press, a culture and a society in which genocide against the Jews, a mere thirty miles away, was neither a fit subject for prolonged concern or sustained action. Its silence is the most eloquent reproach to a society which, because they were Jewish, failed innocent human beings threatened with annihilation.

Notes:

1. Quoted in *Jewish Chronicle [JC]*, 27 April 1945, p. 10.

2. For a detailed account of the newspaper's history, see David Cesarani, *The Jewish Chronicle and Anglo-Jewry, 1841–1991* (Cambridge: Cambridge University Press, 1994.)

3. David Kessler to Ivan Greenberg, 5 January 1940, AJ110/2. Jewish Chronicle Ltd Minute Book, vol. 1, 1 August 1941, Jewish Chronicle Archive [JCMB].

4. Bruno Heilig, the Vienna correspondent was held in Dachau in 1938 and only released through the intervention of David Kessler. Maurice Franks, the British Pro-Consul in Amsterdam and the paper's Dutch correspondent, escaped just ahead of the German army. William Blumberg, the Russian-born Paris correspondent was sent to Drancy and thence to Auschwitz where he was murdered. *JC*, 17 May 1940, p. 1; *JC*, 23 August 1947, p. 13. Information on Heilig supplied by David Kessler.

5. Reports sent from Palestine, mainly about the activities of the Zionist underground, were regularly intercepted by the military censor. News stories generated in London, largely to do with the effect of bombing, were suppressed or left vague in order to deny intelligence to the enemy. *JC*, 20 August 1943, p. 5; 15 October 1943, p. 8; *JC*, 17 October 1948, p. 6; 19 October 1955, p. 6.

6. Tony Kushner, *The Holocaust and the Liberal Imagination* (Oxford: Blackwell, 1994), pp. 123–6, 136–7; Bernard Wasserstein, *Britain and the Jews of Europe 1939–1945* (Oxford: Clarendon Press, 1979), pp. 164–5, 295–9; Michael Balfour, *Propaganda in War 1939–45* (London: Routledge and Kegan, 1979), pp. 31–2, 299–304; Ian McLaine, *Ministry of Morale. Home Front Morale and the Ministry of Information in World War Two* (London: Allen and Unwin, 1979), pp. 166–8; K. R. M. Short, "Hollywood Fights Anti-Semitism, 1940–5", in K. R. M. Short , ed., *Film*

and Radio Propaganda in World War II (London: Croom Helm, 1983), pp. 147–8.

7. Walter Laqueur, *The Terrible Secret* (London: Penguin, 1982), pp. 91–3; Kushner, *The Holocaust and the Liberal Imagination*, p. 136.

8. David Engel, *In the Shadow of Auschwitz. The Polish Government-in-Exile and the Jews, 1939–1942* (Chapel Hill, NC: University of North Carolina Press, 1987) and idem, *Facing a Holocaust. The Polish Government-in-Exile and the Jews, 1939–1942* (Chapel Hill, NC: University of North Carolina Press, 1993.)

9. For examples of reports, see *JC*, 1 March 1940, p. 14; 5 April 1940, p. 20; 7 March 1941, p. 1 and following issues. Editorial comment: 26 January 1940, p. 14; 5 April 1940, p. 20; 26 April 1940, pp. 14–15; 27 September 1940, p. 24; 8 November 1940, p. 10.

10. *JC*, 28 May 1940, p. 9; 6 September 1940, p. 1; 13 September 1940, pp. 10; 18 October 1940, p. 7 and 25 October 1940, p. 1; 1 November 1940, p. 1; 7 and 14 March 1941, p. 1. On the role of US journalists, see Deborah E Lipstadt, *Beyond Belief. The American Press and the Coming of the Holocaust 1933–1945* (New York: Free Press, 1993), pp. 142–9 and 159–60.

11. For the neutral powers' press and diplomats, see Laqueur, *The Terrible Secret*, ch. 2. On 29 August 1941, the *Jewish Chronicle* reported the "International Conference of Jews" held in Moscow on 24 August 1941 to denounce the Nazis and rally world Jewry to the Soviet cause, but its proceedings were vapid. V. M. Molotov, *The Molotov Notes on German Atrocities* (London: HMSO, March 1942); *JC*, 9 January 1942, p. 1.

12. *JC*, 4 July 1941, p. 10; 25 July 1941, p. 12; 22 August 1941, p. 1; 29 August 1941, pp. 8, 10.

13. *JC*, 29 August 1941, p. 10. On the decrypts, see David Cesarani, "Secret Churchill Papers", *Journal of Holocaust Education*, 4:2 (1995), pp. 225–228.

14. *JC*, 24 October 1941, p. 1; 31 October 1941, p. 12. The same pattern was repeated in November and December. At the start of November, the *Jewish Chronicle* simply reported that one-third of Bessarabian Jewry had been "exterminated": *JC*, 7 November 1941, p. 1; 21 November 1941, pp. 1 and 7; 28 November 1941, p. 12. A few weeks later, on 19 December, there was an editorial about a hundred Frenchmen being held hostage

after the killing of a German soldier: *JC*, 19 December 1941, p. 12. Cf. Lipstadt, *Beyond Belief*, pp. 169–74.

15. Richard Bolchover, *British Jewry and the Holocaust* (Cambridge, Cambridge University Press, 1993), pp. 98–99; cf. Bernard Wasserstein, "Patterns of Jewish Leadership in Great Britain during the Nazi Era", in R. Braham (ed.), *Jewish Leadership During the Nazi Era: Patterns of Behavior in the Free World* (New York: Columbia University Press, 1985), pp. 31–2.

16. Engel, *In the Shadow of Auschwitz*, pp. 176–8.

17. Wasserstein, *Britain and the Jews of Europe*, pp. 166–71; Martin Gilbert, *Auschwitz and the Allies* (London: Michael Joseph, 1981), chaps. 2–7; Laqueur, *The Terrible Secret*, chaps 2–4.

18. It is noteworthy that the first leader on this day concerned the United Nations. A subsequent editorial note dealt with the Nazi atrocity at Lidice.

19. Laqueur, *The Terrible Secret*, pp. 73–5; Gilbert, *Auschwitz and the Allies*, pp. 42–3.

20. John P. Fox, "The Jewish Factor in British War Crimes Policy in 1942," *English Historical Review*, 92 (1977), pp. 82–106; Wasserstein, *Britain and the Jews of Europe*, pp. 170–7; Gilbert, *Auschwitz and the Allies*, pp. 94–105; Kushner, *The Holocaust and the Liberal Imagination*, pp. 136–72.

21. On the deportation of Dutch Jews: *JC*, 1 January 1943, p. 1 and 12 November 1943, p. 1; on Auschwitz: *JC*, 12 February 1943, p. 1 and 25 June 1943, p. 1; on the Warsaw Ghetto uprising: *JC*, 7 May 1943, p. 1; 14 May 1943, p. 1; 28 May 1943, p. 1; and 5 November 1943, pp. 1, 9; on Salonika: *JC*, 28 May 1943, p. 1 and 17 December 1943, p. 9; on Belgian Jewry: *JC*, 13 August 1943, p. 7; on Vilna Jewry and Sobibor: *JC*, 12 November 1943, p. 1.

22. On Zygielbojm: *JC*, 14 May 1943, p. 1; 21 May 1943, p. 11. For general responses: Andrew Sharf, *The British Press and the Jews under Nazi Rule* (London: Oxford University Press, 1965), pp. 111–13.

23. Bermuda: *JC*, 2 April 1943, p. 10 and 7 May 1943, p. 8. Palestine: *JC*, 26 November 1943, p. 10; 24 December 1943, p. 10. On the campaign for a Jewish army, see Wasserstein, *Britain and the Jews of Europe*, pp. 273–87 and Bolchover, *British Jewry and the Holocaust*, pp. 126–32.

24. See file 3–4, Papers of Samuel Landman, Jabotinsky Institute in Tel

Aviv, 247P; Papers of Joseph Leftwich, Central Zionist Archives in Jerusalem, A330/116. See also, Aaron Berman, *Nazism, the Jews, and American Zionism 1933–1948* (Detroit: Wayne State University Press, 1990), ch. 4.

25. *JC*, 3 April 1942, 10; 24 April 1942, 10 and almost every week thereafter.

26. Bolchover, *British Jewry and the Holocaust*, pp. 38–9.

27. Weizmann to Weisgal, 29 March 1940, in *Letters and Papers of Chaim Weizmann*, ed. N. Rose (Jerusalem: Israel Universities Press, 1979), vol. 19, *January 1939–June 1940*, pp. 264–5. See *JC*, 1 November 1940, p. 10; 15 November 1940, p. 10; 8 May 1941, p. 8; 30 May 1941, p. 14.

28. JCMB, vol. 1, 16 January 1942 and 29 October 1943. Stein to Greenberg, 4 April 1944; Stein to Greenberg, 20 January 1945, JI, 5–265P; Oppenheimer to Greenberg, 14 October 1944, JI, 5–265P.

29. *JC*, 28 January 1944, 1, 10; 11 February 1944, 8. Gilbert, *Auschwitz and the Allies*, pp. 207–30; Wasserstein, *Britain and the Jews of Europe*, pp. 249–70; Tony Kushner, "Rules of the Game: Britain, America and the Holocaust in 1944", *Holocaust and Genocide Studies*, 5:4 (1990), pp. 382–402.

30. E. Thomas Wood and Stanislaw M. Jankowski, *Karski. How One Man Tried to Stop the Holocaust* (London, John Wiley, 1994.)

31. Kushner, *The Holocaust and the Liberal Imagination*, p.131. See his *The Persistence of Prejudice. Antisemitism in British Society during the Second World War* (Manchester: Manchester University Press, 1989.)

32. Bolchover, *British Jewry and the Holocaust*, pp. 42–53, 103–17.

33. Bolchover, *British Jewry and the Holocaust*, pp. 77–82, 104–8. David Feldman, *Englishmen and Jews* (London: Yale University Press, 1994), pt. 1.

34. *JC*, 11 December 1942, p. 8.

35. Kushner, *The Holocaust and the Liberal Imagination*, p. 132; Bolchover, *British Jewry and the Holocaust*, pp. 31–42; cf. Wasserstein, "Patterns of Jewish Leadership in Great Britain during the Nazi Era", pp. 31–2.

36. See Bryan Cheyette, *Constructions of 'the Jew' in English Literature and Society. Racial representations, 1875–1945* (Cambridge: Cambridge University Press, 1993.)

37. *JC*, 18 December 1942, p. 10; 26 November 1943, 10.

38. See Laqueur, *The Terrible Secret*; Gilbert, *Auschwitz and the Allies*; Wasserstein, *Britain and the Jews of Europe*; Kushner, *The Holocaust and the Liberal Imagination*.

Soviet Journalism

The Holocaust as Reflected in the Soviet Russian Language Newspapers in the Years 1941–1945

Yitshak Arad
Yad Vashem

My subject is the persecution and extermination of the Jews in the occupied territories of the Soviet Union as reflected in the Russian-language Soviet newspapers in the years 1941–1945, that is, since the German attack on the Soviet Union. This study is mainly based upon three newspapers: the Communist Party's *Pravda* (Truth), the Soviet Government's *Izvestia* (News), and the Red Army's *Krasnaya Zvezda* (Red Star). The Soviet press was not a free press. It represented the party and government policy. Everything written and not written there served the Soviet propaganda aims inside the country and abroad, mainly in the allied USA and Great Britain. The articles and the news published in the newspapers consisted of announcements of the Sovinformburo (a party agency created in the first days of the war), announcements of TASS (Telegraphic Agency of the Soviet Union), the newspapers' editorials, and reportage by journalists.

The information reported in the Soviet newspapers about German atrocities against the Jews must be viewed in the context of what was written about the situation of the general population in the occupied territories and how they related to the unique fate of the Jewish population there.

From Hitler's accession to power in 1933, until the German attack on the Soviet Union in June 1941, very little information about Nazi atrocities against the Jews was published in Russian newspapers. One exception was the quite sharp reaction to the riots of '*Kristallnacht*' in November 1938. *Pravda* published an editorial on November 18, 1938, entitled "The Fascist Vandals and Cannibals," describing the brutalities committed against the Jews in Germany. The Soviet newspapers also wrote about protest meetings held in Moscow and other cities against German anti-Semitic policy and about an anti-German declaration adopted at a protest rally in Moscow. This unusual reaction by the Soviet press was generated by anger at Germany's takeover of the Sudetenland in Czechoslovakia and the growing threat to the Soviet Union. Moscow also wanted to be in step with the West's reaction to '*Kristallnacht*' and win public opinion points there against a common enemy, Germany. But, shortly after this unusual reaction, there came a change in Soviet policy in relation to Germany. On August 23, 1939, the world was astounded to learn about the Soviet-German Non-Aggression Pact. In the wake of this agreement, and until the German attack on Soviet Union, reports in the Soviet press about persecution of Jews in Germany, in occupied Poland and in other occupied countries of Europe, ceased entirely. Germany was described in the newspapers as a peace-loving country, while Poland, France and England were aggressors.

Nazi Germany's attack on the Soviet Union changed the tune and direction of the Soviet press concerning Germany, which now became the cruel and murderous enemy, both in reality and in the press. In spite of this, in the first months of the German-Soviet war, very little was written in the newspapers about German atrocities. The information about what was going on in the occupied territories was still limited. There were some articles about Nazi terror in Poland and in the cities of Brest-Litovsk and Minsk, where Jews were mentioned, among other victims.[1]

But the real situation was not yet clear. The first time that the uniqueness of the fate of the Jews was mentioned in the Soviet newspapers was when they published the declaration adopted by the "Meeting of Representatives of the Jewish People," which took place in Moscow on August 24, 1941. Headlined "Brother Jews all over the World!" this declaration said:[2]

> . . . The Slavic nations are being relentlessly annihilated. . .[I]n the occupied countries the bloody fascism has introduced a 'new order' with the help of a knife and gallows, fire and force. But in regard to the Jewish people the bloody Hitlerism has outlined a gangster plan of a full and unrestricted extermination of them.

Already in this declaration, signed by prominent Jewish personalities, the tendency is apparent not to emphasize too much the uniquely different Nazi policy regarding the Jews. All the Soviet newspapers published Stalin's speech on November 6, 1941, marking the 24th anniversary of the October Revolution. He said:[3]

> The Hitlerite rabble is killing and raping the peace-loving inhabitants of our country. . . They are carrying out pogroms in the style of the Middle Ages against the Jews. . . Hitler says . . . that to establish the great German Empire it is first necessary to displace and destroy the Slavic people—the Russians, Poles, Czechs, Slovaks, Bulgarians, Ukrainians, Belorussians . . .

This speech underscores the tendency of Soviet information and propaganda published in the press throughout the war to emphasize that *the Slavic peoples were the target for annihilation.* The reason behind this propaganda thesis was to promote the motivation of the Russians, Ukrainians, Belorussians and other Slavic peoples to fight the Germans. The Nazi atrocities against the Jews could not be omitted, but the truth that they were the only people who faced total extermination, and not the Slavs, was not to be revealed.

Broad coverage was given in the Soviet press to Foreign Minister Molotov's notes which were conveyed to the ambassadors of the states with which Soviet Union maintained diplomatic relations. There were four such notes that referred to the mass murder, terror and devastation committed by the Germans in the occupied territories of the Soviet Union and against Soviet prisoners of war. Each note consisted of dozens of pages. The Jews were mentioned explicitly only in the second note published in the newspapers on January 7, 1942. This note stated:[4]

> . . . The German aggressor carried out a horrific slaughter and pogrom in Kiev, the capital of Ukraine. In the course of several days the German bandits killed and slaughtered 52,000 men, women, old people and children, taking pitiless revenge on all the Ukrainians, Russians and Jews who had shown any devotion to Soviet rule. . . The German occupiers also perpetrated mass mur-

ders in other Ukrainian cities, and this bloody slaughter was directed mainly against defenseless Jews from the working classes. According to incomplete data, in Lvov no less than 6,000 were shot, in Odessa over 8,000 people, in Kamenets-Podolsk around 8,500 people were shot and hanged . . .

It was known in Moscow at that time that the 52,000 people killed in Kiev at the end of September 1941 were exclusively Jews. Yet Molotov, and following him the press, described the victims as Ukrainians, Russians and, only in the third place, Jews. When relating to the mass-murders carried out in other cities, the victims are described as "Jews from the working classes." This implies that there was not a total extermination of the Jews, and that non-working class Jews were not persecuted. There is no mention of Jews at all in *Izvestia*'s January 8, 1942, editorial related to Molotov's note and quoting part of it.

On April 28, 1942, Molotov's third diplomatic note addressing German atrocities carried out in the occupied territories was published in the press. This note cited the murder of 3,000 citizens in Taganrog, 7,000 in Kerch, 6,000 in Vitebsk, 10,000 in Pinsk, 12,000 in Minsk, and 14,000 in Kharkov. There was no mention that all these victims were Jews.[5] The note further stated: ". . . Hundreds of thousands of Ukrainians, Russians, Jews, Moldavians and other nationalities perished at the hands of German butchers in Ukrainian cities."

The uniqueness in the fate of the Jews was not stressed in the note. On January 15, 1942, the Soviet press published an article about a German document captured in the city of Kalinin. It was an order of Field Marshal von Reichenau, commander of the 6th Army, on how the German troops should behave in the occupied Soviet territories. This document was submitted to the newspapers by the Sovinformburo. The German document's opening sentence was:[6] "The essential goal of the campaign against the Jewish-Bolshevik system is the complete destruction of its power instruments. . ." This document, dealing with many issues, such as how to behave with prisoners, partisans, food, captured weapons and other problems, was fully published, with the sole exception of the following paragraph that was omitted:

Therefore, the soldier must have full understanding for the necessity of a severe but just atonement of Jewish subhumanity.

This has the further goal of nipping in the bud rebellions in the rear of the Wehrmacht which, as experience shows, are always instigated by Jews.

This omission was intentional. The information and propaganda policy was to shield the Soviet people and soldiers, as far as possibly, against the trend in German propaganda, directed to their own German soldiers and to the Soviet people, that their war was mainly against the Jews-Bolsheviks (Judeo-Bolshevism), the instigators of the war, and not against the people of the Soviet Union.

Descriptions of Nazi atrocities against the civilian population in the occupied territories were published quite frequently in the press. A declaration signed by intellectuals originally from Lithuania, Latvia and Estonia, about the Nazi terror in their republics, did not mention Jews.[7] An editorial in *Izvestia*, referring to the Ukraine, wrote that 52,000 people were shot in Kiev, 25,000 in Odessa, 10,500 in Dnepropetrovsk and detailed numbers in still other cities. Yet there was no mention that all these people were Jews.[8] A declaration, signed by educators, musicians, physicians and people from other professions, was headlined "We shall defend children from fascist barbarism!" It asked:[9]

. . . Who is annihilating the Slavic people and Slavic children? . . . Hitler . . . By Hitler's order German soldiers kill children . . . In Crimea, in the city of Kerch, the Hitlerites killed 245 Russian and Tatar children. . . .

This declaration makes no mention of Jewish children who were the main victims of Nazi atrocities. The children killed in Kerch were Jewish children, while the Tatar victims were the so-called Krimchaks, who were Jews and the Germans killed them as Jews. (Most of the Tatars in Crimea collaborated with the Germans; in 1944, after the region was liberated by the Red Army, the Soviets expelled them from Crimea.)

The Soviet press constantly concealed the total extermination of the Jews while stressing that the Slavs were the target doomed by the Nazis for extermination. Even the Soviet Jews, to some degree, had to follow this policy. On May 26, 1942, the Soviet press reported about "The Second Meeting of Representatives of the Jewish People," their letter to

Comrade Stalin and their appeal to the "Jews in the Whole World." The purpose and main subject of this meeting, as portrayed in the press, were an appeal by Soviet Jewry to world Jewry to mobilize their political, physical and financial resources in help for the Soviet Union and in the struggle against Germany. Concerning Nazi terror and extermination, the Soviet Jewish appeal to world Jewry declared:[10]

> . . . For the Hitlerites, aside from the Germans, all the nations are "inferior races." They are killing Russians and Ukrainians, Belorussians and Poles. . . The grievance of the Jews is enormous. In the occupied cities the Hitlerites doomed the Jews to a tormented death . . . There are cities and villages . . . where no living Jew was left. . . .

As can be seen in this declaration, even Soviet Jews could not openly refer to the totality of extermination of Jews and the uniqueness of their fate. Whenever they mentioned the extermination of Jews they had to mention the killings of Russians, Ukrainians and others. Without doubt, the Germans murdered many Russians, Ukrainians and others, but it was not a mass and total extermination, like the Jews faced. This reality, the difference between the fate of the Jews and the fate of non-Jews, was blurred in the Soviet press.

On November 1, 1942, *Krasnaya Zvezda* published a short article, headlined "Jews" and written by Ilya Ehrenburg. It dealt with Jewish soldiers and valiant actions carried out by them. Describing the heroic death of David Katz in the defense of Stalingrad, Ehrenburg wrote:[11]

> . . . How not to mention here the old legend about the giant Goliath and little David with a sling. In the past the Jews dreamed about the Promised Land. Now the Jews have a Promised Land: it is the front-line. There they can take revenge on the Germans, for the women, the elderly and children. Great is the love of the Jews for Russia. "For the Homeland," called the Moscow worker Layzer Papernik, while throwing a grenade at the Germans. With these words he died, the devoted son of Russia.

Ehrenburg was able to publish this article because it was part of a series of articles he wrote about participation in battle of different nationalities of the Soviet Union. There were articles headlined "Kirgizians," "Tatars" and the names of other peoples. Ehrenburg's goal in writing the article "Jews" was to confute the anti-Semitic rumors spread among the Soviet population and even among soldiers, that Jews were not fighting, that Jews were not seen at the front-line. But even in this article he felt obliged to introduce sentences like "great is the love of Jews for Russia" or that Leyzer Papernik died as a "devoted son of Russia." It would be more proper to write that Papernik died as a "devoted son of the Jewish people." But Ehrenburg knew very well the Soviet policy in connection with the Jews and the limits within which he could write on this subject. Nevertheless, the Jew Ehrenburg, more than any other publicist, mentioned the suffering of the Jews in his articles.

But the Soviet regime and the Soviet press could not consistently follow this policy of silence about the total extermination of the Jews; there were temporary deviations. On December 18, 1942, the Soviet Union was obliged to publish in the press the Joint Declaration of the Allied Countries, issued simultaneously in Washington, London and Moscow the day before. This declaration said explicitly that in Nazi occupied Europe,

> . . . the German authorities . . . are now putting into effect Hitler's
> oft repeated intention to exterminate the Jewish people in Europe
> . . . Those responsible for these crimes shall not escape retribu-
> tion . . .[12]

The next day following this declaration, on December 19, the Soviet press' front-pages appeared with an announcement from the Foreign Ministry, with the headline "The Realization by the Hitlerite Authorities [of] the Plan of Annihilation of the Jewish People in Europe." This announcement, covering half of the front-page, gave details about atrocities and extermination of the Jews in Nazi-occupied Europe and about the fate of the Jews in the occupied territories of the Soviet Union. This official Soviet declaration stated:[13]

> . . . The cannibalistic plan prepared by Hitler in the beginning
> of this year, foresees to concentrate in Eastern Europe, mainly in
> Poland, until the end of 1942, about 4,000,000 Jews, in order to

kill them . . . the number of Jews murdered already until now . . .
reaches many hundreds of thousands of men, women and children
. . . in the Warsaw ghetto were concentrated 400,000 Jews . . . now
there are hardly 40,000 left there . . .

   . . . [From i]nformation which arrives from the Soviet territories temporarily occupied by the enemy. . . it was verified that in
the Baltic Soviet republics the Hitlerite butchers annihilated tens
of thousands of the best people of Lithuania, Latvia and Estonia,
among whom were citizens of Jewish nationality. . .

   . . . The overwhelming majority of victims in this bloody
rampage are Russian, Ukrainian and Belorussian peasants, workers, employees and intelligentsia. There are appalling [numbers
of] victims among the Lithuanian, Latvian and Estonian people,
among the Moldavians, among the inhabitants of the Karelo-
Finns republic. The Jewish minority within the Soviet population,
in relation to its numerical size, which is not great . . . suffered
particularly severely at the hands of the bestial bloodthirsty
Hitlerite degenerates . . .

The strengthening of the terror against the Ukrainian population in the summer and autumn of this year was marked by a wave
of bloody anti-Jewish pogroms in some settlements of Ukrainian
SSR. During only two days, on August 26–27, the German-fascist
pogrom-makers arranged a bloody slaughter in the following
Ukrainian cities: in Lutsk 20,000 were shot . . . in Sarny this
spring, simultaneously with thousands of Ukrainians and
Russians, 18,000 Jews were executed . . .The suffering of Jewish
old men, women and children in Kiev and Dnepropetrovsk will
never be forgotten: in only these two cities, during the first months
of occupation, the Germans annihilated 60,000 people. . . Heavy
will be the punishing hand of the people who will throw off the
oppression of the German-fascist occupiers. . .

This front-page announcement, in its content, in its length and being
devoted almost exclusively to the Nazi German plan of total extermination of the Jews in the whole of occupied Europe, was the first and the last
of its kind in the wartime Soviet press. It referred to the unique fate of
Jews in Poland, France, Belgium and all the other countries of occupied

Europe. Yet when the announcement related to the fate of the Soviet Jews, their extermination became only a part, and it is combined with the German murderous actions against other nationalities, Russians, Ukrainians, Lithuanians and others, who lived in the occupied areas. So, in spite of the uniqueness of this publication in the Soviet press, there was no basic change in the way the extermination of the Soviet Jews had been described in the past, that the Jews were murdered by the Nazis like other Soviet citizens. The policy to blur the uniqueness of their fate prevailed.

During 1942, the Soviet newspapers sporadically published reports about German atrocities in the occupied territories. These articles were based on information from German prisoners of war, captured letters from German soldiers writing home, as well as from the foreign press, from eyewitnesses in the areas liberated by the Soviet army during the winter offensive in 1941–1942, and other sources. The Soviet army newspaper *Krasnaya Zvezda* published information related to Nazi terror and atrocities in Skvira (south of Kiev), in Vinitsa, in Vielizh (north of Smolensk), in Kursk, in Lithuania, in Berdyansk on the Azov Sea, in Pogorelsk and Karmanovsk in the district of Smolensk, in Minsk, Vitebsk and other areas. Jews were almost not mentioned. Regarding the victims, the newspaper employed the terms "inhabitants", "Soviet citizens", "unfortunates" or "old, women and children."[14] There was a similar editorial policy in other major Soviet newspapers.

After the German defeat at Stalingrad, in January 1943, the Soviet army started its westward advance and almost daily liberated new cities, until the end of the war. What had happened in the liberated areas during the German occupation, the total murder of the Jews there, was now obvious. Did it find an expression in the press?

In January-February 1943, the Soviet army liberated the south-eastern districts of European Russia. This included the Stavropolskii Kray, where at a place called Mineralnye-Vody, the Germans shot 6,000 Jews in September 1942; and the cities of Kharkov and Rostov-on-the-Don, where tens of thousands of Jews were murdered.

Pravda, the leading Soviet newspaper, published announcements from Sovinformburo and articles by their correspondents with information about German atrocities in the liberated areas. These articles included names and ages of hundreds of people murdered by the Nazis. All of them were Russian names; Jews were almost not mentioned.[15]

An article published in *Pravda*, describing the German terror against the local population and the partisan warfare in the area of Kuban, stated:[16] ". . .In Krasnodar, in one day, the Germans shot some thousands of old people, women and children." No mention was made that all these people were Jews. In any place, where Germans shot in one, or even a few days, thousands of "old men, women and children," it was always and only Jews who had been murdered. But the article's author found it important to inform his readers that the "Hitlerites planned target was to annihilate a big part of the Cossaks of Kuban." The reality was that the Germans had related positively to the Cossaks and tens of thousands of them served as volunteers in the German army.

A day after the liberation of Kharkov, *Pravda* wrote in an editorial:[17] ". . .Tens of thousands of Soviet people, Ukrainians, Russians, Jews, were shot, hanged, tortured. . .It is hard to count all the bloody brutalities aimed to annihilate the Ukrainian people, to turn the others into slaves. . ." A *Pravda* correspondent wrote that in Kharkov "a concentration camp was discovered on Kholodnaya Gora where the Germans shot and starved 15,000 people . . .In the area of the Kharkov tractor factory the fascists shot 14,000 Jews. . ."[18]

Sovinformburo published a declaration about the German atrocities in the city of Rostov-on-the-Don. Signed by the city's mayor, some university professors, army officers and workers, the declaration stated:[19]

> After the conquest of Rostov, the [German] city commander, Major-General Kittel, organized the mass annihilation of peaceful citizens of the town. . .They were ordered to appear, together with their children, at collection points, to take with them their valuables and food for 3 days. In the vicinity of the botanical garden and the zoo, the adults were shot and the children poisoned. According the latest data, the German hangmen shot and poisoned 15,000–18,000 people . . .

This was the extermination action of the Jews of Rostov, but the declaration didn't mention the word Jews.

On April 7, 1943, the newspapers carried a front-page editorial and the first announcement of the "Extraordinary Committee to Investigate the German-Fascist Crimes in the Temporarily Occupied Territories of the

Soviet Union."[20] This committee was established by a decree of the Supreme Council of the Soviet Union on November 2, 1942. Local committees, subordinated to the main committee in Moscow, were formed in each Soviet republic, district and liberated city. The first announcement referred to the German atrocities carried out in the cities of Rzev, Viasma and some other cities in the districts of Smolensk and Kalinin, liberated by the Soviet army.

Pravda's editorial related to the announcement quoted Stalin's speech in which he said that the Hitlerites' aims were to turn into slaves or annihilate the people of Ukraine, Belorussia, the Baltic republics, Moldavia, Crimea and the Caucasus. The Extraordinary Committee's announcement covered almost two full pages, with detailed descriptions of German atrocities and killings in many localities, including dozens of names and ages of murdered Russian people. There was only one sentence in the whole announcement which said that 100 Jews were shot in the town of Sychevsk. The announcement included details of brutalities against Soviet prisoners of war, of deportations of Russians for forced labor in Germany and of the destruction by the Germans of housing, schools, institutions and factories.

The announcements by the Extraordinary Committee published in the Soviet press became the main source for information about the Nazi atrocities until the end of the war. Usually, on days when these announcements were published, the editorial of the newspaper was related to them. These announcements give a clear and definite picture of official Soviet policy on how to present the German atrocities in the occupied territories in relation to the people living there and to the Jews.

The following quotations from the announcements by the Extraordinary Committee, relating to some of the largest Jewish communities that came under German occupation, exemplify Soviet practice in reporting the Holocaust, as published in the Soviet press.

The announcement published on July 14, 1943,[21] stated that 6,700 Soviet citizens were killed in Krasnodar, but made no mention of Jews. The editorial quoted a pamphlet issued by the German army, allegedly found in a dead soldier's pocket: ". . .kill every Russian, every Soviet man." It is very doubtful whether such a pamphlet existed, but it stressed again the course of Soviet propaganda, that the Russians were the target for annihilation. In the August 5, 1943, announcement about German atrocities in Stavropolskii Kray (south-east of Russia, the Kuban River area), there was a description of the deportation and murder of 2,000 Jews from Kislovodsk and some thousands from other cities in that area in September 1942.[22]

An editorial and an announcement by the Extraordinary Committee about the murder actions in Kiev and at Babi Yar declared that:[23]

> During the German occupation of Kiev . . . over 195,000 citizens, whose only guilt was being Soviet people, were killed. . . at Babi Yar they threw new-born children into the ravine and buried them alive, together with their killed and wounded parents. . . On September 29, 1941, the Hitlerite bandits rounded up thousands of peaceful Soviet citizens at the corner of Melnik and Dokterev streets and led them to Babi Yar, where they took away from them their valuables and shot them . . .

The omission of the Jews in describing the massacre at Babi Yar was, without doubt, intentional and decided by the highest authorities in Ukraine. It was an expression of Soviet policy in regard to the Holocaust.

On May 7, 1944, the Extraordinary Committee published its announcement about German atrocities in the city and district of Rovno, which had been liberated on February 5, 1944. During 1941–1942, about 28,000–29,000 Jews were murdered in Rovno. The Committee's announcement stated:[24]

> . . . Y. Karpuk, who worked in a German farm . . . told: I saw many times how the Hitlerites annihilated Soviet citizens— Ukrainians, Russians, Poles, Jews. It was carried out in the following way . . .

That was all that was mentioned about Jews in almost a full newspaper page covered by the announcement about Rovno.

On June 14, 1944, the Extraordinary Committee's announcement regarding German atrocities in Odessa and in the district of Odessa was published. The announcement and accompanying editorials referred to 200,000 Soviet citizens murdered by the Germans and Romanians, who had held the region that the Romanians called Transnistria. The announcement described the burning alive of 25,000 people who had been locked inside powder stores in Odessa on October 19, 1941; the killings of 54,000 people in the Bogdanovka camp, in December 1941; and the killing of 22,000 people in the Domanevka camp, and over 35,000 in the area of Mostovsk, between December 1941 and March 1944.

Not a word was said that all these murdered people were Jews. In order to blur the identity of the victims even more, the announcement mentioned the names of 17 people, all of them typical Russian names, like Piotr and Michail Yemelyanov, Georgii and Anna Kolesnykov and others.[25]

On September 20, 1944, the Extraordinary Committee's announcement regarding Minsk was published. In relation to the Jews, the announcement said:[26]

> . . . The Germans sealed about 100,000 Jews in a special ghetto-camp . . . The witnesses . . . stated that the commander of the camp, Ridder, and his helpers . . . abused the prisoners, tortured and shot them without any reason . . .

The announcement also dealt with the "concentration camp" Malyii Trostynets where "peaceful civilians condemned to death were imprisoned." Prisoners were shot in the Blagovshchina grove, about 1.5 km from the camp. In the autumn of 1943, the Germans opened the pits at Blagovshchina and started to cremate the corpses in order to hide their crimes.

Nothing was said about the fact that the 100,000 Jews sealed within the ghetto were totally annihilated, most of them at Malyii Trostynets. An article written by Ponomarenko, the Chairmen of the People's Commissars of Belorussia, said that

> . . . 120,000 people were killed and tortured in Minsk. Among them were peaceful inhabitants of Minsk, prisoners of war and some tens of thousands of Jews who were brought from Hamburg into the ghetto of Minsk . . .

The murdered Jews of Minsk were not mentioned; they were among the "peaceful inhabitants." Yet the killing of foreign Jews, like those from

Hamburg, was mentioned explicitly. This was part of the Soviet propaganda policy in relation to the Holocaust, clearly expressed by the Soviet press.

There were some small deviations from this policy. In the announcement of the Extraordinary Committee about German atrocities in the Lvov district there were descriptions of brutalities against the Jews. About their extermination, it was stated that,[27]

> . . . During the ghetto's existence, from September 7, 1941, until June 6, 1943, the Germans annihilated over 130,000. Part of them were shot inside the ghetto, part in the Janowska camp, [and] the others were deported by the Germans to the death camp of Belzec for annihilation . . .

Jews were also mentioned in the committee's announcements concerning German atrocities in Lithuania and Latvia:[28]

> Hundreds of thousands of Lithuanian citizens were annihilated by the German-fascist butchers. . . They started with the total extermination of the Jews. They planned afterwards to fill the terrible tombs with people of all nations—all who lived in Lithuania.

Descriptions of the murder of the Jews of Riga and Daugavpils were included in the announcement about Latvia.[29]

But these announcements were exceptions. The usual substance of dozens of announcements made by the Extraordinary Committee stressed that Russians, Ukrainians, Belorussians, or the generic "Soviet people," were the principal target of German brutalities and annihilation. Jews were not mentioned at all or in only a few brief sentences, which rarely disclosed the fact that they were totally exterminated.

In July 1943, *Pravda* published some articles about the situation in the occupied territories. One of these articles, written by Y. Kalnberzin, the secretary of the Communist Party of Latvia, stated that "the Hitlerites murdered over 150,000 sons and daughters of the Latvian people." Another article, written by A. Snechkus, the secretary of the Communist Party of Lithuania, declared that "during two years, about 200,000

Lithuanian citizens were killed or tortured to death by the Hitlerites."[30] Not a word about Jews in these countries, even though the overwhelming majority of the victims in Lithuania and Latvia were Jews and the majority among those who participated in killing the Jews there were local Lithuanian and Latvian collaborators.

On July 26, 1943, *Pravda* published an article, "Hitler's War of Annihilation." Some quotations from this article make clear its content and spirit:[31]

> Hitler developed cannibalistic plans to annihilate the Slavs . . . to expel and annihilate Russians, Poles, Czechs, Slovaks, Bulgars, Yugoslavs, Ukrainians, Belorussians. In order to turn Russian, Belorussian, Lithuanian, Estonian, Polish, Yugoslav cities into German cities, their population had to be annihilated. . . [D]uring the first months of their rule, they annihilated tens of thousands of peaceful citizens of Kiev, Odessa, Minsk, Vitebsk, Brest-Litovsk and Lvov. . .

Reading this article, one could think that Jews were not included in Hitler's annihilation plans.

The first war-crimes trial against Germans or local collaborators accused of participation in Nazi atrocities was held in Krasnodar, on July 14–18, 1943. The eleven defendants were local people who served in *SS Sonderkommando 10 A*. Complete proceedings of this trial were published in the Soviet press.[32] In the whole trial record, the word "Jew" was not mentioned. *Sonderkommando 10 A* carried out the murder of thousands of Jews in Krasnodar, some of whom were refugees and evacuees from Ukraine and other places.

The Soviet press also gave full coverage to the second, so-called "Kharkov Trial," which took place during December 15–18, 1943. The defendants were three Germans and one local collaborator. The tragedy of 20,000 Kharkov Jews, who were crowded within the former tractor factory during November–December 1941, and then taken to Drobitsky-Yar and shot, was mentioned at the trial. Nevertheless, the victims were not described as Jews but as "peaceful citizens."[33]

The Soviet press published the proceedings of three other war-crimes trials several months after the German surrender: the Smolensk, Orlov-

Briansk-Bobroisk, and Leningrad trials, in the months of October and December 1945.[34] Jews were not mentioned at any of these trials.

The uprising in the Warsaw Ghetto broke out on April 19, 1943. The Soviet press did not bring this news to the public until almost six weeks later. Only on May 29, 1943, did *Pravda*, in a long article, headlined "The Rear of 'Fortress Europe' Is Not Strong," mention the Warsaw Ghetto Uprising. The article discusses the partisan and anti-Nazi underground struggle inside occupied Europe, with descriptions of partisan warfare in Yugoslavia, Greece, France and Poland.[35] As for the Warsaw Ghetto Uprising,

> The persistent struggle of the Warsaw ghetto Jews against the German cannibals has lasted about a month. The Hitlerites decided to wipe the ghetto from the face of the earth and kill hundreds of thousands of people there. But this time the Hitlerites met fierce resistance. The people encircled in the ghetto are fighting with great courage. They don't have enough arms and take up stones, they blew up houses entered by German police, they turned the ghetto into a fortress and many German Gestapo and policemen found their death there during its siege.

A short notice by the TASS news agency from London, carried in *Pravda* under the headline, "Hitlerite Terror in Warsaw,"[36] stated that

> information has reached London, that for over 3 weeks, [German] SS and army units are besieging the Jewish ghetto in Warsaw and are shelling it with artillery. German planes are dropping bombs on the ghetto neighborhoods. The people of the ghetto are striking back, setting fire to industrial enterprises and German military stores.

Not displayed with any prominent headlines that would draw readers' attention, the news about the Warsaw Ghetto Uprising could easily be overlooked.

Contemporaneously with the Warsaw Ghetto revolt and for months following, the Soviet press engaged in polemics about the Katyn massacre of thousands of Polish army officers. On April 13, 1943, the

Germans announced that mass graves had been discovered in the Katyn Forest, near Smolensk, in the German-occupied territories of the Soviet Union. The graves contained bodies of thousands of Polish officers. The Germans charged the Soviets with murder and asked the International Red Cross to appoint a multinational medical commission to probe the matter. The Polish government-in-exile in London agreed to the investigation by the International Red Cross, while the Soviet Union came out against this demand.

On April 19, 1943, the day when the Warsaw Ghetto Uprising started, *Pravda* published a front-page editorial with the headline "Polish Collaborators with Hitler." The article claimed that the Katyn massacre was carried out by the Germans themselves, and that the Polish government was collaborating on this issue with Germany. To prove the Soviet claim, the article mentions the German atrocities against civilians and against Jews particularly. It said:[37]

> The base fabrications of the Hitlerite butchers have a definite aim—to erase the footprints of their monstrous crimes . . . [F]eeling the enormous anger of progressive mankind about their atrocities against defenseless peaceful civilians, especially against the Jews, the Hitlerites are trying with all their might to direct light-minded and naive people against the Jews. For this purpose they invented some mythical Jewish "commissars," as if they participated in the killing of 10,000 Polish officers. . . .

The presentation of Jews in this article, as victims of German atrocities and as those accused by the Germans of participation in the murder at Katyn, was intended by Soviet propaganda for world public opinion. The Soviets believed that this would strengthen their claim that the Germans were the killers of the Polish officers and put in an embarrassing position the Polish government, which rejected the Soviet argument that the Germans were the murders at Katyn. The Soviet press continued to use the killing of Jews in the controversy over of the Katyn massacre. On April 21, 1943, *Pravda*, in an article headlined "Poland the Hitlerite House of Death," attacked the Polish government-in-exile, calling them "Polish collaborators with Hitler." But the main theme of this article was the German atrocities against the Polish people, in order to portray the

Katyn massacre as part of this German policy. In relation to Jews, the article stated:[38]

> The Czechoslovak foreign minister Masaryk, in his speech in London in January, announced that Germany admits officially, that in Poland 1,600,000 Jews have disappeared . . . The German barbarians see their task as to annihilate totally the entire Jewish population, not only in Poland, but in all the European countries. . .

Further in the article is a description of what was going on at Treblinka. Treblinka A was described as a concentration camp for Polish people. Regarding Treblinka B:

> Treblinka B was constructed in 1942. . . . [T]his camp is called 'the central house of death'. . . . It is a place where mass executions are conducted daily. People are murdered here by steam compressed into hermetically sealed chambers. . . .

While Treblinka A was characterized as a concentration camp for Poles, nothing was said to specify that Treblinka B was a death camp where only Jews were killed. By giving more publicity to German atrocities in Poland and stressing the Nazi policy of total extermination of the Jews, the Soviet propaganda apparatus sought to divert world public opinion from the Katyn massacre to the German terror and thus accept the Soviet version about Katyn. But the outspoken publication about the uniqueness of the fate of the Jews was a temporary, tactical deviation in the Soviet propaganda policy regarding the Holocaust.

On August 11, 1944, *Pravda* published an article, "A Camp at Majdanek."[39] The article declared that ". . . here were driven for death . . . people of all nationalities, all ages, men, women and children. Poles, Russians, Jews, Ukrainians. . ."

The Communist Party's daily returned to the theme of Majdanek on September 16, 1944, with an editorial and an announcement by a Polish-Soviet Extraordinary Committee about Majdanek. The announcement described the atrocities carried out in the camp against people of different European nationalities, including Jews. Regarding the single largest extermination action there, the Committee stated that "on November 3,

1943, 18,400 people were shot in the camp."[40] Not a single word explained that all those shot that day were Jews. On that day 42,000 Jews in all were shot in the camps of Majdanek, Trawniki and Poniatów, all of them in the Lublin area. The Germans called this murder action "*Erntefest*" (harvest festival).

Auschwitz was mentioned a few times in *Pravda*. On October 27, 1944, a TASS communiqué appeared about testimonies of people who had escaped from the camp. According to their testimonies, tens of thousands of people from all over Europe, of different nationalities,—Czechs, French, Poles, Jews, Soviet prisoners-of-war and others—were being brought there for annihilation.[41] Five days after the liberation of the camp in January 1945, *Pravda* published an article about Auschwitz.[42] The article said that transports with people, doomed to die, arrived at the camp from the Soviet Union, Poland, France, Yugoslavia and so forth; but there was not a word about the ethnicity of these people.

On May 7, 1945, *Pravda* published an editorial and an announcement from the Extraordinary Committee about Auschwitz. It was stated that[43]

> . . . in the Auschwitz camp the Germans had annihilated over 4 million citizens of the Soviet Union, Poland, France, Belgium, Holland, Czechoslovakia, Yugoslavia, Romania, Hungary and other countries. . .

The word *Jews* was not mentioned in the two pages of the newspaper. With this official announcement was started the story of 4 million victims of Auschwitz. In such a number, the Jews were a minority among the victims. Now it is known that the number of the victims of Auschwitz was around 1.5 million and that about 90 per cent of them were Jews.

Conclusions

The Soviet press was controlled by the Communist Party and the Soviet government and everything published there, without any exception, was an expression of the policy dictated by the official organs of the state. Questions related to the ideological and propaganda policy, whether in the army, among the civilian population and for use outside the Soviet Union, were decided by the highest party and government organs. A.S. Shcherbakov, the secretary of the Central Committee of the party and the

Head of the Main Political Department of the Soviet Army, held regular meetings with the chief editors of the central Soviet press; officially to discuss common problems, but actually to instruct them in what to write and what not to write. In the main Soviet newspapers the same official announcements were published in all of them on the same day. The difference came in the articles written by the newspapers' own correspondents, but they also were guided by the official policy line. Therefore, the way the Holocaust in general and the Holocaust of the Soviet Jews in the occupied territories was reported in the leading Russian language newspapers had a uniform character. Coverage in those newspapers gave their readers the following picture of the German policy against the population in the occupied territories, among them the Jews: Nazi-German terror is directed mainly against the Slavic peoples (Russians, Ukrainians, Belorussians, Poles) with the aim to enslave and annihilate them. Jews are persecuted and murdered, in some localities even totally, but as Soviet citizens, not just because they are Jews. There is no uniqueness in their fate.

The total extermination of the Jews was blurred, especially when it was related to the Soviet Jews. Even in the most important and explicit announcements about German extermination of the Jews, published by the Soviet newspapers on December 18 and 19, 1942, the uniqueness of their fate was blurred by saying that the overwhelming majority of the victims in the occupied territories of Soviet Union were Russians, Ukrainians, etc.

Even from the beginning of 1943, and until the end of the war, when the Soviet army began to liberate occupied territories and found no living Jews there, the total extermination of Jews was never clearly reported in the Soviet press. There were some reasons for this policy. Communism did not relate to and define the Jewish people as a normal nation, with the need and right to exist in a Communist society. Instead, Jews would have to assimilate and disappear as a nation. This gave the Soviet propagandists and press an ideological excuse to use the term "Soviet citizens" or "people in Lithuania" or of other republics, or just "the elderly, men, women and children" when the victims were *Jews*.

An important role in shaping this Soviet policy was played by German propaganda. The latter constantly stressed that Germany was not fighting against the Russian, Ukrainian and other peoples of the Soviet Union, but against Judeo-Bolshevism and against the Jews who were the ruling caste in the Communist state. Because of the deeply rooted popular anti-Semitism among the Soviet people, this propaganda fell on fertile soil. By publishing the truth, that the Jews were the only people being totally annihilated, the Soviet press would in some way confirm and serve the German propaganda. Therefore, in order to strengthen their motivation to fight against Germany, the Soviet propaganda and press stressed that the Russians, Ukrainians and other Slavic peoples were the main target of the Nazi terror and extermination. Conversely, the Soviet press also conducted the policy of blurring the truth about the total murder of Jews.

Last but not least, there were also anti-Semitic reasons behind this policy, growing out of the anti-Semitism that prevailed among the Soviet leadership. The very fact that this policy of suppressing the unique fate of the Jews was continued after the war, even after Germany's defeat, when there was no more German propaganda, allows the inference that the anti-Semitic factor, the indifference to the fate of the Jews, influenced the Soviet publication policy concerning the Holocaust even during the war.

Notes:

1. *Vechernaya Moskva*, Aug. 4, Aug. 9, 1941.
2. Ibid., Aug. 25, 1941. Such national meetings were also held by representatives of other nations in the Soviet Union.
3. *Pravda, Izvestia* and other newspapers, on November 7, 1941.
4. *Pravda, Izvestia*, January 7, 1942.
5. *Pravda, Izvestia*, April 28, 1942.
6. Ibid., January 15, 1942.
7. *Izvestia*, January 22, 1942.
8. Ibid., February 2, 1942.
9. Ibid., April 21, 1942.
10. Ibid., May 26, 1942.
11. Ibid., November 1, 1942.
12. *Izvestia, Pravda*, December 18, 1942.
13. *Pravda, Izvestia, Krasnaya Zvezda*, December 19, 1942.
14. *Krasnaya Zvezda*, 1942: April 17, May 9, May 25, June 2, June 16, Oct. 4, Oct. 16, Oct. 23.
15. *Pravda*, 1943: Jan. 18, Jan. 23, Jan. 24, Jan. 26, Feb. 3, Feb. 8, Feb. 9.

16. Ibid., February 10, 1943.
17. Ibid., February 11, 1943.
18. Ibid., February 28, 1943.
19. Ibid., March 13, 1943.
20. Ibid., April 7, 1943.
21. Ibid., July 14, 1943.
22. Ibid., August 5, 1943.
23. Ibid., March 1, 1944.
24. Ibid., May 7, 1944.
25. Ibid., June 14, 1944.
26. Ibid., September 20, 1944.
27. Ibid., December 23, 1944.
28. Ibid., December 20, 1944.
29. Ibid., April 5, 1945.
30. Both articles were published in *Pravda* on July 21, 1943.
31. Ibid., July 26, 1944.
32. Ibid., July 15–19, 1943.
33. Ibid., December 16–20, 1943.
34. Ibid., October 16–19, 1945; December 27–31, 1945.
35. Ibid., May 29, 1943.
36. Ibid., June 2, 1943.
37. Ibid., April 19, 1943.
38. Ibid., April 21, 1943.
39. Ibid., August 11, 1944.
40. Ibid., September 16, 1944.
41. Ibid., February 2, 1945.
42. Ibid.., Feb. 2, 1945.
43. Ibid., May 7, 1945.

The Soviet Yiddish Press: *Eynikayt* During The War, 1942–1945

Dov-Ber Kerler
Indiana University

The almost immediate association that comes to mind when the Soviet Yiddish press and the Holocaust are mentioned is the organ of the Soviet Jewish Anti-Fascist Committee, *Eynikayt* (7 June 1942–21 November 1948), by then the only Yiddish newspaper and, as fate would have it, the most nationally-oriented Soviet Jewish periodical.

To be sure, between 1933 and 1941 a variety of Yiddish periodicals and dailies existed in the Soviet Union. A detailed study of the Soviet Yiddish press coverage of the rise of Nazism in Germany, the fate of German and Polish Jews and many other relevant issues of the pre-war years will uncover a complex interplay between the news *per se* and the ongoing Soviet ideological and political constraints conditioning, restricting or blocking their coverage (cf. Greenbaum 1979: 213). The same, of course, applies to any form of public Jewish expression in the Soviet Union since the 1930s.

The ultimate, eventually fateful results of these constraints were becoming evermore conspicuous by the end of the 1930s. The central Soviet Yiddish daily *Der Emes* that appeared in Moscow since 1920 was closed down in 1938 after its editor Moishe Litvakov was imprisoned in 1937. He perished in 1939. The pre-Soviet Yiddish press in the parts of Poland, the Baltic States and Romania that were annexed to the USSR between September 1939 and July 1940, underwent a rapid process of liquidation and overwhelming sovietization (Levin 1989: 137–146). According to Dov Levin (1989: 146) about nine Yiddish dailies appeared in the annexed territories, of which only one, the new Soviet *Bialistoker Shtern*, existed for 20 months until the German invasion in June 1941.

The only surviving daily in the whole of Lithuania between February and June 1941 was the Kovno-based *Der Emes* (see Levin 1977).

As for the Yiddish press in the Soviet Union proper, the two dailies— *Oktyabr* in Minsk and *Shtern* in Kiev (both established in 1925)—were running on borrowed time until the invasion in the summer of 1941. Even *Birobidzhaner Shtern* in Birobidzhan, hardly the most likely region to be reached by the rapidly advancing German Army, ceased publication in the years 1941–1944 (see Shmeruk 1961: 345, No. 3567).

Until 1939, the general Soviet press reported on the inside pages on the fate of Jews in Germany, while the same coverage was allocated a significantly more prominent place on the frontpages of the Soviet Yiddish press (see Altshuler et al. 1993: 208, no. 12; cf. also Pinchuk 1976). However, after the 23 August 1939 Soviet-German pact this coverage as well as any public criticism of the Nazi policies was stopped. It has, therefore, become customary to refer to the years 1939–1953—i. e. the years between the Molotov-Ribbentrop Agreement and Stalin's death—as "The Black Years of Soviet Jewry" (Gilboa 1972; Pinkus 1986: 249–340).

And yet, the establishment of the Soviet Jewish Anti-Fascist Committee with its newspaper *Eynikayt*, in the wake of the German invasion into the Soviet Union, was a major development in the public life of Soviet Jewry. In line with the Slav and other public pressure-group committees, the Jewish Anti-Fascist Committee was brought to life to serve the immediate and vital propagandistic and military needs of the Soviet Union during the critical first years of the War. The name of the Committee's official organ, *Eynikayt* (Unity), is very significant (cf. Gilboa 1972: 37). It encapsulates the call of the Soviet Jews to all Jews abroad (primarily in the USA and Britain) to unite in a common struggle against the Nazis by providing every possible material, moral and political assistance to the Soviet Union. Six years later, in the wake of the so-called *Zhdanovshchina* which started in 1946 and within the Cold War context, the Jewish Anti-Fascist Committee was conveniently treated as the principal nest of dangerously hostile nationalistic "anti-Soviet" activities, which had to be eradicated, paving the way for the ultimate solution of the Jewish question in the Soviet Union (on the 'liquidation' of the Central Yiddish Publishing House "Emes" in 1948, see Y. Kerler 1977: 43–48; on *Eynikayt* and the Jewish Anti-Fascist Committee's archives in today's Russia, see Sandler 1995).

The establishment of the Jewish Anti-Fascist Committee was a pragmatic de-facto reversal of the classical Stalinist perception of Jews. It also sharply contrasted with the situation in which Soviet Jews found themselves since the 1939 Nazi-Soviet Agreement. This complete about-face may be summed up with the Yiddish proverb *"az me darf hobn a ganev - nemt men im arop fun der tliye* (when a thief is needed, he's brought back down from the gallows)."

The first issue of *Eynikayt* appeared on 7 June 1942. Its last, 700th issue is dated 20 November 1948 (cf. Shulman 1991). At first it appeared every ten days in Kuibyshev where at the time the central Government offices and agencies were stationed. In July 1943 *Eynikayt* moved to Moscow where it became a weekly. Later, from 24 February 1945, the newspaper appeared three times a week.

As for circulation, there are indications that the supply and distribution inside the USSR did not match the demand. In early 1943 only 2,000 copies were available for retail sale in the whole of the Soviet Union (Redlich 1982: 48). In July 1943 *Eynikayt* announced that the newspaper's production quotas for the year 1944 were filled up, therefore no new subscriptions for the next year could be accepted (3/7/44, 91, p. 4). After the War the circulation was estimated at 10,000 copies, "of which a considerable quantity was sent abroad." At the same time the number of potential buyers in the USSR alone was estimated at over 50,000. Yet from the very beginning *Eynikayt* received a significant amount of readers' mail, more than 16 letters a day on average. During the first year (June 1942—March 1943), a total of 5,112 letters were received (15/3/43, 28–29, p. 3; Litvak 1966). They arrived from readers in various parts of the Soviet Union including many from soldiers in the Red Army.

The establishment of the newspaper was of course a reviving breath of life for many Yiddish writers, journalists, scholars, educators and other "linguistically unassimilated" members of the Jewish intelligentsia. During the first year the paper managed to attract 300 correspondents comprising both Yiddish and some Russian journalists and writers whose articles appeared in the newspaper. Moreover, according to Shimon Redlich's examination, the number of special *Eynikayt* reporters in 1942–1945 rose from 9 to 95; of these about a third "were military ones, reporting from all parts of the Nazi-Soviet front" (Redlich 1982: 195, n. 21; a partial list of these reporters in Redlich 1987: 83–87). The editorial

board of the newspaper consisted of some of the most prominent personalities of Soviet Yiddish culture who also played a vital role in the work
of the Jewish Anti-Fascist Committee, including: Dovid Bergelson
(1884–1952), Yekhezkl Dobrushin (1883–1953), Shmuel Halkin
(1897–1960), Shloyme Mikhoels (1890–1948), Leyb Strongin (1896–?),
Itzik Fefer (1900–1952), Leyb Kvitko (1890–1952) and Aron Kushnirov
(1890–1949). The editor-in-chief was Shakhno Epshteyn (1883–1945)
and, after his death, Hersh Zhitz (1903–1954) was appointed to this post.

The major issues covered in the paper during the War were:

- news from the front
- mobilization of world Jewry to ensure the Red Army's victory
  over the Nazis (including reports on the work of the Soviet Jewish
  Anti-Fascist Committee)
- prominent featuring of the Jewish participation in the Red Army
  and the partisan movement
- reports on the mass murder of Jews in the Nazi-occupied territories
- Jewish life and culture in the Soviet Union
- Soviet life
- international news
- Jewish news from abroad and especially from the Nazi-occupied
  Europe

It is difficult to say with certainty what prominence was given to each
of these major issues. We have, however, an important thematic list of
communications and correspondences with which *Eynikayt* and the
Jewish Anti-Fascist Committee supplied the foreign press and media during its first year (15/3/43, 28–29, p. 3; Litvak 1966: 223). This list and the
number of items for each topic seem to reflect the overall news-coverage
practices of the newspaper itself (see Table 1 below).

Obviously this list cannot include certain topics which appeared in
the newspaper, such as the news from the front (provided by the main
Soviet news agency), and the foreign-news items many of which were
about Jews abroad especially in Nazi-occupied Europe. Moreover, it cov-
ers only the first year of the *Eynikayt*'s activity. However, both the listing
of the main topics and the number of items that were sent out are also
characteristic of the coverage and reporting that appeared on the pages of

---

Table 1: List of communications and correspondences sent by Eynikayt and the Jewish Anti-Fascist committee to the foreign press and media, June 1942–March 1943.

Items
1. Participation of Jews in the Red Army and their heroism   — 568
2. Jews in the partisan movement   — 108
3. Life and work of the [Soviet] Jewish people in the hinterland — 275
4. Jewish culture [*yidishe kulturboyung*] in the Soviet Union — 256
5. Fascist atrocities [*akhzoryesn*] against the Jewish population — 426
(Source: *Eynikayt* 15/03/43, 28–29, p. 3)

---

the newspaper throughout the War. Prominent featuring of Jewish heroism in the Red Army and (somewhat later on) the partisan movement was the paper's clear policy from the very beginning. The first issue of *Eynikayt* concludes with a call to its readers to gather and forward information on the heroic participation of Jewish soldiers in the war against the Hitlerite occupants. Reports, portraits and articles on this topic were often given under the heading "Our Heroes" or "Our Sons and Daughters". The prominence given to this issue was a clear-cut refutation of the persistant rumors that the Jewish contribution to fighting was negligible for "Jews were hiding in the deep hinterland." These rumors were usually attributed to the Germans. One wonders, however, to what extent, if at all, they were refuted in the general Soviet press.

In 1942 Shakhno Epshteyn "was planning to write a book on the contribution of Soviet Jews to the armed struggle against the Nazis" (Redlich 1982: 198; *Eynikayt* 5/7/42, 4). In March 1943, after it was announced that 32,067 Jews had received military awards, Ilya Ehrenburg (1891–1967) suggested that statistics alone were not enough, and around that time a plan surfaced to prepare a special collection in Russian on the Jewish participation in the Red Army and the partisan movement, dubbed the *Red Book* (cf. Pinkus 1986: 320–321; 1988: 188; Altshuler et al. 1993: 218, n. 38). The book never materialized, yet *Eynikayt* itself provided rich material for such a collection. (It is possible that some new information on the *Red Book* project can be found in the archive collection of the Jewish Anti-Fascist Committee in "The Russian Republic State Archive" in Moscow, see Sandler 1995; on the participation of Soviet Jews in the war against Nazi Germany, see Arad 1994.)

Far better known is the *Black Book* project of the Jewish Anti-Fascist
Committee (Kon 1967–8; Gilboa 1972: 51–54; Kermish 1980; Smolyar
1981; Yelin 1984; Pinkus 1986: 319–320; Pinkus 1988: 187–188;
Altshuler and Ycikas 1992). It was often referred to in *Eynikayt* and this
remarkable collection, together with a wealth of other material which was
not included in the original version, survived both the long delay in publication in Israel and the Soviet regime itself (see Grossman and
Ehrenburg 1980; Arad and Altman 1993). Though it was readied for
press, the *Black Book* was never allowed to be published in the Soviet
Union.

To reiterate: the many publications that appeared on the pages of
Eynikayt provided some of the earliest descriptions, testimonies and
details on the mass murder of Jews in various localities of the occupied
Soviet Union and its "new" territories that were annexed between 1939
and 1940.

The fate of the *Black Book* is analogous to the remarkably different
attitudes to the reporting of the Holocaust by the Yiddish paper on the one
hand and by the general Soviet press on the other hand. With a few exceptions the Soviet Russian press skillfully avoided direct references to the
mass annihilation of the Jews, referring when needed to "the innocent" or
"peaceful, civilian Soviet population." Pinkus (1988: 187, cf. also 1986:
318–319) explains this in part by the unwillingness of the Soviet authorities to be too closely identified with the Jewish cause thereby upholding
in the eyes of its citizens the Nazi equation between Jews and
Communists. However, in the case of *Eynikayt* the authorities had to concede even if only for temporary political and vital propaganda reasons.
Hence, a degree of hitherto unprecedented freedom in Yiddish. Soviet as
it was, *Eynikayt* was for a time given enough rope to become the most
Jewish-oriented of all Soviet Yiddish periodicals.

In the earlier mentioned list of press-communications forwarded by
Eynikayt to the foreign media, the issue of Nazi atrocities against Jews
appears last. However, the number of items forwarded by March 1943
(426 items) makes it the second most reported topic. The same logic by
which the mass murder of the Jews had to be referred to in order to mobilize world Jewry for a common struggle, also allowed for a focused and
unmediated reporting of the terrible events in the Nazi-occupied Soviet
territories. There was also substantial reporting on the Jews in other parts

of occupied Europe, both as news in-brief given under such general headings as "From the Fascist Hell," "Jewish News from Abroad" (sometimes simply "Jewish News" or even "From Abroad"), as well as in longer foreign press communications (e.g. "Di englishe prese vegn dem oysrot funem yidishn folk mitsad di hitleristn," 27/12/42, 21, p. 4). The first description of the Warsaw ghetto uprising (April, 1943), which appeared on 15 May 1943 (No. 35, p. 4) provided a remarkably detailed account written by Ber Mark, whose later book (in its various editions) on the subject bore the same title, "Der ufshtand in Varshever geto." Also noteworthy are his other articles devoted to Jewish resistance in Lodzh ("Der ufshtand in Lodzher geto," 30/12/43 (60), p. 2), Bialystok ("Letster kamf fun Bialistoker geto," 01/06/44 (82), p. 2) and Luninets (West Belorussia, "Ufshtand fun di Luninetser yidn kegn di daytshishe talyonim," 17/07/43 (40), p. 2). A number of signed articles describing or referring to the fate of European Jewry under the Nazis can be found among the many contributions by such authors as Bergelson (eg. "Af tsepukenish," 15/08/42 (8), p. 2; "Dos hobn geton di daytshn," 17/08/44 (93), p. 5), Ehrenburg ("Faran far vos nekome tsu nemen!," 17/12/42 (20), p. 4) and Fefer ("Rotskhisher epos," 01/05/43, 33–34, p. 5).

The importance of these reports and references for gauging the newspaper's and its readers' awareness of the pan-European scale of the Holocaust is self-evident. However, the bulk of reports, bylines and detailed accounts of eyewitnesses was devoted to the Soviet Union, Poland and Lithuania. It is noteworthy that the photos published in *Eynikayt* provided these reports with some of the earliest and most gruesome evidence of persecutions and mass murder. A future systematic index of *Eynikayt* should also include a detailed list of its photographic materials [the earliest ones appeared in the following issues: 17 June 1942 (2), p. 2; 28 June 1942 (3), p. 4; 25 July 1942 (6), p. 2; 25 September 1942 (12), p. 2; 17 December 1942 (20), p. 2; 27 December 1942 (21), p. 2].

The sharp contrast between *Eynikayt* and the Soviet press in referring to the Holocaust can be detected in the Yiddish newspaper itself, for it also published many official Soviet or Soviet-approved communications and press releases on the Nazi policy of mass murder of the "peaceful population." The important press communication of the People's Commissariat of Foreign Affairs published 27 December 1942, perhaps one of the frankest official Soviet references to the Holocaust, it was released in conjunction with the joint allied Governments' statement condemning the mass murder of the Jews. Yet, one need not be a great stylist to detect that even here, in a press communication devoted entirely to the subject, there is a strong tendency to keep references to the Jewish identity of victims to a minimum. It is therefore hardly a surprise that *Eynikayt* had to print in boldface the document's first reference to Jews as the principal Nazi-victims—a reference which appears half-way down the second paragraph. When the Red Army began the fight for Vilna, on 13 July 1944, *Eynikayt* published on its front-page an article by Iustas Paletskis, the Chairman of the Upper Soviet of the Lithuanian Soviet Republic, entitled "Teg fun groyser freyd." Describing Nazi atrocities in the Lithuanian capital, Paletskis also mentions the 100,000 "inhabitants of Vilnius" [=*vilnyuser aynvoyner*] shot to death by the Germans. Compare it with Avrom Sutskever's article "Tsu der bafrayung fun Vilne," that appeared a week later, where the Yiddish poet and partisan says:

> *Un in bren fun ot der heyliker freyd fargesn nit di toyznter un toyznter Vilner zeyer tifn troyer, vos ot di barimte shtot zeyere, a shtot mit a groyser yidisher alt-ayngezesener un hoykh-kulturel-er bafelkerung, iz durkh di daytshn farvandlt gevorn in eynem fun di shreklekhste masn-kvorim far undzere brider un shvester.*
>
> [And in the midst of the great holy happiness, felt by thousands of Vilnerites they also sense a deep sorrow, for their city with its age-old and highly-cultured Jewish population was turned by the Germans into one of the most horrible mass graves of our brothers and sisters.]
>
> (*Eynikayt*, 20/07/1944, 89, p. 2)

The press release by Polpress on Majdanek of 19 August 1944 was published 24 August. Its first paragraph reads:

> In the vicinity of Lublin, in the death-camp Majdanek, the German occupants annihilated Soviet POWs as well as Poles, Frenchmen, Czechs, Jews, Belgians, Hungarians, Serbs, Greeks and people of other nationalities from Europe, who were kept imprisoned in this camp.
>
> (*Eynikayt*, 24/08/1944, 94, p. 2)

Two days before the Polpress press release, *Eynikayt* published Dovid Bergelson's article "Dos hobn geton daytshn!" devoted to Majdanek. Throughout this article Bergelson focuses on the German perpetrators and on Majdanek as the most brutal and vicious affront to humanity. However, in the concluding paragraphs he turns to the question of the victims' identity saying the following:

> *Iz ver ken den in aza moment avekshteln zikh tseyln, vifl por shikh af ot dem feld hobn gehert tsu yidn, un vifl hobn gehert tsu polyakn, tsu rusn, tsu ukrayiner, tsu grikhn, tsu frantsoyzn, tsu holender, tsu norveger un tsu serbn?*
>
> *Undz yidn?. . .*
>
> *Kimat biz eynem hot er oysgerotn undzere brider in di okupirte gegntn. A pust ort hot er undz gelozt dort, vu gelebt un geshafn hobn poylishe, litvishe, letlendishe yidn un mit a vildn tsinizm hot er arayngeshribn in ot der pustkayt:*
>
> *— Vilne on yidn!*
>
> *— Kovne on yidn!*
>
> *— Varshe on yidn!*
>
> *Un dokh, nit mir aleyn kenen zayn bekoyekh optsutsoln far undzer groysn brokh, un nit bloyz undzere aleyn iz di plog, vos heyst "daytsh,"—zi iz di plog fun a gantser velt.*

[So who can in such a moment turn to calculations, to endeavor to count how many pairs of shoes on this particular field belong to Jews and how many to Poles, Russians, Ukrainians, Greeks, Frenchmen, Dutchmen, Norwegians or Serbs?

How many belonged to us, Jews? . . .

Almost to the last one he murdered our brothers and sisters in the occupied regions. He left us a hollow place where once Polish, Lithuanian, Latvian Jews lived and created. And with wild cynicism he engraved in this hollowness:

— Vilna without Jews!

— Kovna without Jews!

— Warsaw without Jews!

And yet, not just we alone are capable of avenging our great disaster, and not just ours alone is the affliction whose name is the German. This is also the plague of the whole world.]

(*Eynikayt*, 17/08/1944, 93, p. 2)

The discrepancy between the two attitudes—between the official Soviet and Jewish reference to the same events—is self-explanatory. Small wonder then, that many, if not most of Ilya Ehrenburg's articles on Jews, that were published in *Eynikayt* and possibly in other languages abroad, *did not* appear in their original in the Soviet Russian press.

Surprising as it may sound to an outsider, the Holocaust in the Soviet Union is a relatively little researched area. Yitshak Arad's important article, entitled "On the Holocaust of the Soviet Jews," which is in many respects a pioneering study, appeared quite recently, in 1991 (see also Altshuler 1983). A systematic collation, comparison and analysis of various testimonies on this subject still appear to be "a matter of the future" (cf. Reuven Shapiro's study on the relevant *Yizkor-bikher*, Shapiro 1995). Therefore, many testimonies and eyewitness accounts that appeared in *Eynikayt* during and immediately after the War sometimes furnish vital information on particular events and localities. Thus, Dovid Bergelson's article "Gedenkt!" of 5 September 1942 (No. 10, p. 2) provides us with the earliest recorded eyewitness account on the annihilation of the Jews in Vitebsk. There is, to my knowledge, only one other testimony on Vitebsk (see Arad 1991a: 113–114). However, even if the same events and details can be found in other sources, the importance of testimonies and reports published by *Eynikayt* for the study of the Holocaust in the Soviet Union, eastern Poland and the Baltic countries cannot and should not be overlooked (for more details see Appendix I).

It is, however, important to note that by far not all valuable materials on the mass murder of Jews or Jewish resistance found their way to one of the four pages of the only Soviet Yiddish newspaper. One of the *Eynikayt* reporters was the Yiddish poet Naftole-Herts Kon (= Cohen, 1910–1971; see Ravich 1945: 215–217, Lengil 1978). A man of tragic fate who was many times imprisoned in three countries (in Romania, and twice each in the Soviet Union and Poland, cf. Altshuler 1993: 59–60, n. 51). As a reporter of the Soviet Yiddish newspaper, Kon, until his second Soviet imprisonment in 1948, traveled across Ukraine, Belorussia, Moldavia and other parts of the USSR, where he managed to find Jewish survivors and non-Jewish eyewitnesses and record their accounts (see Redlich 1982: 48 and 195 n. 23; 1987: 79). Some of these accounts appeared in *Eynikayt* (eg. "Di lebngeblibene dertseyln," 27/03/1945 (134), p. 3); others were sent to the compilers of the *Black Book* (see Arad and Altman 1993: 203–207, Nos. 35 and 36). Later, his records were confiscated and subsequently "lost" during his 1948 imprisonment. Nevertheless, Kon, thanks to his previous "experiences," had decided to copy his records and hide them (Kon 1973: 205–206). As a result he managed to save some of these survivor and eyewitness accounts, which are now kept in Yad Vashem (see Klibanski 1990: nos. 961–964, 966–971) together with the manuscript of his memoirs on the *Black Book* (Kon 1967–8). In Israel, where he lived from 1965 until his death, Naftole-Herts Kon managed to fully restore and publish (in Hebrew) only one of these accounts concerning "passive and active resistance by Jews in the forests of Eastern Galicia" (Klibanski 1990: no. 969; see Kon 1973).

Of course, *Eynikayt* is first of all a source for gauging Soviet Jewish public reaction to the Holocaust in a short period of optimal ideological ease. To be sure, the usual Soviet-type constraints remained in force and since the 1930s every Soviet Yiddish author knew or at least thought he knew the fundamental rules of the game, whereby many central issues still remained off limits or could be dealt with only in a certain officially endorsed way. Moreover, certainly not every writer and journalist was a closet dissident and some trusted "old-guard" engineers of human souls skillfully followed and managed various curves and turns of the Soviet "general line" (official policy). The best example of such a "politically correct" and "ideologically responsible" worker was the first editor-in-chief of *Eynikayt*, Shakhno Epshteyn, who was also the Secretary of the Jewish Anti-Fascist Committee (see some of his articles, especially the programmatic "Dos vidergeburt fun a folk," 8 November 1944, 105–106; cf. Litvak 1966, Redlich 1982; on Epshteyn see also Vaksberg 1995). However, the most important articles which *Eynikayt* published were by **Dovid Bergelson**, one of the great Soviet Yiddish novelists; by **Ilya Ehrenburg**, the influential Soviet Russian author and poet, who foresaw the Holocaust in his famous novel *Khulio Khorenito* in 1922; and by **Itsik Fefer,** one of the leading and ideologically most faithful Soviet Yiddish poets. These articles together with the printed speeches of **Shloyme Mikhoels** are the most emphatic and moving examples of the outspoken public Soviet Jewish response to the greatest catastrophe of European Jewry. Many of them also take pride in Jewish resistance and in the substantial Jewish contribution to the military war against the Nazis. They were read by many thousands in the USSR and abroad, and their message was communicated by word of mouth to thousands of other Jews in the Soviet Union. Many of these articles, as well as a number of those written by Perets Markish, Der Nister, Avrom Sutskever and the Russian Jewish writers Vassily Grossman and Vl. Lidin, are important documents of enduring literary and historical value (for a partial list see Appendix II).

An annotated and critically selected collection of these articles (as well as the relevant speeches and articles by Shloyme Mikhoels) would be a most worthy and effective testimony to the real-time Jewish reaction to the Holocaust in the Soviet Union as well as to Soviet Yiddish literature mobilized to transgress the bounds of purely artistic expression in order to furnish moral support, comfort, and inspiration. Such a collection would also complement the Soviet Yiddish fiction and poetry on the Holocaust which began to feature prominently in the works of such masters as Der Nister, Dovid Bergelson, Perets Markish, Dovid Hofshteyn, Shmuel Halkin and others (many of which were included in the authoritative anthology of Soviet Yiddish belles-lettres *A shpigl af a shteyn*, Shmeruk 1964; see also Shmeruk 1968).

Despite its unprecedented Jewish outspokenness and its propagandistic role in mobilizing Jewish aid to the Soviet Union (appealing to international Jewish solidarity), *Eynikayt* was after all a Soviet newspaper. A number of overpowering restrictions and constraints were operative even in the more liberal years 1942–1945. Cautious formulations and lip-service was obligatory for most articles including a number of those written by the newspaper's principal literary contributors. Certain sensitive issues were bound to stay untouched. One can only guess how painful it must have been to keep silent on the role of the Lithuanian and Ukrainian collaborators. Particularly complex was the issue of foreign contacts, though the most extraordinary 1943 mission of Mikhoels and Fefer to the USA, Canada, Mexico and England was a remarkable success, which fed the illusion of enduring ties between Jews on both sides of the proverbial curtain (see Redlich 1982 and Vaksberg 1995). The official rather than pragmatic de-facto recognition of international Jewish unity was also a delicate matter, which was bound to undergo revision in Shakhno Epshteyn's articles in October–November 1945 and in many ensuing publications almost immediately after the War (including those by Itsik Fefer). The same of course applies to cooperation with, and official recognition of, the Zionist *Yishuv* in Palestine (see Epshteyn's article of 8 November

1944 [105–106], p. 2, and cf. Litvak 1966, Gilboa 1972, Greenbaum 1979, Pinkus 1986: 288–289, 1988: 163–164).

Especially unbearable was the inability to write openly about growing anti-Semitism in the Soviet Union and the liberated territories. This issue is referred to obliquely (almost cryptically) in Epshteyn's editorial of 5 October 1944 in order to minimize or dismiss these "minor temporary difficulties" as rapidly disappearing "remnants of the Nazi occupation." The plight of the Jews (including survivors) returning to their homes was a major concern of the Jewish Anti-Fascist Committee and it is well known that the Committee tried many times to intervene on this matter without any success (e.g. see Mikhoels' and Epshteyn's letter in Vaksberg 1995: 194; Arad forthcoming). These problems already began to surface in 1943, although no trace of them can be found on the pages of the newspaper until at least May 1945. (The fatal ideological tribulations and campaigns, as these were reflected in *Eynikayt* in the post-War years, are discussed in detail in Pinkus 1986: 259–265; 1988: 145–150.)

The first issue of *Eynikayt* opened with Shloyme Mikhoels's passionate call to mobilize direct financial aid that would pay for 500 bomber-planes and 1,000 tanks. By March 1943, in addition to their contribution to the general Soviet fund-drives, Soviet Jews had donated 3,294,000 rubles to the Red Army. In April 1944 the newspaper reported—to cite just the most significant sums—that about $12,100,000 was raised in the USA, £10,000,000 in Great Britain, $750,000 in Palestine, $600,000 in South Africa (see *Eynikayt*, 13/04/1944 [75], p. 3). It seems that both financially and politically the Committee's and its newspaper's mission abroad was a tremendous success. At home very little, if anything, could be achieved to improve Soviet Jewry's plight in the wake of the Holocaust. The many attempts to intervene made by the Jewish Anti-Fascist Committee were later deemed by the authorities a "diversionist" anti-Soviet activity on behalf of American military interests. The Committee's suggestion to rebuild the pre-war Jewish region in Crimea in order to accommodate displaced Soviet Jews away from the growing anti-Semitism especially in Ukraine (cf. Altshuler 1993) was in 1948 conveniently interpreted, to use an anachronism, as a kind of a mid-1940s "Cuba-type-operation" in reverse. In January 1948 Shloyme Mikhoels, the Chairman of the Committee, was killed by KGB agents on direct order from Stalin (for some important details, see Vaksberg 1993 and

1995: 235–272, especially pp. 268–270). In November 1948 the Committee was closed down, and its members, among them six leading Yiddish writers of world-stature, one outstanding Yiddish actor and one distinguished Yiddish scholar, were imprisoned and all but one member of the Committee either died in prison before the trial or were executed on 12 August 1952 (see Vaksberg 1993 and 1995: 273–353, Shmeruk 1995a and 1996b, Naumov 1994). However, during the period in question and in fact until late 1948, the Jewish Anti-Fascist Committee was seen by Soviet Jews and by many of its leaders and activists as their official representative institution.

The Committee's organ, *Eynikayt*, was the most nationally outspoken Soviet Yiddish newspaper, which chronicled the Holocaust of Soviet Jewry, the Jewish resistance and contribution to the War against Nazism, and the defiant creativity of Soviet Yiddish writers, actors, scholars, artists and scientists. It is of paramount value to the history of the Holocaust in the Soviet Union and of Soviet Jewry in the fateful interim period between the Nazi Holocaust and the Stalinist liquidation of Jewish and Yiddish culture in the USSR.

APPENDIX I

Larger Reports, Testimonies, Bylines, and Signed Articles
on the Nazi Persecution and Mass Murder of Jews in
Eynikayt, 7 June 1942–15 May 1945
(incomplete)*

Germany and Nazi-occupied Europe (other than Poland)

25/11/42, 18   Fridrikh Volf [Wolf?], "Yidn in Marsel" [Marseille], p. 3
27/12/42, 21   "Vi azoy di hitlerishe makht . . ." —see under USSR
15/09/42, 11   Elye Vatenberg, "'Yidn shtarbn tsu langzam'," p. 2
25/09/42, 12   Elye Vatenberg, "Dray yor 'naye ordenung' in eyrope," p. 2
18/01/43, 23   I. Yuzefovich, "Di rezultatn fun der 'nayer ordenung' in mayrev-eyrope," p. 2
01/05/43, 33–34 Itsik Fefer, "Rotskhisher epos" [secret German Army Bulletins boasting" that 65,000 Jews in Slovakia, 800,000 in Hungary, 60,000 in Croatia were "disposed of" and that Bessarabia is "free of Jews"], p. 5

*This is a preliminary list. With a few exceptions, shorter digests from foreign press and 'news in brief' were not included.

21/10/43, 50	S. Khaykin, "Di Shvedishe gezelshaftlekhkayt un di yidishe pogromen in Denemark (iberzikht fun der shvedisher prese)" [Sweden and Denmark], p.4
13/01/44, 62	Kh. Esterman, "Der goyrl fun di Slovakishe yidn" [Slovakia], p. 4
13/04/44, 75	B[er] Mark, "Di Ungarishe yidn in toyt-gefar" [Hungary], p. 3
10/08/44, 92	S. Khaykin, "Der goyrl fun di Ungarishe yidn" [Hungary], p. 2

Poland

15/07/42, 5	Henrikh Diamant, "A shvartser indzl" [on Warsaw ghetto], p. 2
15/10/42, 14	Elye Vatenberg, "Vi di natsis 'likvidirn' di yidishe getos" [Sabibor, Lublin, Lemberg, Stanislav, Zlochev, Bzhezhan, Zborozh, Pshemishlyan . . . , Vilne, Kovne, Baranovitchi, Cracow, Warsaw], p. 2
17/12/42, 20	Stefan Yendrikhovski, "Yidish-poylisher vidershtand kegn fashizm," p. 2
27/12/42, 21	"Vi azoy di hitlerishe makht . . ." —see under USSR
18/01/43, 23	E. Sarin, "Yidn in Poyln vayzn aroys a vidershtand di fashistn," p. 2
25/03/43, 30	A briv fun Varshe: "Di hitleristn ayln zikh oysrotn di yidn in Poyln," [unsigned letter from Warsaw], p. 2
15/05/43, 35	B[er] Mark, "Der ufshtand in Varshever geto," p. 4
27/05/43, 36	"In der letster minut: Der ufshtand in Varshever geto flakert nokh," [p. 1]
07/06/43, 37	Elye Vatenberg, "Felker-frayntshaft tsebrekht geto-vent" [Warsaw ghetto, clandestine Polish and Yiddish press], p. 2
14/10/43, 49	"Di yidishe getos in Poyln un Lite 'likvidirt'" (includes: "Ufshtand fun poylishe yidn inem Trembliker kontsentratsye-lager," "Vifl yidn zaynen nokh geblibn in Poyln," "Likvidirt' di geto in Bendin"), p. 2
30/12/43, 60	B[er] Mark, "Der ufshtand in Lodzher geto," p. 2
27/04/44, 77	Dertseylt fun a lebedikn eydes: "Di shlakht in Varshever geto" [the witness' name is not given], p. 2
17/08/44, 94	Dovid Bergelson, "Dos hobn geton di daytshn" [Majdanek], p. 2

24/08/44, 94   "Di shoyderlekhe tragedye in Lublin" [Soviet-edited press release on Majdanek], p. 2

21/09/44, 98   Hershl Polyanker, "Der genem af der velt" (fun undzer front-korespondent) [on Treblinka], p. 3

01/02/45, 117   Yefim Hekhtman, "Tsvishn di khurves fun Varshe" (fun undzer militerishn korespondent), p. 2

15/02/45, 119   Y. Doresman, "Di blutike tragedye fun der yidisher geto in Lodzh,"p. 2

Ibid.   Dovid Notkin, "Af di vegn kin Berlin" [also about ghetto Lodzh], p. 2

10/03/45, 127   Y. Kats, S. Talalayevski, "Oshventshimer toyt-lager" (fun undzere militerishe korespondentn), p. 2

Baltic States

17/06/42, 2   G. Erman, "Der fashistisher gehenem in Lite," p. 3

15/10/42, 14   Elye Vatenberg, "Vi di natsis 'likvidirn' di yidishe getos"—see under Poland

25/10/42, 15   E. Bilevitshius, "Di shoyderlekhe retsikhes fun di fashistn iber di yidn in Lite," p. 2

27/12/42, 21   "Vi azoy di hitlerishe makht..."—see under USSR

14/10/43, 49   "Di yidishe getos in Poyln un Lite 'likvidirt'" (includes: "Der sof fun Yerusholayim deLite"), p. 2

11/05/44, 79   A[vrom] Sutskever, "Der vidershtand in Vilner geto," p. 3

08/06/44, 83   A[vrom] Sutskever, "Tsvey taybelekh zaynen ibern vaser gefloygn" [on the murder of the singer Lyube Levitsky in the Vilna ghetto], p. 3

20/07/44, 89   A[vrom] Sutskever, "Tsu der bafrayung fun Vilne," p. 2

27/07/44, 90   Ilya Erenburg, "Der veg keyn Daytshland" [with the Red Army in Minsk, Rakov, Smorgon, Vilna; Ponar, meeting the young Jewish partisans in Vilna], p. 3

17/08/44, 93   L. Shaus, "Af di khurves fun Kovner geto," p. 2

Ibid.   A. Molotkov, "Geratevete kultur-oytsres (a briv fun Vilne)," p. 2

31/08/44, 95   "Lebn geblibene dertseyln" [from a collection of letters that arrived from the liberated Lithuania to the Jewish Anti-Fascist Committee: the murder of rabbis of Lithuania; Stoklishki; the mass murder in Utyan; who helped (to save Jews)], p. 2

19/10/44, 102   B. Hertsbakh, "Dos kapitl Rige (farshribn loyt di dertseylungen fun yidn vos zaynen antlofn fun Rige)" [cf. the same author's contributions to *The Unknown Black Book*: see Arad and Altman (eds.) 1993: 325 and 332], p. 2

22/02/45, 120   Sh[merke] Katsherginski, "800 yidishe froyen geratevet fun Toruner kontsetratsye-lager," p. 2

USSR and occupied parts of Poland and Rumania

17/06/42, 2   Vl. Lidin [= Vladimir Gamberg], "Yidishe pleytim," p. 3

15/07/42, 5   "Ot azoy rot Hitler oys di yidishe bafelkerung" [from the materials received by the JAC; Belorussia, Ukraine, Crimea], p. 2

15/08/42, 8   [Sofia Ozerskaya,] "Di hitlerishe inkvizitsye in Minsk" (dretseylt fun der lerern Sofia Ozerskaya, vos hot zikh geratevet fun Minsk, farshribn fun S. Rodov), p. 2

15/08/42, 8   L[eyb] Kvitko, "Vos der partizaner Yakov Uzdinski dertseylt" [mass murder of 800 Jews in Leltshits (Mozyr), and 500 in Yelsk; the partisan movement in Mozyr-Turov area], p. 3

05/09/42, 10   Dovid Bergelson, "Gedenkt!" [on Vitebsk; cf. also Arad 1991a: 113–114], p. 2

15/09/42, 11   "Shoyderlekhe masn-shkhite iber yidn in Velizh" [Vitebsk region; information received by the Jewish Anti-Fascist Committee], p. 2

15/10/42, 14   Ilya Erenburg, "Gebentshte erd" [Kharkov, Pervomajsk, Babi Yar, Urechye, Chkalov, Lubni; mostly based on information and documents found on German POWs], p. 2

Ibid.   S. Kikitiev, "Mir veln nit fargesn un nit fargebn" [digest from a small book published in Kalinin right after its liberation, includes testimony of the annihilation of Jews in Kalinin, April 1942], p. 4

25/10/42, 15   L[eyb] Kvitko, "Der ufgeshtanener fun keyver dertseylt" [Kerch, Yosif Vayngortn's testimony; see the same account also in *Dos Shvartse Bukh*, Grossman and Ehrenburg (eds.) 1984: 295–299], p. 2

25/10/42, 15   Kuzma Tsharni, "Di daytshn hobn oysgerotn di yidishe bafelkerung in Vaysrusland," p. 2

21/11/42, 18   L[eyb] Kvitko, "Bentshik lebt!" [continuation of Yosif
                 Vayngortn's testimony, see L. Kvitko 25/10/42, 15], p. 3
17/12/42, 20   M. Sivolobov, "In Bobruisk," [reprinted from "Pravda,"
                 the article is dated: White Russia, October-November
                 1942], p. 2
27/12/42, 21   *"Vi azoy di hitlerishe makht firt durkh dem plan fun oys-*
                 rotn di yidishe bafelkerung fun Eyrope": "Der folks-
                 komisaryat far oysern-inyonim hot in zayn reshus
                 absolyut zikhere informatsye, vos bavayzt, az af di teri-
                 toryes fun di lender fun eyrope, velkhe zaynen okupirt
                 durkh di daytshish-fashistishe farkhaper, iz di letste tsayt
                 umetum tsu merkn a naye farshtarkung funem hitlerishn
                 rezhim fun blutike masn-hariges iber der fridlekher
                 bafelkerung. [...] Di hitleristn un zeyere mitfarbrekher
                 firn derbay durkh mit intensive tempn zeyer spetsyeln
                 plan fun **oysrotn ale biz eynem di gantse yidishe**
                 bafelkerung af der okupirter teritorye fun eyrope." -
                 emphasis in the original; Jews from the rest of Europe
                 brought for annihilation into Poland, the situation in
                 Poland and occupied Soviet territories at the end, signed:
                 Informbyuro fun folkomoysern), p. 2
25/03/43, 30   Itsik Fefer, "Der eydes Rokhl Kuznets" [Usviat,
                 Smolensk region], p. 2
Ibid.   Dovid Bergelson "Heysblutike brider" [Jews of
                 Bessarabia], p. 2
05/04/43, 31   Mikhl Tanklevski, "Der Kiever khurbn" [recounted by
                 Mikhl Tanklevski—one of the survivors], p. 2
25/06/43, 38–39 Mire Zheleznova, "Blut far blut" [Legoysk, 28 July
                 1941], p. 6
17/07/43, 40   B[er] Mark, "Ufshtand fun di Luninetser yidn kegn di
                 daytshishe talyonim" [Western Belorussia], p. 2
31/08/43, 42–43 M. Ben, "Vi di daytshn hobn gebalebatevet in Kharkov,"
                 p. 2
09/09/43, 44   H[ershl] Polyanker, "Di dray shkhites iber di yidn in
                 Oryol," ["from our military correspondent"; cf. the offi-
                 cial press release—16/09/45, (45), "Di retshikhes fun di
                 daytshis-fashistishe farkhaper in Oryol un Oryoler

gegnt," p. 2—in which the Jewish nationality of the victims is not stated], p. 2

30/09/43, 47 Ye[?]. Mar, "Der Oryoler khezhbn" [anihilation of the Jewish population of Oryol, May 1942, testimony of "the only surviving representative (forshteyer) of Oryol Jewry"—Ana Spiridonovna Zhukova], p. 2

21/10/43, 50 S[emyon] Rabinovitsh, "Di shoyderlekhe shkhite in Tatarsk" [Tatarsk, Mohilev region; "from our military correspondent"; incl. official testimonial/ "akt"], p. 3

28/10/43, 51 Dovid Bergelson, "Dnepropetrovsk," p. 2

18/11/43, 54 M. Tsunts [Zunz?], "Di tragedye in Klimovitshi" [Belorussia; from the official testimonial/ "akt" compiled and signed by the citizens of the city of Klimovichi], p. 2

18/11/43, 54 Yankl Yosade, "Lebn geblibene" [Jewish survivors in small towns and villages in White Russia (?)], p. 2

02/12/43, 56 H. Shlyommin, "In Homel," p. 3

06/01/44, 61 [Ber Mark], "A gerateveter fun Lvover geto dertseylt" [farshribn: B. Mark; testimony on the Lvov ghetto], p. 2

10/02/44, 66 Y[ekhiel] Falikman, "Der lebediker eydes" [on the German attempt to destroy the evidences of mass murder in Babi Yar; dates: January 1944], p. 3

23/03/44, 72 B. Shokhat, "Rokhele Yankovski" [Western Belorussia, a Jewish girl from Velizh saved in Simonyata; hundreds and thousands of Jewish soldiers in the front liberating Belorussia; finds in Simonyata a bundle of *Eynikayt*], p. 2

13/04/44, 75 Sh[muel] Persov, "Di shkhite in Brisk," p. 3

25/05/44, 81 Khayim Hekhtman, "Mayn heym-shtetl Brayilov," p. 3

01/06/44, 82 B[er] Mark, "Letster kamf fun Bialistoker geto," p. 2

06/07/44, 87 Uri Finkel, "Minsk iz bafrayt," p. 2

Ibid. Leyzer Katsovitsh, "Minsk - mayn heymshtot," p. 3

27/07/44, 90 Ilya Erenburg, "Der veg keyn Daytshland"—see under Baltic States

31/08/44, 95 M[oyshe] Altman, "Kishenev un der kamf fun di besaraber yidn," p. 2

07/09/44, 96 Y. Herts, "Megiles Lvov (fun di materyaln 'Tsum shvatrtsn bukh')" [cf. with the testimony of Y. Herts and

Naftole Nakht in *Dos Shvartse Bukh*, Grossman and Ehrenburg (eds.), 1984: 129–142], p. 2

21/09/44, 98   D. Stonov, "Kayn yuden gibn zikh nit unter" [liberation of Simferopol], p. 3

29/09/44, 99   Avrom Kahan, "Moyshe Kaharlitski un zayn mishpokhe" [a Jewish family from Kiev saved], p. 3

19/10/44, 102   Leyzer Katsovitsh, "Bagegenishn in Minsk" [Jews saved by non-Jews and Soviet POWs rescued by Jews], p. 2

19/10/44, 102   Y[ekhiel] Falikman, "Yanover lager" [in the suburb of Lvov/Lemberg], p. 3

07/12/44, 109   Noyekh Lurye, "Der Stalindorfer martirolog," p. 2

04/01/45, 113   Meyer(?!) Shternberg, "Vos di Rumenishe fashistn hobn geton mit di yidn," p. 2

17/03/45, 130   B. Lempert, "Kishenever shkhite," p. 3

27/03/45, 134   N. H. Kon [Naftole-Herts Kon], "Di lebngeblibene dertseyln" ("fun undzer Tshernovitser korespondent") [Bogdanovka, Pervomajskij Rajon], p. 3

APPENDIX II
A Preliminary List of Some Important Articles
Published During the War in *EYNIKAYT*

A) Principal Contributors

Bergelson, Dovid (1884–1952)

17/06/42, 2   "Ver?," pp. 3, 4

05/07/42, 4   "Eskadriliye 'Felker-frayntshaft'," p. 2

25/07/42, 6   "Zol di velt zayn an eydes," p. 2

15/08/42, 8   "Af tsepukenish," p. 2

05/09/42, 10   "Gedenkt!," p. 2

25/09/42, 12   "A gut gesheft (kleyner felyeton)," p. 4

06/10/42, 13   "Af le fir (kleyner felyeton)," p. 4

07/11/42, 16–17   "Der yunger sovetisher yid," p. 6

25/11/42, 18   "Ikh ze dikh!," p. 3

05/12/42, 19   "Der goyrl vert bashlosn," p. 2

07/01/43, 22   "Zeyer khezhbn mit yidn," p. 3

23/01/43, 23   "Dos iz er!," p. 3

07/02/43, 25	"Velt-tribune far yidishe sovetishe shrayber" [tsum tsveytn plenum], p. 4
27/02/43, 26–27	"Akh, du liber Avgustin...," p. 5
25/03/43, 30	"Heysblutike brider," p. 2
01/05/43, 33–34	"Kiev," p. 3
27/05/43, 36	"Undzerer a mentsh," p. 3
07/06/43, 37	"In eyn heldn-rey," p. 2
25/06/43, 38–39	"Tsvey yor foterlendishe milkhome un di yidishe sovetishe literatur," p. 6
27/07/43, 41	"Opmekn fun der erd!," p. 3
23/09/43, 46	"A folk—a giber," p. 3
30/09/43, 47	"Bafrayt Sholem-Aleykhems shtot," p. 2
28/10/43, 51	"Dnepropetrovsk," p. 2
11/11/43, 53	"Undzer Kiev," p. 3
18/11/43, 54	"Frayntshaft," p. 3
30/12/43, 60	"Mikhoels tsurik in zayn Tevye-geshtalt," p. 3
30/03/44, 73	"Dray plenums)," p. 3
17/08/44, 93	"Dos hobn geton di daytshn," p. 2
15/02/45, 119	"Sdom brent!," p. 3
22/02/45, 120	"Der yomtev fun felker," p. 2
17/03/45, 130	"Oysrotn zey!," p. 2
10/05/45, 152	"Zig un nekome," p.3

Ehrenburg, Ilya (1891–1967)

28/06/42, 3	"Farvos hasn azoy di fashistn di yidn," p. 2
15/07/42, 5	"Mir veln opshlogn," p. 1
15/10/42, 14	"Gebentshte erd," p. 2
07/11/42, 16–17	"Ot azoy shlogn zikh yidn," p. 6
17/12/42, 20	"Faran far vos nekome tsu nemen!," p. 4
27/12/42, 21	"Di henker funem yidishn folk veln gemishpet un bashtroft vern," p. 3
01/05/43, 33–34	"Friling 1943 yor," p. 5
25/06/43, 38–39	"Undzer ort," p. 4
04/11/43, 52	"Di daytshishe fashistn torn nit lebn blaybn!," p. 2
27/07/44, 90	"Der veg keyn Daytshland," p. 3
05/10/44, 100	"Der mentsh vet zign," p. 2

Epshteyn, Shakhne (1883–1945)

28/06/42, 3	"Undzer shtolts," p. 2
07/11/42, 16–17	"Alts far alts," p. 5
17/12/42, 20	"S'vilt zikh azoy lebn un lebn," p. 2
07/02/43, 24	"Erev dem tsveytn plenum fun yidishn antifashistishn komitet [. . .]," p. 2
11/11/43, 53	"On peyrushim," p. 3
05/10/44, 100	"Hundert numern 'Eynikayt'," p. 1
08/11/44, 105–106	"Dos vidergeburt fun a folk," p. 4
10/05/45, 152	"Freyd un hofenung," p. 3

Fefer, Itsik (1900–1952)

26/06/42, 3	"Yisroel Fisanovitsh, der held fun ratnfarband," p. 3
25/07/42, 6	"A mekhtiker opklang," p. 2
15/08/42, 8	"Nit tsurik in geto, nor foroys in shlakht!," p. 2
07/11/42, 16–17	"Yidn un heymland," p. 7
05/12/42, 19	"Shloyme Garelik der held fun Sovetnfarband," p. 2
27/03/43, 24	"Heldn un pakhdonim," p. 3
07/02/43, 25	"Alo, es redt Kuybishev!," p. 3
25/03/43, 30	"Der eydes Rokhl Kuznets," p. 2
01/05/43, 33–34	"Rotskhisher epos," p. 5
13/01/44, 62	"Fun Moskve keyn Moskve," p. 2
30/03/44, 73	"In vos geyt do?', p. 2
20/04/44, 76	"Yidn in oysland in kamf kegn fashizm; fortrog afn dritn plenum funem yidishn antifashistishn komitet in FSSR" (vert gedrukt loyt a gekirtster stenograme), p. 2
15/06/44, 84	"Der mentsh mitn tshemodan," p. 3
20/07/44, 89	"Azoy zaynen di daytshn gekumen keyn Moskve," p. 2
05/10/44, 100	"Azoy shlogn zikh yidn," p. 2
11/02/45. 114	"Unter a literarisher maske," p. 2
15/03/45, 129	"Mir monen!," p. 2
24/03/45, 133	"Sof ganev letliye," p. 2
10/05/45, 152	"Mazltov!," p. 2

Mikhoels, Shloyme [= Vovsi] (1890–1948)

07/06/42, 1	"1000 tanken, 500 bombardirer!," p. 1
25/03/43, 30	"Der khoyv farn folk," p.1
30/12/43, 60	"Azoy hot tsu mir geredt der lebediker Sholem-Aleykhem," p. 3
30/03/44, 73	"Dervayzt dos, brider!', p. 2
20/04/44, 76	"Di nesye funem anifashistishn komitet in FSSR iber di Fareynikte Shtatn, Kanade, Meksike un England; fortrog afn dritn plenum funem yidishn antifashistishn komitet in FSSR" (vert gedrukt loyt a gekirtster stenograme), p. 3
05/10/44, 100	"Eynikayt in nekome," p. 1
10/05/45, 152	"Gezigt hobn felker, gezigt hot der mentsh," p. 3

Mikhoels, Shloyme and Itsik Fefer

18/02/44, 67	"Undzer rayze keyn Amerike (veg-ayndrukn)" [translated and reprinted from "Vojna i rabochij klass," 2 (1944)], p. 2

B) Some Other Contributors

Der Nister [Pinkhes Kahanovitsh] (1884–1950)

09/12/43, 57	"Di muter fun der rusisher heldn," p. 2
29/06/44, 86	"Has," p. 3

Dobrushin, Yekhezkl (1883–1953)

25/08/42, 9	"Me tor nit farshpetikn," p. 2
15/03/43, 28–29	"Tsayt un stil," p. 7

Grosman, Vasily

25/11/43, 55	"Ukrayine on yidn," p. 3, continued: 02/12/43, 56, p. 3

Kon, Naftole-Herts

13/01/44, 62	"Yidl Adler," p. 3
27/03/45, 134	"Di lebngeblibene dertseyln," p. 3

Kovnator, R[okhl]

25/10/44	"Di yidishe natsyonale partizaner-makhne num[er] 106," p. 3

Markish, Perets (1895–1952)

08/06/42, 3	"Heroyik un patriotizm fun yidishe roytarmeyer," p. 3

07/06/42, 1   "Di hazkore in reykhstag," p. 3
27/02/43, 26–27 "Yidn heldn fun sovetnfarband," p. 3

Nusinov, Yitskhok (1889–1950)
28/06/42, 3   "Der yidisher inteligent in shlakht," p. 2
05/08/42, 7   "Dos yidishe vort vet ufgerikht vern," p. 2
08/11/44, 105–106"Di sovetishe yidishe kultur," p. 8

Polyanovski, Nokhem
31/08/44, 95   "Anatoli Belskis partizaner makhne," p. 3

Shefer, A. [= Itsik Fefer? (See Greenbaum 1979: 217 and 221 n.19.)]
05/08/42, 7   "Di shvue fun frayhayt," p. 2
05/09/42, 10   "Di shlakht traditsyes funem yidishn folk, di krigs-
                        heldntatn fun di uralte yidn (ershter kapitl), p. 2
07/11/42, 16–17 "Yidn in di shlakhtn far der oktyaber-revolyutsye,"
                        p. 5
07/01/43, 22   "Di shlakht traditsyes funem yidishn folk, di krigs-
                        heldntatn fun di uralte yidn (tsveyter kapitl), p. 3
27/02/43, 26–27 "Yidn in der royter armey," p. 5

Shternberg, Yankev
15/09/42, 11   "Zey hobn geshendt Sholem-Aleykhems erd," p. 2

Simonov, Konstantin
15/06/44, 84   "A bagegenish mitn Tshernovitser rov," p. 3

Sutskever, Avrom
12/10/44, 101   "Vos mir hobn geratevet in Vilne," p. 3
20/07/44, 89   "Tsu der bafrayung fun Vilne," p. 2
08/06/44, 83   "Tsvey taybelekh zaynen ibern vaser gefloygn," p.
                        3

Zaslavski, David
28/06/42, 3   "A yor milkhome," p. 2
07/11/42, 16–17 "Dos rusishe folk un di yidn," p. 7
27/02/43, 26–27 "Di royte armey—di bafrayern fun felker," p. 3
25/06/43, 38–39 "Di retung funem yidishn folk," p. 4
10/05/45, 152   "A nay blat in der velt-geshikhte!," p. 2

Zheleznova, Mire
25/06/43, 38–39 "Blut far blut," p. 6

WORKS CITED

Altshuler, Mordechai

1983   "Hapinui vehamenusa shel hayehudim miByelorusia hamizrahit bitkufat hashoa" ["Evacuation and Flight of Jews from Eastern Belorussia, June–August 1941"] in *Yahadut zmanenu—shnaton le'iyun ulemehkar* [*Contemporary Jewry, A Research Annual*], The Hebrew University, vol. 3, pp. 119–158.

1984   "The Jewish Anti-Fascist Committee in the Light of New Documentation" in *Studies in Contemporary Jewry* 1: 253–291.

1993   "Antisemitism in Ukraine toward the End of the Second World War" in *Jews in Eastern Europe* 3 (22): 40–81.

Altshuler, Mordechai and Sima Ycikas

1992   "Were there Two "Black Books" about the Holocaust in the Soviet Union?" in *Jews and Jewish Topics in the Soviet Union and Eastern Europe* 1 (17).

Altshuler, Mordechai, Yitshak Arad, and Shmuel Krakowski

1993   (Eds.) *Sovetskie evrei pishut Il'e Èrenburgu 1943–1966* [=*Soviet Jews Write to Ilya Ehrenburg 1943–1966*], The Centre for Research and Documentation of East-European Jewry, The Hebrew University and Yad Vashem, The Holocaust Martyrs' and Heroes' Remembrance Authority: Jerusalem.

Arad, Yitshak

1991a   (Ed.) *Unichtozhenie evreev SSSR v gody nemeckoi okkupacii (1941–1944), sbornik dokumentov i materialov*, [*Annihilation of the Jews in USSR during the German Occupation (1941–1944), Collection of Documents and Testimonies*] Yad Vashem, The Holocaust Martyrs' and Heroes' Remembrance Authority: Jerusalem.

1991b   "Shoat yehudei brit-hamo'atsot" in *Yad Vashem—kovets mehkarim*, 21: 1–40.

1994   "Yehudei brit-hamo'atsot bamilhama neged Germania hanatsit" in *Yad Vashem—kovets mehkarim*, 23: 51–89.

[forthcoming]   "The Situation of the Jews in the Liberated Territories of the Soviet Union and the Attempts to Renew Jewish Life, 1944–1948," paper presented at The Tenth International Historical Conference [devoted to the topic] "The Jewish People at the End of World War II," Yad Vashem, The International Center for Holocaust Studies, Jerusalem, Ocober 10–12, 1995.

Arad, Yitshak and Il'ia Altman et al.

1993   (Eds.) *Neizvestnaia chernaia kniga* [= *The Unknown Black Book*], Yad Vashem, The Holocaust Martyrs' and Heroes' Remembrance Authority, Yad Vashem and the State Archive of the Russian Federation, GARF: Jerusalem and Moscow.

Ben-Yosef, Avraham

1960   "Bibliografia shel sfarim vekitvei-'et beyidish shenidpesu bivrit-hamo'atsot beshanim 1941–1948" offprint from *Yad Vashem— kovets mehkarim*, 4; separate pagination, pp. 39–75.

Gilboa, Yehoshua A.

1972   *Hashanim hashhorot, yahadut brit-hamo'atsot 1939–1953* [= *The Black Years of Soviet Jewry*], Am Hasefer Publishing: Tel Aviv.

Greenbaum, Avraham

1979   "Toda'a leumit yehudit bepublitsistika hasovietit bitkufat ha"Einikait" ["National Consciousness in Soviet journalism during the *Eynikayt* period"] in *Dapim leheker tkufat hashoa* I: 213–221, Institute for the Research of the Holocaust Period, Hakibuts Hameuhad: Tel Aviv.

Grossman, Vasily and Ilya Ehrenburg,

1980   (Eds.) *Chernaya kniga. O zlodejskom povsemestnom ubijstve evreev nemecko-fashistskimi zakhvachikami vo vremenno-okkupirovannykh rajonakh Sovetskogo Sojuza i v lageryakh unichtozheniya v Pol'she vo vremya vojny 1941–1945 gg.*, Yad Vashem and Tarbut publishers: Jerusalem.

1984   (Eds.) *Dos shvartse bukh*, tsunoyfgeshtelt un redagirt: Vasili Grosman un Ilya Erenburg, Yad Vashem Institut farn ondenk fun umkum un gvure: Jerusalem.

Kerler, Yoysef

1977   *12 oygust, 1952* [= *12 August 1952*], "Eygns": Jerusalem.

Kermish, Yoysef

1980   "Tsu der geshikhte fun shvartsn bukh" in *Di Goldene Keyt* 102: 121–129.

Klibanski, Bronia
1990   *Collection of Testimonies, Memoirs, and Diaries* (Record Group 033), Part I, Yad Vashem Central Archives: Jerusalem.

Kon, Naftole-Herts
1967–8 *"Naphtali-Hertz Cohen*, Details of the origin of the "Black Book" edited by Ilya Ehrenburg and Vassili Grossman, about the murder of Jews in Russia and their fight in the ranks of the partisans and in the Red army against the Nazis," no. 1026 in Yad Vashem Central Archives; see Klibanski 1990: 171–172.

1973   "Yehudei haya'arot" [= "Forrest Jews"] in *Dapim leheker hashoa vehamered*, Second Series, Second Collection, pp. 203–343, Ghetto Fighters House: Hakibuc Hameuhad.

Lengil, Anna
1978   "Naftole Herts" in *Yerushalayimer Almanakh* 10: 186–190.

Levin, Dov
1977   "Ha"Emes" haaharon vesofo: ha'itonut hayomit beyidish belita hasovietit, 1940–1941" [= "The Last "Emess" and its Demise"] in *Shvut* 5: 38–48.

1989   *Tkufa besograim: 1939–1941, tmurot behaiei hayehudim beeizorim shesuphu levrit-hamo'atsot bithilat milhemet ha'olam hashnia [= The Jews in The Soviet Annexed Territories]*, Ghetto Fighters' House: Tel Aviv and Jerusalem.

Litvak, Yosef
1966   "Hava'ad hayehudi haantifashisti (1942–1948)" in *Gesher* 47–48: 218–232.

Mogilevsky, Solomon
1991   "The Liquidation of the Newspaper *Eynikayt* and Repressions in Leningrad, Testimony of Solomon Mogilevsky" in *Jews and Jewish Topics in the Soviet Union and Eastern Europe* 3 (16): 57–59.

Naumov, V. P.
1994   (Ed.) *Nepravednyj sud, poslednij stalinskij rasstrel, stenogramma sudebnogo processa nad chlenami everjskogo antifashistkogo komiteta*, "Nauka": Moscow.

Redlich, Shimon

1982   *Propaganda and Nationalism in Wartime Russia, The Jewish Anti-Fascist Committee in the USSR, 1941–1948*, East European Monographs, No. CVIII, East European Quarterly: USA.

1987   "Hav'ad hayehudi haanti-fashisti bivrit-hamo'atsot vehahit'ore-rut hayehudit bashanim 1944–1948" in Benjamin Pinkus 1987: 67–87.

Pinkus, Benjamin

1986   *Russian and Soviet Jews, Annals of a National Minority* [in Hebrew], Ben Gurion University.

1987   (Ed.), *Yahadut mizrah eiropa bein shoa letkuma*, Ben Gurion University.

1988   *The Jews of the Soviet Union, The History of a National Minority*, Cambridge University Press: Cambridge.

Pinchuk, Benzion

1976   "Emtsa'ei hatikshoret bivrit-hamo'atsot veredifat hayehudim beshtahim kvushim 'al-yedei hanatsim, 1939–1941" [= "Soviet Mass Media and the Persecutions of the Jews in the German Occupied Territories, 1939–1941"] in *Yad Vashem—kovets mehkarim*, 11: 172–180.

Ravich, Melekh

1945   *Mayn leksikon, yidishe dikhter, dertseyler, dramaturgn in poyln tsvishn di tsvey groyse velt-milkhomes*, vol. 1, Montreal.

Sandler, Boris

1995   "A flek af di lider" [= "A Stain on the Poems"] in *Di Pen* (Oxford) 11: 35–36.

Shapiro, Reuven Moshe (Robert Moses)

1995   "Yizker-bikher iber yidishe yeshuvim in sovetishn vaysrusland un ukrayne" [="Memorial Books for Jewish Communities in Soviet Belorussia and Ukraine"] in *Oksforder yidish* (Oxford Institute or Yiddish Studies), vol. III: 701–716.

Shmeruk, Khone

1960   "Sifrut yehudei brit-hamo'atsot byimot hashoa veahareha" off-print from *Yad Vashem—kovets mehkarim*, 4; separate pagination, pp. 3–38.

1961   (Ed.) *Jewish Publications in the Soviet Union 1917–1960* [Yiddish and Hebrew], Bibliographies compiled and arranged by

Y. Y. Cohen with the assistance of M. Piekarz, introductions by Y. Slutski and Kh. Shmeruk, edited by Kh. Shmeruk, "Galuyot" Series, The Historical Society of Israel: Jerusalem.

1964   (Ed.) *A shpigl af a shteyn, poeziye un proze fun tsvelf farshnitene yidishe shraybers in ratn-farband* [An Anthology of Poetry and Prose by Twelve Soviet Yiddish Writers], "Di Goldene Keyt" and I.L. Perets Publishing House: Tel Aviv.

1968   "Yahadut polin besifrut yidish bivrit-hamo'atsot" [= "Polish Jewry in Yiddish Literature in the Soviet Union"] in *Dapim leheker hashoa vehamered*, Second Series, First Collection, pp. 136–151, Ghetto Fighters House: Hakibuc Hameuhad.

1995a   "Der shoyder-protses" [= "The gruesome trial"] in *Di Goldene Keyt* 140: 28–41.

1995b   "The Unjust Trial" in *Jews and Jewish Topics in the Soviet Union and Eastern Europe* 2 (27): 72–79.

Shulman, Moini

1991   "Kh'bin geven baderbay" [= "I witnessed it"] in *Sovetish Heymland*, 11–12: 123–127.

Smolyar, Hersh

1981   "Dos verk fun shvartsn nekhtn af haynt un ledoyres" in *Yerushalayimer Almanakh* 12: 9–15.

Vaksberg, Arkady

1993   *Neraskrytye tajny*, Moscow.

1995   *Stalin protiv evreev* [= *Stalin against the Jews*], Liberty Publishing House: New York.

Yelin, Meyer

1984   "In un arum 'Dos shvartse bukh'," in *Di Goldene Keyt* 114: 178–184.

German Journalism

Adjusting to Catastrophe:
The German Jewish Press (1933–38)
and the Debate over Mass-Emigration

Henry R. Huttenbach
The City College of New York

I

Measuring the effectiveness of the mass media in shaping public opinion remains, at best, a very soft science based largely on ephemeral polls, however statistically "scientific." In the absence of these, the problem of linking the press to the behavior of its readers becomes that much more speculative. And yet, a modicum of causal relationship exists no matter the difficulty in establishing it.

The task of assessing the character and role of the German Jewish Press *vis-à-vis* the issue of mass emigration was not taken up fully by Herbert Freeden's 1987 monograph, *Die Jüdische Presse im Dritten Reich*.[1] Despite its brevity, it touches on the central issues, including the editorial directions taken on emigration from Germany. But it does not ask the key question, namely, of the effectiveness of a press *in extremis*, a press whose editors, despite wide theoretical differences spanning the spectrum of Jewish philosophical and political attitudes in Germany, were equally thunderstruck by a political revolution whose consequences from start (Hitler's coming to power and his first radical, racist anti-Semitic legislation) to finish (the Final Solution) they were obviously unable to anticipate. Whether writing for *Der Schild* (the voice of pro-German Jewish ultra-patriotism) or for *Die Jüdische Rundschau* (the organ of German mainstream Zionism), all were intimately bound to German society and/or culture, including the Orthodox, whose official publication was *Die Laubhütte* (The Sukkah).[2] Thus from the very outset, all Jewish publications found themselves "*dans une condition déracinée*," in a psycho-

logical vacuum, that is, robbed of their German cultural, social, and political underpinnings. Traumatized, the German Jewish press corps had to
confront the issue of staying or leaving Nazi Germany.[3] The question of
remaining or leaving Germany was then and remains now (for historians)
the ultimate one. While Freeden devotes a large segment of his book to
this central topic, he leaves unasked the obvious question: Did the editorial policies for or against emigration have any impact on the readers? Not
surprisingly the multi-faceted German Jewish press was initially not of
one mind, but neither were its readers. Yet mass emigration took place
almost immediately across the German-Jewish social spectrum,[4] raising
academically the intriguing question: Who influenced whom?

Given the context of sudden disorientation, what may fairly be asked
of this disparate collection of publications in light of the Holocaust climax which is known *now* through hindsight but was then, as of 1933, con-
ceptually light years away? Is it fair to subject the German Jewish press
to a set of questions predicated on an event in the making? Beyond asking "What did the German Jewish press do to alert its readers?" may one
decently, as outsiders, also pose the potentially judgmental question
"What should it have done?" as compared to "What could it have done?"
and "What did it actually do and accomplish in the light of the unknown
future?"

Freeden outlines what it did do: 1) it grappled non-stop with the critical problem of emigrating versus staying; 2) it confronted the issue of
continuing to cultivate a strictly *German* Jewish identity as against
embracing a strictly Jewish one *in* Germany; and 3) it raised the question
of whether to stress *aliyah* to Palestine over immigration to any other
country. Nevertheless, this still leaves open the central question whether
the German Jewish press, through its editorials and articles, exercised
much influence on the decision making of its readers, if only by creating
a supportive climate of opinion as individuals privately made up their own
minds.

In evaluating the publications of the German Jewish press individual-
ly and collectively, one has to keep in mind that it was forcefully termi-
nated by the end of 1938. Consequently, its relationship to the Holocaust
qua Final Solution is essentially what amounts to its prelude, to the period of Nazism's legal assault,[5] the legislative severing of the Jewish population's close ties to German society. Though the threat of physical vio-

lence was always present as a background of potential terror, except for individual cases of brutality (usually perceived as exceptions), the overall reality between January 30, 1933, and November 9, 1938, was one of a tidal wave of anti-Semitic decrees, systematically undoing a century of enlightened emancipation granted by the state and enthusiastic Jewish grassroots assimilation into German culture and society.

One of the on-going editorial tasks of each Jewish publication was to assess the direction and accumulating significance of this ceaseless barrage of anti-Jewish government decrees, against which there was no appeal. Because these statutes came sporadically, there were moments when the absence of new official rules and regulations briefly raised hopes that the worst was over and that one could, if necessary, adjust and live with the onerous restrictions imposed to date; several publications pointed to the case of the Jews in Eastern Europe who had learned to cope with repressive decrees, to live among inhospitable populations, and to survive under hostile regimes. Some Jewish commentators consoled their readers with such comparative observations while others used historical analogy, insisting a Thermidorean Reaction was just around the corner; Germany's Jews just needed to be patient. There were no strident prophet-like German Jabotinskys—only a mild, avuncular Rabbi Leo Baeck who, though he concluded as early as 1933 that the end of Jewish history in Germany was at hand,[6] had no inkling how quickly and lethally that end would descend and how brutally catastrophic it would be for those Jews who planned on delaying emigration or remaining indefinitely in the Third Reich. On the contrary, while an emergency was sensed by all, its genocidal potential was not perceived until it was too late; and by then there was no German Jewish press to give advice.

II

Its end came abruptly and violently. In the wake of the nation-wide assault on the Jewish community on November 9-10, 1938, the Nazi regime literally dissolved all autonomous Jewish institutions, among them all weekly, bi-monthly, and monthly news and informational publications.[7] Thereafter, any publication issued in the name of Jewish organizations in Germany contained almost exclusively information originating from the government. The sole vehicle after 1938 was the *Judenblätter* or *Jüdische Nachrichten*. What had been a *bona fide* multi-faceted Jewish press in Germany was suddenly transformed, overnight, into an organ of the state to facilitate its post-*Kristallnacht Judenpolitik* (Jewish policy). This period was to last from December 1938 until Spring 1943, when even these rump publications ceased, the Third Reich, beginning with Berlin, having been officially declared *Judenrein* (free of Jews). If that was the case, then, logically, no more publication for Jews was necessary.

Those last five years with a single state-controlled publication under a supposedly Jewish banner were, at best, a time of a parody press. The *Jüdische Nachrichten* was published and distributed by the *Reichsvereinigung* (the 1939 Berlin-based Nazi-imposed centralizing organization), that bore no resemblance to its predecessor, the *Reischsvertretung* (the pre-1933 freely-formed umbrella federation of Jewish organizations of various persuasions and of other autonomous Jewish groups operating in Germany). The former was an imposed product of the Nazi policy of consolidation, *Gleichschaltung* (literally synchronization), whereas the latter, a free creation of pre-Nazi Germany, bore all the characteristics of the multifarious, though troubled, faction-riddled, pluralistic society of the Weimar republic, of which Jewish organizations were a constituent part.

That era of vibrant civil pluralism after World War I changed radically on January 30, 1933, with the ascent of Hitler and the rapid emergence of an anti-democratic, mono-party, anti-Semitic, racist regime. Like much of German society—whether the Communist Party or the Christian churches—the Jewish press was caught totally off-guard and unprepared psychologically and philosophically. Events moved ever more swiftly, and editorial policies had difficulty catching up, let alone adjusting to the crisis and the emerging catastrophe as far as foresight permitted. That the German Jewish press managed to survive the storms of the post-1933 years until the lighting bolt of November 1938 struck it down was an admirable achievement in itself, one of courage and tenacity in the face of unprecedented material and emotional decline and obstruction, such as the precipitous irreversible economic and demographic decline of German Jewry, and the rising tide of state-induced anti-Semitic persecution and terror.

Its purpose was twofold *vis-à-vis* the Jewish community: *Ausschaltung,* the exclusion and isolation of all Jews from mainstream German society, thereby rendering them superfluous; and, simultaneously, *totale Auswanderung*, wholesale state-induced mass emigration. It was in this context that the German Jewish press had to function and find a meaningful role. It meant, in brief, shifting *volte-face* from an orientation based on the assumption of the *permanence* of Jewish residency in Germany to one acknowledging the reverse premise, namely, the fact of a radically *curtailed* Jewish presence in Germany, that Germany was no longer a friendly or tolerant host country, but one bent on ridding itself of all Jews, no matter how culturally and otherwise assimilated into the German mainstream.

It is this psychological readjustment, a revolutionary reorientation, which commands attention when assessing the role played by the German Jewish press in the first five years of the Third Reich. This re-attunement to the idea of emigration, ironically, was the very same one that the Nazi regime sought to induce and impress upon the Jewish leadership and its rank and file, namely, to make them feel unambiguously unwanted and rejected and to act accordingly. Initially, in 1933, this fact was resisted, or, at least, the crisis was not perceived as so acute as it already was in fact. By October 1938, however, the complete psychological conversion had taken place; by year's end there was an overall resignation among *all* German Jews[8] that there was neither a long term nor a short term Jewish future in Germany,[9] except, perhaps, by a few die-hard holdouts, largely elderly men dating back to the pre-World War I Wilhelmine days, elderly widows, and single women with no place to go.

By then, the Nazi regime seemed permanently entrenched and not just a passing political phase as some had hoped in the earlier years. The militant and violent anti-Semitism, once falsely perceived as a tactic of a regime legitimizing its power, a policy, some had hoped, that would eventually be abandoned, or at least softened, remained unrelentingly in force with no sign of cessation. The oft expected National Socialist Thermidor never came, despite the false hopes generated during the well-orchestrated 1936 Olympic Games and the beginning of Göring's Four Year rearmament plan, which briefly led to a spate of employment opportunities for Jews. Instead, year by year, the legal and economic strangulation of German Jewry continued remorselessly. All of this negative news, along with occasional alternating short episodes of raised hopes followed by dashed expectations, was accurately disseminated by the German Jewish press, which increasingly stressed its bleak implications. This overall trend in Germany had profound cumulative impacts on the various editorial staffs looking for guidelines to navigate their readers through times they themselves barely fathomed.

In order to gain some perspective on the circumstances within which the German Jewish press had to operate, one need only look at the stark turn taken by the non-Jewish German press. Almost simultaneously, publishers and editors supinely toed the party line, largely through self-censorship. The once free press—that which was not purged or closed by the new regime—quickly adopted the propaganda menu of the state, substituting it for independent reporting. Both foreign and domestic affairs were almost totally portrayed through the prism of National Socialism. The peculiar racist terminology of National Socialism became standard press vocabulary, in particular the language of anti-Semitism. If not in the brazen style of the SA's *Der Stürmer*, it was, nevertheless, sufficient to expose the German reader to a daily diet of racist vocabulary, with particular reference to a Manichaean world in which the Aryan was at mortal odds with the Jewish race in its midst. There were no opposition national newspapers, however moderate, no buffer between the supine, state-intimidated German press and the isolated, friendless Jewish news and opinion publications. Within a few weeks after the Nazi seizure of power, the Jewish press in Germany was under perpetual siege, a lonely vehicle of communication, desperately looking for a clarification of its mission in the midst of an on-going crisis it never fully grasped as sociopolitical events frustratingly kept ahead of full comprehension. It was a classic case of unrelieved near-dysfunction.

Ironically, the Jewish press in Germany remained free in as much as it did not have to conform to the demands of the National Socialist "philosophy" inflicted on the German press. On the whole, while its writers naturally had to be circumspect, they had a fairly free range of choice of subjects and expressions of views. In many ways it was more accurate in its reporting, freed from having to spout the government's one dimensional propaganda. In a very real sense, its Jewish readers were better served than the German public by its hopelessly compromised national and regional newspapers. At least the Jewish readers were exposed to honest, fundamental debates about their past, present and future. And a central part of this soul-searching was the painful theme of emigration: of whether to leave Germany, of where to go, of who should go (first), of who should remain, and of *why* one ought (must) leave.

III

Before tracing the editorial paths taken by the German Jewish press through the mid-Thirties, specifically in terms of the emigration debate, several words need to be clarified. The term "German Jewish press" poses some difficulty. Even the word "Jewish" is problematic: on the one hand it presupposes a regular publication of contemporary information sponsored by a Jewish organization based in Germany. However, in Nazi parlance, "Jewish" press also referred to non-Jewish sponsored newspapers, ones either founded, owned and/or editorially supervised by Jewish editors, such as, for example, *Die Frankfurter Allgemeine*. One of the first acts by the new regime was to "dejudaize" (*entjuden*) these publications by forcing their Jewish owners, stockholders, editors and writers off the board and staff. Thus, former "Jewish" newspapers had to be "Aryanized" before they qualified as *bona fide* German. As these papers metamorphosed, they quickly lost their Jewish subscribers who increasingly turned to the Jewish press which most German Jews had not taken too seriously prior to 1933. Equally problematic is the term "press." What precisely does it embrace? Newspapers only? There were no Jewish dailies, only weekly, monthly and quarterly publications. Do only national publications qualify for inclusion? Then what about the regular, though more modest, regional newsletters and community bulletins? Some of the latter, for example those of Berlin and Frankfurt, not only reached a large proportion of the Jewish readership in Germany but contained similar types of content as the Jewish national papers. They included influential opinion editorials, from analytic essays on contemporary problems to announcements and advertisements of immediate use to a readership increasingly dependent for guidance and information on an array of problems—including emigration—serving a readership rapidly disoriented, fragmented, and demoralized.

Thus, since community service by disseminating vital data and potentially influential editorial opinion—ranging from news from abroad to facilitate emigration to news from within Germany to update each Jew on developments of the crisis—became the common denominator of all publications, one should also take stock of some of the major *Mitteilungsblätter* (information bulletins) of the larger *Landesverbände Israelitscher Religionsgemeinde* (Provincial Associations of Jewish communities) as well as of the larger *Gemeindeblätter* (community newsletters) of the major urban centers with a significant Jewish population concentration. This may be stretching the traditional concept of press, but it does highlight the emergency needs served due to the catastrophic crisis that had descended on German Jewry in January 1933. Consequently, the normal pre-1933 distinction between the weekly national newspapers, *e.g.* the *Central-Verein Zeitung*, and the weekly, monthly, or quarterly *Blätter* dissipates in the light of the revolutionary change of circumstance that the Nazi regime initiated.

In his monograph *Die Jüdische Presse im Dritten Reich*, Herbert Freeden is even more inclusive and generous in his definition of what constitutes the press. He counts such publications as occasional reports by Jewish welfare organizations as well as specialized, one issue publications aimed exclusively at target readers such as rabbis, cantors, Jewish craftsmen, women's groups, artists, the deaf, athletes, schools, etc. Some of these items appeared but once or very infrequently and sporadically. And while they no doubt represent a part of Jewish life in Germany, they by no means fall within the range of anything resembling a traditional press, no matter how loosely defined, if only because of their restricted readership and infrequent appearance.

Traditionally, "press" presumes at least a measure of regularity and frequency aimed at a sizable proportion of the targeted reading public on a national, regional and local level. It is also presumed that the bulk of the contents consists of reportage on contemporary issues. While Freeden was correct in concluding the basic commonality of all categories of Jewish publications between January 1933 and November 1938, he nevertheless blurs important distinctions by so doing. Consequently, for this article, the focus will be on major publications, those reaching the widest readership, if only because of their greater potential influence and increasing authority as possible molders and exponents of German Jewish public opinion as it grappled for answers to the emigration question. This group breaks down into the following categories:[10]

I.   Politically Oriented Newspapers (estimated circulation in 1934):
      1. *Central-Verein Zeitung* (center left) : (40,000) weekly
      2. *Jüdische Rundschau* (Zionist): (37,000) bi-weekly
      3. *Israelitishes Familienblatt* (traditional): (36,000) weekly
      4. *Der Schild* (assimilationist, nationalist, center right): (20,000) weekly

II. Religious Papers:
   1. *Jüdische Allgemeine Zeitung* (Liberal)
   2. *Der Israelit* (Zionist)
   3. *Die Laubhütte* (Orthodox)

III. Community Newsletters (estimated circulation):
   1. Berlin: (50,000) weekly
   2. Württemberg: (22,000) bi-monthly
   3. Frankfurt: (8,000) monthly
   4. Prussia: (7,500) monthly
   5. Breslau: (7,500) bi-monthly
   6. Hamburg: (5,000) monthly
   7. Munich: (4,500) monthly
   8. Leipzig: (4,000) monthly

IV. Other regular publications
   1. *Jüdisches Kulturbund*: (28,000) monthly; contained news of opportunities abroad and of artists who had emigrated.
      Berlin: (18,000)
      Cologne: (5,000)
      Frankfurt: (3,500)
      Hamburg: (1,500)
   2. *Der Makkabi*: (44,000) monthly; was very Israel/Palestine oriented.
   3. *Palästina Nachrichten*: (5,000) monthly; became one of the most consulted publications in regard to emigration.

The largest newspaper, the *Central-Verein Zeitung*, printed in Berlin, by 1933 a weekly, enjoyed a circulation of 40,000 (down from 50,000), but experienced a 230% growth in page size between 1932 and 1936, half due to an increase in personal announcements and advertising. The significance of this latter development is that it assured the paper's financial independence. Given the June 1934 law that no more publications were to be distributed free of charge, this quantitative growth proved a bonus, especially for the community bulletins because it allowed each publication to keep its price at a minimum while enjoying a relatively high income growth rate, thereby safeguarding financial independence.

The same trend was true for the *Jüdische Rundschau,* which underwent a 325 per cent enlargement without losing subscribers (37,000
annually) between 1934 and 1937. The popular *Hamburger Israelitisches
Familienblatt* also retained a steady readership (36,000) while attaining a
75 per cent growth overall and a 100 per cent growth in advertising.
Another example of dramatic growth in size was the influential *Berliner
Gemeindeblatt* which expanded 250 per cent and more than tripled its
advertising. Its growth was due to a rapid shift in population from the
provinces to the major cities *(Binnenwanderung)* and a rapid growth of
membership on the part of thousands of formerly unaffiliated Jews who
had need of some social bonding if only to acquire crucial information to
facilitate their emigration. This, of course, greatly enhanced its possible
influence, the basic question raised in this article.

IV

As repeatedly stated, this study seeks to assess what role and influence (if any) the German Jewish press played and exercised upon its readers between 1933 and 1938, a short but critical five years, during which
more and more of Jewish life revolved around existential issues (in particular the decision to emigrate); hence the expansion of topical coverage
to reach new categories of readers via special sections aimed at house-
wives, schools, sport enthusiasts, cultural groups, above all at prospective
emigrants in general and those opting to go to Palestine in particular.

Some of the major publications had already enjoyed long and distinguished careers: *Der Israelit* (Zionist) dated back to 1860; *Die Laubhütte*
(The Sukkah, Orthodox) to 1884; *Die Jüdische Rundschau* (Zionist) to
1896; the *Hamburger Israelitisches Familienblatt* to 1898; *Der Makkabi*
(Zionist) to 1898. More recent papers, national in scope, were *Die
Central-Verein Zeitung* established in 1922 and *Der Morgen* in 1925. The
informative monthly *Palästina-Nachrichten* (Palestine News) with a first
circulation of 7,500 appeared appropriately in 1933.

Given the constraints of space, what can be concluded in broad brush
strokes about the Jewish press and mass emigration that was given even
shorter shrift by Freeden?

Over the course of the five years, 1933 to 1938, there was a surprising degree of growing editorial if not unanimity, then growing consensus
favoring mass emigration, as German Jewry passed various critical

stages. Between 1933 and 1938 there were three such defining moments after the initial assumption of power and the constitutional granting of emergency power to Hitler: 1) the March 1933 statute evicting all Jews from the civil service; 2) the September 1935 Nuremberg Racial Laws, which rendered an official definition of who was a Jew and deprived all Jews of German citizenship;[11] and 3), the 1937 Aryanization policy, which was designed to strip Jews of their personal property and wealth. With each one, there was a commensurate convergence of priorities and views, especially with respect to the imperative of emigration.[12] At the heart of all ideological and political disputes lay the questions whether to stay or leave Germany and where to emigrate: to Palestine or elsewhere.[13] These became the two most fundamental burning issues confronting German Jewry. It involved every segment of Jewish society and spanned the entire range of Jewish political, religious and cultural opinion.

As the first five years progressed, virtually all publications—after considerable ideological and theoretical argumentation—accepted mass emigration as an imperative forced by circumstances. All increased coverage on promoting and facilitating emigration, no matter what their reasons. Initially there was a profound rift between the Zionists (who argued that *aliyah* be adopted as a Jewish *obligation* [*mitzva*] now that Nazism had come to power) and the mainstream assimilationists (who eventually also stressed the need, however reluctantly, to plan on leaving Germany). In due time, even the *Central-Verein Zeitung* not only pushed for large-scale emigration in general but regularly included information about the benefits of settling in Palestine if only as an emergency transitional step. Over the years, the *Central Verein-Zeitung* argued less from an ideological point of view than from a purely pragmatic vantage point. However, in the same manner, Zionists, recognizing the impossibility of all Jews going to British-controlled Mandatory Palestine, encouraged their readers to consider other parts of the world, arguing that this was just part of the experience of exile that would, ultimately, perhaps in their lifetime, culminate with their reaching *Eretz Israel.*

This convergence of editorial policies over emigration, in favor of carefully planned mass emigration, was, in retrospect, the correct position to take. By November 1938, about 160,000 to 180,000 German Jews, nearly 30 per cent, had already left the country. But had they been influenced by the German Jewish press? Or was the influence in the other direction? That is, had they left in response to the circumstances created by the Nazi regime, requiring little convincing from the Jewish leadership whether to stay or to leave? Chronologically, the mass exodus of Jews began early in 1933, coinciding with Hitler's seizure of power, and continued through 1935, even as the Jewish press heatedly debated the issue. Every congregation and organization felt the qualitative and quantitative consequences of this extraordinary exodus. There is reason to believe the initial policy against mass-emigration in some of the mainstream German Jewish press such as the *Central Verein-Zeitung* was eroded by the undeniable fact of the grassroots movement out of Germany, to both Palestine and elsewhere, often with a minimum of ideological motivation. In many instances, Zionists ended up in the United States, and non-Zionists in Palestine, individual decisions taken due to the dire external circumstances and not as a result of personal desire. In the absence of polls and detailed studies, there is no way of accurately and definitively resolving the question, who influenced whom. But no one can deny that the Jewish press quickly disseminated more and more critical information to help prospective *émigrés* make timely and informed decisions.

Since, in retrospect, emigration lay at the heart of survival from Nazism, the German Jewish press fulfilled that function well. There is no better proof than the speedy exodus of yet another 30% of German Jewry from the *Alt-Reich* (pre-1938 Germany) after *Kristallnacht*, most of them between November 1938 and September 1939. All of these people had been nourished by a wealth of information, news, and editorial opinions that had accumulated in the German Jewish press between 1933 and 1938. Practically all publications, no matter what ideological orientations, eventually encouraged a speedy departure from the Third Reich long before these newspapers and bulletins were banned by the Nazi government, a time when German Jews had to rely on the emigration offices set up by the German government in Berlin and Vienna to expedite the policy of forced (*zwang*) mass emigration.

Prior to November 1938, the cumulative effect of greater editorial consensus must have helped somewhat the psychological readjustment of the Jewish population that had to uproot itself, if only by articulating cogent arguments to do so. Herein lies the effectiveness of the press: if it can *repeatedly* stress a particular editorial policy, the key being repetition. There must be (as there was) sufficient editorial commitment to keeping a theme uppermost in the readers' minds in order to stimulate thought and action. By giving the theme of mass emigration the highest priority over all other issues, the bulk of the German Jewish press, until its tragic demise, did exactly what it *should* have done. There literally was no Jewish publication that ultimately did not adopt the promotion of mass emigration as its primary topic.

Though unaware of the ultimate catastrophe, through its unambiguous commitment to emigration (regardless of political, cultural and ideological differences), the Jewish press in Germany achieved what other Jewish presses elsewhere failed to do as well in the 1930s. That over 60 per cent of German Jews (including the author) in the *Alt-Reich* (pre-1938) were out of Germany by September 1939 speaks for itself. Some immeasurable credit must be given to the Jewish press, which, throughout the mid-Thirties remained multifarious in opinion but, after 1935, united more and more in a single conclusion regarding mass departure from Germany. The only analogy that springs to mind is the broad spectrum of conflicting views of the politically diverse underground literature issued in the Warsaw Ghetto and the eventual consensus over the need to resist, no matter the reason. But whereas this show of singleness of purpose came too late (during World War II) to rescue the Jews of Poland, the German Jewish press' pre-World War II recognition of the singular plight of German Jewry and its exhortations that they flee were both timely and, overall, successful.

There was, of course, a tragic irony in this historic drama. It was not simply a dialogue between the German Jewish press and their Jewish readers in Germany, a heated intra-communal debate over the issue of personal and group identities, and the logic of staying or leaving the country of one's birth. One could argue that both the German Jewish ideological leadership writing in the press and the equally diverse-minded German Jewish population evolved in tandem, neither one influencing the other. Both, one could conclude, responded *less* to each other (if in fact they did in matters of mass emigration) than they acted in response to a *third* actor in the drama of the mid-1930s, namely, the Third Reich and its hostile *Judenpolitik*. Its stated goal in 1933–34 was to elicit in Jews a mental revolution, the abandonment of their German patriotism and symbiotic attachment to German culture and society. Its purpose was to install, by all available means, a realization that there was *no* place in Germany for Jews, and that all arguments to the contrary were futile.

This was a powerful reality which, in the end (1938), tolerated little intellectual resistance. German Jews and their leadership, in the long run, simply could not withstand the logical conclusion that flew from the rejectionist Nazi *Judenpolitik*. A combination of rejectionist legislation and a steady dose of psychological and physical terror intimidated the minds of Jewish leaders and rank file alike. By November 1938, prior to *Kristallnacht*, German Jews were not only of one mind regarding mass emigration, they were well on the way literally to abandoning their beloved *Heimat*. By *Kristallnacht* almost all had put in requests for emigration to countries all over the world. That not all had left by September 1939 was not a reflection of a stubborn refusal to leave but a tragic fact caused by stringent immigration laws, limited transportation opportunities, the absence of sponsoring relatives abroad, and family and financial constraints. It is time to put to rest the cruel myth of German Jewry's blindness to the dangerous political reality that swept over them. All too often it is said that their bond with Germanness kept them tied to Germany. That flies in the face of the incontestable evidence. Not only did they vote with their feet in disproportionate numbers compared to other Jewries, but their leadership, via the Jewish press, wisely supported them in their decision to emigrate.

Notes:
1. (Frankfurt am Main: Athenäum). See also an earlier work by Herbert A. Strauss, in *The Jewish Press That Was* (Tel Aviv: World Federation of Jewish Journalists, 1980). [Editor's note: Cf. the Yiddish version of Strauss' chapter "Jewish Press in Germany 1918–1938," in *Di Yidishe Prese vos iz geven* (Tel-Aviv, 1975), pp. 494–541.]
2. The strong bond of all Jewish groups to Germany and its culture was correctly pointed out by Lucy Dawidowicz, (New York, 1975), pp. 170–172. See also *Jüdische Rundschau*, 13 April 1933, for the Orthodox stance: "The historical ties of centuries are not so easy to dissolve."
3. Initially, of course, traditional values and assumptions were shrilly upheld. Thus, in the *Central-Verein Zeitung* (*CV-Z*) on 9 March 1933, ". . .

no one can rob us of our homeland." Or, a prominent youth leader called for a patient retention of German identity: Heinz Kellermann, "Ende der Emanzipation?" *Der Morgen,* 9 August 1933, pp. 173–177. Similarly, ". . . as Jews, we reaffirm a life in Germany and for Germany." Heinrich Stern in *Der Morgen*, 9 August 1933, pp. 165–172. The *CV-Z* was equally forceful: in February 1933, "We are convinced no one will dare violate our constitutional rights," and on 13 July 1933, it proclaimed, "We shall continue to follow a German path."

4. 37,000 left in 1933, about 8 per cent of the Jewish population.

5. See Joseph Walk, *Das Sonderrecht der Juden im NS-Staat* (Karlsruhe, 1981).

6. He made this remark on 13 April 1933 before a conference of the Jewish communities assembled in Berlin. For purposes of this article, Rabbi Leo Baeck quickly recognized the potential of the Jewish press as a transmitter of vital information, but also as a vehicle to bind German Jewry into a more coherent whole. Leo Baeck, "Gedenken an zwei Tote," in *Deutsches Judentum. Aufstieg und Krise* (Stuttgart, 1963), p. 310.

7. Between 1933 and 1938, there were several short periods when individual publications were briefly interrupted due to government intervention. Max Gruenewald, "The Beginning of the Reichsvertretung," in *Leo Baeck Institute (LBI) Year Book* I (1956), p. 60.

8. This is according to a census of German Jews taken in 1939. The documents are in Yad Vashem's archives. According to the questionnaires practically everyone had initiated emigration procedures.

9. The slowest to embrace the idea of emigration was the organ of the German Jewish Veterans of World War I, *Der Schild*. By 1937 its c. 35,000 members were reconciled to the crisis facing all Jews. See Ulrich Dunker, *Der Reichsbund Jüdischer Frontsoldaten 1919–1938* (Düsseldorf, 1977).

10. Information based on 1936 statistics. Herman Saunter, "Die Jüdische Presse in Deutschland" in *Berliner Jüdisches Gemeindeblatt* (23 August 1936). See also *Lexicon des Judentums* (Gütersloh, 1967); and *Philo-Lexicon* (Berlin, 1934 edition and 1937 edition). Further, consult the Hans Hinkel file, copies in Wiener Library (London).

11. Actually the *CV-Z* made its official rejection of the idea of the synthesis between Germanness and Jewishness on 4 April 1935 *before* the

Nuremberg Laws were announced in September, but it did not embrace the idea of unqualified mass emigration until *after*, on 7 December 1938.

The 15 September 1935 Nuremberg Racial Laws served as a catalyst in the Jewish press in Germany. Thereafter, their diverse editorial policies quickly converged, increasingly stressing large-scale emigration as against individual departures. While the *CV-Z* tended to argue along pragmatic lines, the Orthodox minority pointed out the fundamental correctness of its ideological stance, namely, the futility of assimilation and, especially, the unreliability of emancipation. See Herbert Freeden, *Jüdische Presse im Dritten Reich* (1987), p. 77. See also *CV-Z*, 22 November 1935 and *JR*, 15 November 1935.

12. Initially, the Jewish press waged a bitter polemical battle, each blaming the other: the Orthodox for having resisted assimilation; the mainstreamers represented by the *CV-Z* for having placed trust in the state; the Zionists for having resisted emancipation. See: *Der Schild*, 14 September 1933, and *JR*, 15 November 1934.

13. The brief debate over the primacy of emigration to Palestine after 15 September 1935 was one of minor, almost semantic, issues. Thus, the *Jüdische Rundschau* warned since 1933 that life in Palestine would be difficult; expectations should be realistic. *JR*, 20 October 1933. The less committed ought to continue a life of exile (in the *galut)*.

The Austrian Press and the Third Reich: Contradictory Views from a Neighbor

Bruce F. Pauley
University of Central Florida

Austria enjoyed a unique vantage point from which events in the Third Reich could be observed. With language being no barrier, Austrian anti-Semites could observe with approval the enactment of anti-Jewish legislation that Austrians had merely discussed for over half a century. Austrian Jews were painfully aware that if Hitler were ever to fulfill his dream of uniting the two German-speaking countries they would be subjected to the same discriminatory laws as their brethren across the Inn River. Therefore, events in Germany affecting the Jews dominated the pages of Austria's newspapers, especially its Jewish newspapers, at least in 1932 and 1933. To be sure, when a dictatorship was established by Chancellor Engelbert Dollfuss in March 1933, the press in Austria began to be censored. However, the censorship was largely confined to reports involving the Austrian government itself. There is no evidence that it colored reporting on Nazi Germany.[1]

This relative freedom extended to the press organs of political factions within the Jewish community such as *Die Wahrheit*, which represented the assimilationist Union of Austrian Jews, *Die Stimme,* the mouthpiece of mainstream Austrian Zionists, and *Jüdische Presse*, the organ of Austrian Orthodox Jews. In fact, much to the outrage of Austrian anti-Semites, these and other Jewish newspapers, along with the political factions they represented in the *Israelitische Kultusgemeinde* (Jewish Communal Organization), survived to the very end of the First Austrian Republic (1918–38), when German troops occupied the country in March 1938 and carried out the so-called *Anschluss*, annexing the country to the Third Reich. In the meantime, overtly anti-Semitic and Nazi party newspapers, along with all the Austrian political parties, except the government-sponsored umbrella organization, the Fatherland's Front, had been outlawed in 1933 or 1934.

Austrian Anti-Semitism Before Hitler's *Machtergreifung*

Austria had an anti-Semitic tradition of its own that far predated Hitler's takeover of power. This heritage predisposed both anti-Semites and Jews to respond to events in Germany in fairly predictable ways. Catholic journals and newspapers in the First Republic and earlier were filled with articles denouncing Jews in very traditional terms. Such denunciations could be found in almost every issue of the prestigious weekly magazine, *Schönere Zukunft*. Founded in 1925, it was far from being considered an extremist publication featuring as it did commentaries on current events by Catholic bishops, professors of theology, and leading Catholic politicians, not only from Austria but from Hungary and Germany as well. The editor of *Schönere Zukunft*, the German-born Josef Eberle, considered the Jewish question to be the most important of all questions and was himself a frequent contributor of anti-Jewish articles, introductions, and editorials.[2]

Eberle proved to be one of the major moving forces of Catholic anti-Semitism. His primary function was advocating the cause of traditional Catholicism, including traditional Catholic anti-Semitism. In one of the early issues of *Schönere Zukunft*, Eberle claimed that the Talmud predicted future wealth for Jews. This creed had created a type of person who was dangerous to those tolerating him. The one-sided approval of wealth, property, and power by the Jewish religion gave Jews an advantage over Christians, who sanctioned these things only to a very limited extent.[3] To fight this "menace," Eberle published articles calling for boycotts of Jewish department stores.[4]

Anti-Semitic articles and editorials were also commonplace in such newspapers as the *Grazer Volksblatt*, the *Salzburger Volksblatt, Der Bauernbündler*, the *Klerus Zeitschrift für soziale Arbeit*, the *Kleines Kirchenblatt* (aimed at Roman Catholic youth), and countless other Catholic newspapers, as well as journalistic organs of the conservative and pro-Catholic Christian Social party. By far the most important of their periodicals was the *Reichspost*. However, its circulation of 50,000 made it only the fourth largest newspaper in Austria after 1925. In fact the

Reichspost's inferior circulation, which caused financial difficulties, and the absence of journalists comparable to those of the great Jewish-owned Viennese newspapers, doubtless accounted for some of the *Reichspost*'s anti-Semitism.[5] Since the first year of its publication in 1894, the paper dealt with all aspects of the Jewish question in a way designed to evoke an emotional response. The attacks were always aimed against Jews in general, rather than in Jews in particular in order to avoid violating libel laws.[6]

Anti-Jewish articles were endemic in the *Reichspost*, especially in the early postwar years. In 1919 it claimed that six million (ethnic) Germans in Austria were being ruled by a tiny percentage of Jews who belonged not only to a different nation but also to a different race. Other articles dealt with the overrepresentation of Jews in Austrian schools and universities, the supposed prominence of Jews in the Austrian government, and the need for expelling the recent Jewish immigrants from Eastern Europe, the so-called *Ostjuden*.[7]

A favorite topic for the *Reichspost* was the alleged effort by "the Jews" to take over the world, a thesis that the paper tried to prove with contradictory evidence and illogical arguments. Jewish mastery of the world was portrayed not as a question, a possibility, or even an eventuality, but as an established fact. Not surprisingly, therefore, the paper ended an article about the *Protocols of the Elders of Zion* by speaking of their "shocking nature" even though the beginning of the same article expressed doubt about the very authenticity of the *Protocols*.[8]

Not all of the articles in the *Reichspost* that dealt with Jews were negative, at least not superficially. The paper consistently supported Zionism. It favored the same policy of "dissimilation" advocated by the Zionists. However, unlike the Zionists, it was not interested in protecting the rights of a minority, but instead in limiting Jewish influence in the state. Essentially, it wanted to revoke the Jews' equal rights. It favored special laws for Jews that would have limited their freedom of choice in business and the professions as well as where they lived; it also wanted to prevent Jews from holding public office or even from voting.[9]

Christian Social and Roman Catholic newspapers were by no means the only ones espousing virulent anti-Semitism in the First Austrian Republic. Social Democrats and Communists often used anti-Semitism as a club with which to embarrass their capitalist enemies even though their party platforms officially rejected the prejudice. Although as Marxists, the Social Democrats were theoretically opposed to all capitalists without distinction, in practice they frequently gave the impression of being opposed only to Jewish capitalists. They called on the "real anti-Semites" to join them to fight Jewish capitalism. In order to avoid offending their own Jewish constituency, however, Socialists confined their attacks to big Jewish businessmen and ignored small Jewish shop owners.[10]

Examples of such attacks on the big Jewish bourgeoisie in the Socialist press are legion. The March 16, 1921, issue of the party's official mouthpiece, the *Arbeiter-Zeitung*, claimed that the Jewish bourgeoisie did not even mind students, officers, and members of the petite bourgeoisie carrying out violent, anti-Semitic demonstrations because the supposedly anti-Semitic parties never passed any anti-Semitic legislation. The Aryans and the big bourgeoisie knew how to stick together on important issues. In September 1922, the same newspaper called Chancellor Ignaz Seipel a "puppet of the Jews" who wanted to turn Austria over to the enslavement of Jewish international finance capital by signing the Geneva Protocol, which gave Austria a loan of $126 million.[11]

Socialist publications were fond of using terms like *Bankjuden, jüdische Borsenpresse* (Jewish stock-market press), and *Borsenjuden* (stock-market Jews) to describe Jewish capitalists. Opponents of the Socialists were often caricatured in cartoons as looking like Jews. In some Socialist publications and posters even Orthodox Jews were ridiculed. The attacks served to reinforce the stereotype of Jews being money grubbers and manipulators and caused confusion in readers' minds as to whether their real sin was being capitalists or being Jewish.

Unlike either the Marxist parties or, for the most part, the Christian Social party, the *Grossdeutsche Volkspartei* (GDVP), or Greater German People's party, advocated the racist form of anti-Semitism and the establishment of a *Volksgemeinschaft* or racial community which would exclude "parasitic" Jews. Verbal anti-Semitism was not enough to restore the people's community; the Jews had to be treated as a separate nation. The GDVP was a middle-class coalition of seventeen nationalistic splinter parties and organizations left over from the monarchy. It was founded in 1920 by groups that came together more out of necessity than conviction. Because it was created from "above" it had no strong organization. It does not figure prominently in the history of journalistic anti-Semitism because it had no major newspaper of its own, although until the middle 1920s the *Deutsch-österreichische Tages-Zeitung* supported its views. By the time the Nazis had come to power in Germany, most members of the GDVP had been absorbed into the Austrian Nazi party.[12]

Far more vicious than Marxists or even the most extreme Catholic publications were those of the *Antisemitenbund*, the abbreviated name of the German-Austrian Defensive League of Anti-Semites. The League was an umbrella organization consisting of members of all the bourgeois parties and paramilitary formations of Austria including the *Landbund*, a peasant party; the *Heimwehr*, a right-wing paramilitary formation based in the provinces, especially Styria, Upper Austria, Carinthia, and the Tyrol; the League of Front Fighters (*Frontkämpfervereinigung*), another paramilitary formation concentrated in Vienna and Lower Austria; and at times the Austrian Nazi party.

The *Antisemitenbund* was founded during the height of the anti-Semitic hysteria following the First World War, and thereafter its success mirrored the rise and fall of anti-Semitic feelings in Austria. Its first task, and the element that made it unique among anti-Semitic organizations in Austria, was its desire to assemble all anti-Semites into one organization in order to protect them from the alleged economic, social, and political influence of the Jews. The *Antisemitenbund* stood squarely in favor of the racial principle; it defined as a Jew anyone having one Jewish great-grandparent, a definition far more inclusive that that found in the legal commentaries of the Nuremberg Laws of 1935.[13]

In general the *Antisemitenbund* wanted a legal separation of Jews and non-Jews in education, administration of justice, and social welfare. More specifically it wanted to expel all Jews who had immigrated since 1914; forbid all future Jewish immigration; identify as "Jewish" all newspapers and businesses where Jews worked; establish a *numerus clausus* (cap based on proportional representation) for Jews in the arts; exclude Jews from the professions of law, medicine, and teaching; take away their right to vote; and deny them the right to hold public office and to own land.[14]

The *Deutschösterreichische Tages-Zeitung* in Vienna maintained close ties with the *Antisemitenbund*, as did the *Reichspost* (which advertised its meetings), the *Deutsches Volksblatt*, and the *Neuigkeits-Weltblatt*. However, the official newspaper of the organization until 1932 was *Der eiserne Besen*. Founded in Vienna in 1921, it was forced to move its editorial offices to Salzburg in 1923. Its circulation remained quite small, never exceeding six thousand. Even by the low standards of predominantly anti-Semitic newspapers, the contents of *Der eiserne Besen* were primitive; its specialties were detailed descriptions of private sex scandals involving Jews and stories about alleged Jewish ritual murders. It also liked to list the names of Jewish shops together with the names of their "Aryan" customers.[15]

The most infamous of the anti-Semitic organizations of Austria was without doubt the Austrian Nazi party. But once one looks beyond the party's popular reputation it becomes clear that its ideas and methods of propaganda were in no respect completely novel. It is even doubtful whether its Jewish policy, prior to the *Anschluss*, was much more extreme than that of the *Antisemitenbund*, the right-wing of the Christian Social party, or the Greater German People's party. Only in their greater willingness to use violence against Jews did the Nazis differentiate themselves to some extent from other Austrian anti-Semites [16]

The Nazis were more consistent in their anti-Semitism than their rivals. Their "scientific" racism and aggressive opposition to Jews avoided the semi-religious, semiracist, and theoretically "defensive" anti-Semitism of most Christian Socials. Unlike the Socialists they denounced all Jews, not just those who were capitalists; and unlike the *Heimwehr* and the Christian Socials, they did not accept money from Jewish financiers. In contrast to all their anti-Semitic rivals, except Greater Germans and the *Antisemitenbund*, Nazis were not supposed to associate with even baptized Jews.

Although the Austrian Nazis were ultimately the most successful in exploiting traditional Austrian anti-Semitism as well as current events and problems in which Jews were associated or at least alleged to be associated, they employed mostly the traditional techniques of anti-Semites. These techniques ranged from attacks on the alleged cultural influence of Jews to boycotts. As a matter of fact, the Nazis went out of their way to prove that their anti-Semitism was *not* something new or unique. The *Deutsch-österreichische Tages-Zeitung*, which moved toward the Nazi camp in the mid-1920s, announced at least as early as 1926 that the greatest thinkers of all nationalities had been anti-Semites.[17] The violently anti-Semitic newspaper, *Der Stürmer*, asserted that hatred of Jews dated back to ancient times and existed wherever Jews had lived. Even the famous American automobile manufacturer, Henry Ford, subscribed to the principle, as did the Ku Klux Klan, according to the paper.[18]

The Nazis' solutions for the Jewish "problem" were equally shopworn and included such things as reducing Jewish representation in the professions and academic life to their proportion of Austria's (or Vienna's) population and expelling the Jews, or at least the Jewish newcomers from Eastern Europe. As early as 1925, the party's official organ, the *Deutsche Arbeiter-Presse*, demanded that Vienna's second district, Leopoldstadt, be made a ghetto for all Viennese Jews as a prelude to their being expelled from the country.[19]

A favorite tactic of Nazi newspapers was scandal mongering. For example, in the provincial capital of Graz, *Der Kampf*, the official organ of the NSDAP in Styria, accused a Jewish-owned clothing firm by the name of Rendi of failing to pay income taxes and investing money in Switzerland.[20] Such articles could sometimes boomerang, however. When *Der Kampfruf*, the party's official mouthpiece in Vienna, warned its readers against patronizing the Phönix Insurance Company because it had Jewish directors, the newspaper was flooded with angry letters from the company's non-Jewish employees who complained that a boycott would threaten their jobs.[21] The ultimate Jewish scandal and proof of Jewish destructiveness, so far as the Nazis were concerned, was the *Protocols of the Elders of Zion*. Despite the growing evidence that the *Protocols* was a crude forgery, Nazi newspapers, including the *Deutsche Arbeiter-Presse*, *Der Kampf*, and especially *Der Stürmer*, continued to maintain its authenticity, claiming that its prophecies had come true.[22]

Austria's Anti-Semitic Press and the German Nazis

To a very large extent, Austrian anti-Semitism was a war of words fought between the anti-Semites themselves. No political party of any significance entirely ignored the idea for long. Anti-Semitism was a political weapon that every party adapted to its philosophy in order to embarrass its enemies and to integrate its own followers more closely to its organization. The rise of the Nazis to power in Germany, therefore threatened to steal this issue from every Austrian party except the country's Nazi party. After January 1933, the latter enjoyed the enviable position of being able to say that their comrades in Germany were actually doing something about the "Jewish problem" whereas Austrian anti-Semites had seldom done more than talk. In the Reich, Jewish influence was being eliminated from the civil service and cultural life of the country. By 1935, German Jews had been deprived of their full citizenship rights and were being stripped of their wealth.

The rise and triumph of National Socialism in Germany appeared particularly threatening to the Christian Social party. The Austrian Nazis' unscrupulous anti-Semitic propaganda threatened to lure away many of the party's younger members. Anti-Semitism had formed an important part of the Christian Socials' *Weltanschauung* from the party's very beginnings in the 1890s. Even though it became less important after 1922, it remained a significant integrating factor in the heterogeneous party. Indeed, there had to be serious doubts in the minds of the party's leaders whether the party could survive if denied this political tool. Members of the Roman Catholic hierarchy were anxious to convince young people that the church had been anti-Semitic centuries before anyone had heard of National Socialism.

The approach many Catholics took in this competition was that the Germans were too weak or too insincere in their anti-Semitism. Josef Eberle made this point in one of the early issues of *Schönere Zukunft* in 1926, long before the Nazis had become a serious factor in German politics. German Catholics were allegedly not really aware of the Jewish question because their own Catholic press ignored the issue and even accepted advertisements from Jews. Shallow humanism and dangerous tolerance would only benefit Jews at the expense of Christians. Hatred and pogroms were not necessary, but Jewish influence had to be limited to their relative numbers.[23]

Eberle and *Schönere Zukunft* were only mildly critical of the Nazis' persecution of Jews after Hitler's takeover of power in 1933, even though Eberle had written in 1931 that the Nazis' handling of the Jewish question was both un-Christian and barbaric. *Schönere Zukunft* could agree with the Nazis that the Jewish "race" was inferior, but ultimately could not accept the Nazis' idea about the total depravity of Jews or the even broader notion that race is of decisive importance for whole peoples as well as individuals.[24]

Christian Socials could not help but admire the Nazis' anti-Marxism as well as their passionate opposition to the Paris Peace treaties. The *Reichspost* was therefore generally sympathetic to the new Nazi regime in Berlin but faulted its policy toward Jews. The newspaper maintained in March 1933, that the Nazis had betrayed their own anti-Semitic program. Jewish citizens in Germany were being treated just like everyone else. Then, after the brief boycott of Jewish stores on April 1, 1933, the *Reichspost* complained that Nazi anti-Semitism in Germany was not legal and was disturbing the economic order. Other articles about anti-Semitism in Germany were simply printed without comment by the *Reichspost* and other Catholic periodicals. On the other hand, *Christliche Ständestaat* (a Catholic weekly that employed a number of recent Jewish converts) published an article in 1936, warning against trying to take the wind of Nazi sails through the use of anti-Semitism instead of simply rejecting both Nazism and anti-Semitism.[25]

Schönere Zukunft likewise remained critical of the methods, but not the goals, the German Nazis used in "defending themselves" against the "culturally and morally destructive work of the Jews." In May 1933, the weekly magazine claimed that National Socialism had its positive points. Hitler was serious in wanting the German people to preserve their Christian faith. Likewise, the magazine declared its "solidarity" with the German regime after the book burning spectacles of May 10.[26] In November 1933, *Schönere Zukunft* rejected contentions by what it called the "Jewish boulevard press" that anti-Semitism was unpatriotic and a threat to the state. On the contrary, it was patriotic to say when the Jews held too many positions. The "Jewish press," furthermore behaved as if "a few anti-Semitic excesses in the Third Reich were the most disgraceful and terrible crimes in world history."[27]

Both Chancellor Dollfuss and his successor in 1934, Kurt von Schuschnigg, assured foreigners and Jews that they opposed anti-Semitism and were in favor of equal rights for Jews. However, they often tolerated newspapers and organizations that specialized in hate mongering as long as they had no known connections with the illegal Austrian Nazi party. Even *Sturm über Österreich*, the organ of Schuschnigg's own paramilitary organization called the *Ostmärkische Sturmscharen*, talked about the need for a "better anti-Semitism." However, it also said that the "Jewish danger" had to be met with justice, and it rejected the racial anti-Semitism of the Nazi variety. It even went so far as to say that religious and national Jews should not be regarded as enemies. But it added that Austria had to "escape from the evil spirit of Jewish economics."[28]

In general the Nazi triumph and their expropriation of the Catholics' anti-Semitic slogans put most Catholics in the awkward position of being able to do little more than quibble about Nazi racial theories and occasional use of violence if they did not wish to contradict centuries of their own beliefs. Moreover, the official anti-Semitic program of the Third Reich prior to the *Anschluss* in 1938 rarely went beyond that which had been proposed by right-wing Austrian Catholics long before 1933. In short, neither the Catholic clergy nor the Catholic laity managed to denounce either Nazism in general or Nazi anti-Semitism in particular in unequivocal terms. Guenter Lewy's judgment of the Catholic church in Germany is also applicable to Austria: "A Church that justified moderate anti-Semitism and merely objected to extreme and immoral acts was ill-prepared to provide an effective antidote to the Nazis' gospel of hate."[29] The compromising attitude toward Nazism, which characterized the Catholic church after the *Anschluss*, had its origins long before 1938.

It can be no surprise that the *Antisemitenbund* and its journalistic mouthpiece, *Der eiserne Besen*, greeted the rise of the Nazis in both Austria and Germany with undisguised joy. It regarded the Austrian Nazi party as the only genuinely radical anti-Semitic party even after the Nazis had withdrawn from the organization in 1924. After a major Nazi victory in local and state elections in Austria in April 1932, *Der eiserne Besen* described Hitler as the "only politician . . . of the German people who is willing to oppose Jews openly and ruthlessly."[30]

The Austrian Nazi press was outlawed, along with the party itself, following a series of terrorist acts in June 1933. Thereafter, Nazi newspapers either had to be disguised or go underground. For example, two Viennese newspapers, the *Neue Zeitung* and the *Zwölf Uhr Blatt*, were secretly financed by a pro-Nazi German prince, Prince Philipp Josias von Coburg. Far better known and more successful, at least for a time, was the *Wiener Neueste Nachrichten*. Having little else of a legal nature to read, Viennese Nazis subscribed to that paper almost exclusively so that its circulation rose to over 50,000 by July 1934. It too was subsidized from Germany and printed numerous anti-Semitic articles while carefully avoiding any direct criticism of the Austrian government in order to escape censorship. But the censorship of this and other disguised Nazi newspapers, like the *Innsbrucker Nachrichten*, remained so tight that even German diplomats doubted whether it was worth continuing the subsidies.[31]

The most important illegal Nazi newspaper, and perhaps the only one having a national circulation, was the *Österreichischer Beobachter.* Its sixty thousand copies began appearing on July 28, 1936. One of its favorite activities was publishing the name of "Aryan" shops, a practice that had earlier been followed by the legally published *Deutsches Volksblatt.*[32]

In the anti-Semitic "war of words" which gripped Austria for most of the First Republic, but especially in the early 1920s and early 1930s, the Jewish owned and edited newspapers, which were intended to reach a nonsectarian audience, played an almost neutral role. All manner of evils were ascribed by anti-Semites to this "Jewish press," which was above all allegedly responsible for the "decay" of German (-Austrian) intellectual and spiritual life. It was supposedly leading Christian Germans like a "herd of sheep." When the Germans (-Austrians) were about to defend themselves, the Jewish press managed to incite them against each other. The sale of pornographic books was allegedly solely in the hands of Jews and was causing Christians to lose their morality.[33]

It is a fact that the creation of the liberal Viennese press, like much of the metropolitan press in Germany, was largely a Jewish achievement. Jews wrote the leading articles, advertisements, essays, and business news; they were also highly influential in the publication of books and magazines.[34] However, when anti-Semites referred to the "Jewish press," they rarely meant those newspapers which were written by and exclusively for a Jewish audience such as the assimilationist weekly, *Die Wahrheit,* the daily Zionist paper, *Die Wiener Morgenzeitung,* and its successor, the weekly *Stimme.* Because these newspapers exercised no influence over the non-Jewish population, anti-Semites mentioned them only when they might contain a statement that they, the anti-Semites, found damaging to Jewish interests.

Rather it was the secular and liberal press, owned and edited predominantly by Jews, that drew the wrath of anti-Semites. Although they never said so directly, it was actually the liberalism of the Jewish press to which nationalistic anti-Semites objected. Liberal newspapers like the *Neue Freie Presse* certainly depended on well-educated upper-middle-class Jews for much of their readership, but they also could not have survived without a large gentile audience, another fact that infuriated hard-core anti-Semitic editors and politicians.[35]

Far from supporting specifically Jewish causes, the liberal Jewish-owned and edited newspapers of Vienna actually bent over backward to avoid mentioning Jewish issues such as Zionism or Palestine. Even in the liberal causes that Jewish-owned newspapers did support, it may be doubted just how much influence they really had. Liberalism itself was a dying ideology after the mid-1890s and never more so than during the entire First Republic. These papers were occasionally critical of anti-Semitism in both Austria and Germany, but their criticism did nothing to eliminate it. They were staunchly pro-Austrian and anti-Nazi, yet failed to prevent the Nazi takeover in 1938.[36]

A startling contrast to the continuing anti-Semitism of most Austrian newspapers was the articles and editorials published in a weekly Viennese newspaper called *Gerechtigkeit* (Justice). Its editor was a young woman (born in 1900) named Irene Harand who took up the fight against Nazism and anti-Semitism soon after the Nazi electoral success in Germany in September 1930. After giving a number of anti-Nazi speeches and publishing, at her own expense, a brochure in March 1933 entitled *So oder So? Die Wahrheit über den Antisemitismus* (*Either This or That? The Truth about Anti-Semitism*), she founded *Gerechtigkeit* in August of the same year. By December 1936, it had twenty thousand readers in thirty-six countries. A year later it was being published in French, Czech, and Hungarian, in addition to German. In 1935, Harand also wrote *Sein Kampf: Antwort an Hitler* (His Struggle: An Answer to Hitler), a 347–page rebuttal to the ideas that Hitler had laid out in *Mein Kampf.*[37]

Gerechtigkeit was founded in August 1933. In October of the same year, it became the journalistic outlet for a movement with the ambitious title of the World Organization against Racial Hatred and Human Need, popularly known as the Harand Movement. Branches of the organization were established in no fewer than twenty-seven countries.[38] *Gerechtigkeit* was devoted mostly to current events as they involved anti-Semitism and Nazism. When Chancellor Dollfuss was murdered in July 1934, Harand unequivocally declared that the true murderers, who wanted to put the world back a thousand years, were in Berlin and Munich. No government should have further diplomatic relations with Germany. She was apprehensive about the German-Austrian "July Agreement" in 1936, which reestablished normal diplomatic relations between the two countries because it would allow Nazi culture to reenter the country. However, she overoptimistically thought the Austrian government was aware of the problem so that the fears of Jews and Christians were groundless. Likewise, she tried to be reassuring about the Berchtesgaden agreement between Schuschnigg and Hitler in February 1938, which opened the way to the *Anschluss* a month later, calling it a positive step toward world peace.[39]

Although Jewish newspapers like *Die Wahrheit, Die Stimme*, and the American Jewish journal, *B'nai Brith Magazine*, sometimes wrote flattering articles about the Harand Movement, in general Irene Harand did not receive a great deal of support from Jews. The Nazis charged that the Harand Movement was created and financed by Jewish gold from Amsterdam and New York and was led by a Jewish collaborator of Harand named Moritz Zalman. In reality, however, it had only about 3,500 Jewish members and only one Jew in its twelve-member executive committee. Indeed, Harand sometimes complained about the lack of Jewish support. Many Jews, she said, were indifferent to Nazism, including many she had met in Germany in 1932. They were divided into too many organizations and committees. They frequently did not even answer their critics, either out of false shame or false pride. Much of their money was going to Palestine instead of to the resistance against Nazism. It was depressing, she said, to see how they behaved in the face of danger. Their indolence was downright criminal.[40]

The Jewish Press and the Rise of the Nazis

The factionalism of the Jewish community in Austria can be easily seen in the way the press organs of the particular Jewish parties viewed current events in both Austria and in the neighboring Third Reich. Every Jewish newspaper of Austria—meaning only those newspapers that were written exclusively by and for practicing Jews—interpreted events through the prism of its own passionately held ideology. And every paper looked for events that would prove that its group's program was the only one that held hope for the salvation of all Jews in the future.

Die Wahrheit, speaking for those reform Jews who had a strong sense of Austrian patriotism and love of Austrian culture, espoused an optimistic, liberal philosophy which was inclined to put the most hopeful interpretation on the events of the day. For *Die Wahrheit* and the Union of Austrian Jews which it represented, the Hitler movement was no more than a temporary phenomenon.[41]

Hitler's relatively sudden appointment as chancellor of Germany in January 1933, little more than two months after his party had lost over 2 million votes in the parliamentary elections the previous November, came as a terrible shock to Jewish newspapers in Austria. *Die Wahrheit* believed Hitler's chancellorship would be a real testing time for Jews. But it would also be a

> testing time for the Nazis to see if they could actually put their theories into practice. No radical party has ever been spared a contradiction between theory and practice when it took over power. For us Viennese Jews the developments in Germany are nothing new. We went through the same thing during the rise of the Christian Social party (in the 1890s when its leader, Karl Lueger, became the anti-Semitic mayor of Vienna).[42]

When the Nazis won nearly 44 percent of the vote in the parliamentary elections of March 1933, *Die Wahrheit* remained unruffled. Hitler's victory had been expected because of the Nazis' use of terror against opponents, which had prevented the latter from employing their propaganda and had intimidated weaklings. The Unionist organ expressed hope that the anti-Semitic measures of the new German government would be only temporary. Two weeks later, however, *Die Wahrheit* said that there was so much brutality taking place in Germany that it was hard to believe that such things could transpire in the land of poets and thinkers. Why did the German government attack Jews when they had rejected the Communist party so vehemently? Nevertheless, Jews were being equated with Communists.[43]

Just when things appeared bleakest for German Jews in the late winter of 1933, *Die Wahrheit* was greatly encouraged by statements regarding Jews by leading Nazi officials. The paper's hope that current anti-Semitic measures in Germany would soon moderate seemed confirmed by an interview Hermann Göring had with a Swedish newspaper. The Prussian prime minister said that if Jews remained loyal and went about their business as usual they would have no cause to worry. The Nazi government would merely not allow them to lead the Reich. Perhaps even more reassuring was an angry denial by the party's official mouthpiece, *Der Völkischer Beobachter*, that a pogrom was being planned.[44]

A few weeks later, *Die Wahrheit* was able to report even more encouraging news from Germany when Adolf Hitler himself was quoted as saying that he would treat all religions with justice provided only that all religious groups and races fulfilled their legal responsibilities. Göring also told a reporter that no one would be persecuted simply because he was a Jew. The remarks about tolerating the Jewish religion, however, were actually much less significant than they sounded. For years, most racial anti-Semites, including Hitler himself in *Mein Kampf*, had boasted that they were free of religious prejudice and only rejected Jews for their race, not their religion. However, *Die Wahrheit* chose to attribute this apparent change in attitude toward German Jews to the current international boycott of German exports.[45]

Die Wahrheit was much more cautious in interpreting the significance of Hitler calling off the boycott of Jewish shops in Germany just one day after it had been implemented on April 1, 1933. It disagreed with those optimists who thought that conditions would now improve for German Jews. The German government was trying to eliminate the Jews from the country's economic and cultural life, and this had already been largely accomplished. The early end to the boycott did nothing for those Jews who had already lost their jobs in national and local governments, medicine, journalism, teaching, and the arts.[46]

The pessimistic mood of *Die Wahrheit* continued into the fall of 1933, when the paper compared the fate of the German Jews with the fate of Jews in Spain during the Inquisition. The one difference noted by the paper, however, was that in the sixteenth century a Jew could, as a last resort, escape persecution by converting to Christianity (actually this was not entirely true), an option not available in the Third Reich. Even families whose Jewish ancestors had converted to Christianity two generations earlier were being affected by the Nazis' anti-Semitic legislation.[47]

Die Wahrheit's pessimism was nothing, however, compared with that of Zionist newspapers in Austria. Just three days after Hitler's appointment as chancellor on January 30, 1933, *Die Stimme* used events in Germany as a dire warning about the need to join the Zionist cause before it was too late:

The situation of Jews in Germany is deplorable hopelessness, fear, lack of organization, and helplessness. These are the people who did not recognize, or who did not want to recognize, that liberalism had been passed by. They ridiculed the Zionist idea. They did not realize that their desire for assimilation and their cringing made them look silly.[48]

Die Stimme used the burning of 45,000 "Jewish" books on May 10 as the occasion to renew its criticism of assimilated German Jews. Their super patriotism was now coming back to haunt them. They ought to get rid of their past illusions. But if the future of Jews in Germany looked dismal, the future of Zionism was bright. "We are just as certain of final victory as we are sure that culture will always win over barbarism, morality over naked power, justice over the power-politics of despots." The Zionists would never desert the Jews of Germany, but they demanded the same loyalty from the German Jews.[49]

Der jüdischer Arbeiter, the organ of the working-class Zionist Jews in the *Poale Zion*, was a little less moralistic in its assessment of Hitler's takeover, and was more direct and descriptive. The paper remarked that for the first time a government was in power in Germany whose political path was marked by murder and bloodshed and whose party program was characterized by hatred of other races. But *Der jüdischer Arbeiter* also could not resist the temptation to seek political gain. Hitler, it said, could only appear in a capitalist society. The extreme champions of the capitalist order had helped put him in power. After the Reichstag elections in March, the paper noted (with only a slight exaggeration) that it was the middle classes that had voted for Hitler, not the proletariat. [50]

Die neue Welt, founded by Theodor Herzl and belonging now to the Zionist Revisionists, considered Hitler's assumption of power proof that Herzl was right in saying that only the gathering of all Jewish strength on a national basis could resist anti-Semitism. The disaster that was befalling the Jews of Germany was the result of their being politically leaderless, which left them defenseless. Anti-Semitism could be avoided only if German (and by implication, Austrian) Jews did not interfere in the cultural affairs of Christians. Great harm had come when Jewish writers had criticized German artistic taste and morality. The German Jews had been suffering from the illusions of the emancipationist and socialist ideologies that viewed Zionism as unpatriotic and suspect. A few months after dispensing these opinions, *Die neue Welt*, alone among Austrian Jewish newspaper, made the remarkable statement that "Hitler-Germany was preparing to murder hundreds of thousands of Jews,"[51] although the comment was probably intended more as a scare tactic than as a sober prediction.

Jüdische Presse, the organ of Austrian Orthodox Jews, also found it impossible to pass up the opportunity to moralize about the sins of liberal, assimilated German Jews. Their problems were all caused by their not having been given a religious education, the paper editorialized just after Hitler's takeover. "Orthodox Jews in Germany will certainly be negatively affected by Hitler's takeover of power. But it is undeniable that those assimilated Jews who have turned their backs on Judaism will be hurt the most." Other religions were no less endangered than the Jews. The greater part of the first page of this issue, however, was devoted not to events in Germany, but to denouncing the full and equal enfranchisement of women for Viennese Jewish communal elections.[52]

Both the deep pessimism of *Die Wahrheit* and the attention paid to Jewish affairs in Nazi Germany by Zionist papers proved to be short-lived. From 1934 until the *Anschluss*, reports in the liberal paper about the Jewish persecution in Germany became less frequent, and those that were published were considerably more hopeful. The main reason for this relative lack of interest was that, after the initial outburst of persecution in early 1933, life for German Jews settled down into somewhat more tolerable, if uncertain, circumstances. Many Jews who had emigrated in 1933 actually returned after failing to find employment abroad or after encountering more anti-Semitism in their host country than they had left behind in Germany. At the beginning of 1937 there were still 40,000 Jewish-owned businesses in Germany, and some even received government contracts. Unemployment among Jews, about 10 percent, was far higher than among gentiles, where it had practically disappeared, but was well below the 16.9 percent unemployment rate in the United States at the end of 1936. German Jews also experienced little intervention by the Nazi government in the operation of their school system. Jews were not hindered in the practice of their religion or in the functions of their institutions. Therefore, it appeared to many Jews in Germany and Austria that German Jews might be granted a special autonomous position within the Nazi state.[53]

Already by July 1934, *Die Wahrheit* was beginning to regain some of its lost confidence. In that month it expressed pleasant surprise that the recent campaign of the Nazi government to stamp out criticism had ended not with a pogrom, as feared, but with a purge of the *Sturmabteilung* (SA or storm troopers). It expected this "Röhm Purge" to undermine the Nazi regime.[54]

The biggest news to come out of Nazi Germany in the middle 1930s regarding Jews was the publication of the infamous Nuremberg Laws. Approved by the nazified German Reichstag on September 15, 1935, they classified Jews as subjects rather than citizens of the Third Reich. Since the Holocaust, the Nuremberg Laws have been seen as a major step in the Nazis' anti-Jewish program. Far from reacting in horror, however, as one might presume, the reaction of *Die Wahrheit* and many other Jewish newspapers was relatively restrained. Both Jews and non-Jews actually welcomed the new laws as a return of order. The German Jews now at least appeared to have a permanent albeit lowly status. A decree implementing the citizenship law in November narrowed the definition of a full Jew to include only those people who had at least two Jewish grandparents and who practiced Judaism or who had three or more Jewish grandparents if they were nonpracticing Jews. This definition was the least comprehensive of the four presented to Hitler and was designed to make the *Führer* look moderate at a time when a worldwide boycott of the 1936 Olympic Games still seemed likely. Jews were partially excluded from public life and were increasingly isolated from German society; but this merely codified what had long since been implemented.[55]

The Nuremberg Laws were designed first of all to fulfill the Nazi party's original Twenty-five Point Program of 1920 concerning Jews, and secondly to comply, at least superficially, with the demands of German Zionists for cultural autonomy. The German government, in fact, went out of its way to claim that the laws conformed to demands made by a recent Zionist congress in Switzerland. It did not object to Jews as long as they wanted to be members of a separate Jewish *Volk*. *Die Wahrheit* said that the laws only proved that the opposition of the Union of Austrian Jews to declaring Jews a national minority had been justified. The desire of Zionists for such minority status had led to the loss of basic rights for German Jews.[56]

After two months of reflection, *Die Wahrheit* admitted in November that the Nuremberg Laws did not actually involve a worsening of the long-declining status of German Jews. They were mild in comparison to what German Jews had had to endure in practice up to then. The few Jews remaining in lower-level civil service positions had to give up their jobs by the end of 1935 unless they were veterans of the First World War. Jews also lost their right to vote, but that right had been a farce even for gentiles since March 1933. Surprisingly, the laws had already been revised since September so that the minimum age for Aryan women working in Jewish households had been lowered from forty-five to thirty-five in order to preserve some jobs. In sharp contrast to *Die Wahrheit*, however, was the reaction of the bi-monthly Zionist newspaper, *Der Jude*, which denounced the Nuremberg Laws for condemning the German Jews to a death by hunger. The slaves of Abyssinia enjoyed an enviable status compared with the Jews of Germany.[57]

As the Winter and Summer Olympic Games of 1936 approached, the status of German Jews once again faded from Jewish newspapers in Austria. *Die Wahrheit* was not entirely fooled by this diminution of anti-Semitic activity, however. In April 1936, the paper observed that there had been fewer anti-Semitic measures and demonstrations taking place in the Third Reich than at any time since 1933. This happy turn of events, however, could be attributed to the Olympics. The future still looked ominous for Germany's Jews. By November, *Die Wahrheit* already noticed a worsening of the status of the Jews since the end of the Olympics and noted that the Nazi government's policy toward the German Jews was determined by both domestic and international politics.[58]

In 1937, almost nothing was reported in Austrian Jewish newspapers about the status of Germany's Jews. *Die neue Welt* did comment in May, however, that the anti-Semitic measures in Germany had the purpose of destroying the Jews not just economically but spiritually as well. Anti-Semitism had nothing more to do with the so-called cultural Bolshevism and had become a kind of sport.[59]

The events of early 1938 could no longer be ignored by Austria's Jewish press. On January 26, Hitler dismissed his war minister, General Werner von Blomberg, on the pretext that he had recently married a prostitute. Then on February 4, the *Führer* announced the resignation of the commander in chief of the German army, Werner von Fritsch, and Foreign Minister Konstantin von Neurath, both of whom, like von Blomberg, had been outspoken opponents of Hitler's expansionist plans. Hitler now became the supreme commander of all the German armed forces, and the ardent Nazi, Joachim von Ribbentrop, became the new foreign minister.

The *Jüdische Presse*, while admitting that the ministerial changes represented a turning point, thought it was possible that these events would have a favorable result by causing world public opinion to realize the increased danger to peace. The newspaper was even less alarmed by the meeting at Berchtesgaden between Hitler and Schuschnigg at which the Austrian chancellor was forced to make a number of concessions to the Austrian Nazi party. Fears of a "Trojan Horse" arising from the meeting were highly exaggerated, according to the mouthpiece of Austrian Orthodox Jewry. The same fears had existed after the July Agreement in 1936, but the aftermath proved that these fears were unjustified. The new pro-Nazis in the cabinet were friends of Schuschnigg; patriots had no reason to distrust the Austrian chancellor. A week later the *Jüdische Presse* commented that Austria had overcome greater crises in the past than the present one. As long as Schuschnigg was in charge, the Jews were in no danger. *Die Wahrheit* thought that the only purpose of the Berchtesgaden meeting was to restore peace between Germany and Austria. The Germans had assured Schuschnigg that they would not intervene in Austrian affairs and would not support the Austrian Nazis.[60]

The Austrian Jewish Press in Retrospect

The Jewish press of Austria was silenced the same day German troops entered Austria on March 11, 1938. What conclusions can be drawn regarding its reporting on events in Nazi Germany? Certainly its coverage, such as it was, was reasonably accurate. Unfortunately, the interpretations attached to these events often turned out to be wildly over-optimistic. A few months of stability in the treatment of German Jews could produce a spirit of optimism, which then quickly dissipated with the next wave of persecution.[61] However, in general it would appear that there was far less apprehension about Nazi Germany in the Austro-Jewish press at the beginning of 1938 than there had been in the first half of 1933. Even the last few issues of Jewish newspapers on the eve of the *Anschluss* maintained an unrealistic optimism, although this attitude may have been partly motivated by a desire to suppress a sense of panic among their readers. It is entirely possible, of course, that after five years Nazi persecution had lost some of its shock value or news worthiness. It is even more likely, however, that Austrian Jews, like so many Jews and non-Jews outside Nazi Germany, were overly impressed by the comparatively secure and still reasonably prosperous status of the Jews of Berlin and did not realize the extent to which provincial German Jews were subjected to forced "Aryanization" and emigration.

What is more certain is that a large percentage of those articles that had been published during the first five years of Hitler's rule had been designed more to achieve some partisan advantage by proving that the ideology of one's own political faction offered better protection against the Nazi menace than that of one's rival. The persecution of the German Jews had done nothing to bring the Austrian Jews together in a common front. If anything, they were more divided than ever as they were about to face their ultimate challenge.

Much of the optimism of the Jewish press was caused by the conviction that the Nazi persecution of German Jews in the 1930s was fundamentally similar to earlier ordeals through which Jews had passed and survived. Reference has already been made to the apparent similarity between Adolf Hitler and the turn-of-the-century Viennese mayor, Karl Lueger. Soon after the German Nazis became a mass movement in the fall of 1930, *Die Wahrheit* commented that "Judaism has already endured so much that it will also overcome Hitler and Goebbels."[62] In July 1935, *Die Wahrheit* still considered the Nazi regime in Germany no more than a "passing phenomenon" that would not deflect the Union of Austrian Jews from its assimilationist philosophy.[63]

The Unionist organ was not the only newspaper to express such illusions. The *Jüdischer Arbeiter* thought the Jewish "will to live [was] stronger than the hardest blow that can hit us."[64] *Die Stimme* was a little more cautious, saying that it was wrong to say that Jews would endure the present threat because Jews had endured the persecution of Haman (an ancient Persian prime minister) and Torquemada (the head of the Spanish Inquisition in the 1480s). Jews had survived then because they were united, true to their beliefs, and selfless. They would survive again in Hitler's day, but only if they united behind the blue and white flag of Zionism. Divided into parties the Jewish people were nothing. But united they were a mass that could determine their own fate. The Jewish people might be weak, but they were eternal. Jewry had experienced harder times than the present one. Soon there would be a reaction to Hitler.[65]

What most Austrian (and also German and French) Jews forgot was that they had survived popular outbursts of anti-Semitism so often in the past because they had enjoyed the protection of emperors, bishops, abbots, and aristocrats.[66] Under Hitler, however, legal authority changed from being the protector of Jews to their persecutor. The *Jüdische Front*, the organ of the paramilitary League of Jewish Front Fighters, was virtually alone in debunking the idea that Jews would survive Hitler because they had survived so many hardships in the past. This was a dangerous error, the paper warned, that only made the Jews passive. In the past Jews had been able to escape persecution by simply emigrating to another country where there was no hostility toward Jews. This option no longer existed for the Jewish masses because all countries had (in the paper's only slightly exaggerated words) "hermetically sealed their borders."[67]

The harsh realism of *Jüdische Front* was rare among Austrian Jewish newspapers not to mention non-Jewish newspapers regarding events in the Third Reich. All of the Jewish newspapers were blinded by their faith in their own ideology to save them from the approaching disaster. *Die Wahrheit* was the most realistic and had by far the best coverage of events in Germany, but even it was convinced that its liberal belief in the fundamental goodness of man meant that the Nazis represented no more than a passing phenomenon and that soon the historical march toward religious and ethnic tolerance would resume. Mainstream Zionists represented by *Die Stimme* did not allow events in Germany to distract them from their conviction that separation from gentile affairs and working for a Jewish state in Palestine represented the ultimate salvation for Jews. The paper continued its long-standing policy of ignoring all but the most outrageous manifestations of anti-Semitism. Orthodox Jews, as seen in *Jüdische Presse*, also tended to ignore events in the Reich and preached that separation from gentile society and religious purification would save the Jewish people. Above all, Jewish papers used anti-Semitic events in Germany to "prove" that their philosophy was correct and those of their Jewish rivals were shameful and would only lead to disaster.

Traditionally anti-Semitic newspapers like *Die Reichspost* alternated between complaining that German anti-Semitism was not rigorous enough and criticizing it for not being sufficiently "legal." Nazi and pro-Nazi newspapers, of course, gloated over developments in Germany and used them to increase the popularity of the Austrian Nazi party.

Of all the Austrian newspapers, only Irene Harand's *Gerechtigkeit* consistently and unequivocally denounced the outrages which were occurring in the Third Reich. She was "fighting not so much in behalf of the Jews as to save Christians from becoming beasts." Anti-Semitism was an attack on the soul of humanity and a sin against the Savior. Nazism wanted to rob humanity of its reason and every noble feeling. She claimed—probably overoptimistically—that most Christians were not anti-Semites. However, she argued in *Sein Kampf* that it was not enough simply to reject it. "One [did] one's duty only when one actively took part in defense against it."[68] It is doubtful, however, whether her books and small weekly newspaper did much more than preach to the already converted.

Notes:

1. Letter of Avraham Palmon (Jerusalem) to the author, August 20, 1990, pp. 1–2.
2. Peter Eppel, *Zwischen Kreuz und Hakenkreuz: Die Haltung der Zeitschrift "Schönere Zukunft" zum Nationalsozialismus in Deutschland 1934–1938* (Vienna, 1980), pp. 146–47.
3. Josef Eberle, "Umschau: Katholiken und Judenfrage," *Schönere Zukunft* (April 18, 1926), pp. 699, 701.
4. Pfarrer Wilhelm Senn, "Christen—kauft bei Christen!" *Schönere Zukunft* (December 2, 1928), pp. 197–98.
5. Fritz Csoklich, "Presse und Rundfunk," in Erika Weinzierl and Kurt Skalnik, *Österreich 1918–1938* (Graz, 1983), pp. 719–20; Hedwig Pfarrhofer, *Friedrich Funder: Ein Mann zwischen Gestern und Morgen* (Graz, 1978), p. 296.
6. Pfarrhofer, *Friedrich Funder*, p. 16.
7. Elisabeth Streibel, "Judenfrage und Antisemitismus im Spiegel der 'Reichspost' in den Jahren 1918 bis 1923" (University of Vienna, 1981), pp. 15, 92; Anton Staudinger, "Christlichsoziale Judenpolitik in der Grundungsphase der österreichischen Republik," in Karl Stuhlpfarrer, ed., *Jahrbuch für Zeitgeschichte 1978* (Vienna, 1979), p. 30.
8. Streibel, "Judenfrage und Antisemitismus," pp. 94–95, 99.
9. Ibid., pp. 104, 107, 112.

10. John Bunzl, "Arbeiterbewegung, 'Judenfrage' und Antisemitismus: Am Beispiel des Wiener Bezirks Leopoldstadt" in Gerhard Botz, Hans Hautmann, Konrad Helmut, and Josef Weidenholzer, eds., *Bewegung und Klasse: Studien zur österreichischen Arbeitergeschichte* (Vienna, 1978), p. 263.

11. Hermann Holzmann, "Antisemitismus in der österreichischen Innenpolitik 1918–1935: Der Umgang der drei politischen Lager mit diesen Phänomen" (University of Vienna, 1986), pp. 87, 92.

12. By far the best work on the GDVP is Isabella Ackerl, *Die Grossdeutsche Volkspartei* (Vienna, 1967). See especially pp. 46–47, 71, 312–15.

13. Günter Fellner, *Antisemitismus in Salzburg 1918–1938* (Vienna, 1979), pp. 128–30.

14. Ibid., p. 137.

15. *Eiserne Besen* (Vienna), November 22, 1921, p. 1; December 18, 1923, p. 3; October 1, 1931, p. 1; Ernst Hanisch, "Zur Frühgeschichte des Nationalsozialismus in Salzburg (1913–1925)," *Mitteilung der Gesellschaft für Salzburger Landeskunde*, vol. 117 (1977), pp. 374–75; Fellner, *Antisemitismus in Salzburg*, p. 133.

16. Peter G. J. Pulzer, *The Rise of Political Anti-Semitism in Germany and Austria* (Cambridge, Mass., 1988), p. xvi; Roderick Stacklberg, *Idealism debased: From Völkisch Ideology to National Socialism* (Kent, Ohio, 1981), p. 156.

17. *Die Wahrheit* (Vienna), February 5, 1926, p. 1.

18. *Der Stürmer* (Vienna), August 19, 1933, pp. 1, 3; September 1933, p. 3. *Der Stürmer* should not be confused with another newspaper of the same name published in Nuremberg by the infamous Julius Streicher.

19. *Deutsche Arbeiter-Presse* (Vienna), June 6, 1925, p. 1.

20. *Der Kampf* (Graz), August 8, 15, September 26, 1931.

21. Landespressechef Haintz (Linz) to J. Müller (Vienna), January 16, 1933, and several attached letters. Allgemeines Verwaltungsarchiv (Vienna), Nationalsozialistische Parteistellen, carton 8.

22. Holzmann, "Antisemitismus in österr. Innenpolitik," pp. 81–82; *Deutsche Arbeiter-Presse*, July 25, 1925, p. 3; *Der Kampf*, August 13, 1932, p. 1; *Stürmer*, October 14, 1933, p. 5.

23. Josef Eberle, "Umschau: Katholiken und Judenfrage," *Schönere Zukunft*, April 18, 1926, p. 700.

24. Eppel, *Zwischen Kreuz und Hakenkreuz*, pp. 179–80, 184.

25. Heinrich Busshoff, *Das Dollfuss-Regime in Österreich in geistesgeschichtlicher Perspektive unter besonderer Berücksichtigung der "Schöneren Zukunft" und "Reichspost"* (Berlin, 1968), p. 280; Leopold Spira, *Feinbild "Jud": 100 Jahre politischer Antisemitismus in Österreich* (Vienna, 1981), p. 92; Pfarrhofer, *Friedrich Funder*, p. 300; Sylvia Maderegger, *Die Juden im österreichischen Ständestaat 1934–1938* (Vienna, 1973), p. 203; *Wahrheit*, May 1, 1936, p. 1.

26. Hans Eibl, "Lehren aus dem Aufstieg des Nationalsozialismus, II," *Schönere Zukunft*, May 22, 1933, pp. 790–91.

27. [Josef Eberle] "Eine bemerkenswerte Stimme zur Judenfrage in Österreich," ibid., November 19, 1933, p. 206.

28. *Der jüdischer Arbeiter* (Vienna), March 10, 1933, p. 2; *Wahrheit*, July 28, 1933, p. 1; *Die neue Welt* (Vienna), September 23, 1933 p. 1. The quotation is from *Jüdische Information Zentrale*, January 1935, p. 11.

29. Guenter Lewy, *The Catholic Church and Nazi Germany* (New York, 1964), p. 274.

30. *Eiserne Besen*, November 7, 1930, p. 1. The quotation is from April 30, 1932, p. 1.

31. Rieth (Vienna) to the Foreign Ministry, December 12, 1933; National Archives, microfilm T-120, reel 5415, frame K287243; Papen (Vienna) to the Foreign Ministry, May 8, 1935, ibid., frame K287372; Bade (Berlin) to the German Legation in Vienna, June 24, 1936, ibid., frame K287497.

32. *Deutsches Volksblatt* (Vienna), June 22, 1935, p. 12.

33. *Die Juden im Staate Deutsch-Österreich: Veröffentlichungen des Bureaus für Statistik der Juden* (Innsbruck, 1920), pp. 20–22; Edmund Daniek, *Judentum im Kriege* (Vienna, 1919), p. 28; Georg Glockemeier, *Zur Wiener Judenfrage* (Vienna, 1936), pp. 60, 98; Rudolf Ardelt, *Zwischen Demokratie und Faschismus: Deutschnationales Gedankengut in Österreich 1919–1930* (Vienna, 1972), p. 82;

34. Hans Tietze, *Die Juden Wiens: Geschichte, Wirtschaft, Kultur* (Leipzig, 1933), p. 210; Paul Johnson, *A History of the Jews* (New York, 1987), p. 481.

35. Jonny Moser, "Die Katastrophe der Juden in Österreich, 1938–1945—ihre Voraussetzungen und ihre Überwindung," *Studia Judaica Austriaca*, vol. 5: *Der gelbe Stern in Österreich* (Eisenstadt, 1977), p. 79.

36. *Wahrheit*, December 6, 1929, p. 1; Robert Stricker, *Der jüdische Nationalismus: Die wirksame Abwehr des Antisemitismus* (Vienna, 1929), pp. 42–44, 46; Maderegger, *Juden im Ständestaat*, p. 188.

37. *The Anti-Nazi Economic Bulletin*, December 1936, p. 8; Dokumentations Archiv des österreichischen Widerstandes (Vienna), document 11059, 3a; *Die Stimme* (Vienna), November 3, 1933, p. 3; *Gerechtigkeit* (Vienna), September 3, 1936, p. 1; August 12, 1937, p. 1.

38. *The Anti-Nazi Economic Bulletin*, December 1936, p. 8, Dokumentations Archiv des österreichichen Widerstandes, document 11059, 31; Oscar Leonard, "Anti-Semitism Disgraces Christianity," ibid., document 11059, 4.

39. *Gerechtigkeit*, August 2, 1934, p. 1; January 4, 1935, p. 1, February 23, 1935, p. 1; August 13, 1935, p. 1; July 16, 1936, p. 1; February 17, 1938, p. 1l.

40. *Wahrheit*, October 11, 1933, p. 3; *Stimme,* November 3, 1933, p. 1; Leonard, "Anti-Semitism Disgraces Christianity," Dokumentations Archiv des österreichischen Widerstandes, document 11059, 4; "Die Wahrheit über die Harand Bewegung," ibid., document 11059, 3b; Robert Körber, *Rassesieg in Wien: Der Grenzfeste des Reiches* (Vienna, 1939), p. 265; *Gerechtigkeit*, March 14, 1935, p. 1; April 23, 1935, p. 1; May 2, 1935, p. 1; August 19, 1937, p. 1.

41. *Wahrheit*, July 12, 1935, p. 1.

42. Ibid., February 10, 1933, p. 1.

43. Ibid., March 10, 1933, pp. 3–4; March 24, 1933, p. 1.

44. Ibid., March 10, 1933, p. 4.

45. Adolf Hitler, *Mein Kampf* (Boston, 1943), p. 52; *Wahrheit*, March 31, 1933, p. 1.

46. *Wahrheit*, April 10, 1933, p. 3.

47. Ibid., November 17, 1933, p. 1.

48. *Stimme*, February 2, 1933, p. 1.

49. Ibid., May 18, 1933, pp. 1–2.

50. *Jüdischer Arbeiter*, February 3, 1933, p. 1; March 10, 1933, p. 1.

51. *Neue Welt*, February 3, 1933, p. 1; March 31, 1933, p. 1; March 10, 1933, p. 1. The quotation is from August 1933, p. 1.

52. *Jüdische Presse* (Vienna), February 3, 1933, p. 1.

53. Jacob Boas, "German-Jewish Internal Politics under Hitler, 1933–1938," *Leo Baeck Institute Yearbook*, vol. 29 (1984), pp. 3–4.

54. *Wahrheit*, July 6, 1934, pp. 1–2.

55. Karl Schleunes, *The Twisted Road to Auschwitz: The Nazi Policy Toward German Jews, 1933–1939* (Urbana, Ill., 1970), pp. 125–26; Sarah Gordon, *Hitler, Germans, and the "Jewish Question"* (Princeton, N.J., 1984), p. 122; Johnson, *History of the Jews*, p. 484.

56. *Wahrheit*, September 20, 1935, p. 1.

57. Ibid., November 22, 1935, p. 1; *Der Jude* (Berlin, Vienna), October 1935, p. 1.

58. *Wahrheit*, April 6, 1936, p. 5; November 20, 1936, p. 2.

59. *Neue Welt*, May 11, 1937, p. 1.

60. *Jüdische Presse*, February 11, 1938, p. 1; February 18, 1938, p. 1; February 25, 1925, p. 1; *Wahrheit*, March 4, 1938, p. 1.

61. Avraham Barkai, *Von Boycott zur Entjudung: Die wirtschaftliche Existenzkampf der Juden im Dritten Reich 1933–1943* (Frankfurt am Main, 1988), p. 88.

62. *Wahrheit*, April 24, 1931, p. 4.

63. Ibid., July 12, 1935, p. 1.

64. *Jüdischer Arbeiter*, February 2, 1934, p. 1.

65. *Stimme*, June 2, 1932, p. 2; December 22, 1932, p. 1; July 1934, p. 1.

66. Friedrich Heer, "Judentum und österreichischer Genius," in Friedrich Heer, ed., *Land in Strom der Zeit: Österreich gestern, heute, morgen* (Vienna, 1958), p. 297. On the illusions of German and French Jews about Hitler, see Donald Niewyk, *The Jews in Weimar Germany* (Baton Rouge, La., 1980); p. 143; Leonard Baker, *Days of Sorrow and Pain: Leo Baeck and the Berlin Jews* (New York, 1978), p. 180; and David H. Weinberg, *A Community on Trial: The Jews of Paris in the 1930s* (Chicago, 1977), p. 196.

67. *Jüdischer Front*, April 15, 1937, p. 1.

68. *Jüdische Information Zentrale*, January 1935, p. 9; Irene Harand, *So oder So: Die Wahrheit über den Antisemitismus* (Vienna, 1933), p. 2; the quotations are from Irene Harand, *Sein Kampf: Antwort an Hitler* (Vienna, 1935), pp. 277–78.

The Extermination Of The Jews And The Leading Newspapers Of The Third Reich: *Völkischer Beobachter* And *Das Reich*

Franciszek Ryszka
University of Warsaw

Abstract:

Gleichschaltung: The accession of Hitler and the Nazi party to power in Germany in 1933 brought about a dramatic transformation of all mass-media. The newly created Ministry of Propaganda and Popular Education (*Ministerium für Volksaufklärung und Propaganda*) got control over the whole press and radio in the Reich. As a result of such change, a distinction was made between responsibility for financial operations of the publishers and the content they published. Writers and editors were now made responsible for conveying strictly controlled Nazi doctrine. New dailies and journals appeared to follow this aim, and some existing ones, which were ready to comply with the new rules, considerably extended their outreach.

Ideology of Hate: One—but only one—of the important functions of the mass-media was to incite and propagate hatred of the Jews in the whole world, regardless of where in the world they might live. They were continually accused of activities aimed against the German Reich, and against world peace, understood as "*Pax Germanica*," according to Hitler's imperial, expansionist plans. This was something new, unlike the 19th century anti-Semitism well-known in Europe and beyond, which was mostly based on the racial criteria. The new campaign of hatred regarded the Jew as the "objective enemy," possessing innate and ineradicable vicious features.

The New Model of the Press: The Nazi German press was characterized by two main elements: consolidating the conviction that the German Reich was invincible; and propagating the idea that Germany was continuing to fight the mortal enemy of the traditional European values that had prevailed since the Greco-Roman civilization until the 20th century. At the same time, the press was to support the conviction that life in *die Heimat* was running its normal course. Both *Völkischer Beobachter* (hereafter *VB*), addressed to the average reader, and *Das Reich*, aimed at the better-educated public, continued spreading the ideology and arguments for elimination of the Jew. But in neither paper is there yet any explicit indication as to the methods for the physical destruction of the enemy. The main focus was on how the "Jewish world conspiracy" was backed by Bolshevik communism on the one hand and by the American plutocracy on the other. Such reasoning is especially noticeable and becomes the leading theme in *VB*—and more descriptive in character in *Das Reich*, especially after Hitler's attack of the U.S.S.R. The *leitmotiv* is that European civilization found itself in a state of emergency and that Germany has emerged as Europe's staunch defender.

1. *Gleichschaltung:*

Hitler's accession to power was possible, among other reasons, due to crafty political propaganda, involving mainly direct, verbal contact with the masses. At the beginning, the influence of the NSDAP upon the mass-media had been rather insignificant, but the leaders of the party soon realized the potential power of the press and radio. Before 1939 the daily press was rather well developed in Germany, but only a few of the papers had been directly involved in politics (the party papers). Radio broadcasting was already owned by the state and the audience for radio before 1939 placed Germany above the European average (about 20 listeners per radio-set). Hitler's regime promoted energetic development of radio, with the number of radios per capita in Germany becoming the highest in the world. In 1941 there was one radio-set per ca. six persons, and in this way Germany reached the top world ranking. The main reason for such rapid, dramatic increase was, first of all, mass production of the inexpensive *Volksempfänger* (people's receivers). During the war, radio underwent especially strict control. Listening to foreign broadcasts, from enemy countries, was considered a major crime, punishable in extreme cases by death.

The transformation of the press started when central control was introduced with the creation of a new ministry, specially organized for this purpose, the Ministry of Propaganda and Popular Education (March 13, 1933). A month later, the Union of German Newspaper Publishers (*Reichsverband der deutsche Presse*) was dissolved. The party press fell the first victim, starting with the Communist Party (KPD) daily *Rote Fahne*, and followed by all periodicals published by the KPD. Later victims were the Social-Democratic daily *Vorwärts* and the Catholic Center (*Zentrum*) Party's organ *Germania*. Along with the leading papers published in Berlin, local political papers were also forced to shut down their presses. Brutally imposed changes in the editorial boards and in their publishing plans also struck the "quality" papers, such as, for instance *Vossische Zeitung* or *Berliner Börsenblatt* in Berlin and *Frankfurter Zeitung* in Frankfurt. At the same time the majority of the so-called "*Boulevardpresse*" as well as local newspapers, run by the existing press concerns, remained almost intact. In general, the number of titles drastically decreased; but the ones that remained together with the newly created newspapers increased in circulation in a noticeable way. The peak was reached in 1941, with 22.6 million copies published daily.

Until 1933, the most powerful newspaper publisher was the Alfred Hugenberg firm (August Scherl Verlag G.M.b.H.) whose publications were of conservative and nationalistic orientation. Since 1936 this concern had been indirectly changing its ownership, falling victim to the Nazi indoctrination, typified by Franz Eher Verlag in Munich, which was headed by a brutal but quite efficient editor, Max Amann. He served at the same time as director of the Nazi Party's *Zentralverlag*, which published the *Völkischer Beobachter* and other party papers. Amann was very close to Hitler during his entire career and greatly helped Hitler in his financial dealings so that the Nazi leader indeed became a millionaire in the early Thirties. The Franz Eher company headed by Amann had exclusive copyrights for all Hitler's writings and also monopolized publication of all party newspapers. To give an example: this concern's net profit in 1942 amounted to 63.8 million RM (ca. 25.3 million US dollars). The financial success and profit of such a concern could only be explained by the forced demand for its publications; especially profitable was the sale of *Mein Kampf*, with 12 million copies sold by late 1944. Altogether, the Franz Eher company owned about 70 to 80 per cent of the whole German press.

The majority of specialists dealing with Hitler's Germany view Dr. Joseph Goebbels as the sovereign ruler who managed the overwhelming propaganda machinery, especially from the moment he was appointed Reich Minister for Propaganda and Public Information (March 11, 1933). Indeed, Goebbels was a man of great talents, at the same time being disciplined and dynamic. Undoubtedly he was ruthless, immoral and a great cynic. True, he tried hard to get involved personally and directly in management of the gigantic, mass-media Nazi propaganda machinery. He was the author or co-author of a great many innovative propaganda tricks and ideas. But it was simply not feasible for Goebbels himself to be directly in charge of the rapidly expanding tentacles of the propaganda system. He had a staff consisting of loyal and devoted workers, but he also had serious competitors, with whom he had to reckon; not infrequently, he had nothing else left to do but to comply with their autonomous decisions.

The number one man, responsible for the financial operations of the Nazi party press, was the above-mentioned Max Amann. Political supervision was exercized by Dr. Otto Dietrich, whom Hitler appointed as the Reich Leader of the Press and the Reich Press Chief. Dietrich was made personally responsible for what content and how much of it could and should be conveyed to the German public. The selection of information and commentary to be released to the press agents was his sole domain. He was supposed to follow closely Hitler's personal requirements. Every day Otto Dietrich submitted special reports to Hitler, which the German leader highly appreciated. Dietrich's control over the press was, indeed, more efficient than his superior's. Contrary to prevailing arguments, Goebbels cannot be said to have been free of various doubts and he was only too familiar with hanging back. Elke Frölich (1987), editor of the complete edition of Goebbels' diary, speaks about his "tragic fatalism." This is an interesting comment, pointing to Goebbels' awareness of the unachievable victory, the state of consciousness inciting in him a demand for revenge. Such a state of mind would most probably find reflection in his anti-Jewish propaganda, when the ominous Holocaust operation was approaching its tragic end, while at the same time the Reich's armies were retreating on all the fronts.

Interestingly enough, the ministry headed by Goebbels did not exert direct control over the "ideological" press publications intended for the party activists and other personnel directly or only "ideologically" involved in the hideous act of murder. For years these publications had been engaged in preparing grounds for the "desk murderers" (*Schreibtischmörder*), as well as for the actual killers and the representatives of the next generation, who were to inherit the murderers' legacy. Representative examples of such publications, usually monthly magazines, are the *Nationalistische Monatshefte*, an ideological organ of the Nazi Party (NSDAP), edited since 1930 by Alfred Rosenberg; and the weekly *Das Schwarze Korps*, edited by *Hauptsturmführer* Günter d'Alquen, who had previously served as editor of the political column in *Völkischer Beobachter*. *Das Schwarze Korps* fiercely persecuted the so-called "fellow travelers," who were accused of insufficiently breaking with the past or of keeping good relations with the Jews sometime in the past.

Another periodical of this sort was *Wille und Macht*, addressed to leaders of the Hitler Youth (*Hitlerjugend*). The editor was an ex-leader of Hitler Youth, Baldur von Schirach, since 1941 *Gauleiter* in Vienna, where he was personally responsible for deporting 185,000 Jewish inhabitants. Schirach managed to escape proper punishment when he was sentenced by the Nuremberg International Military Tribunal to 20 years in prison. This was only possible because Schirach and his lawyers argued that he had not been aware at the time that deportation of the Jews equaled a death sentence for them. No one could prove anything to the contrary.

A separate place in the panorama of the Nazi German press is occupied by *Der Stürmer*, a weekly, edited since 1923 by Julius Streicher. That it was a mixture of lies and hatred is the least that can be said about this weekly. *Stürmer* was addressed to indiscriminate readers, appealing to their lowest instincts. It was edited in slovenly fashion and was loaded with aggression. Written texts were always illustrated, often with cartoons, specially selected photographs and clichés or slogans. It was also full of erotic motifs, which at that time could be considered sheer pornography. It is not easy to say how *Stürmer* was financed. In all likelihood, most of the funding was from public money coming from Julius Streicher's home region of Franken (Franconia) where he had served as *Gauleiter*. Very widely distributed, *Stürmer* could be found in all sorts of

public places, wherever people were likely to gather: in public and factory canteens, at bus and tram stops, in the parks, all over Germany. There
were the so-called *"Stürmerkästen,"* special window-displays where the
paper could be read by any passer-by free of charge. Such efforts required
substantial funding. It must have been public money, but how much of it,
what percentage it was, is not easy to say. *Stürmer*'s weekly circulation
was 500,000 copies in 1937, though it would decrease by about a half
during the war. But it was long enough for Streicher as editor of *Stürmer*
to make himself a fortune. Thanks to *Stürmer* and Streicher's dirty financial dealings, he could soon claim ownership of 10 different papers in
Franconia. However, as a result of such machinations, the Nazi Party
decided to hold an official inquiry into his dealings, which finally led to
his resignation from all offices in the NSDAP. Nevertheless, publication
of *Stürmer* continued until the end of the war.

2. Ideology of Hate:

Der Stürmer may serve as an example of extreme "ideological
hatred" in its clearest form. Each Jew was meant to be an object of that
hatred. Characteristically, all Jews presented in different illustrations
looked very much alike, in such a way that they would immediately provoke revulsion in the viewer. Next to hideous cartoons, specially selected
photographs were often placed, and such specific collage would usually
occupy about one-fourth of each issue of the paper. All the texts, illustrated in a similar way, from the beginning conveyed the main massage:
that every Jew is a criminal or a potential criminal; and, if this is fact, then
there can be no place for the Jew within the German community.

Writers for *Der Stürmer* hardly ever mentioned any arguments concerning race, because it was too obvious for them. The written texts were
mostly real stories, taken from judicial records and highly dramatized, or
else some sort of cheap fiction. This crafty mixture of fiction and specially prepared real life stories could have, indeed, convinced the less
sophisticated reader that he was being presented with a reflection of truth
and reality. In the same way, a specially prepared cartoon put next to a
photograph could have made him believe that he was being confronted
with only slightly editorially distorted reality. The Jew emerged from that
fictitious reality as the one who was a great menace to the institution of
private property; anybody's property could easily fall prey because of the

Jew. The Jew was a parasite, always ready to deceive, to blackmail, to indulge. The honor and sex of the German or the Aryan woman were always endangered when the Jew appeared. The Jew was always ready to instigate to a crime, finally becoming a murderer himself. The motif of the "ritual murder" often appeared in the columns of *Stürmer*. In 1934, a special issue was published devoted to that topic (*Sondernummer* May 1, 1934). But the presentation was so extreme that the issue was withdrawn from circulation so as not to jeopardize Germany's reputation, a very important consideration for Hitler at that time. The erotic motif appeared most often with accounts of trials for "*Rassenschande*," miscegenation. *Stürmer* was always ready to incite to more repressive verdicts. According to *Stürmer*, the only just punishment for "*Rassenschande*" should have been the death penalty. *Stürmer* had in a way anticipated the restriction of Jews' rights introduced by the Nuremberg Laws of 1935 (Ryszka 1985, pp. 288, 308f), and by subsequent discriminatory rules.

Although *Stürmer*'s propaganda campaigns did not meet with much approval from the ruling elite of the Reich, the paper's activity can be considered effective as far as anti-Jewish discrimination and "*Rassenschande*" are concerned. Particularly instructive was the case of L. Katzenberg and Irene Seidler (*Der Stürmer*, April 2, 1942). From the very beginning, *Stürmer* had insisted on a death sentence verdict for Katzenberg. Two separate indictments were involved: for "*Rassenschande*" and breach of the social parasite law (*Volksschädlinggesetz*). The formulation of this case in the newspaper was almost identical with the court's explication of the verdict.

The role *Stürmer* played in inciting hatred towards the Jews cannot be underestimated, but the paper's appeal to upper class opinion was only a secondary function. More effective was *Stürmer*'s influence upon the lowest social classes, with whom the prevailing stereotypes could be fairly easily strengthened. The general public in Germany had to be presented with more sophisticated arguments to find the "ideology of hatred" towards the Jew appealing. Anti-Semitism had in fact not been either strongly rooted or widespread in Germany before 1933. The majority of Jews inhabiting Germany (ca. 0.6 per cent of the country's population) had been assimilated, but that did not preclude anti-Semitic opinions and attitudes; yet such a moderate type of anti-Semitism would not answer Hitler's purpose. An anti-Semitism with no reference to religious questions (Nipperdey 1976, pp. 144 f) did not seem adequate for the Nazi concept of "ideology of hatred" and its consequences, which were not quite clear at the beginning. Lay anti-Semitism with elements of racial considerations, as it emerged in the specific German doctrine of socio-biological "*völkisch*" nationalism, could in essence be reduced to the following basic assumptions:

- The Jews comprise a closed group despite their deep assimilation and acculturation.
- This group have their own values and interests, which can be historically defined.
- Those interests and values do not correspond with the dominant values and interests prevailing in the whole society.
- Thus, the Jews cannot be made to obey specific laws and regulations, which a given country would consider indispensable.

The above assumptions may be illustrated by the opinions and attitudes of a great many Frenchmen during the Dreyfus case. At that time it became clear for some leading politicians that Jews in international relations might become the enemy. The French would then start speaking about "*les juifs allemands*," who for the Germans corresponded to "*Ostjuden*," and for the Poles to "*Litvaks*," i. e. "Russian Jews." Thus affiliations with an alien culture were almost always held in suspicion, but when there was a conflict of interests, such affiliations might become a strongly negative characteristic.

The type of anti-Semitism characterized above, the original anti-Semitism as we might call it, was close to what the NSDAP members and their specific environment believed, although their condemnation of the Jews was stronger and their conclusions more decisive. (Hitler, however, and his closest followers had still more different ideas about Jews from the very beginning). But, in general, even after the enactment of Nuremberg Laws, the Jew was still considered a human being protected by law, providing the specific legal regulations and rules were taken into consideration. Because of this, Jews were already then regarded as second-class human beings. Continuation of a gradual process of rapid deprivation of their civic and human rights led to the beginning of the genocidal process, i. e. elimination of the ethnic, cultural, religious and human entity. Here two other enacted laws became most operative: the Law on the Citizenship in the Reich (*"Reichsbürger Gesetz"*) which made Aryan blood a requirement of citizenship in the Reich; and the Law for the Protection of German Blood and Honor. Both laws were issued on the same day, September 15, 1935. Genocide, as most pertinently pointed out by the Polish Jewish lawyer, Rafael Lemkin, who coined the term (Lemkin 1944, pp. 76f), does not have to mean an immediate extermination of a nation or a national group. The process may be gradual, but it originates in a carefully planned and complex action, aiming at destruction of national patterns, and consequently completely distorts the normal course of life. The following constituents, integral to such an action, can be discerned:

- abolition of specific social and political institutions,
- destruction of the culture and language,
- prohibiting cultivation of cultural and religious rituals,
- coercive deprivation of the existing ways and means of existence,
- deprivation of personal security and safety,
- restriction and deprivation of freedom of movement and of following a chosen profession,
- deprivation of protection of health,
- deprivation of respect for a human being and his dignity.

All the above mentioned means of deprivation, restriction and oppression were either fully accepted or more often propagated in the columns of the *"gleichgeschaltet"* (coordinated) German press.

Interestingly enough, the newspapers and the radio attempted to present the cases of the persecution of the Jews in such a way that the readers and listeners might get the impression that everything was being done on their own initiative. We may take as an example the boycott of the Jewish shops in April 1933. For instance, in the *VB* of April 10, 1933 (Berlin edition) there appeared some photographs of the Jewish shops, just to guide Germans to where they should not go for their shopping. Other papers published similar photographs. In those pictures we can see the shops being picketed by the uniformed SA Stormtroopers; next to them big posters, carefully prepared in a special way, urging the boycott.

306 Why Didn't The Press Shout?

A boycott of Jewish trade, services and businesses in general had been conducted previously in Germany and in other European countries, including Poland, but not on such a large scale. Now it was presented as some sort of a market game, but with certain restrictions imposed on free choice. Such strategy might be called "malignant or malevolent hostility" (Boulding 1962, pp. 152 f.), that is a "non zero sum game" strategy, where the opponent's losses are intended to be greater than the winner's gains. Such strategy reached the highest level of malignant hostility when Jews employed in factories important to the German economy were nevertheless sent to the gas chambers.

Despite such actions, in official publications nobody yet dared to suggest that Jews were not human. This did not, however, prevent the spread of propaganda in the mass-media depicting the Jew as a second-class citizen. It may be added that not all publications displayed propaganda as drastic as that in *Stürmer*. Goebbels' statement on this question may be regarded as quite instructive. In 1931, in a periodical intended mainly for internal use of party members (*Der Nazi-Sozi*, December, 1931), Goebbels wrote that Jews were living beings, too. But, he continued, no one would argue that the flea was not also a living being, yet nobody could deny that it was harmful for people, a pest. That is why man does not breed fleas, but puts them out of action, concluded Goebbels. (Mosse 1978, p. 185). The above analogy, which might be taken as just one more insult addressed to the Jew, would soon get a tragic connotation, when in the Nazi idiom the following gradation would appear: "*Untermenschen*" (subhumans), "*Unmenschen*" (nonhumans), and "*Ungeziffer*" (vermin, insects). This idiom would permeate the press columns even before the executioners of the mass murder had started devising the most effective means and methods of killing, just like those applied against vermin.

3. The New Model of the Press:

The most important daily in the Reich was *Völkischer Beobachter*. It had originated in 1919, growing out of an anti-Semitic second-rate newspaper, *Münchner Beobachter*. A year later the new daily was bought by Hitler for a ludicrous sum of money, about 600 dollars. Thanks to Max Amann's crafty financial operations, the paper was soon ready to claim no indebtedness, although its debts had been considerable. The current avalanche of inflation was most conducive to the above financial maneuvers. Until the closing days of the Second World War, *VB* was published with its subtitle: *"Kampfblatt der nationalsozialistischen Bewegung Gross Deutschlands"* (Combat paper of the National Socialist movement of Great Germany), in earlier years just *Deutschlands*. Beneath the title appeared a slogan, *"Freiheit und Brot"* (Freedom and Bread). Since 1921, the chief editor of the paper was Alfred Rosenberg, who maintained considerable influence on the paper.

This meant that Goebbels had no monopoly of control over the German press. Even before the Nazis became the second-largest party (with 1,415,000 members in 1932), *VB* was well established on the press market, having nation-wide distribution. The trio of Amann, Goebbels and Rosenberg, assisted by a skillful team of editors, had constructed a new model newspaper: a combination of a widely circulated quality paper and a typical *"Kampfblatt"* (partisan, combative paper), where the latter type had not been over-represented. *VB* liked to boast of its reliability. The editors were always careful to present the world news quickly and to follow it with commentary. Wherever possible, the paper had its own correspondents. At the same time, when the commentary is analyzed more closely, it becomes evident that its dominant features were ruthlessness, indiscriminate doctrinal interpretation, and no arguing with the reader, but feeding him with one-sided, imperative judgments.

There was no column of *"chronique scandaleuse"* in *VB*, although it was a typical feature for *Stürmer* or the Berlin weekly *Der Angriff* (founded by Goebbels in 1927). The anti-Semitic motif was treated in a principal way, and only the most important points were mentioned. The evil ascribed to the Jew was discussed against the background of world international politics. Usually the news column on the first page of the paper would carry something on this topic. This would typically be followed by a one-column editorial, written by Goebbels or by Rosenberg—hardly ever by lesser known writers.

It is interesting to trace the ways the paper reacted to anti-Nazi actions in the world, especially the ones which could be easily publicized. In February 1936, in Davos, Switzerland, a 22-year-old Jewish student, David Frankfurter, shot Wilhelm Gustloff, head of the Swiss Nazi organization; less than three years later (November, 1938), 17-year- old Herszel Grynszpan (Grünspan) mortally wounded a German diplomatic secretary Ernst vom Rath in Paris. The *VB* exploited the two events to show the underground activities of *"Ostjuden"* against Germans, as well as to tell its readers that the *"Ostjuden,"* the Jews from the East (Frankfurter came from Yugoslavia and Grynszpan from Poland), were just tools in international Jewry's hands, part of a world-wide Jewish conspiracy. It was, however, odd that when the case of Grynszpan's attempt on vom Rath's life would later become a pretext for the infamous *Kristallnacht,* the paper did not attempt to exploit the event. Almost simultaneously with the attack on vom Rath, Kemal Atatürk, dictator of Turkey, died and *VB* (of November 9, 1938) devoted much more space to this piece of news than to vom Rath. On the next day, the paper devoted two long columns to the "March on Feldherrnhale" in 1913 and its twenty-fifth anniversary. Vom Rath's case was presented as secondary news, in an article given a symptomatic title: *"Das neueste Opfer jüdischer Mordhetze"* (The newest victim of the Jewish incitement to murder). In the commentary to this report, it was implied that the instigators of what *VB* called *"Die jüdische Bluttat von Paris"* (The Jewish bloody deed of Paris), "were two Jewish emigrants: Georg Bernard and Emil Ludwig." The pogrom of *Kristallnacht* had found no reflection in *VB* except for the comment that "the whole of Germany seeks compensation" from the Jews (*VB*, November 11–13, 1938). The editorial written by Goebbels (November 12, 1938) again underlines the role played by the "secret perpetrators" (*"Hintermänner"*), "who go unpunished." It may be concluded that the murder of vom Rath was presented exactly according to the favorite model promoted by *VB*.

The circulation of *VB* reached its peak during the war. Although its total press run was never made public, it may be assumed that in 1941–42 the three parallel editions of *VB* (Berlin, Münich and Vienna) reached as many as 8 million copies, which corresponded to the wartime membership in the NSDAP. The paper reached both the front and wherever any Germans could be found serving in the occupation administrative and economic systems. The readers everywhere received the paper quite promptly, with only slight delays. Most space in the paper was now devoted to the news from the war front. Everyday, the front-pages carried a special news bulletin from the *Oberkommando der Wehrmacht*, the military high command. Further columns were devoted to recent military promotions, honors and medals, where the texts were always accompanied by photographs of the heroes, often provided with biographical notes. The middle pages of every issue were devoted to domestic and local news. An attempt was made here to show to the reader and to convince him that life and work in the *Heimat* ran their normal course. Fairly much space was reserved for entertainment: sport, film, theater and some local news. Interestingly enough, there was little advertising in *VB*, which may be explained by the financial well-being of the paper. At the end, often in the last column, the readers could find humor. It was there that the reader could encounter most Jews. Characters in the anecdotes or in cartoons were usually presented in political context and with reference to the ongoing war. The style of presentation was not quite as extreme as in *Stürmer*, but something in a similar mode.

We might then conclude that the Jewish motif did not take as much space in the paper as one might have expected. More of it appears after June 22, 1941, and the invasion of the Soviet Union. In the Sunday edition, carrying the above date, the prime story is a report on the visit of Alessandro Pavolini, Italian Minister of Culture, in Germany at the personal invitation of Goebbels. On the next day, in the Monday issue, when the war against the Soviet Union had already been fought for 24 hours, it eventually became the prime news story. The whole issue was devoted to the war. A big headline on the front-page, in the lead column, read: "*Grossdeutschland Wehrmacht in Osten angetreten*" (Great Germany Military in Action in the East). The principal space in the paper was given to Hitler's appeal, which had been read by Goebbels himself in a special broadcast of the *Grossdeutsche Rundfunk* at 5.30 a.m. on the same day. In the opening part of Hitler's speech we find the phrase warning against the Jewish-Bolshevik attempts to rule over the whole world ("*die jüdische-bolschevistische Machthaberschaft*"). In the early weeks of the war (*VB* of July 3, 9, 10, 12, 1941), we find descriptions of "Jewish-Bolshevik machinations" and "Jewish-Bolshevik crimes;" the order of the components here, with "Jewish" in the first place is quite telling. The tone was maintained in such stories as "*Der Bolschevismus enthüllt sein jüdisches Gesicht*" (Bolshevism reveals its Jewish face), or "*Litvinov-Finkelstein tritt hinter der Kulisse hervor*" (Litvinov-Finkelstein appears behind the scenes). Next to articles with the above titles there appeared reports of the just uncovered victims of Soviet mass murders in Lvov and in Luck (facts, álas). In the commentary to the reports we read about the "shameless Jewry," because the Soviet propaganda accused the Germans of the crimes.

In late July (July 25, 1941), a new series appeared in *VB* entitled *"Erlebnisse hinter der Sovjetfront"* (Experiences behind the Soviet front). Here we find descriptions of the living conditions in Russia, with direct accusation of the Jews, who were blamed for the prevailing poverty, for propaganda lies, and for the terror raging under the Soviet regime. The dominant content of the writings, however, is the euphoria caused by the successes at the war front and boasting of the supposed "unity of mind" at the home front (*"Heimat und Front"*). Even when the offensive on Moscow was halted, the pattern of the news and commentary in *VB* remained almost unchanged. Obviously there was now less talk about the successes and there appeared fewer photographs of "Jewish-Bolshevik subhumans," who were carefully selected from among the prisoners of war. There was now more said about the "heroism and the power of resistance of the German soldier" and about the ways the *Heimat* was supporting the war front, for instance, by organizing collections of heavy clothing for the soldiers who had to fight in bitter winter cold.

Interestingly enough, very little appeared in *VB* about Jews in the spring and summer of 1942, exactly when the mass murder of the Jews was in full swing. Obviously, one could expect neither a news report nor even a slight hint about the matter, for disclosure of the awful secret meant serious consequences for anyone who dared. Probably the only exception involved Kurt Gerstein, an SS officer who witnessed the sending of Jews to the gas chambers at Bełżec, probably in August 1942, and attempted to make it public. (Henkys 1967) The *VB*'s restraint in writing on the Jewish question would suggest that perhaps after the "final solution" there was no need to deal with this matter much longer, especially in the face of rapid progress on the eastern front and recent successes in Africa. In July and August 1942, when the *"Endlösung"* grew to horrifying proportions (including the liquidation of the Warsaw and Lvov ghettos), *VB* presented the current reports from the war front but dealt most extensively with the following topics: the opening of the great exhibition of German art in Munich (July 5, 1942); the German Soccer Championship (July 6, 1942); the Germany-Bulgaria Soccer Match (July 16, 1942); and a series of war correspondents' reports, *"Zwischen Berlin und Wjasma,"* that included a report from occupied Poland (the General Government) and scenes from Warsaw—but with not a single word about the Warsaw ghetto (July 16, 1942), from which 300,000 Jews were deported between July 22 and September 12, 1942 (Yahil, p. 378).

The picture *VB* had tried to convey, of harmony in *die Heimat*, where law and order were supposed to prevail (with not a word on the terrifying court trials over violations of the Nazi war laws) was somehow blurred by the bombing of the major German cities: Hamburg, Cologne, and other cities in the Rhineland. But very little was published on the damages inflicted by the bombardments and on the actual victims. Instead, there was much written about the meetings Goebbels had with inhabitants of the bombed cities to cheer them up (*VB* July 25–27, 28; August 13, 18, 1942). Fairly optimistic reports on the "German deed" across the occupied eastern territories could be found in *VB* (July 17 and August 16, 1942). Characteristically, there is not a word published in those reports that there used to live certain people called Jews on those territories.

The above conclusions are drawn on the basis of a close analysis of carefully selected pieces on news and commentary published in *Völkischer Beobachter* during the tragedy of Holocaust. In the following months, until the Battle of Stalingrad, the same editorial pattern for publishing the newspaper was preserved. After Stalingrad, when the awareness of defeat reached Germany (although only one lost battle was mentioned) and the German retreat started, strong anti-Jewish propaganda was revived again. It was now dominated by two main motifs: the Jewish-Bolshevik threats for the future, especially in the face of the recent demonstration of Bolshevik strength, and the Jewish-American plutocracy. Presented as most dangerous, though, were the tight links between the two groups. For instance, in *VB* of February 4, 1943, we find the following editorial: "Our answer—fight with the Bolshevik barbarism and . . . their Jewish-plutocratic allies." The United States of America is now portrayed as being ruled by the Jews. In the newspaper's commentaries we now often find photographs of President Roosevelt's associates with specially prepared biographical notes to identify people like Brandeis, Frankfurter, Morgenthau, and very often "*der Jude Davies*," the former American Ambassador to Moscow. (*VB* April 16, 1945) A British intellectual, Harold Laski, would often join the American Jews in the columns of *VB*. The Jewish generals in the Red Army (*VB* April 11, 1943) are often presented next to "American capitalists and gangsters" (*VB* May 18, 1943). The Katyń case, which did not leave the columns of *VB* for almost a month (April 16–May 13, 1943), was depicted as "the work of destruction performed by the Jewish butchers" (*VB* April 17, 1943). Interestingly, the Polish motif ends with news about the creation of the Polish army division in the U.S.S.R., headed by "a Jewish colonel, Berlin;" of course, his real name was Berling.

Whenever threats to European values, culture and historic monuments are discussed in *VB*, the uppermost place is given to Jews, who are to be blamed for all the evil. For instance, the bombardment of Rome was called by *VB* (July 27, 1943) *"jüdisch-sadistische Zerstörungswut"* (Jewish sadistic lust for destruction), a barbarous act committed by the "British and American air gangsters." In due course, the language used in *VB* to describe the military operations of the Allies turns more malicious and insulting. The "direct clashes" with the Jews in the years before the war had broken out are now recalled. During August 4–6, 1943, the *Völkischer Beobachter* carried a series called "The Jews Who Are Not to Be Forgotten," mentioning some well known figures in art and in politics of the Weimar Republic years, such as the assassinated Walther Rathenau. The conclusion: "this is the way one should deal with the Jews." At the same time not a word about the "Final Solution" was published. The only exception during the whole of 1943 was an extensive report from Sofia (March 9, 1943), where we find a blunt statement that "the Jewish problem in Bulgaria has to be solved uncompromisingly." As is well known, Bulgaria did not join in the Holocaust, insofar as its own Bulgarian Jews were concerned.

Analysis of the content published since 1940 in the weekly *Das Reich*, subtitled "German Weekly Newspaper," and edited by Goebbels himself, confirms the existence of the same editorial pattern, typical for the Nazi press. In this case, the fact that the weekly was addressed to better educated people did not make much difference. For the price of 30 Pf. the reader would get about 26–28 columns every week, containing essays, news reports, news on cultural and academic life, and book reviews. Goebbels himself contributed to almost every issue with editorials on general topics. His writing published in *Das Reich* was far less aggressive than his texts appearing in *Völkischer Beobachter*. Goebbels really cared for *Das Reich* and tried to maintain its elite character. Typical content included articles on "The War Front," that is military actions but seen in a larger political context; and *"Heimat,"* revealing the German contribution to European culture, but seen from the European perspective. A third element was propaganda against the enemy, but, again, more moderate than in the daily press. As an example, we might take an article by Dr.

Hochberg, from the Institute of History of the New Germany (*Institut für Geschichte des neuen Deutschland*) under the title *"Perspektiven den Judenfrage"* (Perspectives on the Jewish Question) (*Das Reich* no. 39, September 28, 1941). The main argument developed in the article concerns the emancipation of the Jew according to the model developed by the French Revolution. The conclusion is that such emancipation had been harmful to those countries, which decided to carry it out.

Goebbels himself, who wrote in *Das Reich* on a variety of subjects, often pondered the future of European culture, obviously perceived according to the Nazi mold, where there certainly was no room for the Jew. From time to time, *Das Reich* invited foreign authors and welcomed their contributions. Such contributions would usually come from the countries occupied in the West or from the neutral ones. There hardly ever appeared any reports from the countries occupied in the East. One such example describes life in German-occupied Poland (*Das Reich*, no. 44, November 2, 1941: W. Oehlman, *"Verwandelter Osten. Reise in Generalgouvernement"* [Transformed East. Travel in the General Government]). The article includes extensive references to Polish culture; an isolated case, because generally, according to the image presented by German mass-media, the Polish culture never existed. Like several previous examples cited above, there are only slight references to Jews to be found. Here the article's author laconically states that they live in "isolated quarters" (mention is made of Lublin), but the word "ghetto" is not used. This may be very typical for the weekly *Das Reich*. In general, *Das Reich* may be regarded as a specific case of mass-media manipulation; not much more that might interest the reader curious about the fate of the Jews can be gained from the analysis of this weekly. *Das Reich*'s role with regard to the Jewish question is only secondary.

Comprehensive review of the whole Nazi press would require extensive and long-range studies. An analysis based on a limited selection leads one to a rather banal conclusion, that the media were skillfully manipulated and used as an important instrument of power. Already before the war's outbreak, the German press had played its part in preparation for mass murder of the Jewish people. The war only provided further arguments for the necessity of getting rid of the Jew. But the papers always tried to present the question in such a way that the German people could be assured of their "civilizing mission" and that their deep-rooted convictions would remain intact. This does not mean, however, that the mass-media were inclined—even for a moment—to give up their campaign of spreading hatred. The horrors and atrocities remained well covered, and all the blame was ascribed to the enemy, but millions of Germans were directly or indirectly confronted with such experiences, first at the war front and later on the home front. The mass-media never directly called for murdering Jews, but they provided enough arguments to make the public feel collective hatred for the whole Jewish community. That hatred easily leads to crime is a banal but unquestionable truth.

WORKS CITED

Boulding, Kenneth. *Conflict and Defense: A General Theory*. New York, 1962.

Fröhlich, Elke. "Joseph Goebbels und sein Tagebuch. Zu den hand-schriftlichen Aufzeichnungen von 1924 bis 1941," *Vierteljahreshefte für Zeitgeschichte*, 35 (1987), no. 4, pp. 489–522.

Henkys, Reinhard. *Die nationalsozialistischen Gewaltverbrechen. Geschichte und Gericht*. Stuttgart-Berlin, 1964.

Lemkin, Rafael. *Axis Rule in Occupied Europe: Laws of Occupation: Analysis of Government: Proposals for Redress*. Washington, D.C., 1944.

Mosse, George L. *Toward the Final Solution: A History of European Racism*. New York , 1978.

Nipperdey, Thomas. *Gesellschaft, Kultur, Theorie. Gesammelte Aufsätze zur neuren Geschichte*. Göttingen, 1976.

Ryszka, Franciszek. *Państwo stanu wyjątkowego. Rzecz o systemie państwa i prawa Trzeciej Rzeszy* (The State of Martial Law: A Study of the Juridical System of the Third Reich). 3th ed. Wrocław-Warszawa, 1985.

Schwarzwäller, Wulf C. *Hitlers Geld. Bilanz einer persönlichen Bereicherung*. Rastatt, 1986.

Yahil, Leni. *The Holocaust*. New York, 1991.

Italian Journalism

An Italian Jewish-Fascist Editor:
Ettore Ovazza and *La Nostra Bandiera*[1]

Alexander Stille
New York City

An Italian Jewish-Fascist magazine called *La Nostra Bandiera* (Our Flag) was published between 1934 and 1938. The idea of a Jewish-Fascist magazine may sound like an oxymoron to contemporary ears, but was hardly so in the context of the Italy of the 1930s. Mussolini had gone to some pains to distinguish himself from his German protégé and Italian Fascism had been in power for sixteen years before officially embracing anti-Semitism in 1938. There were at least five Jews among the 119 souls who participated in the meeting that founded the Italian Fascist party in 1919. Some 229 Jews were awarded the March on Rome Certificate given to those who made an exceptional contribution to the Fascist revolution. To a conservative-minded Jewish Italian, of strongly nationalistic sentiments, there was nothing unusual about supporting the Fascist cause.

Among the 229 Jews who were awarded the March on Rome certificate was a man named Ettore Ovazza, a young Jew from the city of Turin. Ovazza was from a wealthy banking family that had thrived in the newly-unified Italian State and had ties to Italy's royal family (also from Turin). For the Ovazzas, patriotism was almost a second religion. Indeed, family patriarch Ernesto Ovazza (Ettore's father and the president of the Jewish community of Turin) had the words "Fatherland, Faith and Family" placed on his tombstone. Ettore Ovazza (like his brothers) fought in World War I, participated in the disastrous Italian defeat at Caporetto and enthusiastically joined the Fascist cause when it appeared that Italy might be the site of a second Bolshevik revolution.

By the 1930s, roughly one third of Italian Jewish adults were members of the Fascist party, about the same proportion as the rest of the

Italian population and there was no particular reason for Jewish Fascists to differentiate themselves from other Italian Fascists.

The creation of a formal Jewish-Fascist movement in Italy in 1934 followed on the heels of the rise to power of Hitler in Germany in the previous year. In fact, it is my contention that the Italian press's handling of anti-Semitism in these years mirrored quite closely Mussolini's often shifting foreign policy concerns. The ebb and flow of anti-Semitism between 1933 and 1938 can generally be understood as following the ups and downs of Fascist Italy's somewhat ambivalent relationship with Nazi Germany. Naturally, as the relationship solidified between 1936 and 1938, the tide of anti-Semitism in the press appeared to gain momentum preparing the way for the laws of 1938. External events and cynical geopolitical calculation—the wars in Ethiopia and Spain, the axis alliance with Germany—determined the regime's attitude toward Italy's Jews. And yet, Ettore Ovazza and Italy's Jewish Fascists were deeply convinced, and were encouraged to believe, that it was the behavior of the Italian Jews—their manifestations of loyalty or disloyalty toward the regime—that would determine the Jewish policy of Mussolini's government.

Initially, Mussolini greeted Hitler's victory with mixed emotions. On the one hand, it was a confirmation of his own movement, and yet he could not help expressing certain reservations about the excesses of the Nazi movement, in particular its obsession with the Jews. In his widely publicized conversations with German Jewish journalist Emil Ludwig in 1933, Mussolini made a stinging criticism of Nazi racial theories, saying, for example, "National pride has no need of the delirium of race." The Nazis, in turn, referred to the Italian regime as promoting "kosher Fascism."

The eventual alliance between Hitler and Mussolini hardly seemed inevitable. Germany had been Italy's enemy in World War I and many Italians were nervous about pan-German expansionism. Hitler's ambitions to annex Austria would place the Third Reich at Italy's northeastern border and threaten the regions of Italy with substantial German-speaking populations.

At home, Mussolini's policy toward the Jews was equally ambiguous. On the one hand, he opened Italy's borders to several thousand German Jewish refugees, provided they kept their noses out of politics. On the other, he allowed the more fanatic pro-German Fascists to start a small but insistent anti-Jewish campaign. The most prominent of these were *Il Regime Fascista* of Roberto Farinacci, and *Il Tevere* of Telesio Interlandi. They did not espouse biological racism but inveighed against the Jews on national political grounds. The Jews could not be trusted because they were an unassimilated cosmopolitan group, whose strong international loyalties to other Jews around the world made them suspect on patriotic grounds. Many of their attacks were directed at Zionism, which seemed the purest expression of the so-called "Jewish International."

The new anti-Semitic rhetoric fell largely on deaf ears: several prominent Fascists came out strongly in the Jews' defense, and a few months after Hitler's election as chancellor of Germany it seemed to die down. But the campaign was revived by a news story that appeared on the front page of most Italian newspapers on April 1, 1934, announcing the foiling of a "Jewish anti-Fascist plot" against the regime.

The incident itself was minor. Two young Jews from Turin (one of whom was actually only half-Jewish) were caught at the Tresa Bridge trying to smuggle anti-Fascist literature from Switzerland into Italy. Subsequently, another fourteen of their Turinese friends and acquaintances (nine of them Jewish) were arrested for anti-Fascist activities.

The fact that the incident was reported at all in a society where news of dissent was generally suppressed and that many newspapers picked up the anti-Jewish theme was an alarming signal to a Jewish public already nervously scanning the controlled Fascist press for signs of Hitlerian influence. In all likelihood, Mussolini permitted a debate on Jews and Zionism to be stirred up because, in this period of rapprochement between Italy and Germany, he felt that he might have to align his racial policies with those of Hitler or wanted at least to create the ideological preconditions for this option.

But Ettore Ovazza took the propaganda at face value and blamed anti-Fascist Jews for bringing the threat of anti-Semitism to all Italian Jews. As soon as he learned of the arrests, Ovazza fired off the following telegram to Mussolini in choppy telegraphic style:

> In this most sad hour for the Jews of Turin, while a handful of renegades go to their well-deserved, severe punishment, I recall sacrifice Italian Jews for the greatness of Italy and send to our

great and most beloved Duce expression profound pain and scorn confirming the unshakable devotion to the cause of the Fascist Fatherland.

Although some Jews had the self-possession to protest the fact that a single incident was being exploited to tar an entire people, a large number, like Ovazza, felt that it was necessary to make a show of public penitence. In a flood of petitions, open letters to newspapers, and telegrams to Mussolini, prominent Jews throughout Italy expressed shock, outrage and anger at the so-called anti-Fascist elements within their community and begged the dictator not to blame the great majority of loyal Jews for the sins of a few. A number of local Jewish communities (Turin, Milan and Verona) went so far as to make generous donations, as if to expiate some collective guilt.

The Jews' public breast-beating did not mollify the extremist, pro-German wing of the Fascist party, which adopted a new, menacing, inquisitorial tone. A month after the arrests, Farinacci's *Regime Fascista* wrote:

> We do not exclude the possibility that there are good Jews, but it is also our right to demand clarity.
>
> Does there or does there not exist a Zionist movement in Italy?
>
> To deny it would be to lie. The existence of a newspaper in Florence [the Zionist magazine *Israel*] should cut short any discussion. And so these others who claim to be anti-Zionists, what are they doing to fight the other Jews who believe they have another Fatherland that is not Italy?
>
> So far, nothing.
>
> Therefore, it is necessary to decide. We have reached a point at which everyone must take a position. Because he who declares himself Zionist has no right to hold any responsibilities or honors in our country.

The editors of *Israel* responded in an unruffled, dignified manner.

> With all due respect to *Regime Fascista*, we must ask . . . What new has happened to make something that up until yesterday,

until today, was perfectly acceptable, suddenly intolerable and prohibited?

Regime Fascista gives the impression of having discovered that there a Zionist movement exists in Italy, stating rhetorically, "to deny it would be to lie." Whoever denied it?

While the Zionists of *Israel* had the presence not to be drawn into this specious debate, Ovazza and many of his friends in Turin felt that they had to meet Farinacci's challenge by fighting "the other Jews who believe they have another Fatherland that is not Italy." He and other patriots led a coup d'état in the government of Turin's Jewish community; the old administration resigned en masse (as if they were somehow responsible for the incident), and Ovazza became acting administrator until a new council could be elected. At the same time, he founded *La Nostra Bandiera*. Ovazza was convinced that the surest way to ward off the threat of anti-Semitism was to loudly and publicly assert the absolute loyalty of Italy's Jews to the national cause.

Ovazza's front-page editorial announcing the birth and purpose of the paper was a strident call to arms, entitled "An End to Ambiguity:"

We are soldiers, we are Fascists. We feel equal to all other citizens, especially in our duties toward the Fatherland . . .

Ovazza alluded to the arrests of the so-called "Jewish anti-Fascists" but the bulk of his polemical energies were spent attacking Italy's small Zionist movement—despite the fact that they were completely extraneous to the Turin arrests. In fact, *La Nostra Bandiera* was needed, he explained, to balance the negative and unpatriotic image of Jews created by the Zionists' newspaper, *Israel*.

The attitude of a group of Zionist-nationalist intellectuals who, strangers in Italy, make much noise because they have a newspaper of their own, made it necessary, we thought, to have one of our own.

Otherwise our prolonged silence might be interpreted as either indifference or tacit consent.

Ovazza, interestingly enough, did not condemn "philanthropic" Zionism, charitable aid to Jewish settlers in Palestine escaping persecution in Europe; what he rejected was political Zionism, the creation of an independent Jewish state. "We clearly reject the Zionists who live . . . with one eye looking to Rome and the other to Jerusalem," he wrote, calling Zionism "the greatest ally of racist policy."

Following the logic of Farinacci, Ovazza demanded that all Italian Jews clarify their position and declare their "full and absolute adhesion to the Fatherland." Finally he insisted that whoever does "not feel the sacred and obligatory love for the Fatherland where he is born should remove himself from his own country."

This extreme position—almost advocating the expulsion of Zionist Jews from Italy—went far beyond anything Fascism had ever articulated. Ovazza and the *"Bandieristi"* divided the Italian Jews into bitterly warring camps precisely at a time when they faced an extremely dangerous common threat.

Although based in Turin, the *Bandiera* movement had prominent followers throughout Italy. During its first months, the magazine had a weekly circulation of about 2,800 copies and had 1,100 regular subscribers. If its actual readership was somewhere between the two figures, one can infer that roughly 2,000 or about 15 percent of Italy's 15,000 Jewish households received the paper.

While the bulk of their contributors were highly assimilated middle- and upper-middle class Jews like the Ovazzas, a number of Italian rabbis also wrote for the paper.

In June 1934,—the month after starting his magazine—Ovazza organized special elections to form a new governing council for Turin's Jewish Community. In true Fascist style, there was only one electoral list, composed of prominent Jewish Fascists, who were elected almost unanimously (733 out of 741 votes were favorable, with fifty-seven percent of eligible community members voting). A number of Jewish communities in other cities—Rome, Genoa, Ancona and Livorno—followed Turin's lead and elected Fascist administrations in tune with the *Bandieristi*.

But just as external events (the rise of Hitler) had created the crisis, they acted again to dissipate it, if only momentarily.

When Ovazza telegraphed Mussolini in June of 1934 to announce the triumph of the militant Fascists in the Turin elections, the dictator was reeling from his first encounter with Hitler, which Mussolini described as a "collision." A few days later, Mussolini was shocked to hear that Hitler had arranged the murder of many of his closest followers in the infamous "Night of the Long Knives"—a crime that went far beyond anything ever contemplated by Mussolini's black shirts. On July 24, pro-Nazi conspirators murdered the premier of Austria, Engelbert Dolfuss, who was a Mussolini protege, in an attempted coup d'état. Mussolini was beside himself with rage and immediately sent Italian troops to the Austrian border at the Brenner Pass and prepared for war.

Mussolini now regarded Hitler as his greatest menace. "It would mean the end of European civilization if this country of murderers and pederasts were to overrun Europe," he told one foreign diplomat at the time. With this souring of German-Italian relations, the polemical debate over Jews, Zionism and Fascism quickly evaporated. In fact, Mussolini began actively courting the leaders of the international Zionist movement. "I am a Zionist, myself," he told Nahum Goldmann of the World Jewish Congress.

For a time, Mussolini believed that the Zionists might serve as his beachhead in the Middle East and as a useful ally in Italy's plans to wrest control of the Mediterranean from the British. In his meetings with Goldmann, he actively tried to outbid the British for the Zionists' loyalties: "You must have a real state, not the ridiculous National Home that the British have offered you. I shall help you create a Jewish state."

The sudden reflowering of relations between Mussolini and the Jews took the wind out of the Jewish-Fascist movement's sails. In fact, the government began leaning on Ettore Ovazza to close down *La Nostra Bandiera* in November 1934, the same month that Mussolini met with Goldmann. As documents in the Italian State Archives reveal, the government asked Ovazza to stop publishing *La Nostra Bandiera*, a move that Ovazza had to lobby hard to avoid. Ovazza wrote a formal appeal to the government:

Shutting down this newspaper while allowing the weekly paper Israel in Florence to continue, would allow the (fortunately) small groups of anti-Nationalist and Zionist-nationalist Jews to regain their breath and cry victory.

As a face-saving compromise, he was able to continue publication by agreeing to transform the paper from a political weekly paper into a bi-weekly publication that would deal mostly with Jewish culture.

The fact that the Jewish Fascists were being muzzled by the government while the Zionists continued to publish freely never caused Ovazza or any of his chief associates to rethink their relation to Fascism. They never grasped the fact that Mussolini's policy toward the Jews was pure-ly expedient: it depended on larger political interests and not on the loy-alty or disloyalty of the Italian Jews. The crisis over Zionism and the Jews' supposed double-loyalty had been manufactured for political pur-poses and for the same reasons had been made to disappear. Now that Mussolini had decided the Zionists could be useful, the government regarded the ideological fervor of the *Bandieristi* as an embarassing nui-sance.

The next major international event that affected relations between the regime and Italy's Jews was the invasion of Ethiopia. Initially, it seemed to bring about even greater closeness, as most Italians—Jews and gen-tiles—seemed to rally around the Italian cause, which was acting in defi-ance of international sanctions. Synagogues and churches across Italy organized special ceremonies for the so-called "Day of Faith," in which Italian women were supposed to donate their gold wedding rings to be melted down for the war cause.

A number of Jewish communities, including Turin, went beyond the official request and offered the most precious gold and silver religious objects from their synagogues to be melted down for the Fatherland. The national Union of Jewish Communities tried to check their enthusiasm to insure that the synagogues were not mindlessly stripped. The rabbis con-sulted the Talmudic texts and drew up lists specifying which objects could and could not be destroyed for their metallic value.

Mussolini himself expressed great satisfaction with the Jews' solidar-ity: "In these great days for the Italian nation I declare that Italian and Jewish ideals are fully merged into one," *La Nostra Bandiera* proudly quoted him as saying in December 1935.

For Ettore Ovazza and the Jewish-Fascists, the conquest of Ethiopia was the fulfillment of a longstanding dream of Empire. Because Ethiopia had an ancient Jewish community, the Italian Jews felt that they had a spe-cial civilizing mission of their own, parallel to Fascism's. The *"falascia"* (as the Ethiopian Jews were called in Italian) were the descendants of Jews who had migrated to Africa several centuries before Christ and had lived cut off from the rest of the Jewish world since then. *La Nostra Bandiera* saw the invasion of Ethiopia as a war of liberation. After a series of Italian victories during the spring of 1936, the Jewish community was encouraged to send rabbis to establish contacts with the so-called *falascia*. This was the kind of ideal fusion of religion and nationalism that Ovazza and the *Bandieristi* envisioned.

In fact, the Italian foreign ministry published a pamphlet called "The Jews of Italy," advertising Italy's liberal treatment of the Jews in an attempt to combat the international condemnation of the Ethiopian invasion.

Initially, Mussolini saw the war as a new opportunity to strike a deal with Zionism to take control of the Mediterranean. He secretly offered to create a Zionist settlement in Ethiopia as the first step toward a Jewish state in Palestine. When the Fascists took over the Middle East, the Jews would get the Land of Israel and the Italians would keep Iraq and Syria. The leaders of the Zionist movement were justifiably skeptical of this plan and it never acquired any concrete reality.

Mussolini even enlisted the help of Italian Zionists to try to reverse the negative international reaction to the Italian invasion. At the behest of the Fascist government, Dante Lattes, editor of *Israel* (the bete-noire of Ovazza's *La Nostra Bandiera*) flew to London to plead with Zionist leaders to intercede on Italy's behalf with the British government. "But since Jewish influence on world politics was a mere fable," Lattes later wrote, "our efforts . . . had no concrete result whatever."

This courtship was based on Mussolini's distorted view of the Zionist movement as a kind of all-powerful Jewish cabal. When they failed to change French and British policy, the romance ended.

Despite enthusiastic support of most Italian Jews, the Ethiopian war helped to push Italy closer to Nazi Germany and therefore toward anti-Semitism, something that Hitler had shrewdly predicted. "The Italian people, too, will recognize at the end of this struggle that there is a Jewish question," he said just two days after the invasion of Ethiopia. "Let us leave it to the future to reveal how the Jew has had his finger in this pie."

By pitting Italy against its former allies, France and Great Britain, the war pushed Mussolini into the arms of Hitler, and polarized Europe into

Fascist and anti-Fascist blocks. With the imposition of economic sanctions the Fascist regime turned up the heat of its anti-democratic rhetoric and gave legitimacy to various paranoid, conspiracy theories. Any Italian setbacks were explained in terms of the insidious efforts of its enemies: the plutocratic democracies, international capitalism, and the like. Because the Zionist colony in Palestine operated under the aegis of the British Empire, "International Jewry" was now portrayed in the Fascist press as a British agent harmful to Italian interests. Soon enough, the old Masonic-Jewish and Judeo-Bolshevik conspiracy theories were taken out of mothballs and dusted off by the right-wing press. And indeed, in 1936 the hook-nosed caricature of the Jew reappeared in Italian vignettes side-by-side with the octopus of International Plutocracy and the Masonic-Bolshevik hydra, both shown wrapping their tentacles around the Italian nation.

While the Italian Jews greeted Mussolini's Declaration of Empire in May of 1936 with the same kind of patriotic fanfare that had accompanied the invasion, the climate surrounding the Jews had changed in the intervening seven months. *La Nostra Bandiera* published an anguished letter from a young woman describing an anti-Semitic incident at one of the Imperial celebrations.

> Just as my heart palpitated with the most ardent love and pride, when my eyes wept tears of joy, when my soul echoed the sublime words of the Duce . . . a little voice next to me, called out the ignoble phrase . . . Damn the Jews!

With the return of anti-Semitism, the rift among the Jews widened again. In the same issues in which *La Nostra Bandiera* welcomed the Italian triumph, the paper also renewed its assault on the Jewish Union. In typically schizophrenic fashion, the Jewish-Fascists alternately criticized growing anti-Semitism and denounced the leaders of the Italian Jewish establishment for their suspect loyalty and their ties to International Jewry.

Ovazza and *La Nostra Bandiera* did not ignore the danger of anti-Semitism. They paid close attention to developments in Germany, Eastern Europe and answered anti-Semitic critics within Italy. One of the sad ironies of Ovazza's life is that he was more acutely sensitive than most to the dangers of anti-Semitism, but his blind attachment to Fascism prevented him from attributing the anti-Jewish attacks to their true source. More often than not, Ovazza blamed the growth of anti-Semitism in Italy on the Jews themselves rather than on Fascism's growing alliance with Hitler.

The situation, however, was highly confusing. Publicly, Mussolini and the regime never uttered an anti-Semitic word, and occasionally expressed words of support, while those who attacked the Jews appeared to act on their own. This barrage of conflicting messages put Italy's Jews in what studies of schizophrenia have called the "double-bind." The Italian Jews became increasingly disoriented by a society that simultaneously reassured and attacked them.

The Fascist Jews tried everything to please Mussolini, giving increasingly large sums of money to help develop the new Italian colonies and renouncing all ties to the international Jewish community. The Turinese Jews began a second major offensive against the Jewish establishment. They prepared a booklet, published by *La Nostra Bandiera*, called "For the Fulfillment of Jewish Duty in Fascist Italy," which proposed to radically reform Italian Judaism along Fascist lines. It proposed ousting the current leadership, to set up a new centralized governing body with authoritarian power, prohibit contacts with Jewish groups overseas and limit religious observance to its purely ritual functions. Absorbing much of the rhetoric of anti-Semitism, the booklet even accused the official Jewish leadership of "old Masonic roots" and "international links" with subversive, anti-Italian elements.

Once again, the Jewish-Fascists' aggressive attack on the Union did not win them praise from the regime. Instead, the Ministry of the Interior privately rebuked the editors of *La Nostra Bandiera*. A May 1, 1936, dispatch from the Ministry to the Prefect of Turin read:

> The magazine, "La Nostra Bandiera," in its latest issues has published articles criticizing the delegation from the Union of Italian Jewish Communities for having participated in the Conference of the World Jewish Congress, held in Paris in February.
>
> Since the Union was able to use that conference to inform Jewish public opinion about Italy and make it appreciate the atti-

tude of our country toward its Jewish citizens, we ask your excellency to explain to the editors of the magazine "La Nostra Bandiera" the inappropriateness of these kind of articles.

Increasingly, the *Bandieristi* found themselves being whipsawed from the other side. After Mussolini had joined Hitler in sending troops to fight in the Spanish Civil War, Farinacci's newspaper, *Il Regime Fascista*, attacked the Jewish Fascists viciously for failing to act against their subversive Zionist brethren:

> Why do they do nothing concrete to disassociate themselves from all other Jews in the World, the ones whose only goal is the triumph of the Jewish International? Why have they not yet risen against their fellow Jews who are perpetrators of massacres, destroyers of churches, sowers of discord, audacious and evil killers of Christians? . . . There is a growing feeling that all Europe will soon be the scene of a war of religion. Are they not aware of this? We are certain that many will proclaim: we are Jewish Fascists. That is not enough. They must prove with facts to be Fascists first and then Jews.

In May 1937—as Fascist and Nazi officials shuttled back and forth between Rome and Berlin preparing a German-Italian alliance—anti-Jewish propaganda took a quantum leap forward. An important Fascist publicist, Paolo Orano (a member of parliament and Rector of the University of Perugia) published an attack on Italian Jews thinly disguised as a disinterested scholarly analysis. More disturbing was the fact that virtually all the Italian papers, including Mussolini's own *Popolo d'Italia*, used Orano's book, *The Jews of Italy*, as a pretext to raise the so-called "Jewish Question."

The book helped create a specifically Italian Fascist brand of anti-Semitism, based not on biology and eugenics, but on historical, religious and national considerations. Orano, while speaking warmly of several individual Jews (particularly Ettore Ovazza), argued that the Jews were a fundamentally subverversive, revolutionary people who inevitably sought to control and undermine the nations in which they settled. He dedicated an entire chapter to Ovazza, incorporating his critique of Zionism and then extending it to apply to all Jews. While calling Ovazza "the most frank" of the Italian Jews, Orano accused him of suffering from some of the worst traits endemic to his race: "vanity, pride, sense of superiority . . . presumption of belonging to a chosen people . . . "

For Ovazza, the book's publication must have been particularly painful. Orano was a good friend with whom he corresponded regularly. Even as he was preparing the psychological terrain for the Jewish persecutions, Orano never failed to demonstrate affection and respect for Ovazza and his family in their private correspondence. Incredibly, their friendship survived the publication of Orano's book with no loss in cordiality. That a leader of the Jewish community should be on close personal terms with one of the country's leading anti-Semites is highly emblematic of the paradoxical and contradictory nature of the relationship between Jews and Fascist Italy.

Their friendship did not prevent Ovazza from returning Orano's fire in a book entitled *The Jewish Problem: Response to Paolo Orano*. Probably the most interesting of Ovazza's writings on the Jews, it is a cry of desperation written in the shadow of the impending persecutions, a strange mix of blindness and insight. Some of his passages dealing with Zionism sound like anti-Semitic tracts: "An openly Zionist movement operates in Italy which, while headed by organizations established in Italy, is in fact dependant on the headquarters in London and Palestine. This Zionist activity . . . is hostile to the interests of Italy and extraneous to the soul of the Nation."

At the same time, Ovazza makes a passionate and heart-felt defense of the Jews. Hurt and moral indignation take precedence over his anti-Zionist polemic. He makes a blistering attack on the cynicism and intellectual dishonesty of the new Italian anti-Semitism:

We are the masters of Europe? And so why are we having so much difficulty resolving the Zionist question in Palestine? Why are the Jews in Russia oppressed and tyranized? (Aren't they supposed to be in charge?) Why is Poland trying to send its three million Jews into exile? Why is the Jew in Germany no longer a citizen? Why in many of the Balkan states are the Jews shoved aside and treated like animals? . . . On the one hand we are supposed to be the dominators of Europe, taking control of society's nerve centers, millionaires and communists; on the other "incapable of creating, lacking in initiative . . ." I would like to say to . . . the prosecutors and to the Judges: If you want to put Judaism and the Jews on trial get together and decide what the charges are.

Ultimately, however, Ovazza accepted Orano's premise that it is reasonable for the regime to distinguish between good Jews and bad Jews, Fascists and Zionists: "Congressman Orano, I am an Italian Fascist, without reservation, Mussolinian and totalitarian." Ovazza's book unwittingly played into the hands of the propagandists of anti-Semitism; its title alone gave credibility to the notion that there was in fact "a Jewish problem." Ovazza's publisher was the same as Orano's and was instrumental in orchestrating the "debate" on the Jews. Indeed, the publisher marketed the two books together, offering a special price for the reader who bought both. By insisting on the distinction between loyal and disloyal Jews, Ovazza and *La Nostra Bandiera* fell right into a trap laid for them by their persecutors and unwittingly provided ammunition for the regime when it decided to pass anti-semitic legislation.

Logic would seem to dictate that as soon as the Fascist regime openly embraced anti-Semitism during the summer of 1938, Jews would have, in turn, automatically turned against the regime. In fact, this did not happen right away. The council of the Turin Jewish Community, after much agonized debate, voted to maintain its position of unqualified support for the government.

During the fall of 1938, the Italian Jews held their breath and waited to see how far the regime would go. Some still hoped that they might still move Mussolini to leniency. Ovazza and some of his followers devised a desperate plan to grab the regime's attention and remind Mussolini of the Jews' unswerving loyalty. He proposed leading a squad of Jewish Fascists to burn down the offices of the Zionist paper, *Israel*, in Florence. This bizarre, para-military adventure was Ovazza's final political act.

As monstrous as it seems, the attack was, in a sense, a natural—if extreme—extension of the logic of the whole "*Nostra Bandiera*" movement. For years the Fascist hard-liners (like the newspaper *Regime Fascista*), had been goading the Jewish Fascists to "rise up against their fellow Jews," to do something "concrete" in order to "prove with facts that they are Fascists first and Jews second." Fascism had always stressed the importance of action over words and had risen to power by taking to the streets in rebellion against the impotence of parliamentary democracy. The action against *Israel* was a deliberate echo of the early revolutionary days of Fascism when black-shirted Fascist squads had sacked the offices of opposition newspapers. Although it was carried out, the attack seems to have elicited no official response—final proof that the government had little interest in these professions of faith.

After the harsh new racial laws of November 1938, the remnants of the *Nostra Bandiera* movement were swept from positions of leadership in Turin. Ettore Ovazza went a step farther, actually withdrawing from the Jewish community itself, protesting what he perceived as the Jewish community's insufficient Fascist rigor.

By this point, Ovazza was politically out-of-tune not only with the Jewish community but even with the rest of his family. When his two brothers left the country for the U.S. and Argentina, he would not even say good-bye to them. Ovazza remained in Turin throughout the war. Only with great reluctance did he leave the city at the time of the German occupation of Italy in September 1943. But he did not leave the country. He and his family checked into a resort hotel in Gressoney, under their real names. In one of the strange ironies of history, the Ovazzas were among the first Jews who were hunted down and killed by the Nazis after the invasion. They did not even bother to deport them. They shot them, cut up their bodies and burnt them in the stove of a local schoolhouse. In his suitcase, Ovazza carried with him photographs of Mussolini personally autographed to him, convinced, evidently, that these signs of loyalty would protect him from all harm.

Notes:

1. This article is based on research published in Alexander Stille, *Benevolence and Betrayal: Five Italian Jewish Families* (New York: Summit Books, 1991; Penguin, 1993), pp. 17–89 and source notes on pp. 351–352.

"DISCRIMINARE NON SIGNIFICA PERSEGUITARE"[1] (DISCRIMINATION DOES NOT MEAN PERSECUTION)

Lynn M. Gunzberg
Brown University

From the time of consolidation of the Catholic religion on the Italian peninsula, the relations between Jews and the Church have varied from antagonistic to merely strained, but at least until the Second Vatican Council in 1965 they have always been uneasy. Since until the mid-late 1800s the Italian peninsula was politically divided into a crazy quilt of kingdoms and duchies, many belonging to foreign rulers, with a substantial block of central Italy answering directly to the pope, communications between regions were never easy to establish. For the Jews in particular, whose numbers never exceeded approximately one-tenth of one percent of the overall population, geography coupled with their low numbers and general poverty contributed to their lack of political power and cultural influence as a group.

Once the last ghetto closed—in Rome in 1870—all of Italy's Jews were free to mix with the Christian population. And mix they did, assimilating in great numbers and, through much-decried intermarriage and raising of children in the dominant religion, decreased their numbers still further. Jews were also free to take their deserved place in society, with some rising meteorically to positions of prestige and power: as minister of war, the treasury, secretary of state, and so on. At the outbreak of World War One, the influential Jewish journal, *Il Vessillo Israelitico,* exhorted its readers:

> The hour has come. Our Italy has declared war . . . and we will
> dedicate ourselves entirely to her. For us any sacrifice will seem

sweet and every privation our duty. We Jews will give all of ourselves to our country . . . our sons, our possessions, our lives. Italy
has the right to expect everything from us and everything is what
we will give her. Her honor is at stake and [with it] our honor. Our
country must win, . . . even if we must die.[2]

Later, in 1919, when Mussolini organized the Fascist movement,
nationalistic Jews were once again afforded the opportunity to manifest
their devotion, though in time their allegiance would prove to be ironic at
best and, in many cases, tragic. Among the "founding fathers" of Fascism,
Mussolini counted six Jews, and three Jews were enshrined among the
early "martyrs" for the Fascist revolution. Fascist ideals found resonance
among Italians who were intensely nationalistic and anti-socialist as was
the almost solidly bourgeois Jewish community—despite the fact that the
prominent socialists, Modigliani and Treves, were Jews.[3]

Since almost every Italian was Catholic, the Church enjoyed enormous cultural control over daily life. Yet, in 1870 Unification had stripped
the Church of its considerable political power, and it was up to Mussolini
to restore some of that influence while shoring up consensus for his
Fascist regime by officially declaring Catholicism the State religion in
1929 through the mechanism of the Lateran Pacts. Religion was taught in
State schools and politics were often preached in church. A determining
factor for the Church in forging the alliance with Mussolini was that, with
the power of the Regime behind them, the Pope and his minions could
effectuate the country's return to the unchallenged (and, of course, nonexistent) time when Italy was a "model Christian society."[4] The Church
could, therefore, play a major role in the creation of the "new" (read:
quintessentially Fascist) Italian.[5]

A recent discovery has added to our notion of the effective weight of
the Church's vision for Italy, or at least of its influence over the popular
expression of its relations with the Fascist State. In June of 1932, the four-
teenth volume of the fifth edition of the *Enciclopedia italiana* (known as
the "Treccani") was readied for publication. The volume contained a
short doctrinal article entitled "Fascism" which was signed by Mussolini
but in reality written by Giovanni Gentile, the leading philosopher of
Fascism and editor of the encyclopedia. The article had been leaked to
Corriere della Sera and other mainstream newspapers and was read by

Pius XI. Incensed over its content, he summoned De Vecchi, the Italian Ambassador to the Vatican, and through him informed Mussolini of the unacceptability of his notions that "nothing either human or spiritual" could exist outside the State, that the State defined itself as the "educator and promoter of spiritual life," and that it sought "unchallenged" authority over the Fascist soul. The article must be rewritten, he told Mussolini, on pain of excommunication. Unable to modify a text already diffused in the popular press and bearing his signature, Mussolini added a lengthy coda stating that while Fascism did not have religious pretenses of its own, it recognized its mission to "defend and protect" "that positive religion that is Italian Catholicism." The article was then submitted to the Pope for his approval, and while not entirely satisfied with it, he allowed its publication.[6]

Such a conquest by the Church was not without its price, however. Much of the Church's mission to communicate the Word of Christ and its ramifications in modern life was accomplished through a well-established network of daily newspapers and periodicals, as well as diocesan publications and seasonal pastoral letters. After the attack on Mussolini on October 31, 1926, citing 'public safety' the Regime effectively shut down the opposition press and imposed censorship on all remaining titles. The Church press did not escape the increased scrutiny by the State. Nor would the Lateran Pacts accord the Church any special immunity in this regard. Indeed, in a speech to the Chamber of Deputies on May 13, 1929, Mussolini warned:

> The Regime is vigilant and misses nothing. Let no one assume that even an insignificant rag printed in some remote parish won't eventually be known to me. We will never allow the parties and organizations[7] that we destroyed to be resurrected. Don't ever forget that when the Fascist regime takes on a battle we see it through to the end and leave behind us a desert.[8]

Even if truly systematic surveillance had been practicable, the threat of a desert where the press once flourished was a gross exaggeration. In fact, there remained a myriad of Catholic publications, though many journals and newspapers were forced to accommodate a major change in editorial direction or to cease publication. But the survivors have been correctly described as "practically paralyzed by seizure and other forms of persecution."[9] For most publications, the Thirties were years of "sleep, or marking time until things got better."[10] As we know, however, after 1938 things only got worse. The Catholic press 'awakened' as it were in 1938 when faced with Mussolini's pact with Hitler, but by 1942 most titles were closed by the rigors of war.

A few others went underground[11] and still others followed anti-Fascist priests into exile and were printed in France or Switzerland.[12] Occasionally, entrusting its fate to the inefficiency of the Regime's overseers, a paper like the *Eco di Bergamo* would print an anti-Fascist article. The Vatican newspaper, *Osservatore romano,* remained more independent, and was solidly against "Fascism's pretense of controlling all educational endeavors, and against the growing strength of the myth of racism."[13] In fact, it was the only newspaper to contradict the Regime, and as such provided a focal point for Catholics and non-Catholics alike.[14] But we shouldn't make too much of that. The point is that the Catholic press reflected the point of view of the majority of Catholics. And the majority of Catholics, who were, after all, the overwhelming majority of Italians, were solidly Fascist, at least up until the Second World War.

Even with the suppression of so many Catholic and other newspapers, a very large number remained, too many to consider here, indeed too many to review outside of the most encyclopedic sort of inquiry. Those which I have chosen to include in this brief report are: *L'Italia*, a daily newspaper begun in 1912, published in Milan; *Civiltà Cattolica*, which since 1850 has been and continues to be published monthly by the Jesuits in Rome; *Vita e Pensiero,* the organ of the Catholic University in Milan; *Studium*, also published in Milan; and *L'Amico del clero*, a professional publication for the clergy.

Given the exiguousness of the Jewish population in Italy and the pervasiveness of Catholicism in all parts of Italian life, one might assume that the mighty Catholic press was not particularly concerned with the Jews except perhaps in time of crisis. In fact, there was a long-standing tradition of discussing the Jews: their actions, their characteristics, or rather the stereotypes which took the place of solid knowledge about Jews, and their recalcitrance when exhorted to convert to Catholicism.

Civiltà Cattolica had been, in essence, critical of the Jews since its inception. Throughout the Thirties, as in the eighty previous years, it had

published articles about various aspects of Jewish ritual and culture, usually presenting the chosen topic in marked antithesis to Christian practice.
In 1938, that simple antithesis became anathema. Beginning in
September of that year, *Civiltà Cattolica* reprinted a series of articles
from 1890 on "The Jewish Question in Europe: Causes, Effects,
Remedies."[15] The vitriolic articles from forty years earlier had been
inspired by the phenomenon of years of massive and, they felt, invasive
Jewish assimilation. Their reprinting was similarly "inspired by the spectacle of Jewish encroachment and arrogance" and satisfaction in the
Church's "struggle in defense of Christian people against a *'foreign*
nation among the nations in which it dwells and the declared *enemy* of
their well-being.'"[16] These lines from 1890, *mutatis mutandis*, could easily have been written in 1938. In August of 1938, Roberto Farinacci, one
of Italy's most rabidly racist journalists, congratulated *Civiltà Cattolica* in
the pages of his newspaper, *Regime Fascista*, for having "stated the *problem of race* before it was necessary to do so."[17] Embarassed by adulation
from *Regime Fascista*, *Civiltà Cattolica* tried to soft pedal by stating that
the opinions expressed in 1890 belonged to a bygone era. Oddly enough,
however, the "remedies" for 'Jewish offensiveness and obstinacy' suggested in 1890 remained substantially the same in 1938 and resembled
the provisions of the Fascist racial legislation: declare the Jews foreigners
and confiscate their property. But such draconian measures, the Jesuits
argued, contradicted the norms of Christian charity, and represented a
departure from the *modus operandi* of the Church. Confinement and
interdiction, like in the old days—a clear reference to the three centuries
of Jewish ghettos in Italy—was the only way to "defend both Jewish and
Christian interests, with laws not hateful but just, with discrimination not
persecution which would be mutually advantageous."[18] And indeed, they
congratulated themselves and their fellow churchmen that, in the nearly
half-century since the article of 1890, the Church had "committed no violence—neither in the spirit of vengeance nor struggle—against the Jews,
despite their overbearing nature."[19]

The silence of the Church regarding what was happening in Germany
was, of course, more troubling than any of its anti-historical mythology
of good, or at least just, relations with the Jews. It should be understood
that I am referring to the pre-war period before the German occupation of
Italy and therefore before individual clergy and other religious figures

mobilized to rescue Jews. The great historian of the Church, Giovanni Miccoli, rightly states that in the Thirties, the notable indifference toward the plight of the German Jews together with the Church's "unwillingness to defend the Jews" derived in large measure from "its more or less latent antipathy toward the Jews."[20] While the Church under Pius XI maintained a certain distance from National Socialism and its bogus theories about history and race, nonetheless the Church press shored up "that anti-Semitism which was willing to be manipulated by the Church, as evidenced by their use of popular slogans against the Jews which were projected onto an image of the new authoritarian and fundamentally Christian society."[21] Thus, as early as 1933, in an article entitled "Hitler and the Jews," *L'Amico del clero*, the professional journal for priests, clearly blames the Jews for the violence unleashed against them, for being unwilling to practice their religion and go about their business without disturbing others "in which case nobody would disturb them. It is the Jews who promote the worst sort of anticlericalism . . . in their attempt to undermine Christian society. . . . A nation, like an individual, has the right to use force against force so as to avoid that the malice of the wicked might bring harm to the good."[22]

Indeed, in 1933 one could find clearly positive judgements on Hitler in the Italian Church press, brought on, of course, by the refusal of the Jews to speak out against the persecution of Catholics in Germany. One such article, for instance, bears the title "Jewish Slyness and the Extreme Generosity of Catholics."[23] In 1934, *L'Amico del clero* was still railing against the Jews because of the threat they posed to Germany and to all civilized societies. "Judaism," they said, "is a nightmare for so many nations, especially now that Germany is trying barbarously to be rid of its Jews and is scattering them like gifts to neighboring countries." The use of the word "barbarously" here is telling, but its presence does not connote much in the way of concern about the methods used against the *Jews*. Rather, after the attacks of June 30, 1934, which targeted *Catholics* as well as Jews, the clergy feared "another invasion of the Huns, against which we shall of course have to defend ourselves if we do not want to witness the collapse of all of *Christian* civilization. . . ." It had also become clear that those who hoped for the success of the German Concordat of 1933 would be bitterly disappointed.

As time went on, though, even *L'Amico del clero* softened its tone somewhat and abandoned its support for Hitler, preferring instead to condemn the racist policies of the Nazis. For most of the Church press, German racist policies signalled a movement in that country often referred to in Italy as *Neopaganesimo* (new paganism) meaning anti-Catholicism, indeed a new religion to supplant Christianity, which was considered a 'non-German' faith. Articles decrying the "new paganism" began appearing in *Osservatore romano* and other publications in the mid-Thirties.[24] The wave of the 'new German religion' was so powerful, indeed, that according to the journal *Studium* it had managed to capture even Hitler, who "in his heart was not really a persecutor, but who was swept up by the force of the current."[25] According to *L'Amico del clero*, racial anti-Semitism was "an idiotic thing that would only occur to a German." But beyond "idiotic," the violence it provoked posed a clear danger to the many German Catholics, and any public intervention in defense of the Jews, it was felt, would put Catholics at further risk. In 1936, *L'Amico del clero* warned that though they had no sympathy for Germany's persecution of the Jews, the Jews themselves had better understand that "were they to stir up the fire, they might get burned and few people, if anyone, would try to douse those flames."[26] The Church's brand of anti-Semitism, however, was a legitimate defense of a country's moral and economic life[27] and "it was perhaps not a bad idea for the clergy to keep an eye on the Jews and in so doing limit the terrible threat that they pose to our neighbors, though as yet not so much to Italy, thanks to special circumstances and the provisions we have taken."[28]

But though the Church declared itself unwilling to speak out on behalf of German Jews, relations between the Vatican and Berlin grew increasingly more strained, and never more so than in March 1937, after the publication and reading in German churches of Pius XI's encyclical *Mit brennender Sorge* in which the pontiff condemned the nationalist and racist (though not specifically anti-Semitic) foundations of National Socialism, declaring that "whoever takes race, or the concept of a people, or the State . . . and creates around them a cult of idols . . . falsifies and undermines the order of things created by God."[29] Germany's persecution of the German Catholic Church was, he said, aimed at nothing less than the total destruction of Christianity in that society.

As Italy and Germany began to move closer to an alliance, the Church expressed fears that the anti-Christian and anti-clerical ideology of Nazism might make inroads into Italy. One harbinger of trouble to come was the publication in April 1937 of Paolo Orano's book *The Jews in Italy,* a direct attack on the Jews accusing them of anti-Fascism, lack of patriotism, and anti-Catholicism. The book was an instant success in Fascist and many Catholic circles and was followed, in 1937 and 1938, by several imitations. The *Protocols of the Elders of Zion*, translated by Jew-baiter Giovanni Preziosi and first published in 1921, was once again a subject for debate. This time, the Catholic press proclaimed its spuriousness immediately, and *Scuola cattolica*, a publication for religious schools, condemned the book for offering "abundant material to justify the actions of Hitler's regime against the Jews."[30] Then, on July 14, 1938, the *Manifesto of Racist Scientists*, published in *Il Giornale d'Italia*, clearly stated that the racial question in Italy was purely a biological matter, without any philosophical or religious overtones.[31] The *Manifesto* declared categorically, however, that the fact of difference between races did not imply that one race was superior or inferior to another, because Italy "did not wish to introduce German theories of race."[32] Nonetheless, in a speech to the students of Propaganda Fide in July of 1938, the Pope denounced unbridled nationalism and racism and he expressed his displeasure that Italy had launched a campaign of anti-Semitism in clear imitation of Germany. Mussolini's reply was immediate and unequivocal: Italian anti-Semitism was purely Italian and not an imitation of anyone! To be on the safe side, however, the Ministry for Popular Culture, which controlled both the Church and the lay press, prevented the publication of the speech, which was later published in Belgium. Ciano, the foreign minister, summoned the papal nunzio to make it quite clear that since Italy was now an imperial power, having conquered Ethiopia "Mussolini considered the racial question absolutely fundamental."[33] In his diary, Ciano added that he outlined the principles behind Italian anti-Semitism quite clearly and was pleased to find that the nunzio was himself solidly anti-Semitic.[34] As the anti-Semitic campaign advanced, Mussolini had to shore up conformity in public discourse regarding racism and the Jews, especially in light of the coming legislation that would deprive Jews of their civil rights. Thus, on August 16, 1938, the Regime and the Holy See came to an agreement: the government would ease its pressure on *Azione*

Cattolica—an activist movement within Catholicism that Mussolini had long suspected of being anti-Fascist—if churchmen, including the Pope, would refrain from public pronouncements concerning treatment of the Jews.[35] For the time being, government plans for the Jews were to remain a dirty little secret.

But not for long. For although the *Informazione diplomatica* #14 (*Diplomatic Dispatch* #14) on February 16, 1938, had stated that "the Jews as Jews" would not be the objects of "political, economic or moral measures against them,"[36] immediately after, *Osservatore romano* called its readers' attention to the last phrase of that dispatch in which the Regime vowed to defend the nation against the so-called 'overwhelming Jewish influence'[37]in Italian cultural and economic life out of all proportion to the size of the community. This so-called "defensive anti-Semitism" had, in one form or another, been a staple of the Church press for a number of years. And the August 4 edition of *L'Italia* had carried a small, boxed notice on its front page stating: beginning with the school year, Jewish students of foreign birth would no longer be allowed to attend Italian schools. Then, on August 5, *Informazione diplomatica* #18 was published in the lay and ecclesiastical press, with a sibylline declaration that while the government was not specifically planning future measures against the Jews, it must be understood that "discrimination does not mean persecution."[38] No one, said *L'Italia*, had any intention of persecuting the Jews, though the inappropriateness of their influence in Italian life was unmistakeable. Despite Mussolini's desire for secrecy, however, to those readers willing to suspend disbelief the trickle of anti-Jewish legislation enacted by the Great Council of Fascism, which quickly became a stream and then a veritable waterfall beginning in the autumn of 1938, was discernible in the laconic reportage in the Church press along each step of the way.

On September 1, 1938, citing public safety, the government forbade "foreigners of the Jewish race to establish permanent residence on Italian soil, in Libya, or in Italy's Aegean possessions" and on September 7 revoked the "concession of Italian citizenship to Jews contracted after January 1, 1919," and gave them six months to leave the country. Some six thousand Jews were forced to emigrate.[39] *Civiltà Cattolica* carried this notice in their issue of September 17. Along with it, they reprinted the legislation of September 2, which denied access to, or new or continued employment in, Fascist schools to anyone, student or teacher, of the "Jewish race" beyond the date of October 16, 1938.[40]

But just who was a member of the Jewish race? On October 7, *L'Italia* published a handy guide to race that had been outlined by the Great Council of Fascism the day before. Jews were people born of two Jewish parents (even if the parents professed another religion); of a mixed marriage; of a Jewish mother and an unknown father; of a "mixed marriage between Italians who later embraced the Jewish faith." Anyone born of Italian citizens who did not practice the Jewish religion by October 1, 1938, was *not* to be considered a Jew. The Church was clearly favorable to this provision, because such legislation appeared to "substitute Fascist racial criteria with religious practice as a basis for discrimination"[41] and that could only please the Church which, traditionally, hoped for nothing better than the conversion of the Jews.

On November 7, 1938, Herschel Grynszpan assassinated vom Rath in Paris and the brutal retaliation known as *Kristallnacht* swept Germany during the night between November 9 and 10. Although some Catholic papers expressed their dismay over the event,[42] far too many were silent. Relatively quick to report the death of vom Rath "an unknown and peaceful bureaucrat" and to condemn Grynszpan in an article on November 10 for his "lack of Christian love" toward his victim, *L'Italia* made no mention, then or after, of the tragic pogrom that signalled the beginning of the Holocaust.[43]

On November 17, the Great Council of Fascism passed law #1728, the first of four "Provisions for the Defense of the Italian Race," which robbed Jews of the bulk of their remaining civil rights. The Church, incredulous and indignant, reacted swiftly, but not, unfortunately, on behalf of the Jews. For the new laws affected the Church right along with the Jews. On November 10, a law had been passed forbidding marriages between Italian Aryans and members of any other race, and declaring null any such marriages that might be contracted in defiance of the law. But article #34 of the Concordat had expressly assigned the marriage of Catholics to the governance of canon, not secular law. Taking its lead from *Osservatore romano*, in its December 3rd issue *Civiltà Cattolica* explained:

> The Church prohibits marriage between Catholics and non-Catholics, of whatever race, but permits marriage between two

Catholics of whatever race. . . . If there is no impediment to marriage between two Catholics, the Church may not deny them the sacrament of marriage on account of race. The Church's holy mission requires this as do the rights given by God through the Church to all His children without discrimination. [44]

To infringe on the Church's sacred mission in this way was to inflict a grave wound, a *vulnus*—as the Church referred to it—on the Concordat and on the Church itself. By its interference, this law was a repudiation of the very nature of the catholic, that is, universal Church, in which religion, not race, determines the relationship between the individual and the Church.[45]

After the racial laws were announced, article after article in the Church press complained about them—but primarily because of the *vulnus*. According to Valerio Marchi, *L'Italia* was, for instance, certainly well aware of the existence of the concentration camps "which, even if they had not yet become extermination camps, were already doing their damage," but *L'Italia* chose to rail instead against the *vulnus*, and defended the Jews only when referring to baptized Jews.[46]

But the Church was not completely silent about the tragic events in Germany. On November 13, in reaction to *Kristallnacht*, Cardinal Schuster—Italian despite his German name—had pronounced a homily in the Duomo of Milan condemning German racism as "un-Roman heresy,"[47] and "no less dangerous for the world than bolshevism."[48] But from the homily, which was reprinted in its entirety in *L'Italia* two days later, one easily deduces that, once again, the emphasis was not on the fate of the Jews, but on the divinization of the State under Nazism which effectively shut out spirituality, that is, the influence of the Church. Goebbels denounced the homily as sabotage against the Axis,[49] and the Fascist authorities ordered *L'Italia* to change its editorial policy or shut down.

Pius XI had been denouncing racism for a long time, though after August 6 he tailored his comments against the racist policies of the regime to meetings with foreigners or Italians who, like *Azione Cattolica*, were already out of favor with the government. Thus, in September of 1938, immediately after the announcement of the criteria for Italian citizenship (prior to January 1, 1919), before a group of pilgrims from

Belgian radio, the Pope denounced anti-Semitism as "a movement that no Christian should have anything to do with" and, harking back to the Judaic origins of Christianity, declared: "spiritually we are all Semites."[50] In reporting the speech, *Osservatore romano* and the entire Italian mainstream Church press chose to omit the part containing Pius' expression of his concern for the Jews.

In June, the Pope had commissioned three Jesuits—an American, a Frenchman, and a German—to help him compose an encyclical against racism and, in particular, anti-Semitism. Undaunted but seriously ill, the Pope pressed on with his encyclical. It was ready in the fall and the Pope corrected it and chose the title, *Humani Generis Unitas*, the unity of the *human* race: a text which proclaimed the brotherhood of all humankind without regard for race. The encyclical was to be made public to the bishops assembled for the tenth anniversary celebrations of the Lateran Pacts, on February 11, 1939. But Pius XI died on February 10, and it was left to his successor, Pius XII, to publish the *Humani Generis Unitas* or put it aside. Pius XII opted for caution, in this as in so many other ways, publishing his own encyclical, *Summi Pontificatus*, in October 1939. The text of Pius XI's encyclical had been considered lost until mid-September of 1995, when it was discovered in France. One of the most interesting aspects of this and Pius XII's *Summi Pontificatus* is Pius XII's affirmation that: "in light of the unity of rights and the fact of the entirety of humankind, individuals do not appear to us to be disconnected from each other . . . and certain groups of people who, evolving in accordance with their own culture and circumstances, have differentiated themselves from other groups, will not inevitably destroy the unity of human life but rather enrich it."[51] While he is accused of hiding Pius XI's incendiary text,[52] it is possible that Pius XII incorporated concepts from it in his encyclical. What we do know is that under Pius XII, the Church press became ever more silent until, finally, burdened by war, much of it ceased publication altogether.

Notes:

1. From *Informazione Diplomatica*, no. 18.
2. *Vessillo Israelitico* 63, no. 10 (1915), p. 1.
3. For a numerical history of Jewish membership in the Fascist party, see

R. De Felice, *Ebrei sotto fascismo* (Turin: Einaudi, 1961), p. 75.

4. B. Bocchini Camaiani, "Chiesa cattolica italiana e leggi razziali," in *Qualestoria* XVII, 1 (1989), p. 43.

5. See, for instance p. A. Gemelli, "L'unità nell'educazione," *Vita e Pensiero*, XXV, 1 (1939), p. 7.

6. G. Belardelli, "TRECCANI, Il papa censurò Mussolini: Pio XI minacciò la scomunica e il duce riscrisse la voce *Fascismo*," in *Corriere delle Sera* (17 November 1995), pp. 1, 3.

7. The principal organization to which Mussolini was referring was probably Azione Cattolica, thought by the Regime to be a front organization for the antifascist Partito Popolare.

8. Cited in G. Licata, *Giornalismo cattolico italiano (1861–1943)* (Rome: Editrice Studium, 1966), p. 120.

9. Licata, p. 127.

10. Licata, p. 130.

11. Among these were *La Democrazia* (Milan), *Il Popolo* and *La Punta* (Rome), *Per il domani* and *La Vedetta della democrazia subalpina* (Turin), *Il Momento* (Vicenza), *La Libertà* (Padua), *Voce operaia* (Catholic Communists), *L'Uomo* ("Spiritual Movement" organization), and *L'Azione* (Catholics of the Left).

12. The better known of these were *Il Pungolo* (France) and *Il Corriere degli Italiani* and *La Libertà* (Switzerland).

13. A. Mayo, *Storia della stampa cattolica in Italia* (Milan: Nuove Edizioni Duomo, 1987), p. 186.

14. Mayo, p. 185.

15. R. Ballerini, "Della questione giudaica in Europa: Le cause (p. 5), Gli effetti (p. 385), I rimedi (p. 641)" *Civiltà Cattolica*, Series XIV (1890), rpt. *Civiltà Cattolica* LXXXIX, 3 (1938), 559–561.

16. Cited in *Civiltà Cattolica*, LXXXIX, 3 (1938), 561.

17. R. Farinacci, in "Un tremendo atto di accusa," in *Regime fascista* (30 August 1938), went so far as to state that "Fascism is far gentler, in its intentions and their execution, than *Civiltà Cattolica*."

18. "La questione giudaica e la *Civiltà Cattolica*," *Civiltà Cattolica*, LXXXIX, 4 (1938), p. 8.

19. Ibid.

20. G. Miccoli, "Santa Sede e Chiesa italiana di fronte alle leggi antiebraiche del 1938," in *La legislazione antiebraica in Italia e in*

Europa, Atti del Convegno nel cinquantenario delle leggi razziali (Roma, 17–18 ottobre 1988) (Rome: Camera dei deputati, 1989), p. 176.

21. Ibid.

22. "Hitler e gli ebrei," *L'Amico del clero*, XV (1933), p. 228, cited in Miccoli, p. 178.

23. "La furbizia degli Ebrei e l'estrema generosità dei Cattolici," *L'Amico del clero*, XV (1933), p. 299. See also *La Liguria del popolo* for 1933.

24. G. Dalla Torre, "Il sol levante del neopaganesimo," XXI (1935). See also "La nuova fede tedesca," in *La scuola cattolica* LXIII (December 1935), 667–697; Bendiscioli, *La Germania religiosa del III Reich* (Brescia, 1936) and *Neopaganesimo razzista* (Brescia, 1937).

25. Found in the regular column "Vitae ecclesiae," *Studium*, XXXIII, 4 (1937), p. 280, cited in Bocchini Camaiani, p. 45.

26. "Per lo 'strangolamento dell'Italia,'" *L'Amico del clero* XVIII (1936), p. 154, cited in Miccoli, p. 240, n. 53.

27. "Gli ebrei in Austria," *L'Amico del clero* XVII (1935), p. 504, cited in Miccoli, p. 179.

28. "Il 'giudeo rosso' di Francia dopo le batoste tedesche," *L'Amico del clero,* XVIII, 4 (1936), pp. 262–264, cited in Miccoli, p. 240 n. 52.

29. Cited in S. Friedlander, *Pio XII e il Terzo Reich* (Milan: Feltrinelli, 1965), p. 93.

30. "*I Protocolli dei Saggi di Sion* sono una falsificazione," in *Scuola cattolica* LXVI, 2 (1938), p. 115, cited in Miccoli, p. 198.

31. See A. Martini, S.J., "L'ultima battaglia di Pio XI," in *Studi sulla Questione romana e la Conciliazione* (Rome: 1963), 175–230, in particular p. 181; also, A. Cavaglion-G.F. Romagnani, *Le interdizioni del Duce. A cinquant'anni dalle leggi razziali in Italia (1938–1988)* (Turin: 1988), pp. 19–26.

32. Cited in Miccoli, p. 189.

33. G. Ciano, *Diario, 1937–1938* (Milan: Rizzoli, 1938), p. 162, cited in Miccoli, p. 185

34. Ibid.

35. See Martini, p. 187; Miccoli, pp. 184–187, 211, 214; Bocchini Camaiani, p. 57.

36. Cited in Miccoli, p. 189.

37. "Tre punti," in *Osservatore romano* (March 10, 1938), p. 2; see also N. Orlandi, "L'invasione ebraica anche in Italia," in *L'Amico del clero* XX, 3 (1938), pp. 114ff.

38. Ibid.

39. A. Spinosa, "Le persecuzioni razziali," in *Il Ponte* 9 (1953): 1079; R. De Felice, *Ebrei sotto fascismo* (1972), p. 276. De Felice attributes this assertion to Ciano, *Diario*, entry for July 4, 1938, p. 209.

40. *Civiltà Cattolica* LXXXIX, 3, pp. 559–561.

41. G. Miccoli, *Santa Sede e Chiesa Italiana,* cited in V. Marchi, *"L'Italia e la 'questione ebraica' negli anni Trenta,"* *Studi Storici* , XXXV, 3 (1994), p. 840.

42. See, for instance, R.M., "Questione di coscienza," *L'Avvenire d'Italia*, Bologna, November 11, 1938.

43. "Nostalgia dell'amore" *L'Italia* , November 10, 1938, 1, cited in Marchi, p. 841. On the reluctance of much of the Church press to report the pogrom, see A. Fleury, *La "Croix" et l'Allemagne (1930–1940)*, (Paris: 1986).

44. *Civiltà Cattolica* LXXXIX, 4 (December 3, 1938), pp. 473–474.

45. See OK, "Una soluzione italiana," *Civiltà Cattolica* , LXXXIX, 3 (1938), p. 1.

46. Marchi, p. 842. See also, Miccoli, p. 214.

47. Cited in Mayo, p. 188.

48. See *L'Italia* for November 15, 1938; see also, Miccoli, p. 222.

49. Miccoli, p. 222.

50. See Miccoli, p. 211.

51. Cited in D. Del Rio, "Vade retro, Hitler" *La Stampa* , CXXIX, 258 (1995), p. 16.

52. A. Cazzullo, "Pio XI, ecco l'enciclica scomparsa. La difesa degli ebrei nascosta da Pacelli?" in *ibid.*

L'Osservatore romano and the Holocaust, 1933–45

Andrea Grover
New York University

Introduction

The Vatican's position on the Holocaust has been controversial. The consensus view has been that the Vatican was acquiescent, if not unsympathetic, to the plight of the Jews.[1] The vast literature on this subject is practically devoid of references to the Vatican newspaper, L'Osservatore romano, the one exception being the oft-cited message that Pius XII penned for the October 29, 1943, edition, in which—it is generally assumed—he referred obliquely[2] to the Nazi round-up of one thousand Roman Jews.

L'Osservatore romano is the newspaper of the territorial see of the Papacy and therefore a state organ. As such, it is read by state departments as well as Church officials. In addition to news of religious interest, L'Osservatore romano (hereafter referred to as the O.R.) publishes documents, papal addresses, and reports and comments on political and social events throughout the world. The O.R. is considered an official organ only for documents and addresses; for all other content, it is deemed semi-official. A daily founded in 1861, its editors are laymen whom the Pope appoints and over whom he wields final editorial discretion.

To test the validity of the prevailing view and to shed new light on the question of the Church's attitude toward the systematic slaughter of European Jewry, I read the O.R. from January 1,1933 to June 30, 1945. In examining the paper, it was my intention to get at issues of the Holocaust—specifically the Vatican's stance during the period under discussion.

The O.R. is a useful tool for getting at these questions because it reflects the Church's position not only on theological issues but on political and social ones as well. Moreover, it has the imprimatur of the Pope. The position of the *O.R.* on the persecution of the Jews by the Nazis was complex. It changed over time in response to a number of factors: Church animosity toward the Jews; Church misunderstanding of Nazi racial anti-Semitism and how it differed from Church religious anti-Semitism; Vatican-German relations; Vatican diplomatic interests, particularly in relation to Palestine; fear of communism; personal attitudes of the popes; and subservience to Italy during the war.

In his book *The British Press and the Jews Under Nazi Rule,* Andrew Sharf notes that the press may at once try to mirror public opinion and to mold it. It is probable, he says, that both editorial approach and selection of news are the result of a complicated interaction between those two processes.[3] Deborah Lipstadt's *Beyond Belief,* a survey of American press reaction to the Holocaust, is particularly attuned to the mechanics of newspaper coverage: In interpreting how an article resonates, she attributes much import to its length, placement, and to the size of its headline.[4] My research touches on all these variables. My conclusions, however, are based as much on the lack of coverage as on what it consisted of.

My presentation here is chronological, with emphasis on the themes stated above. I have distinguished three periods: from Hitler's rise to power in January 1933 to *Kristallnacht* in November 1938; from *Kristallnacht* to the death of Pius XI in February 1939; and from the investiture of Pius XII in March 1939 to the end of the war in Europe in May 1945.

1933 to *Kristallnacht*

At first glance, the *O.R.*'s position on Nazi anti-Semitism during this period appears contradictory. Anti-Semitic events in Germany are reported, but German justifications for these actions are often given space; Nazi exaltation of race is condemned, but not Nazi anti-Semitism. Additionally, traditional Church anti-Jewish dogma appears frequently.

In March 1933, the *O.R.* began to report on a series of anti-Semitic events in Germany. During March and April 1933, it published dispatches from Berlin nearly every day chronicling the anti-Semitic campaign. They contained news that German Jews had been removed from public and semi-public offices, that Jewish doctors had been dismissed from hospitals,[5] and that Jewish judges and lawyers had been transferred from the criminal to the civil court.[6] In March, a release from Berlin on the *O.R.*'s last page told of the establishment of a concentration camp at Dachau for 5,000 Communists and other "enemies of the German people."[7] The headline called the internees "Communists and the like," assuming its readers would identify the latter as Jews. In doing so, the newspaper perpetuated the stereotypical linkage of Jews with Communists. It would do so again in 1935, when an article on the Nuremberg laws included Hitler's assertion that almost all Communist agitators were Jewish.[8] As we will see, this trend continued throughout the war years.

A hallmark of early *O.R.* reporting on Nazi anti-Semitism was the justification of German measures against the Jews. When growing concern for the safety of German Jews prompted foreign governments, such as the U.S. and Britain, to open official investigations, the *O.R.* gave space both to the investigations and to the German responses. The British Foreign Secretary, Sir John Simon, was quoted as having been reassured of the safety of English subjects by the German foreign minister.[9] The newspaper reported that in a speech responding to the U.S. investigation, Goering had stated: "no Jewish businesses have been destroyed nor any cemeteries or synagogues vandalized."[10] Another article, datelined Washington, reported that anti-Semitic violence in Germany had ended as a result of the U.S. investigation.[11] Hitler's reassurances that a "religious and moral healing" had begun[12] were found in the same edition that reported that Jews in Bavaria had been expelled from a part of the state at the end of March 1933.[13]

The *O. R.* was hardly impartial in reporting news of a planned German boycott of Jewish businesses, doctors, and lawyers. "The boycott is purely a defensive action, directed exclusively against the German Jews," stated the paper.[14] There were no words of concern for the victims of the boycott, although it received daily coverage. A story from Berlin noted that a Nazi manifesto blamed the boycott on the foreign press' negative attitude toward Germany and said that this attitude would hurt the very people it sought to help.[15] That the *O.R.* voiced no opposition to the boycott should not be surprising, in light of traditional Church doctrine on Jewish commerce. (For that matter, articles in February and August, 1943—when the Church already knew what was happening to "deported" Jews—were still referring to the "insatiable voraciousness" and "greed" of fifteenth-century Jewish usurers.)[16] Another headline on the April 1933 boycott of Jewish businesses revealed how the Church's self-interest prevented it from understanding Nazi racist anti-Semitism. It read: "How the anti-Jewish boycott—even against converts—will proceed."[17]

The previous two months' events in Germany did not prevent Pope Pius XI from holding a private audience with Vice-Chancellor von Papen and Minister Goering in April, 1933. The *O. R.* reported that the German leaders also met with the Vatican Secretary of State, Eugenio Pacelli.[18]

Coverage of the anti-Semitic campaign in Germany continued during the summer and autumn of 1933, as it had since the campaign's inception. A May release stated that Jews were no longer allowed to represent Germany in Davis Cup tennis competition.[19] But these last page items were only a few lines long and were reported without comment. Moreover, no editorials on German anti-Semitism appeared. Indeed, Jews, such as Albert Einstein, who had been offered a chair at Oxford,[20] were portrayed as free to leave Germany and establish themselves elsewhere. It was not until the summer of 1935 that anti-Semitic events in Germany again took center stage and, consequently, became front-page news.

The *O.R.* was still offering justification for Nazi behavior toward Jews when mobs of unruly Germans beat up Jews in Berlin in July 1935. In an article headlined "Renewal of Anti-Semitism in Germany," appearing on the front page on July 17, 1935, a new wave of anti-Semitism was said to have led to the transfer of Jews to concentration camps for their own protection. Two incidents were recounted in which Jews were publicly humiliated. One reported that a Jewish butcher had been dragged through the streets with a sign around his neck: "This Jew bastard demanded that a German S.A. salute him."[21] The editorial decision to include these emotional incidents might have sprung from a desire to differentiate between the lawlessness of a segment of the German population and the legal behavior of the German leaders, who put Jews in camps for their own protection. Another possible reason for the inclusion of these articles is more subtle and harks back to the Church's traditional policy of vilification and humiliation of the Jews. For centuries the Church had forced Jews to endure the mockery and violence of the masses at the carnival games in Rome and to run naked in the Palio.[22]

The *O.R.*'s ambivalence *vis-à-vis* Nazi racism was still evident in September 1935, when the Nuremberg Laws disenfranchised Jews and classified them as non-citizens. A last-page article briefly discussed Nuremberg, reporting, without comment, that Hitler felt the new law on nationality rendered a service to the Jews because it provided them with the only reasonable way to live their own ethnic life.[23]

The Church, however, was becoming concerned with Nazi racism, but not because of the ravages it had inflicted on the Jews. Rather, a new offensive against Germany can be traced to Nazi outrages against Catholics. The Vatican retaliated in the pages of the *O.R.*, accusing the Nazis of contravening the 1933 Concordat between them.[24] This policy of condemning Nazi persecution of Catholics and not of Jews was also in evidence when Germany occupied Austria in 1938. Although the *O.R.* reported arrests of Austrian Jews and Catholics, Cardinal Innitzer, the archbishop of Vienna, replied only to Nazi provocations against Catholics.[25] He did not mention the Jews.

On March 21, 1937, Pope Pius XI issued the encyclical *Mit brennender Sorge*. Written in German, it was the Church's first official statement against German racism and nationalism since Hitler's rise to power four years earlier. The encyclical did not, however, explicitly condemn Nazi persecution of the Jews. (In fact, the Pope characterized Jews as wayward souls chosen, despite themselves, to accomplish a divine mission. Christ, he went on to say, received his "human nature" from a people destined to crucify him.)[26] The *O.R.* reported on March 23 that parish priests read the encyclical aloud throughout Germany on Palm Sunday.[27] The next day, a report on activities at the Fascist Cultural Institutes appeared in *Cronaca di Roma,* a section of the newspaper dealing with events in Rome. It related that anti-Semitism and the conversion of the Jews had been the topic of a talk given the previous week at one of the institutes.[28]

Though it might seem that during the period from 1933 to *Kristallnacht* the O.R's position on Nazi anti-Semitism was contradictory, on closer examination there is a principle that explains this paradox: The Church distinguished between racism and anti-Semitism. In the April 1933 report on the German boycott of Jewish businesses it was clear that the Vatican did not fully understand the distinction between Nazi racial anti-Semitism and the religious anti-Judaism of the Church. The understanding of this distinction changed over time. With *Mit brennender Sorge*, Pius XI clearly justified the persecution of Jews by religion but not by race. This stance left the door open to disagreement even within the

Church's own ranks. The homily delivered by the bishop of Cremona in January 1939 attests to this divergence. Printed by the *O.R.*, the homily sought to defend the Church against accusations that *Mit brennender Sorge* favored Jews at the expense of Catholics. Calling upon perennial theological arguments, the bishop, Monsignor Cazzani, stated: "The Church has always considered it dangerous to cohabit with Jews, as long as they remain Jews."[29]

Similarly, a story from Warsaw appearing in the *O.R.* in June 1938 reported that the Polish Party of National Unity differentiated between Nazi racial theories and the "legal and necessary" defense of Polish culture from Jewish influence. Racism, stated the Party, was completely contrary to the Catholic religion and its practices and therefore unacceptable; anti-Semitism, on the other hand, was both legal and necessary.[30]

In keeping with this distinction was the *O.R.*'s reportage on Italy's enactment of racial laws against its Jews in the autumn of 1938.[31] Although numerous articles on the measures appeared, none was critical of the Italian action. A scant year and a half earlier Pius XI had condemned Nazi racism in *Mit brennender Sorge*.

Pope Pius XI finally spoke out against anti-Semitism at a private audience with a group from the Belgian Catholic Radio. "Anti-Semitism," he stated, "is unacceptable. Spiritually we are all Semites."[32] Although recorded for posterity by a participant, these words were not included in a summary of the meeting appearing in the September 9, 1938, edition of the Vatican newspaper.

Kristallnacht—February 1939

During this period the Vatican continued to vacillate concerning German racial anti-Semitism, but was moving toward more forthright condemnation. Its position was determined in part by German treatment of Catholics, and by concern about Jewish immigration to Palestine (presumably because of an underlying concern for relations with the Arabs).

After *Kristallnacht*, *O.R.* coverage of Nazi anti-Semitism stepped up. Articles about the pogrom appeared on the front-page for much of November 1938. One such article contained remarks made by Churchill, Roosevelt, and others denouncing in no uncertain terms the behavior of the German people and their leaders.[33] The *O.R.* carried Goering's response. He stated that the struggle against the Jews would continue until their extermination.[34] The word extermination can leave no doubt about German plans for the Jews. The placement of this article on the last page is perplexing. If the intent was to minimize the import of Goering's statement, why print it at all? Once the decision to print it was made, however, surely Goering's threat to exterminate the Jews belonged on the first page. Another last-page headline stated that the anti-Semitic campaign in Germany was growing harsher.[35]

At the end of 1938, Pius XI began to mount a campaign for American support against the Reich. This can be surmised by the coverage afforded such items as discussions on the Jewish issue between Roosevelt and the American ambassadors to Italy and the Reich,[36] and Roosevelt's December 1938 speech on the Jewish question.[37] Indeed, the last few months of 1938 signaled a turning point in *O. R.* coverage of religious persecution in the Reich. No fewer than forty articles, news releases and editorials alike underscored pervasive German anti-Semitism, friction between the Vatican and Nazi Germany over persecution of Catholics, and the Church's attempts to line up supporters of its cause, specifically the United States.[38]

As part of the attempt to enlist the aid of the United States, the Vatican newspaper kept close tabs on the growing tension between Berlin and Washington. Front-page headlines of both editorials and news releases fanned the flames. "Washington speaks out on anti-Semitism," headlined an editorial that contained excerpts from a speech by Interior Secretary Harold Ickes, in which he spoke of the "thousands of unhappy Jews, robbed and tortured by a brutal dictatorship."[39] A story from Berlin quoted a note by the German *chargé d'affaires* in Washington. Any improvement in U. S.—German relations was impossible, said the German, as long as Washington put Jewish interests above all others.[40] A Roosevelt message to Mussolini on the issue of European Jewry and its possible solutions appeared in the Italian news section.[41]

The escalation of the *O.R* 's coverage of the Jewish problem in the Reich paralleled a growing concern in the Vatican both about attacks on German Catholics and a possible river of Jewish refugees flowing in the direction of Palestine. Whatever the reason for this shift, the increasingly anti-German tenor of the coverage appears to corroborate what we now know: Pius XI planned to issue an encyclical strongly condemning Nazi anti-Semitism. The encyclical, *Humani Generis Unitas,* clearly spelled out the link between racism and anti-Semitism. It stated that "the struggle for racial purity ends by being uniquely the struggle against the Jews." But the Pope could not leave well enough alone. After censuring the Nazis for stripping Jews of their basic rights as citizens, thereby creating a sea of wandering and destitute exiles, he offered ammunition to the very anti-Semites he had condemned. The encyclical (as quoted in Frederick Brown's review of *L'Encyclique "cachee" de Pius XI* [The "Hidden" Encyclical of Pius XI] by Georges Passelcq and Bernard Suchecky) went on to propose that Jews be quarantined lest they infect Christians with their dreams of "temporal conquest" and "material success," "their unbelief" and "hostility to Christianity," and their promotion of "revolutionary movements bent on upsetting the social order and tearing souls away from the knowledge and love of God."[42] It is probably fortunate that *Humani Generis Unitas* never saw the light of day.

As early as 1938, the Church understood that there was no hope for peace in Europe until the Jewish question was settled. This issue was closely linked to the Church's fear that Jewish emigration would go exclusively to Palestine. The Vatican was particularly anxious about a large influx of Polish Jews; a substantial increase in the Zionist population would tip the scales, both militarily and politically, in favor of the Jews.[43] In mid-July 1938, *Acta Diurna*, a news of the week in review column that mirrored Church policy, posited that the "Reason(s) for new riots in Palestine" was "Zionist immigration" and suggested that the latter be limited.[44]

Editorials and news items in early 1939 highlighted Church concern about Jewish emigration: Romania declared its intention to encourage Jewish emigration from Romania to overseas territories;[45] Polish Jews were expelled from Germany, and Poland and Germany were bickering over who was to receive their assets;[46] in Poland the National Jewish Committee for Emigration and Colonization voted to encourage correligionists to emigrate to countries, in addition to Palestine, that were suitable for colonization.[47] The Holy See would have undoubtedly welcomed a satisfactory solution of the Jewish problem, especially if it entailed no further Jewish immigration in Palestine.

On February 12, 1939, Pope Pius XI died. His Secretary of State, Eugenio Pacelli, the former papal nunzio in Munich and Berlin whom many considered a Germanophile,[48] succeeded him on March 2, taking the name Pius XII. During Pius XI's pontificate, the semi-official organ of the Holy See reported persecution of the Jews by the Reich and its allies. Yet no editorials or messages from the Pope explicitly condemned anti-Semitism. Nor did the *O.R.* publish his remarks on anti-Semitism delivered to the pilgrims from Belgian Catholic Radio.

March 1939–May 1945

During this last period the *O.R.* reported less on the Jewish question even as the 'final solution' got underway. This policy was determined by a Germanophile Pope, subservience to Italy (which entered the war in 1940), continued hostility to Jewish settlement in Palestine, and, as seen in *Mit brennender Sorge* and *Humani Generis Unitas*, the Church's religious anti-Semitism.

The Vatican's policy regarding the Jewish question did not change in the new papacy. Articles about the expulsion of foreign Jews from Italy,[49] the warning to Jews in Bohemia that they would have the same destiny as in the Reich,[50] laws concerning the Jews in Hungary,[51] the Italian Racial Laws,[52] an announcement of the reaffirmation of the Italian-German alliance,[53] and news from Prague about the arrests of Jews and Czechs in Prague all appeared,[54] without comment, in Pius XII's first month in office.

A front-page editorial on Jewish immigration in Palestine appeared early in the new pontiff's tenure. Discussing limits on Jewish immigration in Palestine enacted by the British for the purpose of appeasing the Arabs and thus restoring order,[55] the writer missed a perfect opportunity to speak out on the plight of Europe's Jewish refugees. The Vatican's interest in finding the refugees a home other than Palestine was evident in such articles as that of May 1939, in which the *O.R.* reported from London that Jewish emigration might be diverted to British Guyana.[56] This policy persisted even after it had become abundantly clear that very few places were willing to admit Jews. As late as November 1944, a boldface headline read: "Jewish Terrorism in Palestine."[57] Not coincidentally, this headline came on the heels of an item reporting that English Jews had asked Britain to proclaim Palestine a Jewish state.[58]

Pius XII attempted a rapprochement with the Reich early in his tenure.[59] This decision determined *O.R.* policy even after Germany invaded Poland on September 1, 1939. In fact, the *O.R.*'s first report on the fate of the Polish Jews appeared only on November 4, 1939, over two months after the German invasion.[60] Through the end of the year, the newspaper chronicled—without comment—the anti-Semitic "campaign" in Poland: Polish students damaged stores and homes in the Jewish quarter, Jews were deported from Katowice and their assets confiscated,[61] the Jews of Poland, Germany, Bohemia and Moravia were being relocated to Lublin to remove debris from the bombed areas,[62] all Jewish-owned shops were shuttered, Polish Jews were separated from the rest of the population and were obliged to wear a yellow badge, and 25,000 Jews were reported to have fled to Russia.[63] In a manner reminiscent of earlier coverage of anti-Semitic incidents in Germany, the *O.R.* justified the German actions: "If Poles are hungry it is the fault of Jewish speculators. German troops and authorities have every right to see Jews as their adversaries." The *O.R.* took this quotation from the *National Zeitung,* a German newspaper.[64]

Angered by German atrocities against such Polish Catholics as the Bishop of Lublin, the Pope retreated momentarily from his policy of appeasement. In his first encyclical, *Summi Pontificatus,* issued on October 20, 1939—only fifty days after the invasion—the Pope declared: "The blood of countless human beings, even noncombatants, raises a piteous dirge over a nation such as Our dear Poland, which, for its fidelity to the Church, for its services in the defence of Christian civilization . . . has a right to the generous and brotherly sympathy of the whole world[.]"[65]

Although there was very little news of the fate of the Polish Jews—and usually another country was the source of what news there was—the tone of the articles changed. Several even evinced compassion. A story from Paris spoke of "Forced labor for the Jews in Poland."[66] The Dutch press referred to the events regarding the Jews in Poland as "painful and tragic" and reported that the deadline for Polish Jews to declare property worth more than two thousand zlotys had passed.[67] These were the first sympathetic words about the Jews to appear in the *O.R.* since Pius XII's investiture. An article originating in Geneva reported that the Germans had threatened to relocate the Lodz ghetto Jews if they did not make a payment of several million zlotys.[68]

Italy's June 10, 1940, declaration of war against Great Britain and France and its invasion of France marked the end of this interlude.[69] First, the veiled attacks on Germany stopped, and, second, Italy's entrance into the war as an ally of Germany placed international news permanently on the front-page. Beginning in August 1940, the lead item in the international news was generally either glowing news from the Reich or Italian-German relations. News about the Polish Jews virtually dried up. From mid-1940 to July 27, 1941, not one article on Poland appeared.[70] This policy was not determined by Italian censorship. Mussolini had recognized papal sovereignty over the Vatican in the 1929 Lateran Treaty.

As the campaign against the Jews spread and intensified, the *O.R.*'s coverage shrunk. An inverse proportion developed between what was occurring and what was being reported. The murder of approximately twenty thousand Jews in Iasi and Bialystok went unreported.

It was not until July 1941 that the *O.R.* reported Jews had been killed. The front-page headline, however, read "Serbian Communists Shot." One needed to continue reading to find out that Jews as well as Communists had been shot for sabotage.[71] There was no sense either in this article or in others to follow that Jews were being killed simply because they were Jews. On the contrary, typical of these reports was the inclusion of a rationale—usually sabotage—for the shootings. The choice of words is always important; in this case it was extremely important for it completely misled the reader. Jews were Communists and saboteurs in Serbia, terrorists in Palestine, and revolutionaries in the secret encyclical *Humani Generis Unitas*. They were never referred to as freedom fighters or partisans, much less innocent victims.

An early indication of such slanted reportage can be seen in an April 1933 report from Berlin, headlined "New laws against terrorism." Only a few months after Hitler's election, the *O.R.* had chosen to lump together under one headline three seemingly unconnected news items from Germany: the passage of new laws against terrorism, new economic accords between the Reich and several states, and a law prohibiting kosher slaughter by Jews.[72] The reader is left to make the inference that kosher butchering is somehow in league with terrorism.

The link between Jewish fatalities and sabotage or treason was a continuing theme of *O.R.* coverage. Numerous examples include: the deaths in Croatia of twenty Jews and Serbs charged with sabotage,[73] the arrest of 350 Communists and Jews in Budapest for treason,[74] the accusation that Jews, Freemasons and Communists impeded the reprovisioning of

France,[75] and the death of fifty more Croatian Jews and Communists accused of sabotage.[76]

The year 1942 witnessed the deportation of almost sixty thousand Slovak Jews, the construction of the extermination camp Sobibor and its use beginning in May, the round up of fourteen thousand Jews in Vienna and their deportation to Theresienstadt, the deportation of French Jews to Auschwitz, mass deportations from Warsaw (300,000), the release of information on the plans to exterminate European Jewry by Rabbi Stephen Wise, and an Allied declaration condemning the Nazis' "bestial policy of cold-blooded extermination."[77] The *O.R.* did not report these events. In contrast, the Inter-Allied Information Committee's report had a profound effect on the British press. The *News Chronicle* of December 18, 1942, carried the following editorial: "There is no room for doubt that the German Government is responsible for ordering the wholesale slaughter of Jewish people throughout Europe on a scale, and with a degree of inhumanity which makes its actions one of the foulest horrors in recorded history."[78]

Nevertheless, there was no change in the Holy See's policy regarding the treatment of Jews in Nazi-occupied Europe. In the new year, the *O.R* reprinted parts of a speech made recently in Germany. "The victims of Bolshevism will be those people and countries that, clinging to Judaism, have brought about their own end by Bolshevism's poison."[79] This coupling of Judaism with Bolshevism, reminiscent of *Humani Generis Unitas* and "Communists and the like," lends weight to the explanation, offered by some scholars, that the Vatican remained silent on the Holocaust because it feared a Nazi victory less than a Soviet one.[80]

During the period immediately after Mussolini's overthrow on July 26, 1943, the *O.R.* reflected the indecisiveness of Vatican foreign policy. Four days after Mussolini's ouster, Roosevelt's words appeared on the first page. "The Allies," he said, "fight for personal, religious, economic, and political freedom."[81] Soon thereafter, the Germans occupied Rome. Within a week, the *O.R.* printed the text of a radio message by Mussolini—recently installed as the puppet head of the Nazi-controlled Republic of Salo'—that exhorted the Italians to continue fighting along-side Germany.[82]

After the Germans occupied Rome, they turned their attention to the city's Jewish population. The Gestapo gave the Roman Jews until

September 28 to deliver a levy of fifty kilos of gold. As the deadline approached, Pius XII remained silent. Instead, a front-page article in the *O.R.* entitled, "The Pope Defends Himself," stated that His Holiness had always defended all those who believed in the salvation announced and attained by He whom the Pope represents.[83] Obviously this did not include the Jews of Rome. In fact, a month before this incident, the newspaper had carried the article cited above, in which the Jews were called greedy usurers.

The Badoglio government declared war on Germany on October 13, 1943.[84] Between October 16 and 18, the Germans rounded up and deported to Auschwitz over one thousand Roman Jews. The *O.R.* did not report these events. On October 29, a message by Pope Pius XII appeared on the front page. Entitled "The heart of the Sovereign Pontiff for the victims of the war"—and issued over ten days after the deportations—the wording of this message was so vague and formulaic[85] as to render it ineffective. Scholars agree that the Germans, initially anxious about the Pope's response to the deportations of Italian citizens right from under his nose, were relieved by the mildness of his message.[86]

The November 30, 1943, decision by the Salo' authorities to place all Italian Jews in concentration camps was condemned by the *O.R.* in two front-page editorials. The writer voiced concern for the innocent women and children, for the elderly, and for the sick. The newspaper's strongest response, however, was to the persecution of Catholics, those detainees born to parents who had converted from Judaism many years ago.[87] The appearance of these editorials was in striking contrast to the newspaper's total silence on the November round-ups and deportations of Italian Jews in Genoa, Florence, Milan, Venice and Ferrara, during which, in a remarkable display of viciousness, hard-line Fascists removed Jews from hospitals and old-age homes and deported them to Auschwitz.

The *O.R.* devoted much space to Hungarian anti-Semitic measures during the last stages of the war in Europe. But by July 22, 1944, when it carried the story that in response to the protests of many governments and the International Red Cross, all Hungarian Jews with visas for Palestine could leave Hungary, about 437,000 had already been deported to Auschwitz.[88] According to Dr. Gerhart Riegner of the World Jewish Congress, Vatican action in Hungary saved many Jewish lives.[89] Yet there is no hint of that in the July 22 *O.R.* article. As we know, the pressure from foreign governments and the Red Cross prompted Miklos Horthy, the Hungarian regent, to order an end to the deportation of Hungarian Jews in July 1944.

On November 26, 1944, all major American newspapers carried the War Refugee Board's report of the eyewitness account of Auschwitz. "Not since *Kristallnacht* had a story been so widely featured or prompted such extensive comment," writes Deborah Lipstadt in *Beyond Belief*.[90] The *O.R.* did not carry the story. Certainly fear of German reprisal was no longer a factor in Vatican policy; Rome had been freed by the Americans on June 4, 1944.

The *O.R.* released four stories in April 1945 on Buchenwald. They offered, however, no substantive information and no mention of Jews.[91] In June, it was reported that eight hundred Polish priests had been liberated from Dachau. The O.R. news item did not report on Jewish survivors of the camp.[92] "The Holy See backs the Romanian Jews" headlined a story in May 1945.[93] Ironically, the war was over before the Vatican newspaper printed unqualified words of support for the Jews.

Conclusion

During the period from January 1933 to May 1945, in over forty-three hundred editions of the *O.R.*, there were approximately two hundred articles about the fate of the Jews in Europe. Given the events of these years—and in comparison to the coverage of America and British newspapers—this is a meager number indeed. But it is not only the paucity of coverage that is shocking. Long after it knew the truth about the cold-blooded murder of entire Jewish communities, the most influential newspaper in the Catholic world, in both its selection of news and editorial policy, consistently misled its readers as to the true nature of Nazi anti-Semitism. It failed to report eyewitness accounts of the death camps, or, for that matter, to even mention that death camps existed. It failed to follow the lead of such papers as *The Manchester Guardian*, which reported in October 1942 that between one and two million Jews were believed to have already been destroyed.[94] In twelve years of reportage, from 1933 to 1945, a few hundred Jews lost their lives in the *O.R.*'s pages. Moreover, and more importantly, long after it knew the truth about what was happening to the European Jewish world, the *O.R.* continued to spew out traditional Church anti-Jewish teachings.

A careful reading of the *O.R.* during the years 1933–1945 leads one to conclude that it ignored the almost total annihilation of European Jewry. For the reader of the Vatican newspaper, the Holocaust did not occur.

Notes:

1. See, for example, Rolf Hochhuth, *The Deputy* (New York: Grove Press, 1964); Saul Friedlander, *Pius XII and the Third Reich* (Oxford: Octagon Books, 1980); Avro Manhattan, *The Vatican in World Politics* (New York: Gaer Associates, 1949); John F. Morley, *Vatican Diplomacy and the Jews During the Holocaust 1939–1943* (New York: KTAV Publishing, 1980); Guenter Lewy, *The Catholic Church and Nazi Germany* (New York: McGraw Hill, 1964); Robert G. Weisbord and Wallace P. Sillanpoa, *The Chief Rabbi, the Pope, and the Holocaust* (New Brunswick, N.J.: Transaction Publishers, 1992).

2. *O. R.* , October 29, 1943, "Il Sommo Pontefice per le vittime della guerra." The only words in the Pope's message that can be construed as referring to the deported Roman Jews are: "senza distinzione di nazionalita', di stirpe, o di confessione religiosa." This front-page message by Pius XII is virtually the only example of *O.R.* reportage cited by scholars of the Italian phase of the Holocaust.

3. See Andrew Sharf, *The British Press and the Jews Under Nazi Rule* (London: Oxford University Press, 1964.)

4. See Deborah Lipstadt, *Beyond Belief* (New York: The Free Press, 1986.)

5. *O.R.*, March 20–21, 1933, "Gli Israelitici allontanati dagli uffici."

6. *O.R.*, March 22, 1933, "La questione semitica in tribunale."

7. *O.R.*, March 22, 1933, "Un campo di concentramento per 5 mila comunisti e simili."

8. *O.R.*, September 16–17, 1935, "Il Discorso di Hitler davanti al Reichstag." Hitler stated: "gli agitatori comunisti sono quasi tutti ebrei (.)" In another article on Nuremberg (*O.R.*, September 15, 1938, "Le Feste di Norimberga"), Hitler called communism "di ispirazione ebraica."

9. *O.R.*, March 30, 1933, "La sorte degli Israeliti inglesi dimoranti in Germania."

10. *O.R.*, March 25, 1933, "I pieni poteri concessi ad Hitler."

11. *O.R.*, March 27–28, 1933, "Le violenze antisemitiche terminate."

12. *O.R.*, March 25, 1933, "I pieni poteri concessi ad Hitler." The *Führer* announced "una intensa attivita' di risanamento religioso e morale del popolo, dichiarando le confessioni cristiane come base di questa elevazione. Le altre religioni, purche' rimangano nell'ambito della disciplina statale, troveranno obbiettiva giustizia."

13. *O. R.*, March 25, 1933, "La lotta antisemita." This article reported the first expulsion of Jews since Hitler's rise to power: "L'espulsione dal Palatinato dei Israeliti (particolarment polacchi) che vi risiedevano dal 1 agosto 1918 ha anticipato ordini ufficiali emessi dal commissario del Reich per Bavaria."

14. *O.R.*, March 30, 1933, "Boicottaggio contro gli Israeliti." The statement read: "Il boicottaggio e' una pura misura di difesa, diretta esclusivamente contro gli Israeliti tedeschi."

15. *O.R.*, March 31, 1933, "Le disposizioni del partito nazionalsocialista per il boicottagiio antisemitico."

16. *O. R.*, February 20, 1943, "Il Primo fondatore dei Monti di Pieta'," and *O.R.*, August 21, 1943, "La Cappella dell'Arco del Monte ed i Monti di Pieta'." Both articles were about the Monti di Pieta', the loan banks established in the sixteenth century by the Franciscans. The earlier article was written on the occasion of the beatification of Michele Carcano, a sixteenth-century Jesuit priest and founder of the Monti.

17. *O.R.*, April 1, 1933, "Come si svolgera' il boicottaggio contro gli Ebrei anche se convertiti." For the Church, the important words in this headline were "anche se convertiti."

18. *O.R.*, April 13, 1933, "Nostre Informazioni" and "Il vice-cancelliere Von Papen e il ministro Goering visitano il Santo Padre." There were two articles about the visit, a sure indication that the Vatican considered it important.

19. *O.R.*, May 13, 1933, "La questione semitica nel campo sportivo."

20. *O.R.*, July 28, 1933, "Proposte a favore degli Israeliti nella Camera dei Comuni."

21. *O.R.*, July 17, 1935, "Ripresa di antisemitismo in Germania." Riots were said to have led to "...il trasferimento degli ebrei nei campi di concentramento per garantire la loro sicurezza."

22. See Anna Foa, *Ebrei in Europa: Dalla peste nera all'emancipazione*

(Rome: Laterza, 1992), p. 57. Of particular interest in this context is the chapter on the Church and the Jews.

23. *O.R.*, September 16–17, 1935 "Hitler e gli Ebrei." Hitler interpreted the new law on nationality thusly: "un servizio reso agli Israeliti. . . che permette agli Ebrei di vivere la propria vita etnica in tutti i campi."

24. *O.R.*, July 15–16, 1935, "Questioni concordatarie in Germania."

25. *O.R.*, March 24, 1938, "La situazione religiosa nell'Austria."

26. *The Papal Encyclicals 1903–1939*, ed. Claudia Carlen (Raleigh, N.C.: McGrath Publishing, 1981), Vol. 3, p. 528.

27. *O.R.*, March 23, 1937, "Dopo l'Enciclica sulla Chiesa in Germania."

28. *O.R.*, March 24, 1937, "L'antisemitismo e le conversioni degli Israeliti."

29. *O.R.*, January 16–17, 1939, "Un'Omelia del Monsignor Cazzani, Vescovo di Cremona."

30. *O.R.*, June 15, 1938, "Il problema ebraico in Polonia."

31. *O.R.*, October 8, 1938, "Le deliberazioni del Gran Consiglio."

32. Alberto Cavaglion and Gian Paolo Romagnani, *Le interdizioni del Duce*, Torino: Albert Meynier Editore, 1988, p.131.

33. *O.R.*, November 12, 1938, "Dopo le manifestazioni antisemite in Germania."

34. *O.R.*, November 13, 1938, "Dopo le manifestazioni antisemite in Germania." The word Goering used was "sterminio."

35. *O.R.*, November 26, 1938, "Inasprimento della lotta antisemita in Germania."

36. *O.R.*, November 28–29, 1938, "Gli ambasciatori in Italia e nel Reich conferiscono con Roosevelt."

37. *O.R.*, December 5–6, 1938, "Roosevelt parlera' oggi sul problema ebriaco."

38. During this period, the O.R. never directly attacked Germany. Rather, it reported incidents that were unfavorable to the Nazis, and quoted speeches, such as Ickes' (see note 39 below) in which they were portrayed as villainous.

39. *O.R.*, December 30, 1938, "Tensione fra Berlino e Washington." Signed G.G. (Guido Gonella) This editorial appeared under the rubric *Acta Diurna*. Appearing intermittently, and often signed, these editorials were read by cognoscenti in order to monitor fluctuations in the Vatican's position on important issues.

40. *O.R.*, January 1, 1939, "Un'informazione berlinese sulle relazioni tedesca-americane."
41. *O. R.*, January 6, 1939, "Un messaggio di Roosevelt a Mussolini sulla questione semitica."
42. Frederick Brown, "The Hidden Encyclical," *New Republic*, April, 15, 1996, p. 31.
43. A doctinaire concern informed Vatican efforts to divert Jewish emigration from Palestine. As killers of Christ, Jews had been banished from the Holy Land to wander in expiation of their guilt. A return to Jerusalem was untenable for the Church before the Jews had accepted Christ. On this doctrine rested the Vatican's support of the Arab cause in the Holy Land.
44. *O.R.*, July 10, 1938, "Ragioni dei nuovi disordini palestinesi: Limitazione dell'immigrazione sionista," an *Acta Diurna* editorial.
45. *O.R.*, January 4, 1939, "Nuovi orientamenti danubiani." (Signed G.G.) An *Acta Diurna* editorial.
46. *O.R.*, January 15, 1939, "Le conversazioni polacco-tedeschi per gli ebrei polacchi."
47. *O.R.*, January 18, 1939, "Le recenti deliberazioni dal comitato ebriaco polacco."
48. Friedlander, p 4.
49. *O.R.*, March 17, 1939, "L'allontamento degli ebrei."
50. *O.R.*, March 17,1939, "Le ripercussioni degli avvenimenti in Boemia."
51. *O.R.*, March 26, "Le leggi ebraiche approvate dalla camera ungherese."
52. *O. R.*, March 20–21, 1939, "Dopo i provvedimenti della razza."
53. *O.R.*, March 23, 1939, "Riaffermata adesione nella politica dell'"Asse."
54. *O.R.*, March 24, 1939, "Misure antiebraiche in Boemia."
55. *O.R.*, March 18, 1939, "Gli ebrei non ammetterebbero le proposte britanniche per la Palestina."
56. *O.R.*, May 14, 1939, "Immigrazione di ebrei nella Guiana britannica." This news was probably tied to Britain's issuance of the MacDonald White Paper, which severely restricted Jewish immigration in Palestine.
57. *O.R.*, November 19, 1944, "Il Terrorismo Ebraico in Palestina."
58. *O.R.*, November 6–7, 1944, "La questione palestinese."

59. Friedlander, pp. 13–17.
60. *O.R.*, November 9, 1939, "Notiziario Polacco."
61. *O.R.*, November 8, 1939, "Notiziario polacco."
62. *O.R.*, November 29, 1939, "La 'riserva' ebraica di Lublino."
63. *O.R.*, November 19, 1939, "Notiziario polacco."
64. *O.R.*, November 15, 1939, "Notiziario polacco." The quote from the German newspaper (translated into Italian) said: "Se la popolazione polacca soffre la fame . . . la colpa e' degli speculatori ebrei(.)"
65. *The Papal Encyclicals 1939–1958*, ed. Claudia Carlen (Raleigh, N.C.: McGrath Publishing, 1981), Vol. 4, p. 19.
66. *O.R.*, January 17, 1940, "Il lavoro obbligatorio per gli ebrei in Polonia."
67. *O.R.*, February 5–6, 1940, "Notiziario polacco." Dutch press called the situation of Jews in Poland "dolorose e tragiche."
68. *O.R.*, February 10, 1940, "Nuovi provvedimenti contro gli ebrei di Polonia."
69. Friedlander, p.17.
70. See Lucjan Dobroszycki, *Reptile Journalism* (New Haven: Yale University Press, 1994.) According to Dobroszycki, news from Poland was available, not only from the underground press but from the "legal" Polish press as well.
71. *O.R.*, July 26, 1941, "Fucillazioni di comunisti in Serbia."
72. *O.R.*, April 6, 1933, "Nuovi leggi contro il terrorismo."
73. *O.R.*, August 13, 1941, "La situazione in Croazia."
74. *O.R.*, August 15, 1941, "Esecuzioni e arresti nei Balcani."
75. *O.R.*, September 7, 1941, "Politica di Vichy."
76. *O.R.*, September 25, 1941, "Condanne del tribunale speciale croato."
77. *Encyclopedia of the Holocaust* (New York: Macmillan, 1990), 4: 1769–1775; Lipstadt, p. 186.
78. Sharf, p. 94.
79. *O.R.*, March 28, 1943, "Documentazione: Germania."
80. See Susan Zuccotti, *The Italians and the Holocaust* (New York: Basic Books, 1987), p. 133; Friedlander, p. 236; Weisbord and Sillanpoa, p.48.
81. *O.R.*, July 30 1943, "Dichiarazione di Roosevelt."
82. *O.R.*, September 20–21, 1043, "Un radiodiscorso di Mussolini."
83. *O.R.*, September 27–28, 1943, "Il Papa si defende."
84. Marshal Pietro Badoglio was chief of staff from 1925 to 1940. In July

1943, when the Fascist government fell, he was appointed head of state by King Victor Emmanuel III.

85. See note 2 above.

86. See Zuccotti, p. 131; Michaelis, p. 371; Friedlander, p. 208.

87. *O.R.*, December, 3 and 4, 1943, "Carita' civile."

88. *O.R.*, July 22, 1944, "Ebrei ungheresi in Palestina."

89. See John T. Pawlikowski, "The Vatican and the Holocaust: Unresolved Issues," in *Jewish-Christian Encounters Over the Centuries*, eds. Marvin Perry and Frederick M. Schweitzer (New York: Peter Lang, 1994), pp. 293–209.

90. Lipstadt, p. 263.

91. *O.R.*, April 27, 1945, "Una relazione sul campo di Buchenwald."

92. *O.R.*, June 1–2, 1945, "Sacerdoti polacchi a Dachau."

93. *O.R.*, May 30, 1945, "La Sante Sede in favore degli Ebrei in Romania."

94. Sharf, p. 93n.

Hungarian Journalism

The Hungarian Press, 1938–1945

Randolph L. Braham
City University of New York

The Holocaust clearly demonstrated the validity of the maxim that the pen is at least as mighty, if not mightier, than the sword. The power of the word was exploited by the Nazis and their accomplices all over Europe, as evidenced by the emphasis they placed on propaganda. The Nazis' propaganda campaign aimed to create a climate of opinion that would make their diabolical plans for the "solution of the Jewish question" acceptable. This was clearly reflected in the prosecution statement in the Nuremberg trial of Julius Streicher, the publisher of the rabidly anti-Semitic *Der Stürmer*:

> No government in the world, before the Nazis came to power, could have embarked upon and put into effect a policy of mass extermination without having a people who would back them and support them. It was to the task of educating people, of producing murderers, educating and poisoning them with hate that Streicher set himself. . . He made these crimes possible which could never have happened had it not been for him and for those like him. . .[1]

Like other countries in Nazi dominated Europe, Hungary too was cursed with many journalists and xenophobic intellectuals agitating in Streicher's vein. These were associated with ultra-Rightist political movements and parties that had at their disposal a large number of anti-Semitic press organs. Collectively, they fostered a climate of opinion that conditioned the Hungarian public to acquiesce in the increasingly severe anti-Jewish policies of the various governments, including those enacted during the Holocaust.

Although the tone of the anti-Jewish drive became particularly abrasive following the adoption of the first major anti-Jewish law in 1938, the climate of intolerance was created after the end of World War I. The disintegration of the Austro-Hungarian Empire and the truncating of Hungary not only put an end to the relatively short-lived "Golden Era" of Hungarian Jewry,[2] but eventually also brought to power a fundamentally anti-Semitic counterrevolutionary regime that ruled the country until the end of World War II. This regime was supported primarily by disgruntled officers who had lost their positions, the fixed-income middle and lower middle classes that were severely hit by the ever steeper inflationary spiral, and the large number of public servants and property owners who escaped from or were expelled by the authorities of the Successor States.[3] These disgruntled elements were susceptible to being swayed by demagogic intellectuals placing the blame for their suffering on the "alien" Jews. As the authors and embodiments of an ideology which came to be known as the "Szeged Idea" (*A szegedi gondolat*)—a nebulous amalgam of political propagandistic views incorporating the concepts of anti-Bolshevism, anti-Semitism, chauvinistic nationalism, and revisionism— these Rightist intellectuals were in fact the forerunners of Hungarian proto-Fascism. Many among them were journalists and editors associated with a variety of anti-Semitic press organs.

The real strongholds of power supporting the champions of the Szeged Idea were the many secret and semi-clandestine patriotic associations and paramilitary organizations that were not only tolerated, but actively encouraged and secretly supported by the counterrevolutionary governments. Using their groups' press organs, the leaders of these associations and organizations arrogated to themselves the power and responsibility to defend "the Magyar cause" by spreading the virulent seeds of revisionism, irredentism, anti-liberalism, and, above all, anti-Semitism. They depicted Jews as "aliens" hostile to the Christian body politic and inimical to the national interests of Hungary. Through the press organs to which they had access, they helped propagate the Nazi myth about the Jews by depicting them as being at once exploiters and revolutionaries, both plutocrats and Bolsheviks. After the collapse of the multinational Hungarian kingdom, the Jews emerged as the most vulnerable minority group. In contrast to the so-called Golden Era when the Jewish question was politically and officially suppressed, in Trianon Hungary the Jews, having lost their importance as statistical recruits to the cause of Magyardom, found themselves exploited as scapegoats for the country's political and economic disasters.

The anti-Jewish campaign gained considerable momentum in 1932–33 with the almost simultaneous acquisition of power by Gyula Gömbös in Hungary and Hitler in Germany. The foremost representative and leader of the Hungarian Radical Right, Gömbös managed during his four-year tenure as prime minister (1932–1936) to tie Hungary's destiny almost irrevocably to Nazi Germany's. He brought Hungary's foreign policy into line with that of the Third Reich and made possible the subsequent penetration and direct involvement of the National Socialists in practically every aspect of the country's life. By replacing large segments of the civil and military bureaucracies of the state apparatus with his own protégés and packing the upper army hierarchy, including the General Staff, with younger, highly nationalistic Germanophile officers, Gömbös brought about the establishment of a collaborationist power base in Hungary which later proved fatal to Hungarian Jewry.

Perhaps the most successful achievement of the Nazis during the Gömbös period was the radicalization of the press. The Third Reich was quite generous in supporting the publication of a large number of vitriolically anti-Semitic dailies and weeklies like *Új Magyarság* (New Magyardom), *Magyarság* (Magyardom), *Virradat* (Dawn), *Magyar Futár* (Hungarian Courier), *Nemzetör* (National Guard), *Összetartás* (Unity), and *Pesti Ujság* (Journal of Pest). The journalists and editors of these publications spewed an incessantly pro-Nazi and virulently anti-Semitic propaganda barrage that poisoned Hungarian public opinion and prepared the ground for the general acceptance of the increasingly severe measures adopted against the Jews.[4] Toward the end of the 1930s, the Jewish question became a major national obsession, frequently rivaling revisionism in the intensity of feeling it aroused. Emulating its Nazi counterpart, the Hungarian radical press became ever more shrill in depicting the Jews as naturally unpatriotic, parasites sapping the energy of the nation, and agents of both Soviet communism and Western capitalism. The propaganda campaign was soon coupled with demands for a definitive solution of the Jewish question. The suggestions offered by the radicals ranged from legal restrictions on the Jews' professional and economic activities to their orderly "resettlement" out of the country.

The anti-Semitic press also played a leading role in crystallizing the ideas and championing the cause of the various Right-radical movements and parties that challenged the legitimacy of the ruling elites on whom the Jews depended for their survival.[5] Having embraced the Third Reich for its opposition to Bolshevism and support for Hungarian revisionism, Hungary's conservative-aristocratic governments were soon compelled to come to grips with the ever more influential Right radicals at home. While they despised and feared these radicals perhaps even more than they did the Jews—the Hungarian ultra-Rightists had advocated not only solving the Jewish question, but also bringing about a social revolution to end the inherited privileges of the ruling elites—the governmental leaders felt compelled to appease them. In fact, they soon looked upon the Right radicals' preoccupation with the Jewish question as a blessing in disguise, for it helped deflect attention from the grave social-agrarian problems confronting the nation.

While opposing the domestic political and socio-economic agenda of the Right radicals, the ruling aristocratic-conservative forces shared some of the ideas advanced by them. These included the issue of territorial revisionism, the pursuit of national-Christian, anti-Bolshevik policies, and the urgent need to "solve" the Jewish question. But while the ruling elite adopted a relatively moderate Italian-type semi-Fascist position, the Right radicals were eager to embrace the German brand of National Socialism. This division in the political Right was reflected especially in the approach to the "solution" of the Jewish question. The aristocratic-conservative-dominated ruling wing, which had good connections with the Jewish upper class, attempted to implement a "civilized" anti-Semitic program calculated not only to gradually diminish and eventually eliminate the Jews' influence from the country's economic and cultural life, but also to appease the Right radicals at home and the National Socialists abroad. While recognizing the danger of German expansionism, this group felt a need to keep on good terms with the Third Reich, primarily for the advancement of Hungary's revisionist objectives. The Right radical wing, on the other hand, was politically and ideologically attracted and firmly committed to Nazism. It wholeheartedly embraced the National Socialist program not only because of its anti-Semitism, though this was its most attractive aspect, but also because of its emphasis on social and political reforms that agreed with their own platform.

Whatever the differences in domestic and foreign policy objectives and tactics, a common denominator in the ideologies of these two wings of the political Right was their preoccupation with the "solution" of the Jewish question. The official press organs of the ruling Hungarian Life Party (*Magyar Élet Pártja*—MÉP)—including *Függetlenség* (Independence) and *Esti Ujság* (Evening Journal)—and those of the Government (*Pester Lloyd* and *Magyarország* [Hungary]) were often as nauseating on this issue as the openly Nazi papers. This stance reflected primarily the position of the Right wing of the ruling elite, which the "moderates" often also felt compelled to adopt for reasons of political expediency.

Despite the deteriorating anti-Jewish climate and the close coopera- tion with the Third Reich, which enabled Hungary to fulfill some of its revisionist ambitions,[6] the aristocratic-conservative government permit- ted the publication of several opposition newspapers. The most important among these were *Népszava* (People's Voice), organ of the Social Democratic Party, the independent *Magyar Nemzet* (Hungarian Nation), *Mai Nap* (Today), the liberal *Pesti Napló* (Journal of Pest), *Ujság* (Journal), *8 Orai Ujság* (The 8 o'Clock Journal), and *Esti Kurir* (Evening Courier), which often provided objective and balanced accounts of the major issues confronting the country.

A fateful turn for the worse came early in 1938, when Hungary adopt- ed the first major anti-Jewish law. Among other things, the law restricted the proportion of Jews employed in the free professions, including jour- nalism, to 20 percent. Under the second major anti-Jewish law, adopted a year later, the proportion was reduced to six percent. Both laws were adopted with the wholehearted support of the Christian Church leaders. The reaction of the press to these anti-Jewish measures was predictable: the Rightist press supported them enthusiastically, hailing the beginning of the drive designed to end the alleged Jewish domination over the coun- try's cultural and economic life. The opposition press deplored the mea- sures and hinted at the influence of the Third Reich in their adoption. Its tone, like the protest by some of Hungary's leading writers and artists, was considerably less critically assertive with regard to the second anti- Jewish law than with regard to the first, although the second one was much more restrictive. Under the provisions of this second anti-Jewish law, Jews were prohibited, among other things, from holding leading positions in the non-Jewish press. The prohibition affected reporters, editors, responsible editors, and publishers of newspapers and periodicals. Following the adoption of this law, the opposition press generally restricted itself to the publication of the major provisions of the law and of the decrees relating to its enactment, without taking real editorial positions against them.

The press-related anti-Jewish measures were adopted on the initiative of the Press Division (*Sajtóosztály*) in the prime minister's office, which had since the end of 1938 been under the leadership of Mihály Kolosváry-Borcsa.[7] A notorious anti-Semite, Kolosváry-Borcsa was a member of the lower house of the Hungarian Parliament, representing Pest-Pilis-Solt-Kiskun County, and served as the editor of *Függetlenség*, one of the ruling party's official organs. Under his leadership, the Press Division was used as a vehicle to curtail not only the Jewish journalists but also those associated with the relatively weak liberal and leftist press. It enthusiastically implemented the provisions of Press Law No. XVIII of 1938, under which the licenses of newspaper publishers were subjected to thorough political scrutiny designed to curtail and eventually eliminate the Jews' role in the press. This measure, coupled with the introduction of prior censorship and strict supervision of newsprint utilization, compelled 430 mostly smaller newspapers to end publication by early 1939.[8] In addition, a large number of Jewish journalists and editors lost their positions by being purged from membership in the Press Chamber (*Sajtókamara.*) In 1941, only 1,572 of the 3,435 applicants for membership in the Press Chamber were admitted, with hardly any Jews among them.[9] The drive against Jewish journalists was also pursued through the cooperation of the ministry of defense, which drafted many of them into the military forced labor service system. Many of these journalists, including some of the most influential figures of the Hungarian press, were assigned to labor service companies that were deployed in the Ukraine and Serbia. Only a few managed to return home after the war.[10]

The opposition press was generally ineffective in counteracting either the anti-Jewish measures of the government or the anti-Semitic onslaught of the Right radical press. This impotence was also the hallmark of the small and increasingly restricted Jewish press, which followed a generally assimilationist, pro-Magyar, patriotic, anti-Zionist line. One of the first victims of the anti-democratic press policies of the Hungarian authorities was *Egyenlöség* (Equality), the country's largest Jewish weekly. Launched in 1882, the weekly was supported primarily by the non-Orthodox strata of Hungarian Jewry. It ceased publication in December 1938 and was succeeded a month later by *A Magyar Zsidók Lapja* (Journal of Hungarian Jews). The new weekly followed the editorial stance of its predecessor, reflecting the assimilationist patriotic posture of the central leadership of Hungarian Jewry. After the outbreak of World War II, *A Magyar Zsidók Lapja* became, for a time at least, Hungarian Jewry's only newspaper. All the other Hungarian- or Yiddish-language papers were compelled to cease publication. The ban affected the Jewish press in the territories acquired by Hungary both before and after the outbreak of the war as well.[11] In 1940, however, the government permitted the publication of a new Hungarian-language Jewish weekly—*Képes Családi Lapok* (Illustrated Family Journal)— that appeared in Budapest. Its title notwithstanding, the weekly was basically non-illustrated and, in accordance with the new regulations, had to identify itself in the subtitle as a "Jewish Journal" (*Zsidó Lap*). This weekly occasionally challenged the policies of the Jewish leaders and devoted more space to issues of emigration and paid more attention to the social and economic problems confronting the Jewish community than *A Magyar Zsidók Lapja*, but it too pursued a basically assimilationist editorial policy. Both weeklies adopted a generally apologetic stance: they tried to evoke the sympathy of the authorities—and indirectly of Christian Hungarians—by featuring articles on the contribution of Hungarian Jews to the enrichment of Hungary's culture and economy and, above all, on their participation in the country's struggle for independence and during World War I.

While the Jewish press and non-Jewish opposition press were under duress, the influence of the Right radical press grew by leaps and bounds. On the eve of World War II, the Rightist press organs were bolstered not only by lavish support from the Third Reich, but also by the virtual free rein they received from the government of Pál Teleki (February 1939–April 1941). They became ever more vocal in advancing the twin causes of Nazism and anti-Semitism. In the forefront of this campaign were the major national dailies *Magyarság*, *Új Magyarság*, *Pesti Ujság*, and *Virradat*. These were joined during Teleki's first year in office by three equally anti-Semitic weeklies—*Holnap* (Tomorrow), *A Nép* (The People), and *Nemzeti Élet* (National Life). Even more rabid in their pro-

Nazism and anti-Semitism were *Összetartás* (Unity), *Egyedül Vagyunk* (We Are Alone), *Ország* (Country), and the pictorial *Magyar Futár* (Hungarian Courier). The publishers, editors, and journalists associated with these press organs, including Ferenc Rajniss (*Magyar Futár*), Olivér Rupprecht (*Magyarság*), György Oláh (*Egyedül Vagyunk*), Ferenc Vajta (*Ország*), Károly Maróthy (*Pesti Ujság*), Gábor Bornemisza (*Összetartás* and *Virradat*), and István Milotay (*Új Magyarság*), poured out an incessant pro-Nazi and anti-Semitic propaganda barrage that poisoned Hungarian public opinion. By fanning the flames of the anti-Jewish psychosis, they laid the foundation for the acceptance of the draconian measures being adopted against the Jews. After Germany's attack on Poland on September 1, 1939, and the consequent outbreak of World War II, the editorial position of most newspapers became even more pro-Nazi, the editors-in-chief having been warned by the prime minister to keep German foreign political interests in mind.

After Hungary joined the Axis in attacking the Soviet Union (June 27, 1941), the anti-Jewish propaganda campaign became more vicious than ever before. Coinciding with the adoption of the openly racist third anti-Jewish law,[12] the press campaign identified the Jews with all the ills of the country. They were blamed not only for Hungary's involvement in the war, but also for all the domestic evils associated with it, including the shortages of goods and the flourishing black market. The Jews were portrayed as "traitorous, unscrupulous, and cheating" throughout Hungarian history—"an alien race with diabolical skills" that represented a clear and present danger to Hungarian society. They were depicted as foreign agents beholden to both Soviet Bolshevism and Western "plutocratic capitalism."

The anti-Semitic Rightist press demanded the emulation of the Third Reich in the "solution" of the Jewish question and offered specific plans for the "resettlement" of the Jews. Urged on by the venomous press campaign and the many anti-Jewish measures of the government, public opinion took a sharp swing to the Right.

The anti-Semitic climate was also exacerbated by some Catholic publications, which were both theologically and culturally anti-Jewish. These further promoted the anti-Semitic indoctrination of the faithful by dwelling on the issue of deicide, blaming the Jews as a whole for the killing of Jesus.[13]

Following the outbreak of hostilities in June 1941, the opposition press became even more ineffective in counteracting the propaganda impact of the Right radicals. This was also true of the main Jewish press organs, the *A Magyar Zsidók Lapja* and the *Képes Családi Lapok*. Like the non-Jewish opposition press in general, they too failed to inform, let alone alert, their readers about the tragedy that was befalling the Jewish communities in Nazi-dominated Europe. The occasional news items about Jewish communities abroad gave the general impression that while anti-Semitism in Hitler's Europe was more intense than ever before, the communities themselves were not threatened by extinction. On August 14, 1941, for example, *A Magyar Zsidók Lapja* reported that German Jews in French labor camps were allowed to petition for voluntary transfer to German labor camps "where they wish to work." In one of the extremely rare, if not the only, references to the Warsaw Ghetto, it was pointed out in this newspaper that "in the midst of the greatest difficulties and deprivations, there are regular cultural performances there."[14] There is no account about mass starvation and death, or the humiliation and tortures to which the Jews of Warsaw and Poland in general were subjected. There is not even a reference to the Warsaw Ghetto Uprising in any issue.

The same misleading impression is conveyed by the one report in *A Magyar Zsidók Lapja* on the Soviet Jewish prisoners of war (POWs) in German hands. Quoting the *Israelitisches Wochenblatt* (Jewish Weekly) of Zurich, the Hungarian Jewish paper informs its readers that the Germans transferred the POWs to camps in the Third Reich, where, according to a finding by the Red Cross, their situation was not objectionable.[15] The Hungarian Jewish masses could not possibly suspect from this article that many of the Soviet POWs in general and the Jewish POWs in particular were subjected, like the deported Jews in Auschwitz and other death camps, to murderous "special treatment" (*Sonderbehandlung*) by the Germans. A similarly false impression was fostered about the fate of the German Jews. On March 12, 1942, for example, when there were hardly any Jews left in Germany, *A Magyar Zsidók Lapja* selectively cited a dispatch from Frankfurt-am-Main to the effect that Dr. Josef Wohlgemuth, the former rector of the rabbinical seminary of Berlin, had died in the local Jewish hospital. Without any reference to the plight of the German Jews since Hitler's coming to power early in 1933, it leaves the impression that the Jews still had their hospitals and implicitly other communal institutions as well.

Misinformation about the plight of the Jews in the Nazi-dominated parts of Europe extended to inaccurate reporting about the suffering of Hungarian Jewish labor servicemen in the Ukraine and elsewhere. While practically every issue of *A Magyar Zsidók Lapja* contained appeals to help the labor servicemen with money and clothing, at no time did these appeals include any accounts of the barbarous treatment of the labor servicemen by many of their commanders and guards as well as the SS. No space was ever allotted to depicting the liquidation of the Jewish communities in the parts of the Ukraine in which many thousands of Hungarian soldiers and Jewish labor servicemen were stationed. Neither was there any account of the roundup and deportation in the summer of 1941 of close to 18,000 "alien" Jews to near Kamenets-Podolsk, where they were murdered by the SS. The same code of silence was generally observed in connection with the massacres that took place in the Újvidék (Novi Sad) area early in 1942.

Képes Családi Lapok, however, occasionally published news about the suffering and difficulties encountered by Jewish labor servicemen, to the chagrin of the authorities. Upon overstepping the boundaries of censorship in 1943, the weekly was suspended by the minister of the interior.[16]

The general silence of the Jewish press about the realities of the Nazi persecutions was matched by that of the non-Jewish opposition newspapers, including *Népszava* and *Magyar Nemzet*, which were as uninformative about the plight of the Jews in Nazi-dominated Europe as *A Magyar Zsidók Lapja*. While both the Jewish and the opposition organs were quite skillful in occasionally informing their readers about the military reverses of the Axis by using a generally understood coded language, they failed to apply the same technique in connection with the plight of European Jewry. As a consequence the Hungarian Jews, lulled into a state of confidence—they deluded themselves by insisting that "what happened in Poland could not possibly happen in chivalrous Hungary"—were caught totally unprepared when Hungary was occupied by the Germans.

In contrast to the Jewish and non-Jewish opposition press organs, which were basically silent about the anti-Jewish drive in Nazi-dominated Europe, the ultra-Rightist press was engaged in a vast disinformation campaign designed to advance the drive for the "solution" of the Jewish question in Hungary. It dwelt extensively on the Nazis' "resettlement" program in Poland and elsewhere in German-occupied Europe. It projected a positive image of the new Jewish "settlements" in the East, claiming that Jews from all over Europe were involved there in "productive" physical work and no longer depended on "blackmarketeering, swindling, and banking" for making a living. The following January 10, 1942, report by *Magyarság* was typical of the accounts provided by many other central and local newspapers about ghetto life in Poland:

> The houses are the property of the state, but the Jews live in them totally without cost. They live an undisturbed private life and enjoy full self-government. Their food is good and the supply is abundant, receiving the same ration as the Germans deployed in the East; those engaged in heavy labor get extra rations. Each person disposes of the wages received in his own way. The [ghetto dwellers] almost never deal with the German authorities. They have no need for that because everything proceeds just fine . . . It is understandable that one of the Jews complained only about one injustice to our reporter, namely that the other [Jews] are still at home wheeling and dealing in their old ways, and he would like all of them without exception to be here.

The failure to reveal the realities of the Nazis' "resettlement" program and the positive portrayal of ghetto life in Poland played into the hands of the Right radicals. The "positive" press accounts not only mollified large segments of Christians, especially the moderates who had some qualms about the "rumored ultimate" fate of the Jews, but also lulled many of the potential victims into inaction. The disinformation accounts, which Jews also read, reinforced in many the belief that the extermination rumors were nothing but anti-Nazi propaganda.

The inciting, propagandistic, anti-Jewish tone of the Budapest-based major Rightist press organs also became the hallmark of most local and provincial newspapers during the war. This was the case not only of those published in Trianon Hungary,[17] but also of those in the reacquired territories.[18] With the passage of time many of the formerly democratic or moderate local press organs were transformed into mouthpieces of the

Right. The liberal journalists associated with them were either silenced or made to adjust to the new political realities.

The anti-Jewish propaganda of the wartime period was matched by that directed against the Allies in general and the Soviet Union in particular. The press organs vilified the leaders of the Grand Alliance as stooges in the service of the Jews' drive for world domination. Using inflammatory rhetoric, they exploited the themes originally expounded in the *Protocols of the Elders of Zion*, emphasizing the conspiratorial power of the Jews in the anti-Axis alliance. Anti-Allied propaganda included the publication of cartoons, pictures, and articles about Anglo-Saxon "atrocity" bombings of non-military targets, including schools, hospitals, and cultural establishments.

The press campaign against the Jews and the Allies became even more vicious after the German occupation of Hungary on March 19, 1944. With the opposition newspapers eliminated, the ultra-Rightist press became an accomplice in the implementation of the Final Solution program.

The tone and content of the press organs were largely determined and supervised by the newly established Office of the Royal Hungarian Government Commissioner of the Press (*A sajtóügyek m. kir. kormánybiztosa*). The leadership of the office was entrusted to Mihály Kolosváry-Borcsa,[19] then head of the National Hungarian Press Chamber (*Országos Magyar Sajtókamara*). The chamber operated in conjunction with the National Press Council (*Országos Sajtótanács*) and the Press Division (*Sajtóosztály*) in the Prime Minister's Office. The main function of the Press Division and of the affiliated agencies was to:

- monitor the press and political literature published in Hungary;
- inform the press about measures taken by the government and, in certain concrete cases, about the position of the government; and
- provide direction in all matters relating to the press's policies.

In early 1944, the Press Division was divided into two sections. The Section of Press Policy (*Sajtópolitikai Osztály*) assumed most of the responsibilities of the Division; while the Press Administration Section (*Sajtóigazgatási Osztály*) was entrusted, among other things, with the administration of legal matters and the preparation of press-related legislation.[20]

Kolosváry-Borcsa's anti-Jewish propaganda campaign was further orchestrated by two agencies: the Hungarian Royal Propaganda Office for National Defense (*Magyar Királyi Nemzetvédelmi Propagandahivatal*) and the Hungarian Institute for the Researching of the Jewish Question (*A Zsidókérdéstkutató Magyar Intézet*)—the former already in existence before the German occupation, the latter established a few months after it.

The Hungarian Royal Propaganda Office for National Defense was established in April 1942 and served in fact as Hungary's Ministry of Propaganda.[21] With several mass media outlets under its direct control and generously supported by the government, it was primarily concerned with molding public opinion along Axis lines. The Propaganda Office's anti-Jewish tone became especially virulent after the German occupation, when it operated with seven departments. Of these, by far the most important were Department I (National Policies, *Nemzetpolitikai Ügyosztály*), which dealt with propaganda and the molding of public opinion, and Department III (Information, *Tájékoztató Ügyosztály*), which monitored public opinion and guided the press organs involved in shaping it.

The Hungarian Institute for the Researching of the Jewish Question was established in April 1944 and formally inaugurated on May 12.[22] Launched with the advice and guidance of *SS-Hauptsturmführer* Ballensiefen, a Nazi expert on anti-Jewish propaganda, the Institute was placed under the leadership of Zoltán Bosnyák, a notorious Hungarian anti-Semite. According to article 3 of its bylaws, the Institute was to "study the Jewish question in Hungary in a systematic and scientific manner, collect and scientifically process the related data, and inform Hungarian public opinion about the Hungarian and general Jewish question." Its major vehicle for the latter purpose was *Harc* (Battle), a vehemently anti-Jewish weekly modelled after the German *Der Stürmer*.

The anti-Jewish tone and content of the Budapest newspapers and periodicals were echoed by those published in the provinces. They applauded the measures adopted by the post-occupation quisling government against the Jews. They printed and gleefully commented on the increasingly severe decrees relating to the isolation, expropriation, ghettoization, and concentration of the Jews. Most of the local newspapers became the mouthpiece of the pro-Nazi regime, enthusiastically supporting all anti-Jewish policies. Many of their feature articles focused attention on loopholes in the existing anti-Jewish legislation, often calling for ever harsher restrictions. Virtually all newspapers praised the "positive" impact of the anti-Jewish measures in the country and aimed to reassure their readers about the ultimate fate of the deported Jews. Many of the articles dealt with the healthier lifestyle that was reportedly created for the Jews in the new "settlements in the East." After the Jews were deported from the various "operational zones,"[23] the anti-Semitic press became preoccupied with issues relating to the spoliation of Jewish property.

With new and more stringent censorship laws fully enforced after the German occupation, *A Magyar Zsidók Lapja* was also transformed into an instrument of the Nazis and their Hungarian accomplices.[24] As the only "official" organ of Hungarian Jewry—the Jews were urged to subscribe to it—the weekly was exploited by the Nazis to lull the Jews into accepting all the measures that were enacted against them.[25] It printed not only the decrees and orders issued by both the Hungarian and the Nazi authorities, but also the reassuring messages of the central leadership of the Jewish community. The appeals for calm and submission emanating from the leaders of the Jewish Council of Budapest were reinforced by those issued by some of the country's top rabbinical figures. In the virtual absence of any other source of information,[26] the Jewish masses, isolated and uninformed about the realities of Auschwitz, accepted the measures that had been adopted against them. It is one of the great tragedies of the Holocaust era that the provincial Jews of Hungary were liquidated on the eve of Allied victory, when leaders of the world, including the Jewish and non-Jewish leaders of Hungary, were already familiar with the Nazis' Final Solution program. Kept in the dark about the secrets of the death camps, the Hungarian Jews accepted the draconian measures that were enacted against them with the fatalism that characterized the behavior of the other Jewish communities in Nazi-dominated Europe. For the Nazis and their Hungarian accomplices who recognized that the Axis had lost the war against the Allies, the liquidation of Hungarian Jewry represented the last major victory in the genocidal war against the Jews. The anti-Semitic indoctrination and propaganda to which the Hungarian people were subjected during the war years conditioned them to accept the speed, effectiveness and fanaticism with which the deportations were carried out. The genocidal "victory" was made possible not only by the ruthlessness of the SS and the Hungarian gendarmerie and police, but also by the anti-Semitic press.

Notes:

1. Robert E. Conot, *Justice at Nuremberg* (New York: Harper & Row, 1983), pp. 384–85.
2. For some details on the Golden Era of Hungarian Jewry, see Randolph L. Braham, *The Politics of Genocide. The Holocaust in Hungary*, 2d ed. (New York: The Rosenthal Institute for Holocaust Studies of the City University of New York, 1994), pp. 1–39. (Cited hereafter as Braham, *Politics*).
3. Under the impact of the depression of the 1930s, the Right radical movements also gained the support of a sizable number of industrial workers and landless peasants who were swayed by the demagogic promises of social and economic reforms.
4. Among the most notorious of these Right-radical journalists were Gábor Bornemissza, Ferenc Fiala, Kálmán Hubay, Károly Maróthy, Ferenc Mikes, István Milotay, Árpád Oláh, Ferenc Rajniss, Oliver Rupprecht, and Ferenc Vajta. For some details on these ultra-Rightist journalists and the newspapers they worked for, consult Róbert Major, *25 év ellenforradalmi sajtó, 1919–1944* (Twenty-Five Years of Counterrevolutionary Press, 1919–1944) (New York: Magyar Zsidók Világszövetsége, 1972).
5. For some details on these Right-radical movements and parties, see Braham, *Politics*, pp. 57–70.
6. Hungary acquired the so-called *Felvidék* (Upper Province) in November 1938, and Carpatho-Ruthenia (*Kárpátalja*) in March 1939, from Czechoslovakia; Northern Transylvania from Romania in August 1940; and the so-called *Délvidék* (Bácska) area from Yugoslavia in April 1941. Its Jewish population, consequently, increased from 400,000 to more than 820,000, including the approximately 100,000 converts identified as Jews under the Nazi laws in effect during the Holocaust.
7. For some specific functions of the Press Division, see below.
8. *Magyar Sajtó* (Hungarian Press), official organ of the Hungarian Press Chamber (*Magyar Sajtókamara*), as quoted by Pëter Róbert, "A Holocaust a magyar sajtóban" (The Holocaust in the Hungarian Press), in Studies on Hungarian Jewry, ed. Randolph Braham (forthcoming; manuscript, p. 16.)
9. Ibid., p. 22.
10. Among the journalists drafted into the labor service system were such

Why Didn't The Press Shout?

well-known journalists and writers as Viktor Brassai, Ernö Ligeti, Iván Erdös, Soma Braun, Ernö Salamon, and Béla Zsolt.

11. Among the newspapers banned in Northern Transylvania, for example, were *Új Kelet* (New East), the largest circulation daily published in Kolozsvár (Cluj), and *Népünk* (Our People), published in Nagyvárad (Oradea).

12. Enacted on August 2, 1941, the third anti-Jewish law was clearly based upon the Nuremberg Law of 1935.

13. Historically, many of the Christian denominational journals and periodicals were in the forefront of the anti-Judaism and anti-Semitic agitation. Among the worst offenders were the Catholic *Egyházi Közlöny* (Church Gazette) and *Magyar Kultura* (Hungarian Culture). The March 20, 1943, issue of *Magyar Kultura*, the leading periodical of Catholic intellectuals, for example, carried an article by József Takács titled "Krisztus és a zsidóság" (Christ and Jewry). He asserted that the Jews deserved their fate for having murdered Jesus Christ: "The entire people, Jewry as a whole is guilty for this. . . . Since then they do not constitute a chosen people. Since then there is only a cursed people!" György Kis, *Megielölye Krisztus keresztjével és Dávid csillagával* (Identified by Christ's Cross and David's Star) (Budapest: The Author, 1987), pp. 228–229. On the anti-Jewish character of Christian press organs, see also pp. 210, 224–225, 229–231, 241 and 254–255. See also Róbert, p. 35.

14. *A Magyar Zsidók Lapja*, October 11, 1941, p. 2.

15. Ibid.

16. The suspension was noted without comment by *A Magyar Zsidók Lapja*. Péter Robert, "A Holocaust a magyar sajtóban," p. 35.

17. Among the most influential local press organs in Trianon Hungary were *Györi Nemzeti Hirlap* (National Journal of Györ), *Debreceni Ujság* (Newspaper of Debrecen), *Reggeli Hirlap* (Morning Journal) of Miskolc, and *Dunántul* (Transdanubia), the regional organ.

18. Among the most important local Rightist newspapers in Northern Transylvania, for example, were *Esti Lap* (Evening Journal) of Kolozsvár, *Szamosvölgye* (Szamos Valley) of Dés; the daily *Székely Nép* (The Szekely People) of Sepsiszentgyörgy, the largest provincial paper in Hungary; the weekly *Gyergyói Lapok* (Gyergyó Papers) of Gyergyószentmiklós; and three Kolozsvár periodicals: *Hitel* (Credit), *Pásztortüz* (Shepherd's Fire), and *Katolikus Status* (Catholic Status).

19. Mihály Kolosváry-Borcsa had previously served as Chief of the Press Department in the Béla Imrédy government (1938–39). He was appointed to this new position on April 7, although the announcement was not made until April 15. *Budapesti Közlöny* (Gazette of Budapest), April 30, 1944, pp. 5–6. He was relieved of the position on September 9, 1944, i.e., two months after the mass deportations were halted.

20. For details on the structure, functions, and personnel of the Press Division, the Hungarian Press Chamber, and the National Press Council during the 1942–44 period, see *Magyarország tiszti cim- és névtára* (Title and Name Register of Hungary) (Budapest: Magyar Királyi Allami Nyomda), vol. 49, 1942, pp. 26, 32; vol. 50, 1943, pp. 27, 33–34; vol. 51, 1944, pp. 27, 34–35; and vol. 51, 1944 (Supplement), p. 8.

21. Between April 1942 and August 1944, the Propaganda Office was headed by István Antal, who also served as minister of justice and acting minister of religious affairs and education.

22. The founders included Kolosváry-Borcsa, Zoltán Bosnyák, László Endre, and Ákos Doroghi Farkas—notorious anti-Semites who played a leading role in the destruction of Hungarian Jewry.

23. The deportation of the Jews began on May 15, 1944, and by the time it was halted on July 9, all of Hungary (with the notable exception of Budapest) was already *Judenrein*.

24. A short while after the occupation, the name of the weekly was changed to *A Magyarországi Zsidók Lapja* (Journal of the Jews of Hungary). This was in tune with the new political climate in the country that no longer identified the Jews as "Hungarian" but merely as living in Hungary.

25. For some details, see Braham, *Politics*, pp. 462–78.

26. Almost immediately after the occupation, the Jews were prohibited from having radios and telephones, forbidden to travel, and compelled to wear a Yellow Star.

Romanian Journalism

The Romanian Press:
Preparing the Ground for the Holocaust and Reporting on its Implentation

Radu Ioanid
United States Holocaust Memorial Museum

Preparing the Ground for the Holocaust

Pointing out that Romanian anti-Semitism did not develop into genocide accidentally, Lucretiu Patrascanu (Minister of Justice in the first government that succeeded the Antonescu regime and a Communist who was executed in a show trial in 1954) wrote sometime between March 1942 and September 1943: "For years Romanian public opinion had been poisoned by an infamous anti-Semitic press campaign. The lie, the calumny, the falsehood up to the most shameless demagogy—everything had been used."[1] This press campaign corrupted many minds and its arguments served as justification for many acts of cruelty perpetrated by Romanian fascists. Patrascanu continued:

> Official pogroms were organized, the soldiers and the state organs being ordered to carry them out. Thousands and tens of thousands of individuals, men and women, children and old people who were made to cross the Dniester in the winter were condemned to certain death through the hunger and the cold that ravaged those deserted regions.[2]

Between the two World Wars, Romania had one of Europe's largest Jewish populations; its 759,930 Jews in 1930 constituted the largest Jewish community after the Jewries of Poland and the Soviet Union. In 1923 a new Constitution adopted under the pressure of the Western powers granted citizenship to almost all members of the ethnic minorities living in Romania. This juridical situation remained in place until 1938.

Anti-Semitism was one of the main ideological components of the Romanian extreme right. Before 1938, when the royal dictatorship of King Carol II dissolved all political parties, the League of National Christian Defense (LANC) and Iron Guard theoreticians systematically presented the Jews as the ruling economic class in Romania, as the major threat to the existence of the Romanian state, being spies, Communists, agents of Soviet Russia, and generally as the principal enemy of the Romanian people. They argued that the Jews were guilty of promoting communism, syphilis, alcoholism, prostitution, abortion, divorce, pederasty and feminism. For many years, day after day, the Iron Guard and LANC newspapers disseminated hatred and violence against the Jews, paving the road to the Holocaust.

A. C. Cuza, the leader of LANC, wrote that "The elimination of the kikes from within the other nations where they live as dangerous parasites for their existence is the sole possible solution—according to science, the Christian religion and humanity—of the Jewish problem."[3] C.Z. Codreanu, leader of the Iron Guard, emphasized in a programmatic book for his legionnaires, that "The historical mission of our generation is the solving of the Jewish problem. Our struggle of over fifteen years had this scope and all our future efforts will have this scope."[4]

Very often the Romanian fascists presented all Jews as being Communists. For example, C. Z. Codreanu wrote about the relation between Jews and communism, declaring that "every kike, tradesman, intellectual, banker or capitalist in his sphere of action was an agent of these revolutionary anti-Romanian ideas."[5] In fact the Romanian Communist Party (RCP) was extremely small. In June 1940, there were 4,210 registered members of the RCP. According to post-World War II testimonies another 5,917 people were considered "under the influence" of the RCP.[6] Romanian anti-Semites who equated Jews with communism were never able to reconcile the very well known truth of the weakness of the RCP with the very large number of Romanian Jews.

Ernest Bernea, a theorist of the Iron Guard, emphasized the programmatic priority for his organization to solve the "Jewish problem":

We had [the year] 1877 which saved us from the Turks. When will we have another 1877 which will save us from the Jews and their Communist seeds[?] We need a second independence.

Because we are not with the masonic Communist and Jewish France, we are Hitler's followers.[7]

Mircea Eliade, a preeminent Iron Guard propagandist, openly assumed the consequences of his anti-Semitic writings: "I know very well that the Jews will shout that I am a hooligan or a fascist. . . I am not upset when I hear the Jews shouting 'anti-Semitism', 'fascism', 'Nazism'."[8]

When the fragile political balance of post-World War I Europe was destroyed, the Romanian governments felt free to cancel the laws emancipating the Romanian Jews.

King Carol, who viewed the National Christian Party (PNC—successor of LANC) of Goga and Cuza as a lesser evil than the Iron Guard and installed it in power for a few months, explained his intentions and feelings toward the Jews in an interview given to A.L. Easterman of the London *Daily Herald* on January 10, 1938:

> What happened was something in the nature of an invasion of Galician and Russian Jews who came illegally. Their number was exaggerated: some say as many 800,000 but the maximum was about 250,000 who invaded the villages and are not a good element. . . . Can people be regarded as good citizens who entered the country by fraud? . . . There is no question of expulsion. But the public feeling is such that we cannot give political rights to the invaders. There is no reason for anxiety abroad in this matter. We shall not be rabid.[9]

Four days earlier, Octavian Goga, the newly appointed Prime-Minister talked to the journalist Easterman about "500,000 vagabond people whom we cannot regard as Romanian citizens" and detailed his plans to "ban 500,000 Jews from citizenship and try to expatriate them."[10]

What were the concrete proposals of the Romanian fascists for solving the "Jewish problem"? On January 10, 1938, Octavian Goga, under obvious Nazi influence, proposed (in an interview given to the French daily *Paris Soir*) the deportation of all European Jews to Madagascar which would be surrounded by the warships of the League of Nations to make impossible "the escape of the Jews. . ."[11] Also in 1938, Alexandru Razmerita, a high school teacher, criticized the position of a priest who wanted to drown the Jews in the Black Sea, arguing that this solution would make the Romanian fleet unavailable. Razmerita described in detail "a plan for the total elimination of the Jews" in the cities and their deportation to the countryside for forced labor. According to Razmerita, the Jews ought to be deprived of the right to have recourse through the justice system. Attempts to escape the work camps ought to be punished by execution. He also proposed introducing little village camps containing 24 to 40 men, with forced labor applying also to children older than ten. The children were to be separated from their parents and their identity papers were to contain only the name of the "owner" to whom they were assigned.[12]

On January 21, 1938, Royal Decree no. 169 signed by King Carol II and Prime Minister Octavian Goga, established "revision" of the grant of citizenship to the Jews. In clarifying the reasons for this decree, Minister of Justice V. Radulescu gave as fundamental motivation for this law "the invasion" of the Jews into Romania after 1918. The Constitutional Law of February 27, 1938, emphasized "the proclamation of the law of the blood" and also "the juridical and political distinction between the Romanians having Romanian blood" and "other" Romanian citizens. In a similar vein, on December 1, 1938, Gheorghe Alexianu, Royal Resident (Governor) of Suceava district (who three years later became the Governor of Transnistria) also issued a decree (adopted in order "to protect the public property and to maintain the public order and security") forbidding the Jewish population "to use any other language than Romanian in places of businesses, factories, banks, industrial establishments, professional offices, industrial and commercial enterprises, in the halls of the Palace of Justice, in general in all public places."[13] Article 3 of this decree specified: "The Jews who will continue to speak some other language than Romanian on the streets and in public places will thereby prove that they are not Romanian citizens and will not be able to enjoy the privileges of Romanian citizenship."[14]

One month before General Antonescu took power, the Gigurtu government of King Carol II passed severely anti-Semitic legislation openly inspired by the Nuremberg racial laws. On August 8, 1940, Carol signed the decree-law no. 2650 concerning the juridical situation of the Jews living in Romania (also signed by Prime Minister Ion Gigurtu and the Minister of Justice Ion V. Gruia.) On the same date, another law (no.

2651) was published, forbidding marriages between "Romanians with Romanian blood" and Jews. These two laws are important in the analysis of the Romanian fascist anti-Semitic legislation because they remained in force and were a permanent reference point for the subsequent Antonescu-Sima (September 1940–January 1941) and Antonescu (January 1941–August 1944) governments. The last period of the royal dictatorship had strong fascist characteristics and these laws, which preceded the Antonescu-Sima fascist government by one month, clearly were the first Romanian fascist "racial" laws. From August 1940 until May 1942, hundreds of anti-Semitic decrees and administrative decisions were adopted in Romania. These regulations covered all aspects of economic, political and social life.

A violent anti-Semitic press campaign developed in Romania at the beginning of the rule of General Antonescu, who took power with the Iron Guard on September 6, 1940. This press campaign asked for stronger anti-Semitic laws, approved the deportations to Transnistria and eulogized the ghettos as the only "solution for the Jewish problem." Especially in *Porunca Vremii*, but also in other newspapers, violent and injurious hate toward the Jews was a daily subject. The Jews were presented once again as the main source of Romanian difficulties, as traitors, as the people who started the war. This anti-Semitism was racial, economic and religious. Ion Antonescu was himself a fanatical Jew hater. On September 28, 1940, three weeks after taking power, in an interview granted to the Italian newspaper *La Stampa*, he emphasized that solving the "Jewish problem" was one of the most important among the tasks of the new government.[15]

During the Antonescu regimes (Antonescu ruled with and without the Iron Guard), the racist aspects of the Iron Guard and Antonescu's propaganda intensified. In 1940 Traian Herseni, theorist of the Iron Guard's racism, adopted the slogan of another member of the Iron Guard, Constantin Papanace, who proposed to use racial purification against the Jews, Greeks and the Gypsies:

> We need eugenics laws and eugenic practices. Reproduction cannot be left to hazard . . . [C]ertain people must not be allowed to reproduce themselves and inferior races must be completely isolated from the [main] ethnic group. The sterilization of certain

categories of people must not be conceived in a stupid manner, as a violation of human dignity but as a eulogy to beauty, morality and perfection.[16]

Traian Herseni also advocated "the elimination of the Jews because they belong to an inferior race."[17] Another supporter of eugenic laws was P. Tiparescu who wrote in 1941 about "racial diseases" and maintained that the Jews "are the most dangerous carriers of infectious diseases because of their dirtiness" yet without being themselves infected.[18]

Romanian fascist theorists who were also members of Antonescu's administration proposed eugenics laws and practices including steriliza-tion of the Jews.[19] The Romanian racist Toma Petrescu wrote that mar-riages between Jews and Romanians are a danger for the biological health of the state: "Jews are degenerate people because they have a great num-ber of insane individuals." Furthermore, "all the Jewish women married to Christians are working as spies for foreign powers." Toma Petrescu proposed that "all the state clerks in Romania be prohibited from marry-ing Jewish women [and proposed] to apply forced sterilization for the bastards born from these marriages."[20] Ion Chelcea, professor at the University of Iasi, advocated the same solution for the Gypsies.[21]

At the end of January 1941, during the Iron Guard rebellion against its former ally, General Antonescu, Iron Guard members savagely killed 120 Jews in Bucharest and devastated over one thousand Jewish proper-ties. General Antonescu, hitherto the savior of the legion and the nation, was now labeled by the rebels as an agent of "Judeo-Masonry" and of "English espionage." For his part, Antonescu accused the legionnaires (previously "his children") of being Communists. The legionary masses were thrown into battle against the Romanian army to cries of "Down with the Freemason," "Long live Horia Sima," and "Death to the Kikes."

Iron Guard propaganda clearly indicated that the authors of the con-flict between the legionary movement and General Antonescu were the Jews. A leaflet signed by Viorel Trifa, president of the Iron Guard student organization that was protesting against the assassination of the German Major Doering by an Intelligence Service agent, blamed the assassination on the Jews and asked "for the removal of all masonic and pro-Jewish per-sons from the government."[22] An article published in the Iron Guard newspaper *Cuvantul*, signed by Serban Milcoveanu, emphasized that

"Today as yesterday we have before us all the kikes and the robbers of this country."[23] A leaflet signed by Dumitru Groza, chief of the Iron Guard workers, targeted as their main adversary "the cursed masonic Hydra who is showing his fangs through the sinister grin of the pro-Jewish Riosanu."[24] (Riosanu was a high ranking official at the Ministry of Internal Affairs trusted by Antonescu in his fight against the Iron Guard.) Another Iron Guard call to arms, published by *Cuvantul* under the title "How the Judeo-Masonic Plot Was Organized," appealed for unity between the legionary movement and the army: "If it is necessary to use weapons let's not fire at each other; we know very well whom to shoot at. The kikes and the free-masons are taking advantage of this misunderstanding."[25]

Reporting on the Holocaust.

At the end of June 1941, over 8,000 Jews were killed in Iasi and in two death trains. The pogrom of Iasi, which started on June 28, 1941, was organized by the leadership of *Serviciul Special de Informatii* (SSI), the Romanian agency in charge of espionage and counter-espionage, in close collaboration with Section II of the Romanian Army General Headquarters. There was also some German involvement in the organization of the pogrom.

In the city of Iasi Romanian and German military units, Romanian police and gendarmerie units, former Iron Guard members and local mobs perpetrated the killings. The heaviest responsibility lies with the local Romanian military authorities and with the Romanian and German commanders of the units in transit through Iasi toward the front line. There was no *Einsatzgruppen* involvement in the pogrom of Iasi where scenes of unbelievable cruelty took place. Jews were killed with iron bars and machine-gunned in the streets or in the courtyards. After the killings, two trains were sealed and many deportees perished due to lack of air and water. At least 2,594 Jews died in the two death trains. The officially issued communiqué on the pogrom of Iasi acknowledged that 500 Jews died, and went on to explain:

> The Soviets are trying in every possible way to inspire sabotage, disorder, and aggression behind the front. To this end they parachute spies and terrorists from airplanes. Once on land, the

enemies contact local agents in Romania and Judeo-Communists, jointly organizing acts of aggression. Some agents have been caught and punished for attempted acts of aggression. In Iasi, 500 Judeo-Communists, who had fired from houses at German and Romanian soldiers, were executed. All further attempts to disturb peace and order will be mercilessly repressed.[26]

Porunca Vremii and other newspapers used this communiqué in order to launch a new anti-Semitic campaign and to praise Ion Antonescu for his determined attitude against the Jews.

The events in Iasi were followed by many other mass killings, especially in Bessarabia and Bukovina and by the deportation of the entire Jewish population from Bessarabia and of almost all Jews from Northern Bukovina. German involvement in the killing of Romanian Jews began after Romania entered the war in June 1941, but this involvement varied in magnitude. Sometimes, as in the cases of the mass killings in Balti and Chisinau, *Einsatzgruppen* units and Romanian army and gendarmerie units acted together. On the other side of the Bug, where the Romanian jurisdiction ended, the Germans killed Romanian Jews handed over from Transnistria by the Romanian administration. In the case of the mass killings in Odessa and in the Golta district the Romanian responsibility was overwhelming while the Germans' was minimal.

The destruction of the Romanian Jews was systematic in Bessarabia, Bukovina and Transnistria especially at the beginning of the war; but unsystematic in the Old Kingdom, that is Romania in its pre-World War I borders. Almost all the Jewish population from rural areas of Bessarabia and Bukovina was wiped out by Romanian and German armies during the first weeks of the war. Before 1940 approximately 300,000 Jews lived in Bessarabia and Bukovina. Several sources indicate that some 130,000 retreated with the Red Army or were deported to Siberia by the Soviet authorities just before the beginning of the war. According to Raul Hilberg over 27,000 Jews were killed in July and August 1941, especially in Bessarabia and Bukovina (over 10,000 in July shootings, about 7,000 in August in transit camps, and about 10,000 in Transnistria). Between 140,000 and 160,000 Jews were seized for deportation in Bessarabia, Bukovina and Dorohoi, and at least 118,000 of them had reached the eastern shore of the Dniester during the Fall of 1941. Two years later, only 50,741 of the Bessarabian, Bukovinian and Dorohoi Jewish deportees were left alive in Transnistria. From within Old Romania, 10,000 to 12,000 Jews were deported from Dorohoi county by the Romanian authorities to Transnistria but only 6,000 came back. Also deported from Old Romania to Transnistria were about 2,000 Jews, including political prisoners, people who tried to escape forced labor, and families who before the war had wanted to emigrate to the Soviet Union. In Transnistria, Romanian authorities were also responsible for the killing of approximately 150,000 indigenous Jews in the Odessa area and Golta. About 25,000 Gypsies were also deported from Old Romania to Transnistria; only a few thousand returned. The deportations of all the Jews from Bessarabia and Bukovina were ordered by Ion Antonescu. The vice-president of the Romanian government, Mihai Antonescu, super-vised the elaboration of the anti-Semitic laws and regulations implement-ed in Bessarabia and Bukovina. Both Antonescus considered the Jews from Bessarabia and Bukovina to be traitors, Soviet agents and Communists. The pretext was the fact that these Jews had lived one year under Soviet occupation in Bessarabia and Northern Bukovina and that some of them welcomed the Red Army and showed hostility toward the retreating Romanian armies in 1940. In fact the old dream of Romanian nationalists to have these provinces free of Jews and other minorities seemed feasible at the beginning of World War II. Consequently, in the autumn of 1941, after the reoccupation of these provinces by the Romanian Army, the military units and the police carried out the depor-tation of the remaining Jews to Transnistria.[27]

Once the war against the Soviet Union began, the Romanian fascist propaganda very often employed the theme of Jewish espionage. The Jews were consistently presented as "Bolshevik agents," as mortal ene-mies of Romania. A former member of the Iron Guard, Constantin Virgil Gheorghiu wrote, reporting from the Eastern front about "all the Jews, lit-tle children and old people included [who] are spying for the Bolsheviks . . . These deadly enemies of our country day and night carry information about the positions of our armies."[28]

The first wave of deportations of the Jews at the very beginning of the war was also reflected by the Romanian press. From a news report pub-lished on July 6, 1941:

On the roads of Moldova I encountered numerous convoys of carriages and whole trains of wandering Jews. They came [to Moldova] with bundles on their backs and they left in the same way. And the women and the children who are still in shtetls and towns wear as a distinctive sign on the right arm a yellow armband on which is sewn the Jewish star. Now they are completely isolated from Christianity.[29]

Antonescu responded by letter on October 14, 1941, to Wilhelm Filderman, the President of the Union of Jewish Federations, who had begged him not to deport the Jews from Bessarabia and Bukovina: "Even before the appearance of the Soviet troops, the Jews of Bessarabia and Bukovina spat upon our officers, tore off their epaulets, ripped their uniforms and, when they could, beat and killed our soldiers like cowards."[30] In the same letter Antonescu blamed the Jews for the resistance of the Soviet troops that opposed the Romanian armies: "In return for our generous reception and treatment given them, your Jews who have become Soviet Commissars drove the Soviet troops ahead in the Odessa region into unheard-of terror, as confessed by Russian prisoners; [they] resorted to useless massacre, only to cause us further losses."[31] This letter did not remain private, but was released to the Romanian press which started a new and extremely violent campaign against the Jews. Newspapers like *Actiunea, Unirea, Gazeta Tarii, Opinia Capitalei* and especially *Porunca Vremii* used this pretext in order to launch a new and heavy anti-Semitic campaign.

Many of these anti-Semitic attacks again presented Antonescu's point of view justifying the deportations and praised him for the deportations. For example, Ilie Radulescu, director of *Porunca Vremii*, on October 27, 1941, published an article entitled "Long Life to Marshall Antonescu":

Marshall Antonescu yesterday replied to the repeated insinuations of Dr. Filderman . . . What did the kikes do in Bessarabia and Bukovina, not to mention their demented outbursts on this side of the Prut in Iasi for example? They spat on the Romanian officers, they tore their uniforms, killed our soldiers with sticks in 1940 in order to receive the Bolsheviks with flowers. . . . *The Jewish problem has started to be solved in a radical and defini-*

tive way in Romania. The first groups of kikes are sent to the ghettos from the Bug.[32]

An anonymous author in *Opinia Capitalei* also praised the ghettoization in Transnistria:

The order for ghettoization on the Bug is a tolerant order, an order of mercy and of profound humanity. One cannot imagine a more tolerant treatment toward the people who showed hatred of the ultimate enemy and the savage cruelty of those about whom the fuhrer Adolf Hitler said that they are not human beings anymore but beasts.[33]

A similar theme was treated by Stefan Anghelescu in *Porunca Vremii*:

Our force of cleansing and of getting rid of the parasitic creatures who lived so long on the body of this nation grows to true dimensions. The kikes are leaving. They are leaving toward the Bug. The ghettos of a new century emerge, of the twentieth century.[34]

In the same issue of *Porunca Vremii*, I.P. Prundeni wrote:

Jewry went down without glory and it is only a cadaver that we have to evacuate as soon as possible. But we cannot have pity. We were not created to take care of the sorrow of Jewry. We respond to hate with hate. The country must be disinfected. The convoy of our oppressors goes nobody knows where and we salute this somber procession as a liberation. [35]

The director of *Porunca Vremii*, Ilie Radulescu, wrote on October 30, 1941:

The dice have been thrown. The liquidation of Judaism has entered its final and decisive phase in Romania: the exodus, the elimination of the Jews from the nation's community becomes reality. . . . The rest, the phases of the liquidation are only a formality. The great and definitive liberation of Romania was pro-

Why Didn't The Press Shout?

mulgated and this is the merit of the Marshall [Antonescu]. To the joy of the liberation is added the pride of being a pioneer and road opener in solving the Judaic problem in Europe. From the satisfaction with which the German press records the words and the decisions of the Marshall we understand that today's Romania is anticipating the historical decisions of tomorrow's Europe in the Jewish question.[36]

One day later Ilie Radulescu also wrote:

The divorce between us and the kikes having been a priority for a long time is today definitively and irrevocably decided. Especially after the public response given by Marshall Antonescu to Filderman, there is no Romanian or kike to not understand that the separation is a simple question of procedure, a reality with its last forms to be filled. Between us and the kikes a deep ravine was dug which cannot be filled in, not even let's say [by] an impossible victory of England.[37]

The summer and the fall of 1942 represented a critical time for the Jews of the Old Kingdom and Southern Transylvania. During this period Romanian authorities made the decision to deport all Romanian Jews to the German death camps and a schedule of trains for the transports was established. But due to international pressures, intervention by the leaders of the Romanian Jewish community, and by several Romanian politicians, clergymen, as well as the Royal Palace, Antonescu postponed the deportation to the spring of 1943. During November and December 1942, despite strong German pressure Romanian authorities became more and more elusive about this matter, as they started to understand that the Germans could lose the war. In addition to defamation and violence, opportunism was another main feature of Romanian anti-Semitism. If at the beginning of the war, the German authorities were dissatisfied by the *ad hoc* nature of the Romanian killing of the Jewish population, in 1942 they were strongly displeased by the Romanian refusal to deport Romanian Jews to the Nazi death camps. This was not the first clash between Romanians and Germans in Jewish matters. During the summer of 1941 the Germans protested several times because the Romanian units did not bury their Jewish victims, thus creating the danger of epidemics and possibly damaging the image of both armies. Another conflict arose in July-August 1941 when the Romanians tried to push thousands of Jews across the Bug River in an attempt to have them killed by *Einsatzgruppe D*. Busy with the killings of the Jews of Ukraine, the Germans pushed the Romanian Jews back into Bessarabia.

The Allies, especially the United States, were pretty well informed about the treatment of the Jews in Romania. Romania broke its diplomatic relations with the U.S. in December 1941. Until that date the American Legation in Bucharest sent fairly accurate reports on the pogrom of Iasi and the deportation of the Jews from Bessarabia and Bukovina. In the fall of 1941, *The Record* (published by the United Romanian Jews of America, a World Jewish Congress affiliate) reported on the Bucharest pogrom[38] of the previous January, under the title "Mass Execution of Jews—Why Does Washington Remain Silent." Quoting diplomatic sources from Ankara, Turkey, as well as the London *Evening Standard* and the Jewish Telegraphic Agency in Lisbon, in June 1942 *The Record* further described the massacres of Bessarabia and Bukovina in 1941, the ghettoization of the Jews in those regions, their deportation to Transnistria and the typhus epidemics in that region.[39]

In September 1942, on Rosh Hashanah, a rumor circulated in Bucharest: the American Secretary of State Cordell Hull's declaration of sympathy toward the European Jews, which was allegedly broadcasted from New York. This "declaration" had a broad impact in Romania. Vasile Mares, a friend of Antonescu used it as a pretext for refusing a position in the Antonescu government. Even the intensely anti-Semitic journalist I.P. Prundeni of *Porunca Vremii* mentioned Cordell Hull's declaration and wrote using a milder tone:

> In the overflow of our hate there is a discreet sentiment of admiration for all this stubbornness in believing shown by the Jews, for this calculated resignation and this outstanding robustness which is shown in the acceptance of the suffering and the persecutions. The fundamental merit of Jewry is this unusual power to begin anew after all catastrophes. These are the dimensions of the problem, the way in which it should be seen after eliminating from the waves of hate the adjectives which never resolve anything.[40]

One week later the Romanian newspapers mentioned the round up of 4,000 Romanian Jews in Paris.[41] Arrested because of the lack of Romanian consular protection over them, they were interned in Drancy, from which most were sent to Auschwitz. A press release from the Romanian Ministry of Propaganda announced in November 1942 that bookshops were forbidden to sell the works of 45 Jewish authors, including Camil Baltazar, Emil Dorian and Tristan Tzara, among others.[42]

Romanian authorities intensely implemented the policies of genocide at the beginning of the war and ended them gradually in 1943. For the Romanian authorities, the Jews became a bargaining chip during 1943, a possibility for gaining some sympathy from the Allies and perhaps some money, too. Historian David Wyman writes:

A dispatch from C.L. Sulzberger in London disclosed that the Romanian government had offered to cooperate in moving 70,000 Jews from Transnistria to any place of refuge chosen by the Allies. The Romanians suggested Palestine and offered to provide Romanian ships for the voyage. In return Romania asked to be paid transportation and related expenses amounting to 20,000 Romanian lei (about £130) per refugee, along with additional funds should Romanian ships be utilized.[43] . . . On February 16, [1943,] three days after it published Sulzberger's distpach the *New York Times* carried a three-quarter-page advertisement with the large headline "For sale to Humanity 70,000 Jews." Its sponsor was the Committee for a Jewish Army of Stateless and Palestinian Jews.[44]

The change in the attitude of the Romanian authorities toward the Jews was reflected in the Romanian newspapers, too. I.P. Prundeni wrote in May 1943, in *Porunca Vremii*, the most anti-Semitic Romanian newspaper, that: "The anti-Semitic movement in Romania is so old. Nobody's head was cut, not one synagogue was devastated, not one cemetery was desecrated. . . . The human being was defended . . ."[45]

Despite his own anti-Semitism, in 1943 General Antonescu allowed several thousand of the surviving Jews in Transnistria to return to Romania. This repatriation began at the very end of 1943 and continued through the spring of 1944. A few thousand orphans from Transnistria were allowed to emigrate to Palestine. Altogether, about 300,000 Romanian Jews survived the war. In the meantime, denial of the Romanian Holocaust started in Bucharest from the very top of the regime.

Ion Antonescu issued a statement published on January 1, 1944, with the title "In front of history, the people and the enemies, I am responsible for you." The dictator brazenly declared:

> We did not deport anyone and you did not stab anybody in the chest with a dagger. Innocent people were not thrown into and are not interned in our prisons. Everybody's faith and the political beliefs of everyone were respected. We did not displace either people or families from their settlements for our political or national interests.[46]

On June 4, 1945, the sentences of fourteen journalists tried before the Romanian People's Court as war criminals were announced. The journalists were all accused of contributing to pro-Axis, anti-Allied and anti-Semitic propaganda before and during the war. Seven of the fourteen were tried *in absentia*. Two of the accused were condemned to death, seven were sentenced to life imprisonment at hard labor, one to penal servitude for life, another to three to twenty years at hard labor, and one to twelve years of severe imprisonment. To these penalties were added the loss of civil rights for varying periods and the confiscation of property. Appeals were filed for all and none of the death sentences was carried out.[47] The president of the People's Court asked one defendant, "Is it true that by your articles you supported the extermination of Romanian citizens and of the civilian population for racial and political reasons through collective and individual excesses?"[48] Ilie Radulescu, the director of *Porunca Vremii*, answered: "If you are alluding to the Jewish problem—because that is the only instigation you can talk about—I always argued, before and after 1941, in favor of solving the Jewish problem through elimination. The only support I gave was the mass executions in Iasi."[49]

Notes:

1. Lucretiu Patrascanu, *Problemele de baza ale Romaniei* (Bucharest: Socec, 1945), p. 211.

2. Ibid.

3. A.C. Cuza, "Doctrina Nationalista Crestina, Apararea Nationala," an VI, no. 16, April 15, 1928, in *Ideea care ucide, Noua Alternativa* (Bucharest, 1994), pp.194–195.

4. C.Z. Codreanu, *Circulari si manifeste* (Madrid, 1951), p. 199, in Leon Volovici, "Ideologia nationalista si "problema evreiasca"" in *Romania anilor '30* (Bucharest: Humanitas, 1995), pp. 82–83.

5. C.Z. Codreanu, *Pentru legionari* (Sibiu, 1936), p. 10, in Leon Volovici, *Ideologia nationalista*, p. 84.

6. Archive of the Central Committee of the Romanian Communist Party/Archives of the General Staff of the Romanian Ministry of Defense, folder 238, June 12, 1974.

7. Ernest Bernea, "Hitlerismul nostru," *Rinduiala*, an I, no. 4 (1935), in *Ideea care ucide*, p. 224.

8. Mircea Eliade, "Pilotii orbi," *Vremea*, X, no. 505, September 19, 1939.

9. A.L. Easterman, Interview with King Carol II, *Daily Herald*, London, January 10, 1938.

10. A.L. Easterman, Interview with Prime-Minister Octavian Goga, *Daily Herald*, January 6, 1938.

11. *Paris Soir*, Jan. 10, 1938.

12. Alexandru Razmerita, *Cum sa ne aparam de evrei, Un plan de eliminare totala* (Minerva, Turnu Severin), pp. 65–69.

13. *Documents Concerning the Fate of Romanian Jewry During the Holocaust*, ed. Jean Ancel (New York: Beate Klarsfeld Foundation, 1986; hereafter DCFRJDH), vol.1, p. 248.

14. Idem.

15. *La Stampa*, September 28, 1995.

16. Traian Herseni, "Rasa si destin national," *Cuvantul*, XVII, no. 91, January 16, 1941.

17. Traian Herseni, "Mitul singelui", *Cuvantul*, XVII, no. 41, November 23, 1940.

18. P. Tiparescu, *Rasa si degenerare* (Bucharest: Bucovina, 1941), p. 8.

19. Traian Herseni, "Rasa si destin national", *Cuvintul* (January 16, 1941); and Toma Petrescu, *Ni se pierde neamul—Actiunea jidanilor*

impotriva natiei romanesti (Bucharest: Cugetarea, 1940), 124.

20. Toma Petrescu, *Ni se pierde neamul—Actiunea jidanilor impotriva natiei romanesti*, Cugetarea (Bucharest, 1940), p. 33.

21. Ion Chelcea, *Tiganii in Romania—Monografie etnografica* (Bucharest: Institutul Central de Statistica, 1944), pp.100–101.

22. DCFRJDH, 2:155.

23. Serban Milcoveanu, "Ai incredere in noi, vom merge pina la capat capitane," *Cuvantul*, January 24, 1941, in DCFRJDH, 2: 163.

24. Ibid., 2:156.

25. Cuvintul, "Cum a fost organizat complotul iudeo-francmasonic," Jan. 24, 1941, DCFRJDH, 2:159.

26. *Universul* (Bucharest, 2 July 1941).

27. Raul Hilberg, *The Destruction of the European Jews*, Revised Edition (New York, 1985), pp. 304–7, 374–5, 758–96.

28. Constantin Virgil Gheorghiu, *Ard Malurile Nistrului* (Bucharest, 1941), p.8.

29. *Curentul*, no. 4808, July 6, 1941.

30. Enclosure no. 4 to Dispatch No. 2108 of November 4, 1941, from the American Legation in Bucharest, Romania, in DCFRJDH, 5: 349.

31. Idem.

32. Ilie Radulescu, "Traiasca Maresalul Antonescu," *Porunca Vremii*, October 27, 1941, in DCFRJDH, 5: 116.

33. Anonymous, "Ghetourile de pe Bug—Ce trebuie sa inteleaga evreii din Romania," *Opinia Capitalei*, October 28, 1941.

34. Stefan Anghelescu, "Ghetourile de pe Bug," *Porunca Vremii*, October 29, 1941.

35. I.P. Prundeni, "Marele rechizitoriu," *Porunca Vremii*, October 29, 1941, in DCFRJDH, 5: 122–123.

36. Ilie Radulescu, "Lichidarea iudaismului," *Porunca Vremii*, October 30, 1941, in DCFRJDH, 3: 315.

37. Ilie Radulescu, "Lichidati domnilor," *Porunca Vremii*, November 1, 1941, in DCFRJDH, 3: 323.

38. See Robert St.John, "Reporting the Romanian Pogrom of 1940/41," in this volume.

39. DCFRJDH, 4: 54–60.

40. I.P. Prundeni, "Intelesul unui mesagiu," *Porunca Vremii*, September 13, 1942, in DCFRJDH, 4: 186.

41. "Arestarea evreilor romani la Paris," *Poporul*, September 19, 1942.

42. "Vinzarea operelor scriitorilor evrei interzisa in librarii," *Universul*, November 5, 1942.

43. David S. Wyman, *The Abandonment of the Jews* (New York: Pantheon Books, 1984), p. 82, citing *New York Times*, Feb. 13, 1943.

44. Wyman, p. 84, citing *New York Times*, Feb. 16, 1943.

45. I.P. Prundeni, "Omenie romaneasca," *Porunca Vremii*, May 16, 1943.

46. Ion Antonescu, "In fata istoriei in fata poporului si a dusmanilor raspund eu pentru voi," *Ecoul*, January 1, 1944, in DCFRJDH, 4: 712.

47. American Jewish Archives, fond World Jewish Congress, 8A/2, OSS report 2469.

48. "Ziaristii fascisti in fata tribunalului suprem," *Scinteia*, June 2, 1945.

49. Idem.

Polish Journalism

Polish Press Reporting About the Nazi Germans' Anti-Jewish Policy, 1933–39

Anna Landau-Czajka
Polish Academy of Sciences Historical Institute

The Polish press in the years 1933–1939 gave its attention to the troublesome Jewish question in Poland, as well as to the political movement of National Socialism in neighboring Germany. Since the struggle against the Jews was one of the most visible elements of Nazism, these two themes were often connected in articles by Polish journalists.

What attitude did the Polish press display towards the German policy regarding Jews? One would assume that, in all likelihood, the more anti-Semitic journals that were connected with the nationalist camp would more keenly support the German anti-Jewish laws and Hitler's policy aimed at ousting the Jews from public life. On the other hand, periodicals connected with the democratic or leftist groups, in accord with the logic of their programs, should more or less energetically have opposed the German policy. The ecclesiastical press, in view of the then-prevailing doctrines in Catholicism, was clearly prejudiced against the Jews. However, one would assume that the Catholic press would come out against active persecution of Jews in accordance with the principle of brotherly love.

But it should be remembered that the logic of political programs is sometimes at variance with common sense—and so it was in this case. Press organs of the nationalist parties, even the most radical ones, for example *Falanga*, *Szczerbiec* (Jagged Sword) or *Przełom* (Crisis), were reluctant to admit frankly that they were supporting Hitler's policy towards Jews. This was due to at least three factors. Most Polish nationalist groups descended from the National Democrats (Narodowa Demokracja, Endecja), who were traditionally more disposed towards alliance with Russia and looked with suspicion on all things coming from Germany, even when they were consistent with the rest of the Endecja program. Secondly, the nationalists, more than other political parties, feared that the German policy would cause a rapid influx of German Jews into Poland. Thirdly, all national movements tend to be reluctant to admit to following a foreign model; hence, the widespread contortions of nationalist writers, who supported the German policy, but did not want to be seen as sympathetic to Germany or supportive of its ways. Such Polish nationalists claimed that Nazi policies regarding the Jewish question were actually founded on ideas invented earlier by the Polish nationalist movement. These journalists also supported all the anti-Jewish activities and legislation in Romania and Hungary.

Of course, not only a journal's immediate opinions about Hitler's policy can help to deduce what that periodical's attitude was towards the anti-Jewish laws in Germany. Sometimes, the way events were described was sufficient, even without any explicitly expressed opinion, to infer an attitude. It may be valuable to point out that the various partisan newspapers did write about the Nazi policy towards Jews, but almost never transmitted to their readers full information about the scope of that policy.

After looking over the periodicals of different parties, one gets the impression that each of them wrote about another Germany and other Nuremberg laws. Opponents of the anti-Jewish policy concentrated on depicting how it was implemented, while the advocates of anti-Jewish policies described nothing but the formal legal provisions. Thus, writers who disapproved of the German policy layed stress on the violence and acts of terror being committed in Germany. They very often called readers' attention to the cases of suicide committed by German Jews, but rarely referred to the few instances in which German officials were killed by desperate Jews. On the other hand, most authors who supported the Nuremberg laws passed over in silence the use of force, concentrating on German administrative actions such as confiscation of property, excluding Jews from certain professions, inducing them to emigrate.

In articles written by those opposed to Nazi policy, Germany was portrayed as a country of rampant lawlessness, where not only Jews, but also other groups (for example Catholics) could not feel safe. In contrast, rightists portrayed Germany as a land of law-abiding people complying with legislation good for the genuine citizens of the country. At times, though rarely, rightist authors did criticize what they felt were excessively radical methods. However, while direct use of force against people met animosity, it was seldom condemned by the rightists. Other forms of violence, for example breaking windows in Jewish shops or burning piles of books, were criticized in lesser degree. Such violence against Jewish books generally met with the approval of the nationalist and ecclesiastic Polish press.

Relatively uncommon were the opinions expressed by the most ardent nationalists who approved both the idea and the methods employed by Hitler against the Jews. Hitler's Germany was depicted by them as an example of a suitable solution of the Jewish problem. These radical writers usually presented the argument about lawful defense of the nation against the Jewish invasion.

Interestingly, no Polish newspaper, irrespective of its opinions about Hitler and his regime, published fundamental articles concerning the policy of Nazi Germany towards the Jews in general. The press limited itself to references, not too numerous, rather than detailed description and analysis of events in Germany. Why was this so? In the case of parties supporting the Nazi principles, but not their methods, the answer seems clear. All of these Polish groups were deeply attached to Christian values, even if they themselves propagated anti-Semitic slogans, and regarded Germany as knowing how to deal properly with the Jewish problem. If the press informed readers that Germany's actions against the Jews required the use of force, it could stir up animosity and opposition against importing those methods onto Polish soil.

The problem becomes more complicated when analyzing the Polish press edited by opponents of the Nuremberg laws, who were mainly on the left. One might expect to find in such periodicals not only information about individual acts of terror, but also an account of the anti-Jewish legislation in general, so as to make the readers sensitive to the potential for implementing similar principles in Poland. Yet there were virtually no such articles. Readers of the left-wing press had little chance to be informed about the exact content of the Nuremberg laws. They could only infer from individual references that accused Polish nationalists of seeking to follow the German model (for example, the so-called Aryan paragraph). The newspapers of the moderate left, as well as those of the right, certainly sought to sway their readers to their ideologies, but they feared to stray too far from the opinions already held by those readers. Thus, one can conclude that the writers and editors of Polish journals tacitly assumed that the methods used by the Nazis were unacceptable for the majority of Polish public opinion. Therefore, the right-wing press did not write explicitly about Nazi methods. The journalists assumed, however, that the German legal regulations employed against the Jewish population could find some support in Poland. As a result, the leftist press, opposed to such "legal methods," preferred not to describe them.

The Polish press also reflected how opinions about the German state's actions against the Jews changed in the course of time. In general, Nazi German anti-Jewish initiatives were supported more often during 1936–38, years when Polish-German relations were moderately good and when Polish-Jewish conflicts intensified at the same time. The year 1939 brought substantial change because the German threat persuaded even the explicitly anti-Semitic press to cease regarding the Jewish minority as Poland's principal enemy and to concentrate on the real menace.

How did the German policy towards the Jews look as judged by the press of different political orientations? To start with the leftist newspapers, they are conspicuous not exactly for condemning the German policy towards the Jews, but by their declared lack of understanding of this policy. This is in substantial contrast to the press of all the other political trends, which—even when condemning the Germans—underscored how justifiable were the motives of the anti-Jewish policy.

While not all of the leading periodicals can be examined here, some newspapers can be taken to represent the main political currents of interwar Poland. The left-wing press relatively rarely dealt with the Jewish problem. However, as war approached, the plight of German Jews was touched on more and more frequently, in contrast to the other newspapers. In July 1933, a socialist daily wrote:

> The barbarous treatment of the Jewish population in Germany by the Nazi regime, depriving them not only of political and civil rights, but also taking away from them any possibility of social and material existence, has again brought the Jewish problem, that unfortunately still exists, into the foreground of social problems internationally.[1]

References to the position of the Jews in Germany were rather sporadic up to 1937, but increased in 1938, after the *Anschluss* with Austria.

Robotnik (Worker), the central organ of the Polish Socialist Party, tried above all to convince its readers that all that the Germans were saying and writing about Jews was only a propaganda ploy, and had nothing to do with reality.[2] In the July 1938 article, "The Jew Is To Blame for Everything" ("Wszystkiemu winien jest Żyd"), the author referred to an interview given by a Nazi dignitary to a Swedish daily. The Nazi allegedly confirmed that all the German allegations regarding the Jews were only a trick to raise passions, a propaganda ploy which could be exploited in the future for political purposes. The author of the Polish socialist article commented that the followers of Hitler were doing the same thing, exploiting the instincts of impoverished and desperate masses for their own purposes.[3] *Robotnik* also demonstrated to its readers how absurd were regulations founded on racist principles, since pure human races did not exist in Europe.[4]

Nevertheless, until 1939, *Robotnik* rarely referred directly to Hitler's policy of anti-Semitism. Only in 1939 did such references begin to grow in frequency. Prior articles tended to be rather mild explanations that anti-Semitism and anti-Jewish laws, in Germany and elsewhere, were baseless. In 1939, the socialist daily's articles became more intense. Paradoxically, the left-wing newspaper employed the Catholic Church's positions and the principles of the Christian faith as the main reasons to oppose Germany's anti-Jewish politics.[5] The authors emphasized that eminent priests, cardinals and popes, and especially the current Pope Pius XI, had come out against anti-Semitism. The socialist daily's writers pointed out that Christian principles were not observed in Hitler's Germany and that the Old Testament, also a Christian holy book, was condemned by the Nazis as a Jewish invention. Both Catholics and Jews were being persecuted in Germany; Christians ought to condemn both campaigns of persecution, declared writers in the Polish Socialist Party's newspaper.

Robotnik had a solidly negative opinion about how the Jewish question in Germany was being solved, but that opinion was expressed in a restrained manner. It wanted not only to condemn the German methods, but above all to convince its readers that those methods were morally unacceptable and that the prejudice against Jews had no real foundation.

Another leftist publication, *Czarno na białem* (Black on White), a weekly connected with the democratic opposition (Polish Socialist Party and Peasant Party) and later with the Democratic Party, expressed much more emphatically not only condemnation, but plain disgust with Nazi German ideas and methods. This journal was addressed to the intellectual left, so it had no need to convince its readers that anti-Semitism was not a just and reasonable attitude. Dealing with the Jewish question in Germany, it concentrated on fighting against those advocating implementing the Nazi solutions in Poland and on revealing the Nazi German barbarity. *Czarno na białem* thundered above all against the groups seeking to transfer German models into Poland. Benedykt Hertz warned that: "Nothing can be invented by aping the patterns of the Black Hundred or by the racist rubbish of Hitlerism. . . . However the present influx of Judeophobia excited by the racism of Germany can have the most disastrous effects."[6] In "Invasion of the Anthropoids," Jan Karol Wende noted that: "The epoch of Hitlerism also turned the morality of a certain section of society upside down among us. The worst meanness grows today into a virtue, and troublemakers are named national heroes."[7]

In time, the tone of articles in *Czarno na białem* became more and more alarming. The authors emphasized that the Nazi methods were being accepted in one country after another—Hungary, Italy, Romania and Czechoslovakia; actions directly modeled after Nazi ideology were emerging in Poland, too. Thus, there were the demand that Jewish professors be removed from Poland's universities and Sejm Deputy Franciszek Stoch's proposed law to deprive Jews of civil rights in Poland. An April 1939 article in *Czarno na białem* concluded that: "For a pretty long time, the terrible venom of the Hitlerite philosophy of life, the negation of all the values of universal culture, has been penetrating certain circles of our youth."[8]

No other political trend's periodicals expressed condemnation of Nazism as resolutely as the leftist press. Although one cannot claim that all the other movements and periodicals accepted or supported Nazi policy, in place of the leftist tone of harsh censure one finds a tone of mild regret connected with a certain degree of understanding. This was the case with two political currents, the Christian Democrats and the Conservatives.

Conservatives had no common program concerning the Jews, and the Jewish question was not their main interest. The only exception was the Vilna daily *Słowo* (Word), or, more exactly, its ideologue and main publicist Stanisław Cat-Mackiewicz. Other Conservatives expressed their opinion regarding the Jews only sporadically, on the occasion of current events, while Cat began in 1933 to develop his own program for solution of the Jewish question in Poland. He did not conceal the fact that his program was founded on certain examples taken from Hitler's Germany.

After the introduction of the anti-Jewish laws in Germany, *Słowo*'s first impulse had been indignation. Its journalists quoted protests by the League of Nations and ecclesiastical dignitaries against the persecution. But already in May 1933, an article by Cat-Mackiewicz appeared, in which he called reports about the persecution of Jews in Nazi Germany exaggerated. Cat declared that he had met no one in Germany who had seen the persecutions with his own eyes. Instead, he himself had seen many Jewish shops, open and prosperous. In his view, ". . . what has been written about the persecution in Germany is full, if not of exaggeration, then of pathos arising from justifiable compassion and indignation."[9]

However, any tone of compassion or indignation gradually vanished from Cat's articles. In 1937, he declared that all that had happened in Nazi Germany was fully comprehensible and resulted from the occupation by Jews of the most lucrative positions in Germany. Although he still could not reconcile himself to the methods used by the Nazis, he became more inclined to understand the Nazi reasoning and to accept the purpose they were serving: removal of the Jews from the country. He stated, "I'm not an advocate of transferring the Nazi means of fighting against the Jews onto Polish soil, although I consider the principle of racism to be logical."[10] Cat considered all the anti-German propaganda in the Polish press to be Jewish manipulation. He himself drew evidence for his clearly anti-Semitic articles from the anti-Jewish expositions organized in Germany.

In the beginning of 1938, Cat published the article "Nazwisko" ("Surname"), in which he most broadly expressed his opinion on the German policy towards the Jews and on transferring that policy to Poland. On the one hand, he insisted that the hatred and contempt felt by the Nazis for the Jews were alien to him. On the other hand, he favored applying some examples of Nazi legislation in Poland. It is worth quoting an extended fragment from this article:

Be forewarned: I will refer to Hitlerism. . . . What I shall write
about is connected with Hitlerism, because it strives for isolation
of the Jewish nation and for separating from it. . . . What Hitler is
doing, aiming frankly for the specific separation of Jews and
Germans by legal means, will not seem ridiculous to a man who
seriously ponders over these problems. . . . Finally, I declare one
thing: Even when I admit that I am prepared to recommend certain patterns of Nazi legislation, the Nazi hatred and contempt for
the Jews are alien to me personally.[11]

The views of Cat-Mackiewicz on the Jewish question changed
abruptly in the second half of the Thirties under the influence of changes
occurring in Germany as well as in Poland. While he was disposed to
approve with enthusiasm and to recommend certain Nazi legislative solutions, we need to emphasize that he, as well as the newspaper run by him,
looked with extreme anxiety at all the violent anti-Jewish assaults. Thus,
when describing Germany's anti-Jewish policy after 1935, the aspect of
violence inherent in it was neglected.

Another major conservative journal was *Dziennik Poznański* (Poznan
Daily), published in Poznan in Western Poland. The attitude of the
Poznan conservatives towards the German policy was determined by the
memory of former German rule and efforts at Germanization. Their prejudice against the Germans did not allow them to become fascinated by
Nazism as happened with Cat. Thus, *Dziennik Poznański* used the word
"bestiality" in depicting the activities of Nazis in 1933.[12] Later, however,
Dziennik Poznański avoided any mention of the situation in Germany,
evidently unwilling to praise it, because of the paper's anti-German bias,
but also unwilling to condemn it, in view of the newspaper's growing
antipathy for Jews. Instead, the Poznań conservatives repeatedly
expressed their support for the Romanian government and, above all, for
the anti-Jewish legislation introduced by Premier Octavian Goga, imitating the German policy toward Jews. The example of Romania, flourishing as they believed thanks to these laws, ought to show Poles their great
significance for the state.[13]

Still another conservative organ, *Czas* (Time; in Kraków until 1935,
then in Warsaw), was the least interested in the Jewish question. However,
after 1935, when the Jewish question became so important that all the

political groups had to take a position concerning it, *Czas* began to print articles directed against anti-Semitism and racism, especially against violent anti-Jewish attacks. The situation in Germany was depicted as a negative example. The persecution of eminent personalities because of their Jewish descent was described with irony and disbelief.[14]

Readers of the peasant press could learn little about the situation of the Jews in Germany. While the Jewish question itself was touched upon relatively often in the columns of the papers designed for the rural countryside in predominately agrarian Poland, the focus was only on Polish affairs. Probably, the situation of Germany's Jews was considered so remote a subject that it was not expected to arouse the peasant readers' interest. It is impossible to find in these newspapers any full description of the situation in Germany. Occasionally, one could find an evaluation of some German policy, but only as to whether such methods were worth employing in Poland.

The weekly *Piast* presented more about the situation in Germany than other peasant periodicals. Although at first, in 1933, *Piast* described the Jews as the support of every dictatorship, both Bolshevik and Fascist, this trend did not persist.[15] A year later, an author presented Germany as a pattern to be followed, pointing out that the Germans considered the Jews to be their enemies though the Jews were much less numerous there than in Poland. He added that the Germans knew what they were doing, because the Jews were their former friends.[16] However, after 1936, *Piast* was of the opinion that Poles had to resolve the Jewish question independently, imitating no foreign patterns and avoiding the use of force. This meant not adopting any German-style anti-Jewish laws.

A reader of the Christian Democratic journals, *Głos Narodu* (Voice of the People) and *Zwrot* (Return), could learn a little more about the German Jewish situation, although in this case it would be extremely difficult to form a homogeneous opinion on the basis of these papers. *Głos Narodu*, being moderately critical found certain excuses for the German policy, while *Zwrot* was firmly opposed to the Nazi policy. *Głos Narodu*'s reports from Germany changed radically in the course of time. Thus, in 1935, *Głos Narodu* did not veil its indignation at the persecution in Germany of eminent physicians and Nobel Prize laureates.[17] Some articles were dedicated to proving that racism was nonsense, and that the pure Jewish race did not exist.[18] *Głos Narodu*'s editors were concerned by the developments in Germany, but not because of the suffering of the Jews; they feared mass emigration of Germany's Jews to Poland. Yet the tone of articles in the Christian Democratic paper changed totally, so that in 1937 readers could learn that the Jews in Germany were doing well, that they frequented the cafés, and were running their shops. What had been a serious and anxious tone in *Głos Narodu* was replaced by face-tiousness, as the daily life of Nazi Germany's Jews was depicted in an almost humorous sketch.[19] In 1938, *Głos Narodu* leaned visibly towards the opinion that Hitler's purposes were good; only his means were evil.

Meanwhile, the readers of *Zwrot* were informed that excessively concentrating on the Jewish question and propagating anti-Semitism was in the interest of Germany. In April 1939, *Zwrot* recapitulated the declaration by the widely known priest, Rev. Stanisław Trzeciak, praising Germany for reintroducing such old canon law concepts as a ghetto and a yellow patch for the Jews. The Christian Democratic writers stated that they could not believe their eyes when they read the report in the widely circulated Catholic *Mały Dziennik* (Little Daily). Referring to the priest's eulogies of the German anti-Jewish laws, the authors of the article in *Zwrot* wrote:

We are deeply convinced, as Catholics, that Rev. Trzeciak has become seriously ill because of laborious research. Therefore, he ought to rest and, after returning to mental equilibrium, he will undoubtedly rouse himself from the influence of the Talmud and of medieval history and he will return to Christianity and to the 20th century.[20]

Such discordant opinions expressed by Catholic publicists in the Christian Democratic press are not to be wondered at, considering that the Catholic Church in Poland did not have a uniform opinion worked out on this matter, despite the papal encyclical directed against fascism. While certain publicists connected with the Catholic newspapers condemned the use of force, if not the German anti-Jewish policy itself, other Catholic journalists portrayed the German solutions of the Jewish question as a pattern to be followed in Poland.

The most frequently presented opinion in the Catholic press was approval of the policy of ousting the Jews from different fields of life in favor of the "aboriginal" German nation. At the same time, the Polish ecclesiastical press distrusted the German methods, which they considered to be too violent. Such attitudes were presented in *Mały Dziennik* (Little Daily), *Przegląd Powszechny* (Universal Review) and *Pro Christo* (For Christ). In describing the plight of the German Jews, these newspapers' writers had no doubt that the position of Jews in Germany had decidedly deteriorated, but they considered it to be a just and comprehensible change. They tried to convince their readers that the German Jews were themselves responsible for the present German policy, because they occupied too much space in the social, cultural and political life of Germany; they had to be removed from the normal life of the nation.[21] In *Przegląd Powszechny*, E. Kosibowicz expressed this point of view most distinctly:

> It became evident from the official specifications and returns that the Jews in Germany have taken great advantage of the period of their freedom. Promoting assimilation, they assimilated not themselves, but above all the Germans, filling all of German culture with their ideology. There came a brutal, in many cases inhuman impulse, but its foundations were easily understood. Just as in the past, when the Spanish Inquisition tried to defend Christian culture against the invasion of Eastern Jewry, so the Hitlerite organizations united under the battlecry of the defense of German culture.[22]

A similar opinion could be read in *Pro Christo*:

> . . . Hitlerite anti-Semitism is indeed something new in XX century Europe. It sometimes manifests itself in wild, barbarous forms, but—if we accept in principle the very inclination to purify the nation from alien and destructive accretions and to deliver it from the foreign and hostile element living a harmful and parasitic life in its bosom—we must state that it is a wholesome and normal tendency.[23]

Clearly, these Church affiliated journals approved of the purpose of Nazi activities, and at least understood the methods used. While the immediate use of force was generally disapproved by the Catholic publicists, some of them saw in it nothing evil or exceeding Christian principles. Thus, a writer in *Pro Christo* in July 1934 declared:

> We don't condemn everything in the Hitlerites, and their *vigorous self-defense* against the Jewish pest least of all. If any excesses or abuse of physical force occurred, it was *caused by the necessity of self-defense* and doesn't deserve condemnation by Christians.
> . . .[24] [emphasis in original]

In general, however, measures aimed at elimination of the Jewish community from Germany's daily life, and particularly from German literature and culture, were the best understood and accepted among Catholic journalists. Even rough means were appreciated. The author of an October 1935 *Mały Dziennik* article concerning the ousting of the Jews from culture remarked with satisfaction that "The whole world observes the battle of German culture against the Semitic germ."[25] *Przewodnik Katolicki* (Catholic Guide) presented this outlook even more distinctly, pointing repeatedly to the book burning as the example to follow. One author rejoiced in May 1934: "Hitler is like he is, but he taught the German and Jewish piglets a lesson. He has burned up their books, and expelled a great part of their scribblers abroad."[26] Four years later, *Przewodnik Katolicki* told its readers:

> . . . [I]n a certain state that is on friendly terms with Poland, all the Jewish filth, licentious papers and songs were burned at the stake, and the Jewish films were banned. When shall we follow our "friends"?[27]

Even in May 1939, the same newspaper referred to the burning of books by Jewish authors as "the fresh, benign breath of air passing through the German land" and regretted that it was not continued.[28]

Alas, it is much more difficult to find in the interwar Catholic press articles expressing unequivocal condemnation of the Nazi policy toward Jews. Though the respectable periodicals, such as *Kultura* (Culture) or *Przegląd Powszechny*, regretted the brutality used by Germans in ousting the Jews from the country's society, compassion for the oppressed was nowhere to be found. Only the Jesuit *Posłaniec Serca Jezusowego* (Messenger of the Heart of Jesus), although not as friendly towards the Jews, wrote frankly in a January 1939 article about the Jewish tragedy in Germany, the Draconian laws and the persecution. It was, it appears, the only honest description of the plight of the German Jews to be found in the Catholic press and the only one expressing such a decidedly negative opinion about the German methods:

> The strangest phenomenon in all that anti-Jewish campaign is the burning down of synagogues. If Jewish banks and gambling dens, Jewish cinemas and brothels were burned in this obsession of hatred, it could be understood; but burning down the synagogues? . . . [The] German way of struggle against the Jews must be condemned by everybody![29]

The periodicals described above presented opinions of the political opposition or were ecclesiastical magazines independent of the government. Much more difficult was the position of the press of Poland's ruling camp. When describing the plight of Jews in Germany, the ruling camp's press had simultaneously to take into account official foreign policy and the official policy towards Poland's own national minorities.

Up to 1939, the main organ of the ruling group, *Gazeta Polska* (Polish Gazette), reported about the plight of the German Jews only in small notices, without editorial commentaries. The difficulties endured by the German Jews and the growth of German anti-Semitism were not kept secret. Although this subject was not emphasized, *Gazeta Polska* was one of few newspapers from which a careful reader could more or less learn about the actual position of Jews in Germany and what legislation the Nazi government introduced. However, when the matter concerned the internal politics of Germany, there were no editorial commentaries—neither condemning, nor approving the German anti-Semitism. The only exception was the Gdańsk (Danzig) question. *Gazeta Polska* wrote with animosity about all the anti-Jewish regulations in this territory. Nevertheless, the newspaper's attitude towards the German policy concerning Jews can be deduced only indirectly. From 1937, *Gazeta Polska* began publishing articles concerning Romania, Hungary and Italy—countries which decided to implement anti-Jewish laws modeled after the

German ones. Editorial commentaries appeared, explicitly favorable to the legal changes introduced. *Gazeta Polska*'s editorial arguments here resembled those in the Christian Democratic and ecclesiastical press, that the Jews themselves are responsible:

> The government of Mr. Goga indeed has a visibly anti-Semitic aspect, but it is not racist, for it is fighting not against the principle of equal rights for the ethnic minorities, but against abuse of the liberties vested in these minorities. . . . The battlecry, "Romania for the Romanians," is not xenophobia. It is only an expression of the aspiration to make Romanians the masters in their own country.[30]

While the various journals of the governing circles sometimes expressed a certain amount of approval for anti-Jewish laws, in general they did not support the German policy in totality, and they assumed a particularly unfavorable attitude towards the use of force. Quite different were the periodicals connected with the extreme nationalist groups, who were decidedly sympathetic to Hitler's purposes and to the means used by the Nazis. Such papers wrote often, and with pleasure, about the "proper order" introduced in Germany and regretted only that Poland was so backward in that respect.

It should be noted that the numerous and noisy extreme nationalist press had relatively few readers in comparison with the press representing the larger and more serious political currents. There was a striking difference in how National Socialism was dealt with in the extreme nationalist press in comparison with the rest of the Polish press. The prevailing majority of authors in the Polish press did not support the Nazi ideology as a whole, irrespective of their judgment on the German policy in the Jewish question. On the other hand, the Polish nationalist press repeatedly expressed its fascination with Fascism and National Socialism as truly nationalist political systems. Unlike most of the Polish groups that supported German anti-Semitism, the extreme nationalists' acceptance of the German policy towards the Jews was consistent with their approval of the totality of Germany's domestic policies.

The press of radical nationalist groups like OWP (Camp of Great Poland) or ONR (National-Radical Camp) did not extensively discuss the Jewish question in Germany, treating it as one of the elements in the system which ought to be imported to Poland. They gave no description of the plight of Jews in Germany. All negative opinions concerning National Socialism and its attitude towards the Jewish minority were treated as the result of a Jewish or Jewish-Masonic plot aimed at slandering Germany.[31] In April 1933, a writer in *Szczerbiec* (Jagged Sword) frankly admitted envy of the Nazis:

> But even if what Jews are writing now about what is happening in Germany is entirely true, it cannot distort our judgment on the present events in Germany. These crimes and outrages (if they happened at all and if they are something more than isolated pranks) . . . are only a scum floating over the surface of the mighty and clear stream. What is happening in Germany now is a beautiful trend of revival. It is a purification of German life from the secular intoxication with the venom of decay . . . by Jewry, which increased like cancer in its body. We are looking at the essence of what is happening in Germany not only without condemnation and horror, but with envy.[32]

Another author, also writing in *Szczerbiec* in mid-1933, suggested that:

> Nationalist Germany has understood how dangerous it is to allow the Jews into their families, and their offspring into offices. Today they are removing from national and social life not only the Jewish sons, but also the grandsons. The same should be done in Poland.[33]

The Nuremberg laws promulgated in September 1935 were accepted by many radical nationalists as the example to follow. They claimed that the German Jews would at last be locked inside ghettos thanks to these laws, and from there they would do no more harm to the German nation. A journalist in *Ruch Młodych* (Movement of Youths) argued that, "Such legislation takes its example from the legislation of the period which had the wisest policy towards Jews—the Middle Ages—and from the teaching of the Catholic Church."[34]

The only common element uniting exponents of the different opinions referred to above was denial of the ideology of racism, which was the very foundation of the German policy. Both Polish supporters and opponents of anti-Jewish laws introduced in Germany noted in the main that a distinct Jewish race does not exist; depending on their political convictions, they added that the concept was "scientific nonsense" and "an invention by madmen" or "a poetic conjecture." While adversaries of anti-Semitism demonstrated how groundless separating Jews from society was, the supporters of anti-Semitism proposed to ground the plan of elimination of Jews on a broader principle than merely racism.

Recapitulating, we can agree with Włodzimierz Mich's proposition that for Polish anti-Semites Nazism was, above all, encouragement and proof that the plan to get rid of Jews is more than a mere utopia.[35] For the political groups well disposed towards the Jewish minority, Nazism was a warning, that the Polish anti-Semitic slogans about ousting the Jews out of the country were not merely propaganda catch phrases but warnings of a real menace.

In any event, no reader of the interwar Polish press—whether rightist, middle or leftist—could get fully and precisely informed as to what the plight was of the Jews in Germany between 1933 and 1939.

Notes:

1. J. Arnold, "Kwestia żydowska a 'klasy pośrednie'," *Robotnik*, 3 July 1933, no. 230, p. 2.
2. "Źródła antysemityzmu," *Robotnik*, 28 Oct. 1938, no. 307, p. 4.
3. B.D., "Wszystkiemu winien jest Żyd," *Robotnik*, 29 July 1938, no. 208.
4. "Hitlerowcy i Żydzi są . . . rasowo spokrawieni," *Robotnik*, 24 Aug. 1938, no. 236, p. 3.
5. Examples: K. Cz., "Zakłamanie, Chrzescijaństwo a posiew nienawiści," *Robotnik*, 7 Jan. 1939, p. 3; P. Hulka-Laskowski, "Antysemityzm niemiecki ongi i dzisiaj," *Robotnik*, 14 Feb. 1939, no. 45, p. 4; B.D., "W matni antysemickiego zakłamania," *Robotnik*, 20 July 1939, no. 200, p. 5.
6. B. Hertz, "Na rozum," *Czarno na białem*, 10 July 1938, no. 28, p. 7.
7. J. K. Wende, "Inwazja antropoidów," *Czarno na białem*, 3 Apr. 1938, no. 14, p. 4.
8. "Stronnictwo Demokratyczne o zajściach na wyższych uczelniach," *Czarno na białem*, 11 Apr. 1939, no. 24, p. 7.

9. S. Cat-Mackiewicz, "Polscy Żydzi w Berlinie," *Słowo*, 11 May 1933, no. 127, p. 1.

10. S. Cat-Mackiewicz, "Naród, z którym normalnej wojny prowadzić nie można," *Słowo*, 8 Aug. 1937, no. 217, p. 1.

11. Cat, "Nazwisko," *Słowo*, 15 Feb. 1938, no. 45, p. 1.

12. "Odpowiedż hitlerowców na bojkot żydowski," *Dziennik Poznański*, 29 Mar. 1933, no. 73, p. 2.

13. In 1937, an article appeared in *Dziennik Poznański* in which the author presented a project for implementing anti-Jewish legislation in Poland, patterned after the German laws. S. Okoniewski, "Aryjskie rozważania," 27 June 1937, no. 197, p. 1.

14. "Rasizm i medycyna," *Czas*, 27 Mar. 1935, no. 75, p. 3.

15. "Podpory dyktatury. Rzut oka na politykę Żydów," *Piast*, 26 Mar. 1933, no. 13, p. 5.

16. "Jasno i wyrażnie," *Piast*, 17 June 1934, no. 31, pp. 1–2.

17. "Przeciw najwybitniejszym przedstawicielom niemieckiej medycyny," *Głos Narodu*, 22 Feb. 1935, no. 52, p. 7.

18. St. Sikorski, "Antropologia i rasy. Żydzi pod względem rasowym," *Głos Narodu*, 28 Apr. 1935, no. 115, p. 4.

19. J.F., "Żydzi w Berlinie czują sie dobrze" [Jews in Berlin Are Feeling Good], *Głos Narodu*, 17 Nov. 1937, no. 316, p. 6.

20. "Rozprawki. Potwórność z 'Małego Dziennika'," *Zwrot*, 2 Apr. 1939, no. 13, pp. 6–7.

21. Among others: "Dwie różne sprawy," *Mały Dziennik*, 14 Aug. 1935, no. 89, p. 3; "Z powrotem do Ghetta," *Mały Dziennik*, 22 Sept. 1935, no. 128, p. 5.

22. E. Kosibowicz, "Sprawy Kościoła. Rzut oka na dzieje 'żydowskiej kwestii'," *Przegląd Powszechny*, Jan. 1934, no. 601, p. 149.

23. "Na froncie walki," *Pro Christo*, May 1933, no. 5, p. 308.

24. M. Wiśniewski, "Z rozmyślań czerwcowych," *Pro Christo*, July 1934, no. 7, p. 490.

25. "Hitler przeciw sztuce żydowskiej," *Mały Dziennik*, 10 Oct. 1935, no. 146, p. 3.

26. "O polskich żydzietach, o francuskich prosietach i o pewnej złośliwej pannie,"*Przewodnik Katolicki*, 27 May 1934, no. 21, pp. 330–331.

27. "List Starego Macieja," *Przewodnik Katolicki*, 22 May 1938, no. 21, pp. 350–351.

28. Wuj z Baranowa, "Gawęda świąteczna," *Przewodnik Katolicki*, 28 May 1939, no. 22, pp. 364–365.

29. "Z frontu religijnego," *Posłaniec Serca Jezusowego*, Jan. 1939, no. 1, pp. 21–31.

30. S. Werner, "Rewolucja narodowa, czy tylko zwrot na prawo?," *Gazeta Polska*, 12 Jan. 1938, no. 11.

31. For example, W.K. Borski, "Wygodna moralność," *Akademik Polski*, 1 Dec. 1934, no. 2, p. 4.

32. "Chwalimy czy ganimy," *Szczerbiec*, 25 April 1933, no. 13, pp. 1–2.

33. T. Kaminski, "O polskość Polaków," *Szczerbiec*, 10 June 1933, no. 19, pp. 5–6.

34. Untitled, *Ruch Młodych*, [1935?] vol. 10, no. 1, p. 2.

35. W. Mich, *Obcy w polskim domu* (Lublin, 1994).

The Polish-Language Jewish Press and Events in the Third Reich, 1933–1939

Daniel Grinberg
University of Białystok

Publications dealing with the events which took place in Nazi Germany in 1933–1939 today comprise an enormous multi-language library which an individual scholar is simply unable to exploit to the full. Nonetheless, the reflection of these events in the press of neighboring countries has up to now attracted astonishingly little attention. This fact could be explained, to a certain extent, by the retarded development of research on the history of the daily and periodical press and by an insufficient familiarity with modern research techniques which make it possible to embark upon a multi-faceted analysis of the contents of the press. The sheer number and availability of other sources which refer to historical reality in a more direct manner certainly did not favor concentration of attention on the contemporaneous press in adjacent countries.

The historian's creation of a fundamental network of facts is succeeded by questions of a more general nature such as those concerned with the prevalent spiritual atmosphere, state of consciousness, the language of description and its relation to reality, as well as the circulation of information and the degree of trust towards that information, so essential for study of the Holocaust. Research into the press could throw more light onto each of the above listed issues, thus altering our vision of the situation. Such studies should constitute an independent and extremely essential object of research per se, if only due to the role played by the press in twentieth century politics, culture and education.

In the case of the Polish-language Jewish press in the Second Republic (1919–1939), we are dealing with a phenomenon of such dimension and significance for the comprehension of processes that occurred within the largest and probably most differentiated European Jewish community, that the call for the historian's attention to focus on the press does not require special justification. One could merely express astonishment that so little has been written on the subject.[1] More than half a century later, we still do not have copious syntheses and monographic studies on select examples of the interwar Polish Jewish press, but only a handful of articles and laboriously prepared lists of titles, that are probably still incomplete.[2] There are equally incomplete collections of basic periodicals, scattered among Polish and foreign libraries. In this situation, it hardly comes as a surprise that studies on the history of the national minorities' press in Poland, including that of the Jewish community, are treated as marginal or outright ignored.[3] We have at our disposal, therefore, more of a set of inquiries and unverified hypotheses than ready solutions.

Even such a fundamental issue as the assessment of the scale and degree of the uniqueness of the Jewish press in Poland, in comparison with other minorities, gives rise to impassioned controversies. Jewish authors' intuitive premises, presented already prior to 1939, emphasized the exceptional nature of the Jewish press in the Second Republic, as an unparalleled phenomenon both within Poland and in comparison with the publishing activity of Jews living in other parts of Europe.[4] Yet those assumptions remain at odds, at least quantitatively, with collective information cited in generally accessible syntheses on the history of the Polish and German inter-war press.[5]

Naturally, it is not the intention of the author of this paper to resolve such dilemmas. Basically, the focus here will be on the manner in which leading Polish-language Jewish newspapers, of diverse political orientations, described and commented upon events in Nazi Germany. Information and opinions contained in socio-cultural periodicals and the "yellow" press will be cited only upon certain occasions. The analysis will, of course, exclude such leading Yiddish dailies as *Haynt* (Today) or *Moment*, as well as almost the whole Bund press, essential for shaping Jewish public opinion. The obvious need for a comparison with the interpretation of the same problems by the Polish press is hampered by the absence of more extensive studies on this topic. At any rate, the limited comparative material used by the author does not allow extensive generalizations.

Before embarking upon the basic topic, some general remarks are needed on the conditions in which the Polish press functioned in the 1930s, since they exerted a prime impact upon the possibilities and forms of presenting politically "delicate" topics, indubitably including the German and Jewish questions. Like many other domains of social life, freedom of the press was subject to certain limitations already in 1926, in the wake of Piłsudski's *coup d'état*. During the 1930s, the ruling camp clearly sought not only to subjugate the politically loyal press grouped in concerns steered by the state, but also to expand considerably its range of influence over publications issued by the opposition. Confiscation of some issues, blank spaces on newspaper pages caused by the intervention of censors, or even administrative decisions about closing down a given newspaper all primarily affected the left-wing press or publications representing the radical wing of the rightist National Democracy movement that opposed the Piłsudski camp. The oft-repeated suggestions that it was precisely the Jewish press which was the target of mounting repression remain unconfirmed by the accessible comparative data concerning the number of confiscations; although, naturally, the press organs of the extreme left were frequently threatened with such forms of harassment.

The Jewish press, which *en masse* represented the most loyal of all the national minorities, was nonetheless very carefully read and scrutinized, since each of its language versions reached foreign readers and contributed to molding generally held opinions about Poland and its system of government. The "protection of the supreme interests of the state," as implemented by the censors, to a great measure followed the binding directives of both the Ministry of Internal Affairs and the Ministry of Foreign Affairs for which the Jewish question in Poland and the world played a prominent role.

In the concrete realm of Polish-German relations, a press agreement was signed on February 24, 1934. It closely followed a political convention that normalized Poland's relations with the Third Reich, obligating both parties to impede publications containing contents insulting to the signatories of the agreements, as well as excessive criticism of foreign policies or the domestic situation in the neighboring country. Under the impact of the agreement, a considerable part of the Polish press changed, at least for a certain period of time, the tone of its statements on the German question. Interventions by the German embassy in Warsaw, that referred to the pact, perceptibly softened critical comments in the press at a time when Poland's western neighbor was repudiating the decisions of the Versailles Treaty, as well as during the 1936 Olympic Games held in Berlin. Additional restrictions were introduced in the autumn of 1938 when official relations with Hitler's state deteriorated. The "Decree on the Protection of Select State Interests," issued in November 1938, made it feasible to interfere in texts which could inflame tension in Polish-German relations. The decree was particularly frequently cited during the intensification of diplomatic activity from March to the second half of August 1939, i.e. until after the signing of the Ribbentrop-Molotov pact, when it was decided to disclose to society the whole truth about the menacing situation.

In the light of these facts, and comparing the information about Germany in the years 1933–1939 contained in a press intended basically for Poles and Jews,[6] one feels tempted to declare that the vagaries of foreign policy had a much slighter impact on the Jewish press (regardless of its language.) Throughout the entire period of interest to us, the Jewish press spoke in a strident tone which would have little or no chance to be employed by other periodicals, rarely so critical towards the Third Reich. Censors sometimes even ignored attacks launched against the leading figures of Nazi Germany, despite the fact that such forays always met with decisive reactions on the part of the German embassy and Wilhelmstrasse. Apparently, the Jewish press, in contrast to its rivals, enjoyed a slightly more unbridled freedom in formulating its descriptions and evaluations of events taking place beyond the western border. This is by no means surprising if we realize that the same paradox occurred to an even larger degree in Germany itself. Herbert Freeden has shown that, for an amazingly long time (up to 1939) the Jewish press in Germany was not subjected to regulations enforcing Nazi indoctrination, and so retained its vitality and a certain range of liberty in depicting gloomy Nazi reality. [7]

The manner in which this margin of freedom was put to use was adversely affected by hampered access to information. In this respect the Jewish press, even publications with solid financial foundations, found itself in a particularly difficult situation. From 1933 to 1934, the majority of Jewish correspondents in the Third Reich had ceased to write. Many had emigrated to Palestine, while others resigned under the pressure of various obstacles. In time, Jewish newspapers were forced to rely to a growing extent on information services provided by the Jewish Telegraphic Agency (*Żydowska Agencja Telegraficzna* , ŻAT), the Polish Telegraphic Agency (*Polska Agencja Telegraficzna*, PAT) and, to a lesser degree, the Havas and Reuter agencies. In these conditions, reports from Germany grew increasingly similar even in the publications of ideologically divergent camps. This tendency probably explains the relatively small part played by the German question in the turbulent and persistent ideological debates conducted by competing groups through the medium of their leading periodicals. In reports on "the successive excesses of the Nazi hordes" and in a characteristic language brimming with invective, which concealed helplessness and despair, Jewish socialists, Folkists and Zionists were more alike than when their reflections were concerned with the coming communal elections, Polish domestic policy or even an assessment of British imperialism. Although there was no lack of mutual charges about an exaggerated or inadequate appraisal of various events or phenomena, this particular topic was rarely treated as a convenient platform for launching an attack against ideological opponents.

Undoubtedly, long before 1933 the Jewish press had all possible reasons for anxiously following the development of events in the Weimar Republic and the advancement of the National Socialist movement. In 1932, the election successes of the NSDAP and attempts at confiscating Jewish property (to be granted to the unemployed) carried out by the *Land* government imposed over Prussia in July, meant that news from Germany dominated the front pages of some of the papers. From the very outset, the leading Polish-language Jewish newspapers were Warsaw's *Nasz Przegląd* (Our Review) and the Lwów-based *Chwila* (Moment).

Chwila, a journal devoted to "political, social and cultural problems" appeared uninterruptedly from 1919. It was edited by Henryk Hescheles and represented liberal, democratic and anti-assimilation tendencies. The daily's circulation exceeded 30,000 copies, at the relatively high price of 20–25 *groszy* per copy. Already on February 7, 1932, the front page of *Chwila*, referring to PAT news from Berlin, reported that Adolf Hitler expected to be nominated chancellor, while the accompanying commentary naively explained this striving as a wish to accelerate the decision to grant the Austrian-born Hitler German citizenship.[8] A mixture of facts, suppositions and fiction was to become a constant feature, although in varying proportions, of a considerable part of the reported news from

Germany. The sensational character of the actual events made it extremely difficult to distinguish half-truths and inventions from reliable information fully attested by facts.

Legislation portending the confiscation of the property of "*Ostjuden*" was forced through the Prussian *Landtag* in the summer of 1932. On July 3, Henryk Hescheles, who at the time also headed *Chwila*'s political section, reacted in an article entitled "Protest against Barbarity." He emphasized the particular anxiety engendered among the Polish Jewish community by "this trend which has set forth on a speedy march across Germany."[9] The next day, demonstrations were held in Lwów against "the barbarousness and anti-Semitism of Nazi Prussia."

For quite some time, at least up to the middle of the following year, other Jewish and Polish newspapers perceived the course of German events as a chaotic tangle devoid of inner logic.[10] In contrast, some leftist periodicals (although not orthodox Marxist ones), as well as (at the other end of the political spectrum) Hescheles' *Chwila*, harbored ominous forebodings about the uniqueness of the events they were witnessing, that were the inauguration of a new tragic era. On July 13, news about street fighting and martial law courts in Saxony induced *Chwila* to assure its readers about the "new era" which Germany was entering. For the next weeks, reports from Berlin and Munich, exhibiting a certain grandiloquence and exaggeration, were almost constantly on the front pages. Having begun on this high note, *Chwila* rapidly reached the highest registers. On July 22, its front page carried the alarming headline, "Civil War in Germany," referring to the introduction of temporary martial law (in force until July 28) in Berlin and Brandenburg in connection with the imposition of the federal commissioner regime in Prussia. When Hitler actually came to power half a year later, *Chwila*'s editor was at a loss for new words to portray fully the gravity of the moment and stimulate necessary mobilization.

The horizon of the "black scenarios of events," which already at that time were regarded as highly realistic, is well illustrated by a ŻAT article in *Chwila* on July 20. "What Can the German Jews Expect after the Rise of Hitler to Power?" was based on an interview with Dr. Wilhelm Solmann, a Social Democrat and former minister in the Weimar Republic. Attention is called not only to the rather swift coming to terms with the perspective of the Nazi seizure of power which in the not-so-distant past was regarded as pure intellectual speculation. The ŻAT interviewer foresaw, i.a., the possibility of spontaneous pogroms carried out by mobs of Hitler's supporters incited against the Jews, although ultimately he did not regard them as the greatest danger. "The German Jews should anticipate in a Hitler dictatorship the forsaking of all gains from their emancipation. Exceptional taxes will ruin them economically." He also took into consideration the eventuality of a "quiet" boycott of Jewish entrepreneurs, traders, physicians and lawyers, as well as difficulties created for Jewish artists. This vision, close to the nightmare of the first years of the Third Reich, is accompanied, however, by a belief that " . . . Hitler's dictatorship in Germany is possible for only a short duration."

Growing tension was at times countered by press reports—usually of little reliability—whose purpose was to instill some hope into the anxious hearts of the readers. On August 9, 1932, *Chwila* mentioned, for instance, a secret pact for the reinstatement of the German monarchy. On 13 January 1933, PAT reported a mutiny within the Nazi ranks. Equally compelling was a series of *Chwila* articles entitled "Jews in the Service of German Culture," that recapitulated the historic accomplishments of German Jews in all domains of the arts, achievements usually ignored by Nazi and radically nationalist propaganda.

Nasz Przegląd, published in Warsaw from 1923 as an "independent press organ" of clearly pro-Zionist sympathies, was the most popular Jewish daily in Polish. It had an imposing staff, a forcefully edited weekly illustrated supplement, and special inserts for young readers and sport fans. In its treatment of events in Germany, *Nasz Przegląd* adopted a line similar to the one pursued by *Chwila* although expressed in even stronger terms. Systematic reports came in from the paper's own correspondents in Berlin (including B. Zynger) and Bavaria (Engineer F. Recher). Much space was devoted to reprints of appeals made by leading Jewish associations in the Weimar Republic.

In an interview published in *Nasz Przegląd* on 1 July 1932, Nahum Sokołów, President of the World Zionist Organization, condemned acts of barbarity which he correctly judged to be "a foretaste of what everyone can expect if Hitler were to assume power." Such a possibility was regarded seriously up to the November elections to the *Reichstag* that ended with the first decline in votes for the Nazi Party. A commentary published on November 8 by N.S. (probably Natan Szwalbe) declared that ". . .

plans of winning indivisible rule in the state, cherished by Hitler, had finally collapsed." The style in which the *Nasz Przegląd*'s front page informed readers about current events is testified by a title from the same issue, "A Paralytic Succeeds the Blind," referring to the victory of Franklin D. Roosevelt over Herbert Hoover in the American presidential election.

Nasz Przegląd Ilustrowany (Our Illustrated Review), which appeared on Sundays, devoted an exceptionally large amount of space to German issues. It drew particular and strange satisfaction from presenting photographs from German army maneuvers, provocative visits of the German fleet in Gdańsk (Danzig) or Nazi demonstrations. Material of this sort was obviously supposed to act as a warning. From 1933 the paper's tone changed and accent was placed on the exaggerated force of the anti-Nazi opposition and the enormity of losses for the culture, science and economy of the Third Reich caused by the mass exodus of eminent "non-Aryan" public figures. Photographs illustrating the rising military and political threat were at times accompanied by curious depictions of the "poverty of the German village" and the fragility of the "supposed" industrial power of Hitler's state.

Completely different contents and tone can be found in the leftist press of the period. *Nowe Pismo* (New Writing), a weekly published from October 30, 1932, by the socialist left wing close to the Bund, evaluated events exclusively from the point of view of class struggle. The progress of Nazism was explained in a manner similar to the one employed by the official doctrine of the III International—by pointing to the *petit bourgeois* character of the electorate, the "surrender" of big capital and, last but not least, the tactical errors committed by the Social Democratic Party (SPD). The situation of the German Jews was never discussed, and the theme of anti-Semitism was treated with great caution. An article by Bundist leader Wiktor Alter addressed this topic in *Nowe Pismo* number 18 (2 April 1933), portraying Hitler as "a zoological anti-Semite." But the article's title refers to a threat to the working class at large. The weekly was involved in a debate with *Robotnik* (Worker), the leading organ of the Polish Socialist Party which, as regards the German question, shared the opinion of the Socialist Workers International, and was accused *inter alia* of a non-critical attitude to the reformism of the German Social Democrats.

Naturally, Hitler's nomination to be Germany's chancellor in January 1933 did not pass unnoticed, although one could get the impression that journalists writing for Polish-language Jewish periodicals remained unaware of the significance of changes initiated by that nomination. *Opinia*, a new "socio-political and literary weekly," published its first issue at the end of January 1933, as Hitler was coming to power. *Opinia* proclaimed itself to be "a platform of Jewish national thought." In its program article, "What Is Europe Heading Towards?",[11] the new Jewish weekly noted that Hitler's coming to power denoted the liquidation of the aftermath of the November revolution of 1918 and marked the beginning of "hard times" for the Jews. Nonetheless, it simultaneously expressed the conviction that the need to take into consideration coalition partners "makes it impossible for Hitler to dare to realize his insane 'Jewish program'." The article's author was of the opinion that a program of this sort was purely propaganda; he foresaw the intensification of chaos and decisive action on the part of the League of Nations. *Opinia*'s outstanding staff included distinguished journalists, men of letters (Szalom Asz [Asch], Uri Cwi Grinberg [Greenberg], Roman Brandstaetter), historians (Majer Bałaban, Ignacy Schipper, Mojżesz Schorr) and Zionist politicians. The weekly could boast of the most interesting political commentaries. Originally published in Warsaw, from 1936 it appeared in Lwów as *Nasza Opinia* (Our Opinion). The choice of Leon Feuchtwanger's *Der jüdische Krieg* (The Jewish War) as the first novel approved by the editorial board to be serialized was highly symptomatic for the journal's trend of influencing public opinion. It was not by accident that it was *Opinia* which embarked upon the harshest critique of the attitude of a sizable part of the German Jewish community that tried at all cost to find a place in the "national revolution" steered by the NSDAP.[12]

Illusions about the possibility of a rapid downfall of the coalition cabinet, or the diversion of its program to a "civilized" course, were originally shared by almost the entire press. In his comments on the first weeks of Hitler's rule, J. M. (a special correspondent for *Chwila*), accented the unpredictability of the further course of events. He feared civil war, an open *coup d'état* and swindles at the polls. On the other hand, he did not notice the threat posed by the consolidation and legalization of the Nazi system with the aid of measures sanctioned by law.[13] Citing the opinions of the Italian press, *Nasz Przegląd* was convinced that the presence of von Neurath, German Minister of Foreign Affairs, was decisive for the retention of political continuity. The editorial stressed constitutional legality and the moderate tactics of the first moves made by the new cabinet.[14] The author of the commentary (Natan Szwalbe) expected, not without justification, a quick elimination of the Communists, but similarly to many other observers of the period he anticipated that the future would follow a course modeled on the Italian events of 1922–1924. PAT dispatches mentioned universal enthusiasm and joy. According to the Berlin correspondent of the PAT agency: "The German Jews believe that Hitler would not have the courage to violate laws fortified by the constitution . . . The slogan of the German Jews is: calm persistence."[15] The German Jews' *Zentral-Verein* (Central Association of German Citizens of the Jewish Faith) asserted that though it harbored "the greatest distrust" towards the National Socialist government, it would opt for "biding time."

Doubts were dispersed extremely swiftly and in a manner whose vehemence took the majority of observers by surprise. By the very nature of things, the reaction of the Polish-language Jewish press to the establishment of a Nazi dictatorship must have been more intense and concentrated on the persecution of the "non-Aryan" population than the reaction of the rest of the Polish press. The reports of dailies intended primarily for the Polish Christian reader as a rule opted for a calmer and more distant tone and a language less bristling with invective. The National Democratic periodicals even, occasionally, praised the solution applied by the new leaders of Germany to the "Jewish question," thus provoking a series of polemical articles warning against a Polish variety of fascism.

For the larger part of 1933, sensational and ominous events in "the land of Hitler," announced by loud and vivid headlines, did not leave the front pages of the Jewish press. Almost on a daily basis, new reports talked about persecutions, decrees or plans aimed not only against *"Ostjuden"* who lacked German citizenship, but also directly against the assimilated and deeply patriotic native German Jews. Zionist periodicals, engaged in a battle against assimilationism, conceived this situation as an ideal argument confirming the correctness of their own stance. Nonetheless, *Nasz Przegląd* and *Opinia* referred to it very carefully, probably not wishing to give the impression of preying on the tragic fate of others.

The alarmist tone of the reports in the Polish-Jewish press was not solely the outcome of the very scale of the persecutions and the speed with which the supporters of the *Führer* were capable of transforming the German state, which Jews traditionally held in high esteem, into a totalitarian and cowed Third Reich. It was also an attempt at arousing counteraction, as well as a reaction to the passive attitude of the Polish government, the inertness of public opinion, and the absence of suitable resonance in the global press. Lastly, it was an expression of a growing fear of isolation in the face of a ruthless enemy. It is not surprising that Jewish journalists often perceived the threat gathering over their nation in suprahistorical categories, fitting it into universally known archetypes of persecutions suffered by the adherents of the Mosaic faith, familiar to all their readers. At the same time, they tended to lose the specificity of current events. Occasionally, the tendency towards inserting "history unleashed" into old, one-sided paradigms produced extraordinarily acute interpretations, but more often it favored erroneous, shortsighted assessments which strike today's reader, endowed with the knowledge of hindsight, as particularly inapt. Sharp language, full of invective, initially tolerated by censorship, protested against the course of events and reflected the helplessness of their witnesses.

Already in March 1933, *Nasz Przegląd* ceased hoping that Hitler could be halted by forces inside Germany. In his commentary on the situation in mid-March, prominent Kraków Rabbi Dr. Ozjasz Thon, a leading member of the Zionist Organization, concluded that Hitler had escaped from under the control of Hindenburg and Hugenberg, and instead totally dominated them. Nevertheless, Thon remained convinced that although the German Chancellor lacked all restraint, he presented a real danger only at home.[16]

Already then, Hitler was at times compared to Haman, and the fate of the German Jewish brethren was described as "martyrdom." The mood of the news reports from Germany is well reflected in titles like "Wild Anti-Jewish Brawl" or "Hitler's Hordes on the Rampage." Interestingly, at the same time *Nasz Przegląd* also ran articles about daily life in Berlin and discussed, for example, the revival of the top hat in the city streets. On the day after the solidarity protest held by the largest Jewish organizations in Poland, the March 28, 1933, issue printed the first tragic list of 51 persons killed or assaulted in Germany—Polish citizens of Jewish descent who fell prey to the terror perpetrated by Nazi Stormtroopers. In April the periodical no longer deliberated about whether Hitler would manage to stay in power. It now posed a symptomatic question of a totally different nature: "Is Polish Nazism Possible?"[17]

Relatively little space was devoted to a critical appraisal of the attitude of the SPD or the German Jewish organizations seeking accommodation with National Socialism. Attention was rather called to the mobilization of the widest possible front of protest against terror and the boycott campaign aimed against the Jewish community. This front was increasingly clearly abandoned by the Bund whose publications, led by the Yiddish daily *Folkstsaytung* (People's Newspaper), attacked the Jewish press for ignoring social conditions that promoted anti-Semitism and the Nazi movement.

The leftist press interpreted the consolidation of German fascism from a decidedly more partisan perspective, and despite a certain ideological proximity launched mutual accusations of tactical mistakes, passivity and even cowardice. Strong emphasis was placed on the absence of resistance on the part of German society, and on the "inevitability" of an imperialist war in Europe which had to end in a new "great carnage." Oskar Lange, commentator of *Nasza Walka* (Our Struggle) and at the time a young theoretical economist who did not conceal his socialist sympathies, linked the successes of the "brown-shirt tide," that was making its way across Europe, with a crisis of socialist ideals.

Another typical feature of the left-wing press was its inclination towards far-reaching simplification and "strong" language. Well-known commentators did not recoil from such expressions as "the dictatorship of an oaf," "the talons of brown-shirt thugs," and so forth. Upon occasion, they used a similar vocabulary for describing the situation in Poland, a tendency which must have led to blurring the basic quantitative differences and losing the very essence of Hitler's version of fascism. Branding the religiously orthodox and politically conservative views of the Agudat Israel party as "an open and official exposition of fascism in Jewish society,"[18] for instance, could not contribute to comprehending the nature of the phenomenon of fascism. With the exception of extremely few Polish-language publications connected with the Bund or the Zionist left wing, such as the Poale Zion, the contents of the Jewish left-wing press, addressed to readers fluent in Polish, did not differ significantly from that in the general Socialist press of Poland.

Relatively objective reports can be found in articles published in 1933 by the weekly *Opinia*. A series of articles by Ignacy Schipper, entitled

"The Jewish Contribution to German Culture," was accompanied by an in-depth analysis of the new legal situation of Germans of Jewish descent or the interesting reflections of Dr. F. Rotenstreich about the foreign policy of the Third Reich.

The passage of time and adjustment to the new reality caused the news from Germany to grow less sensational. Reports were gradually relegated to the back pages of dailies and weeklies despite the fact that their content was no less terrifying than those from the previous period. At the end of June 1934, attention was stirred up once again, albeit this time briefly, by the "Night of the Long Knives."

The lowering of the rhetorical volume was caused not so much by a weariness with the subject but by the activity of censors, intensified at the beginning of the year, who were now compelled by treaty to oppose all slander directed against Hitler and Göring, as leaders of a neighboring country with which Poland wished to retain correct relations. A certain role was also played by the effectiveness of Goebbels' propaganda which attempted to present the Third Reich as the embodiment of stability and peace. After 1934 the number of reports from Germany published in *Opinia* and *Chwila* was further restricted. Information provided by the papers' own correspondents ceased appearing. Commentaries were now based to a growing extent on generally available dispatches offered by the main press agencies. Even such events as the violation of the Versailles Treaty resolutions, the militarization of the Rhineland or the passing of the Nuremberg laws did not produce reactions comparable with those which dominated two and three years earlier.

Nasz Przegląd remained most persevering in its treatment of the German theme that up to 1938 appeared in other publications on a very irregular basis. For example, interesting analyses of anti-Jewish economic steps, written by sociologist and educator Dr. Arje Tartakower, were published by *Nasza Walka*, an ephemeral weekly published by Zionist socialists in 1935.

In the mid-thirties, *Chwila* ascribed decisive priority to the Palestine question. The German problem made relatively rare appearances on the front page, usually in the form of reprints of material published earlier by the *Morning Post* or other British and French periodicals. Relatively considerable space was devoted, however, to particular events such as the July 1935 appeal made to President Roosevelt by the American Jews who urged not only a verbal condemnation of the barbarity and persecutions committed under the sign of the swastika but also a boycott of the Berlin Olympic Games, as well as international sanctions against the Third Reich to be imposed by the League of Nations, and the refusal to sign any bilateral agreements with Hitler.[19] Needless to say, none of these demands was ever implemented.

We also come across information which cannot be viewed as reliable or which even bears the marks of intentional disinformation produced by Goebbels' Ministry of Propaganda. The reduction of independent sources of information forced commentators to speculate upon the basis of data provided by official sources; consequently, they tended to ascribe excessive importance to hearsay and information of unknown origin. This led to the proliferation of news reports about supposed personal conflicts, a pro-Jewish atmosphere in the *Wehrmacht* or preparations for a fundamental change of the heretofore domestic policy line. At the same time, there is no lack of interesting analyses of the effects of economic outreach or attempts at penetrating the far-reaching plans of the *Führer*.[20] The growth of the military power of the Reich was closely followed with great uneasiness. The concealed menace, however, was counterbalanced by the editors' strongly expressed belief that the excessive tempo of armament led the Reich to the verge of a great economic crisis. In 1937–1938 petty, third-rate information was perceived as symptoms of a profound depression which inevitably would affect the whole country.

In the second half of the 1930s, the interpretation of German domestic and foreign policy was influenced by news from Spain and the Soviet Union. The second context, in particular, systematically accompanied all analyses of past Polish-German relations as well as the appraisal of the very nature of the revolution experienced by Poland's western neighbor. This topic was mentioned already in 1932 in the article, "Hitler - Poland - Soviet Union," printed by the socialist weekly *Nowe Pismo* which drew attention to the fact that the eventual victory of fascism in Germany would, paradoxically, increase the security of Soviet borders.[21] A year later, critical remarks on the situation of Soviet Jews in Birobidzhan, presented by Gerszon Wolf in *Nasz Przegląd* on 9 February 1933, drew a bold comparison with the Third Reich. From the very beginning of the Moscow trials, such analogies were made increasingly frequently in the entire Jewish press free of Comintern orthodoxy. A summary of the trials in *Nasza Opinia* (probably by Dr. Abraham Insler) described them as a "nightmare" and "Dante's Inferno," stressing similarities with the administration of justice in the Third Reich.[22] True, *Chwila* remained skeptical about the unavoidable conflict between Nazi Germany and the Soviet state,[23] but on October 5, 1937, citing the opinions of French specialists apprehensive about the new claims made by Hitler, it suggested the necessity of "coming to terms with the hammer or the anvil." Ewrein Carlebach, a journalist writing for *Chwila*, described the trial of Bukharin as a "fraud" and ridiculed accusations which claimed that Trotsky was a Nazi agent.[24] *Nasz Przegląd* and *Chwila* sporadically resorted to the term "totalitarianism" in characterizing features and practices common for both powerful neighbors of the Polish Second Republic.

The shock brought about by the 1938 Munich crisis and the events which took place immediately afterwards (the expulsion from Germany of about 25,000 Polish Jews and *Kristallnacht*) could be deciphered from the empty spaces left on newspaper pages after the ejection of articles questioned by censors in consecutive editions of the leading titles of the Jewish press. The situation of the German Jews, arson, pogroms and violence—all these topics returned once again to the front pages of Polish-language dailies. For censorship reasons, this information was rarely accompanied by more profound reflection on the true meaning of the events, which would have been an attempt at deciphering the extensive plans pursued by Hitler as regards the Jewish people. Quite possibly, a complete awareness of the impending danger—total extermination—transcended the cognitive horizon of the majority of the commentators of the period. Seeking refuge in a world of illusion appeared to be the need of the moment. Hence the references, made in good faith, to calculations by foreign astrologers and mathematicians which infallibly demonstrated that Hitler would die in 1939, or the serious assurances about "the total defeat of the Axis in a war of nerves" proclaimed on the very eve of the Ribbentrop-Molotov pact which came as a shock not only to the Jewish readers.[25]

Censorship and official optimism, imposed from above, meant that the Polish Jews, like the majority Christian Poles, found themselves insufficiently prepared by their press for coping with current challenges. Recollections about the "mild" occupation from the days of World War I created an additional hindrance for a correct orientation in the new reality. Ideological "rabidness," a feature shared by the majority of the press, apparently played a smaller role than is usually assumed in the years before September 1939.

Notes:

1. Next to Marian Fuks' monograph *Prasa żydowska w Warszawie 1823–1939* (The Jewish Press in Warsaw 1823–1939) (Warszawa, 1979) and the article by Aleksander Hafftka in the prewar publication *Żydzi w Polsce odrodzonej* (Jews in Reborn Poland) (Warszawa 1933), vol. II, I would also like to mention the series of publications by M. Fuks in the *Biuletyn Żydowskiego Instytutu Historycznego (BZIH)*; as well as the review by Andrzej Notkowski, "O działalności wydawniczej Żydów warszawskich w XIX i XX w." (On publication activity of Warsaw Jews in the nineteenth and twentieth century), published in *Przegląd Historyczny*, vol. LXXII, no. 4/1981, pp. 722–746; and Michael Steinlauf, "The Polish Jewish Daily Press," *Polin* 2 (1987), pp. 219–246.
2. I. Szajn (prep. by M. Fuks), "Bibliografia dzienników i czasopism żydowskich wydawanych w Polsce w latach 1918–1939 w języku polskim" (Bibliography of Polish-language Jewish Dailies and Periodicals Published in Poland in the Years 1918–1939), *BZIH*, no. 78 (1971), pp. 107–132 (subsequently supplemented by lists of youth and communist press); Paul Glikson, *Preliminary Inventory of the Jewish Daily and Periodical Press Published in the Polish Language* (Jerusalem, 1983); and A. Cała, "Bibliografia żydowskich periodyków polskojęzycznych"(Bibliography of Jewish Polish-language Periodicals) (manuscript).
3. It is totally omitted by A. Notkowski in his book, *Polska prasa prowincjonalna II Rzeczypospolitej (1918–1939)* (The Polish Provincial Press in the Second Republic [1918–1939]) (Warszawa-Łódź, 1982). Other authors of syntheses are content with brief concluding sketches that echo universally accepted opinions and findings.
4. Cf. e.g. A. Hafftka, op. cit.; Z. Jamiński, *Prasa żydowska w Polsce* (The Jewish Press in Poland) (Warszawa, 1936).
5. In his *Prasa polska w latach 1918–1939* (Polish Press in the Years 1918–1939) (Warszawa, 1980), pp. 343–362, Andrzej Paczkowski

demonstrates that one minority periodical was published per 130,000 Belorussians, per 40,000 Ukrainians, per 24,000 Jews and only 7,100 Germans, with a national average of 1 copy for 12,600 persons. For every 100 representatives of an ethnic minority in Poland, 12.7 Germans, 10 Jews, only 0.6 Ukrainians and not a single Belorussian had his own copy of a daily newspaper. Data about the circulation of Jewish periodicals in Germany, cited by Herbert Freeden, *The Jewish Press in the Third Reich* (Oxford, 1993), also indicate greater publication effort and readership in proportion to this population group.

6. One should keep in mind, however, that this is a slightly imprecise distinction since part of the Polish-language Jewish press reached the Polish reader and a considerable number of the Jewish intelligentsia read general Polish publications, as well.

7. H. Freeden, op. cit., chapter 1.

8. *Chwila*, no. 4623a, 7 Feb. 1932.

9. *Chwila*, no. 4768a, 3 July 1932.

10. This trend of thought was pursued mainly, but not only by such tabloids as *5 Rano* (5 o'Clock) or *Ostatnie Wiadomości* (Latest News), but originally also by more serious publications such as *Opinia* (Opinion).

11. *Opinia*, no. 1, 1 Feb. 1933, p. 1.

12. Cf. ibid., no 5, 5 March 1933, article: "Flames over Berlin."

13. *Chwila*, no. 4986, 9 Feb. 1933 .

14. *Nasz Przegląd*, 1 Feb. 1933.

15. *Nasz Przegląd*, 1 Feb. 1933.

16. *Nasz Przegląd*, 15 March 1933, the article "Hindenburg - Hugenberg - Hitler."

17. 1 April 1933. Earlier, on March 21, the author S.H. expressed his astonishment at the symptoms of pro-fascist sympathies among the Polish right wing ("The Hitlerite Eclipse of Poland.")

18. *Nasza Walka*, IV, August 1931.

19. *Chwila*, 25 July 1935 (second edition, after confiscation).

20. Cf. the article "Plans of Today's Germany - How Does Hitler Keep the German People in Check?" which referred to the publication by Bontemps, *Chwila* no. 6253 (14 August 1936).

21. *Nowe Pismo*, no. 7, 20 Dec. 1932.

22. *Nasza Opinia*, VI, no. 135 (262) , 13 March 1938.

23. Cf. the article "Is There a Possibility of War Between Germany and the Soviet Union?," *Chwila*. no. 6122, 7 May 1936.

24. *Chwila*, 5 Oct. 1937.

25. *Chwila*, 8 July 1939.

The Jews in the Polish Clandestine Press, 1939–1945[1]

Lucjan Dobroszycki
Yeshiva University and YIVO Institute for Jewish Research

The German occupation of Poland brought about a situation without precedent in the history of the Polish press. Indeed, it had never before been the case that an invading power forbade the publishing of newspapers and periodicals throughout the entire land. By comparison, under the Partitions, the Poles had been able to publish their own papers, and in the Polish language. Often the papers were inspired or censored by the Prussian, Russian, and Austrian authorities, but they did exist. We can find this type of censored press in almost all of the countries occupied by the Germans during World War II, in Bohemia, Moravia, Denmark, Norway, Belgium, Holland and France. But in all of these countries, German policy sought to win the good will of the local population, hence the readiness to make concessions. One of the features of this policy in western Europe was a relatively liberal attitude toward the mass media. In some countries, Nazi press policy was much more liberal than in Germany itself. The newpapers and periodicals in the Protectorate of Bohemia and Moravia or in France remained largely in the hands of the prewar publishers, with the exception, of course, of the Jewish publishers.[2]

In Poland it was otherwise. Here, terror, forced labor, and the plundering of the national wealth set the tone for Nazi policy. The total liquidation of the Polish press was only one of its elements. In Great Poland, Pomerania, and Silesia, the territories directly incorporated into the Third Reich, all printing houses owned by Poles and Jews were already confiscated in accordance with the nationalities program of the N.S.D.A.P. Racial Policy Office of November 25, 1939:

[In the territories incorporated into the Reich] there will be no
Polish newspapers, and no Polish books or periodicals will be
published. For the same reason, Poles may not own radio sets or
gramophones.[3]

The situation in the so-called 'General Government', which consisted of Kraków, Radom, Lublin, Warsaw, and—after 1941—Lwów
provinces, was somehow different. Here, from the strictly formal point of
view, publishing activity was not forbidden. The German regulations
referred only to the need for the consent of the authorities, but in practice
such permission was never granted, and almost all of the publishing
establishments were taken over by the Germans. Soon thereafter, in all of
occupied Poland, the publication of newspapers and periodicals, as well
as books, fell into the hands of the Germans. However, almost at the same
time that the first issues of the German press in the Polish language started to appear, an underground Polish press came into being. Underground
publications had a long tradition in Poland, but never before had they
appeared on so large a scale as they did during the Second World War.
Studies on the underground press which I published in 1962 and 1963 list
more than 1,500 titles of newspapers and periodicals.[4] As a basis for
comparison between Poland and other occupied countries, it should be
noted that in the Netherlands there were 1,200 titles, in France 1,200, in
Denmark 550, and in Italy 545.[5] To be sure, of those 1,500-plus titles in
Poland there were many which had no more than a few single issues. We
can, however, set aside a sizable number of papers which continued to
come out for several years. Among the underground papers published in
occupied Poland, about 400 came out for about two years, 145 for three
years, 65 for four years, and 41 for five years. Finally, three papers were
published almost without interruption from the end of 1939 until January
1945, which marked the end of the German occupation of former Polish
territory. These were *Szaniec* (The Rampart), *Biuletyn Informacyjny*
(Information Bulletin), and *Dziennik Radiowy* (The Daily Radio News).

All of this underground publishing activity in Poland during the war
was accomplished despite the very difficult and dangerous conditions
under which the papers had to be produced. The work had to be done in
secret, and the least lack of discretion could result in arrest, deportation
to concentration camps, or even execution. When the Germans discovered

an underground printing shop or distribution center, they applied the principle of collective responsibility, terrorizing whole buildings, streets, and even entire neighborhoods. The underground press touched on almost all problems, for there were no forbidden topics in the Polish underground press. Each publisher, aside from the danger that threatened him from the Germans, considered himself free to express his own views. The opinions of one publisher could and often did arouse the disagreement of another. This led to the growth of widely diversified political writing. In the underground, the people were free, and so was its press.

It might be expected that the entire underground press, which had to produce its work with such effort and with such great risk, and which was almost without exception anti-German, would have been also, if not pro-Jewish, then at least sympathetic to Hitler's first victims, and that, in a country where the entire population was treated worse by the Germans than anywhere else in occupied Europe, there would have been a basis, again, if not for a common struggle against a common enemy, then at least for putting an end to anti-Jewish propaganda. As we will see, it did not happen this way. The underground press in Poland was put out by all the parties, organizations, and groups which had existed before the war, and even the new parties and organizations that came into being during the war were patterned on the prewar social and political movements. Thus, the press constituted a mosaic of opinions and attitudes, ranging from the far right to the far left. At one extreme, there were the publications of the nationalist radicals and conservative organizations; at the other, those of the democratic, socialist, peasant, syndicalist and communist parties. All these parties and their press during the war were divided over such issues as who was responsible for the Polish defeat in 1939, how the struggle against the Germans should be conducted, what the attitude toward the Western Allies and the Soviet Union should be, what the form of government in Poland after the war should be, and what the policy towards Poland's national minorities should be. Here, the proper attitude towards the Jews both during the war and afterwards was one of the most widely discussed problems.

To begin from the right side of the political spectrum, there were four organizations: *Szaniec* (The Rampart), *Pobudka* (The Awakening), *Konfederacja Narodu* (The Confederation of the Nation), and *Narodowe Siły Zbrojne* (The National Armed Forces). All of them grew out of prewar parties that had until 1939 openly sympathized with the Nazi movement in Germany and Italy. The German invasion of Poland put an end to this friendship. For the Germans, even the Polish fascists were first of all Poles and therefore *Untermenschen*. Neither then, nor now, after over 50 years have passed, could one calmly read what these extremist underground groups published on the Jews during the German occupation. What I present are not quotations taken out of context, but fragments of much longer pieces written in the same vein on issues that kept recurring over and over again, from the first day of the German occupation to the last.

"The Germans and the Jews have set the world on fire; therefore they must burn together," wrote the Confederation of the Nation in its paper, *Do Broni* (To Arms), at the time of the mass deportation from the Warsaw Ghetto in 1942, when over 300,000 Jews were sent to the death camp in Treblinka. Another paper from the same group, *Barykada* (The Barricade), featured an editorial in March 1943 in which we find the following: "The liquidation of the Jews on Polish soil is of great significance for our future development, since it will free us from several million parasites. The Germans have greatly aided us in this matter." And here are parts of an article entitled "The Essence of the Social Changes in Poland," which appeared in the monthly *Pobudka* (Reveille), dated September 1943:

> Before the war, the Jewish question was a matter of propaganda. Now the situation has changed radically. The measures taken by the Germans have removed the Jews not only from our territories but most importantly from our mentality. The Poles—peasant, landlord, merchant, and industrialist—have seen for themselves how they can survive on their own without help from the Jews, even under the worst kind of conditions created during the occupation. In this way, the foundation has been set for a real solution of the Jewish problem.

The papers put out by these organizations were not the only ones to carry such articles. One finds similar attitudes expressed in the publications of the National Democrats and Christian Democrats. But while the extremist organizations had been on the margin of the political scene in Poland both before and during the war, the National and Christian

Democrats had constituted a major political and social movement ever since the end of the nineteenth century. As soon as the Second Polish Republic was founded in 1918, they became part of the governing coalition and at least until 1928 they had the largest number of seats in the Polish Parliament. Traditionally anti-Jewish, they did not change their policy during the German occupation, a fact which they often emphasized in their writing. They even boasted that they had seen through the Jews long before Hitler came to power in Germany. Let me quote parts of only two articles, one from *Naród* (The Nation), a paper issued by the Christian Democrats, and another from *Walka* (The Struggle), published by the National Democrats. The first one, entitled "The Jews Must Emigrate," appeared in January 1942. The article was written in connection with plans to create a federation of all Slavic countries after the defeat of Germany. To quote:

> The Jewish Question is now a burning issue. We must tell ourselves that the Jews cannot regain their political rights and the property which they have lost. Moreover, they must in the future entirely leave the territories of our country. The matter is complicated by the fact that once we demand that the Jews leave Poland, we will not be able to tolerate them on the territories of the future federation of Slavic nations. This means that we have to cleanse all of central and southern Europe of the Jewish element, which amounts to moving some 8 to 9 million Jews.

In another article, the author tries to solve the problem of where these Jews are to emigrate. Palestine is, for him, out of the question. It is too small and, moreover, England is raising objections. He then writes: "As Christians, we must demand that the Holy Land, which constitutes half of Palestine, be handed over to Christians, since we cannot permit the Jews to settle there." The second article, from *Walka*, entitled "The Danger of an Apparent Solution," came out when the extermination of the Jews of Europe was at its peak and after the suppression of the Warsaw Ghetto Uprising. To quote:

> From a biological point of view, the Jews have been greatly undercut. The decline of Israel, in which Roman Dmowski, the

founder of the National Democratic Party, once believed, has unexpectedly come much closer because of the biological defeat of that nation, namely, the destruction of millions of its most racially pure representatives.

The author also takes issue with those who think that after the war there will be no Jewish question anymore. According to him, two problems will still remain: one will concern property left behind by the Jews, to which Jews from abroad will lay claim. The other will have to do with the political influence of the Jews in the international arena. Elsewhere in a paper issued by that same party, *Warszawski Dziennik Narodowy* (Warsaw National Daily), we find the following: "It will do us no harm if our Western Allies are weakened by the war. Then their role as tools in the hands of Jewish Freemasonry will be of lesser significance for Poland."

Though less violently and less openly expressed, similar attitudes towards the Jews were voiced in many other publications close to the National Democrats and Christian Democrats. Only one of its groups made an open break with the traditions of the movement. I have in mind the organization founded by the Polish Catholic writer Zofia Kossak-Szczucka under the name *Front Odrodzenia Polski* (Front for the Restitution of Poland). It brought together members of the Polish Catholic intelligentsia who already before the war had been strongly influenced by the rationalism of Francois Mauriac. The Front's task concerning the Jews was not easy, and its stand on the Jewish question was at the beginning somehow divided. Partly because of its own views but mostly because it did not wish to become completely cut off from other Catholic groups, the Front in some of its publications asserted that the fate which had met the Jews was a well deserved punishment, since God does not permit injustice and since the Jews from the time of Bar-Kokhba had been parasites on the body of the European nation, and so on. In this respect, the Front shared the views proclaimed by the rest of the movement, but its main argument, repeated from the day the group was founded until the last day of the German occupation, was that the Christians bore the blame for what the Jews were and that, moreover, at a time when the Jews were being destroyed by the Germans, it was the duty of every Christian to give them moral and active support. Zofia Kossak-Szczucka founded and headed the Council to Aid the Jews, ŻEGOTA,[6] a joint organization that included representatives from almost all Polish liberal, socialist and democratic parties, in addition to delegates from the Home Army. Also on the Council were two representatives from the Jewish resistance movement, Adolf Berman from the Zionist movement and Leon Feiner from the Bund. The underground press put out by all of the groups under the umbrella of Kossak-Szczucka's organization published quite a large number of papers. Special attention should be given to the press published by the Polish Socialist Party, the WRN, *Barykada Wolności*, as well as to the main publications of the Home Army, particularly its *Biuletyn Informacyjny* and *Wiadomości Polskie*. *Biuletyn* was the weekly with the highest regular circulation, about 45,000 copies, high indeed considering the conditions of that time. It was also, as already mentioned, one of the three papers published almost without interruption from 1939 to 1945. Its editor-in-chief was Aleksander Kamiński, the well-known Polish educator and Scout leader, who before the war maintained close contacts with the Zionist *Halutzim* in Poland. It was during this time that he made friends with Mordechaj Anielewicz, who later headed the Jewish Fighting Organization and was commander of the Warsaw Ghetto Uprising in April 1943. *Biuletyn* gave up-to-date information on the situation of the Jews in Poland, condemned the crimes perpetrated by the Germans, appealed to its readers to help the victims, and warned that measures would be taken against those who collaborated in any way with the Germans in the extermination of the Jews.

While speaking of the pro-Jewish press in Poland, one cannot omit two papers that were published in Warsaw in the underground. One was *Abecadło Lekarskie* (The Physician's ABC), the other *Nowy Dziennik* (The New Daily). In the first months of the war, when the ghettos were being created and the Jews were being thrown out of their homes, workshops and offices, *Abecadło Lekarskie* appealed to Polish doctors not to take over the offices of their Jewish colleagues without their permission; in case they were forced to do so, the paper continued, they should try to do everything possible to keep the property of the Jewish physician intact, and, whenever possible, help him financially. In the spring of 1941, the Germans initiated a widely publicized anti-Jewish campaign in Warsaw. Posters with the slogan "Jews, Lice, Typhus" appeared on walls and fences all over Warsaw. In response to this campaign, *Abecadło Lekarskie* published a scientific analysis of the origins of typhus in the ghetto in a well documented article entitled "The Ghetto and the Epidemic." The author and co-editor, Dr. Ludwik Rostkowski, wrote, "The Nazis, just like the well-known British scholar Topley, have conducted an experiment by introducing healthy individuals into a contaminated environment on a mass scale and studying the development of this epidemic. But Topley made his experiment on rats." After a detailed description of the conditions created by the Germans in the ghetto, Dr. Rostkowski made the following appeal:

> The Poles and the Jews should regard each other as allies in the struggle against a common enemy. The medical community in particular should oppose the harmful anti-Jewish propaganda that seeks to give a scientific basis to its political aims. A physician, whose primary duty is to give help to a man without regard for his race or nationality, must reject racism and its inhuman methods. In everyone who is suffering and sick a doctor should see, first of all, a fellow human being.[7]

While *Abecadło Lekarskie* was a periodical which appeared irregularly and was meant to be read by a rather narrow group of people, *Nowy Dziennik* was one of the underground daily papers published in occupied Warsaw. It covered events on both sides of the wall, as they were taking place. Such was the case during the Warsaw Ghetto Uprising in April and May of 1943. One of the *Nowy Dziennik* reporters was Aurelia Wyleżyńska, a well-known Polish writer. I will quote a fragment of her article entitled *"Gloria victis,"* published on May 14, 1943, two days before General-SS Jürgen Stroop reported, "The Jewish Quarter in Warsaw is no more!"

> *Gloria victis!* May 14, 1943. Pockets of resistance are still holding on in the hopeless battle. I approach the front line. It is rather one great cemetery. No natural disaster has ever produced such a mass grave. Near the freshly demolished wall, some German soldiers are practicing target shooting. Haven't they practiced enough? The defense of Warsaw's Nalewki Street will pass into history alongside the defense of Saragossa, Alcazar, Westerplatte, and Stalingrad, every one of them held with blood. The defend-

ers of the ghetto succumbed not only to the brutal violence and overwhelming strength of the enemy. They have gone through an inferno of suffering, through every torment that man can inflict on man. They depart, victims of a total and complete burning. The civilized world will remember them forever.

Thus far I have limited myself to representing different points of view as they were expressed in publications issued by parties and groups that were virulently antisemitic and by those who stood by the Jews in thought and deed. To determine which of the two attitudes was predominant in the underground press is not an easy task. Simply to count the relevant numbers of publications of titles or articles is clearly not adequate. One would have to take into consideration at least such factors as the circulation of each of the papers; the rank, size, and importance of the parties and organizations that put them out; the names of the writers, newsmen, and editors; who wrote what and where; and finally, and this might be the most difficult question, what the readership and perception of the underground press were. Not all of the questions can be answered at this point of research. Three things, however, can be said. First, the Polish underground press was a very powerful instrument in shaping public opinion, and at the same time a faithful reflection of it. Second, the parties that had always been pro-Jewish remained so during the war, while the others, for whom antisemitism had been one of the basic premises of their policy in prewar times, continued to wage war, with pen and word at least, against the Jews: in the ghettos, during the deportations, and even when there were almost no Jews left in Poland. Third, the anti-Jewish writing of such respectable parties as the National Democrats and the Christian Democrats, to say nothing of the Polish Fascist organizations, even if it had no effect on the policies of the Germans, contributed to an unfriendly and hostile attitude toward the Jews in occupied Poland, and made extremely difficult the work of Polish groups, organizations and individuals who sought to help the Jews escaping from the ghetto, escaping from transports to the death camps, trying to remain on the Aryan side, or trying to hide in the forest. While German propaganda in occupied Poland was on the whole ineffective, there were a few areas in which it found some response. One of them was its anti-Jewish theme, for there were no great differences between what was written in the Nazi press and in the underground press of the National Democratic and Christian Democratic parties, not to mention the press of the extreme right organizations.

Notes:

1. This chapter originally appeared in *The Jews in Poland*, ed. Andrzej K. Paluch (Kraków: Jagiellonian University Research Center on Jewish History and Culture in Poland, 1992), vol. I, pp. 289–296. It is reprinted with the kind permission of Dr. Dobroszycki's wife, Felicja Dobroszycki.

2. L. Dobroszycki, *Die legale polnische Presse in Generalgouvernement, 1939–1945* (Munich: Institut für Zeitgeschichte, 1977), p. 209. [Ed. Note: Cf. L. Dobroszycki, *Reptile Journalism The Official Polish-Language Press under the Nazis, 1939–1945*, trans. Barbara Harshav (New Haven: Yale University Press, 1994).]

3. See Wetzel-Hecht memorandum entitled: "Die Frage der Behandlung der Bevölkerung der ehemaligen polnischen Gebiete nach rassenpolitischen Gesichtspunkten." The text in the original language was published by K. M. Pospieszalski, *Hitlerowskie "prawo" okupacyjne w Polsce*, part I (Poznań, 1952), pp. 2–28.

4. L. Dobroszycki, *Centralny Katalog Polskiej prasy Konspiracyjnej, 1939–1945* (Warsaw, 1962); L. Dobroszycki, "Zaginiona prasa Konspiracyjna z lat 1939–1945," *Najnowsze Dzieje Polski: Materiały i Studia z okresu II wojny światowej* 7 (Warsaw, 1963), pp. 173–196.

5. S. Płoski, Foreword to Dobroszycki, *Centralny Katalog Polskiej prasy Konspiracyjnej, 1939–1945*; L. Dobroszycki, "Studies of the Underground Press in Poland, 1939–1945," *Acta Poloniae Historica* 7 (Warsaw, 1962), pp. 96–102.

6. For more about ŻEGOTA, see T. Prekerowa, *Konspiracyjna Rada Pomocy Żydów w Warszawie, 1942–1945* (Warsaw, 1982).

7. L. Dobroszycki, "Konspiracyjne 'Abecadło Lekarskie'," *Polityka*, 1962, no. 42, p. 11.

The Warsaw Ghetto Underground Press
A Case Study in the Reaction to Antisemitism[1]

Leni Yahil
Hebrew University in Jerusalem

In almost all the countries that Germany occupied during World War II, resistance found its first expression in the underground press. The need for information about the war and its political implications was so pressing that people were ready to take the risk involved in gathering news, producing papers, distributing them, and—last but not least—reading them. Nowhere was German vigilance able to stop the underground flow of information. The clandestine press thus became one of the most powerful tools of the various resistance movements in their efforts to promote their points of view and to stiffen the opposition to the occupation and its collaborators.

The Jews incarcerated in the Warsaw ghetto were in an especially precarious situation with regard to the gathering and distributing of reliable information—as they were in everything. The 30 dailies and 130 periodicals in Yiddish, Hebrew, and Polish that they were accustomed to had been abolished in 1939, and they were even forbidden to read German newspapers. In 1940 the German administration, the General-gouvernement, started to publish a weekly paper, *Gazeta żydowska* (Jewish Gazette), which contained only the orders and news the German authorities wanted to communicate to the Jews and the lies by which they intended to deceive them. The situation became even more difficult after the ghetto was closed in November 1940. After that, the several hundred newspapers of the Polish underground press were not easy for the Jews to obtain.

However, the Jewish underground press of the Warsaw ghetto continued to provide not only information but a focus for the Jews' determination to hold on despite tribulation. It is no accident that most of the editors of these publications were leading members of the various prewar organizations, carrying on their activities in the underground. Many of the very young were active in the youth movements and later would be outstanding figures in the ghetto revolts in Warsaw and elsewhere.[2] Thanks to Emanuel Ringelblum's secret archive, Oneg Shabbat, a considerable number of these newspapers have been saved, found after the war in containers buried beneath the ghetto's shambles. Not all containers were discovered, however, and no complete runs of these papers survive. Yad Vashem undertook to publish the 250 issues—comprising 2,933 pages—of fifty-two papers that were preserved. They were put out by eighteen different organizations, ranging from Revisionists to Troskyists. Written in Yiddish, Hebrew, and Polish, they are now being published in Hebrew with an appropriate scholarly apparatus. Three of the projected six volumes are currently in print.[3] They cover the period from May 1940 to October 1941—1,488 pages of seventy-five publications issued by ten different organizations. Some of these papers have only a few pages, while others are the size of a booklet; the largest consists of eighty-nine pages in print.[4] All but one were originally copied by mimeograph, since the Germans had closed down all printing shops. Lack of printing equipment was but one of the many technical handicaps these publications faced; above all was the permanent threat of detection by the Gestapo. The publication of these papers has to be seen as an act of resistance.

According to Joseph Kermish, the editor of the Yad Vashem collection, these papers are being published "in order to perpetuate the memory of the emotional and spiritual world of the underground people, with their various ideological strains representing many different currents, parties, and youth movements, and thereby immortalize their struggle."[5] Some features are common to almost all the papers, however, in spite of their different political outlooks and different languages. They usually start with an editorial or other article indicating the subject the editor wishes to emphasize. Here, of course, the different approaches and convictions of the sponsoring organizations find their specific expression. Yet all the Jews are in the same traumatic situation; they live and act under the same dangerous conditions in confrontation with the deadly enemy. Their interpretation of the present and the future, their reactions to misery, humiliation, and lack of defense in the face of an inexorable fate vary in content but not in character and quality. They all try not only to hold out but are determined to preserve their human dignity and to wrestle, at the same time, with the intellectual clarification of their beliefs. Their beliefs, like their reactions, are not identical, but there is one axiom they all share: in the end, Hitler will be defeated, and afterwards, a better world will rise out of the destruction he perpetrated. They all profess hope against hope. This is their inspiration, the faith that keeps them going. Each one, however, looks at the present and pictures the future according to what was thought and believed in the past, before the catastrophe struck. This is their strength—and their weakness. It is the purpose of this essay to analyze their reasoning as they attempted to reconcile their convictions with the overpowering reality they faced.

Who are these people? To which strata of the prewar Polish-Jewish society did they belong? Half of the political organizations represented in the first three published volumes were affiliated with various brands of socialism. The most important among them, and the largest underground organization of the Warsaw ghetto, was the Jewish Socialist party, the Bund. With its youth section, it is represented by the greatest number of papers published in the current Yad Vashem collection—twenty-eight issues, or 37 percent. The two other Jewish-oriented socialist parties represented in the three volumes belonged to the Zionist movement; they are Poalei Zion (ZS)[6] in the right wing of the Zionist labor movement, and Left Poalei Zion. Three small sections of socialists represented were affiliated with Polish parties; they are Jewish communists, Trotskyists, and Polish socialists affiliated with the left-wing Polish Socialist Party of the same name (PPS).

The other five organizations represented in these three volumes are Zionist youth movements. Three of them were affiliated with the labor movement and belonged to the worldwide pioneer organization Halutz, each connected with a specific kibbutz movement in Eretz Israel (then still Palestine). They were Dror he-Halutz, Gordonia, and Hashomer Hazair.[7] The nonsocialist Noar Ziyyoni (Zionist Youth) also belonged to the Halutz. Distinct from them was Betar, the youth movement of Vladimir Jabotinsky's Revisionist party.

Thus, with the exception of Noar Ziyyoni and Betar, all these organizations were socialist but represented different currents and held divergent ideologies. The main dissension, however, manifests itself between the radical socialists and the Zionists even though most of the latter combine Zionism with socialism.

War and Ideology

The papers dealing with the general political situation and military developments are accurate in their information, but in their interpretation they are very clearly influenced by their respective ideologies. The Bund papers devote the most space to these subjects. Here the information itself is often detailed and surprisingly correct considering the difficulties entailed in listening to the international radio and in obtaining not only copies of local Polish clandestine papers but also news published abroad. The very first item of the collection, the Bund's *Biuletyn* (Bulletin) of May 1940, describes the situation on the Western Front, mentioning specific places and incidents in battles in France, the Netherlands, Belgium, and Norway. British Prime Minister Winston Churchill's new cabinet is reported as including eleven members of the Labour party, with Clement Attlee, Arthur Greenwood, and Herbert Morrison mentioned by name. Yet the report is one-sided, making more of German casualties than of German victories. President Franklin D. Roosevelt is quoted as hinting at the possibility of the United States' entering the war and giving orders for mounting military preparations. To this information the paper adds: "The thought of taking part in the war becomes more and more accepted in America. The anti-German mood is increasing."[8] This exaggeration reflects more wishful thinking than reality.

A month later, in June, the paper allots much space to Italy's entry into the war and analyzes Benito Mussolini's intentions. There is a note of disillusionment in the statement: "America and Roosevelt did not declare war even after Italy joined the war." But there is some consolation: "What does America do? She provides war material to the Allies. The American munitions industry is working unremittingly."[9] In contrast to the hope *Biuletyn* pins on the West and the French people, who will not acquiesce in Philippe Pétain's "Fascist Betrayal,"[10] the paper is very critical of the Soviet Union in general and of Stalin in particular. In this respect the Bund differs widely from all the other radical socialists with whom it shares the conviction that capitalist society is doomed. Viewing the situation in the Balkans in July, the paper reminds its readers of Russia's occupation of the Baltic countries Lithuania, Latvia, and Estonia and of Bessarabia, and North Bukovina, annexed from Romania. It continues: "The Swiss press relates that these annexations were preconceived in accordance with the pact concluded between Germany and Russia in 1939 . . . . The annexation stirred up great tension in the Balkans. Hungary and Bulgaria also claim territorial demands from Rumania."[11]

The Bund's youth movement Tsukunft (Future) had its own Yiddish newspaper *Yugnt-Shtime* (Voice of the Youth), which generally promulgated the same thoughts and slogans as *Biuletyn*. Under the headline, "We the Young Guard," the editorial of the October 1940 issue proclaims: "We know: Capitalism in the Fascist form is undertaking the last trial. This is the effort of the moribund condemned to die. Out of the birth pangs of suffering mankind new life is born."[12] Under the headline, "The Soviet Union and the War," the paper pronounces its harsh verdict on Stalin's policy. Russia is criticized not only for remaining neutral but for strengthening Hitler with huge deliveries of fuel and food. Soviet propaganda is castigated for using every occasion to prove that it was not Germany that started the war, and socialist leaders are denounced as warmongers. Moreover: "It is clear: if Hitler will succeed in the West, he will try to realize his dreams of supremacy in Eastern Europe also." The countries Russia occupies are described as Hitler's gift to Stalin's dictatorship for its attitude in the war. However:

Hitler is not giving anything free of charge. For the "voluntary" annexation of the said countries [mentioned above] the Soviet Union will be charged a costly price. Hitler likes to give and afterward to take back with interest added. The price which the Soviet Union will have to pay will be enormous.[13]

In September 1940, *Płomienie* (Flames), the Polish newspaper of the Zionist youth movement Hashomer Hazair, sums up the first year of the war. Its radical socialist conviction makes it unwavering in its justification of the actions of the Soviet Union. "We are witnessing events that will determine the fate of the world." The decisive campaign that is approaching is fought over who will rule the world. Tricky and deceitful Britain, the stronghold of the old order, now appears as the defender of freedom, but her victory will not bring freedom to the millions of subjugated colonial slaves. Like the First World War, this is an imperialistic war about raw materials and markets. Those who suffer are the common people who do not understand what is really going on. Once these common people will revolt, the strong and victorious army of the proletariat (i.e., the Red Army) will move and destroy the tottering strongholds of the reaction.[14] A month later, in a new summary, the paper explains that England is holding out, but her empire is disintegrating; the United States is lying in wait to take over. Russia is in a strong position, for economic advantages, discussed in detail, are being offered to her by the Allies and the Germans alike, as each tries to draw her to its side.[15]

The socialist ideology of the Left Poalei Zion, though similar to that of Hashomer Hazair, is even more radical. In January 1941, the Yiddish paper of the party's youth movement, *Yugnt-Ruf* (Call of the Youth), explains that the Hitler regime ascended to power in order to save the declining capitalistic class but will go under together with it. "This is the first historic axiom: Hitlerism—notwithstanding the present jubilation over its victories—is doomed." The war, the paper asserts, is being fought between the two "capitalistic-imperialistic blocs: the 'satiated' imperialism with the British Empire at its helm, and the 'hungry' imperialism of fascism." The war, in this view, is a more loathsome and disastrous repetition of the First World War; the "ideological" slogans of both sides are nothing but deceit. "The arch-reactionary Churchill calls for neither more nor less than 'fight for democracy' and 'progress' and 'social reform.'" After both sides have spent their force in the fight, the working class, with the proletarian state at its head, will have the final word.[16] Together with those inclined to fascism, such as Romania and Poland (*sic!*), the Western powers are responsible for the attitude of the Soviet Union because, "until the last moment, all these states did not renounce their dreams of anti-Soviet intervention:" And therefore:

> The Soviet policy is conducted in the realm of armed neutrality, ready for battle. The proletarian state understood that she should not, even that she is forbidden, to side actively with one of the capitalist blocs. She is obliged to defend her vital interests and not let any of the imperialists impair her boundaries ... At the same time, the independent and revolutionary proletarian power has to get ready in every respect to enter the battlefield of the world as soon as the conditions are ripe.[17]

The same pragmatic, Marxist explanations are put forth in *Dror* (Freedom), the Yiddish paper of the youth movement Dror heHalutz. Obviously, there is some discussion within the organization about Russia's policy. The author of an article in the October 1940 issue says:

I have some things to say about the Soviet Union. Several comrades have presented unjustified arguments against the foreign policy of the socialist state. Policy is not connected with morality. Policy works to create the most convenient conditions under given circumstances. It was not difficult to instigate war between the Soviet Union and England or between the Soviet Union and Germany. If this did not happen—and for the time being there seems to be no direct danger to the socialist country [the Soviet Union] and the great socialist upbuilding she has accomplished— it is only because of her policy of "divide and rule."[18]

The author is Yitzhak Zuckerman, a leading figure of the movement who survived to become one of the founders of Kibbutz Lohamei haGetaot (Ghetto Fighters). The article is, of course, signed with one of his many pseudonyms, as all writers in the underground press guarded their anonymity by using either fictitious names or initials. However, the editors of the Yad Vashem collection have gone to great lengths to establish the identity of even the most obscure writers, an article sometimes being the only memory left of a person.

Confrontation with Reality

Politics is neither the only nor the most important subject of an article in the same issue of *Dror*, whose headline reads, "What We Are Preparing For." Originally this was an address to a meeting of more than one hundred pioneers preparing themselves in groups for *aliyah* (immigration) to Eretz Israel by doing work in special agricultural-training farms called *hachsharah*. The meeting took place in Warsaw in October 1940. Because of the article's importance, it is related in detail.[19]

The speaker asks himself and his audience if all their dealings with their special problems are not futile in light of what is going on outside in the street.

The street is enmeshed in disaster and agony; the street is full of horror. Does this meeting, with its visions of the future, have any meaning for the gray daily life in the street? May it not be that these visions are nothing but weakness, an escape from this life into the mind? Perhaps someone thinks that we should not have convened today, since our thinking will not in any way determine anything and our talking will not change the order of the world. We are so few. The great socialist family is divided and split. And we—young Jews and young socialists—are a splinter of a people headed for destruction and a tiny splinter of the already split socialist movement. Those who measure our inner strength by our present situation, who do not see anything but our weakness and are not strong enough to see something else, may agree with this perspective. We who know the strength of the *avant-garde*, however, who are aware of the meaning of pioneering, we understand the impact of our discussions. We sit here among ourselves, and we think to ourselves[:] Toward what shall we educate? What have we to prepare? The shortsighted who maintain that tomorrow will be like today have nothing to prepare for. We, however, know that we have much to lose by apathetic thinking, because then we will not understand the future. The force behind our considerations will show itself and become meaningful as the driving force of ideas pierces the walls that keep tomorrow from our sight.

In the following section "Antek" (Zuckerman's clandestine name) explains the three factors of the future that, in his opinion, "are the most important for the realization of our national and socialist aims." First is "Eretz Israel's political consolidation as a state after the war." On this issue Zuckerman does not want to comment because direct communication with Palestine has been severed by the war. "However, it is possible that after the war we shall be able to claim the right to the country on surer ground than we can today." Second is the belief he shares with all the other socialists that the socialist revolution will take place in Europe after the war. Third is his concern for "the moral and spiritual character of the Jewish communities in the occupied countries that are today exposed to the fire of the war." After the war, when the fate of the nations will be fixed, it will be of paramount importance whether the Jewish people will be able to use the opportunity, or will miss it. Elaborating on this point, he says:

> The present, with all its dangers, is menacing us. It breaks our courage, robs our belief, weakens our resistance, and throws us into the grip of desperation and apathy. Where is the vigor that was inherent in the life of the Jewish community in Poland? The whole life of this community has become dependent on philanthropy.
>
> We have to take upon ourselves the responsibility for the fate of this community. We are responsible for the young generation that is educated under the war conditions, lest without surveillance and without defense, they tumble into the abyss of demoralization.
>
> Our movement comes from the people, and it is meant for the people. The essence of our being and its meaning must not and cannot be determined by mere proclamations of loyalty. We are made for action. Every deed, every positive doing, is a revolutionary act. They want to deprive us of the image of man; they want to break us mentally; they are sowing horror among us; and they are harvesting the destroyed life of Jews. By the force of our belief, by the unshaken force of our will, let us do all we can. Nothing is not important. No deed is too little. We have to educate the young generation and as many strata of the people as possible. We have to get ready in earnest for tomorrow. As much as we can, let us stop the rolling wheel that drags all of us into the abyss. This is our duty today.

The political orientation of Dror was identical with that of Poalei Zion (ZS). The only issue of Poalei Zion's paper *Bafrayung* (Liberation) published so far is that for December 1940. It opens by recalling the ideology and image of the party's founder, Ber Borochov, "the man who created an era in the history of the struggle for the Jewish people's national and social redemption.[20]

Under the headline "WHY," a long article discusses German anti-Semitism. Using irony like a fine chisel, the unidentified author says:

Looking at the huge apparatus Nazi Germany has erected against us, seeing how much time and energy are invested in order to invent evernew tortures to use against us, one could become filled with a little pride. Common sense could suggest that we are the most important element in this war, that we have infiltrated deep into the enemy's bones. How, otherwise, to explain his zealotry, his burning hate of us?

All this, the author goes on, in these days when the enemy has quite enough other things to worry about. After all, lots of other nations are sworn enemies of the Germans.[21]

Citing the German propaganda's exaggeration of the Jewish influence, the author states that "the entire Jewish people stands today on one side in the war, though we do not have an army of our own. But, it is clear to all that there is no correlation whatsoever between the impact the Jews have and the wicked tortures they are suffering today... *The measuring-rod applied to Jews is completely different from that applied to others.*" This "different measuring-rod"—the author goes on—was not invented by Adolf Hitler; it is as old as the Diaspora. Various explanations have been proposed; today it is said:

The Hitler regime uses the Jews to fool the German masses. . . . He wants to turn their minds by telling them that they are the best, the crown of the world, and therefore he oppresses and slanders the Jews so that the German masses may measure their fictitious "superiority" by the low stature of the Jews. . . . In any case, it is clear that he needs the Jews' misery, their suffering, and their blood for his own purposes.

But, the author stresses, the main question remains, Why always we Jews? Are we different from all the others? In reply he asserts: "Yes, we are different; *we are not like all the nations.*" We are not better and worse than other people, and we are not different but in one respect: "*We are the only people in God's world that wanders without a home.*" This is the basic cause of all the calamities we have to bear. This root of our difference is not concealed from sight; Zionism disclosed it long ago. The author concludes:

The enemy is sucking the marrow of our bones. No doubt we shall emerge from this bitter experience considerably weakened. However, notwithstanding the weakness, we will have to concentrate what is left of our energy in one direction: to abolish, to erase completely the homeless situation, to be "as all the nations:" Perhaps, because of the Hitler catastrophe there will be no repetition of the satanic phenomenon that a multitude of social organizations of Jews oppose [as in the past] the erection of a home for the Jewish people.[22]

Nevertheless, for the people of the Warsaw ghetto, there was no escape from reality. In all the papers the people of the underground are conscious of the disastrous consequences implied in the current situation and are especially worried about their influence on the youth. In the September 1940 issue of *Płomienie*, Hashomer Hazair reaches conclusions similar to Dror's about the necessity of thought. The war, says *Płomienie*, has an overpowering influence. "It is infiltrating into the pores of our soul. Who can face this situation and teach [the people] how to resist this influence, if not the young? In all the hard times, the youth have been the faithful and the basis for resistance. But not now."[23]

Among the youth, the struggle for existence has the top priority. One has to get a piece of bread—and nothing more. The prevailing slogan among the young is, "Eat and drink. Today we are alive. Who knows what will happen to us tomorrow? Let's enjoy life as long as we can. Why should we strain our brain with farfetched thoughts? What is to be expected will come anyhow—in spite of us!" The author adds:

At the same time, the head is bowing and the slave-soul is in the making. Our young learn to take off their hats in front of Germans, to smile the smile of obedience and slavery. Inside the heart there whisper envy and deep admiration for brutal fascist haughtiness. And deep down in the heart the dream is hidden: to be as one of them—handsome, elegant, strong, self-possessed. So that we, too, may hit without a trial, strike, loot, despise others as they are now despising me.

Moreover, the young loathe the stripe attached to their right arm that marks them as Jews. "It burns like fire. It is such a great calamity to be born a Jew! If only it would be possible to escape Jewishness.[24]

The author ponders: The Germans took away the schools, the libraries. Why? Is it not because they are afraid that books might promote thought? Shouldn't the young initiate resistance by *thinking*? It is necessary to think clearly and coldly and to study so that one may analyze historical events accurately. Fascism promotes the low instincts. We have to overcome them in our hearts, to believe, even today, in the good in men, in human solidarity. Reminding readers of Hashomer Hazair's ideology, the author asserts: "We have to understand that the structure of compulsion and oppression will be destroyed according to the inevitable force of history. Our enemies are pitifully deceived people; with their blood they are buying profits for the capitalists." And he concludes:

> We are able to preserve our human and national pride, to walk erect, with our back straight not bowed. We have no reason to escape Judaism . . . . There are pleasures in life that are not vanishing—the pleasure of thinking, of struggle, of revolt.
> *Thinking—this is the slogan and this is the task.*[25]

The Past, the Future, and the Ghetto

The Revisionist youth movement Betar is here represented by only one issue of its fortnightly magazine *Hamedinah* (The State). This is the only Jewish clandestine paper that was actually printed. It came out in August 1940 and is dedicated to the memory of the founder and leader of the Revisionist movement, Vladimir Jabotinsky, who died in New York on August 3, 1940. Jabotinsky's death was a bitter blow for the movement and especially for its young members, who were left incarcerated in Warsaw after most of their elder leaders had fled before the Germans arrived. It must be noted that this loss of leadership was typical for most of the Polish-Jewish organizations, parties, and youth movements, although some of these leaders later returned. By and large, the young had to shoulder new and greater responsibilities in this unforeseen and catastrophic situation, a necessity that had decisive influence on the development of the underground in the ghetto, where young leaders came to the fore.[26]

The young Revisionists' shock at Jabotinsky's death is very much evident in *Hamedinah*, though they try hard to restrain themselves. In accordance with the military form of organization of Betar, the magazine, written in Yiddish, opens with "the order of mourning" in Hebrew, fixing the rules the members have to observe during the mourning period of thirty days. There follow words where words seem to be of no avail:

> We have no words to express our sorrow. . . . Nor can we express it in deeds, because our hands are tied up; nor in tears because he has forbidden it. Only keeping silent, grinding our teeth, with tired eyes burning, choking from the knot in our throat—may we somehow express our pain that has no words and our mourning that has no end.[27]

The story of Jabotinsky's life and his dedication to his vision of the Jewish state are recounted, and passages from his speeches and articles of 1935 and 1936 demonstrate how he anticipated great dangers and called for the evacuation of millions of Jews from Eastern Europe to Eretz Israel. (He thought this evacuation would take two generations.) There is some bitterness in the recounting, for the prophecies have come true while Jabotinsky's plea "to evacuate in order to rescue" went unheeded. The reason, the paper maintains, is to be found in Jewry itself.

> As there is no event that came over us similar to the holocaust, there is nothing similar to the inner situation of the [Jewish] people just before the catastrophe. The most terrible period in our history found the masses unprepared, divided, and without a leader. Bewildered peoples were facing an inevitable storm.[28]

The young Revisionists were not the only ones complaining that the elder generation did not understand the omen of their time. A publication of Hashomer Hazair lamented:

> Who would have said that we—children of the twentieth century—would be turned into slaves? Who would have thought that we should be confronted with the walls of the medieval ghetto? Alas, about that our fathers did not dream and our mothers did not sing to us . . . . Why did you not answer the call fifty years ago [when Zionism was proclaimed]? Why, instead of redeeming

yourselves and us, did you remain serfs so that we are now thrown back into the Middle Ages? . . . Why, standing on the brink, did you not see the abyss?

This outcry of agony is, however, followed by the vow to end servitude: "The generation to come will not know anymore the dwellings of the ghetto. We shall build a big Jewish settlement that will know to defend itself; we shall erect a just world that will have no room for the villain."[29]

This is part of the Hebrew opening of *Iton ha-tnuah* (The Paper of the Movement), the most extensive publication of the Hashomer Hazair, 111 mimeographed pages, written alternately in all the three languages. It was published at the end of 1940 and beginning of 1941 and must be understood as a concentrated reaction to the situation after the closing of the ghetto in November, prepared in spite of the tumultuous days of the incarceration. Apparently the intention was not only to summarize the sixteen months of the war, but to provide a historical analysis and outline the tasks and possibilities of the movement in the present situation and toward the unknown future, including the circumstances prevailing in the formerly Polish provinces that had now become occupied Russian territory. Thus, the editors implemented their belief that the way to promote resistance to the catastrophic situation was to stimulate thinking connected with learning. They dealt with the following subjects.

First, there is a review of political and military developments since the beginning of the war, starting with a historical analysis of the reasons for the Nazis' ascent to power. This analysis is complemented by a special explanation of the demographic-historic situation in the Balkans, with emphasis put on Yugoslavia's and Russia's strategic interests there.[30]

Second is an extensive discussion of the socialist movement—its history, ideology, policies, auspices, and, of course, the role of the Soviet Union in it.[31] In spite of the intention to justify her internal and foreign policies, the disappointment about her relation to the Jews is evident, especially in connection with the oppression of everything Jewish in the newly occupied territories. In these discussions among the members there are even some remarks critical of the Soviet Union.

Third, much space is allotted to the problems and ideology of the movement itself. The current situation is perceived as not only the fate of the Jewish people in the war but of mankind in general. Nothing in the long history of suffering of the Jewish people is similar to the present situation. "This time the effort is made to destroy us completely." Not only their own movement, Hashomer Hazair, in Poland and elsewhere is menaced, but the entire Jewish people is threatened with destruction. The local conditions of Hashomer's branches in the various places affected by the war are surveyed. Yet, in spite of the war, "We must already now make preparations for the peace to come. Our comrades have to be ready for any situation that may evolve." With the coming of the war, a wave of flight erupted, mostly over the Soviet border, which disrupted the movement's organization. Messengers sent from Warsaw to all branches helped to restore communications, and, with great effort, the organization was maintained. With the closing of the Warsaw ghetto, these contacts were interrupted again, but new emissaries were sent to all the branches in order to guide their work on the spot. "This entailed enormous difficulties, but we knew to overcome them." The main thing was not to yield to circumstances, no matter how obstructive they may be.[32]

Fourth, in a section called "Milieu," these circumstances are described in all their harsh reality, starting with the horrors of the war and its tribulations, including the flight over the Soviet border.[33] The precarious situation of Hashomer Hazair's comrades under Soviet rule is openly discussed, and their underground struggle to keep the movement alive is emphasized. In Vilna, where these efforts are centralized, a great accomplishment is detailed: forty-seven members of the Halutz managed to get away from this overcrowded and starving city and to go "on *aliyah*" to Eretz Israel.[34]

There is a major emphasis on education problems: Did the movement's educational method prove adequate to the catastrophic conditions? The answer is in the affirmative: "Our people, starving, in rags, persecuted, harassed, and fearful of the tomorrow, are also troubled by internal ideological debates.—Everyone who saw them thus steadfastly adhering to their principles perceived for the first time how powerful the impact of our education has been."[35]

Still, it was inevitable that the revolutionary and shattering experience of the ghetto would provoke emotional reactions of different kinds in young people. In addition to those already mentioned, there are two of special significance. Youngsters whose lives had been focused around the movement, very often in open opposition to their parents, were suddenly physically and emotionally thrown back on their families. In the ghetto they lived together in overcrowded dwellings, starved together, and did not know what would happen next. Thus, a new sense of belonging and responsibility to the family developed in these young people, which was expressed as follows:

> Sadness at home. I know my parents . . . . I revolted against them; my thoughts transgressed their world's circle. However, a deep feeling emanating from the bottom of the soul is never blurred . . . . Our movement, being born out of the young generation's revolt against the grown-ups, overacted more than once in its relation to the family and thus even provided an example of unsocial behavior.

But perhaps the most powerful trauma the young experienced was the confrontation with death, at that time mostly death from hunger. The young people wanted to hold on to life and loathed the defilement and constant degradation of human dignity. Two quotations are characteristic:

> Wherever you look, there is tragic poverty. I wonder why those people do not want to die. . . . Does death ask for greater heroism than the life of extreme poverty and endless humiliation? Perhaps men like their chains? Still, there is a way for people to defend themselves. Even in the most inhuman circumstances there is something that remains to beautify human life, something people are able to fight for . . . . If we renounce our abused right to struggle, we break our only force, the moral impetus, the self-respect.

In another piece a girl writes:

> You know how terrible is the thought that soon the day will arrive when masses of men will die, knowing for sure that redemption is not coming from anywhere, and that this is the end . . .
>
> What, then, shall be the reaction? True, people with empty stomachs do not ponder about ideals, but this eventuality is bound to provoke a revolt against reality . . . .
>
> Our reaction, too, will be intensified revolt, for we know the reason and the goal. Aren't we the vanguard? . . .

> And this is what I think: when we shall face death by starvation and shall probe our life's meaning, lest we have wasted it, we shall be able to say with full certitude that we did not forfeit life, that we lived as we were obliged to live by our conscience. This is very important.[36]

These are the thoughts of anonymous members of Hashomer Hazair in Warsaw, two years before the Warsaw Uprising.

The ghetto was now their daily reality, and its misery and torment were their way of life. The papers always deal, of course, with this subject, but it does not preponderate. All try to free their readers from those destructive influences, to lift them out of their incessant struggle to keep life going, to demonstrate the truth of the biblical saying that "man doth not live by bread only."[37] Cultural subjects are discussed primarily by the Zionists. The anniversaries of Hebrew and Yiddish writers and poets provide these papers with the opportunity to consider and quote from their work. Poems of living poets like Yitzhak Katzenelson and others are frequently published, and cultural activities, such as the performances of a dramatic circle, are reported. The ghetto itself is reviewed in a historical perspective.[38]

Nevertheless, the piercing realities of ghetto life could not and would not be neglected. Certain subjects stand out, one way or the other, in all the papers. These include hunger and the trials of overcoming it; the unbearable constraint of overcrowded living quarters; the deterioration of public health and the ensuing deaths; the agony of slave labor; and, more than anything else, the deadly torture in the labor camps. Harsh criticism is heaped on the *Judenrat*. In addition to all the suffering of about half a million Jews in Warsaw, there is disastrous news coming in from throughout occupied Poland.[39] Often these themes converge, as in the following article from the May 1941 issue of *Dror*:

> As for Jewish existence, the situation is unbearable. The sealed walls have a double impact: From the moral point of view, they depress, break, and degenerate the soul. From the economic point of view, they deprive most everyone of the possibility of sustenance. The consequences are to be seen everywhere. Add to these the demoralization of public life that spread between the walls of

the ghetto [as manifested by] the impudent violation of all moral rules by our "tribunes" and "defenders" [the *Judenrat* and the Jewish police], and the trade in human life and health in every respect.[40]

The final accusation here refers to the fact that people could free themselves from coercive labor duty by paying money to the *Judenrat*.

In one of the next issues of *Dror*, there is a detailed description of "The Situation in the Warsaw Ghetto." Included are statistics on the numbers of people coming in and going out of the ghetto; figures on the refugees arriving in Warsaw from near and far, with stories of their desperate situation; figures on the numbers of cases of spotted fever among Jews in the first year of the war; and a comparison between the food rations for the general population and the smaller allotments for the people in the ghetto, an inequality that has necessitated widespread smuggling. The inflated prices for bread and other essentials are listed, together with the taxes that have to be paid for ration cards. The final figure is for the number of funerals each month, which rose from 360 in August 1939 to 1,608 in March 1941, a total three times higher than that for December 1940, immediately after the closing of the ghetto.[41]

The most devastating conditions, however, were in the slave-labor camps, and they also raised the most violent denunciations. Under the headline "Summary of Bloodshed," *Yugnt-Shtime* describes the operation of these camps in 1940. The people slept on bare planks in barns without windows, often without lights, sometimes without a roof. Ten were crowded into a "room" of five by six meters. Water was scarce, and sometimes the inmates were unable to wash or change their underwear for months. They were plagued by insects, vermin, and diseases. Medicines were unavailable, and sickrooms, if they existed at all, were not much different from the lodgings. "The people," the paper continues, "were literally barefoot and naked. Many sold their clothing for a piece of bread." In addition to living in such conditions, they had to do hard labor in swamps, on highways, and the like. The guards were mostly SS men.[42]

As the labor units were recruited by the *Judenrat*, the people held it responsible for their suffering—and that was exactly what the Germans intended. At the end of the article in *Yugnt-Shtime*, a passage from a letter someone in a labor camp sent to the *Judenrat* of Warsaw is quoted:

"Our fate and our life are dependent only on you; you are responsible for everything, and you will not be spared the punishment you have earned. We have made a ceremonial vow that we will take a bloody vengeance at the first opportunity."[43]

In a similar vein, in the May 1941 issue of *Proletarisher Gedank* (Proletarian Thought), Left Poalei Zion reports, under the headline "The Hunting Season for People":

> In the beginning of April the recruitment of people for the infamous labor camps started. The German Labor Office demanded thirty to forty thousand people from the *Judenrat* of Warsaw, mainly to work on the irrigation of rivers. Under what conditions this work is performed the Jews of Warsaw still remember from the camps of last year, which cost the lives of hundreds of young people.[44]

Again the *Judenrat* is held responsible.

In the beginning of 1941 the young Zionists thought that it would be possible to avoid the labor camp by projecting agricultural *hachsharah* on Jewish or Polish farms where members of the Halutz would work during the summer, something they had successfully organized the year before.[45] The Bund attacked the project fiercely. In March 1941 *Biuletyn* reports the German demands, warns of the catastrophic consequences, and threatens the *Judenrat*. The main attack is, however, directed against the Zionists, though without calling them by name: "In connection with this disastrous decree, in connection with this catastrophe of the 'labor camps,' irresponsible groups have put forth, at this most trying moment, the slogan of 'agricultural *hachsharah*.'" The Jewish "nationalists" are accused of exploiting the "Hitlerist opportunity" and the difficult situation of the Polish farmers, many of whom had been deported as cheap labor to Germany. According to the Bund's way of thinking, it is opportunism to save "several thousand youngsters from being taken to the labor camp. This will not diminish the amount of people languishing in the camps."[46]

This is only one example of the ideological controversies among the different parties in the Jewish public. The Bund defames the Zionists by calling them "strangers to the authentic national interests of the Jewish masses in Poland"[47] and "the young emigrationist organizations."[48] The Bund sees the true interest of the Jewish masses indisputably connected with the future of the Polish proletariat. Only by the alliance with the Polish socialists can the Jews secure their own existence. In the Bund's eyes, the Zionist aspiration at building a Jewish state in Palestine is not only unrealistic but a betrayal of socialism. The Jewish Question will be solved in the classless proletarian society of the future. Therefore, the separate agricultural training of the Halutz is denounced as bourgeois nationalism.

The Zionists attack the Bund as neglecting the true interest of the Jewish masses that lies in the erection of their own national home. Those who believe, however, that the future Jewish commonwealth must be founded on socialist principles attack the Revisionists as "fascists."[49] This internecine struggle among the different parties, inherited from the controversies preceding the war, had tragic consequences at this crucial time, and only after the catastrophe of the major deportation was a way found to cooperate in defense.[50]

From May 1 to June 22, 1941

The various socialist convictions found their most concentrated expression in the different periodicals dedicated to the First of May. All declare their unshaken faith in the final victory of socialism, but the kind of socialism each movement has in mind is determined by its basic philosophy. Most continue to profess their belief in the Soviet Union's righteousness and strength; only the Bund is unshaken in its criticism of communism: "The communist movement is absent from the front. It disappeared from the surface of Europe. Corroded by the tactics of the Comintern, an obedient tool in the hands of the Soviet diplomacy, it did not stand the trial of history."[51] The editorial of *Yugnt-Shtime* addresses itself solely "To the Masses of Workers in Poland," praising them for choosing the right way, which led them "to stubborn resistance . . . in all fields of life." Among Hitler's evildoings, "the massive deportations of people toward famine and destruction and the crime of the ghetto" are singled out, but the Jews as such are not explicitly mentioned.[52]

This time the voice of a communist group in the ghetto, *Sierp i Młot* (Hammer and Sickle), is heard. In the First of May issue of its short weekly *Morgn-Fray* (Tomorrow Free), it calls for unity: "No chosen races, no classes and privileged cliques. People, only people." At this moment, all differences must vanish. The fighters for freedom are all on one side of the barricades; "on the opposite [side] are our enemies and their helpers."[53] Among the enemies they include the community (i.e., the *Judenrat*) because it is sending the people to the labor camps.

On this occasion Hashomer Hazair extensively reviews the movement's principal conceptions, political views, and actual observations. After describing the mood prevailing in the starving ghetto, the editorial proclaims:

> To this stiffling atmosphere of prison, degradation, and poverty, our paper will bring a different blast of wind, alien to it. To the voice of despair and doubt we shall respond with our steadfast belief. To the voice of degradation, with the message about a different kind of life, and to the voices of escape from reality, we shall reply by looking straight into its face.[54]

Dealing with the war situation after the German victories in the Balkans, Hashomer Hazair's Polish periodical *Neged ha-zerem* (Against the Current) emphasizes the danger threatening Palestine: "Victory of Germany implies not only the destruction of European Jewry but to a great extent also a death penalty for the Jewish settlement in Eretz Israel.[55]

Left Poalei Zion is exaggerated in its praise of the Soviet Union and its denunciation of the "Reformist Social Democracy." Moreover, *Proletarisher Gedank* denounces "Bourgeois Zionism and its collaborators, the socialist Zionists." In its perspective, the hope of the Jewish workers for social and national liberation depends exclusively on the world's proletariat. This hope "is not based on empty optimism but on Marxist realistic evaluation of the situation in general."[56]

Dror, too, voices socialist hopes in its editorial: "On the First of May, the workers' file will continue to march, albeit in the underground." The paper assures its readers, "As no force in the world will sever us from the fight for a new social regime in the world, no one will sever us from the country of our hope."[57] The feature article points out that on the First of May, more than on any other day, we have to prove "where, after all, we stand in the world." The author then weighs the pros and cons of the present situation in the socialist movement and concludes that only by force will the people, fighting for their freedom, be able to overcome fascism, but this inevitable clash will be possible only after Hitler has suffered his first defeat.[58]

Although the Bund had anticipated that Hitler would eventually turn against the Soviet Union and massive troop movements had been observed in the Generalgouvernement,[59] the German onslaught on Russia on June 22, 1941, must have come as a shock to the people in the ghetto, especially to the faithful believers in the Soviet Union's political wisdom—all the more so because of the German army's initially quick advance. The Bund, however, claimed not to be surprised and again denounced the German-Soviet pact of 1939: "This was the first stab of the Stalinist dictatorship in the back of the Western countries, in the back of the working class, and also—as we see today—in the back of the Soviet Union itself," writes *Yunge Gvardye* (Young Guard), a new periodical of the Bund, in July 1941. The paper adds that the official announcements of Joseph Stalin and V. M. Molotov give the impression of helplessness and that more than anything else they want to prove that they did not start the war. But "the great failure of the Soviet Union was exactly that she did not attack fascism but waited until it fell upon her."[60]

In a similar vein, the Trotskyite paper *Czerwony Sztandar* (Red Flag) writes in an editorial called "Our War" in July 1941: "Hitler's military action against the Soviet 'ally' was inevitable. We anticipated it at the time, as nothing seemed to trouble 'the friendship' between Stalin and Hitler."[61] The steadfast believers in the Soviet Union, however, try to overcome the shock by reiterating their ideologies and interpreting events accordingly. In August 1941, Left Poalei Zion's *Nasze Hasła* (Our Slogans) defends the "tactical maneuvers and concessions" of the Soviet Union, whose intention was "to avoid the start of the inevitable struggle under unsuitable conditions." Now, however, "the great historical hour arrived, the enormous battle started, that will determine the fate of the human race for generations to come."[62] In September, *Proletarisher Gedank* writes in a similar vein and quotes at length the August 22 communiqué of the Soviet information bureau. In its conclusions it says, "The plan to destroy the Red Army in five or six weeks failed—the war will go on for a long time."[63]

In an editorial written in July and published in August, Hashomer Hazair's *Neged ha-zerem* is also sure that the German attack has collapsed. It asserts that the resistance of the Red Army was not broken and the Germans "did not gain a single one of the territorial aims of the onslaught." The paper is adamant in its conviction that "in the end the victory of the Red Army and the deliverance of the world from the Hitlerite nightmare will come."[64]

The three volumes in print so far include a few issues of *Słowo Młodych* (Word of the Young), the Polish periodical of Gordonia. In an editorial in the July 1941 issue, Hitler's war is compared to that of Napoleon. Now, as then, "the way to London goes through Moscow." The paper indicates that the Red Army is much more powerful than most people had the impression after its winter campaign against Finland.[65] In September the headline of the political and military survey reads: "In the East: 'Nothing New'."[66] Still, the main focus of the paper is its view of Zionism and socialism. Theodor Herzl and the national poet, Hayyim Nahman Bialik, are quoted extensively, especially in connection with the anniversaries of their deaths in the summer.[67]

Shaviv (Spark), the periodical of the Noar Ziyyoni, was not concerned about socialist ideology. The editorial of its June-July issue deals with the spiritual and psychological corruption endangering the Jews in addition to the threat of physical destruction that they face. To forestall this depravation of Zionist belief, the whole issue is dedicated to Herzl and Bialik.[68] Meanwhile, something occurred that was different from all that the Jews in the Warsaw ghetto had experienced until that time. Bit by bit trickled in the hair-raising news of the mass slaughter of Jews in German-occupied territories formerly held by the Russians. In an article entitled "Documents of Fascist Bestiality," the September 1941 issue of *Proletarisher Gedank* describes the brutal deportations of the Jews from several towns in western Poland to the Generalgouvernement, the savage expulsions over the Russian border, and individual acts of sadism, all of which occurred during the last year. To this the paper adds: "However, the tragedy [of the victims of these atrocities] is nothing but child's play compared to the mass murder of the Jewish population in the recently occupied territories of Białystok, Brisk, Vilna, and Lwów.[69]

This news was first received in July. *Słowo Młodych* reports in the editorial of that month's issue: "Immediately after the crossing of the [river] Bug the blood of thousands of innocent victims stained the streets of Białystok, Lwów, Brisk, and many other towns."[70] At the time, these acts were still seen as local pogroms, and it was not clear who started them and to what extent the Polish population took part in them. By October it was known that the Germans perpetrated the killings and atrocities together with the newly formed Polish *Hilfspolizei* (auxiliary police) recruited from members of anti-Semitic organizations who had been in jail under the Soviet rule.[71]

The most accurate information was received by Hashomer Hazair. One of the movement's members escaped from Vilna and arrived in Warsaw on October 16. His story is told in the September-October issue of *Neged hazerem* under the headline "The Days of Blood in Vilna." It includes an accurate description of the massacre in the forest of Ponary and reports on the disastrous situation in the ghetto. The ghetto had been divided into two sectors, one for the skilled workers and their families and the other for the people the Germans called "unproductive." The number of people killed after three months of German occupation is given correctly as 35,000 of the 70,000 Jewish inhabitants of Vilna prior to the arrival of the Germans.[72] Yisrael Gutman, examining the same source, concludes: "Neither the article itself, however, nor the rest of the description gleaned from the witness suggests that the events in Vilna are symptomatic of the danger hovering over all the Jews trapped within the Nazi occupation.[73]

Biuletyn, however, arrives in the same month at an overall conclusion. "Hitlerism and the Jewish Problem" analyzes an article published in the official German organ, *Das Reich*, which deals with the solution of the Jewish Question. Its author differentiates between the ghetto of the Middle Ages and the modern one: While in the Middle Ages the Jews performed necessary economic functions, Hitler's state intends to remove the Jews from Europe altogether. The ghetto is only a temporary device. After the victory, the final solution will be implemented. There is also a hint at what this solution entails. No doubt aware of the news from the occupied Russian territory, *Biuletyn* concludes:

> In simple human language, the meaning is: physical extermination of the Jews in the shortest time and the cheapest manner. We can imagine that the Jews themselves will have to finance the penal commandos of German gendarmes who will expel the Jews from Europe, and the Jews themselves will have to dig mass graves for their brethren; everywhere in Europe the mass graves will signify "the new order."[74]

Conclusion

In hindsight, the Bund's relentless analysis of the facts often presents the most penetrating view of the political and military situation. In contrast, the socialist Zionists' orthodox Marxist interpretation of the facts, no matter how true, and the almost unwavering justification of the Soviet Union's politics blur their political insight and refute their claim of "Marxist realistic evaluation."[75] All the socialists, however, have one element in common. While relying on the doctrine and on renowned authorities, they feel the need to recall other revolutionary events; the two outstanding events mentioned are the Paris Commune in 1871 and the uprising of the Schutzbund in Vienna in 1934.[76]

The Paris Commune is mentioned, on the occasion of its seventieth anniversary in March 1941, by both the Bund and Left Poalei Zion, despite the vast difference between the Social Democratic approach of the former and the left-wing socialist conviction of the latter. *Yugnt-Shtime* presents a short historical survey opening with the statement that the French workers were the first in history to venture a campaign of liberation and seize power, even if only for a short time. The article concludes: "As the reactionaries could then not uproot the spirit of freedom among the workers of France, the hangmen of today will not uproot the iron will of the working class to overcome the evil and to establish freedom "[77]

Proletarisher Gedank analyzes the reasons for the defeat of the uprising and adds: "The Commune held out for only seventy-two days, but to this day *its memory is precious and holy* to the international proletariat, which is inspired by the heroism and learns the lesson of the errors."[78]

The Bund, Dror, and Hashomer Hazair all mark the anniversary of the revolt of the Schutzbund, which had happened in their time and was aimed against their own enemy—fascism. *Yugnt-Shtime* asserts: "The day after the defeat of the February uprising, the workers' marvelous socialist public in Austria . . . continued their fight for their ideals. *In the underground thousands went on to struggle clandestinely* for socialism and against the fascist slavery."[79]

Dror printed the recollections of the wife of Koloman Wallisch, one of the leaders of the uprising. She explains the failure by the fact that only some of the workers, about 30 percent, were ready to fight and quoted her husband as saying to her at the time of the outbreak: "*I am sure that this struggle is organized suicide* . . . . I also know that after the defeat I shall be one of the victims. Better that my end will come quickly than to live such a life."[80]

Hashomer Hazair printed the most extensive description and discussion. *Neged ha-zerem* includes the whole story of Austrian Social Democracy, pointing to the successes and criticizing the errors that led to the failure. Still, the paper is full of praise.

> Indeed, the workers of Austria proved their unequaled dedication to socialism and *their readiness to die in its defense*. They proved readiness to pay the price of their errors with their blood. But the sacrifice of their blood will not be in vain if we will learn its lesson so *that we shall know how to prepare for our [finest] hour to come, and come it will!*[81]

An additional feature article discusses the development of the European socialist movement between the two wars and culminates in the oft-expressed belief that the end of the current war will bring the great revolution.[82]

History did not bear out these prophecies, but this "unrealistic" revolutionary vision of the Jewish underground fulfilled a crucial function in the history of the Warsaw ghetto and of many other communities in the occupied territories. Let us recollect the movements' incredible efforts in not only keeping up their organizations but in preserving the fighting spirit of their members, their dedication and their hope for the future, and especially in taking care of the children and the young,[83] all this in declared defiance of the physically weakening and morally debauching conditions of the ghetto. To this end comes the conviction of the Zionist movements that they have to fulfill a Jewish national task. The youth movements, in particular, see themselves as the vanguard of "the state under way." Again and again they emphasize: Eretz Israel is our goal and our hope. Moreover, Eretz Israel needs us.

With all their faith in their combined national and social mission, they cannot completely avoid conflicts between their socialist ideologies and their national commitment; which is rejected by Marxism in theory and in practice. There are occasional doubts about the Soviet Union, while, on the other hand, the discord provokes the violent attacks of the Bund. Time and again, the socialist Zionists try to overcome the discord by certain intellectual acrobatics. Hashomer Hazair, for instance, proclaims that

Eretz Israel has to become a Jewish-Soviet state. Most of the time, however, both points of view are interwoven.[84]

Thus, the fighting spirit of the Jews in the Warsaw ghetto, constantly nourished by thinking, was preserved for more than three years of ever-worsening conditions and increasing dangers and fears. The Warsaw Uprising was not born of nothing. Indeed, all the elements admired in the Paris Commune and the revolt of the Schutzbund became alive: "Thousands struggled clandestinely in the underground"; it was "organized suicide" undertaken with the knowledge that "the end will come quickly"; there was "readiness to die in the defense of their conviction"; thus, when the hour came, they were "ready for the sacrifice of life" believing that it would not be in vain.

History bore out their "unrealistic" view. The uprising, which was crushed like the two revolutionary paradigms, left a "precious memory" and the legend of outstanding heroism and dedication. This did not and could not efface the terrible fact of the murder of the defenseless millions. But the Jewish underground's reaction to the Holocaust helped after the war, like a kernel of grain, to ferment the spirit of renewal in the Jewish people and became thus an agent in the evolution of history. The underground press of the Warsaw ghetto describes the unremitting struggle by which the uprising was prepared for and made possible.

For Yisrael Gutman

Notes:

1. Originally published as "The Warsaw Underground Press," in *Living with Antisemitism: Modern Jewish Responses*, ed. Jehuda Reinharz, © 1987 by The Trustees of Brandeis University. Reprinted with permission of University Press of New England.

2. Among these editors were Yitzhak Zuckerman and Mordechai Anielewicz, leaders of the Warsaw Uprising, and Mordechai Tenenbaum-Tamarof, known for his activities in Vilna and Bialystok.

3. Editor's note: Since this article was written, all 6 volumes of the Yad Vashem Hebrew edition of the Warsaw Ghetto Underground Press have been published. The sixth volume of *Itonut ha-mahteret ha-yehudit be-Varshah*, edited by Israel Shoham, appeared in 1997. The set presents a total of 247 surviving underground publications.

4. Joseph Kermish, ed., *Itonut ha-mahteret ha-yehudit be-Varshah*, vols.1–3 (Jerusalem, 1979, 1984). For general survey of Oneg Shabbat and the underground, see Yisrael Gutman, *The Jews of Warsaw, 1939–1943: Ghetto, Underground, Revolt* (Bloomington, Ind., 1982), pp. 144–54. Material for the Yad Vashem collection also came from the archives of the Halutz movement and the Bund. Most underground papers ceased with the great deportations from Warsaw to the extermination camps of Treblinka and Sobibor in July through September 1942. See Gutman, *Jews of Warsaw*, passim.

5. Kermish, preface to *Itonut ha-mahteret*, 1:vi.

6. ZS stands for the Zionist Socialists, a party that merged with Poalei Zion.

7. *Dror* (Freedom) was adopted as the name of two youth movements— Fraihait and He-Halutz Hazair—that merged in 1938. Together they comprised 350 branches in all of Poland, including the area occupied by the Soviet Union. See *Itonut ha-mahteret*, 1:112 n. 8. The movement was connected with Hakibbutz Hameuhad in Eretz Israel. Gordonia—after A. D. Gordon, one of the founding fathers of the kibbutz movement— belongs to Hever Hakwuzot. The kibbutz movement of Hashomer Hazair was and is to this day Hakibbutz Haartzi.

8. *Biuletyn*, May 1940, in ibid., p. 9. *Biuletyn* was a Yiddish monthly, one of twelve publications the Bund issued until 1942. The editorial explains Hitler's attack on the West as motivated by the need to show new victories and to secure raw materials. Therefore "Hitler hastes."

9. Ibid., June 1940, in *Itonut ha-mahteret*, 1: 14.

10. "Fascist Betrayal" is the headline of the editorial in the July 1940 issue of *Biuletyn*, in ibid., 1: 21.

11. Ibid., 1: 29.

12. *Yugnt-Shtime*, October 1940, in ibid., 1: 117. *Yugnt-Shtime* (transcription according to the Yiddish spelling) was a monthly; this is issue number 11.

13. Ibid., 1:124.

14. *Płomienie*, September 1940, in ibid., 1: 89–90. *Płomienie* was the publication of one of the units of Hashomer Hazair in Warsaw; this is the first issue.

15. *Płomienie*, October 1940, in ibid., 1: 134.

16. *Yugnt-Ruf*, January 1941, in ibid., 1: 396. The quotation marks, indi-

cating irony, are in the original. This is the first issue of *Yugnt-Ruf*, which did not appear again until October 1941.

17. Ibid., 1: 397–98.

18. *Dror*, October 1940, in ibid., 1: 105–6. This is the fourth issue of *Dror*.

19. *Itonut ha-mahteret*, 1: 103–7; quotations on pp. 104, 106–7. For information about the meeting, see p. 113 and n. 8.

20. *Bafrayung*, December 1940, in ibid., 1: 178. Under the headline "The Labor Movement at the Crossroads," the paper analyzes the present situation and the future chances of the socialist movement, concluding that the proletariat will decide the future of mankind but until now has failed completely in every historic test. Ibid., pp. 182–85.

21. Ibid., p. 179.

22. Ibid., pp. 180–82, italics in original.

23. *Płomienie*, September 1940, in ibid., p. 90.

24. Ibid., p. 91. The "Jewish badge" in Poland was usually a white armband with a Star of David on it, worn on the right sleeve. Requiring it was a matter of local initiative until the order of November 23,1939, of Hans Frank, governor of the Generalgouvernement.

25. Ibid., p. 92, italics in original.

26. See Gutman, *Jews of Warsaw*, pp. 120–21.

27. *Hamedinah*, August 1940, in *Itonut ha-mahteret*, 1:64. The original has sixteen pages. Ibid., pp. 63–74.

28. Ibid., p. 68.

29. *Iton ha-tnuah*, December 1940–January 1941, in ibid.; quotations on p. 261.

30. Ibid., pp. 264–71, 292–97.

31. Socialism is discussed in ibid., pp. 272–83. Included in the discussion on Socialism are references to and quotations from socialist leaders like Karl Marx, Friedrich Engels, V. I. Lenin, Georgi Dimitrov, and Otto Bauer. Central events and decisive meetings are also reviewed. The discussion on the Soviet Union is on pp. 289–93.

32. Special emphasis is put on Ber Borochov's ideology and on the problem and teaching of Jewish national socialism in opposition to the socialist ideology's negation of the Jewish nationality. Ibid., pp. 285–89. The situation of the movement during the war is described on pp. 297–310; quotations on pp. 301, 304.

33. Ibid., pp. 310–49.

34. On Vilna, see ibid., pp. 318–22; on the *aliyah*, p. 347. For a detailed description of events in Vilna, see Yitzhak Arad, *Ghetto in Flames* (New York, 1982), passim.

35. A special session was held to clarify the educational problems created by the ghetto and to draw practical conclusions. *Iton ha-tnuah*, December 1940–January 1941, in *Itonut ha-mahteret*, 1:337–45. Reviewing the impact of the ghetto situation on their educational system, the participants in the discussion found their education adequate in spite of many obstructions. Ibid., pp. 343–44.

36. Ibid., pp. 327, 328, 334.

37. Deut. 8:3.

38. *Yugnt-Shtime*, November 1940, in *Itonut ha-mahteret*, 1:152–53; ibid., December 1940, in *Itonut ha-mahteret*, p. 221; "The Jewish Ghetto: A Historical Summary;" *Bafrayung*, December 1940, in ibid. pp. 198–202; "Historical Summary in the Wake of the Erection of the Warsaw Ghetto," *Yugnt-Ruf*, January 1941, in ibid. pp. 404–5.

39. The May 1940 issue of *Biuletyn* brought news about German atrocities in Lublin and information about the ghetto in Łódź, which had just been closed. Ibid., pp. 4–5. Later, *Biuletyn* and *Yugnt-Shtime* both included a regular column called "Jewish Chronicle," which reported news from other Jewish communities. Thus, for instance, the March 1941 issue *Biuletyn* describes the expulsion of Jews from the western provinces of Poland into the Generalgouvernement and their being driven from place to place; the deportation of Jews from Vienna to the Generalgouvernement is also reported. Ibid., 2:94–96. See also *Yugnt-Shtime*, in ibid., pp. 219–20. In the January–February 1941 issue of *Dror*, Yitzhak Zuckerman reminds his readers of "the hundreds of Jewish townlets that still wait in great fear for what may be at stake. . . . In places where ghettos have not been erected, massive expulsions have taken place." Ibid., 1:353–54.

40. *Dror*, May 1941, in ibid., 2:309.

41. Ibid., May–June 1941, in ibid., pp. 418–23. This double issue is sixty-four pages in the original. Ibid., pp. 380–441. In addition to feature articles, it includes a wealth of literary material. For more on the situation in the Warsaw ghetto, see Gutman, *Jews of Warsaw*, chap. 3.

42. *Yugnt-Shtime*, April 1941, in *Itonut ha-mahteret*, 2: 217–18, quotation

marks in original. Another detailed description of a labor camp, written by Yitzhak Zuckerman, is in *Dror*, May–June 1941, in ibid., pp. 425–30. Its epigraph is a quotation from Dante. The likening of the Holocaust to Dante's description of Hell is also frequently found in survivor accounts.

43. *Yugnt-Shtime*, April 1941, in ibid., p. 218.

44. *Proletarisher Gedank*, May 1941, in ibid., pp. 295–96.

45. See Yitzhak Zuckerman in *Dror*, January-February 1941, ibid., 1:355–56.

46. *Biuletyn*, March 1941, in ibid., 2:140–42; *Yugnt-Shtime*, March 1941, ibid., pp. 109–10. Actually, only some hundred could avail themselves of the opportunity. See Gutman, *Jews of Warsaw*, pp. 139–40, 442 n. 33.

47. *Yugnt-Shtime*, March 1941 in *Itonut ha-mahteret*, 2:110. A similar wording appears in ibid., July 1941, in ibid., 3:13. Here the Zionist youth movements are classified as "soft bourgeois," disregarding their socialist commitment.

48. Ibid., October 1941, in ibid., 3:464–65. The paper again blames the Zionist youth movements: "They Are Trading in the Youth's Life," the headline says. The reference is to courses in agriculture and gardening, organized in the ghetto with the help of a society called Toporol and with German consent. The vegetables grown were distributed to the needy. In this connection also the *hachsharah* was organized and blamed by the Bund. See also Kermish's explanation, ibid., n. 25, and Gutman, *Jews of Warsaw*, pp. 139–40.

49. Left Poalei Zion, proclaiming radical socialism, attacks the Bund for its criticism of the Soviet Union and the Revisionists because they neglect the revolutionary task of the proletariat. *Yugnt-Ruf*, October 1941, in *Itonut ha-mahteret*, 3:477–79. Hashomer Hazair states that the Bund (without calling it by name) has nothing to offer the impoverished masses at this time of great calamities, in spite of its high standard of organization. *Iton ha-tnuah*, December 1940–January 1941, in ibid., 1:262–63. In Hashomer Hazair's Polish periodical, *Neged ha-zerem*, Revisionism is denounced as "the Jewish fascism." *Neged ha-zerem*, February-March 1941, in ibid., 2:57. It must be said, however, that on the whole the Zionist papers did not that much emphasize the discussion with the Bund and did not use the same acid language in these polemics that the Bund's papers used.

50. See Gutman, *Jews of Warsaw*, chap. 10.

51. *Yugnt-Shtime*, May 1941, in *Itonut ha-mahteret*, 2:282.

52. Ibid., p. 278.

53. *Morgn-Fray*, First of May 1941, in ibid., pp. 300–301.

54. *El-Al, Iton ha-zofim* (Upward, Paper of the Scouts), April 1941, in ibid., pp. 226–27. This is the first issue of this Polish periodical.

55. *Neged ha-zerem*, March-April 1941, dedicated to the First of May, in ibid., pp. 163–90: quotation on p. 183.

56. *Proletarisher Gedank*, May 1941, in ibid., pp. 290, 292.

57. *Dror*, First of May 1941, in ibid., pp. 268–69.

58. Ibid., pp. 270, 272.

59. See the communist paper, *Morgn-Fray*, June 15, 1941, in ibid., p. 455.

60. *Yunge Gvardye*, July 1941, in ibid., 3:3, 6. This is the paper's first issue. See also the editorial in *Biuletyn*, August 1941, in ibid., p. 131; and the editorial in the Bund's Polish *Za Naszą i Waszą Wolność* (For Our and Your Freedom), in ibid., p. 246: "The Soviet-German marriage, doomed to failure, has been a nightmare to us."

61. *Czerwony Sztandar*, July 1941, in ibid., issue p. 45, quotation marks in original. This is number 6 of the Trotskyite periodical, the only one in the Yad Vashem collection. It contains an extensive survey and analysis of political and military affairs.Ibid., pp. 45–64.

62. *Nasze Hasła*, August 1941, in ibid., pp. 202–3. The periodical was published in Polish; this is issue number 3.

63. *Proletarischer Gedank*, September 1941, in ibid., pp. 311–27 passim; quotation on p. 317.

64. *Neged ha-zerem*, August 1941, in ibid., pp. 95,.99. The German-Soviet agreement is justified on p. 98. Some of Hashomer Hazair's factual observations are meant as encouragement. Thus *El-Al* explains in the editorial of its third issue, August 1941, that Germany cannot afford a long war. One feature article envisions how all the troubles will end: The day will come when the revolting armies will point their armor against those who gave it to them and the starving millions will turn toward the Kremlin. Then will come the moment for which it is worthvhile to live and to suffer. The walls of the ghetto will crumble and the Russian soldiers who will enter the sunny streets will address the inhabitants as comrades. Ibid., p. 186.

65. *Słowo Młodych*, July 1941, in ibid., p. 66; this is year 4, issue number 5.

66. *Słowo Młodych*, September 1941, in ibid., p. 331. The headline is a paraphrase of Erich M. Remarque's famous novel about World War I, *Im Westen Nichts Neues* (1929). Because of his sharp criticism, Remarque had been deprived by the Nazis of his German citizenship in 1938. Eventually he became an American citizen.

67. *Słowo Młodych*, July 1941, in ibid., pp. 69–91. Socialism is dealt with in a historical survey. Ibid., pp. 91–94.

68. *Shaviv*, June-July 1941, in ibid., 2:482–517; this is issue number 5.

69. *Proletarisher Gedank*, September 1941, in ibid., 3:320–23; quotation on pp. 322–23. On deportations and expulsions, see also n. 37 above.

70. *Słowo Młodych*, July 1941, in ibid., pp. 68–69. The original text reads "attained" for "stained"; this printer's error has been corrected here. Left Poalei Zion's *Awangarda Młodieży* (Young Pioneer) publishes details from a story of a Jewish worker from a factory in Białystok who escaped. "The facts that this worker tells about what was going on in the regions near the Soviet border are horrifying." *Awangarda Młodieży*, October 1941, in ibid., pp. 437–39; quotation on p. 437. This is issue number 6–7.

71. In ibid., p. 439.

72. *Neged ha-zerem*, September-October 1941, in ibid., pp. 403–6.

73. Gutman, *Jews of Warsaw*, p. 162.

74. *Biuletyn*, October 1941, in *Itonut ha-mahteret*, 3:420.

75. "The Proletarian Palestineism during the Second World War," *Proletarisher Gedank*, March-April 1941, in ibid., 2:148. "Marxist realistic evaluation" is implemented with: "This sober evaluation bestows on the Jewish worker of Marxist understanding the faith in the general liberation that will come following the present world war, as well as in the full social and national liberation of the Jewish workers." The consequence must be "socialist territorialism brought to life as proletarian Palestineism." Ibid.

76. See Karl Marx, *The Civil War in France* (London, 1871); Otto Leichter, *Zwischen Zwei Diktaturen: Österreichs Revolutionäre, 1934–1938* (Vienna, 1968).

77. *Yugnt-Shtime*, March 1941, in *Itonut ha-mahteret*, 2:111–13.

78. *Proletarisher Gedank*, March-April 1941, in ibid., pp. 151–52; quotation on p. 152, my italics.

79. *Yugnt-Shtime*, January-February 1941, in ibid., 1:427, my italics. The article compares the present situation with the underground of the

Schutzbund and includes a quotation from Marx's *Civil War in France*.
80. *Dror*, January-February 1941, in ibid., p. 371, my italics. Wallisch
was condemned to death and executed, together with several other leaders of the uprising. See Paula Wallisch's report in ibid., pp. 371–73.
81. *Neged ha-zerem*, February-March 1941, in ibid., 2:29–35; quotation
p. 30, my italics. This article was originally published in the movement's
Hebrew periodical on March 1, 1934, and now translated into Polish.
82. "Some Problems of Socialism: Thoughts on the Memorial Day of the
'Schutzbund,'" ibid., pp. 35–46.
83. A separate article would be needed to describe the efforts concentrated on saving the young generation from moral and intellectual ruin. The
suffering of the children and their tragic situation are apparent. *Neged ha-
zerem*, for instance, is worried about the change the young are experienc-
ing: "A leap was done from childhood, from the world of dreams into
reality, whose conditions forced upon the children the character of grown-
ups—dwindling, despairing [like them]." May 1941, in ibid., p. 353. In
the same vein, *Słowo Młodych* describes the child that smuggles food into
the ghetto for the family. September 1941, in ibid., 3:347. See also
Gutman, *Jews of Warsaw*, pp. 69–70. *Bafrayung* describes the child begging for bread in the street. December 1940, in *Itonut ha-mahteret*,
1:205–6.
84. *Neged ha-zerem*, August 1941, in *Itonut ha-mahteret*, 3:95. The article calls: "For: The victory of the Red Army! Worldwide socialist revolution! National and social redemption of the Jewish masses in Soviet Eretz
Israel!" An earlier discussion within Hashomer Hazair, however, reveals
an awareness of the conflict: Eretz Israel cannot develop without immigration; Russia will not concede *aliyah*; so what shall we do at the time
of the-hoped for-Soviet victory and Russian rule? *Iton ha-tnuah*,
December 1940-January 1941, in ibid., 1:308.

The Polish Clandestine Press' Treatment of the Warsaw Ghetto Uprising

Paweł Szapiro
Warsaw, Poland

> *It's burning, brothers, it's burning!*
> *Help depends only on you.*
> *If the town is dear to you,*
> *Take the tools, quench the fire.*
> *Quench it with your own blood.*
> *Show that you can do it.*
> *Don't stand there looking on, brothers,*
> *With folded arms.*
> *Don't stand there, brothers,*
> *Quench the fire,*
> *Our little town's aflame!*
> *Mordechai Gebirtig, 1938[1]*

The Warsaw Ghetto Uprising was an extraordinary event. It was the greatest Jewish armed upheaval in the galaxy of the Third Reich, the greatest military action in Polish territories since the invasion in 1939, and also the first uprising in a city in Nazi-occupied Europe. That April 19th of 1943 was also the first time in almost two thousand years that Jews stood up against a regular army as the people of Israel.

Today, this event is described and considered worthy of the highest respect. People talk about it using words like "first" and "most." Today, this way of speaking about the Warsaw Ghetto events is conventional and typical, though there are exceptions.

Has it always been like this? Can we identify our judgments with the judgments of people at the time? How was the Warsaw Ghetto Uprising presented and evaluated by the witnesses? With a considerable degree of certainty we can expect that—at least until the fighting started—Poles at the time had very different ideas than today regarding Jewish resistance and passivity.

Contemporary witnesses to the Warsaw Ghetto struggle were compelled to pay attention by the very fact that the event was occurring in the very midst of the Polish capital. In contrast, our attention is freely focused, which means that it is directed by purposeful, active intention. And this intentional focus is different than that of fifteen or twenty years ago. This difference will turn out to be very significant.

Originally, for Polish witnesses, the Jewish uprising was a dramatic problem not pictured or conceived in the way that we see it today. Precisely what the event was is not important. It was, however, important that the event demanded response, either by action or intentional inaction.

Polish witnesses to the ghetto uprising could make a decision, withdraw it, postpone it or even just not act on it. The circumstances of time and place demanded, however, concrete solutions. Not only was the Warsaw Ghetto Uprising the greatest conflagration in the history of Warsaw (until 1944); it took place not in some far off land, but within the sight and hearing of Warsaw's citizens. Above all, it was an immense struggle on common territory against a common enemy.

Within only a few weeks, the situation practically ceased to be an issue of day to day life. The ghetto uprising had failed, had been suppressed. Thereafter, the question of fighting Jews was no longer a problem that had to be solved or dealt with. Once the ghetto fighting ceased, the uprising became and remains merely a question of knowledge about the past. It should be examined in detail, while remembering not to judge the views and attitudes of fifty years ago by today's standards.

The fundamental problem can be summarized in three questions: What was the attitude taken by the Polish population *en masse* towards the Warsaw Ghetto Uprising? What reasons, evaluations, norms and principles of that time and place determined the attitude taken by Poles toward the uprising? What was it that allowed the Polish witnesses to declare that their attitude towards the Jewish insurgents was in fact such as it should have been ethically and morally?

Looking within the contemporaneous Polish clandestine press, as well as in post-war Polish historiography and publications, both in Poland

and abroad, it is impossible to find voices questioning the appropriateness of the attitude taken by the Polish population towards the Jewish uprising.

To determine the attitude of the general Polish population toward the ghetto uprising requires the examination of three issues: degree of interest and information about the uprising, its interpretation and the issue of assistance extended to struggling Jews. In the latter instance, of course, I am not referring to real aid, but to how it was seen, understood and experienced at the time.

I have left out certain issues beyond the sphere of this essay. To mention only a few: Poles' attitude towards the idea of the Jewish uprising, the appreciation of armed struggle waged by Jews[2] or a change in attitude towards the Jewish community *in toto*, which resulted from the armed resistance.[3] There are many other issues. I have selected only those that would constitute a relatively complete answer to the question implied in the title of this essay.

II

After the huge deportation action in July-September 1942, some 70 thousand Jews remained within the walls of the Warsaw Ghetto. The number of deported victims (about 250 thousand) and the pace of the action led Poles to conclude that the Nazi German scenario of the destination for all Jews had been finally determined and entirely achieved, with scarce exceptions. The few remaining Jews were considered helpless survivors, unable to take any action, passively awaiting the execution of the unavoidable sentence.[4] Although informed by the clandestine press about armed actions in the ghetto at the end of 1942 and at the beginning of 1943, and about the breakthrough in the attitudes of its inhabitants regarding active resistance, Polish public opinion paid no particular attention. The Polish population, its elites and organizations were focused on other issues that were more narrowly Polish.[5]

In the spring of 1943, the frontlines of the Second World War were still more than 1000 kilometers distant from Warsaw. The escalation of anti-Polish terror and resistance against murderous German actions were considered to be the most important issues in occupied Poland. Clandestine activities, consisting so far of collaboration with the anti-Nazi coalition, were changing slowly but systematically, into an independent struggle for the biological survival of the Polish nation.

Armed action conducted by the underground Polish state was animated. In the course of only six months (October 1942–March 1943), immediately prior to the ghetto uprising, there were at least seventy skirmishes in the streets of Warsaw. This was three times the number during the preceding past three years.[6]

At the end of 1942 the atmosphere was heated by reports on the brutal 'pacifications' of villages and reprisal actions in south-eastern Poland. In view of the similarity in methods used by the Germans in destroying Jews, by the beginning of October 1942, the clandestine press carried hundreds of articles proclaiming a new danger: *It will be the Poles' turn after the Jews.*

At the end of 1942 and the beginning of 1943, Poles were the first to become aware that this time it was not the murdering of Jews, but the murder of *all* Jews. Maybe for this reason, there was a general feeling, attested to by numerous articles carried by the clandestine Polish press, that *Jews went like sheep to the slaughter.*

That assumption was rejected on April 19, 1943.

III

Rumors circulated a day earlier that a huge police action would be held in the ghetto. It was expected that it would resemble the previous summer's action. Anyway, rumors regarding this issue had been circulating for weeks. Nevertheless, the underground press from the last ten days of April unequivocally reflects complete surprise and confusion in public opinion.[7]

All Poles now confronted the necessity to perceive and appreciate Jews from an entirely new perspective. Jews had invaded territory alien to them: armed struggle. It need not be added that, by taking up arms, the Jews placed themselves at the crux of the world conflict. It is for this reason that the events within the ghetto walls were accompanied not only by the reflection of Polish passers-by but also by meticulous consideration by the Polish elites. Echoes of emotions related to the armed upheaval in the ghetto can be sought in the clandestine Polish press.

The ghetto developments became the subject of numerous Polish underground press statements, and would be discussed long after the conclusion of battle. From the outbreak of the uprising until the end of the German occupation, some 700 articles alluding to the Warsaw Ghetto

Uprising were carried by the clandestine press. A majority of them have survived, but of course not all. A total of 556 articles, reports, notes and references have been found regarding the struggles of Warsaw's Jewry. Only part of them, 455 to be precise, are original texts; the remainder are discussions and reprints. They were published in 153 different clandestine papers: dailies, weeklies, monthlies and others.[8] These periodicals were published in 21 different cities and localities throughout the country.[9] They were press organs of 37 clandestine organizations including the most important ones.[10] It would be fair to say that they represented the entire political and ideological spectrum of the underground Polish state.

Most of these periodicals, as many as 113 that reported or commented on the ghetto uprising, were published in Warsaw itself: the battlefield, the metropolis, for Poles still the capital of Poland, the seat of the highest civilian and military authorities of the underground state, and significantly the center of the clandestine publishing movement. A total of 600 periodicals were published there during the five years of German occupation.

The German occupation authorities said nothing publicly about the ghetto battles. Even the *Nowy Kurier Warszawski*, published in Warsaw by the Germans in Polish, was mute. Such licit periodicals were not published for Poles to provide them with news. In fact, the clandestine press filled this gap, with effective assistance by radio programs broadcast in Polish from Great Britain.

It appears to be true that not all papers wrote about the uprising. However, there is no complete certainty in this respect, since not every issue of the clandestine press has survived. Nevertheless, the underground papers informed Poles in the whole country about developments in the Warsaw Ghetto. Involved in this effort were the editorial boards of major papers, representing the principal underground military and civilian organizations, with large circulation, and disseminated throughout the country.

They included *Agencja Prasowa* (Press Agency) and *Biuletyn Informacyjny* (Information Bulletin). *Agencja Prasowa* was a weekly with a circulation of 200 numbered copies, meant only for the editorial boards of affiliated clandestine papers. All the local papers were obligated to reprint specially signed articles. They usually pertained to programs, dealt with key political and social problems of the country, and at the same time presented the position taken by the Chief Headquarters of the Home Army with respect to these issues. The chronicle of developments in the country carried by *Agencja Prasowa* was one of the principal sources of information for local papers.

Biuletyn Informacyjny, a weekly with a circulation of 25 thousand copies, was the most important newspaper of the Polish underground. At the same time, it was a model periodical for all the local papers. Subjects for lead articles were taken from it; articles were reprinted *in extenso* or rewritten, leaving intact the leading thought. This applied also to texts expressing assessments of developments in the country.

All the papers mentioned above were employed by the Office of Information and Propaganda of the Home Army to present a uniform propaganda line throughout the country. Interventions were made in case of political or propaganda errors committed in affiliated publications. Therefore, it can be assumed that decisions regarding reports on ghetto fighting were taken at the highest level.

In this context, more than striking is the case of *Wiadomości Polskie* (Polish News). We have all 117 issues of this bi-weekly newspaper, one of the six major papers published by the Office of Information and Propaganda of the Chief Headquarters of the Home Army. With a circulation of eight thousand copies, it was intended for commanders and intelligentsia of the Home Army, to provide them with information on the political and military situation. It was recommended for editors of the clandestine press. Texts could not be reprinted word for word, but were the basis for independent articles written for a large readership. The articles were suited to the level of readers with a certain political knowledge. It can be assumed that the silence of *Wiadomości Polskie* was not incidental and was significant for skilled readers. It seems that a decision on this matter could not have been taken merely at the level of the editorial board.

IV

Consider all the terms employed to describe the events that took place in the Warsaw Ghetto after April 19, 1943. I deem this important since, in accordance with William Isaac Thomas' rule, people react not only to objective features of a situation but also, and maybe mostly, to its significance. Once a meaning is attributed to a situation, it defines subsequent behavior and consequences.[11]

The Polish word ***powstanie*** (uprising) means an armed upheaval in the name of freedom and liberation.[12] This term not only carries a denotative meaning but also a connotation of high status, even nobility. In Polish history, it is applied to struggles like that of Kościuszko in 1794 or the January 1863 rising against the Russians.

In underground press references, the Warsaw Ghetto developments were most frequently, in over 230 instances, referred to as a **"fight"** or a **"revolt."** In over 100 publications we find the word **"resistance"** employed, qualified as armed or first. Events in the ghetto were also described as the **"liquidation,"** characterized as final, last.

The character of the struggle imposed the use of the word **"defense."** A number of times **"self-defense"** was employed. Martial references included use of the words **"war"** and **"front."** The war was "Jewish-German," the battle of "Ghettograd" was the "third front". In this group of terms we can include: **battle, fortress, siege, attack, stronghold.** These terms were used scores of times.

Not even once have I mentioned the word **uprising** (*powstanie*) used in the clandestine press in regard to the Warsaw Ghetto. This does not mean that the term was not used in the clandestine press regarding the Jewish struggle. It was used, but rarely; to be precise, it was employed only 24 times in 10 articles carried by 11 papers belonging to 9 clandestine organizations. This enables me to state that Polish public opinion did not use the expression "Warsaw Ghetto Uprising." Why?

Those papers that did use the term **uprising** were mostly published by leftist organizations. In general, these organizations promoted an immediate all-Polish uprising directed against the Germans. This could explain why the majority of underground papers, that represented another option for when to begin the general uprising, did not use this term, precisely so as not to provoke a premature outbreak.

Maybe the ghetto event was too insignificant. In the eyes of Poles, brought up in the tradition of the great national uprisings in the 19th century, the fighting in the Warsaw Ghetto did not meet the standard territorially, in numbers, size or duration. The universally accepted Polish tradition of terminology reserved this word, **uprising**, for a grander event. One might think, and this is yet another hypothesis, that for Poles at that time, the term **uprising** was being saved for a very concrete event. The Command of the Home Army planned to start an **uprising** at the simultaneous moment of military failure of the Third Reich on the Eastern front and the exhausting of the Red Army's offensive power. It was an event expected in 1943, anticipated throughout Poland, and, what is most important, expected to bring a Polish victory. Only the status of an ally would make Jews equal in the eyes of Polish public opinion.

Thus, perhaps **uprising** was a sacrocanct term for Poles at that time. If it were to take place in their territory, it could only be applied to ethnic Poles, and never to strangers, that is, to Jews.

V

The history of the press is not only about what was written in the press, but also why it was written. What is most surprising is that none of the papers of the Home Army tried to vindicate or defend—neither in 1943 nor in 1944—any of the numerous aid actions carried out by its own armed soldiers. Understandably in this situation, no mention was made of actions carried out by other groups.

One of the expert historians of the ghetto uprising, Michał Borwicz, even says that, since the newspapers remained mute, Warsaw citizens did not know about actions conducted by Home Army patrols at the walls of the Ghetto.[13] I would agree with this statement, but only with a minor reservation. Warsaw citizens could hear and even, as it turned out, read about shots fired near the ghetto. But they could not be sure as to who fired them.[14]

Why did the so-called "opinion-makers," the underground newspaper editors, decide to remain silent, to confuse Polish public opinion, and very likely allow the Home Army's merits to be discredited by other organizations? It must be borne in mind that the balance of forces, at the time and subsequently, impeded any meaningful aid that could significantly change the position of the fighting Jews. Attacks near the ghetto were, therefore, a manifestation of what was possible under the circumstances and, above all, an act of solidarity whose price could be human life.[15] Who was anxious to make this immense moral value known or to conceal it? And why?

Not much light is cast on this enigma by the statement of an indubitably competent person, namely the commander of the Warsaw district of the Home Army, Antoni Chruściel. Chruściel ("Monter") wrote the scholar Ber Mark that:

The Home Army's clandestine press did not mention these actions for understandable reasons. Both the people and Germans knew who was capable in Warsaw of launching such actions and it would be superfluous to publicize it. Though there was a part of the population, luckily scarce, whose attitude towards aid actions for Jews was unfavorable or even adverse.[16]

Mark considered the first argument hardly convincing. He wrote that newspapers of all the clandestine organizations, including those of the Home Army, frequently and willingly published information about even less significant actions. (The second of Chruściel's arguments will be dealt with below.)

It is worth knowing that this statement is valid only from a certain moment of great significance for this analysis. Initially, the Home Army carried out actions that were intentionally attributed to other subversive forces in order to protect people from reprisals. Such assaults most frequently simulated the presence of Soviet guerrillas and parachutists. Only with the order dated January 22, 1943, did the Commander of the Home Army direct that subversive actions be conducted in the Home Army's own name.

Documents seem to prove unequivocally that "Monter's" testimony, or rather interpretation of events, is incomplete and clearly confusing. To be precise, his statement contains truth and only truth, but not the whole truth. In view of the Home Army Commander's January 1943 order on taking credit for attacks, it cannot be doubted that hundreds of Home Army affiliated newspapers throughout the country applied an embargo on reporting information regarding all armed actions near the ghetto walls.

This is a statement entailing such serious research consequences that it requires the examination of all the circumstances in favor and against it. Assuming that the order of the Commander of the Home Army was disobeyed, that could happen only with his consent or due to a conspiracy of silence on a matter of considerable significance not only for the fighting Jews, underground soldiers and the population of the occupied capital at the time, but also for us today.[17] The hypothesis of a coincidental convergence of views or of a conspiracy can be rejected out of hand as absurd and not feasible in the case of the underground military's press. Editors and writers constituted a part of the clandestine army and had to promote a given political program; they were by no means to be a clandestine free political platform.

Therefore, we can and should consider whether a directive of silence issued at the top was feasible in the conditions of the clandestine publication system. Of course, it was. The clandestine press, as a phenomenon, enjoys an undue reputation of having been exceptionally independent. When we look at how it operated, we see that nothing seems to attest to any greater or lesser independence than that enjoyed by a legally published press. This comment applies *in extenso* to the Polish clandestine press.

We cannot forget a significant element of the situation, namely the civilian Polish population's own knowledge about the Warsaw Ghetto fighting. Maybe this knowledge was incomplete, as the diarist Ludwik Landau demonstrates,[18] but a position had to be taken, attention drawn in a desirable direction, in order to prevent gossip. That could be achieved only with the spreading of confusion, and namely through the dissemination of vague general or false information.

And this is how it was. *Biuletyn Informacyjny* carried reports that Jews had already initiated a number of attacks, as a result of which there were victims near the Warsaw Ghetto walls. For example, at the intersection of Bonifraterska and Konwiktorska streets, a five-man German police patrol was killed.[19] As a matter of fact, near the crossing of those two streets, an action was carried out on April 19 by a sapper unit of the Warsaw District of the Home Army commanded by Captain Józef Pszenny ("Chwacki").

Weakly echoed was another action carried out on April 23 by a group of the Communist People's Guard (Gwardia Ludowa, GL). *Biuletyn Informacyjny* published a report on ghetto fighting stating that "During fighting on the 23rd of this month . . . a bomb was thrown in the evening under a German car in Freta Street. A number of SS-men and two civilians died."[20] The information could in practice have been comprehended only by inhabitants of the capital. Only Warsaw's inhabitants, and not all, knew that Freta Street was outside the ghetto. Moreover, the use of an impersonal verb form makes it impossible to identify participants in the action.

It is high time to ask a question whose answer could turn out to be the key to the problem of aid that interests us: Why was the directive of silence applied with regard to armed attacks carried out by underground soldiers near the walls of the ghetto?

The principle of conspiratorial activity is not to announce one's own action. Therefore, silence while the Ghetto Uprising was actually under way, when solidarity actions were being planned and executed, must be deemed understandable. But can we consider this explanation satisfactory? Most certainly not, for since the beginning of 1943, the principle of anonymity with regard to its own already executed actions ceased to be binding in the Home Army's press, with the apparent notable exception of the Warsaw Ghetto Uprising.

Let us recall, therefore, that "Monter" mentions attitudes adverse to Jews. The historian Mark accepts this element without reservation and develops it into a categorical statement, that

> the main reason for public silence with regard to its armed actions in solidarity with the fighting Ghetto was fear that the Home Army's command would be accused by NSZ, the extreme National Democracy and other similar elements with being favorable to Jews. It is interesting that the Office of the Delegate did not even mention these events in all the reports sent to London. [21]

The groups of the extreme right were carriers of hostility towards Jews; and maybe so was the Office of the Polish Government-in-exile's Delegate. But the Chief Headquarters of the Home Army is free of this accusation. At the same time, there is apparent a significant, if not a decisive, influence exerted on the underground Polish state's propaganda policy by groups whose program included anti-Semitism.

But we also know about tensions in the Chief Headquarters of the Home Army with regard to the idea of aid for the ghetto. Perhaps the explanation has to be sought at this level. Nor is there doubt that the outlooks of the Jewish ghetto fighters and of the Home Army were divergent. In 1943, the Polish side did not want an uprising in Warsaw, and so the silence with regard to its actions was intended to prevent a pro-uprising anxiety among the citizens of Warsaw and among its own soldiers. But was that all?

Kronika Polska (Polish Chronicle), published by the rightist National Party in July 1944, wrote:

> . . . The Armed Forces in the Country [=Armia Krajowa, Home Army] decided to extend aid to the besieged Jews. Diversionary units were ordered to attack the German ring surrounding the ghetto, in a number of places. Rank and file soldiers of diver-

sionary units, recruited from the Polish proletariat, the most disciplined element of the Armed Forces in the Country, tested in many actions against the overwhelming forces of the adversary, in this instance—failed. They simply did not show up for the assembly.[22]

Unfortunately nothing concrete is known about this action.

VI

A summary: Sometimes in extremely difficult conditions, circumstances occur in which the rejection of universally accepted values becomes necessary for survival. Striving to survive at any price is a biological imperative, a manifestation of the survival instinct, but by no means is this the outlook consistently respected by thinking men and women. For this reason, after the fact (and also during the course of events) we seek every possible method to achieve at least an illusion of having acted in accord with universally accepted ethical norms. So long as we do not perceive and reject this illusion, we shall not learn the truth. As a result, the work of the historian will be increasingly difficult, but by the same token increasingly interesting.

Notes:

1. Gebirtig's Yiddish song, "Undzer shtetl brent" (Our town is burning), was composed in 1938, in the wake of an epidemic of pogroms in prewar Poland. This partial translation is based on the Yiddish and English texts in Ruth Rubin, *Voices of a People: Yiddish Folk Song* (NY, 1963), pp. 430–431. For the full Yiddish text, see Eleanor Gordon Mlotek, *Mir Trogn a Gezang!* Second Enlarged Edition (NY, 1977), pp. 231–232.

2. Ludwik Landau noted in his diary on April 23, 1943, that: ". . .this fight was appreciated earlier, gave rise to compassion towards Jews even in milieus hardly accessible to them, especially with regard to the unequivocal position taken by the press . . ." Ludwik Landau, *Kronika lat wojny i okupacji* (Warsaw, 1961–62), vol. II, p. 362.

3. The problem of transformation of the appreciation of the Jews by the ethnic Polish community, when Jews were entrapped in the mechanism of

Annihilation, is entirely known. There was a negative evaluation until a certain time of Jews' passivity toward the Germans. For illustration, see an excerpt from an article carried by a socialist paper: "[. . .]when liquidating Jews the brutal occupant comes across a similar reaction, and not like the passiveness so far, equivalent in many cases to degradation." *Wolność - organ PPS* (WRN, Kraków), 24 Apr.1943, No. 510. The uprising contributed to the expansion of the collection of phrases by which to construe an opinion about Jews, such as, for example, "Jews raised themselves from [being] a helpless herd, murdered by German criminals, to the level of a fighting nation." *Myśl państwowa* (KON, Warszawa), 30 Apr. 1943, No. 37. After April 19, 1943, descriptions of Jewry expressed appreciation for the first time. Developments in the Warsaw Ghetto are even compared to the defense of Thermopylae, the defense of the Polish capital in September 1939, or the epic of the Polish garrison holding Westerplatte near Danzig in September-October 1939. Of course, attempts were also made to discredit the Jewish armed effort and hostile opinions were heard in general.

4. This was the opinion of the Commander-in-Chief of the Home Army General Stefan Rowecki-Grot even at the beginning of 1943. On January 2, he cabled to London:

> Jews from all kinds of groups, including Communists, have turned to us lately asking for arms, as if we had depots full of them. As an experiment, I took out a few revolvers. I have no assurance that they will use these weapons. I shall not give out any more weapons, for you know that we ourselves have none. I am awaiting another shipment. Apprise me of what contact our Jews have with London.

Quoted after Y. Gutman, *The Jews of Warsaw, 1939–1943* (Bloomington, 1989), p. 256.

5. Indubitably, the Jewish resistence movement, especially the fighting in January 1943, resulted in a breakthrough in the attitudes of the leadership of the Polish underground organizations (Home Army) with regard to Jews and of the Jews towards the Germans. The latter change was a phenomenon of great importance although unknown or unnoticed by the Polish community. Any armed action within the ghetto depended as much on attitudes within the Jewish community as on the willingness of the Polish underground to cooperate. For the first three years of the occupa-

tion, Jews were outside the sphere of interest of the underground Polish state.

6. Tomasz Strzembosz, *Akcje zbrojne podziemnej Warszawy 1939–1944* (Warsaw, 1983), pp. 264–265.

7. This is confirmed by Landau's diary:

... Something is going on in the Ghetto. Nobody knows what. [. . .] War is waged beside us, a true war with shooting, fires, and even with the use of tanks and some small cannons—a modern *Jewish war* which provides episodes worthy of the writing of Josephus Flavius [. . .]. The Warsaw which lives with the problem of the war, the *Jewish-German war*, of the *third front*, as somebody called it . . . (Landau, *Kronika*, 2: 322.)

8. For the entire underground press material regarding the Warsaw Ghetto Uprising, see Paweł Szapiro, *Wojna Żydowsko-Niemiecka, Polska prasa konspiracyjna 1943–1944 o powstaniu w getcie Warszawy* (The Jewish-German War, The Polish Underground Press 1943–1944)(London, 1992.)

9. Warsaw (113 papers), Kraków (10), Lwów (8), Częstochowa (2), Legionowo (2), Białystok, Boby, Garwolin, Grodzisk Mazowiecki, Jelna (Rzeszów province), Łódź, Ostrów Wielkopolski, Puławy, Rzeszów, Tarnopol, Tarnów, Trzydnik, Wadowice, Wilno, an unidentified locality in Kielce province and another unidentified locality.

10. Twenty-five papers were published by the Home Army (AK); 18 by the Office of the London government-in-exile's *Delegatura* in occupied Poland.

11. See R.K. Merton, *Social Theory and Social Structure* (NY: Free Press, 1947), p. 398.

12. *Słownik języka polskiego* (Warsaw: PWN, 1983), vol. II, p. 875. *Słownik frazeologiczny języka polskiego*, ed. Stanisław Skorupka (Warszawa, 1985) defines *powstanie* as "taking up of arms, insurrection."

13. Michel Borwicz, *L'insurrection du ghetto de Varsovie* (Paris, 1966).

14. Tomasz Strzembosz writes that "During only six months (October 1942–March 1943 . . .) at least seventy skirmishes were noted in the town . . . " (op.cit., pp. 264–265.)

15. A participant in the event, Zbigniew Młynarski ("Kret"), concludes his report with a significant statement: "I have an impression that I will not commit an error if I say that tonight they were the first victims in the

defense of Jews sealed in the Ghetto." Quoted after B. Mark, *W piętnaste rocznice powstania w getcie warszawskim* (Warsaw, 1958).

16. Letter of A. Chruściel to B. Mark, January 25, 1958. Quoted after B. Mark, "Ruch oporu i powstanie w getcie warszawskim," *Biuletyn ZIH*, 1963, No. 45–46, p. 34.

17. Tomasz Strzembosz, op. cit., pp.280–281

18. Landau, *Kronika*, 2: 322. See the quote in note 7 above.

19. *Biuletyn Informacyjny*, (AK, Warsaw), No. 17(172), 29 Apr.1943, article "Obrona getta warszawskiego." Reprinted in *Przegląd prasowy* (GL, Warsaw), No. 24, 5 May 1943, article "Stosunek do walki czynnej".

20. *Biuletyn Informacyjny*, (AK, Warsaw), No. 17[172], 29 Apr.1943, article "Obrona getta warszawskiego".

21. B. Mark, *W piętnaste rocznice powstania w getcie warszawskim* (Warsaw, 1958), p. 35.

22. Paweł Szapiro, *Wojna żydowsko-Niemiecka*, p. 408.

Dziennik Polski (The Polish Daily), The Official Organ of the Polish Government-in-Exile, and the Holocaust, 1940–1945[1]

Piotr Wróbel
University of Toronto

Polish-Jewish relations during World War II belong to the most controversial subjects in the entire history of Poland. Fiercely discussed and diversely interpreted, the topic strongly affects postwar contacts between the Poles and the Jews. Thousands of books and articles have been devoted to this important subject, but the dimensions and significance of the Holocaust still motivate historians to re-examine every aspect of its history.

Various Polish institutions, social groups, and individuals had different attitudes towards the Jews during the last world war. It is hard to decide which attitudes and elements of historical realities are most important to a general interpretation. There was, however, one institution that was recognized by a majority of the Poles as their representation and leader: the Polish government-in-exile. It formulated Polish policy during the war, directed the underground state in occupied Poland, maintained relations with the anti-Nazi coalition, and designed plans for the future. "For all of these reasons," writes David Engel in the introduction to his book *In the Shadow of Auschwitz*, "it seems sensible to begin an investigation into the responses of the Polish leadership to the Holocaust of Polish Jewry with an examination of the Jewish policies of the Polish government-in-exile."[2]

This examination is not an easy task. The government-in-exile worked in very difficult conditions, under heavy pressure from the Allies and Polish public opinion. It consisted of representatives of various political orientations: the Polish Socialist Party, National Democratic Party,

Party of Labor (Stronnictwo Pracy, SP), Peasant Party, and some representatives of the prewar regime. Their worldviews and attitudes towards
the Jews differed. Confused and overwhelmed by the war, they were far
from compromise on several issues. Survival of Poland was at stake, and
they did not consider the Jewish question the most important problem. In
Jewish matters too, their activities were frequently chaotic and inconsistent. There is, however, a procedure that can help to establish what was
the most important general line of the government's policy towards the
Jews, and to determine how the Polish leaders saw their war situation and
the postwar future of Poland. From 1940, the Polish government-in-exile
in London published its official organ, *Dziennik Polski* (The Polish
Daily). This newspaper was to perform many important functions. It
announced and explained decisions of the government, published government documents, and tried to shape Polish public opinion not only in
Great Britain but also in the entire Polish war diaspora. Because this
newspaper served as the voice of the most significant Polish leadership
during the Second World War, analyzing the material published in it is the
best indicator of the content and intent of official policy regarding Jews.

An Englishman once said that where there are three Poles, at least one
newspaper must be printed.[3] This ironic statement reflected intense cultural activities among the Polish refugees in Great Britain during the war.
After the debacle of France in June 1940, about 25,000 Polish soldiers
and a large group of civilians landed in England. In 1943, the Polish community in the Great Britain reached about 60,000 people.[4] Most of them
followed the vicissitudes of the war with great excitement, but they did
not know English and felt isolated. In addition, unlike the 1939–1940
immigrants to France, the Poles who came to England between 1940 and
1945 were predominantly from the intelligentsia. Consequently, a great
demand for Polish newspapers appeared.[5]

The Polish soldiers evacuated to England were placed at different
military camps. Waiting for a German invasion, they had much time on
their hands. They received some money and wanted to read.
Spontaneously, almost every larger Polish unit started publishing its own
periodical. Even some ships' companies brought out their own newsletters.[6] Altogether, about 150 periodicals and newspapers were published
by and for the soldiers. The largest, and chronologically the first Polish
newspaper for soldiers and others was *Dziennik Żołnierza* (The Soldier's

Daily). Its first issue was printed in a tent at a camp in Douglas, Scotland, as early as June 29, 1940. Later, the newspaper was read by Polish soldiers everywhere in Great Britain, and was extremely popular.[7]

Civilian journalists were very active, too. Soon, numerous Polish papers appeared. No official British license was necessary to print a periodical. Quite a few editorial staff of Polish papers published in France in 1939–1940 managed to escape to England. The last Paris issue of the leading periodical of the 1939 Polish emigration, *Wiadomości Polskie* (Polish News), was dated June 23, 1940. Its first London issue appeared on July 14, 1940. Every political orientation, many professional groups, and representatives of important geographical regions of prewar Poland tried to publish a paper in order to participate in political life of the war emigration, to express their opinions, and to fight for their interests. All those newspapers and periodicals, like papers published by the soldiers, included mostly what the Poles called *publicystyka* (essays, reviews, and discussions). The articles represented very diverse worldviews, and were frequently sharply critical of the Polish government-in-exile.[8]

The largest Polish newspaper and periodical publisher in Great Britain was the government-in-exile itself. Each of its ministries published at least one major periodical and several minor ones. The most active in this respect was the Ministry of Information and Documentation. Originally organized as the Center for Information and Documentation (Centrala Informacji i Dokumentacji) in France, in the fall of 1939, it was reshaped into a ministry on September 11, 1940, in England and was directed subsequently by Stanisław Stroński (Sept. 11, 1940–March 15, 1943), Stanisław Kot (March 18, 1943–Nov. 24, 1944), and Adam Pragier (Nov. 29, 1944–July 1945). The ministry's aim was to gather, elaborate, and disseminate information and documentation on Polish affairs. It controlled the Polish Telegraphic Agency (Polska Agencja Telegraficzna, PAT) and the Polish Radio, operated its own monitoring of international broadcasting, and published several periodicals devoted to political, military, and economic matters, that reviewed newspapers published in England, the Soviet Union, Germany, and other countries. The largest and the most prestigious among these publications was *Dziennik Polski* (The Polish Daily).[9]

Dziennik Polski, whose first issue appeared in London on July 12, 1940, constituted a continuation of an official organ of the Polish government-in-exile in France, *Głos Polski* (The Polish Voice). It was edited by a group of journalists who had worked before the war mostly for newspapers and periodicals of the Party of Labor, Socialist, and Christian-Democratic movements. Between July 12 and August 15, 1940, the editorial staff of *Dziennik Polski* was directed by Jerzy Szapiro and Jan Tabaczyński. Before the war, Szapiro had directed *Robotnik* (The Worker), the organ of the Polish Socialist Party, as well as Warsaw's *Kurier Codzienny* (The Daily Courier) and *Przełom* (The Turning Point) published by the left-of-center Union of Reform (Związek Naprawy). During 1939–1940, Szapiro was editor-in-chief of the socialist *Robotnik Polski we Francji* (The Polish Worker in France).[10] Tabaczyński had directed the Christian-Democratic *Polonia*, published by Wojciech Korfanty in Katowice during the interwar period.[11] Between August 15, 1940 and July 1, 1943, *Dziennik Polski* was edited by Marceli Karczewski, a journalist who had worked for Warsaw's *Kurier Polski* before the war. Karczewski was one of the main columnists of *Dziennik Polski* until an unfortunate polemical article about one of Churchill's speeches forced him to resign.[12] He was succeeded by Stanisław Sopicki, an activist of the Party of Labor who, before the war, edited Warsaw's *Nowa Prawda* (The New Truth), an organ of his party, and then worked for *Polonia* in Katowice.[13] On December 15, 1943, after Sopicki became a member of the government, the editor-in-chief position of *Dziennik Polski* was taken by Zygmunt Lityński, one of the most active columnists of the newspaper and a Paris correspondent of *Ilustrowany Kurier Codzienny* (Illustrated Daily Courier) before the war.[14]

As a result of a government crisis in the fall of 1943, *Dziennik Polski* and *Dziennik Żołnierza* were merged and, from January 1, 1944, appeared with a new title: *Dziennik Polski i Dziennik Żołnierza* (The Polish Daily and Soldier's Daily). The merger was variously interpreted. It seems that the government of Stanisław Mikołajczyk wanted to control or even liquidate the most popular army newspaper because it was too anti-Soviet and opposed Mikołajczyk's policy towards the Soviet Union.[15] The new paper, which looked almost identical to *Dziennik Polski*, was edited by Mieczysław Szerer and, after the fall of Mikołajczyk's cabinet in November 1944, by an outstanding journalist, Jan Czarnocki. Czarnocki made the paper more patriotic and national during the government of Tomasz Arciszewski.[16]

From 1940 to 1943, between 10,000 and 15,000 copies of the paper were printed and distributed through 55 sales agencies in Great Britain. The price was one penny per copy, which was rather inexpensive. The newspaper was also distributed in the most important centers of the Polish war diaspora. *Dziennik* explained the government policies, discussed the opposition, and tried to shape Polish public opinion according to the government's plans. Prime Minister Sikorski's administration believed that the entire Polish war diaspora should gather around the government-in-exile. On November 22, 1940, during a controversy over the anti-Semitic periodical *Jestem Polakiem* (I am a Pole), it announced:

> The Polish Government has decided that for the purpose of national unity during the present war, there must be published here, in exile, one political newspaper only, namely, *Dziennik Polski* (The Polish Daily).[17]

Nicely printed at St. Clement Press in London, the paper had four pages divided into five columns, and included illustrations, photographs, and maps. The first page was devoted to the most important international and Polish affairs, including news from the occupied home country. The second and the third pages included comments, essays, important speeches, and documents. The last page contained short news and advertising. The newspaper appeared six times a week, with one issue for Saturdays and Sundays.[18]

Dziennik Polski had a large group of well-known contributors. Minister of Information and Documentation Stanisław Stroński frequently published his essays and comments there. Stroński collaborated with the paper so closely that he became almost a super-editor-in-chief. Tadeusz Katelbach specialized in German affairs. Witold Czerwiński, director of a division in the Ministry of Information and Documentation, and Józef Retinger, a gray eminence of the government-in-exile and personal advisor of Premier Sikorski, wrote for the newspaper, too. A group of outstanding journalists and writers of the interwar period, such as Karol Zbyszewski, Zbigniew Grabowski, Wacław Solski, Eugeniusz Hinterhoff, Tadeusz Zabłocki, and Zygmunt Nowakowski, filled the pages of the paper with their articles. The group of collaborators was so large that, as one of them once said sarcastically, when somebody from the émigré political establishment had nothing to do, or the government did not know what to do with such a person, he or she was usually made a member of the paper's editorial staff.[19]

From their first days in England, the Poles had many British friends and enthusiastic supporters; at the same time however, the Polish government-in-exile and the Polish press were attacked from various sides. The accusations, used against them most frequently, were anti-Sovietism, anti-Semitism, political irresponsibility, and chauvinism. These arguments were directed with different intensity against all Polish political groups and periodicals active in the Great Britain during the war, including *Dziennik Polski* whose editorial staff consisted, among others, of socialists and persons of Jewish background. Most Poles did not understand why, after their evacuation to England, the Jewish issue in Poland became so widely discussed in Great Britain.[20] The Poles were certain that Soviet agencies, including the Communist Party of Great Britain, sponsored or organized the attacks, and that anti-Semitism was deliberately used and tied to anti-Sovietism by anti-Polish and pro-Soviet forces in order to create a convincing negative image of the Polish nation and to weaken the Polish diplomatic defense of the prewar eastern borders of Poland.[21] Already on August 20, 1940, a month after the evacuation of the Poles to England, when only some Polish newspapers had begun to appear, a Communist MP Gallacher made the following statement in the House of Commons:

> In this country the most filthy, vile and slanderous anti-Soviet propaganda is being published, some of it under the auspices of the Ministry of Information. Take, for instance, the Polish Press published in this country. In one of the Polish papers, the so-called Foreign Secretary declares that the Polish Government in this country is conducting a war against the Soviet Union. One of these Polish papers is continually filled with anti-Soviet and anti-Semitic propaganda. You could not get anything more Fascist than that propaganda, and it is supported by the Ministry of Information. . . .[22]

Several days later, Labor MP Josiah Wedgwood stated that "certainly the feeling of Poles towards Jews can be paralleled by the feelings of

Germans towards Jews."[23] Wedgwood, his party colleague Sidney Silverman (who simultaneously was a vice-president of the British Section of the World Jewish Congress), the Communist Gallacher, and a group of other MPs constantly repeated their attacks in the House of Commons. They accused the Polish Army in the West of anti-Semitic harassment of its Jewish soldiers and demanded that British censorship should control Polish periodicals and limit their number.[24] On December 4, 1940, Gallacher

asked the Under-Secretary of State for Foreign Affairs why the Polish Forces are being rapidly armed by His Majesty's Government, in view of the fact that the Polish Government claims to be in a state of war with the Soviet Government, and that in their recent proposals to the Soviet Government His Majesty's Government promised not to render assistance to any Power or Powers engaged in war against the Soviet Union.[25]

After the German invasion of the Soviet Union, these attacks became more intense.[26] The problem of the Polish soldiers of Jewish origin returned several times to the British Parliament, where the Communist Gallacher spoke about "the vicious character" of the Polish press. The *Daily Worker* sneered that the Polish army was "something between a gang of brigands and a music-hall . . ." and called the Mikołajczyk cabinet "the utterly unrepresentative émigré band which does duty as the Polish Government in London."[27] Even English conservative newspapers published anti-Polish cartoons.[28] The British government pressed the Poles to find a compromise with the Soviets and to end press polemics with them.[29]

On the other hand, especially after the signing of the Maisky-Sikorski Agreement of July 30, 1941, the situation of the Polish government and its press was getting harder, due to intense activities of the Polish political opposition and to Polish anti-Semitic publications. In the fall of 1940, the case of the anti-Semitic paper *Jestem Polakiem* (I am a Pole), published by former members of the prewar National Radical Camp (Obóz Narodowo Radykalny, ONR), became widely discussed.[30] The government issued the statement that only one Polish political paper should be published and announced that

The publication *Jestem Polakiem* (I am a Pole) which was not
supported by any of the political parties composing the national
unity, did not concur. This is harmful and must be condemned as
a violation of national discipline.[31]

Eventually, *Jestem Polakiem* was forced to close in May 1941.
Manipulating with paper control and in cooperation with the British
administration, the government-in-exile also suspended several other
periodicals, including the outstanding *Wiadomości Polskie* (The Polish
News) which opposed the government's policies, especially those concerning Polish-Soviet relations and the eastern borders of Poland.[32]

Many Polish periodicals, political organizations, and individuals criticized *Dziennik Polski*. They questioned its quality and claimed that the
supervision by the Minister, Stroński, paralyzed the initiative and limited
the freedom of the editorial staff. According to the paper's critics, because
it was run by representatives of various allied governing parties, it was
inconsistent and lacked a clear ideological profile. *Dziennik* was ridiculed
for being too flattering towards the government. Many Poles did not trust
the paper, claiming that it added to the overwhelming confusion of the
émigré society, was too optimistic, included too many platitudes, and
resembled the over-confident propaganda of the prewar Polish regime.
Some journalists left the paper because it was unpopular and, allegedly,
too pro-Soviet. Others objected to unfair attacks published by the paper
against such outstanding personalities as General Kazimierz Sosnkowski,
who succeeded Sikorski as Commander-in-Chief, or journalist Zygmunt
Nowakowski, who left *Dziennik*, cooperated closely with *Wiadomości
Literackie*, and sharply criticized General Sikorski's successor, Stanisław
Mikołajczyk.[33]

Dziennik Polski could have been better edited, and some of its critics
were right. But in spite of all the criticism and pressure from many sides,
the paper was not bad. It gave its readers quick and generally reliable
information, and most of its comments were reasonable. Unfair evaluations, superficial generalizations, and traditional Polish stereotypes happened on its pages, but all these diversions did not define the profile of the
paper. The same applies to the way in which *Dziennik* wrote about Jewish
matters.

The "Jewish question" did not belong to the most important problems
of the government-in-exile. It devoted much more time and energy to

other issues, such as the war with Germany, the international situation, Polish-British and Polish-Soviet relations, the eastern borders of Poland, the Polish refugees, and Polish army units in the West. These priorities were reflected in the official governmental press organ, especially during the first years of the war, when the German plans towards the Jews were not so clear as after 1941. The coverage of the Jewish issue by *Dziennik* looked different in different periods of the war.

The first of these periods lasted from the evacuation of the Polish government and the Polish Army from France to England in June 1940, until the outbreak of the Soviet-German war in June 1941. During this time, *Dziennik* published between five and eight news articles or commentaries on the Jewish situation every month. Usually, these were unsigned short articles of about 300 words located on the second or third page, mostly about anti-Jewish persecutions in occupied Poland and other European countries, especially France.[34] Longer articles (one-third of a page and more), interviews, or open letters appeared only about ten times during this entire year.[35] As a result, information about Jews was overshadowed by many other topics. Nevertheless, readers of *Dziennik Polski* could find in it relatively recent and accurate information about the most important changes in the Jewish situation in Poland.

In October 1940, the paper published several notes about the establishment of the Warsaw ghetto and the exchange of population between the Jewish and the "Aryan" sides.[36] On November 30, 1940, fourteen days after it had actually happened, the paper reported that the Warsaw ghetto was sealed. The same article listed other kinds of persecutions directed against the Jews of Warsaw, Kraków, and Łódź. Two weeks later, *Dziennik* gave some information on the Jewish administration and the Jewish police in the Warsaw ghetto.[37] The matter of the Jewish police and ghetto administration was later discussed several times.[38] On February 22, 1941, *Dziennik* reprinted the entire front page of *Nowy Kurier Warszawski*, published in Warsaw under German control. The reprint included the order of the Nazi governor of Warsaw about the establishment of the ghetto and a map of the ghetto. *Dziennik* added a comment about the terrible conditions of life in the sealed district.[39] Later, short articles about the ghettos of Łódź, Kraków, Tarnów, Bochnia, Kielce, and Otwock appeared, including a map of the "Jewish district" of Kraków and a reprint of the German order concerning the segregation of the population in that city.[40] *Dziennik* discussed rumors about a planned Jewish reservation in the Lublin area, and showed how the Germans antagonized the Polish and the Jewish population by intense propaganda about an alleged Jewish role as an economic exploiter of the Poles and about infectious diseases spread by the Jews.[41]

Most information from Poland came from the Swedish press and from analyses of Polish and German newspapers published in occupied Poland and in Germany. Before December 1940, there was no radio communication with the anti-Nazi underground in Poland. For example, a review of a long article about the "Development of Administration in the General Government," published in *Voelkischer Beobachter*, concluded correctly that there were four categories of population in occupied Poland: the best one, the Germans; the second best, the Ukrainians and the *"gorale"* (highlanders from the Tatra Mountains); the third category, the Poles; and the worst and special one: the Jews.[42]

Dziennik summarized the statements of several British MPs about anti-Semitism in the Polish Army in England and, previously, in France where, allegedly, the Polish-Jewish refugees had been forced by the Poles to join the Polish Army against their will.[43]

In order to clear this issue, the paper published an order of the Commander-in-Chief, General Sikorski, of August 5, 1940, and an open letter of a Polish officer of Jewish origin, who protested against the offensive anti-Polish statements in the House of Commons.[44] The order obliged officers of the Polish Army to prevent any ethnic discord, and stated that every soldier who had fought for Poland was a good Pole, regardless of his religion and ethnic background.[45]

In order to build a bridge between the Poles and the Jews, *Dziennik* quoted several statements of Ignacy Schwarzbart, a representative of the Jewish national minority in the Polish National Council (Rada Narodowa), a Parliament-in-exile. Schwarzbart also wrote for the newspaper and emphasized that, although anti-Semitic events used to happen in Polish society and the Polish Army, the parties of the governing Polish coalition strove against anti-Semitism. The Polish Jews, according to Schwarzbart, were loyal towards Poland, their fatherland, and would fulfill their obligations as Polish citizens. Schwarzbart had visited several Polish military camps, had interviewed soldiers and officers, and expressed his satisfaction about the situation in the army.[46] Initially, probably until 1942, Schwarzbart believed that the Jews and Poles suffered together and hoped that this "common fate" ("wspólnota losu") would help to build a democratic multi-national Polish state after the war.[47]

Dziennik Polski wrote frequently about Polish-Jewish cooperation. For example it reported on a large meeting organized by the Council of Polish Jewry in Great Britain (Międzystowarzyszeniowa Rada Żydostwa Polskiego w Wielkiej Brytanii) and the Organizational Committee of the Polish Jewry Representation in London (Komitet Organizacyjny Reprezentacji Żydostwa Polskiego w Londynie) on November 3, 1940.[48] Four ministers of the Polish government-in-exile, the vice-president and leading representatives of the National Council, and a group of generals representing the Polish military leadership, took part in this meeting. Among several pronouncements and lectures of Polish and Jewish leaders, there was an important speech by the Minister of Labor and Social Welfare, Jan Stańczyk. He condemned racism and anti-Semitism, and talked about a common fight of all Polish citizens against the Nazi aggressors. On behalf of the Polish government, he assured the Jews that they would enjoy equal rights with all other Polish citizens, and would be able to cultivate their culture, religion, and language after the war in liberated Poland. The next issue of *Dziennik Polski* quoted formal telegrams expressing support and loyalty towards Poland which the leaders of the Council of Polish Jewry had sent to the President of Poland and to the Polish Commander-in-Chief after this meeting.[49] On March 26, 1941, during a session of the National Council, Ignacy Schwarzbart stated that Stańczyk's declaration was very important and constructive in terms of Polish-Jewish relations. Schwarzbart emphasized that the Polish Jews participated in the struggle for Poland and they expected that the future Polish authorities would abandon the prewar "evacuation" and mass emigration policy. *Dziennik* published a long and detailed summary of Schwarzbart's speech.[50]

The paper also devoted a lot of space to the official visit of General Sikorski to Washington in April 1941. After his return to London, the government-in-exile met several times to discuss the premier's report on his trip. The Jewish issue belonged to the most important topics addressed at these meetings, since Sikorski's visit had provoked very diversified repercussions in the American Jewish press, including unfriendly comments about Polish anti-Semitism. In response, during his visit, Sikorski had again condemned the anti-Semitic *Jestem Polakiem*, and stated that freedom of religion, freedom of speech, freedom from fear of attack, freedom of information, freedom of the press, and freedom from want were the most important principles of his government, and that the Jews would have equal duties and equal rights in postwar Poland. Sikorski repeated this declaration on June 4, 1941, during one of the government meetings that reviewed his trip to Washington. The government issued a special formal statement approving this declaration and condemning anti-Semitism. *Dziennik* gave the full text of this statement on its first page, right below the paper's title.[51]

Dziennik also reported about cooperation between Polish and Jewish organizations in the United States[52] and about a banquet organized in London by the Jewish Relief Fund (Komitet Pomocy dla Uchodźców Żydów z Polski) to honor a similar Polish Relief Fund (Polski Komitet Pomocy). During the banquet, the chief rabbi of Great Britain and several Jewish-British leaders gave friendly pro-Polish speeches.[53] The paper also summarized a formal letter sent by the representative of Polish Jewry in the National Council, Ignacy Schwarzbart, to Vice-Premier Kazimierz Sosnkowski, on the eve of the anniversary of the Constitution of May 3, 1791.[54]

Several times, however, the paper assumed an ambiguous attitude, or published articles that could not be appreciated by the Jews. Some of them stated that the Jews had enjoyed a privileged status at the beginning of Soviet occupation of the Eastern Polish provinces.[55] Later, two articles explained that the Jewish situation in the Soviet-occupied territories had worsened.[56] In the summer of 1940, the paper published a strange note forbidding the British press to criticize the anti-Semitic *Jestem Polakiem* and to apply British standards ("if not British-Jewish standards") to Poland.[57] In April 1941, *Dziennik* reversed its attitude: it condemned the anti-Semitic periodical and quoted the above mentioned official statement of the Polish government.[58] In January 1941, however, a controversial note had appeared on the front page. Entitled "Those, who suffered the most," it described the fate of the Poles of Christian religion and Jewish background, who were persecuted as converts and traitors in the Warsaw ghetto by its Jewish administration.[59] Four days later, on the third page, the paper published a protest letter from Ignacy Schwarzbart, who called the information unbelievable and offensive to the Jews. The paper's editorial answered that *Dziennik* could not limit itself to descriptions of suffering of only one section of Polish society, namely Jewish, and had to write about the Poles, too. This answer was grossly unfair, considering that a clear majority of sad news from Poland was devoted to the calamities of the Poles.[60]

The Nazi aggression against the Soviet Union opened a new chapter in the history of the Polish government-in-exile and its press. The entire war situation of Poland changed dramatically. On July 30, 1941, the Polish government, intensely pressed by the British, signed a treaty with the Soviet authorities. Poland and the Soviet Union became allies. A large part, if not a majority, of Polish public opinion reacted very unfavorably to the signing of the Maisky-Sikorski Treaty, and believed that it threatened the Polish eastern border.[61] The representatives of the National Democratic Party left the government coalition. After the Nazi invasion, the Soviet Union seemed to be very close to final defeat and disintegration. In late June, July, and August 1941, *Dziennik Polski* and all other Polish papers printed in England were dominated by reports about these matters, and Jewish news appeared rarely, at most two or three times a month.[62]

In September and October 1941, *Dziennik* returned to its customary coverage of Jewish matters. The paper reported on the activities of Jewish organizations in Great Britain[63] and told of their support for Poland.[64] Several articles brought new details about life in the Polish ghettos.[65] However, a new, gruesome tone characterized these articles. *Dziennik* reported on deportations of German Jews to Poland, and about the Slovak Jews who were sent in an unknown direction and virtually disappeared.[66] Also, in several Polish towns, only the last Jewish remnants survived, and entire communities were deported.[67] On October 31, 1941, the paper reported that, by the end of August, the Germans had organized a new labor camp between the villages of Czyżewo, Zaręby and Kościelna, not far from Łomża. Six thousand German Jews were transported to this camp and machine-gunned in large ditches. The name of the camp was not mentioned, but this appears to have been one of the first press reports about Treblinka.[68]

From the spring of 1942, the Home Army operated better clandestine transmitters and improved greatly its contact with the government-in-exile. It received more information about the mass extermination of the Polish and the Jewish population in Poland than before and, at a special session on June 6, 1942, it prepared an alarming note to the Allies. The note stated that suppression of war crimes, committed by the Germans in Poland, and punishment of war criminals should be made one of the main war goals. On June 9, 1942, General Sikorski, in a speech that was aired by the BBC, described German atrocities in Poland.[69] *Dziennik* summarized Sikorski's speech, which concentrated on Polish suffering but also included a paragraph devoted to the Jews. The Premier stated clearly that there was no doubt that the Germans were going to murder the entire Jewish population of occupied Europe, and that tens of thousands of Jews had already been killed or had starved in the ghettos of Lublin, Vilna, Lwów, Stanisławów, Rzeszów, and Miechów.[70]

The BBC speech of General Sikorski in June 1942 opened a new period in the coverage of Jewish affairs by *Dziennik Polski*. At least two or three times a week thereafter, the paper published information about the Jews; frequently, three or more articles appeared in one issue. As in the previous periods, *Dziennik* tried to improve Polish-Jewish relations. It described the help given by American Jewish organizations to the Poles in the Soviet Union, and claimed that the Polish Jews in Russia were not neglected by Polish relief organizations. It reported that the British MPs who had attacked the Poles in 1940 and 1941 had abandoned their negative attitude. The paper described how warmly Minister Stańczyk was received by the Federation of the Polish Jews on June 25, 1942, and how cordially Rabbi Stephen S. Wise, President of the World Jewish Congress, thanked Stańczyk for his speech on that occasion which condemned anti-Semitism, and emphasizing the long lasting Polish-Jewish ties.[71] *Dziennik* continued to report on the activities of the Jewish representatives in the Polish National Council, Ignacy Szwarzbart and Szmul Zygielbojm, and the Jewish leaders in America and Great Britain.[72]

However, from early summer 1942, most "Jewish" news reports were devoted to the annihilation of Polish Jewry. In late October, November, and December 1942, articles about the Holocaust were published almost every day. In June, *Dziennik* reported about an epidemic of typhus and about hunger in the Warsaw ghetto.[73] The paper described how the ghetto of Kraków was shrinking.[74] On June 30, 1942, the paper published on the front page a story about the murder of one million Jews, including 700,000 Polish Jews, in occupied Europe. Several days later, *Dziennik* wrote that all the Jews of Poland had been concentrated in large ghettos by the German occupiers. The paper published comments of Schwarzbart and Szmul Zygielbojm (who had joined the Polish National Council in January 1942), on this news. These explained that this operation was undertaken to make the extermination of the Jews easier. Zygielbojm, who had come to London from occupied Poland and issued a special memorandum on the situation of the Polish Jewry, reported that about 6,000 Jews died every month in the Warsaw ghetto alone.[75] The paper quoted newspapers published underground in occupied Poland on the mass executions of Jews and Poles. It also reported on the deportations of Jews from Western Europe to Poland, and on the genocide of Romanian Jewry.[76] *Dziennik* analyzed publications of the Swedish press, which described German extermination operations in Poland, confirmed that about 700,000 Jews had been killed in Poland, and stated that altogether about 4 million people had disappeared in Poland since the beginning of the war.[77]

On July 29, 1942, seven days after the beginning of the large deportation of the Warsaw Jews to Treblinka, *Dziennik* published on the second page the following somewhat vague note under the heading "The Jews of Warsaw are deported to the East":

An order was issued concerning a deportation of 6,000 Jews from the Warsaw ghetto. (. . .) Till now, two trains [full of Jews] were sent for execution (Dotychczas wywieziono już bez wieści 2 pociągi na stracenie). This news caused despair and numerous suicides in the ghetto. The Polish Police was removed and replaced by the Lithuanian shaulis, Latvians, and Ukrainians. Constant shooting is heard in the streets and houses of the ghetto.

It seems that, initially, the Polish underground, the government-in-exile, and the *Dziennik Polski* editorial staff were not certain about the character of the German activities in the Warsaw ghetto. The quoted news was received in London on July 26 and probably described "the beginning of the annihilation."[78] Later, the Germans sent several trains a day to Treblinka from the Warsaw ghetto; but, for reasons difficult to explain, *Dziennik* did not write about it. Finally, in the last days of November 1942, *Dziennik* published several front-page articles on the liquidation of the Warsaw ghetto. Only 40,000 Jews survived out of 433,000, informed

a major article. It went on to describe precisely how the German operation was organized, and added that the smaller ghettos of the Warsaw
regions (Falenica, Rembertów, Nowy Dwór, Kałuszyn, and Mińsk
Mazowiecki) were also liquidated, and that only one ghetto survived in
the Vilna region. The paper repeated several times that the German goal
of total extermination of the Jews was beyond any doubt and that about
one million Polish Jews had been killed by the end of October 1942.[79]

Dziennik also reported on Polish official reaction to the Holocaust. A
long front-page article described General Sikorski's participation in a
large protest demonstration organized by the Board of Deputies of British
Jews at the Royal Albert Hall in London on October 29, 1942. There,
Sikorski again condemned the genocide of the Jews in Poland and, on
behalf of the Polish government, assured the Polish Jews that "in common
with all Polish citizens, they shall reap all the benefit from the victory of
the Allied Nations."[80] The paper reported that the Polish National Council
devoted several meetings to the Jewish Holocaust in Poland. During one
of these meetings, Vice-Premier Stanisław Mikołajczyk gave a speech.
He protested against the genocide, asked the Allies for help, and stated
that the Poles were unable to stop the German crimes. A similar resolution from the National Council was published by *Dziennik Polski* as a
message from the official representatives of Poland to the Allied
Nations.[81] A week later, the Polish Minister of Foreign Affairs, Edward
Raczyński, sent a special, eleven-page memorandum to the governments
of the Allied Nations. The memorandum, summarized by *Dziennik*,
emphasized that one-third of Polish Jewry had already been murdered by
the Germans, and that the Polish government-in-exile had warned the
governments of the Allied Nations repeatedly about the genocide of the
Jews in Poland. Raczyński repeated his message in a speech given on the
Home Radio Service on December 17, 1942.[82]

Later, *Dziennik Polski* reported with satisfaction that the Raczyński
message was discussed by the *Times*, in the British Parliament, and by the
Swedish press, and that it had persuaded the Allied Powers to sign a joint
declaration condemning the Holocaust.[83] *Dziennik* wrote about a week of
mourning announced by the Chief Rabbi of the British Empire, in memory of the killed Jews of Poland, and about an exchange of telegrams
between Minister Raczyński and the president of the World Zionist
Organization, Chaim Weizmann, who thanked the Polish minister for his

words of support and friendship.[84] The paper also summarized a telegram, "an appeal of desperation," sent by Zygielbojm to Churchill and Roosevelt, begging them to save the remnants of Polish Jewry.[85]

The period of very intense, almost daily coverage of Jewish matters by the *Dziennik Polski* continued into 1943. Most news about the Jews looked like nightmarish obituaries. *Dziennik Polski* quoted the Nazi paper *Ostland* to the effect that successive Polish regions were becoming *Judenrein* as a result of the German activities. *Ostland* listed 41 open *Judenwohnbezirke* and 13 closed ghettos in the General Government by the end of 1942.[86] An article in the *Krakauer Zeitung* indicated that the Lublin ghetto had been liquidated, wrote *Dziennik Polski*.[87] A local German radio station in Zeesen broadcast a talk by a German journalist who visited Kraków and noticed a visible improvement of food supply in that city, due to the fact there were no more Jews there.[88] This information was confirmed by the Polish underground: the Germans killed thousands of Jews during the liquidation of the Kraków ghetto in March 1943.[89] *Dziennik* quoted the Swedish press on the massacres of the Jews in the Vilna region, and on the miserable life of the last remnants of the Warsaw ghetto.[90] *Dziennik* also quoted the American and Turkish press. In February 1943, one of the Istanbul newspapers published a long article titled "Poland—the graveyard of the Jews."[91] These sometimes chaotic reports given by the *Dziennik Polski* assumed a terrible sequence: first, according to *Ostdeutscher Beobachter* about 130,000 Dutch Jews were deported to the ghettos of Poland; according to British intelligence, the Jews of Salonika were deported to Poland; then, according to the Swedish press, the entire ghetto of Rowne, about 30,000 people, was sent into an "unknown direction."[92]

In the first months of 1943, information about particular events was published rather promptly. On January 20, two days after the German attempt to liquidate the last remnants of the Warsaw ghetto, *Dziennik* published a front page article, right beneath the paper title: "Days of Horror in Warsaw. Sent to the East in the sealed train cars." This article of 120 words, printed with spaced out font and subtitled "The Germans deport thousands of Poles to new concentrations camps," included information about the Polish and Jewish population of Warsaw. The last one third of the article stated:

There is an atmosphere of horror in Warsaw. Thousands of families were separated. The most cruel rumors about the fate of arrested people circulate in Warsaw. The horror is intensified by the news from the ghetto. On the night of January 17/18 and on Monday, shooting was heard from the ghetto. There is a conviction in Warsaw, that the Germans are liquidating the rest of the Jews in the ghetto. As we already know, out of 450,000 inhabitants of the Warsaw ghetto in July [1942] only 33,000 were left there on January 1[, 1943].

The same issue of January 20, 1943, also included a second-page article "55 Jewish camps of torture in Poland." These articles were followed later by several more specific descriptions of the extermination of the Warsaw Jews and, finally, by news on the Warsaw Ghetto Uprising. *Dziennik* wrote about the gas chambers of Treblinka, that killed 7,000 people a day, and quoted a message from Poland that only 200,000 Jews seemed to have survived the large liquidation actions of 1942 and early 1943.[93]

Dziennik Polski also discussed the Soviet communiqué which stated that Henryk Erlich and Wiktor Alter had been executed for allegedly anti-Soviet activities, cooperation with the Polish intelligence, and defeatism. The Erlich-Alter affair, which moved public opinion troughout the world, also evoked a profound response from the Poles in England. *Dziennik* described protest meetings and resolutions of the Polish National Committee and the Polish Socialist Party.[94] The paper also wrote much about the suicide of Szmul Zygielbojm on the night of May 11, 1943. *Dziennik* gave a detailed curriculum vitae of Zygielbojm, and described his attempts to save Polish Jewry. The paper reported on Zygielbojm's funeral and noted the reactions of the Polish government-in-exile, and of Polish and international public opinion.[95] *Dziennik* published the letter left by Zygielbojm in its entirety. This letter included fragments unpleasant to the Polish government:

The responsibility for the crime of murdering the whole Jewish nation in Poland falls first of all upon the perpetrators but, indirectly, also on the entire mankind. [. . .] I have to state that although the Polish government did a lot to mobilize world public opinion, yet the government did it in an insufficient way and was not able to do something extraordinary, something which would be adequate to the dimension of the tragedy that took place in the Country.[96]

Between June 1942 and the spring of 1943, most articles about the Jews appeared on the first and the second pages, together with the most important political and military information. Several times, articles about the extermination of the Jews constituted the most important news of an issue. It was so on July 29, October 30, November 26 and 30, and on December 11, 1942 (the largest or the second largest title directly under the name of the newspaper, between one-sixth and one-third of the front page).

From the late spring of 1943, Jewish issues were getting less and less visible. Other dramatic events overshadowed the news about the last remnants of the Jewish community in Poland. First, it was the discovery of the Katyn graves in April 1943, then the death of General Sikorski on July 4, 1943, the breaking off of Polish-Soviet diplomatic relations, deteriorating Polish-Soviet contacts, and clear indications that Stalin had new plans for Poland: the creation of the Union of Polish Patriots and of the communist-controlled Polish army in the Soviet Union. In 1944 and 1945, the Poles in England were getting desperate. It was obvious that Poland, theoretically a member of the victorious alliance, practically would lose the war. A large part of the Polish refugees in England, particularly those who left Russia with the Anders army in 1942, were from Poland's prewar eastern territories which by the end of the war were incorporated into the Soviet Union. The Poles from Eastern Poland knew that their world was disappearing.

From the summer of 1943, the coverage of the Holocaust in *Dziennik Polski* returned to its pre-1942 intensity. Every month, there were between four and nine articles or longer notes on specifically Jewish issues. In addition, *Dziennik* published general articles on the concentration and extermination camps, on gas chambers, medical experiments, hunger, deportations, economic exploitation, arrests, public executions, and numerous other terrible aspects of the Nazi New Order. The intention of these general articles was to show the sufferings of the entire population of occupied Poland, and the Jews were barely mentioned in them.

The Jewish subject was once more overshadowed by Polish news. The paper published long lists of names of people killed by the Germans. Almost always these were names of Christian Poles.

Among the articles devoted specifically to the Jews after the summer of 1943, the most numerous category was devoted to the martyrdom of the last Jews in Poland. *Dziennik* described the last Polish ghettos and their liquidation, German plans for the emptied ghettos, German cover-up of the Nazi crimes, the gas chambers, the camps of Auschwitz, Majdanek, Treblinka, Bełżec, Sobibór, Starogard, Potulice, Kosów Podlaski, Trawniki, Pomiechówek.[97] By the end of 1944, *Dziennik* quoted estimates that only about 450,000 Jews survived in Poland.[98]

After the summer of 1943, critics of Polish anti-Semitism and the Polish-Jewish polemics once more became visible and intense. A polemic provoked by the Yiddish *Morning Journal* (New York) was quite typical. The paper stated that the government-in-exile was not able to represent the Polish Jews because it did not include any Jewish ministers. When *Dziennik* named ministers Ludwik Grosfeld and Herman Lieberman, the Yiddish *Morning Journal* answered that Grosfeld could not be considered a real Jew because he belonged to the Polish Socialist Party and was assimilated.[99] The readers of *Dziennik Polski* read about Polish Jews who, allegedly persecuted in the Polish Army, deserted and joined the British Army, and about a session of the British Parliament devoted to this issue.[100]

Relatively numerous articles reported on the fate of the Jews outside Poland: in other countries occupied or controlled by the Nazis and their allies, in Denmark, France, Hungary, Czechoslovakia, and in Germany itself. There was even an analysis of the situation of Algerian Jewry.[101] Another category of articles reported on activities of the Jews in Great Britain, America, Palestine, and other countries of the free world.[102]

From its first days, *Dziennik Polski* tried to build a bridge between the Poles and the Jews. Frequently, it showed the sufferings of the Poles and the Jews, and their fight against the Nazis, as a source of a future Polish-Jewish rapprochement and fraternization.[103] The paper quoted the *Gauleiter* of Upper Silesia, Bracht, to the effect that the Poles and the Jews should be treated equally.[104] Several articles described the participation of Polish Jews, living in England, in Polish national and governmental activities.[105] The paper wrote proudly about those Poles in the occupied homeland who helped the Jews, and about the Committee for Aid to Jews (*Żegota*).[106] A number of articles described with satisfaction instances of cooperation between the Polish government-in-exile and various Jewish organizations in America and England, and told about Jewish soldiers fighting in the Polish Army.[107] *Dziennik* reported on the Jewish holidays and celebrations in the Polish Army and outside it,[108] and criticized anti-Jewish articles published in some Polish periodicals in England.[109] On the first anniversary of the 1943 Warsaw Ghetto Uprising, the paper published a special article, and summarized an anniversary letter written by the Prime Minister Mikołajczyk.[110]

There were many waves of political emigration in the history of Poland, but never before had any Polish emigrant group produced so rich a literature and so many periodicals. Polish soldiers and civilian refugees in Britain after 1939 had a strong conviction that propaganda was an important part of the war effort.[111] Polish émigré newspapers and periodicals participated in the national debate on a program for Poland's future. The Jewish and national minorities questions were an important part of this program.

Yet, the coverage of the Holocaust by *Dziennik Polski* was not fully adequate and satisfactory. Some information could have been published earlier, in a clearer and stronger way. From December 1940, the government-in-exile had a direct radio contact with the anti-German resistance in Poland. Yet, a large part of all the telegrams (sometimes 50%) sent from Warsaw were lost or were not quite understandable. In London, the messages from the home country were transmitted to the press through the Ministries of Interior and Information and Documentation. It meant that, to a great extent, communication with Poland was controlled by politicians from the peasant movement who were frequently not friendly towards the Jews.[112] Quite often, the Poles in London thought that the tragic news from Poland was exaggerated. Some Polish journalists and politicians were afraid that the news about the sufferings of the Jews would make the Polish martyrdom pale. Ignacy Schwarzbart believed that between July and October 1942, during and immediately after the liquidation of the Warsaw ghetto, Mikołajczyk, the Minister of Interior at that time, deliberately blocked information on the extermination of the Jews. Several ministers and influential émigré politicians were afraid that Polish public opinion both in England and in Poland would consider the government-in-exile pro-Jewish (the Jews were the only national minority represented in the National Council).[113] On the pages of *Dziennik Polski* the genocide of the Jews was overshadowed by news about the extermination of the Poles. On occasion, the death of a well-known Polish personality was described better than the annihilation of an entire Jewish ghetto. Some editors of the *Dziennik* were not friendly towards Jews and published articles that irritated or offended them. The "Jewish policy" of the paper resulted from many political forces, disagreements, pressures, and war chaos.

On the other hand, however, analysis of *Dziennik Polski* demonstrates that there was no "conspiracy of silence" on the part of the Polish government-in-exile and such evaluations as David Rosenthal's statement that "During all of 1942, news about the destruction of Polish Jewry was given only a few sentences altogether in official government communiqués"[114] are plainly untrue. Not a single anti-Semitic article appeared in *Dziennik Polski* during the entire war. The way in which the newspaper reported about the Holocaust was different in different periods of the war. Less intense before the summer of 1942 and after the summer of 1943, it was very diligent during this crucial period in the history of the Holocaust in Poland. Simultaneously, between 1941 and 1943, the National Democrats were not members of the coalition that formed the government-in-exile, having left the coalition in protest against the Maisky-Sikorski Pact. As a result, the National Democrats, who were far less friendly towards the Jews than their former colleagues from other government parties (Polish Socialist Party, Peasant Party, Party of Labor), were unable, during this critical period, to influence the way the government periodicals covered the Holocaust. *Dziennik Polski* was read by tens of thousands of Poles, by Czechs whose press was much less developed in England, by employees of the English and Soviet Foreign Offices, and by members of the British intellectual elite who knew Polish, such as Louis Namier.[115]

With all their twists and mistakes, Polish governmental publications in Britain, including *Dziennik Polski*, were very important when it came to informing the West about the killing of the Jews in German-occupied Poland.

Notes:

1. This is a revised version of the paper originally presented at the Yeshiva University Conference on Journalism During the Holocaust. A somewhat different version was also published in the Tel-Aviv University journal of Polish Jewish history, *Gal-ed* 17 (2000), pp. 57–85.

2. David Engel, *In the Shadow of Auschwitz. The Polish Government-In-Exile and the Jews, 1939–1942* (Chapel Hill and London, 1987), p. 9.

3. Jan Hulewicz, "Polski ruch wydawniczy w W. Brytanii w latach wojny 1940–1945," *Twórczość* vol. 2, no. 7–8 (July–August 1946), p. 181.

4. Marian Marek Drozdowski, "Polonia a powstanie w getcie warszawskim," *Przegląd Polonijny*, vol. 5, no. 1 (1979), p. 21.

5. Ksawery Pruszyński, *Nasi nad Tamiza* (Kraków, 1966), p. 222.

6. Stanisław Strumph Wojtkiewicz, *Książka szła za emigrantem* (Wrocław: Ossolineum, 1963), pp. 384–388.

7. J. Hulewicz, op. cit., p. 185, 188; Stanisława Lewandowska, *Prasa polskiej emigracji wojennej 1939–1945* (Warsaw, 1993), pp. 51–55; *Literatura Polska na Obczyźnie 1940–1960*, vol. 2, ed.Tymon Terlecki (London, 1965), p. 479; K. Pruszyński, op. cit., p. 223.

8. Hanna Świderska, "Z dziejów polskiej prasy opozycyjnej w Londynie 1941–1945," *Zeszyty Historyczne* no. 101 (Paris, 1992), p. 58; S. Lewandowska, op. cit., pp. 69–78; J. Hulewicz, op. cit., p. 190; *Catalogue of Periodicals in Polish or Relating to Poland and Other Slavonic Countries Published Outside Poland since September 1st, 1939*, ed. by Maria Danielewicz and Barbara Jablonska (London, 1971); Rafał Habielski, "Emigracja i polityka. *'Wiadomości Polskie'* wobec dylematów wychodzstwa 1940–1944," *Kwartalnik Historii Prasy Polskiej* vol. XXV, no. 3, pp. 57–86; Stanisław Mackiewicz, *Październik 1941. Fakty i Dokumenty* (London, 1941), pp. 22–28; Stanisław Mackiewicz, *Czarnym atramentem* (London, 1942), pp. 4–23.

9. *Literatura Polska na Obczyźnie*, pp. 503–505; S. Lewandowska, op. cit., pp. 62–69; J. Hulewicz, op. cit., pp. 189–193; R. Habielski, op. cit., pp. 57–59.

10. S. Lewandowska, op. cit., p. 64.

11. Ibid., p. 64.

12. Ibid., p. 64.

13. Ibid., p. 64–65; Eugeniusz Duraczyński, *Rząd Polski na uchodzstwie 1939–1945* (Warsaw, 1993), pp. 104, 418.

14. S. Lewandowska, op. cit., p. 64–65.

15. Witold Leitgeber, *W Kwaterze Prasowej. Dziennik z lat wojny 1939–1945* (London, 1972), p. 252, 275, 283; S. Lewandowska, op. cit., p. 73–74; *Literatura Polska na Obczyźnie*, pp. 508–509.

16. S. Lewandowska, op. cit., p. 73–74; *Literatura Polska na Obczyźnie*, p. 503.

17. *Poland in the British Parliament 1939–1945*, vol. 1, eds. Wacław Jędrzejewicz and Pauline C. Ramsey (New York, 1946), p. 459.

18. S. Lewandowska, op. cit., p. 66; J. Hulewicz, op. cit., pp. 189–190.

19. S. Lewandowska, op. cit., p. 64–65; J. Hulewicz, op. cit., pp. 189–190.

20. W. Leitgeber, *W Kwaterze Prasowej*, p. 66.

21. Ibid., p. 116; H. Świderska, op. cit., pp. 60–65.

22. *Poland in the British Parliament 1939–1945*, vol. 1, p. 433.

23. Ibid., p. 438.

24. Ibid., p. 438–463.

25. Ibid., p. 449.

26. H. Świderska, op. cit., pp. 60.

27. *Poland in the British Parliament 1939–1945*, vol. 2, eds. Wacław Jędrzejewicz and Pauline C. Ramsey (New York, 1959), p. 262.

28. Witold Babiński, "Prasa angielska w sprawach Polskich na przełomie lat 1943–1944," *Zeszyty Historyczne*, no. 20 (1971), pp. 3–33.

29. Ibid., pp. 60–65; Edward Raczyński, *In Allied London* (London, 1962), pp. 134, 201–203, 210–213, 251–253; *Poland in the British Parliament 1939–1945*, vol. 2, pp. 232–233, 262–265.

30. David Engel, *In the Shadow of Auschwitz*, pp. 71–74; J. Hulewicz, op. cit., p. 190; Zygmunt Nagórski Senior, *Wojna w Londynie. Wspomnienia 1939–1945* (Paris, 1966), p. 76; Dariusz Stoła,"Kwestia żydowska w Radzie Narodowej RP (1939–1945)," *Więź* (Warsaw), no. 4, 1992, p. 92.

31. *Poland in the British Parliament 1939–1945*, vol. 1, p. 459.

32. H. Świderska, op. cit., pp. 59, 60–75; R. Habielski, op. cit., p. 85; J. Hulewicz, op. cit., p. 191; Marian Marek Drozdowski, "The Attitude of Sikorski's Government to the Tragedy of the Polish Jews (1939–1944)," *Acta Polonia Historica*, no. 52 (1985), p. 150.

33. J. Hulewicz, op. cit. pp. 189; S. Lewandowska, op. cit., pp. 63–65; S. Mackiewicz, *Październik 1941*, pp. 25–26; S. Mackiewicz, *Czarnym atramentem*, pp. 5, 21; Z. Nagórski Senior, *Wojna w Londynie*, pp. 76–77;

Babiński, *Przyczynki Historyczne do Okresu 1939–1945* (London, 1967), p. 269; E. Duraczyński, *Rząd Polski*, p. 245.

34. *Dziennik Polski*, July. 22, 29; Aug. 13; Sept. 17–19; Oct. 3, 16, 17, 23, 24, 25, 28, 29; Nov. 30; Dec. 12, 1940; Jan. 3, Feb. 13, 22, March 4, 15, 26, 29, April 4, 5, 24, May 1, 3, 9, 22, 24, June 5, 9, 10, 20, 1941.

35. *Dziennik Polski*, Aug. 27; Sept. 25, 28; Nov. 5 (two articles) 1940, Jan. 18, Feb. 22, April 4, 12, June 20, 1941.

36. *Dziennik Polski*, Oct. 17, 23, 25, 28, 29, 1940.

37. *Dziennik Polski*, Dec. 12, 1940, p. 2.

38 *Dziennik Polski*, Jan. 3, May 1, 1941.

39. *Dziennik Polski*, Feb. 22, 1941, p. 3.

40. *Dziennik Polski*, March 15, 1941, p.2; March 29, 1941, p. 2; May 1, 1941, p. 2; June 5, 9, 20, 1941, p. 2.

41. *Dziennik Polski*, March 26, 1941, p.2; May 3, 22, 1941, p. 2.

42. *Dziennik Polski*, Sept. 28, 1940, p. 2.

43. *Dziennik Polski*, Aug. 27, 1940, p. 2.

44. *Dziennik Polski*, Sept. 25, 1940, p. 2.

45. *Dziennik Polski*, Aug. 19, 1940, p. 3.

46. *Dziennik Polski*, Aug. 8, p. 2; Oct. 16, 1940, p. 2; April 31, 1941, p. 1.

47. Dariusz Stola, *Nadzieja i zagłada. Ignacy Schwarzbart—żydowski przedstawiciel w Radzie Narodowej RP (1940–1945)* (Warsaw, 1995), p. 66.

48. *Dziennik Polski*, Nov. 5, 1940, pp. 2–3.

49. *Dziennik Polski*, Nov. 6, 1940, pp. 2.

50. *Dziennik Polski*, April 4, 1941, p. 2.

51. *Dziennik Polski*, June 12, 1941; M. M. Drozdowski, "Tragedy of the Polish Jews," pp. 150–151; Kazimierz Iranek-Osmecki, *He Who Saves One Life* (New York: Crown Publishers, 1971), pp. 182–185.

52. *Dziennik Polski*, May 24, 1941, p. 2.

53. *Dziennik Polski*, Jan. 18, 1941, p. 2.

54. *Dziennik Polski*, May 9, 1941, p. 2.

55 *Dziennik Polski*, July 31, 1940, p. 2.

56. *Dziennik Polski*, Jan. 3, 15, 1941, p. 2.

57. *Dziennik Polski*, Aug. 27, 1940, p. 2.

58. *Dziennik Polski*, April 12, 1941, p. 2; April 15, 1941, p. 1.

59. *Dziennik Polski*, Jan. 9, 1941, p. 1.

60. *Dziennik Polski*, Jan. 13, 1941, p. 3.

61. W. Leitgeber, op. cit., p. 136; Witold Babiński, *Przyczynki historyczne do okresu 1939–1945* (London: B. Świderski, 1967), p. 78.

62. *Dziennik Polski*, July 17, 25, Aug. 2, 4, 1941.

63. *Dziennik Polski*, Sept. 20, 1941, p. 1.

64. *Dziennik Polski*, Sept. 2, 1941, p.2; Nov. 20, 1941, p. 2.

65. *Dziennik Polski*, Sept. 26, Oct. 31, Nov. 5, 15, 17, Dec. 3, 27, 30, 1941; Jan. 23, Feb. 7, March 4, April 20, May 29, 1942.

66. *Dziennik Polski*, March 18, 1942, p.2; May 23, 1941, p. 2; June 3, 1942, p. 3.

67. *Dziennik Polski*, March 7, 1942, p. 2.

68. *Dziennik Polski*, Oct. 31, 1941, p. 1.

69. E. Duraczyński, *Rząd Polski*, p. 206; M. M. Drozdowski, "Tragedy of the Polish Jews," pp. 152–154; K. Iranek-Osmecki, *He Who Saves One Life*, pp. 186–188.

70. *Dziennik Polski*, June 10, 1942, p. 1–2.

71. *Dziennik Polski*, June 15, 23, July 2, Oct. 28, 1941.

72. *Dziennik Polski*, July 10, 24, 1941, p. 1.

73. *Dziennik Polski*, June 23, July 2, 1942.

74. *Dziennik Polski*, July 9, 1942, p. 2.

75. *Dziennik Polski*, June 39, July 9, 10, 1942.

76. *Dziennik Polski*, July 29, 1942, pp. 1–2; Aug. 5, 24, Oct. 6, 22, 1942.

77. *Dziennik Polski*, Oct. 22, 26, 1942.

78. Dariusz Stola, "In the Shadow of the Facts," *Polin. Studies in Polish Jewry*, 8: 339.

79. *Dziennik Polski*, Nov. 20, 26, 27, 1942.

80. *Dziennik Polski*, Oct. 30, 1942, pp. 1–2; M. M. Drozdowski, "The Tragedy of the Polish Jews," pp. 154–155.

81. *Dziennik Polski*, Nov. 28, 30, Dec. 11, 1942.

82. *Dziennik Polski*, Dec. 11, 18, 1942.

83. *Dziennik Polski*, Dec. 11, 14, 16, 18, 1942.

84. *Dziennik Polski*, Dec. 14, 17, 18, 1942, p. 2.

85. *Dziennik Polski*, Dec. 17, 1942, p. 2.

86. *Dziennik Polski*, Jan. 11, 20, 1943.

87. *Dziennik Polski*, March 2, 1943, p. 2.

88. *Dziennik Polski*, March 26, 1943, p. 1.

89. *Dziennik Polski*, April 12, 1943, p. 2.

90. *Dziennik Polski*, Jan. 16, May 18, 22, 1943.

91. *Dziennik Polski*, Feb. 19, 1943, p. 2.

92. *Dziennik Polski*, April 13, June 9, 22, 1943.

93. *Dziennik Polski*, March 19, May 15, 22, June 5, 1943, front pages only.

94. *Dziennik Polski*, March 5, 6, 17, April 5, 19, 1943.

95. *Dziennik Polski*, May 14, 20, 22, 25, June 2, 1943.

96. *Dziennik Polski*, June 2, 1943, p. 2.

97. *Dziennik Polski*, July 22, Aug. 7, 10, 23, Oct. 3, 8, 9, 23, Nov. 8, 19, 1943, *Dziennik Polski i Dziennik Żołnierza*, Jan. 27, Feb. 28, March 17, 27, June 1, 13, July 13, Aug. 17, 31, Sept. 16, Dec. 13, 1944, Jan. 12, March 17, April 23, 1945.

98. *Dziennik Polski i Dziennik Żołnierza*, Dec. 29, 1944.

99. *Dziennik Polski*, July 22, 27, 1943.

100. *Dziennik Polski i Dziennik Żołnierza*, April 6, 13, 18, 27, May 8, 10, 1944.

101. *Dziennik Polski*, March 4, 1943, pp. 2–3; *Dziennik Polski i Dziennik Żołnierza*, March 31, May 2, June 9, July 5, Dec. 4, 1944, April 5, 25, 26, May 5, 1945.

102. *Dziennik Polski*, Sept. 8, Oct. 7, 1943; *Dziennik Polski i Dziennik Żołnierza*, April 25, July 15, Sept. 5, Nov. 28, 1944, Jan. 16, March 21, 1945.

103. *Dziennik Polski*, Jan. 23, 1943; *Dziennik Polski i Dziennik Żołnierza*, May, 2, 1944.

104. *Dziennik Polski*, Feb. 4, 1943, p. 2.

105. *Dziennik Polski*, July 19, Aug. 10, 1943; *Dziennik Polski i Dziennik Żołnierza*, Jan. 15, 20, 21, Sept. 6, 1944.

106. *Dziennik Polski*, Aug. 3, 1943; *Dziennik Polski i Dziennik Żołnierza*, Jan. 12, May 13, 27, 1944.

107. *Dziennik Polski*, Sept. 8, 1943; *Dziennik Polski i Dziennik Żołnierza*, Dec. 22, 1944.

108. *Dziennik Polski*, Oct. 6, 1943; *Dziennik Polski i Dziennik Żołnierza*, Oct. 20, 1944.

109. *Dziennik Polski*, Oct. 7, 1943.

110. *Dziennik Polski i Dziennik Żołnierza*, April 20, 1944, p. 2.

111. S. Strumph Wojtkiewicz, *Książka szła za emigrantem*, pp. 361–362.

112. Andrzej Friszke, "Rząd na obczyźnie wobec państwa podziemnego w kraju," *Władze RP na obczyznie podczas II wojny światowej 1939–1945*, ed. by Zbigniew Błażyński (London, 1994), p. 565; D. Stola, *Nadzieja*, pp. 155–156.

113. D. Stola, *Nadzieja*, pp. 160, 179–181.

114. David Rosenthal, "Shmuel Zygielboim's Suicide in Protest," *Midstream*, June-July 1993, p. 21.

115. H. Świderska, op. cit., pp. 64–82; W. Leitgeber, *W Kwaterze Prasowej*, p. 110, 235.

Ukrainian Journalism

"This Is the Way It Was!" Textual and Iconographic Images of Jews in the Nazi-Sponsored Ukrainian Press of Distrikt Galizien

Henry Abramson
Florida Atlantic University

The destruction of the Jews in Western Ukraine was almost total.[1] Figures for Eastern Galicia and neighboring Volhynia indicate that roughly ninety-eight percent of nearly a million Jews perished during the war.[2] The Jews of L'viv (Lwów, L'vov, Lemberg), the principal city of the region, suffered similar devastation. The late historian Philip Friedman calculated that he was one of the 823 survivors out of some 180,000 Jews present at the time of the Nazi conquest.[3] The aim of this paper is to examine the nature of one aspect of the German propaganda machine that contributed to this mass murder: the Ukrainian-language Nazi press. To a large extent, the anti-Jewish content of this press conformed to the paradigm that was replicated in many of the propaganda organs in other regions under German control. Several small differences exist, however, and these nuances shed some light on Nazi policy towards both Jews and Ukrainians.

Eastern Galicia had an ethnically heterogeneous population, divided principally between Poles, Ukrainians, and Jews, the latter being especially prominent in the urban sphere.[4] The region became part of reborn Poland after World War I, and was the principal battleground between Polish and Ukrainian nationalists during the interwar period. Jews often found themselves caught between "the hammer and the anvil" in this conflict, and occasionally suffered violent attacks if one group felt that the

Jews showed excessive sympathy for the rival cause.[5]

When the Nazis and the Soviets divided up East Central Europe according to the terms of the 1939 Molotov-Ribbentrop pact, Eastern Galicia fell into the Soviet zone. The region suffered nearly two years of rapid, forced Sovietization, a period in which the Ukrainian intelligentsia was persecuted severely.[6] Rightly or wrongly, the perception of many Ukrainians was that Jews figured prominently in the invading Communist movement, most heinously in the dreaded NKVD.[7] When the Nazis invaded in June of 1941, the Soviet prisons were opened up to reveal the mutilated bodies of many arrested Ukrainian leaders, sparking a massive outrage in the Ukrainian population. Pogroms erupted, some spontaneous and others organized by the Nazis, and Jews were taken to the prisons and forced to perform the difficult task of removing the bodies and cleaning up the human gore. On several occasions the pogromists vented their fury by executing these Jews, "in revenge" for the crimes of their hypothetical coreligionists.[8]

The Ukrainian nationalist leadership had placed much trust in the Nazis, hoping that they would sponsor the establishment of a state, and in fact the Ukrainians issued a declaration of independence on 30 June 1941. The Nazis, however, responded by promptly arresting the principal leaders, and the region was annexed to the General Government to the northwest (hence Galicia "District").[9] The Ukrainians soon began to feel the edge of the Nazi blade.[10]

The General Government had a functioning "Department for Public Enlightenment and Propaganda," headed by Joseph Goebbels, which published in German, Polish, Russian, Ukrainian, and even Yiddish.[11] Several papers were soon established in L'viv, the most prominent Ukrainian-language daily being *L'vivs'ki visti* (L'viv News).[12] While the paper acted as a conduit for Nazi propaganda, it delved deeply into areas of Ukrainian concern, particularly in literature and the student movement. The characterization of a sister publication generally holds true for *L'vivs'ki visti*: it "was not a German paper in the Ukrainian language, rather it was a Ukrainian paper, edited in the German reality," i.e., bearing in mind the reality of the German presence.[13] It was edited by Osyp Bondarovych, a prominent Ukrainian activist who had a long history of involvement in Ukrainian journalism.[14] Circulation in 1941 was 124,000, climbing to 296,000 in 1942 and 238,000 in 1943, and then dropping to 93,000 in

1944.[15] It was probably distributed at no cost to readers.[16]

A typical edition of *L'vivs'ki visti* was four to six pages long. Despite the official designation as a "daily," it generally appeared only six days a week, with the Sunday and Monday editions combined into one issue. News of the war featured prominently, and for the most part dominated the front page. An editorial devoted to some issue of special concern would also appear on the front page, and sometimes would continue on page two. Short news items from around the world as well as news from the countryside appeared, and the paper often published serial articles dealing with Ukrainian issues. Regular columns included sports news, a community calendar (which sometimes announced the mandatory registration of Jews, alongside theatrical performances and other local cultural events), and occasional reviews of new Ukrainian-language books. An entire issue was devoted to the writer Taras Shevchenko,[17] and a selection of non-war news items include an article condemning home-brewed alcohol,[18] women's fashions ("Pretty and Practical: A Discussion on the Theme of Women's Summer Clothes")[19] and, indicative of difficult living conditions, an illustrated article on how to make home-made shoes.[20] Each issue concluded with classified ads, along with a few commercial advertisements for light bulbs and so on. Amidst the horrors of the Holocaust—which are not directly discussed in its pages—*L'vivs'ki visti* strove to present a depiction of normality and even cheerfulness under the Nazis. The Easter issue for 1942 was decorated, for example, with pictures of cute little bunnies.[21] Political cartoons appeared frequently but not in every issue, and not always in the same location. In general, however, *L'vivs'ki visti* was edited according to a predictable formula that changed only slightly from time to time.

Information on Jews appeared in three basic forms in *L'vivs'ki visti:* short news articles about Jews around the world, major articles on Jews and Jewish influence, and cartoons. The brief news items carried stories from Nazi press agencies, and described pernicious Jewish influence (as perceived by the Nazis) in, for example, Romania,[22] France,[23] Australia,[24] British Palestine,[25] and so on. They were often misleading and sometimes completely untrue.[26]

The longer articles contained, naturally, more detailed expositions of anti-Semitic theory. A series of exceptionally virulent articles appeared in the summer of 1943 both in *L'vivs'ki visti* and *Krakivs'ki visti*. John-Paul

Himka studied the correspondence of the editors of the latter paper, and has shown that these articles were specifically ordered by their Nazi supervisors.[27] He theorizes that this command came as a response to the recent military setbacks as well as uprisings in several Jewish ghettos, including L'viv. It is worth noting at this point that the earliest issues of *L'vivs'ki visti* were not overtly anti-Semitic, lending support to the thesis that the anti-Jewish editorial policy was imposed from above.[28]

The cartoons provide the most vivid source of information on Jews in *L'vivs'ki visti*. While less sophisticated than the longer articles, they appeared with much greater frequency and repeatedly stressed a basic set of anti-Semitic ideas that were readily accessible to all. This would be especially important with the illiterate and functionally illiterate population of the region. By the fall of 1942 it was more common to find cartoons on the front page along with the major news items, an indication of their greater significance. The themes of the cartoons were exceptionally repetitive and showed little originality. Taken together, these sources of information presented a simplistic, and not entirely coherent, model of anti-Semitism that stressed the following three points:

- Jews wield undue power in world affairs, and use this power for financial gain and general oppression of non-Jews;
- the Western Allies (particularly the United States, Britain, and the Soviet Union) are the unwitting dupes of the Jews, although they sometimes openly collude with them for financial gain;
- and the Jews are most closely identified with the Soviet Union and its leader, Joseph Stalin.

Let us illustrate each point in turn. The notion of a world Jewish conspiracy appears often in *L'vivs'ki visti*, most notably in the 25/26 July 1943 edition when the article, "Jewish Plans To Rule the World," reporting on a story in the *Voelkisher Beobachter* in Germany, was published on the first page in the top left hand column, a space normally reserved for the lead war story.[29] The article, which discusses the potential "Jewish-capitalist World Republic," is somewhat unusual for *L'vivs'ki visti*, which preferred to express these views in a less blatant manner in other articles. Furthermore, while the articles taken or adapted from German sources reflect a world conspiracy with considerable emphasis on Jewish power in the United States, the editorials written specifically for the readership of *L'vivs'ki visti* tended to stress the importance of the Jews in the Soviet Union. For example, "The Struggle With World Jewry" (14 July 1943), an unusually long editorial, devotes only one short paragraph on the second page to the notion that the "Jew-capitalist and the Jew-Communist are not only identical in their Jewishness, but also identical in their aims . . . the Jewish triumph and dictatorship of the entire world."[30] The majority of the article deals with Jewish involvement with Marxism and the Soviet Union, including a brief list of important Jewish members of the NKVD.[31]

The cartoons, however, are much clearer on this point. Images include a Jew seated in a carriage pulled with difficulty by Roosevelt, Stalin, and Churchill (see illustration no. 1),[32] a meeting between Stalin, a Jew, a capitalist, and a Mason, over a map of Europe,[33] and a series of rather unimaginative cartoons which, through use of national symbols (the Stars and Stripes, the Union Jack, the Star of David, etc.) indicate the "hidden hand" of the Jews in world affairs.[34] Occasionally, a motive for this world conspiracy is suggested, such as the image of two capitalist Jews capturing coins from a bleeding globe.[35] The allies sometimes participate in this activity, as Roosevelt and Churchill (who appears in the caption but not in the cartoon) collect money dripping from gun barrels;[36] in another cartoon, Roosevelt and a Jew team up to pick the pocket of an American worker (see illustration no. 2).[37]

Jews are also portrayed as directing the war efforts of the Allies. Roosevelt is manipulated by a Jewish puppeteer, for example.[38] Elsewhere, a Jew is depicted as riding on a wounded British lion with Churchill's face,[39] riding on a wounded soldier,[40] riding Uncle Sam (see illustration no. 3),[41] and walking a vicious dog with Stalin's face (see illustration no. 4).[42] In a mood reminiscent of the early twentieth-century fears that subways were being built to facilitate the underground machinations of the world Jewish conspiracy, two Jews crouch underneath Capitol Hill and discuss their nefarious plans (see illustration no. 5).[43] The Star of David is gratuitously applied to the bodies or clothing of the Allies, even when the cartoon otherwise has no obvious anti-Semitic content.[44] In some cases, the Allies seem to be unaware that they are actually fighting a "Jewish war." Jews laugh as Roosevelt, Churchill, and Stalin try to hold on to each other's noses,[45] and there is a rather repetitive theme of Stalin, Churchill, and Roosevelt standing on each other's shoulders to

No. 1:

Onward "Troika!" 7/8 June 1942.

No. 2:

WORLD PHARISEES.
Roosevelt to American worker: "My son,
there lies Europe, which wishes to take
advantage of you! 12 March 1942.

No. 3:

Воєнні тягарі „вуйка Сама", (Телепрес)

War burdens of "Uncle Sam." (Telepress) 19 August 1942.

No. 4:

ЖИДІВСЬКА СОБАКА

Конґрес жидів у Москві заявив: „Совєтська політика — це політи жидівства"

JEWISH DOG. Congress of Jews in Moscow declared: "Soviet Politics — that's the politics of Jewry." 14 July 1944.

No. 5: **Розв'язання Комінтерну**

"Йому — спокійно, а нам — не зле!.."
(Рис. Л. Мелік)

The Dissolution of the Komintern. — "For
him, all is well, and for us — not bad!…"
(Lev Melik) 4/5 July 1943.

No. 6:
Untiring old nag. (Telepress)
12 March 1943.

Невтомна шкапа
(Телепрес)

No. 7:

Сензація у небі

С т а л і н перед оркестрою янгелів: „Привіт, від архіепископа Кентерберії! Я переймаю дириген гуру",

Sensation in Heaven. Stalin before the angelic orchestra: "Excuse me, I will take over the role of conductor from the Archbishop of Canterbury." 21/22 June 1942.

No. 8:

Secretary of the former Communist International: "Now no one can stop me from supporting you, as a spokesman for the Russian nation." (Lev Melik) 3 June 1943.

No. 9:

Чиє справжнє обличчя!   (Рис. Лев Мелік)

His true image! (Lev Melik) 13 May 1943.

No. 10: **ТАК ВОНО БУЛО!**

Так воно було перших днів після розгрому большевизму на наших землях! Як дуже зминилися на краще умовини сьогодні. Наше селянство зрозуміло справу, — і такого образу ніколи вже більше не побачите.

THIS IS THE WAY IT WAS! This is the way it was in the first days after the defeat of Bolshevism in our land! How much has changed for the better are conditions today. Our peasantry understands the matter, — and such a sight you will never see again. (M. Yatsysh[yn?]) 1 September 1942.

support a Jew (see illustration no. 6).[46]

The principal enemy of the Ukrainian nationalists, however, was Joseph Stalin and the Soviet Union, and it is here that the Jews receive the most intensive villification. While Roosevelt and Churchill are often depicted as being collaborators with the Jews, they are never portrayed as Jews themselves. Stalin, on the other hand, is quite frequently presented as a caricature of a Jew (fat, bulbous or hooked nose, and often unshaven) (see illustrations no. 7, 8). He is sometimes shown as a king of the Jews, wearing a Star of David atop his crown.[47] In one particularly revealing cartoon, a robed and crowned Stalin looks at himself in the mirror. His reflection, however ("his true image," the caption reads), is of a bearded Jew (see illustration no. 9).[48]

This is the quintessential image of the Jew for wartime Ukrainian anti-Semites.[49] The theme of the Jew as Stalin and/or Communist is the most common element in cartoons drawn by the local Lev Melik, which were apparently not imported from the Nazi Telepress agency.[50] "It is known to all people in all places," begins the October 1943 article, "Jewish Aristocracy in the USSR," "that Jews in the Soviet Union rule over all spheres of people's lives and that they are in their complete control."[51] Ukrainian interests are often depicted as conflicting specifically with Jewish interests.[52] The equation of Jews and the Soviet Union, of course, explicitly includes Jews even when the subject matter at hand is fighting with the Red Army, as in the article "To Battle With the Jew-Commune!"[53] For the most part, the content of these articles runs along the timeworn themes of the Jewish world conspiracy.

To this point little has been mentioned which would significantly distinguish *L'vivs'ki visti* from Nazi anti-Semitic propaganda elsewhere in occupied Europe. It is possible to note, however, three areas of contrast which may reveal some aspects of Nazi policy towards Jews and Ukrainians:

1. *L'vivs'ki visti* contains remarkably little propaganda, comparatively speaking, on the issue of *Rassenschande*, or prohibited sexual relations between Jews and non-Jews. Indeed, *L'vivski visti* was a very conservative paper when it comes to matters of sexuality in general. In the entire run of issues available to me, I noticed only three cartoons of a mildly sexual nature, and none of them explicitly anti-Semitic in orientation. In one, a nude woman bathing is threatened by a snake depicted in stars and

stripes; the caption indicates that this is a comment on US aid to South America.[54] In another, Roosevelt mauls a woman sitting next to him in a movie theatre,[55] and in a third, Stalin molests "Miss Brittania," asking if she believes in his love.[56] Sexuality is otherwise not depicted in the cartoons. This stands in stark contrast to, for example, *Der Stuermer*, in which anti-Semitism, sexuality, and violence against women are an almost inseparable triumvirate. *L'vivs'ki visti* contains nothing even remotely as horrible as *Der Stuermer*'s depiction of Jews binding a nude gentile girl and tearing at her wrists to drink her blood or Jewish abortionists gleefully operating on naked Gentile women.[57]

While *Der Stuermer* is arguably the most offensive of the Nazi organs, the combination of sexuality, violence against women, and anti-Semitism is also to be found elsewhere in Nazi-occupied Europe. French propaganda, for example, depicts lusty Jewish men attacking incongruously nude French women, a theme which was popular in 19th-century Western European propaganda as well.[58] Unlike the Ukrainian variety, Nazi propaganda in France did not hesitate to portray female nudity (and in some cases male nudity as well[59]), particularly in connection with Jewish threats. This could be expressed most commonly as a physical attack on an individual French woman, or as a stylized attack on the French nation as a whole, such as the poster which portrayed a large Jewish vulture (exaggerated, phallic hooked nose and wearing a Star of David) standing on a prone bare-breasted woman partially covered in the French flag.[60] Full frontal nudity, incidentally, was less common.[61] Jewish men are also caricatured as involved in exploiting the sexual desires of French men by pimping.[62]

Why was this theme less prevalent in *L'vivs'ki visti*? One might argue that French culture was more tolerant of nudity in general, and thus an image which would have offended Eastern European sensibilities would not have raised an eyebrow in the West. Furthermore, marriages between Jews and non-Jews were quite common in the West, whereas in Galicia they were statistically insignificant.[63] The possibility of *Rassenschande* in France and Germany was therefore much more relevant.

2. The depiction of the "Judeo-Bolshevik" conspiracy is typically more forceful in *L'vivs'ki visti* than in the West, particularly in the cartoons. Stalin is often depicted as a Jew himself, a relationship of identity.

In Western propaganda, on the other hand, it was more common to depict Stalin as a tool of the Jews (which, as we noted above, also finds expression in *L'vivski visti*). In one typical example of French propaganda, a sinister figure wearing a Star of David lurks behind the US, British, and Soviet flags with the caption, "And behind: THE JEW."[64] Similarly, the Jew stands *behind* a faceless de Gaulle[65] but is not depicted as de Gaulle *himself*; a dog labeled "the Jew" threatens France *alongside* a dog labled "de Gaulle."[66] This identification of Jews with Communism did not need much encouragement for, as noted above, the notion was widespread. Indeed, some of the best examples of this in *L'vivs'ki visti*, such as Stalin looking at his Jewish image in the mirror, were executed by the local cartoonist Melik.

3. One theme conspicuous by its absence in *L'vivs'ki visti* is the depiction of the national hero forcibly evicting the Jew. After the crimes of the Jew in France are exposed, he is taken out by the scruff of his neck,[67] kicked out by an anonymous boot,[68] swept out by a gigantic broom,[69] or driven out by children pelting stones.[70] Two salient observations: firstly, the person or persons driving out the Jews are not nationally identified. Indeed, they are commonly not depicted (the broom, the boot, or children). Secondly, the method of ridding France of the Jews is expulsion (usually to the West, strangely enough).

Why is this motif absent in *L'vivs'ki visti*? It is possible to theorize that this was a reflection of Nazi occupation policy. Jews were, after all, not to leave Eastern Europe at all.

Most of the cartoons published in *L'vivs'ki visti* conform to a general pattern which was repeated in other Nazi organs. One unique exception to this is a cartoon published in September 1942, signed by one M.Yatsyshyn, depicting a premodern form of Ukrainian anti-Semitism (see illustration no. 10). A sinister Hasidic Jew, holding a patched pair of overalls (apparently from an earlier transaction), offers a gramophone and a sewing machine to impoverished Ukrainian peasants, presumably for a small down payment with an extortionate rate of interest.[71] The caption reads:

> THE IS THE WAY IT WAS! This is the way it was in the first days after the destruction of Bolshevism in our land! How much changed for the better are conditions today. Our peasantry understands this—and you will never see such a sight again.

By the time this cartoon was published the truth of this assertion was obvious.

Notes:

1. This paper was prepared with the support of the Program of Jewish Studies of Cornell University while I held the Slovin/YIVO Visiting Assistant Professorship in 1995–1996. I am grateful to Mr. Yoram Szekely and Ms. Julie Copenhagen of Olin Library for their assistance in procuring microfilms and other materials. Mr. Myron Momryk of the National Archives of Canada (Social Cultural Archives Program, Manuscript Division) generously provided me with copies of rare material from the Andry Zhuk Collection (MG30 C167). This paper benefited from the comments of Professors Zvi Gitelman (University of Michigan), John-Paul Himka (University of Alberta), and Steven Katz (Boston University). I am also grateful for the support of Ms. Zella Linn of the History Department at Florida Atlantic University and to three undergraduate students (Danielle Balch, Gedony Fontil, and Wilson Charles) for their work on the images presented in this article. The original photocopies were taken from microfilms of deteriorating wartime newspapers, and these three students spent many hours scanning the images and removing much detritus to make them as clear as possible. All errors of fact or interpretation remain my responsibility.

2. Some 17,000 Jews out of 870,000 survived. See Aharon Weiss, "Jewish-Ukrainian Relations in Western Ukraine During the Holocaust," *Ukrainian-Jewish Relations in Historical Perspective*, eds. Peter Potichnyj and Howard Aster (Edmonton: CIUS/University of Alberta, 1988), 409.

3. This figure includes refugees who initally sought shelter in L'viv as well as those who fled the city. See Philip Friedman, "The Destruction of the Jews of Lwow, 1941–1944," in *Roads to Extinction: Essays on the Holocaust*, ed. Ada Friedman (New York-Philadelphia: Jewish Publication Society, 1980), 244–245, 316–317.

4. According to the 1931 census, Poles made up fifty percent of the population of L'viv (156,000), followed by Jews with 31.9 percent (99,600) and

Ukrainians with 16.3 percent (50,900): A. Figol, V. Kubijovyc, and A. Zhukovsky, "L'viv," *Encyclopedia of Ukraine*, 5 vols., eds. Volodymyr Kubijovyc and Danylo Struk (Toronto: University of Toronto Press, 1984–1993), 3:223. Looking at the region as a whole, however, Ukrainians dominated with over 60 % of the population, followed by Poles, Jews, and other ethnic groups. V. Kubijovyc et al., "Galicia," ibid. 2:12.

5. See for example Frank Golczewski, *Polnisch-Jüdische Beziehungen 1881–1922: Eine Studie zur Geschichte des Anti-Semitismus in Osteuropa*, Series: Quellen und Studien zur Geschichte des Ostlichen Europa 15 (Wiesbaden: Franz Steiner, 1981), 186–188, 216.

6. See Orest Subtelny, "The Soviet Occupation of Western Ukraine, 1939–1941: An Overview," in *Ukraine during World War II: History and Its Aftermath*, ed. Yury Boshyk, (Edmonton: CIUS/University of Alberta), 1986, 5–14; Jan T. Gross, "The Sovietization of Western Ukraine and Western Byelorussia," *Jews in Eastern Poland and the USSR, 1939–1946*, eds. Norman Davies and Antony Polonsky (New York: St. Martin's, 1991), 60–76; Kost' Pankivs'kyi, *Vid derzhavy do komitetu (Lito 1941 roky u L'vovi)* 2nd ed. (New York Toronto: Kliuchi, 1970), 21–28. For a Soviet interpretation of this period, see *Istoriia L'vova*, eds. V. Sekretariuk et al. (Kiev: Naukova Dumka, 1984), 226–246.

7. Even individuals with a positive attitude to Jews were known to participate in this belief. The Ukrainian Catholic Metropolitan Andrei Sheptyts'kyi, who engineered the rescue of some 150–200 children in his monasteries and convents, made negative comments of this nature. See Shimon Redlich, "Sheptyts'kyi and the Jews," in *Morality and Reality: The Life and Times of Andrei Sheptyts'kyi*, ed. Paul Magocsi (Edmonton: CIUS/University of Alberta, 1989). See, however, Jan Gross' thoughtful article on the nature of this widespread perception, "The Jewish Community in the Soviet-Annexed Territories on the Eve of the Holocaust: A Social Scientist's View," *The Holocaust in the Soviet Union*, eds. Lucjan Dobroszycki and Jeffrey Gurock (Armonk, NY, London: M.E. Sharpe, 1993), 155–171.

8. See Friedman, "Destruction," 245–249; David Kahane, *Lvov Ghetto Diary*, trans. Jerzy Michalowicz (Amherst: University of Massachusetts), 5–13; Dr. Ludwig Fleck, "The Lemberg Ghetto," in David Hackett (ed.), *The Buchenwald Report* (Boulder, CO, San Fransisco, Oxford: Westview, 1995), 357–360; Kurt Lewin, *A Journey Through Illusions* (Santa

Barbara: Fithian Press, 1994), 35–40.

9. See Map 1 in Michael Marrus, *The Holocaust in History* (Toronto: Lester & Orpen Dennys, 1987), 61.

10. See Bohdan Vitvitsky, "Slavs and Jews: Consistent and Inconsistent Perspectives on the Holocaust," in Michael Berenbaum, ed., *A Mosaic of Victims: Non-Jews Persecuted and Murdered by the Nazis* (New York London: New York University Press, 1990), 101–108; Bohdan Wytwycky [Vitvitsky], *The Other Holocaust: Many Circles of Hell* (Washington, DC: The Novak Report, 1980), 52–64; Bohdan Krawchenko, "Soviet Ukraine under Nazi Occupation, 1941–1944," in Yury Boshyk, ed., *Ukraine during World War II: History and Its Aftermath*, (Edmonton: Canadian Institute of Ukrainian Studies, 1986), 25–29.

11. Lucjan Dobroszycki, *Reptile Journalism: The Official Polish-Language Press under the Nazis, 1939–1945*, trans. Barbara Harshav (New Haven London: Yale, 1994), 50–55.

12. See Friedman, "Destruction," 318. Over a hundred Ukrainian-language papers were established after the Nazi invasion, yet less than half lasted until the spring of 1942. See Krawchenko, "Soviet Ukraine under Nazi Occupation," 20, 28. Unfortunately, not all the issues of *L'vivs'ki visti* are readily available to Western scholars. This chapter is based on the issues published between February 1942 [23 (147)] and July 1944 [162 (881)] available on microfilm in the Columbia Library system (some small gaps exist in this run) and two issues of its immediate predecessor, *Ukrains'ki shchodenni visti* (27 and 29 July 1941) from the Andry Zhuk Collection of the National Archives of Canada (MG30 C167, vol. 38, files 49 and 50).

13. The reference was made regarding *Krakivs'ki visti* (Cracow News). Volodymyr Kubiiovych, *Ukraintsi v Heneral'nyi hubernii 1939–1941: Istoriia Ukrains'koho tsentral'noho komitetu* (Chicago: Vydavnytsvo Mykoly Denysiuka, 1975), 276, cited in Ivan Khymka [John-Paul Himka], "'Krakivs'ki visti' pro yevreiv, 1943 r.: Prychynok do istorii ukrains'ko-yevreis'kykh vidnosyn pid chas druhoi svitovoi viiny," unpublished manuscript, 3. An English-language version of this paper has appeared under the title "*Krakivski visti* and the Jews, 1943: A Contribution to the History of Ukrainian-Jewish Relations during the Second World War," in *Ukraine: Developing a Democratic Polity, Essays in Honour of Peter J. Potichnyj* (Edmonton: Canadian Institute of

Ukrainian Studies, 1997 [special edition of the *Journal of Ukrainian Studies*, vol. 21: 1–2 (Toronto, Summer-Winter, 1996]), 81–95.

14. Bodnarovych edited the paper from its inception (as *Ukrains'ki shchodenni visti*) until his death in June 1944; M. Semchyshyn took over for the few remaining weeks. Obituaries of Bodnarovych were published on 29 June 1944, ch. 148 (867) ("Redaktor Osyp Bodnarovych") and 2/3 July 1944, ch. 151 (870), 3 ("Ostannia doroha red. O. Bondarovycha"). See also "Bodnarovych, Osyp," *Encyclopedia of Ukraine* 1:251; Pankivs'kyi, *Vid Derzhavy*, 57–58.

15. "L'vivs'ki visti," *Encyclopedia of Ukraine*, 3:242.

16. *L'vivs'ki visti* listed no price on its banner. Under its previous title, the paper sold for 50 kopeks (issue number 19, 27 July 1941), decreasing to 30 kopeks (issue number 20, 29 July 1941).

17. 15 March 1943, ch. 58 (476).

18. "Borot'ba zi samohonom," 10 February 1943, ch. 28 (448), 1.

19. "Harne i praktychne: Rozmovy na temu zhinochykh litnikh ybran'," 11/12 July 1943, ch 154 (574), 6.

20. "Yak samomu zrobyty vzuttia na lito?" 25 July 1943, ch. 168 (586).

21. 3–7 April 1942, ch. 73 (197).

22. 6 February 1942 ch. 25 (149), 2.

23. 14 October 1943, ch. 235 (655), 2.

24. 19 March1942, ch. 60 (184), 2.

25. 20 March 1942 ch. 61 (185), 2; 30/31 August 1942 ch. 195 (319), 2.

26. On false news, see also Khymka [Himka], "'Krakivs'ki visti,'" 4.

27. Khymka [Himka], "'Krakivs'ki visti,'" 5–6.

28. Unfortunately, as noted above, the entire run of *L'vivs'ki visti* was not available for examination. It would be worthwhile to determine the point at which anti-Semitic articles and cartoons first appeared in the newspaper; however, the earliest issues have yet to be microfilmed and made available to researchers working in North America. Issues 1–43 (1941) are held in the Jagiellonian Library in Krakow.

29. "Zhydivs'ki plany panuvannia nad svitom," 25/26 July 1943, ch. 166 (586), 1. The Ukrainian word *zhyd*, like its Polish but unlike its Russian cognate, does not necessarily convey a derogatory meaning. I have therefore translated the term *zhyd* as "Jew," even though the context of its usage might also justify a more colorful expression. On this term, see Henrik Birnbaum, "Some Problems with the Etymology and Semantics of

the Slavic *Zid* 'Jew,'" *Slavica Hierosolymitana* 7 (Jerusalem, 1985) 1–11; and John D. Klier, "*Zhid*: Biography of a Russian Epithet," *Slavonic and East European Review* 60:1 (London, 1982), 1–15.

30. 'Borot'ba z svitovym zhydivstvom," 14 July 1943, ch. 156 (576), 1–2.

31. See also "Vyna zhydiv za teperishniu viinu," 10 June 1943, ch 129 (549), 2.

32. 7/8 June 1942, ch. 124 (248), 5.

33. 29 May 1942, ch. 116 (240), 4.

34. See 19/29 December 1943, ch. 292 (712), 1; 10 December 1943, ch. 234 (704), 1; 7 October 1943, ch. 229 (649), 1.

35. 12 November 1943, ch. 260 (680), 1.

36. 3 November 1942, ch. 250 (374), 1.

37. 12 March 1942, ch. 54 (178), 4.

38. 22 January 1943, ch. 12 (432), 1.

39. 5 June 1942, ch. 122 (246), 4.

40. 11 November 1943, ch. 259 (679), 1.

41. 19 August 1942, ch. 186 (310), 1.

42. 14 July 1944, ch. 161 (880), 4.

43. 4/5 July 1943, ch. 148 (560), 1. On the role of subways, see Norman Cohn, *Warrant for Genocide: The Myth of the Jewish World Conspiracy and the Protocols of the Elders of Zion* (Ann Arbor: Scholars' Press, 1981), 63.

44. See, for example, 31 May/1 June 1942, ch. 118 (242), 5; 4 November 1942, ch. 251 (375), 1; 21/22 June 1942, ch. 136 (260), 5.

45. 30 June 1944, ch. 149 (868).

46. See 17 March 1943, ch. 58 (478), 1; 12 May 1943, ch. 104 (524), 1; 16 October 1943, ch. 237 (659), 1. Interestingly, the order is always the same: USSR on the bottom, then England, the US, and the Jew on top. This theme has precedents in modern anti-Semitism; see for example Eduard Fuchs, *Die Juden in der Karikatur: Ein Beitrag zur Kulturgeschichte* (Berlin: Guhl, 1985 [f.p. 1921]), 240–241.

47. 3 June 1943, ch. 123 (543), 1; see also 21 June 1943, ch. 162 (582), 1.

48. 13 May 1943, ch. 105 (525), 1.

49. For a brief discussion of the changing nature of Ukrainian anti-Semitism in the modern era, see Henry Abramson, "The Scattering of Amalek: A Model for Understanding the Ukrainian-Jewish Conflict,"

East European Jewish Affairs 24:1 (London, 1994), 39–47.

50. See for example 13 May 1943, ch. 105 (525), 1; 21 July 1943, ch. 162 (582), 1; 3 June 1943, ch. 123 (543), 1; 19/29 December 1943, ch. 292 (712), 1 (the uniforms are Soviet); and 4/5 July 1943, ch. 148 (568), 1. I have concluded that Melik lived in the region because he occasionally drew illustrations of local personalities (see, for example, 26/27 September 1943, ch. 220 [640], 4; 2 December 1943, ch. 277 [697], 3: 8 December 1943, ch. 282 [702], 3. It should be mentioned, however, that Melik may have been of Russian, and not Ukrainian, extraction. Credits to his cartoons spell his name with an "i," the twelfth letter of the Ukrainian alphabet, yet an examination of his signature reveals that he signed his name with the Russian equivalent, which is the eleventh letter of the Ukrainian alphabet.

51. T. Ts., "Zhydivs'ke dvorianstvo v SSSR," 3/4 October 1943, ch. 226 (646), 3. See also "Meta bol'shevyzmu nezminna," 6 April 1943, ch. 75 (495), 1–2.

52. "Ukrains'ka national'na solidarnist'," 29/30 March 1942, ch. 69 (193), 1–2; "Vidpir vorozhiyi ahitatsii," 7 February 1942, ch. 26 (158), 1; "Na mistsi zhydiv torhuiut' sil's'ki lehini," 18 August 1942, ch. 185 (309), 3; "Zmora narodu," 21 July 1943, ch. 162 (582), 1.

53. "Do borot'by z zhydo-komunoiu!" 22 May 1943, ch. 113 (533), 1–2.

54. 8–9 February 1942, ch. 27 (151), 2.

55. 28/29 August 1942, ch. 194 (318), 2.

56. While Stalin is depicted here, as usual, with Jewish features, the import of the cartoon is primarily political. 18 June 1943, ch. 134 (554), 1.

57. Reproduced in Dennis Showalter, *Little Man, What Now? Der Stuermer in the Weimar Republic* (Hamden, CT: Archon, 1982), 197, 215.

58. Gerard Silvain, *La Question Juive en Europe 1933–1945* ([Paris]: Jean-Claude Lattes, 1985), 198; Fuchs, *Die Juden*, 230–235, 257, 286–88.

59. Silvain, *La Question*, 142.

60. Pierre Bourget and Charles Lacretelle, *Sur les Murs de Paris et de France 1939–1945* (Coulommiers: Hachette, 1980), 77.

61. Compare Silvain, *La Question*, 312. This example is from German-language propaganda.

62. Silvain, *La Question*, 121.

63. See Krysztof Zamorski, *Transformacja demograficzna w Galicji na tle przemian ludnościowych innych obszarów Europy środkowej w drugiej połowie XIX i na początku XX w.* (Kraków: Uniwersytet Jagielloński, 1991), 73.

64. Bourget and Lacretelle, *Sur les Murs*, 155.

65. Bourget and Lacretelle, *Sur les Murs*, 85.

66. Bourget and Lacretelle, *Sur les Murs*, 76.

67. Silvain, *La Question*, 121.

68. Dominique Rossignol, *Histoire de la Propagande en France de 1940 à 1944: L'utopie Pétain* (Paris: Presses Universitaires de France, 1991), 235; Silvain, *La Question*, 196.

69. Rossignol, *Histoire*, 235; Silvain, *La Question*, 65.

70. Silvain, *La Question*, 59.

71. 1 September 1942, ch. 196 (320), 1. The reproduction on microfilm is less than perfect, and only the letters "M. Yatsysh" are completely legible. The final two letters appear to be "yn," a typical Ukrainian form.

French Journalism

The Jewish Press in Wartime Europe: France, a case study on the role and limitation of the legal and clandestine press in the struggle for survival, 1940–1944

Jacques Adler
University of Melbourne

The German occupation of France marked the end of what had been a wide-ranging Jewish press in the inter-war period.[1] Yet neither the imposition of Nazi rule nor the new French government succeeded in silencing Jewish organizations. A Jewish press totally unlike what had previously existed appeared. The imposed Jewish Council had been ordered to publish a newspaper under Nazi control while reconstructed organizations began to issue illegal publications.[2]

Recent studies of the Holocaust have chosen to refer neither to the Jewish Council's newspaper nor to the clandestine press.[3] Focusing on relief and rescue activities, such studies neglected to examine the underground press' place in the struggle for survival. It is clear that relief and rescue organizations supported and saved thousands of Jews. But these organizations did not function without some relationship to the other socio-political forces operating in the community.

To limit the presentation of Jewish responses to the Holocaust in France to these activities and ignore the existence of the clandestine press is to overlook its specific contribution to the struggle for survival. The publications of such organizations as the Jewish section of the French Communist Party or the mixed Jewish-non-Jewish *Mouvement National Contre le Racisme* (National Movement Against Racism, hereafter MNCR) always proceeded on the basis of an interpretation of the course of events based upon the problems confonting the Jewish population. These organizations committed resources and manpower to the dissemination of information designed to provide an effective contribution to the defense of the Jews. The central brief of these publications was to alert the population. Once the mass deportations had begun they waged a persistent campaign against passivity and urged active defense. Perhaps most importantly, they chose to win over the non-Jews to the struggle out of the firmly held conviction that only with their aid and cooperation was survival possible. While internment and deportation affected only some Jews, these publications concentrated their efforts on convincing the remaining Jews to cast off the illusion that they might yet be spared. Their editorial line reiterated that hope rested in recognizing that a very particular war was being waged against all Jews and therefore one needed to act accordingly. At all times these organizations viewed their clandestine press not only as a source of information, as a warning bell, but also as a mean for organizing solidarity and defense.

Given the interrelationship of this press with the course of events, these publications should be considered as reflecting an analysis of situations to which they reacted and in time came to anticipate. While space does not allow for a detailed study, this paper will, of necessity, have to refer briefly to the context in which that press emerged. In my examination I shall first deal with the legal press' origin, content, function and its public perceptions. Then follows an overview of the clandestine press and its specific genesis, language and content. I shall argue that while we cannot measure the effective contribution of the clandestine press to the survival of the Jews in France, it can however be asserted that it significantly contributed in their defense.

While the survival of over seventy percent of the French Jewish population cannot be attributed to the illegal presses' publications, their campaigns against passivity, their ceaseless insistence on the abandonment of registered addresses, on the need to hide and the call to enter the struggle against Nazism all surely assisted directly or indirectly the Jews' defense. For, and above all else, the clandestine press devoted its efforts to encouraging people to overcome fear, to develop a fighting spirit, and to sustain the hope that deportation to that unknown destination was not inevitable.

1. The Legal Jewish Press:
a. Genesis:
Even before the Jewish population realised that radical changes in the life of the community were about to take place, the authorities had

already begun adopting measures which were to challenge the very basis of its existence. No sooner had the Vichy government been formed than it promulgated laws and adopted measures which unmistakably heralded a xenophobic and anti-Semitic policy. Parallel with Vichy's own programmatic measures, the first concrete step in bringing the status of the Jews of occupied France into line with the European-wide Nazi policy of isolation from the rest of the population was taken in January 1941 by Theodor Dannecker, the *Judenreferent* for France. Limited at first in his capacity to proceed at will by the German military administration, by January 1941 he had successfully manipulated a number of relief organizations into forming the *Comité de Coordination des Oeuvres Juives de Bienfaisance du Grand Paris* (Coordination Committee of Jewish Relief Organizations, hereafter C.C.).[4] The basic framework of a Jewish council had been created. One of Dannecker's earliest orders to the newly constituted C.C. was to publish a community newspaper. As the official voice of the Jewish community it was to be the only legal Jewish newspaper allowed in France after the armistice. It first appeared in Paris on 19 April 1941 under the name, *Informations Juives*. [5]

b. Function:

Why the C.C. was ordered by Dannecker to publish a newspaper became clear to its leadership when two Jews arrived in Paris from Vienna on 18 March 1941.[6] They were Dannecker's answer to what he considered was the procrastination of the C.C. leadership. Armed with the experience of Vienna Jewry's *Kultusgemeinde* (religious community), one of them, Israel Israelowitz, was ordered to "teach" French Jewry how a Jewish council was to function. His immediate task was to ensure that all Jews became members of the C.C. He took in hand the creation and use of a community newspaper which was to serve as the vehicle for the execution by the communities of all of Dannecker's future orders.

It was with the first issue, which appeared on 19 April 1941, that Israelowitz undertook to fulfill Dannecker's objective, the creation of such an organization. His editorial announced: "It will no longer be possible for the C.C. to dispense advice or to give financial aid unless you become members of the Community of Paris."[7]

Yet, his first appeal to the Jews of Paris did not receive the expected results; in fact few people joined the C.C. Frustrated with a poor response, in the following issue of the paper Israelowitz resorted to threats when he declared:

> And those whose heart and reason remain closed to our words . . . , those people will have to bear the consequences. There will be—we all know—decisions taken and changes.

The first issue was sent to 10,000 families, whose names and addresses were culled from the October 1940 census.[8] It was clear for all to see that the aim of *Informations Juives* was to lay the basis and prepare the Jews of Paris for the introduction of a Nazi-type council. Israelowitz did not, however, retain control of the newspaper. By June 1941, as a consequence of Dannecker's continued pressure for the establishment of an active leadership, the C.C. was reorganized. A new leadership emerged, led by native French Jews, which immediately removed Israelowitz from an executive role and succeeded in relegating him to the function of liaison with Dannecker. Right from its formation, it was clearly understood by this new leadership that Dannecker was not interested in the *Informations Juives* becoming a real newspaper. They knew that they would not be given editorial independence nor would the newspaper be allowed to present news of specific interest to the Jewish population. The newspaper was clearly intended to assist in the execution of Dannecker's orders. Its primary organizing purpose was well understood: it was to keep the Jewish population informed of all measures affecting it and, equally significant and already made obvious by the first two issues published by Israelowitz, it had to inform the community that the C.C. was the only organization permitted to represent it to the authorities.

c. Content:

With Israelowitz's removal as editor, the new C.C.'s leadership was determined to ensure that the newspaper would not threaten the community and that its content was to be useful to the community. Compelled to publish, the C.C. leadership filled its pages with historical anecdotes or biblical stories. Lacking substance, the paper nevertheless did fulfill a communal function. It regularly published the addresses of institutions which offered a wide range of services. Whenever new German or French measures were announced the paper endeavored to explain their implications. When access to non-Jewish stores was limited or affected by Allied air raids, the paper informed the Jews of the changes in the prescribed shopping hours.[9] The paper published the addresses of the non-aryanized Jewish stores which allowed Jews unrestricted access.[10] Thus, it acted according to the authorities' orders but also provided information useful to the community.

When in December 1941 the C.C. was dissolved and replaced by a nation-wide French government-supervised council, the *Union Générale des Israélites de France* (General Union of the Israelites of France, hereafter UGIF), the publication of *Informations Juives* was not suspended. At the end of January 1942, after a brief interruption, it reappeared as the *Bulletin de l'UGIF* and retained its former editorial policy. The lead articles remained anecdotal and it continued to publish the texts of the measures affecting Jews. When at the end of 1942 letters began to arrive from those who had been deported to Eastern Europe, the paper published the names of the families to whom they were addressed.[11] Until the end of 1942 it even included a Yiddish language supplement which Israelowitz had initiated in order to reach immigrant Jewry. But by then a large proportion of the East European Jews of Paris had either been deported, gone into hiding or had fled to the Vichy zone, and the Yiddish supplement was discontinued.[12]

The paper was never distributed in the Vichy zone, even after the Allied forces' landing in North Africa in November 1942, when the German and Italian armies occupied the rest of the France. There was an order from Alois Brunner, who had arrived from Salonika to accelerate deportations in June 1943, for a nation-wide distribution of the paper.[13] But this was never carried out by the UGIF leadership. Brunner, too busy organizing deportations, never again referred to the issue.

d. Council Policy and How It Was Viewed by the Population:

With few funds at its disposal during the early months of its existence, the C.C. used its newspaper's pages to appeal to the community for donations to meet communal needs. Given the widely-held popular view that the C.C. was Gestapo-controlled, despite the fact that it was led by well-meaning individuals, its calls for donations received little or negative responses.[14] Further calls for donations, following the May 1941 internment of 4,000 immigrant Jews, once again failed to be supported. The families of interned Jews, in particular, objected to being asked for contributions. They voiced in no uncertain terms their views that the C.C. had not done anything on their behalf.[15] The advertised positions for representatives to collect subscriptions for the newspaper, offering good salaries and a "secure future," were again the object of derision. The calls for volunteers to work for a German company operating farms in northern France, which began to appear in August 1941, accompanied with the promise that the workers would be well fed and that their families would be provided for, were neither trusted nor well received. Isolated, functioning in a community generally critical if not opposed to it, the general Jewish population did not know that the C.C.'s leadership had refused, despite personal threats, to proceed with a selection of who was to go to these farms. Unable to circumvent Dannecker's demand, and in order to avoid reprisals, the C.C. leadership did the next best thing: it called for volunteers through the pages of *Informations Juives*.[16]

Notwithstanding the external and internal limitations on its content, the editorial comments, which followed the publication of the texts of repressive measures, expressed the general political line of the C.C. and later of the UGIF. These editorial comments consistently recommended that readers abide by all regulations, although there is no evidence that the *Judenreferent* ever gave instructions to that effect. There is no doubt that the council, as a controlled organization, did have to generally comply with and work within and around orders given to its leaders. But the question remains: were the well-intentioned UGIF recommendations for strict compliance with the laws in accordance with the interests of the Jewish population ? Did the internments of May, August and December 1941, followed in June and July 1942 with mass deportations, demand that the Jews abide by the laws? Since sales of the news sheet numbered only some 400 copies weekly and it was only available in occupied France, it cannot be argued that it had a wide influence. The fact remains, however, that the content of its pages was widely discussed and known.[17] Throughout the occupation this legal voice consistently pleaded for and advocated the strict observance of all regulations. It was not surprising, therefore, that the illegal press opposed the C.C. and the appointed council which later replaced it. It was no surprise either that the C.C. and the UGIF leaderships were characterized by the clandestine press as agents of collaboration.[18]

2. The Clandestine Press:
a. General Introduction:

While it can be argued, in broad terms, that the Jewish council's newspaper mirrored its strategy, the clandestine press mirrored the positions over a range of issues of those forces directly committed to active defense of the community. The content of these publications reveals these organizations' understanding of the sense and significance of the measures taken against the population. More importantly, a chronological examination of the content of these newspapers reveals the genesis and development of what came to be referred to as the Jewish resistance and the broad strategies its various forces were to adopt.

Characteristics and features of the clandestine press need to be mentioned. In the first place, it was, and remained throughout the occupation, the creation of immigrant Jewry, the Yiddish-speaking organizations. The native Franco-Jewish organizations that engaged in the same struggle never issued illegal publications. They certainly never considered of prime importance the need to disseminate the news of the mass murders taking place in Eastern Europe which were prophetic for French Jewry. They never considered using the press both as a medium for information and as an appeal to the non-Jewish world for help.

Secondly, of all the existing organizations, *Solidarité* (later renamed the *Union des Juifs pour la Résistance et l'Entr'Aide*, Union of the Jews for Resistance and Mutual Aid; hereafter UJRE) was the only organization to regularly issue a wide range of newspapers, leaflets, appeals and pamphlets, in Yiddish and French. The Bund, the Zionist organizations, the *Fédération des Societés Juives de France* (French Federation of Jewish Hometown Societies; hereafter FSJF) and later the *Comité Général de Défense* (United Defense Committee; hereafter CGD) also issued newspapers, leaflets, newsletters and information bulletins. The Zionist movement even circulated reports on Palestine and Jewish life.[19] But all these organizations' publishing efforts were never as regular or as extensive as the range of publications issued by the Communists. Does this indicate that these organizations were only partially convinced of the need to keep the Jewish population informed? Was the decision to limit publication due to fear of the Gestapo's attention and the risk of reprisals? Or was this reluctance to take up the challenge of publishing rather due to other priorities: to focus activities on immediate and practical assistance for the population?

In fact, the non-Communist organizations did consider as their first priority the distribution of material assistance. Nonetheless, their inability to keep the population informed was always bitterly resented. Indeed, all clandestine organizations recognized the need and urgency to keep the Jewish population informed, and to breach the wall of silence. At the end of 1942, the FSJF issued its first appeal to the French people, under the title "Le silence complice du crime."[20] But it was only in December 1943 that the FSJF published a clandestine news sheet, under the name *Quand Même*, in which it chose to express its views in the French language. Addressing itself to the Jewish and to the French population, the FSJF acknowledged the problem created by the imposed silence on the Jewish organizations:

> Among the many pains inflicted on the Jews . . . , silence is perhaps the most painful to our dignity . . . , it is the torture of the imposed silence which we had to bear for three years. *Quand Même* is the first attempt to break the silence, to make known to those who do not recognize the "civilizing" action of the promoters of the new order against women and children, against old and sick Jews; to give a voice to the victims and express their contempt for the new "Europeans."[21]

The delayed appearance of the the FSJF's own newspaper, months after March 1943 when the decision had been taken to abandon legal activities, cannot be explained solely by its inability to overcome publishing difficulties.[22] Two pre-conditions were essential. There had to be both the conviction that a clandestine press was important and an organizational infrastructure put into place. The example of continued publication by the Communists makes the point. Most organizations occasionally issued illegal publications, while others claimed not to have the capacity to do so, but in either case the real enough difficulties were only partially attributable to organizational problems. When in July 1943 the immigrant organizations joined forces and established the CGD, the decision was then taken to publish the CGD's own newspaper. Shortly thereafter, *Unzer kamf* (Yiddish: Our Struggle) appeared. But that decision was only realized as a result of an appeal for help to the only organization which had successfully maintained publication throughout this period, the UJRE.[23]

To publish under clandestine conditions did present real difficulties. It necessitated not only technical facilities, a serious problem for the publication of material in Yiddish, but also a scarce commodity: paper. Furthermore, it required safe premises which were not easely found. Lastly, but central to the purpose, there was the distribution problem. Little imagination is required to appreciate what it must have taken the Communists, for example, to produce not only "printed", as opposed to mimeographed material, which was an achievement in itself, but also lengthy pamphlets, one of which numbered no less than 75 pages.[24] Their capacity to produce and, above all, to distribute a large volume of material, when compared to the other clandestine organizations, warrants reflection. Did it mean that the Communists were a unique group of people ? They certainly had a dedicated membership. But it cannot be argued that its members were more devoted to their movement and cause than members of other organizations. More likely, it would seem that the limited publishing efforts made by all the non-Communist organizations can only be understood in terms of their strategic thinking as to what they perceived were the most suitable forms of resistance.

This line of argumentation finds confirmation in the course of a debate in the ranks of the CGD following a proposal made by the UJRE for the establishment of CGD fighting units. Although a majority of the CGD's executive rejected the proposal to commit the organization to the armed struggle, a compromise solution was adopted according to which the CGD would provide financial assistance to the UJRE's fighting units. The debate over what were to be the main thrusts of the CGD's activities closely parallels the publishing policies of the non-Communist organizations. It would therefore seem that the limited efforts of all the non-Communist organizations as far as clandestine publications were concerned were not solely due to practical problems but more importantly to particular conceptions of resistance and forms of struggle.[25]

Until the mass deportations of July 1942, the content of the published material was taken up with the conditions in the camps in France, and in particular the terrible conditions in the Drancy camp. The virulent anti-Semitic propaganda disseminated in the press and radio, the relentless "aryanization" of properties, the internment during 1941 of over 8,000 men, foreign and French, dominated the clandestine press' coverage. The editorial outrage in the clandestine press culminated in December 1941. In reprisal for the activities of the French resistance, the Germans had ordered the execution of 100 men, including 53 Jews, imposed a massive fine of a billion francs on the Jewish population and arrested 743 Franco-Jewish notables as part of 1,000 Jews to be deported to the East.[26] The voices of the Bund and the Poale-Zion were then silent. It did not mean that they did not understand the significance of this new kind of measure. The most widely publicized and distributed responses came from *Solidarité*'s press. There was simply no other major underground voice, for there were no other organizations committed to large scale underground publishing.

Until the eve of July 1942, the content of the clandestine press, alongside reports on local issues and problems, devoted more and more space to reporting news of the events taking place in the East. The dramatic broadcast of August 1941, from the Jewish Anti-Fascist Committee in Moscow, had unveiled the crimes committed by the German armies on Soviet soil and exposed the Nazis' intention to exterminate the Jewish people. The Moscow appeal could not but exert a radical influence upon the immigrant organizations and their publications. *Solidarité*'s press concluded and warned the population that worse was to be expected.

The Communist press' coverage acquired even more immediacy and relevance following 16 July 1942. Women, children, old and sick had been arrested and deported to that unknown destination and fate. From then on, the illegal press saw its task as two-fold: to exhort Jews to hide and resist arrest by all available means and also to convey hope. For, while no Jew was safe from the threat of deportation, all the clandestine publications considered that their prime task was to provide the necessary advice on how to survive, and how to sustain the collective and individual will to evade deportation.

The mass arrests and deportation of immigrant Jews which began in July 1942 gave a radical impulse to earlier appeals from *Unzer vort* (Our Word) which had called upon the Jews to join the armed struggle against the Nazis. The pain experienced by the men, women and young people who had lost relatives spurred many of them to join Solidarité's fighting units which had been formed in May 1942 under the leadership of the French Communist Party. These Jews did not join the armed struggle because they had been won over to the Communist cause, but as Jews motivated by the tragic loss of their families. The Communist analysis of the situation, as expressed in *Unzer vort* and all related publications, called for the development of a fighting spirit which it considered essential to survival. Not all the clandestine publications which then appeared called upon the Jews to fight. Thus, if only for articulating the view that solely through action, rather than passivity, was survival conceivable, the clandestine press that did call for action deserves a place of honour in the history of the struggle for survival of the Jews in France during the German occupation.

b. Genesis of the Clandestine Press:

The first clandestine publications to appear in the occupied zone of France were issued by the Jewish Communist organization. As an integral part of the French Communist movement it had been banned in September 1939, and its prewar daily, the *Naye Presse* (New Press), no longer appeared. True to their revolutionary tradition, the Communist organizations soon resumed clandestine activities. As a consequence, well before three-fifths of France was occupied in June 1940, the Jewish section was already engaged in clandestine activities. Already then the Jewish Communists had organized illegal printing facilities and had begun publishing. Following the German occupation, their organization reemerged under the name Solidarité. Its former Yiddish newspaper reappeared as *Unzer vort*, and it was to continue to use this name until the liberation in August 1944.[27] The first illegally printed Bundist Yiddish leaflet appeared in Paris. Unlike the Communists, the Bundist organization had not been banned at the eve of the war. Its technical capacity to issue clandestine publications had simply been due to its leadership's foresight in preparing printing facilites as the German armies entered Paris.

While it was essential for organizations to have at their disposal the necessary technical facilites for publication, an infrastructure to ensure distribution was also required. The Communists, with their sizable membership and sympathizers, were able to resolve the problem.[28] As told in the memoirs of one of its leaders, Alfred Grant, Solidarité's organizational structures proved capable of maintaining production and distribution throughout and until the liberation in August 1944. But, as his memoirs indicate, this was only achieved at a high human cost and under extremely difficult conditions.[29]

The volume of Bund material published during the first two years of the occupation was not large, certainly far less than the Communists. Its first leaflet appeared in Paris in January 1941.[30] It was to be the only publication issued from occupied France, for all the others appeared in the Vichy zone where the Bund's leadership had moved. It maintained, however, an information bulletin and a newspaper, *Unzer kamf* (Our Fight), and it retained this name until 1943 when the CGD took over the title for its own publications. But it continued to appear intermittently until liberation as *Unzer shtime* (Our Voice).

In occupied Paris, other forces besides the Communists and the Bund had also considered publishing. In 1940, as the German army was arriving in Paris, the "Comité Amelot" was created by members of the Bund, Zionist organizations and the FSJF. By 1941, with the Amelot Committee firmly established, the Bund representatives proposed publishing a clandestine paper. The proposal was then rejected, considered beyond the Committee's capacity.[31] The Poale-Zion (Left) published occasional issues of its *Unzer shtime* between 1941 and July 1942, in the second half of 1943 an *Informatsye Buletin*, and from November 1943 the *Arbeter Tsaytung* (Workers Newspaper). The CGD published *Unzer kamf* from November 1943 and *Notre Lutte* in the last two months of the war. But no other movement besides the Communists succeeded in maintaining regular publication of newspapers, leaflets and appeals in both Yiddish and French. Throughout the occupation, the Communists, according to A. Rayski, had succeeded in publishing in Yiddish 42 issues of three newspapers under various names and in French 90 issues of twelve different newspapers and 62 leaflets and pamphlets.[32]

c. The Language of the Illegal Press until July 1942:

While addressing themselves to the problems confronting the community, the language used in the Left's publications today appears anachronistic. In the interwar years, the Jewish left-wing's press had adopted and made its own the slogans and terminology which were part and parcel of the political discourse common to all the political parties claiming to represent the working class. Their continued wartime usage must therefore be read and understood in the light of the shared language of the 1930s.

The earliest clandestine publications which appeared both in occupied France and in the whole of France came from the traditional Left: the Communist *Solidarité*, the Bund, Socialists and the Poale-Zion (Left). All appealed to their former constituency, the working class and the "*folks-mentshn*" (the common people) and for some years they continued to share the former political terminology. In November 1940, *Unzer vort* issued a greeting to the Soviet Union at the occasion of the 23rd anniversary of the Revolution. The first Bundist publication, printed in Paris in January 1941, was headed "*Tsu di yidishe masn*" (To the Jewish masses). In its analysis of the situation it contrasted the goals of Fascism and Socialism and their implications for the Jewish working class. This two-page publication concluded with a number of slogans among which we find "*Zol lebn der sotsializm*" (Long live Socialism).[33] It attacked Capitalism and praised Socialism.

In November 1940, Aron Bekerman in his diary referred to *Unzer vort* as the only Jewish revolutionary expression then in existence.[34] While his diary's entry is of historical interest in so far as it shows that there was already then a clandestine Jewish publication, the question, retrospectively, may well be asked: did the Jews, already victims of Franco-German discriminatory measures, need a "revolutionary movement"? On the occasion of May Day 1941, the Bund issued a statement addressed to the Jewish workers calling on them to mobilize their forces in the struggle against Fascism and Capitalism. As late as April-May 1942, the Bund still used the class-language of the 1930s, although by then 8,000 Parisian Jews languished in camps in occupied France, thousands of others in Vichy France and the first deportation to the East had already taken place. Capitalist exploitation was still considered responsible for the war. The Bund and Solidarité, whilst highly conscious of the ever worsening situation were still determined and convinced of the need to continue to propagandize their former ideological positions.

The impact upon the Jewish population of the early German measures, which were preceded and followed by a wave of Vichy laws and decrees, was analysed and conclusions were drawn in the Left's publications in narrowly political terms. As late as June 1943, a leaflet from the Poale-Zion (Left), while urging the Jewish youth to join fighting groups, still referred to Socialism and to the creation of a Socialist *Erets Israel*.[35] In the course of time, the Bundist publications adopted broader formulations as did the Communist publications, so that their only major differences can be found in references to the Soviet Union. The Bundist publications attacked the Soviet Union over the arrest and then the murder of its two leaders, Victor Alter and Henryk Ehrlich. And, until the Liberation, all the publications of Solidarité and the UJRE, while empha- sising communal united action, never failed to praise the Soviet Union and the Red Army.

d. The Content of the Clandestine Press:

Only a few issues of *Unzer vort* from before May 1941 have been pre- served. A. Rayski, one of Solidarité's leaders, has presented excerpts of issues published in September and October 1940. They refer to the Vichy government's policy of keeping in concentration camps Jewish immi- grants who in 1939 had joined the ranks of the French army and had been demobilized in the Vichy zone in 1940. By October, *Unzer vort* attacked the Paris Consistory, alleging that it was attempting to group all Jews into a single organization. These attacks reflected not only existing divisions within the community but also the lack of contacts between immigrant and native French Jewry.[36]

It was with the first internment of immigrant Jews, in May 1941, that Solidarité began a campaign which it was to pursue throughout the war. It called upon the French people to express its opposition to the persecu- tion of Jews. A leaflet in the French language called upon the non-Jewish population to join the Jews in protest. From November 1941, the articles in the clandestine press acquired a note of urgency. From then on issues such as the imposition of a Nazi-type *Judenrat*, the employment of work- ers and artisans in industries working for the German army, businessmen trading with the Germans and calls for resistance acquired more and more space in their pages.

The Vichy decision to establish a national *Judenrat* under the leader- ship of native French Jews, in particular, was strongly opposed by all the immigrant organizations. The earlier opposition encountered by the C.C. in the occupied zone was once more reaffirmed, but in more strident terms. On the eve of Vichy's announcement of the establishment of the Union Générale des Israélites de France (UGIF), *Unzer vort* labeled those notables who were solicited and tempted to accept a leadership role on these councils as "potential traitors":

Will there be in France those who will accept a "shameful col- laboration" with the destroyers of the Jewish people? We cannot believe it, but if there are such people they will be spewed out by the Jewish community, expelled as traitors, considered lepers by the Jewish masses.[37]

The Bund, in *Unzer kamf*, also opposed Jewish participation in an imposed council and declared:

> They want to organize Jewish shame . . . to create a moral ghet-to—to isolate the Jews . . . . [D]uring the Inquisition it was done by "itself;" today it is to be done with Jewish participation. No. A thousand times No !!![38]

In Paris, between September and December 1941, massive strikes of Jewish workers in various industries, involving hundreds of workers, some lasting as long as six weeks, were organized by the Communist-led illegal trade union organization and supported by the Bund. *Unzer vort* and *Unzer kamf* not only called for support of these strikes but also for a broad boycott by the workers of any work useful to the German war effort. Appeals were made to Jewish businessmen and manufacturers not to trade or work for the Germans.[39]

In April 1942, the Bund issued an appeal in *Unzer kamf* to all workers and employers to refuse to work or deal with the Germans:

> Hitler's armies not only need planes and tanks, but clothes, shoes and knitwear. Jewish businessmen! Do not trade with your murderers! Jewish workers and artisans! Do not work for your tormentors!! No one should freely work for Hitler's war machine. Where compelled, destroy, work slowly, the slower the sooner freedom. All means must be used.[40]

By June 1942, Solidarité, as if anticipating what was to come, declared in *Unzer vort* that "The Jewish masses feel that the fate of the community is being decided." This somber warning was reiterated with a note of urgency when Solidarité launched a desperate appeal to the workers to "sabotage production," to "break the machines," to "tear up the clothes."[41]

Until July 1942, the illegal publications had addressed themselves to the terrible conditions prevailing in Drancy, the camp which would soon become the main French transit point to Auschwitz, and to Compiègne from where, in March, the first deportation had already taken place. Appeals to the Jewish population for solidarity and a campaign of protest regarding the conditions in the Drancy camp filled the pages. The introduction of the "Yellow star" in June 1942 was attacked by *Unzer vort* and *Unzer kamf* as a medieval measure.[42] At the end of June, Solidarité issued an appeal calling upon the French to express their solidarity with the Jewish population.[43]

It was early in July 1942 that a special leaflet in Yiddish began to circulate in Paris. Issued by Solidarité, it warned immigrant Jewry that extraordinary large arrests were about to take place. The leaflet announced:

> According to information from impeccable sources the Germans will soon launch immense arrests and deportations of Jews. The extermination of the Jews must act as a warning to the French who oppose the enslavement of their country. . . . To close one's eyes before the tragic reality is suicidal. Open your eyes. Becoming conscious of the danger will lead to salvation, to resistance and to life.
>
> Each Jew confronts the question: what must be done in order not to fall into the hands of the criminal SS ? What must be done to hasten their end and your liberation ? . . . .
>
> 1) Do not wait at home. Hide yourself and in the first place the children.
>
> 2) Once one's freedom is guaranteed, join a fighting patriotic organization to combat the bloody enemy and avenge their crimes.
>
> 3) If you fall into the hands of the criminals, resist by all available means. Block the doors, call for help . . . attempt to flee. Not a single Jew must become a victim. Each Jew free and alive is a victory upon our enemy who shall not and will not succeed in our extermination.[44]

Although rumors of an imminent mass arrest of immigrant Jews in Paris were widespread on the eve of 16 July 1942, Solidarité's leaflet had played its part in informing the Jews. For Solidarité was the only mass organization in Paris capable of widely disseminating the news. Neither the Bundists nor the Zionists had the means to do so. All they could do was resort to word of mouth. But none of their recommendations went as far as Solidarité's. No other organization recommended that Jews barricade their homes, refuse to surrender and join the resistance movement.

July 1942 represents the crucial turning point in the life and death of the Jews in France. It marked the introduction of the Final Solution on French soil. The process of the destruction of French Jewry began with the deportation of the immigrant Jews. The arrest of close to 13,000 men, women and children, which began on 16 July, and continued over a few days, was carried out by the French police. Of an unprecedented nature, this mass arrest heralded a new phase. Until then only men had been arrested. From then on, no Jew was safe, irrespective of age, sex or state of health, and within four weeks this edict extended across the whole of France.[45]

The French police had selected from earlier censuses the names and addresses of 23,000 Jews, but they only succeeded in arresting 13,000. Some 10,000 men, women and children had been able to hide. Yet, despite the rumors, the newspapers and the leaflets, organizations such as Solidarité lost many members. Not even its own members and supporters were prepared to believe that women and children would also be arrested. Solidarité was not the only organization to lose members, as the Bund, the Poale-Zion and the FSJF, all equally well informed, also lost both members and leaders.

The issue of the role and function of the illegal press in the struggle for survival, as exemplified by the warnings it provided on the eve of July 1942, gives rise to an important question: did the arrests of many of its editors, printers and distributors, either as resisters or simply as Jews, warrant the need for continued publication? What evidence and justification did their publishers have of their effectiveness? Yet such questions were never asked. The fact remains that publication was never interrupted. Despite police arrests, organizations such as Solidarité never once considered stopping publication. If anything, the July 1942 events provided its leadership with the renewed determination that its press had an important role to play in the struggle.

Continued efforts were made to inform the remaining Jews of what was taking place in Drancy, of the brutal separation of the children from their parents and their subsequent deportation. Increasingly, news of the mass killings in Poland and other occupied territories was reported. It was

in October 1942 that Solidarité's leadership learned from a Pole recently
arrived from Poland that gas was used to kill Jews. *J'Accuse*, published
by the Franco-Jewish organization MNCR, was the first to publish the
news and it was soon taken up by its other publication, *Fraternité*. The
decision to publish the news in the French language was consistent with
Solidarité's strategy that succor resided in the non-Jewish world, and with
the churches in particular. For, of all the forces likely to aid the Jews, the
churches needed to be won over in their defense.[46] Yet the news of the use
of gas was not given prominence nor emphasized in the underground
press. The decision to print the news was debated by Solidarité's leadership and considered in view of its potential negative impact. The resultant
fear and the despondency the news might induce could not be ignored.
Nevertheless, regardless of its possible negative impact, the decision was
taken to publish. Considered retrospectively, the publication of this new
horror had no impact on the Jewish population in France. It is evidenced
by the fact that no single survivor deported from France to Auschwitz,
including members from Solidarité, has ever reported that he expected to
be gassed upon arrival in the camp. It can nonetheless be argued that
Solidarité's decision to publish was moved by the same sense of historical reponsibility that guided Emanuel Ringelblum when he rejoiced that
his report about the planned extermination of Polish Jewry had reached
the West.[47]

A dominant feature of the underground press, following the mass
deportations which began in July 1942, was the reporting of news of the
mass murders of Jews in the East. However disturbing such news was for
the Jews originally from Eastern Europe, it was the news of the Warsaw
Ghetto Uprising that reached France shortly after its outbreak which had
the most profound impact. By June 1943, all immigrant organizations
knew the fate of Polish Jewry. What astounded most was that the Jews of
Warsaw, the remnants of the largest ghetto in Europe, had been prepared
to die rather than submit. In June 1943, Poale-Zion (Left) issued a leaflet
in which it declared: "A people is losing its blood. Must we let ourselves
be killed like sheep?"[48] In September, Poale-Zion's *Arbeter Tsaytung*
briefed its readers and emphasized the heroism of the ghetto fighters. In
June and again in September, echoing the Vilna underground, it continued
to proclaim that "It is enough: we shall not be slaves."[49] The news of the
Warsaw Ghetto Uprising directly contributed to the unification of all

immigrant forces and indirectly with the organizations representing native French Jews.

In April 1944, *Notre voix*, issued by the UJRE, not only commemorated the Warsaw Ghetto Uprising but also reported the uprisings which had taken place in the Bialystok ghetto and in Treblinka.[50] Until liberation, the clandestine Jewish press continued to urge the Jews to fight back. As late as June 1944, after the landing of the Allied forces and on the eve of the end of the German occupation, this press continually sought to convince the remaining population to hide and to ignore the Jewish council's recommendations to abide by the German and Vichy laws.[51]

Conclusions:

No comparison between the function of the illegal press in the struggle for survival with the practical work of aid and rescue can, or needs, to be made. In the final analysis what mattered above all to the Jewish population which was still free was not information but concrete and effective assistance. Each family, each Jew, knew what was required for survival. What each Jew needed was a safe place to hide, good identity papers and material aid. Considered in such terms the contribution of that press to daily survival is difficult to measure and partially explains why a study of this specific issue has not been previously undertaken.

We can quantify the numbers of Jews who were helped, the material aid distributed, but it is impossible to compare these facts with the role of the underground press. Were the tremendous efforts made by its publishers, and above all by its distributors, to inform the population, to warn it, to seek to convince it of the threat it confronted wasted, misplaced or of marginal importance? To present the issue in such terms is to fail to recognize the indirect but historical contribution to survival made by the Jewish resistance in general and in particular of the significance of the sacrifices made by those who answered the press' call to join the armed resistance. Viewed in such terms we would have to conclude that the clandestine press did contribute to the defense of the Jews.

One criterion by which we can establish the role of the press was its function as a disseminator of information. For a population placed in a ghetto without walls, forbidden to own radios, news was eagerly sought. Each Jew knew that his life depended upon the outcome of the war. Information was essential if people were to retain faith that they would yet live to see freedom. Furthermore, until the Liberation, organizations such as Solidarité were convinced that the fate of the Jews depended upon the assistance of the non-Jewish population and that it would come to the aid of the Jews if it was informed. The campaign of information conducted by the MNCR among the French people and the churches assisted in creating the appropriate climate. In this sense the struggle for the dissemination of information can be said to have been vital.

A further criterion must also be considered: the press as a platform for the presentation and discussion of policies among the Jewish organizations. As Rayski has pointed out, that press was also a laboratory of ideas.[52] It was in the pages of the Communist press that ideas on what it believed needed to be done were presented and developed. Indeed, an organization such as Solidarité used its press to present policies which contributed in raising debates within the ranks of all the immigrant organizations. Its repeated calls for a united front, irrespective of political tendencies, contributed to the creation of constructive dialogues with other organizations. In Paris, in September 1941, its press played its part in influencing a number of immigrant organizations to join forces and create a United Workers Party. This development was the direct outcome of the appeal from the Jewish Anti-Fascist Committee of Moscow. That the United Workers Party proved temporary and only lasted a few months is immaterial. Solidarité's publications' repeated calls for united action were certainly a decisive factor in the forging of the CGD.[53] One can also argue that, in December 1943, it contributed to the creation of the appropriate political climate for a dialogue between immigrant organizations and native French Jewry which resulted in the creation of the *Conseil Représentatif des Israélites de France* (CRIF). The press as a platform for the presentation of policies and the development of debates as to an appropriate course of action found justification in the final outcome, the unification of all the forces.

There is yet another criterion which can be used to evaluate the role of the press. Organizations such as Solidarité, and then the UJRE, had always taken the view that their publications were a medium for organizing. Wherever their publications were distributed they were not only directed at convincing the readers of the need to take steps for their self-protection but also to encourage them to join the organized struggle. Thus, the press fulfilled a wide-ranging agenda: to keep the community informed and also to contribute to the development of organized resistance.

The view that the clandestine press served as a vehicle for information, a laboratory of ideas and as a means of radicalizing the population was only partially recognized by other organizations. Neither the Bund nor any other organization ever perceived their publications in the same terms. Overwhelmed by the situation, they committed their forces to day-to-day activities. They formed committees wherever sizable Jewish communities existed. But instead of seeking to draw more people into their activities and thus develop widespread networks of activists, they fell back on their own small nuclei. These groups were never oriented towards, nor felt the need, to establish organizations with mass participation.

In conclusion, the French Jewish clandestine press deserves to be given the appropriate credit. It deserves to be considered as an integral part of the struggle for survival. It saw itself, above all, as the bearer of a historic responsibility. Like the armed struggle in which hundreds of Jewish men, women and young people gave their lives, there was never any doubt in the minds of the clandestine press' publishers and distributors that they were making a contribution to the defeat of Nazi Germany. The press, just like the armed struggle, was an article of faith. It was an expression of a continued and profound desire to do whatever was possible to make the murderers pay for their crimes and to contribute to the defeat of Nazi Germany. As such, its role and effectiveness cannot and should not be measured by the same criteria used to assess those activities directly involved in the daily protection of the population.

Notes:

1. For a survey of the Jewish press in France during that period, see Z. Szajkowski, "Bibliography of the Jewish Press in France and the Jewish Colonies (with an introduction on: 150 years of the Jewish press in France)," in E. Tcherikower (ed.), *Yidn in Frankraykh. Shtudyes un materyaln* (New York: Yivo, 1942) 1: 236–308. Besides two dailies there were also an extremely wide range of periodicals. For the number of publications issued by political movements, see ibid., 1: 244, table III.

2. The term "clandestine press" shall refer to all publications issued, such as news sheets, internal bulletins, leaflets and pamphlets. All were generally produced by editorial boards made up of former editors, journalists and writers. All translations in the text are by the author.

3. See L. Lazare, *La Résistance Juive en France.* intro. S. Friedlander (Paris, 1987); A. Kaspi, *Les Juifs pendant l'occupation* (Paris, 1991).

4. See J. Adler, *The Jews of Paris and the Final Solution. Communal Responses and Internal Conflicts* (New York, 1985); for a concise presentation of the origins of the C.C., see J. Biélinky, "Colonie Scolaire, Comité de Coordination," in *Journal, 1940–1942. Un journaliste juif à Paris sous l'occupation*, edited by R. Poznanski (Paris, 1992), 277–284.

5. Although all former newspapers had to apply to the German censorship board for permission to print, no former Jewish newspaper did so. In the Vichy zone, French laws did permit all papers formerly published in Paris to apply and be allowed to reappear. *Terre Retrouvée*, Keren Kayemeth's bi-monthly, applied but was refused permission on the ground of "inopportunity;" see "Les organisations sionistes," in *L'Activité des Organisations Juives en France sous l'Occupation* (Paris, 1947), 181–182.

6. Israel Israelowitz and Wilhem Biberstein arrived in Paris on 18 March 1941. For their role in the C.C., see J. Adler, *The Jews of Paris and the Final solution*, 65–72.

7. For a cinematographic, but historically accurate, presentation of the manner by which the first issues of *Informations Juives* were distributed, see the movie, *Mr. Klein* (France, 1977). Collections of the newspaper are held at the Centre de Documentation Juive Contemporaine (hereafter CDJC) and the Library of the Alliance Universelle Juive, both in Paris.

8. See Ruven Grinberg, "Les Juifs à Paris sous l'Occupation allemande," YIVO Archives, Record Group Tcherikower, file 1650.

9. 13 December 1943.

10. 25 December 1942.

11. The first letters from Birkenau arrived on 15 January 1943 and the names of their recipients were published in the *Bulletin* until 25 June 1943.

12. Chief Rabbi P. Hagenauer, writing to A. Baur, then Vice-President of the UGIF, opposed a Yiddish supplement. In a letter of protest he wrote:

> I must say that the Judeo-German insert . . . displeases me even
> more than my faithful. I cannot but think that all our miseries

come from bodies, newspapers and journals which our foreign co-religionists have introduced in France since the Armistice [1918]. It is an error which we must not perpetuate. Hagenauer to Baur, 4 February 1942, YIVO Archives, RG UGIF, LXXXI-II–24, 058. A. Baur, however, did not accept such a xenophobic view. The last Yiddish insert appeared on 12 December 1942. The end of the Yiddish supplement came to reflect the virtual disappearance of immigrant Jewry in occupied France, either through deportations or by going into hiding.

13. See minutes of meeting between Brunner and Baur, 30 June 1943, YIVO Archives, RG UGIF, IV, 4, 0113, during which Brunner demanded that the number of pages be increased and that it be renamed as *Presse Juive* and be distributed throughout France.

14. See J. Bielinky, *Journal, 1940–1942*, entry 22 April, 1941, and endnote 26, on p.107.

15. Ibid., entry 26 August 1941.

16. On the issue of the recruitment of workers to the Ardennes, see Adler, *The Jews of Paris*, 73–76; see also M. Rajfus, *Des Juifs dans la collaboration. L'UGIF 1941–1944*. (Paris, 1980), 219–230.

17. See R. Grinberg's report, "Les Juifs à Paris sous l'Occupation allemande," YIVO Archives, RG Tcherikower, file 1650.

18. The clandestine press' attacks upon the C.C. and the UGIF will be discussed below.

19. See "Les Organisations sionistes" in *L'Activité des Organisations Juives*, 182–183. J. Fisher, on behalf of the Zionist movement, intermittently issued newsletters twice monthly with information from Palestine; see CDJC, CCXX–67.

20. Also referred to as "Le document vert" (CDJC, CCXII–68). For an account of its composition, see H. Hertz "Le document vert," Yad Vashem Archive, P7/4.

21. Reproduced in D. Knout, *Contribution à l'histoire de la Résistance Juive en France 1940–1944* (Paris, 1947), 96. Only three numbers were published of which, besides the excerpt presented by Knout, only the second issue has been preserved.

22. As late as February 1943, the FSJF was still operating legally in the Vichy zone, although already then it combined both legal and illegal activities. It was a founding member of the CGD when established in July 1943; see L. Lazare, *La résistance juive en France* (Paris, 1987) 248, 253.

Its newspaper owed its publication to the assistance of the *Mouvement des Jeunesses Sionistes* (MJS); see A. Rayski, *Le choix des Juifs sous Vichy. Entre soumission et résistance* (Paris, 1992),180.
23. Information kindly provided to the author by A. Rayski.
24. L. Gronowski, *L'Antisémitisme, le Racisme et les Juifs* (Paris, 1941) was issued in 25,000 copies; see J. Ravine, *La Résistance organisée des Juifs en France (1940–1944)* (Paris, 1973), 78. In the course of an interview, D. Diamant, the post-war UJRE archivist, asserted that Jewish Communist publications were generally printed in runs of 3,000 to 5,000 copies, a quantity which seems inordinately high and for which there is no available confirming evidence.
25. For the issue of the debate within the CGD over the question of armed resistance, see J. Ravine, *La Résistance organisée des Juifs en France*, 154. For a brief but incisive comment by a former leader of the Communist movement on this question, see A. Rayski, *Le choix des Juifs*, 180.
26. For the list of Jews executed in December 1941, see S. Klarsfeld, *Le Livre des otages* (Paris, 1979); for the December crisis see, J. Adler, *The Jews of Paris*, 109–110; for the Communist press' analysis of the situation see, *Solidaritet*, December 1941, in *Dos vort fun vidershtand un zig* (Paris, 1949), 69–70.
27. See A. Rayski's memoirs, *Nos illusions perdues* (Paris, 1980), 67.
28. In a personal interview with the author, D. Diamant stated that by mid-1941 Solidarité's membership and supporters in Paris numbered 2,000 people. If such was the case, and we do not have the means of verifying his statement, it certainly had the necessary manpower to ensure a wide distribution of its publications.
29. A. Grant, *Pariz a shtot fun front* (Paris, 1958). For the list of editors of its various publications and their fate, see S. Courtois and A. Rayski, *Qui savait quoi? L'Extermination des Juifs, 1941–1945* (Paris,1987), 118.
30. "Tsu di yidishe masn!," a two-sided leaflet, claims to have been printed in Paris in early January 1941. It already referred to the establishment of a "*Judenrat*" which was formally established on 31 January 1941 (copy kindly provided by Mr.Waiszbrot of the Medem Library, Paris).
31. See Y. Jakobowitz, *Ru Amelot. Hilf un vidershtand* (Paris, 1948), 52; see also Jakobowitz, "Fun aristocrat zu a konspirator," in *Léon Glazer,*

Der kultur un frayhayt-kemfer, ed. C. Tchoubinski (Paris, 1947), 34–38.

32. For a list of the names of the various newspapers and their editors, see S. Courtois and A. Rayski, *Qui savait quoi?*, 118. The figures for the number of illegal leaflets and pamphlets were presented in a paper read by A. Rayski in 1993 at the United States Holocaust Memorial Museum in Washington. The author thanks Rayski for permission to quote.

33. Medem Library (Paris).

34. *Dos vort fun vidershtand un zig*, 37.

35. Leaflet issued in June 1943, CDJC, CDLXX–97.

36. See S. Courtois and A. Rayski *Qui savait quoi?*, 123–125; see also extracts from A. Bekerman's journal, in *Dos vort fun vidershtand un zig*, 31–37. For the pre-occupation period, which refers to *Unzer vort* appearing before the arrival of the German armies, see *Bleter far Geshikhte* (Warsaw) VIII, no.2–3, pp. 59–85.

37. *Unzer vort*, 36, 6/12/1941, French transl. by A. Wieviorka in *Le Monde Juif*, Jan.-Mar. 1987, 125, pp.27–29. Original Yiddish in *Dos vort fun vidershtand un zig*, 65–67.

38. *Unzer kamf*, 1, June 1942, (YIVO Archives, France, II World War, 1–1, 0057–0059).

39. See J. Adler, *The Jews of Paris and the Final Solution*, 184–186.

40. April 1942, in YIVO Archives, France, II World War, 1–9, 005–007.

41. 1 June 1942, in *Dos vort fun vidershtand un zig*, 99–100.

42. *Solidaritet*, no.3, 1/4/1942, in *Dos vort fun vidershtand un zig*, 91–2; *Unzer vort*, in ibid., 107–108; *Unzer kamf*, no.2, June 1942 (YIVO Archives, France, II World War, 1–1, 008–0046).

43. See S. Courtois and A. Rayski, *Qui savait quoi?*, 140–141.

44. Underlining in original; see *Dos vort fun vidershtand un zig*, 105–106.

45. For the evidence of the preparations and the role of the French authorities in the July 1942 mass arrests of immigrant Jews in Paris, see S. Klarsfeld, *Vichy-Auschwitz: le role de Vichy dans la solution finale de la question juive en France, 1942* (Paris, 1983).

46. *J'Accuse*, no. 2, 20 Oct.1942; *Fraternité*, no. 3, Feb. 1943, in S. Courtois and A. Rayski, *Qui savait quoi?*,155–156, 170–174.

47. For the debate over whether to publish or not, see A. Rayski, *Le Choix des Juifs*, 175–177; for E. Ringelblum, see his *Ksovim fun geto*, ed. by J. Kermish (Tel Aviv, 1985) 1: 376–377, entry dated 26 June 1942.

48. June 1943 (CDJC, CDLXX–97).

49. *Arbeter Tsaytung*, September 1943 (CDJC, CDLXX–141).

50. *Notre Voix*, April 1944, no. 71, in *La Presse antiraciste*, 179–189.

51. A leaflet entitled "Les Juifs de France contribueront de toutes leurs forces a l'écrasement de l'ennemi hitlerien," in *La Presse antiraciste*, 213–215.

52. S. Courtois and A. Rayski, *Qui savait quoi?*, 119.

53. For Bundist views, see P. Shrager, *Oyfn rand fun tsvey tkufes (zekhroynes)* (Paris, 1976), 170–171.

Greek Journalism

The Greek Press, 1933–1945:
The Writing on the Walls

Yitzchak Kerem
Aristotle University, Thessaloniki, Greece

The press in Greece, the general public press as well as the Jewish press in Salonika and Athens, presented very informative accounts of the course of events in Nazi Germany from the ascendance of Hitler to power in 1933 and Germany's expansion throughout Europe until the liberation in 1945. Each major step of Hitler was documented from 1933 until the German occupation of Greece in April 1941. Afterward, the pro-German press served as a vicious vehicle of anti-Semitism and incitement, in particular toward the large Judeo-Spanish speaking Sephardic population in Salonika and other parts of Macedonia. The leftist components of the Greek resistance, ELAS-EAM, publicized bulletins calling for the Jews to try to escape from deportation and encouraging the mainstream Greek Orthodox population to protect the Jews. Greece was liberated in fall 1944; by the spring of 1945 the press published items about the horrors that the Jews suffered in the death camps, but the local population had a hard time believing the stories of the survivors.

In the 1930s, the Jewish press in Salonika reported about the Hitler regime, Nazi terror, the 1936 Olympics, *Kristallnacht*, etc. Some of the local Jewish elite were Germanophiles and adherents of German culture. They were aware of the events in Germany and the character of the Nazi regime. The Salonikan Jewish leader Leon Recanati left his birthplace in 1934 for Palestine after a disturbing business trip to Germany before Hitler's accession to power. Despite the Depression, Recanati's business in Salonika was flourishing, but he foresaw danger. In Germany, while going to his hotel in Dresden, he had passed one of the main squares where a huge crowd listened in an impressive silence to a stormy speech by none other than the *Führer*, Adolph Hitler. The latter mapped out his political program and the plan of the Nazi Party. Recanati, who understood German well, thought to himself that if Hitler ever took power, he would have a catastrophic effect on Europe and the Jewish people as well.[1]

At first there was a sense of optimism toward the future of German Jewry in the Salonikan Jewish press, even after the initial outbreak of anti-Semitic agitation and hostilities. *Axion* noted that there was no equality for German Jewry and new legislation differentiated between Jews and Aryans,[2] but the newspaper reported that the German Minister of Justice was going to declare an "armistice" in the recent promulgation of Jewish laws. The Minister of National Economy and the head of the political department of the Nazi Party had addressed an appeal to the general population to abstain in the future from boycotting Jewish businesses. The Justice Minister was reported as saying that, "The problem of the Jews in Germany can be considered as resolved and in consequence all hostile activity must stop and is going to stop."[3] He also was noted as saying that the foregoing point would demonstrate to all the world that the Jews were living in Germany by virtue of the laws and could continue to live in tranquility. He further commented that the Jews could escape their tragedy by the creation of a Jewish State in Palestine. In Geneva, at the League of Nations, when numerous nations discussed the Jewish question, the German representative favored the proposition of the Dutch delegate to form an international organization to come to the assistance of the German refugees. Former United States President Hoover was nominated to head the body. At the League of Nations, numerous nations spoke in favor of easing restrictions on Jewish immigration to Palestine. After the below enumerated Campbell riots in 1931, some 15,000–18,000 Salonikan Jews would immigrate to Palestine by 1938, but British-imposed immigration restrictions hindered thousands of other Greek Jews from moving to *Erets-Israel* and saving themselves from annihilation in the Holocaust at the hands of the Nazis.

The Jewish press in Salonika traced the German steps designed to legitimize German expansion. Articles reported details and usually did not add political or editorial commentary. In 1934, *Axion* publicized Germany's first move to enhance its hold on the Saar region by formulating an agreement with France calling for a popular plebiscite to determine sovereignty.[4] In August of the same year, the newspaper lamented German President Hindenburg's death, recalling that he had made no distinction between Aryans and non-Aryans and was supported by German Jewry in the 1932 elections. The paper also showed a stern-looking picture of Hitler, symbolizing a much different reality.[5]

The aggressive and violent nature of Hitler had already been depicted in the Jewish *Axion*, when it reported the June 30, 1934, massacre ("The Night of the Long Knives") in which scores of prominent Nazis and others were shot and 1,500 arrested at Hitler's order. The SA leader, Ernst Röhm, was executed for treason, though there were also numerous reported suicides.[6] It was also noted that even German army generals and non-aligned politicians like General von Schleicher or the head of the Catholic Party von Klausner had committed suicide. The question of to what extent the terror would continue was posed. The severity of the events was so great that *Axion* even wrote an editorial on the same front page about Hitler's actions. Hitler was viewed as spreading violence but becoming indispensable and a recurrence of past German anti-Semitism since World War I and the economic crisis. The Jews would not return to their past state. By now, the gentile lawyers, judges, doctors, artists, journalists, and so forth, had replaced the Jews and become propagandists against them. The editorial also noted that anti-Semitism existed not only in Germany, but throughout the whole world as a sickness that attacked during war and suffering, or during economic crises that hurt all of humanity. The article stated that currently liberalism was paralyzed as strong or dictatorial regimes prevailed; for leaders like Hitler, Mussolini, Horthy, and Kemal Ataturk, second-class people, like the Jews, were not important. German national chauvinism was pushing itself to the utmost extremes. There was a call for Hitler to go, which would bring upon the Jews great joy and a real Purim holiday, but this was unrealistic and wishful thinking. The issue was further discussed on the back page, where foreign news was typically covered.[7] The main point of the article was that Hitler pretended that he had not ordered the executions. The headline noted that thousands had died that weekend. This seems exaggerated in view of other accounts. Hitler was quoted as saying that the deaths were necessary in order to avoid the spilling of the blood of many thousands of people and soldiers. The German Council of Ministers also approved of the measures taken, called for a state of emergency, and promulgated a law repressing citizens who acted against the country. The article concluded by noting that an absolute state of military dictatorship prevailed in Germany. The local Jews in Salonika, reading such articles, clearly became aware of the terror and brutality that the Hitler regime incited and encouraged.

In March 1935, the Salonikan newspaper *Le Progrés* reprinted a letter that Julius Streicher, editor of the Nazi newspaper *Der Stürmer*, addressed to the French newspaper *Le Currier*.[8] Between the lines, one sees Streicher's hate for the Jews and a concurrent wave of disinformation. Streicher declared that "irresponsible elements had spread the lie" that the "Israelites" had plotted against the life of the *Führer*; leaflets had even been put up to incite the population to a pogrom. Streicher bluntly called for punishment of those who propagated the rumor. Moreover, the Nazi editor called for strict discipline against any irresponsible elements who "commit such imprudent behavior" and who should be expelled from the Nazi Party and arrested.[9]

In 1936, the local Salonikan Jewish French newspapers, *Le Progrés* and *L'Independant*, exposed the evil of the Nazi regime. When the Swiss Nazi leader, Dr. Wilhelm Gustloff, was murdered, *L'Independant* commented that there was no reaction against the Jews, but the paper exposed the lunacy and madness of the anti-Jewish German regime of barbaric Nazis and its potential to harm the German Jews.[10] The editor of *Le Progrés*, Sam Modiano, wrote that the Olympic games prevented the outbreak of anti-Semitism in retaliation for the murder of the Nazi leader Dr. Gustloff at Davos.[11] Not wanting embarrassment at the important Olympic games, the authorities halted retaliatory reprisals against German Jewry. Modiano also noted the efforts of Alfred Rosenberg, the theoretician of racism, and Streicher, editor of *Der Stürmer*, seeking to advance Nazi propaganda abroad, spreading hatred toward the Jews. On the other hand, Streicher and the Nazi Party collected clippings from the Salonikan Jewish press that dealt with the latter's awareness of the development of the Nazi regime and the ensuing anti-Semitism.[12]

James G. McDonald was appointed High Commissioner for Refugees from Germany under the League of Nations in autumn 1933. After two years of frustration, and in the aftermath of the Nuremberg Laws, McDonald tendered his resignation. Salonika's *Axion* reported that in his letter of resignation, McDonald recommended that measures be taken against Germany in order to decrease numbers of emigrants. The article also noted that German Jewry was managing in the midst of its suffering.[13]

The Judeo-Spanish press of Salonika closely followed the developments of German expansionism and the escalation of World War II at the end of the 1930s and in 1940. The two main Judeo-Spanish newspapers, *El Mesagero* and *Axion,* published daily reports of Hitler's proclamations, German diplomatic activity, and the German military conquests drawing on English and French press agencies. Salonikan Jewry read on the front page of *Axion* about Germany's rapid assault and advance into Poland,[14] about the German attacks on Belgium and France,[15] plans to attack Switzerland,[16] Germany's success in conquering Norway,[17] the German sinking of the English destroyer *Royal Oak* and the heavy loss of life,[18] and fears of a German attack on England.[19] Hitler's ambitions for expansion into *Lebensraum* (living space) beyond Germany's eastern borders, so as to include the formerly German peoples, were clearly depicted in *El Mesagero.*[20]

The naiveté of the Salonikan Jewish press resembled that of England's Chamberlain, who was repeatedly fooled by German peace agreements and believed that each additional country assaulted would be the last step. The hope for peace reflected in the Jewish press was highly improbable in light of the continuous German military advances. On January 21, 1940, *Axion*[21] published an article in which Professor Brodetsky of the World Zionist Executive raised the issue of Jewish representation at a Peace Conference. Not only was such an idea farfetched and impractical at that time, but the *Axion* article noted the prospect of Poland's liberation and the need to resolve the minority question in such a state. The article also stated the need for equality and liberty for European Jewry in the future, but seems totally out of place in view of the German advance in Eastern Europe after the *Anschluss* and the ensuing anti-Semitism, arrests, and extension of the Nuremberg Laws. When one notes the Jewish newspaper's coverage of the escalation of German anti-Semitism since 1933, the article seems very out of place and overly utopian in nature. *Axion*'s competitor *El Mesagero* on October 6, 1939, published reports from Berlin affirming that Hitler had no designs for conquering Western Europe. Thus the Greek Jewish press repeated what was part of the German propaganda campaign of disinformation and trickery, weakening better and more critical judgement.[22]

Salonikan Jews also read in their Jewish press about the fate of the Jews of Poland under German occupation. At the end of October 1939, less than two months after the beginning of German occupation, the Salonikan Jewish daily newspaper *Mesagero* reported that 40,000 Jews had died in Lublin.[23] The article noted that the Germans wanted to establish a Jewish state there, although there were other rumors regarding a Jewish state to be established in Galicia to which all the Polish Jews were to be transferred. The Greek Jewish daily further mentioned a Jewish Telegraphic Agency report that a Jewish region would be set up in Poland, to which Jews would be sent from other areas. Gentile Poles residing in the designated Jewish area would be relocated elsewhere.

At the end of January 1940, *Axion* reported that 2,608 Palestinian subjects had been arrested by the Germans in occupied Poland.[24] Salonika's Jews knew little about the establishment of the Warsaw Ghetto where, starting in August 1943, some Greek Jewish prisoners sent from Auschwitz would clear and clean up rubble left after the unsuccessful Jewish revolt.[25]

In following the course of the war, *Mesagero* noted the conditions for peace that Germany set.[26] Hitler's avowed war aims included establishing order in the neighboring countries and providing solutions for the minorities questions in all the countries of Southeastern Europe, as well as making an effort to resolve the Jewish problem, reorganization of commercial and economic life, dealing with Poland so that it could not take action against Germany and Russia, and reorganization of Europe's security. Hitler noted that England rejected these conditions and for this reason the England of Churchill and Chamberlain must disappear. While the ultimate nature of Hitler's solutions for the Jews and occupied Europe could not then be comprehended, the brutally violent character of his continued aggression was apparent.

From Hitler's speech to the Nazi Party for the new year of 1940, *Mesagero* published the following excerpt regarding Jews:[27]

> The Germans have an enemy. Judaism and capitalism are going to proceed against us. And this enemy only has one aim: to endanger Germany and the German people. Despite the attempts to hide this aim, nothing can change their real intentions.

Hitler added that the Jewish agitators and the reactionaries in the capitalist countries had long hoped for this moment; they were prepared and did not want to abandon their projects for destruction of Germany. The article revealed Hitler's deeply embedded anti-Semitism and his vicious incitement and demagoguery. However, most of Salonikan Jewry did not have enough political sophistication and foresight to realize that they were also among Hitler's targets.

The Jewish press in Salonika often followed the military actions of the English forces with great admiration. Britain was regarded as the active power that would stand up to the Germans. During January 1940, there were articles about the possibility that Britain would bomb Berlin, as well as about the British embargo against Germany.[28] The press also reported Hitler's bombastic proclamations and ferocious intentions of defeating the British.[29] On January 26, 1940, *Axion* reported that the British had confiscated as war contraband 25,000 postal items, which had been shipped from the United States to Germany.[30]

The local Jewish Salonikan press had great faith in the Allies and pointed out the magnitude of their efforts. *Axion* noted at the end of January 1940, that in the course of two months the United States had spent five hundred million dollars on munitions and military preparations.[31]

Italy confronted the Greek dictator Metaxas with an ultimatum on October 28, 1940, demanding that Greece surrender. The Hellenes rejected the ultimatum and war broke out between Greek and Italian forces in the region of the Albanian border. The next day, *Mesagero* appeared with bombastic front-page headlines like "G-d is with us" and "We have with us the Allies . . . and Justice."[32] The paper noted that this war was imposed on Greece, and the Greeks would be victorious. As the Greek forces valiantly repulsed the Italians, Salonika's Jews did not envision that the Germans would come to the Italians' aid, invade Greece and impose an occupation that would be catastrophic for the Greek Jews and the country in general.

The Salonikan Jewish press had previously covered the subject of Italian aggression and the role of Italy in the Axis alliance. The Jewish newspapers in June 1940 were open and frank in writing about Italy's declaration of war on France and England[33] and about Allied progress in fighting against Italy,[34] but did not touch on the predicament of Salonikan Jewry in view of their Italian connections and the arrest of numerous Italian subjects by the Greek government when the Albanian campaign began at the end of October 1940. Subsequently, the Italians treated the Jews well during their occupation in Greece; as long as Italian forces were present, the Jews were for the most part not harmed.[35] In Salonika, the Italian diplomatic corps made great efforts to save some 800 Jews from deportation and sent most of them to Athens by Italian military train. After the Italian occupation regime was replaced by the Germans in autumn 1943, most of these Italian subjects and protectees were deported from Athens to Birkenau by the Germans in April 1944.[36]

On April 6, 1940, *Mesagero* announced that new military successes had been achieved along the Albanian front and Greece had improved many of its strategic positions.[37] The article displayed chauvinism and overconfidence in the military capabilities of Greece. The very same day, Greece was attacked by Germany on the Macedonian and Bulgarian fronts.

The situation in Greece during the period prior to the German invasion is described by Leigh White, a reporter for the Jewish Telegraphic Agency, who visited Greece in March 1941. Injured in a Stuka dive-bombing in Patras, White remained in Greece until evacuated by the British enroute to Lisbon on September 15, 1941.[38] He sensed an anti-Italian feeling amongst the people he met; a natural feeling in light of the Albanian campaign during which Greece suffered many casualties in the fighting from October 28, 1940, until April 1941. He also observed the great reverence that the admirers of the Metaxas dictatorship had for the Germans, but he misperceived the nature of the Greek people. Although he judged that they would not fight against the Germans,[39] he was utterly incorrect. White observed that the Greek government was fascist in nature, but anti-fascist against the Italians and pro-Nazi *vis-à-vis* the German regime. This was true, but it did not reflect the nature of the society. During the German occupation of Greece some 700,000 people in a population of 7,000,000 would die fighting against the German army, most of them while fighting on the side of the Communist-leaning leftist ELAS-EAM resistance movement. White was unaware that the same Metaxas government rejected Hitler's request to apply the Nuremberg

Laws to the Jews of Greece, played a key role in assisting illegal immigration to *Erets-Israel*,[40] and was very Zionistic and pro-Jewish.

He met a Jew from Salonika, whom he fictively called Jose Medina. White noted that Medina himself was preparing to escape. He was not panicky; he was simply convinced that it would be quite impossible for 200,000 ill-armed Greeks, even with the assistance of the British, to hold off 350,000 mechanized Germans. If the Germans took Salonika, he knew, they would make short shrift of a Jew as prominent as he was, even if he was a Sephardi and not an Ashkenazi.[41] There were numerous instances of such members of the elite preparing to flee Salonika in prospect of the German conquest and occupation of Salonika. White also remarked that numerous boats along the quay of the Bay of Salonika were being loaded with household goods in preparation for flight from Macedonia, but he did not realize that this was not a Jewish trend. Although the Jews were active at the port, in shipping, and in maritime activities, they would leave Salonika by train to escape the Germans. As a journalist, only consulting a few members of the elite or taking a fleeting glance, White was only able to pick up on isolated instances. Nonetheless, his accounts are important, since he would write about his trips in the press, and he was there as a primary source.

Working in Athens in March 1941, White wrote two pieces for the ONA (Overseas News Agency, which disseminated information about persecuted minorities in Europe). He noted that there was no Jewish problem in Athens, so he really did not have a good reason to be in the region. He had submitted two articles: a survey on the Jews of Macedonia, and a comparison of the climates of Athens and Sofia, having visited the Bulgarian capital at the end of February. He later commented that the articles "had been so mutilated by the censors that it was a waste of money ever to have sent them."[42] He added that the only items he compiled were military reports, but ONA would not syndicate stories of that nature.

White also was moved negatively by the presence of the *Ethniki Neolea*, "the National Youth," that Metaxas founded in imitation of the *Hitlerjugend* (Hitler Youth).[43] He was appalled as he witnessed their March 25, 1941, Independence Day marching, which was requested by King George II, while inferring that Metaxas' successor Korizis, former Governor of the Bank of Greece, did not protest this. Korizis would commit suicide after the April 17 decision to dissolve the Greek army, ten days before the German occupation of Athens. Before his death Korizis disbanded the *Neolea* and it was not revived during the German occupation.[44] White furthermore pointed out that the Greek mainstream had fought in Albania and suffered tens of thousands of deaths and other casualties against the Italians in Albania, but had optimistically waited for two months for a proclamation of democracy; their future turned out otherwise and they would soon face German occupation.

Although White's book was published in 1944, most of his numerous observations from his 1941 Greek visit could not be published in the press due to the war conditions and censorship. Some of his topics included the appointment of Damaskinos as archbishop by the Germans who did not realize his anti-fascist background, that would continue during the occupation and also benefit the Jews; the German seizure of thousands of British prisoners although many British soldiers, including Palestinian Jews, hid out on the mainland; and the collaboration of the Germanophile General Tsolakoglou as head of the quisling government.

Most of the Jewish population of Salonika was very insulated and traditional. They were very naive and conservative. Most accepted the events of the German occupation as they occurred and did not think of resistance. Jewish families were large and the young people did not want to leave their families in order to go to the partisans. Thus, most were deported, but a significant minority numbering between 5,000 and 7,000 escaped Salonika between 1941 and 1943, seeking safer conditions in Athens in the Italian occupation zone.[45] These people had an acute political awareness and did not trust the Germans. Although they were unaware of the existence of death camps, they knew that the Germans were brutally anti-Semitic and instigated terror and havoc. Some of these people were already conscious of German aggression and terror from reading the local press in the 1930s.

Sam Nissim was thirteen years old when he left Salonika on his own, four days before the German arrival in the city, in order to try to escape from the country. Years later, he recalled knowing about the devious anti-Semitic nature of the Germans from reading the local press in the late 1930s; he vowed to himself that he would not remain in Greece for the Germans to harm him. Lacking the necessary funds, means, and resourcefulness, he was lucky enough to meet adults, who helped him depart from

Athens, and then leave Crete for Egypt with the retreating British forces.[46]

On April 11, 1941, two days after the Germans entered Salonika, they halted the publication of all of the newspapers in the city, including the Judeo-Spanish *El Mesagero* and the two French Jewish newspapers, *L'Independant* and *Le Progrés*.[47] *Apoyevmatini* (Afternoon) was the only Greek newspaper allowed to continue publication. The Germans also established a new newspaper, *Nea Evropi* (New Europe), whose editors, Papastratigakis and Lamzakis (Salonika's city engineer), although known for their anti-Semitic character, were not extreme in trying to campaign against the Jews during the first year of the German occupation in Salonika.[48] No orders were given from above by the Gestapo to create an anti-Jewish atmosphere in the press during this time. Both Lamzakis and Papastratigakis were sentenced to death *in absentia* for their crimes during the war.[49]

On April 20, 1941, Hitler's birthday, *Nea Evropi* published an article entitled "Teach Me," that blamed the Jews for Germany's former downfall; in the future, when there would be no more war, with Germany's victory, the Satanic Jew would disappear from political life and from Europe. This was one of the first of many inciting and devious anti-Semitic articles published in the Nazi-sponsored newspaper.[50]

On April 29, 1941, *Nea Evropi* was used by the German authorities to notify the local Jewish population that they must turn in their radios.[51] *Nea Evropi* further exhibited its anti-Semitic character and the whims of its Gestapo sponsors by calling on May 12 for a renewal of the anti-Semitic E.E.E. organization.[52] The organization had been outlawed in the latter 1930s by the dictator Metaxas after it had been responsible for burning down the Campbell neighborhood in 1931, during the regime of the anti-Semitic Republican Eleftherios Venizelos;[53] some 2,000 Jewish fishermen, porters, and laborers had lived in the affected neighborhood with their families.[54] The article in *Nea Evropi* advocated "that the organization must continue in its struggle against the hidden enemies of Greece," referring specifically to Salonika's large Jewish population, whose presence and electoral power had served as a threat to Greek-Orthodox national political hegemony and chauvinist nationalist exclusivity in the past. The E.E.E. had established relations with the Nazi Party after it took power in Germany 1933.

In general, *Nea Evropi* was not very active against the Jews until the summer of 1942. The Nuremberg Laws were not yet enacted in Salonika. Suddenly, on July 8, 1942, the newspaper *Apoyevmatini* [55] published the order that all Jewish males between the ages 18 and 45 had to report to Plateia Eleftherias (Freedom Square) on Saturday, July 11.[56] The notice did not state the purpose of the assembly. When the 9,000 young Jewish men arrived in their Sabbath dress, they were registered for forced labor for the physically excruciating tasks of road and railroad construction for the German authorities directed by the Miller and Todt companies.[57] There, from eight o'clock in the morning until two o'clock in the afternoon under the hot sun, they were tortured, compelled to do exercises, acrobatics, and were badly beaten by the German soldiers and officials.[58]

The next day, *Nea Evropi*, was full of mockery toward the event.[59] Devoting the entire front page to the "important event," photos and cartoons illustrated the Germans' pleasure in humiliating the Jews of Salonika. The newspaper portrayed the joy of the Greek-Orthodox citizens looking on from the side streets as the Jews suffered torment and agony, and explicitly stated that the Christians had but one wish in their hearts, that the drama continue as long as possible. Historian Michael Molho has commented that there was no public condemnation of the persecution; neither by the trade unions, the university, nor by the Greek General Governor, who gave the impression that he saw nothing while assisting the Germans.[60]

Some 4,000 Jews were drafted for forced labor throughout the country, and were subjected to extremely difficult work conditions, typhus, starvation, exhaustion, and even numerous deaths.[61] Following the Plateia Eleftherias incident, *Nea Evropi* did not cease publishing vicious items against the Jews. The campaign was intensive and systematic. Under its bold title on the draft for forced labor, *Nea Evropi* called for enactment of the racial laws in all areas of life; as the first step, the newspaper demanded that the Jews wear a sign in order to differentiate themselves from the other residents of the city.[62] Niko Carmona, a veteran resident of the city (and not one of the vehemently anti-Semitic Asia Minor refugees arriving after the 1922 population exchange between Greece and Turkey), who previously appeared as a friend of the Jews on the eve of World War Two and was looked upon with admiration by them, suddenly began an anti-Jewish campaign. The terms "ghetto" and "means of identification" for the Jews became the most popularly used motifs in the newspaper. Again and again, *Nea Evropi* harped on these themes; as well as inserting into its articles crass anti-Jewish jokes, wicked fabrications, and baseless accusations and assertions.[63]

Elements associated with the press actively assisted the Gestapo and participated in the confiscation of property. Molho gave the following account:

> Langhammer, director of the German Office for Control and Propaganda in Salonika, was assisted by Alleko Orologos, owner of the evening newspaper *Apoyvematini* and one named *Polatos*, who together with several pathetic hack writers turned into a sect of robbers. Their first and daring step was the robbing of paper factories—from the most successful in this branch—from their Jewish owners. On 23 October [1942,] the anti-Semitic journalist Fardis, accompanied by Germans, reported to the paper and carton factories of Solomon Cohen, some of the most flourishing in the city, and demanded that he show them the paper storerooms. This anti-Semitic journalist had always poured out his venom on the Jews. On November 5 Cohen was arrested, and while he was brought to the Pablo Mela camp, the Germans emptied his stores and storerooms and robbed his jewelry treasure and cash. At the same opportunity, they broke into and emptied the iron cash register of the Shalom family, that was kept in the basement of Cohen and contained a real treasure, a remnant of the property of a veteran Jewish family.[64]

The above-mentioned Fardis, one of the Greek-Orthodox refugees from Asia Minor in the 1920s, was the editor of the anti-Semitic daily newspaper *Makedonia*. His frequent exacerbation and baiting of the Jews and against the Maccabi youth sports movement in his newspaper throughout the 1920s and early 1930s created the conditions for the afore-mentioned Campbell riots of 1931.

Between March and August 1943, more than 50,000 Salonikan Jews were deported to Auschwitz-Birkenau and other concentration camps; by autumn, German rule had expanded to the south of Greece. On October 7, 1943, the Athenian newspaper *Eleftheron Vima* published the order of the new commander for Greece, SS General Jürgen Stroop (the German commander who destroyed the Warsaw Ghetto), instructing the Jews to return to their homes of June 1, 1943, and report to the Jewish community office within five days.[65] Jews not adhering to the notice would be shot and non-Jews hiding Jews would face the penalty of imprisonment in a concentration camp or even something more severe. The notice was also posted in the streets. Unlike in Salonika, most of the local population and the thousands of Salonikan Jews that had flocked there to escape the German anti-Semitic measures and deportations did not obey the orders and hid, joined the leftist ELAS-EAM partisan movement, or fled to Palestine via fishing boats to Turkey.[66]

After the war, the Greek press publicized the accounts of those survivors who returned from the camps.[67] The general Greek society, and even Jews who were not deported from Greece to the death camps, had a hard time fathoming the horrors that the camp survivors recalled. Greece was liberated from the Germans in September-October 1944. Most of the surviving prisoners were liberated in April and May 1945, but some escapees arrived earlier in 1945. The Athenian Auschwitz survivor, of Ioaniote extraction, Leon Batish, the first to return, received a very strange reception when he arrived in Salonika in ca. March 1945.[68] Those that he met thought he was telling them stories from another planet. He was written about and photographed widely throughout the general press in Greece, but his depiction of Auschwitz and German behavior toward the Jews was so strange that he was laughed at as if he were crazy. Once Greek Jews and many of the other Greek-Orthodox political prisoners began returning to Greece from the camps, Greek society began absorbing what the Nazis did to their compatriots in the previous two or more years. The Greek press was also quite active in portraying war crimes and trials of Germans and of Greek Orthodox Christian and Jewish collaborators who deported Greek Jews to the death camps or stole Jewish property in Greece.[69]

The Greek press, with access to European press agencies, greatly informed its readers about the rise of Hitler and Nazism. Signs of future disaster were present, but this critical analysis benefits from hindsight. People live in their respective surroundings, and changes on a large scale do not usually take place. People were aware of dangers, but there was little they could do to change their situation. Auschwitz, gas chambers, and the design of the 'Final Solution' were as unknown in Greece as they were in Poland. Nonetheless, Greek Jewry and the general Greek society were aware of German expansionism and military aggression.

Major events like deportations were not published in the press. Jews who escaped Greece and arrived in Istanbul informed the officials of the Jewish *Aliyah Bet* illegal immigration organization about deportations. Nevertheless, the latter officials themselves only learned of the early March 1943 Bulgarian deportations of Thracian Jewry after some two months delay. The Nazi extermination machine was in full swing and possibilities for rescue were slim.[70] The Nazi genocide of European Jewry overwhelmed the world and could only be halted when all of the Allies together finally entered the war and advanced sufficiently militarily. The press provided an outline of Nazi behavior, but the events were so treacherous, numerous, and secluded that they could only be annotated, absorbed, and comprehended many years later.

Notes:
1. Harry Recanati, *Recanati, Father and Son* (Jerusalem: Kane, 1984), p. 22. [Hebrew]
2. *Axion*, Salonika, October 8, 1933, p. 8.
3. Ibid.
4. *Axion*, Salonika, June 7, 1934, Year 6, No. 1443, p. 4.
5. *Axion*, August 9, 1934, No. 1492, Year 6, p. 1.
6. *Axion.*, July 4, 1934, No. 1465, Year 6, p. 1.
7. *Axion*, p. 4.
8. *Le Progrés*, Salonika, 27.3.1935.
9. "Julius Streicher schutzt die Juden," Bundesarchiv, Koblenz, Streicher file AL 28. Streicher wrote:

> Unverantwortliche Elemente haben die Lüge verbreitet, dass die Israeliten sich gegen das Leben des Führers verschworen hatten, und diese deswegen getötet werden mussten. Sie blieben die Sache so weit, dass sie sogar Aufrufe an die Plakatsaulen anschlugen, worin sie die Bevölkerung zu einem Pogrom aufreizten.
>
> In Franken begehle ich, und kein anderer als ich hat dazu das Recht. Ich habe einen Kreisleiter wegen Mangel an Disziplin ver-

abschiedet; ich werde jeden rücksichtslos aus der Partei ausstossen und verhaften lassen, der sich unterfangt, solche unbedachtsame Handlungen zu begehen.

gez.: Gauleiter Julius Streicher.

10. *L'Independant*, Salonika, 10 February 1936.

11. *Le Progrés*, Salonika, 2.2.1936.

12. Bundesarchiv, Koblenz, Germany. Streicher file AL 28, Culture 1935–1938.

13. Leni Yahil, *The Holocaust* (New York: Oxford Univ. Press, 1990), p. 94; *Axion*, 2 January 1936, No. 1916, Year 8, p. 4.

14. *Axion*, 9.9.1939, No. 3095, 11th Year, p. 1.

15. *Axion*, 6.9.1939, No. 3092, 11th Year, p. 1; *Mesagero*, October 17, 1939, No. 1261, 4th Year, p. 1; and June 13, 1940, No. 1477, 5th Year, p. 1.

16. *Mesagero*, October 28, 1939, No. 1271, p. 4.

17. *Mesagero*. 30 April 1940, p. 1.

18. *Axion*, 15.10.1939, No. 3124, 11th Year, p. 1.

19. *Mesagero*, 13 May 1940, No. 1447, p. 1.

20. *Mesagero*, 25 November 1939, No. 1295, p. 1.

21. *Axion*, 21.1.1940, No. 3208, Year 12, p. 1.

22. *Mesagero*, 6 October 1939, No. 1252, p. 1.

23. *Mesagero*, 28 October 1939, No. 1271, 4th Year, p. 1.

24. *Axion*, 25.1.1940, 12th Year, No. 3211, p. 1.

25. Yitzchak Kerem, "The History of the Jews in Salonika in the 19th and 20th Centuries," *Pinkas Kehilot Yavan*, (Jerusalem: Yad Vashem, [in press]) [Hebrew].

26. *Mesagero*, November 18, 1939, No. 1289, Year 4, p. 4.

27. *Mesagero*, December 31, 1939, Year 5, No. 1326, pp. 2,4.

28. *Axion*, January 26, 1940. No. 3212, 12th Year, pp. 1, 4.

29. *Axion*, January 27, 1940, No. 3213, 12th Year, p. 1.

30. *Axion*, January 26, 1940, No. 3212, 12th Year, p. 1.

31. *Axion*, January 30, 1940, No. 3215, 12th Year, p. 1.

32. *Mesagero*, 29 October 1940, No. 1613, 5th Year, p. 1.

33. *Mesagero*, June 11, 1940, No. 1476, 5th Year, p. 1.

34. *Mesagero*, February 17, 1941, No. 1720, 6th Year, p. 1. The article dealt with the landing of English parachutists in Italy during the first half of February 1941.

35. Jonathan Steinberg, *All or Nothing, The Axis and the Holocaust 1941–43*, (London and New York: Routledge, 1990), pp. 85–105.

36. Kerem, "Rescue Attempts," pp. 91–92. See note 57 below.

37. *Mesagero*, April 6, 1941, No. 1768, 6th Year, p. 1.

38. Leigh White, *The Long Balkan Night* (New York: Charles Scribner's Sons, 1944), p. 423.

39. Later in his book, he noted the "guts" and "character" of the Greeks, in combatting the much larger German nation of 80,000,000 and Italy of 45,000,000, even though they knew they could not win. They had a strong national pride based on 5,000 years of wisdom and traditions. Despite past British domination, the Greeks revered Britain for coming to try to combat the Germans in the Peleponese and Crete. Ibid., pp. 389–390.

40. Yitzchak Kerem, "The Greek Connection to Illegal Immigration to Palestine, 1934–1947," *Shoreshim Bemizrah*, Vol. IV (Ramat Efal: Yad Tabenkin, 1998), pp. 241–282.[Hebrew].

41. White, p. 191.

42. Ibid., pp. 195–196.

43. Ibid., pp. 196–199.

44. Ibid., pp. 389–390.

45. Daniel Carpi, "Notes on the History of the Jews in Greece during the Holocaust Period, The Attitude of the Italians (1941–1943)," reprinted from *Festschrift in Honor of Dr. George S. Wise* (Tel Aviv, 1981), pp. 25–62; and Yitzchak Kerem, "The Historiography of the Jews of Greece in the Holocaust", in Menachem Mor, ed., *Crisis and Reaction: The Hero in Jewish History* (Omaha, Nebraska: Creighton University Press, 1995), pp. 229–238.

46. Interview with Sam Nissim, New York City, Spielberg Survivors of the Shoah Foundation, March 1995.

47. David A. Recanati, *Zikhron Saloniki, Gedulata Vehurbana shel Yerushalayim Debalkan*, (Zikhron Saloniki, The Growth and the Destruction of Jerusalem of the Balkans) Vol. I, (Tel Aviv: The Committee for the Publication of the Salonikan Communal Book, 1972), p. 236.

48. Yosef Ben, *Greek Jewry in the Holocaust and the Resistance 1941–1944*, (Tel Aviv: The Institute for the Research of Salonikan Jewry, 1985), p. 36. [Hebrew]

49. Michael Molho and Joseph Nehama, *The Destruction of Greek Jewry,*

1941–1944, (Jerusalem: Yad Vashem, 1965), p. 38. [Hebrew]
50. Ibid., p. 39.
51. Ibid.
52. Ibid., p. 40.
53. George Th. Mavrogordatos, *Stillborn Republic, Social Coalitions and Party Strategies in Greece, 1922–1936* (Berkeley: University of California Press, 1983), p. 255.
54. Yitzchak Kerem, "The History of the Jews of Salonika in the 19th and 20th Centuries", in *Pinkas Kehilot Yavan*, (Jerusalem: Yad Vashem, [in press]). [Hebrew]
55. *Apoyevmatini*, July 8, 1942.
56. Molho and Nehama, p. 46; and Ben, p. 36.
57. Yitzchak Kerem, "Rescue Attempts of Jews in Greece during the Second World War," *Pe'amim*, No. 27, 1986, pp. 77–109.[Hebrew]
58. Michael S. Carasso, pp. 112–382; *Eu Sobrevivi*, (Vitoria, Brazil: Ed. Bahia Blanca, 1994), p. 25.
59. *Nea Evropi*, July 12, 1942, p. 1.
60. Molho and Nehama, pp. 47–48.
61. Mark Mazower, *Inside Hitler's Greece, The Experience of Occupation 1941–1944*, (New Haven and London: Yale University Press, 1993), pp. 239, 402. Mazower cites another estimate that 7,000 Jews were in forced labor. This figure is higher than others in the historiography.
62. *Nea Evropi*, July 12, 1942, p. 1.
63. Molho and Nehama, p. 55.
64. Molho and Nehama, p. 56.
65. Ben, pp. 53–54.
66. See Kerem, "Rescue Attempts," pp. 83–84, 97–100; Martin Gilbert, *Atlas of the Holocaust*, (Jerusalem: Steimatzky, 1982), pp. 180–181.
67. See issues of *Makedonia* (Thessaloniki), Spring 1945; and *Eleftheron Vima*, *Akropoli*, and *Vradini* (Athens), 1945–1946.
68. Interview with Makis Batish, Athens, Spring 1985.
69. Alexander Matkovski, *A History of the Jews in Macedonia* (Skopje: Macedonian Review Editions, 1982), pp. 195–197.
70. Zeev Venia Hadari, *Against All Odds, Istanbul 1942–1945*, (Tel Aviv: Ministry of Defence Israel, 1992) pp. 63–64, 350–356. [Hebrew]

Hebrew Journalism

It Was in the Papers:
The Hebrew Press in Palestine and the Holocaust

Tom Segev
Jerusalem, Israel

Israeli Journalists like to tell each other about the editor of *HaBoker*, a daily newspaper that no longer exists. On the morning of September 2, 1939, so the story goes, *HaBoker* devoted its main headline to a speech made by the Mayor of Tel Aviv. When asked why the main headline on that day was not about the outbreak of the Second World War, the editor is said to have answered: because the Mayor constantly calls my office, and Hitler never does. *HaBoker*'s headline on that day did in fact report the outbreak of the war, but the story is not that far from reality.

Covering the Holocaust, the Hebrew press in Palestine did not do a very good job. Most headlines of the time dealt with the needs of the country, its development, the struggle for national independence and the daily routine of local politics. As a rule the newspapers treated reports on the extermination of the Jews as if they merely represented a local angle of the real drama, namely the war. The press reflected the attitude of the country's communal and political leadership.

Jews living in Palestine were passionate newspaper readers, as Israelis still are today; even then it was a highly politicized society. There were at least a dozen decent Hebrew daily newspapers as well as a multitude of periodicals. This is quite remarkable for a community which at the beginning of the 1930's numbered less than 200,000 and by the end of the war less than half a million. The readers were fairly well informed. Comparing the newspapers with other historical sources of the time, such as official minutes, diplomatic correspondence, etc., it seems that the press rarely overlooked major developments and hardly left any big secrets uncovered. The papers followed the tradition of Jewish newspapers in the Diaspora, but increasingly tended to adopt the professional principles of the British press. Palestine was then under the rule of Great Britain. The two major daily papers were *Davar*, published by the Histadrut Labor Federation, and *HaAretz*, an independent liberal paper. Both still exist today.

To understand the curious, indeed disturbing coverage of the Holocaust, it may be helpful to review just briefly the coverage of three milestones on the road to the Holocaust. They were the rise of the Nazis (1933), the Nuremberg laws (1935) and *Kristallnacht* (1938).

In January 1933, the papers carried a great deal of information on the rise of the Nazis. News from Berlin made the main headlines almost every day. The reports were not always fully accurate, but the general picture they gave was reasonably correct. Readers of *HaAretz* received more information, but less pointed commentary; readers of *Davar* received less information but better background and commentary. Thus, *HaAretz* described the rise of the Nazis in a headline stating "Black Days in Germany."[1] The paper, however, repeatedly tried to reassure its readers: "One must suppose that Hitler's Germany will now renounce terrorist methods: government carries responsibility."[2] British papers held a similar view and so did other newspapers in Palestine. *Davar* was more pessimistic. It described Hitler as a man of hate who would uproot the entire Jewish people.[3] As early as 1933 the papers coined the basic terms that would remain in use ever since: the Jews were said to face the danger of *Hashmada*—extermination; their fate was to be *Shoah*—catastrophe.[4] As early as 1935, the papers quoted a Nazi official to the effect that the Germans were aiming at "a final solution" of the Jewish problem.[5]

Above all, the rise of the Nazis appeared to confirm the historical prognosis of the Zionist ideology: Jews were in danger, always and everywhere, which is why they needed their own independent state. A weekly newsmagazine described the Nazi persecution of the Jews as "punishment" for their wish to be integrated into German society instead of leaving for Palestine while it was still possible to do so. Now they would have to run in panic "like mice," the paper said.[6] Another paper used even stronger language: "The Jews of Germany are being persecuted now not in spite of their efforts to be part of that country, but because of those efforts."[7]

Everyone wondered how the Jewish tragedy in Germany would affect the future of Zionism: the papers expected tens of thousands of new immigrants from Germany and predicted unprecedented advancement and strength. Indeed soon after the Nazis had come to power, the Zionist movement reached an agreement with the German government. Jews could now leave Germany for Palestine, taking with them a substantial part of their property. The so-called *Haavara* (transfer) agreement led to a passionate and painful controversy, which for quite some time overshadowed the coverage of Nazi Germany.

In November 1935 both *HaAretz* and *Davar* covered the Nuremberg convention of the Nazi party. Both reported that the Germans were to announce new laws against the Jews, yet the story received rather hesitant and inconclusive treatment. Neither *Davar* nor *HaAretz* ever put the Nuremberg laws in a main headline, nor did they ever comment on them in their editorials. To be sure, the full wording of the new legislation was to become public only several weeks after its spectacular presentation at the convention. Legislative procedure is not easy to cover. Beyond that difficulty, however, both *Davar* and *HaAretz* failed to realize the unique nature of the Nuremberg laws. From now on Jews were to be persecuted not for anything they had done or chosen to be. They were to be persecuted for what they were, according to a new, racist definition. Neither *Davar* nor *HaAretz* seemed to understand that. Both papers compared the new measures against the Jews to the decrees against the Jewish religion in the Middle Ages. *Davar* presented the ban on mixed marriages and sexual relations between Jews and Aryans as a display of bad taste; the paper commented mainly on the pornographic nature of the act.

Davar did a better job than *HaAretz*. It was first to point out that the Nuremberg laws were only the beginning and that much worse was soon to come.[8] About ten days later the paper stated, "The Jews of Germany have been outlawed."[9] *HaAretz* published an opinion piece written by Itzhak Gruenbaum, a leader of the Zionist movement, who deplored what he described as the unworthy behavior of the Jews in Germany. They should not surrender without at least trying to fight back.[10] Later of course this would be one of the major issues confronting the survivors of the Holocaust: why did you let the Nazis drive you to your death like lambs to the slaughterhouse? Gruenbaum's article of 1935 reads like a forerunner of that accusation. *HaAretz* was not in very good shape at the time. The paper would soon be sold and get a new editor. Born in Germany, Gershom Schocken possessed historical perception and rather sharp journalistic instincts. Covering *Kristallnacht*, *HaAretz* definitely did a better job than *Davar*.

Kristallnacht was obviously a more dramatic story than the Nuremberg laws; hence it was easier to cover. On November 8, 1938, *HaAretz* stated in its main headline, "Desperate Act of a Young Jew." It was a detailed, fairly accurate description of the attack on the secretary of the German Embassy in Paris, vom Rath. There was action in the story, there was color, there was human interest and there was political background. According to the paper, Herschel Grünspan, the assailant, acted out of national motives, following the persecution of his people. His aim was revenge, the paper said. *HaAretz* described Grünspan as an immature, unbalanced and desperate boy; the paper however never condemned the attack itself. In the following days *HaAretz* covered the story in the main headlines and a number of editorials. The paper described the anti-Jewish riots that broke out in Germany in as much detail and color as one could expect. *HaAretz* left no doubt that it was a major story, of historical significance.

Davar on the other hand played down both the attack and its aftermath. The main headline on November 8 said: "Flood Scare in Tel-Aviv." An early editorial strongly condemned Grünspan. The paper said the assault on vom Rath was putting the German Jews in grave danger and was likely to cause them great harm. *Davar* also held that the act was morally wrong: acts of vengeance and of despair contradict the spirit of Judaism, the paper said. The main headlines of the paper continued to deal with local politics, even as the violence against the Jews in Germany and their property reached unprecedented dimensions. This could not have been a coincidence or simple professional failure. The editors of *Davar* must have made a decision: the struggle against the British was more significant at that point in time than the events in Germany. The British press, reported *Davar* on its front page, is full of protest against the barbaric cruelty of the Germans. Living in a glass house, however, one should not throw stones, the paper continued, and asked: what, after all, are the British themselves doing in Palestine?[11]

Commenting on *Kristallnacht* both papers as a rule used very strong language; in fact it was the strongest language available. At first they compared the violence in Germany to the pogroms in Russia. Soon, however, they looked for more powerful metaphors. They described Germany as a jungle, the Germans as cannibals.[12] The papers said Hitler was Satan. The term *Hashmada* (extermination), that had been in use since 1933, appeared again. They also consulted the Bible. Hitler was a modern Pharaoh and Haman: no room for the Ten Commandments in the German Sodom, stated *HaAretz*.[13]

Of course, the wish to put the news from Germany in historical perspective was only natural, as was the need to compare the events with some familiar precedent. Also the tendency to regard the events in Germany as one link in a long chain of anti-Semitic outbursts corresponds to the Zionist view of Jewish history. Then, too, this was a time when the Hebrew language hardly recognized the art and power of understatement: such was the style of the time. Still, the language of 1938 explains at least partly the subsequent treatment of the Holocaust itself.

There were two other striking characteristics and both are similarly relevant to the analysis of the later press. Both *Davar* and *HaAretz* reflected a sense of complete helplessness. Some of the commentary is heartbreaking. "Oh God, dear God, what have you done to us?" wrote a columnist in *HaAretz*, and added, "There is nothing one wants to do, these days, but cry. Just cry."[14]

They felt that there was nothing they could do, and they felt guilty about it, blaming themselves for lack of care and compassion. Why are we silent, why are we indifferent, they asked themselves again and again and demanded at least stronger protest.[15] *HaAretz* based an editorial on Psalm 83: "Do not keep silence, O God ("*Al Domi*"): do not hold thy peace and be still." The paper believed that, unlike the Soviet Union, Nazi Germany was still sensitive to protests from abroad.[16]

Here, then, are three main themes that dominated the coverage of *Kristallnacht*. They were the horror, expressed in the strongest possible language; the feeling of helplessness; and a tendency to blame oneself for insufficient compassion and protest. This now brings us to 1942.

Information about the fate of the Jews filtered into the West on a regular basis from a number of sources, arriving without much difficulty or delay by mail, wire, and phone. There were also reports from eyewitnesses who had escaped from occupied countries: refugees, diplomats, businessmen, various messengers, journalists and spies. Not all reports were reliable. Furthermore, not all information available abroad reached Palestine. Not all information available to the heads of the Jewish Agency immediately reached the press. However, the accumulated information available to a newspaper editor in Tel-Aviv was sufficient to inform his readers that the Nazis were systematically exterminating the Jews of Europe; they knew about the gas chambers, too. As a rule, the papers played down these stories. Few of them appeared in main headlines and many never even made the front pages.

On June 30, 1942, *Davar* reported that the Nazis had murdered a million Jews. The paper put the item on the front page, but did not give it the main headline. From a journalistic point of view, the story contained little fresh news—similar stories had appeared in the paper before. An eyewitness reported the murder of Jews in mobile gas facilities near the village of Chelmno, Poland. The report appeared in *Davar* on page 2.[17] A story on the trucks used to gas Jews had appeared in the paper a few months earlier, without major play. The main headline that day was about the submarine war; the editorial criticized the country's health system.[18] *HaAretz* once ran a detailed and quite gruesome report about the mistreatment of Jews in Kharkov, Ukraine. The item appeared on page 2, under a one-column headline. Immediately above it, in the same column, the paper reported a great victory of a Jewish soccer team in Damascus.[19] Similar examples are easy to point out.

Toward the end of November 1942, the Jewish Agency executive made an official statement on the extermination of the Jews. The statement asserted that the Germans were acting according to an official master plan, designed to kill the entire Jewish population of Europe. By the time it made that statement the Jewish Agency had received information about the systematic murder of Jews carried out in the vicinity of a little town called Auschwitz. The statement did not mention that name, but was otherwise quite explicit.[20]

Years later it would become accepted wisdom that the Jewish Agency announcement had significantly revised the public's attitude to the Holocaust. Until then, according to several writers, people had not been aware of the situation in Europe; they had known what was going on, but had been unable to "internalize" the information.[21] The fact is that the Jewish Agency statement contained little news. The editors of both

HaAretz and *Davar* put the statement on their front pages, yet the main headline for the day reported news from the front near Stalingrad. In the coming weeks, the Jewish Agency organized a series of protests, and the newspapers devoted more space to the extermination of the Jews, including main headlines and editorials. Within a few months, however, they bumped the subject back to the inside pages. From the second half of 1943 onward, the Holocaust was again no big story. Life went on. The newspapers announced fashion shows, end of season sales, sports events, opera performances.

David Ben Gurion once said that no one needed the Jewish Agency to know that Hitler intended to exterminate the Jews—it was all in *Mein Kampf*.[22] Indeed, it was all in the papers, too. The attitude of the Jewish community in Palestine toward the Holocaust lies far beyond the scope of the present discussion; it is a complex and to the present day an extremely sensitive subject. Two points, however, need brief mentioning, before moving on.

The first point is that the Jewish community in Palestine was powerless to prevent the extermination of the Jews. They were able to rescue a few thousands, they may or may not have been able to rescue a few more; they were in no position to save the lives of millions.

The second point is this: A variety of ideological and psychological factors led leaders of the Jewish community in Palestine to disassociate themselves from the tragedy of the Jews. Obviously for thousands of people who had just arrived from Europe, the cities and towns conquered by the Germans were not just names in the news. They represented family and friends who had been deported, lost or killed. For all these people the Holocaust was a personal tragedy; they lived in fear and in mourning. The leading political establishment, however, concentrated its attention on the needs of the Zionist enterprise in Palestine and on the struggle for national independence.

The press shared this attitude. Similar to the country's leadership the papers gave top priority to the events in Palestine. Similar to the political establishment it failed to display as much compassion for the Jews of Europe as one would like to find, in hindsight. Never was the mental gap between the "new Hebrew" of Palestine and the "old Jew" of the Diaspora as deep and as painful as it was in those days.

To understand the coverage of the Holocaust, however, it is not enough to analyze it as part of the Zionist mentality. It is necessary to analyze it also in the context of the professional journalistic practice.

First of all, editors could often not decide whether the information they received about the destruction of the Jews was true or not. "I did not believe it and I had called for others not to believe it either," wrote a member of the *Davar* staff.[23] Some of these editors were old enough to remember the fabricated horror stories that were spread during World War I. They felt a moral and national obligation to publish; if it was not true—they would obviously not publish, but how could they be sure? It was a constant dilemma. From time to time, the papers would accuse one another of overstating the horrors: "What for? Do the Jewish people not have enough problems?" asked one of the editors.[24] Naturally, they also feared that their doubts would lead them to miss a story and get scooped by the competition. So to be on the safe side they often published the stories, but played them down. They often expressed their reservations with the help of a question mark, as in one headline from *Davar*: "Half a Million Jews Exterminated in Romania?"[25] It was not a main headline.

At one point *Davar*'s editor-in-chief, Berl Katzenelson, suggested that there was only little demand for news about the Holocaust.[26] He felt that people had lost their ability and willingness to listen. The year was 1942. Let us remain in Katzenelson's newsroom for a moment. The inclination to believe the worst is part of the Jewish tradition: paradoxically, it also serves as the basis for an intrinsic optimism. Both these traits derive from a long history of persecution, expulsion, and death, including the destruction of entire Jewish communities. They also derive from an equally long history of survival and rebirth. The reports that came from the occupied lands, then, did not immediately go beyond what was already part of the collective memory of the Jewish people; they corroborated the historical analysis of the Zionist ideology. Analyzing the news, reports on the extermination of the Jews seemed to confirm a very realistic assessment of the strategic aims of Nazi Germany and were thus regarded and treated as an integral and inevitable part of the war. The papers tended to accept the official position of the Allies to the effect that the Jews would be rescued with the defeat of the Germans.

Finally, both editors and readers learned to live with the reported horrors stage by stage, each stage preparing them for the next. This is where we need to recall the earlier coverage of Nazi Germany. As early as 1933, the papers had used the term *Shoah*; long before the establishment of the first extermination camp they used the term *Hashmada*—extermination. By 1938 they had described Germany as Sodom and as Hell. Thus the newspapers had brought the story to its journalistic, linguistic and emotional height—long before it actually got there. A story in *Davar* from November 1938 reported that SS men had taken a group of children and dumped them at the Dutch border. The headline read: "Climax of Evil and Cruelty."[27] It seems then that by the time they had to deal with the extermination itself—the strongest language had been used up. The words had lost their power, and so had the mental energy needed to deal with the Holocaust. So they banned the Holocaust from the present and made it part of history, even while it was still going on.

Having experienced the Holocaust as a public and collective tragedy for nearly ten years, leaders of the community started to blame each other and themselves for not having done enough to rescue the Jews. Most of the victims of the Holocaust were still alive. Both leaders of the *Yishuv* (Jewish society in Palestine) and the newspapers seemed to be living in the future. Four weeks after the Nazi invasion of Poland, the political committee of the leading Mapai (Labor) party convened to discuss "what should be done now, after the Holocaust that has come upon Polish Jewry."[28] This was no slip of the tongue: even then, at the beginning of November 1939, they often referred to the situation of the Jews in the past tense. Looking ahead, members of the Zionist executive started to examine the legal and political possibilities to demand reparations from Germany, after the war. Others designed a plan to put up a national memorial for the Jews of Europe. They even thought of a name for the project—*Yad VaShem*. It was 1942: most victims of the Holocaust were still alive.

The newspapers too tended to regard the extermination of the Jews as part of history, even while it had not yet reached its climax, because from a journalistic point of view they had already been there. Thus the first press report on the murder of the Jews in mobile gas chambers appeared in biblical language, and in grammar that alluded to a distant past. "They would put them in a truck, the driver would put poison gas in pipes specially prepared for this purpose . . . voices and dull pounding would be heard from the truck, but after a while all would be quiet . . ."[29] The year was 1942; the Hebrew press in Palestine was missing one of the biggest stories of the century.

Notes:

1. *HaAretz*, 8 February 1933, p. 1.
2. Ibid., p. 2.
3. *Davar*, 1 February 1933, p. 1.
4. *HaPoel HaTsair*, 3 March 1933, p. 1; 26 May 1933, p. 1.
5. *Davar*, 17 November 1935, page 2.
6. *HaPoel HaTsair*, 21 March 1933, p. 1.
7. *Hazit HaAm*, 2 June 1933, p. 2.
8. *Davar*, 3 October 1935, p. 1.
9. *Davar*, 15 October 1935, p. 2.
10. *HaAretz*, 4 October 1935, p. 2.
11. *Davar*, 16 October 1938, p. 1.
12. *HaAretz*, November 12, 1938, p.1; *Davar*, November 13, 1938, p. 1.
13. *HaAretz*, November 15, 1938, (Evening Supplement) p. 1.
14. *HaAretz*, November 16, page 2.
15. *Davar*, November 16, 1938, p. 2; *HaAretz*, November 13, 1938, p. 2.
16. *HaAretz*, November 17, 1938, p. 2.
17. *Davar*, 8 October 1942, p. 2.
18. *Davar*, 25 June 1942, p. 1
19. *HaAretz*, 13 January 1942, p.2
20. *HaAretz*, 23 November 1942, p. 1
21. Tom Segev, *The Seventh Million* (New York: Hill & Wang, 1993), p. 531, note 34.
22. David Ben-Gurion at a gathering of Mapai activists, 8 December 1942, Labor Party Archive, 3/6.
23. *Davar*, 30 November 1942, p. 2.
24. *HaTsofe*, 18 March 1942, p. 3.
25. *Davar*, 10 August 1942, p. 1.
26. *Davar*, 22 April 1942, p. 1.
27. *Davar*, 24 November 1938, p. 1.
28. Mapai Political Committee, 2 November 1939, Labor Party Archive, 23/39.
29. *Davar*, 8 October 1942, p. 2.

Contributors

Contributors

Henry Abramson is an Associate Professor in the Department of History and the Program of Holocaust and Judaic Studies at Florida Atlantic University in Boca Raton. He is the author of *A Prayer for the Government: Ukrainians and Jews in Revolutionary Times, 1917–1920* (Harvard, 1999) and *The Art of Hatred: Images of Intolerance in Florida Culture* (Jewish Museum of Florida, 2001).

Jacques Adler, a native of France, is a Senior Fellow in the History Department of the University of Melbourne (Australia). He is the author of *Face á la persecution. Les organisations Juives á Paris* (1985); *The Jews of Paris and the Final Solution: Communal Response and Internal Conflicts, 1940–1944* (1987, 1991). His more recent articles are "The French Catholic Church and the Jewish question: July 1940-March 1941" in *The Australian Journal of Politics and History*; and "The Jews and Vichy: Reflections on French Historiography" in *The Historical Journal*. He is currently working on "The Holocaust and Pope Pius XII's Silences."

Yitshak Arad is a native of Poland who for for over two decades (1972–1993) was Chairman of the Directorate of Yad Vashem in Jerusalem. He has published dozens of scholarly articles and numerous books on the subject of the Holocaust, including *Ghetto in Flames* about the Vilna Ghetto; *Belzec, Sobibor, and Treblinka: The Operation Reinhard Death Camps*; *A Pictorial History of the Holocaust*; his personal memoir, *The Partisan*; and other books. He is now engaged in the writing of a comprehensive history of the Holocaust in the occupied territories of the Soviet Union.

Randolph L. Braham is Distinguished Professor Emeritus of Political Science at The City College and the Doctoral Program at the Graduate

Center of the City University of New York, where he also serves as Director of the Rosenthal Institute for Holocaust Studies. He is the author of numerous works in comparative politics and the Holocaust, including the two-volume *The Politics of Genocide. The Holocaust in Hungary* (1981; 2d ed. 1994).

Abraham Brumberg is a native of Wilno, Poland, who was educated in the Yiddish secular schools before immigrating to the USA, where he became a prolific scholar in the study of Communism and the Communist regimes in Eastern Europe. Among other publications, he edited *Poland: Genesis of a Revolution* (1983) and *Chronicle of a Revolution: A Western-Soviet Inquiry into Perestroika* (1990). His reviews have appeared in the London *Times Literary Supplement*, and the *New York Times Book Review*, among other journals.

David Cesarani is professor of modern Jewish history and Director of the AHRB Centre for the Study of Jewish/Non-Jewish Relations at the University of Southampton. His publications include *The Jewish Chronicle and Anglo-Jewry, 1841–1991* (1994); and *Arthur Koestler: The Homeless Mind* (1998); and, as editor, *Genocide and Rescue: The Holocaust in Hungary 1944* (1997) and *The Final Solution: Origins and Implementation* (1994).

Lucjan Dobroszycki (1925–1995) was Senior Research Associate at the YIVO Institute for Jewish Research and occupied the Eli and Diana Zborowski Chair in Interdisciplinary Holocaust Studies at Yeshiva University. Author and editor of more than a dozen books, he is most prominently known as the editor of *The Chronicle of the Łódź Ghetto 1941–1944* and as co-editor of *Image Before My Eyes: A Photographic History of Jewish Life in Poland, 1864–1939*. A native of Łódź, he survived over four years in the ghetto, followed by deportation to Auschwitz. In postwar Poland, he was a historian affiliated with the Institute of History of the Polish Academy of Sciences, focusing on both legal and clandestine journalism, as well as diaries, during the Second World War. The anti-Zionist campaign after the Six-Day War ultimately led to his immigration to the United States.

Max Frankel is a distinguished journalist whose career has included serving as managing editor of *The New York Times*. He is the author of *The Times of My Life: And My Life with the Times* (1999).

Daniel Grinberg is a historian born in Łódź, Poland, in 1950. He is on the faculty of the University of Białystok and the Graduate School of Social Research in Warsaw. Between 1990 and 1995, he was director of the Jewish Historical Institute in Warsaw. Prof. Grinberg is the author of numerous works on 19th century history and about the Holocaust. He has also translated into Polish works by Hannah Arendt, Isaiah Berlin and Bertrand Russell.

Andrea Grover is an adjunct associate professor of Humanities at New York University. She is the translator of *The Jews of Europe After the Black Death* (University of California Press, 2000) by the distinguished Italian historian Anna Foa. She has written on Italian Jewish culture for the *Forward*. For both the city of Newark, New Jersey, and Brooklyn Polytechnic University, she has been the keynote speaker for their Annual Holocaust Observence Day. She lectured on *"L'Osservatore romano* and the Holocaust 1939–1945" at the United States Holocaust Memorial Museum in Washington, D.C.

Lynn M. Gunzberg is Associate Dean of The College, Brown University, where she is also Associate Professor of Italian Studies. She is author of *Strangers at Home: Jews in the Italian Literary Imagination* (University of California Press, 1992).

Ron Hollander teaches journalism at Montclair State University in New Jersey where he offers the only course in the country devoted solely to a study of American journalism during the Holocaust. He has lectured widely on the subject.

Henry Huttenbach is Professor of East European History at The City College of New York. He is the founding editor of the journal *Genocide Research* and of *The Genocide Forum*. He is the author of numerous publications in a dozen languages, including *Soviet Nationality Policies*

(1990) and other books. He has lectured on comparative genocide in the USA, Sweden, Denmark, Norway and other countries.

Radu Ioanid is Director of the International Archival Programs Division at the United States Holocaust Memorial Museum. A native of Romania, he has published in Romanian, French and English. Dr. Ioanid is author of *The Sword of the Archangel: Fascist Ideology in Romania* (1990) and *The Holocaust in Romania: The Destruction of Jews and Gypsies Under the Antonescu Regime, 1940–1944* (2000).

Marvin Kalb is executive director of the Washington office of the Joan Shorenstein Center on the Press, Politics and Public Policy. For twelve years, he directed the Center at Harvard University's John F. Kennedy School of Government, where he also taught and lectured as the Edward R. Murrow Professor on Press and Politics. A veteran journalist and commentator, Kalb was the Chief Diplomatic Correspondent for CBS News and NBC News over a distinguished 30-year career. He is author of numerous books, including *Kissinger, Roots of Involvement, The Nixon Memo*, as well as two best-selling novels. His latest book, *One Scandalous Story*, dissects Washington journalism in the breaking of the Lewinsky scandal in January 1998. Mr. Kalb is a Fellow of the American Academy of Arts and Sciences.

Yitzchak Kerem is a historian of Greek and Sephardic Jewry at Aristotle University, Thessaloniki, Greece, and The Hebrew University of Jerusalem. Founder and Director of the Institute of Hellenic-Jewish Relations, University of Denver, he also edits the monthly academic e-mail publication *Sefarad, the Sephardic Newsletter*. Kerem is a documentary filmmaker and exhibit curator on Greek and Sephardic Jewry and the Holocaust. He also sits on the board of the Casa Shalom Institute for Crypto-Jewish Studies, and co-founded the International Forum for Tolerance and Peace.

Dov-Ber Kerler is professor of Yiddish at Indiana University. A native of Russia, educated in Israel and at Oxford University, where he formerly taught, Kerler is a prolific Yiddish poet and linguist. Author of *The*

Origins of Modern Literary Yiddish (1999), Prof. Kerler edited and co-edited *History of Yiddish Studies* (1992), the *Oksforder Yidish* collections (1991-1995), and *The Politics of Yiddish* (1998). With his late father, poet Josef Kerler, he co-edited four volumes of *Yerushalaimer Almanakh, Annual for Yiddish Literature, Scholarship, and Culture* (Jerusalem, 1993-1998).

Anna Landau-Czajka, a graduate of the University of Warsaw, is a researcher at the Historical Institute of the Polish Academy of Sciences. She wrote her doctorate on the ideology of the extreme right in inter-war Poland. She is the author of *W jednym stali domu: koncepcje rozwiązania kwestii żydowskiej w publicystyce polskiej lat 1933–1939* (1998).

Laurel Leff is an assistant professor in the School of Journalism at Northeastern University in Boston. She has worked as a reporter for the *Wall Street Journal* and the *Miami Herald* and as an editor for the *Hartford Courant* and American Lawyer Media.

Haskel Lookstein is Rabbi of Congregation Kehilath Jeshurun and Principal of the Ramaz School. He holds a Ph.D in Modern Jewish History from the Bernard Revel Graduate School of Yeshiva University and is the author of *Were We Our Brothers' Keepers: The Public Response of American Jews to the Holocaust, 1938–1944.*

Bruce F. Pauley, Professor of History at the University of Central Florida, is the author of *The Habsburg Legacy, 1867–1939*; *Hahnenschwanz und Hakenkreuz: Steirischer Heimatschutz und österreichischer Nationalsozialismus, 1918–1934*; *Hitler and the Forgotten Nazis: A History of Austrian National Socialism*; and *Hitler, Stalin, and Mussolini: Totalitarianism in the Twentieth Century.* His book, *From Prejudice to Persecution: A History of Austrian Anti-Semitism* (University of North Carolina Press) won the Charles Smith Award from the Southern Historical Association and the Best Book Prize from the Austrian Cultural Institute.

Franciszek Ryszka (1924–1998) earned his doctorate in law at the University of Wrocław. From 1982, he was professor of political theory at the University of Warsaw and was a member of the Polish Academy of Sciences. Author of 17 books and over 120 scholarly articles in Polish, German, French, English and Russian, he was a visiting professor at universities in Germany and France. Prof. Ryszka's most important works include *The State of Martial Law: The Legal System of the Third Reich* (Polish; 3rd edition, 1985); *In the Circle of Illusions: History of Spanish Anarchism*, 2 vols. (Polish; 1991); and *Nacht und Nebel* (4th enlarged edition, 1997).

Tom Segev is an Israeli journalist and historian. Segev writes for the Israeli daily, *Haaretz*; his weekly column deals mainly with politics and human rights. Born in Jerusalem in 1945, Segev graduated from Hebrew University and received a Ph.D in history from Boston University. He is author of *1949–The First Israelis* (1986); *Soldiers of Evil—The Commanders of Nazi Concentration Camps* (1988); *The Seventh Million—The Israelis and the Holocaust* (1993); *One Palestine, Complete: Jews and Arabs Under the British Mandate* (2000); and *Elvis in Jerusalem: Post-Zionism and the Americanization of Israel* (2002).

Jeffrey Shandler is an assistant professor in the Department of Jewish Studies at Rutgers University. He is the author of *While America Watches: Televising the Holocaust* (Oxford University Press, 1999) and the editor of *Awakening Lives: Autobiographies of Jewish Youth in Poland before the Holocaust* (Yale University Press/YIVO Institute, 2002).

Robert Moses Shapiro is a historian born in Germany to parents from Chrzanów and Sosnowiec, Poland. He edited *Holocaust Chronicles: Individualizing the Holocaust through Diaries and Other Contemporaneous Personal Accounts* (KTAV/Yeshiva University Press, 1999), which was a Finalist for the National Jewish Book Award. His published research has concentrated on the final generation of Polish Jewry, particularly in Łódź. Dr. Shapiro has translated Isaiah Trunk's pioneering Yiddish monograph on the Łódź Ghetto for the U.S. Holocaust Memorial Museum. He teaches history at the Ramaz School and is Adjunct Associate Professor of Jewish Studies at Yeshiva University in New York City.

Colin Shindler is Fellow in Israeli Studies at the School of Oriental and African Studies, University of London, England. He is a former editor of *Jewish Quarterly* and *Judaism Today*. An updated edition of his political history of the Israeli Right, *The Land beyond Promise: Israel, Likud and the Zionist Dream*, was published at the beginning of 2002.

Alexander Stille is a free-lance writer who lives in New York. He is the author of *Benevolence and Betrayal: Five Italian-Jewish Families Under Fascism* (Penguin), which won the 1992 Los Angeles Times Book Award for best work of General Non-Fiction; *Excellent Cadavers: The Mafia and the Death of the First Italian Republic* (Vintage); and *The Future of the Past* (Farrar, Straus & Giroux), an exploration of the cultural impact of technological change and its effect on our relation to the historical past. Stille is also a regular contributor to *The New York Times Arts & Ideas* page as well as to *The New York Review of Books* and *The New Yorker*.

Robert St. John is a celebrated journalist and author. Born in Chicago, St. John was a top Associated Press reporter and NBC commentator, who announced the Japanese surrender in September 1945 on both NBC radio and television. Author of 22 published books reflecting more than 3,000,000 miles of travel as a reporter, Robert St.John was featured in the Smithsonian Institute National Portrait Gallery exhibition, "Reporting the War: The Journalistic Coverage of World War II" (1994). His books include *Ben-Gurion, the Biography of an Extraordinary Man*; *Shalom Means Peace*, about the creation of modern Israel; *Tongue of the Prophets*, the biography of the Hebrew linguist Eliezer Ben-Yehuda; and a biography of Abba Eban.

Paweł Szapiro is a Polish historian in Warsaw, whose research and publications have focused on the period of the Second World War. He edited *The Jewish-German War: Polish Underground Press 1943-1944 on the Warsaw Ghetto Uprising* (Polish; London, 1992); the Warsaw Ghetto diary of Calel Perechodnik, *Czy ja jestem mordercą?* (1993); and co-edited the diary of Basia Temkin-Bermanowa, *Dziennik z podziemia* (2000).

Piotr Wróbel, a native of Poland and graduate of the University of Warsaw, is Professor of History at the University of Toronto. His numerous publications include *The History of the Jews in Poland: 1870-1918* (Polish; 1991); as co-author, *A Contemporary History of the Jews in Poland* (Polish; 1993); and as editor, *Historical Dictionary of Poland, 1945-1996* (English; 1998).

Leni Yahil is Professor Emerita at Haifa University, and member of the Editorial Board of *Yad Vashem Studies*. She is the author of *The Holocaust: The Fate of European Jewry* (Hebrew, 1987; English, 1990); and of *The Rescue of Danish Jewry: Test of a Democracy* (1969, 1983).

Index